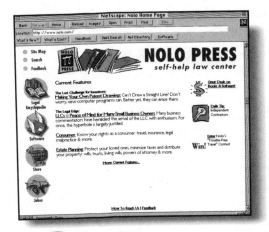

SECOND EDITION

SOFTWARE DEVELOPMENT

A Legal Guide

BY ATTORNEY STEPHEN FISHMAN

BERKELEY   NOLO PRESS

Your Responsibility When Using a Self-Help Law Book

We've done our best to give you useful and accurate information in this book. But laws and procedures change frequently and are subject to differing interpretations. If you want legal advice backed by a guarantee, see a lawyer. If you use this book, it's your responsibility to make sure that the facts and general advice contained in it are applicable to your situation.

Keeping Up to Date

To keep its books up to date, Nolo Press issues new printings and new editions periodically. New printings reflect minor legal changes and technical corrections. New editions contain major legal changes, major text additions or major reorganizations. To find out if a later printing or edition of any Nolo book is available, call Nolo Press at 510-549-1976 or check the catalog in the *Nolo News*, our quarterly publication. You can also contact us on the Internet at www.nolo.com.

To stay current, follow the "Update" service in the *Nolo News*. You can get a free one-year subscription by sending us the registration card in the back of the book. In another effort to help you use Nolo's latest materials, we offer a 25% discount off the purchase of the new edition of your Nolo book if you turn in the cover of an earlier edition. (See the "Special Upgrade Offer" in the back of this book.) This book was last revised in **January 1998.**

Second Edition	JANUARY 1998
Illustrations	MARI STEIN
Cover Design	LINDA WANCZYK
Layout Design	TERRI HEARSH
Index	SHARON DUFFY
Proofreading	ROBERT WELLS
Printing	BERTELSMANN INDUSTRY SERVICES, INC.

Fishman, Stephen.
    Software development : a legal guide / by Stephen Fishman. -- 2nd national ed.
        p.   cm.
    Includes index.
    ISBN 0-87337-397-9
        1. Computer Software--Law and legislation--United States.
    I. Title.
    KF390.5.C66F57   1997
    343.73'078004--dc21   97-17507
                                                                                                  CIP

Acknowledgments

My sincere thanks to:

Nolo publisher Jake Warner for his invaluable editorial contributions, patience and support,

Stan Jacobson for his invaluable research assistance,

Terri Hearsh for her oustanding book design and Linda Wanczyk for her terrific cover,

Ely Newman for preparing the CD-ROM disk.

The following attorneys who provided insightful comments about software contracts (Chapter 17):

- Paul Goodman of Elias, Goodman and Shanks, P.C. (New York),
- Susan Eiselman of TeleLawyer, Inc.,
- Alan Alberts of Alberts and Associates (Placerville, California), and
- Andrew Weill of Benjamin, Weill and Mazer (San Francisco).

Donna Demac, fellow, the Freedom Forum Media Studies Center at Columbia University, for her comments on Chapter 13 (Multimedia Projects),

Vincent S. Castellucci, Associate Director of Licensing, Harry Fox Agency, for reviewing the material on use of music in multimedia programs (Chapter 13),

William Roberts, President, Media-Pedia Video Clips Inc., for patiently explaining the stock footage business.

Finally, I thank Steve Elias and dedicate this book to him. Steve has not only been my indefatigable editor, but my role model as well.

About the Authors

Stephen Fishman received his law degree from the University of Southern California in 1979. After stints in government and private practice, he became a full-time legal writer in 1983. He has helped write and edit over a dozen reference books for attorneys. He is also the author of *The Copyright Handbook* (Nolo Press).

Table of Contents

1 How to Use This Book

2 Introduction to Intellectual Property

3 Copyright Basics

4 Copyright Registration and Notice

Part I. Copyright Registration

Part II. Software Copyright Notice

5 Software Copyright Infringement

6 Trade Secret Basics

7 Establishing a Trade Secret Protection Program

8 Software Patents

9 Trademarks and Software

10 International Software Protection

11 Software Ownership

12 Computer Databases

13 Multimedia Programs

14 Employment Agreements

Part I. Employer's Guide to Drafting Employment Agreements

Part II. Employment Agreements From the Employee's Viewpoint

15 Consulting Agreements

16 Software Licenses

17 Software Development Agreements

18 Help Beyond This Book

Chapter 1

How to Use This Book

This book is about computer software law and contracts (written agreements). It may be used by anyone involved in the software industry, including:

- software developers
- companies and individuals who hire software developers to create software on their behalf, and
- people who work for software developers, whether as employees or independent contractors.

A. How This Book is Organized

Conceptually, this book is divided into four parts:

Chapters 1-10 contain an overview of how to use the book, followed by a detailed discussion of intellectual property protection for software, including copyright, trade secret, patent and trademark protection. Chapter 12 covers protection for computer databases.

Chapters 11, 14 and 15 examine the legal relationship between a software developer and its employees and independent contractors; separate chapters cover employment and independent contractor agreements.

Chapters 13, 16 and 17 cover agreements for the development and licensing of software. Included are:

- a detailed custom development agreement, which governs the development of software for a specific enduser (Chapter 17),

- software license agreements (Chapter 16)
- a discussion of special legal problems involved in developing multimedia programs (Chapter 13).

Chapter 18, Help Beyond This Book, tells you how to do further research on your own and, if necessary, find a software attorney.

Icons Used in This Book

 A caution to slow down and consider potential problems.

 "Fast track" lets you know that you may be able to skip some material that doesn't apply to your situation.

 Information regarding the CD-ROM included with this book.

 This icon alerts you to a tip that may help you negotiate or draft an agreement.

 This icon refers you to helpful books or other sources.

B. Which Parts of the Book You Should Read

Not everyone will want to read the whole book. Which parts you do want to read will, of course, depend on why you bought the book.

Most of you bought the book for one or more of these four reasons:

1. You want a contract you can use with a client, developer, employee or independent contractor.
2. You want to know how to obtain the maximum legal protection possible for your software.
3. You have a specific question or problem.
4. You want a general education in software law.

Let's look at each of these reasons in more detail.

1. You Want a Contract to Use

This book contains a number of sample software contracts. These contracts are also on the forms disk at the end of this book, so you can easily load them onto your computer.

Before you use any contract on the forms disk, read the detailed discussion about it in the book. Most of the contracts contain a number of alternate provisions and you'll need to read the book to know which ones to use. The information in the book will help you decide whether to add or delete material from a contract, or perhaps not even use it at all.

Following are the types of forms in the book and on the disk; a complete list is in Section C, below. You need only read the chapters that cover areas of concern to you:

- Trade secret nondisclosure agreements (in Chapter 7);
- Departing employee's acknowledgment of obligations to employer (in Chapter 7);
- Employment agreements for technical and nontechnical employees (in Chapter 14);
- Independent contractor or consulting agreement (in Chapter 15);
- Software license agreement (in Chapter 16);
- Custom software development agreement (in Chapter 17): and
- Multimedia license agreements (in Chapter 13).

2. You Want Maximum Legal Protection for Your Software

Perhaps the sole reason you bought this book was to learn how to obtain maximum legal protection for the ideas and expression associated with your software. Here's how to proceed:

- First, read Chapter 2, Introduction to Intellectual Property, for an overview of the various forms of protection, and a discussion of how to implement an intellectual property protection plan.
- Next, you can read Chapters 3-10 and Chapter 12 straight through, or whatever portions of them interest you.
- Also, read Chapter 11, Software Ownership, which discusses the ownership issues involved whenever software is

created by an employee or independent contractor.

3. You Have a Specific Question or Problem

If you have a specific question or problem, look for that topic in the table of contents at the front of the book. For example, suppose you want to know whether you need to get permission to use an excerpt from a book in a multimedia program you're developing. By scanning the Table of Contents, you would discover Chapter 13, Multimedia Programs—probably the place to start. And by examining the section headings under Chapter 13, you would find that Section B is the place to start reading. If you didn't find what you were looking for in the Table of Contents, you could search in the index under such terms as "multimedia" and "permissions."

4. You Want a General Education in Software Law

Perhaps you bought this book because you want to learn all about software law. It may come as a surprise to discover that there really is no such thing as software law. Instead, there is a vast body of different state and federal intellectual property and contract laws that, taken together, are used legally to protect software and govern software transactions. Read Chapter 2 for an overview of intellectual property law and then delve into whatever chapters interest you.

C. Using the Forms Disk

All of the forms discussed in this book are included on a CD-ROM disk in the back of the book. This CD, which can be used with Windows, DOS and Macintosh computers, installs files that can be opened, printed and edited using a word processor or other software. It is NOT a stand-alone software program. Please read this section and the README.TXT file included on the disk for instructions on using the forms disk.

Two different kinds of forms are contained on the CD-ROM:

- agreement forms that you can open and edit with your word processing program (see Section 2, below), and
- U.S. Copyright Office registration forms in PDF format you can open and print out only with the Adobe Acrobat Reader application (see Section 3, below). While both Windows and Mac users can use these forms, DOS users cannot.

How to View the README File

If you do not know how to view the file README.TXT, insert the CD into your computer's CD-ROM drive and follow these instructions:

- **Windows 95:** (1) On your PC's Desktop, double-click the My Computer icon; (2) right-click the icon for your CD-ROM drive; (3) click Explore; (4) in the left window, click on the icon for the CD-ROM drive; (5) in the right window, double-click the README.TXT icon.
- **Windows 3.1:** (1) Open File Manager; (2) double-click the icon for the CD-ROM drive; (3) double-click the README.TXT icon.
- **Macintosh:** (1) If the "Software Development" CD window is not open, open it by double-clicking the "Software Development" CD icon; (2) double-click on the README.TXT icon.
- **DOS:** At the DOS prompt, type EDIT D:README.TXT and press the Enter key (substitute the letter of your CD-ROM drive for "D").

While the ReadMe file is open, print it out by using the Print command from the File menu.

1. Installing the Form Files Onto Your Computer

Before you can do anything else, you need to install the files from the CD on to your hard disk. In accordance with U.S. copyright laws, remember that copies of the disk and its files are for your personal use only.

Insert the forms disk and do the following:

a. Windows 95 Users

Follow the instructions that appear on screen.

By default, all the files are installed to the \SFTFORMS\ directory.

b. Windows 3.1 Users

Step 1: In Program Manager, choose Run from the File menu.

Step 2: Enter D:\INSTALL.HLP (substitute the letter of your CD-ROM drive for "D").

Step 3: Follow the instructions that appear on screen.

By default, all the files are installed to the \SFTFORMS\ directory.

c. Macintosh Users

Step 1: If the "Software Development" CD window is not open, open it by double-clicking the "Software Development" CD icon.

Step 2: Select the "Software Dev. Forms" folder icon.

Step 3: Drag and drop the folder icon onto the icon of your hard disk.

d. DOS Users

(These instructions assume that the D: drive is the source you want to copy from and that the C: drive is the location you want to copy the files to.)

Step 1: To create a directory named "SFTFORMS" on your C: hard disk drive, type the following at the DOS prompt:

C: <ENTER>
CD\ <ENTER>
MD SFTFORMS <ENTER>

Step 2: To change to the SFTFORMS directory, type:

CD SFTFORMS <ENTER>

Step 3: To create a subdirectory named "TXT" to the SFTFORMS directory, at the C:\SFTFORMS> prompt type:

MD TXT <ENTER>

Step 4: To change to the TXT subdirectory you just created, type:

CD TXT <ENTER>

Step 5: To copy all the files from the TXT directory of the CD (in your D: drive) to the current directory, at the C:\SFTFORMS\TXT> prompt type:

COPY D:\TXT*.* <ENTER>

All of the files in the TXT directory on the CD will be copied to the\SFTFORMS\TXT directory on your C: drive.

2. Creating Agreements With the Word Processing Files

This section concerns the files for agreement forms that can be opened and edited with your word processing program. (Copyright Office registration forms in PDF format are discussed in Section 3, below). All forms and their filenames are listed below.

All agreement forms come in two file types (or formats):

- the standard ASCII text format (TXT), and
- rich text format (RTF).

ASCII files can be read by every word processor or text editor including DOS Edit, all flavors of MS Word and WordPerfect (including Macintosh), Windows Notepad and WordPad and Macintosh SimpleText or TeachText.

RTF files have the same text as the ASCII files, plus additional formatting. They can be read by most recent word processing programs including all versions of MS Word for Windows and Macintosh, Windows WordPad, and recent versions of Word-Perfect for Windows and Macintosh.

To create your document using a form file, you must: (1) open a file in your word processor or text editor; (2) edit the form by filling in the required information; (3) print it out; (4) save your revised file.

The following are general instructions on how to do this. However, each word processor uses different commands to open, format, save and print documents. Please read your word processor's manual for specific instructions on performing these tasks.

 Do not call Nolo's technical support if you have questions on how to use your word processor.

Ch/Sec.	Form	File Name
7C	General Nondisclosure Agreement	NONDISC1
7C	Nondisclosure Agreement (Prospective Licensee)	NONDISC2
7C	Beta Tester's Non-disclosure Agreement	NONDISC3
7C	Visitor's Nondisclosure Agreement	NONDISC4
7C	Interview Confidential Disclosure Agreement	NONDISC5
7D	Acknowledgment of Obligations	ACKOBLIG
7D	Letter to New Employer	LTRSECRT
9F	List of Patent and Trademark Libraries	PTDLLIST
11C	Copyright Assignment	ASSIGN
13C	Search Request Form	SEARCH
13F	Multimedia Publicity/ Privacy Release	MULTIREL
13G	Multimedia License Agreement	MULTILIC
14F	Employment Agreement for Nontechnical Employees	EMPLOY1
14G	Employment Agreement for Technical Employees	EMPLOY2
15D	Consulting Agreement (Favoring Hiring Firm)	CONSULT1
15F	Consulting Agreement (Favoring Consultant)	CONSULT2
16E	Shrink-Wrap License	LICENSE1
16E	Click-Wrap License	LICENSE2
16F	Negotiated License	LICENSE3
17B	Custom Software Development Agreement	CUSTSFT

a. Step 1: Opening a File

To open a file in your word processor, you need to start your word processing program and open the file from within the program. This process usually entails going to the File menu and choosing the Open command. This opens a dialog box where you will tell the program (1) the type of file you want to open (either *.TXT or *.RTF) and (2) the location and name of the file (you will need to navigate through the directory tree to get to the folder/directory on your hard disk that you installed the files to).

Which File Format Should You Use?

If you are not sure which file format to use with your word processor, try opening the RTF files first. Rich text files (RTF) contain most of the formatting included in the sample forms found in this book. Most current Windows and Macintosh word processing programs, such as Microsoft Word or WordPerfect, can read RTF files.

If you are unable to open the RTF file in your word processor, or a bunch of "garbage" characters appear on screen when you do, then use the TXT files instead. All word processors and text editors can read TXT files, which contain only text, tabs and carriage returns; all other formatting and special characters have been stripped out.

Where the Files Are Installed

Windows and DOS Users
- ASCII text files are installed by default to a directory on your hard disk named \SFTFORMS\TXT\.
- RTF files are installed by default to a directory on your hard disk named \SFTFORMS\RTF\.

Macintosh Users
- ASCII text files are located in the "TXT" folder within the "Software Dev. Forms" folder.
- RTF files are located in the "RTF" folder within the "Software Dev. Forms" folder.

You can also open a file more directly by double-clicking on it. Use File Manager (Windows 3.1), My Computer or Windows Explorer (Windows 95) or the Finder (Macintosh) go to the folder/directory you installed the files to. Then, double-click on the specific file you want to open. If you click on an RTF file and you have a program installed that "understands" RTF, your word processor should launch and load the file that you double-clicked on. If the file isn't loaded, or if it contains a bunch of garbage characters, use your word processor's Open command, as described above, to open the TXT file instead. If you directly double-click on a TXT file, it will load into a basic text editor like Notepad or SimpleText rather than your word processor.

If you do not know how to use your word processor to open a file or document, you will need to look through the manual for your word processing program—Nolo's technical support department will NOT be able to help you with the use of your word processing program.

b. Step 2: Editing Your Document

Fill in the appropriate information according to the instructions and sample agreements in the book. If you do not know how to use your word processor to edit a document, you will need to look through the manual for your word processing program—Nolo's technical support department will NOT be able to help you with the use of your word processing program.

When filling in the forms, follow these simple rules:

- Read the instructions in this book. This book explains key features of all forms and guides you through the process of completing them.
- Look for instructions in brackets and capital letters. The forms indicate where information must be filled in by short instructions contained in brackets, such as "[DATE]." You may want to

search for a left bracket ("[") to find the beginning of each item that must be completed. Remember to delete (or replace) the bracketed instructions after you've read them.

- Modify and delete text only as directed. The clauses are legally sound as designed. If, however, you change important terms, you may affect their legal validity.

- Select alternatives as directed and delete alternatives that don't apply. When you have a choice between two or more provisions, these are referred to as "alternatives." Read the discussion of the alternatives in the book; the text of all alternatives is on the disk only. Each alternative is clearly marked at the beginning "[ALTERNATIVE 1]," "[ALTERNATIVE 2]," and so on. Each alternative ends with a similar marking: "[END ALTERNATIVE 1]," and so on. Delete the markers as well as the alternative(s) that you did not select.

- Optional clauses are marked "[OPTIONAL]." That means it's up to you as to whether or not to include them. Delete the word "[OPTIONAL]" and the subsequent "[END OPTION]" marker if you use the clause. Delete the entire clause and markers if you choose not to use it.

c. Step 3: Printing Out the Document

Use your word processor's or text editor's Print command to print out your document. If you do not know how to use your word

processor to print a document, you will need to look through the manual for your word processing program—Nolo's technical support department will NOT be able to help you with the use of your word processing program.

d. Step 4: Saving Your Document

After filling in the form, do a "save as" and give the file a new name.

If you do not rename the file, brackets that indicate where you need to enter your information will be lost and you will not be able to create a new document with this file without recopying the original file from the CD.

If you do not know how to use your word processor to rename and save a document, you will need to look through the manual for your word processing program—Nolo's technical support department will NOT be able to help you with the use of your word processing program.

3. Copyright Office Registration Forms

Electronic copies of the following Copyright Office application forms are also included on the CD-ROM disk. These forms are in Adobe Acrobat PDF format and you must have the Adobe Acrobat Reader installed on your computer (see below) to view and print the forms. DOS users will not be able to use these files.

Ch/Sec.	Form	File Name
4G	Form TX	FORMTXI.PDF
4G	Form PA	FORMPAI.PDF
4G	Short Form TX	FORMTXS.PDF
4G	Short Form PA	FORMPAS.PDF
4G	Form VA	FORMVAI.PDF
4G	Short Form VA	FORMVAS.PDF
4G	Form ___/CON	FORMCON.PDF
4O	Form CA	FORMCA.PDF
11C	Copyright Office Document Cover Sheet	FORMDOC.PDF.

To complete your document using these files, you must: (1) start Acrobat Reader; (2) open a file ; (3) print it out; (4) complete them by hand or typewriter. You will not be able to complete these forms using your computer.

Where the PDF Files Are Installed

- **Windows Users:** PDF files are installed by default to a directory on your hard disk named \SFTFORMS\PDF\.
- **Macintosh Users:** PDF files are located in the "PDF" folder within the "Software Dev. Forms" folder.

Installing Acrobat Reader

To install the Adobe Acrobat Reader, insert the CD into your computer's CD-ROM drive and follow these instructions:

- **Windows 95:** Follow the instructions that appear on screen
- **Windows 3.1 Users:** (1). In Program Manager, choose Run from the File menu; (2) Enter D:\INSTALL.HLP (substitute the letter of your CD-ROM drive for "D"); (3) Follow the instructions that appear on screen.
- **Macintosh:** (1) If the "Software Development" CD window is not open, open it by double-clicking the "Software Development" CD icon; (2) Double-click on the "Install Acrobat Reader 3.0" icon.

DOS users cannot install Acrobat Reader.

If you do not know how to use Adobe Acrobat to view and print the files, you will need to consult the online documentation that comes with the Acrobat Reader program.

Do NOT call Nolo technical support if you have questions on how to use Acrobat Reader.

Print Quality Counts. The Copyright Office is very particular about how you print out its forms. It says that the forms should be printed head to head (top of page 2 is directly behind the top of page

1) using BOTH SIDES of a single sheet of paper. NOTE: Short forms are one sided. Dot matrix printer copies of the forms are not acceptable. Inkjet printer copies of the forms require enlarging if you use the Shrink to Fit Page option. To achieve the best quality copies of the application forms, it is recommended that you use a laser printer.

The forms submitted to the Copyright Office must be clear, legible, and on a good grade of 8½- inch by 11-inch white paper. The quality of the copyright application forms submitted for registration directly affects the quality of the copyright registration certificate you receive. The Copyright Office produces completed registration certificates through an optical scanning system that utilizes an image scanned from the original application submitted. As a result, copyright applications submitted that are of poor print quality will negatively affect the print quality of the copyright registration certificate you receive. For these reasons, the utmost effort should be made to submit the best quality application form possible.

D. Putting the Agreement Together

After the parties have decided what to include in their agreement, there are some technical details that have to be dealt with. Usually, one party handles this and submits the finished agreement to the other for review and signature.

1. The Process of Reaching a Final Agreement

One of the parties will create a first draft of the agreement. This and all subsequent drafts should be dated and numbered (e.g., "draft #1, October 6, 1998"). In addition, a legend like the following should be placed at the top of the draft to make clear that it is not the final agreement:

PRELIMINARY DRAFT FOR DISCUSSION PURPOSES ONLY—NOT INTENDED AS A LEGALLY BINDING DOCUMENT.

The draft should be sent to the other party to review. Often, the other party will want to make changes. This can be done in several ways. The other party can discuss the changes with the original drafter in person or by telephone; the original drafter will then make the agreed changes and send a second draft to the other party for review. Alternatively, the other side may suggest its changes in writing; this can be in the form of a letter, interlineations to the original draft, or by completely revising the original draft. The original drafter will then review the changes, perhaps make more changes, and then send another draft back to the other side for review. It is common for contract drafts to go back and forth among the parties many times before a final agreement is reached.

a. Keeping Track of Changes

Care must be taken to alert the other side to all changes made in each draft. The normal practice is to underline all additions and to indicate deletions either by leaving them in place with a line drawn through them or using a caret or other sign indicating omissions. This can be easily done with many word processing programs.

2. Print Out and Proofread the Final Agreement

Print out the final agreement on regular 8½-x 11-inch paper. Make sure the pages are consecutively numbered (either at the top right corner or the bottom of each page). Read through the entire agreement to make sure it is correct and complete. Minor changes can be made by hand (in ink only) and initialed. However, it's probably just as easy (and neater) to make any changes on your computer and then print out the agreement again. When you're finished proofreading, print out at least two copies of the agreement.

3. Attach All Exhibits

Attach a complete copy of all exhibits, if any, to every copy of the agreement. Each exhibit should be consecutively numbered or lettered ("A,B,C" or "1,2,3"). Make sure that your references to the exhibits in the main body of the agreement match the actual exhibits.

4. Signing the Agreement

Each party should sign both copies of the agreement (both are originals). The parties don't have to be in the same room when they sign and it's okay if the dates of signing are a few days apart.

It's very important that both parties sign the agreement properly. Failure to do so can have drastic consequences. How to sign depends on the legal form of each party's business.

Sole proprietors. If you or the client are sole proprietors, you can simply sign your own names because a sole proprietorship is not a separate legal entity.

However, if you use a fictitious business name, it's best for you to sign on behalf of your business. This will help show you're an employee of the client.

> EXAMPLE: Chris Kraft is a sole proprietor software developer. Instead of using his own name for the business, he calls it AAA Software Development. He should sign his contracts like this:
>
> AAA Software Development
> By: *Chist Kraft*
> Chris Kraft

Partnerships. If either party is a partnership, a general partner should sign on the partnership's behalf. Only one partner needs to sign. The signature block for the partnership should state the partnership's name and name and title of the person signing on the partnership's behalf. If a partner signs only his or her name without mentioning the partnership, the partnership is not bound by the agreement.

> EXAMPLE: AAA Software Development contracts to perform programmng services for a Michigan partnership called The Argus Partnership. Randy Argus is one of the general partners. He signs the contract on the partnership's behalf like this:
>
> The Argus Partnership
> A Michigan Partnership
> By: *Randy Argus*
>   Randy Argus, a General Partner

If a person who is not a partner signs the agreement, the signature should be accompanied by a partnership resolution stating that the person signing the agreement has the authority to do so. The partnership resolution is a document signed by one or more of the general partners stating that the person named has the authority to sign contracts on the partnership's behalf.

Corporations. If either or both of the parties is a corporation, the agreement should be signed in their corporate capacities. For example, if Joe Jones is President of AcmeSoft Corporation, he should sign on AcmeSoft's behalf, like this:

> AcmeSoft Corporation,
> By: *Joe Jones*
>   Joe Jones

It's best that a corporation's president or chief executive office (CEO) sign the agreement, since he or she will have clear authority to sign for the corporation. For the same reason, if a party is a partnership, it's preferable that a partner sign. If this is not possible, the signature should be accompanied by a corporate resolution or partnership resolution stating that the person signing the agreement has authority to do so.

5. Save the Agreement

Each party should keep one original signed copy of the agreement. Make sure to store it in a safe place. You might want to make additional photocopies to ensure against loss. ■

Chapter 2

Introduction to Intellectual Property

This chapter introduces the concept of intellectual property and discuss how a software developer may implement a simple plan to preserve and protect its intellectual property.

A. What Is Intellectual Property?

"Intellectual property" is a generic term used to describe products of the human intellect that have economic value. Computer software is just one of the many forms of intellectual property. Other examples include books, music, movies, photographs, artwork, records and other works of authorship; inventions that qualify for patent protection; product names, logos, slogans and packaging; and valuable information that is kept secret.

Intellectual property is "property" because, over the past 200 years or so, a body of laws has been created that gives owners of such works legal rights similar in some respects to those given to owners of real estate or tangible personal property (such as automobiles). Intellectual property may be owned and bought and sold the same as other types of property. But in many important respects, owning intellectual property is very different from owning a house or a car.

Anybody who develops real estate would be a fool not to know something about real estate law. Similarly, everyone who creates software, or hires others to do so, should have a basic understanding of intellectual property laws. These laws define exactly what a software developer owns and doesn't own, what it can sell and what it can and cannot legally take from others.

A software developer or owner that makes wise use of the intellectual property laws maximizes the value of its software. In contrast, a developer or owner that pays little or no attention to intellectual property may end up throwing away potentially valuable assets or find itself at the wrong end of an expensive lawsuit.

B. Using Intellectual Property Laws to Protect Software

There are more ways to legally protect computer software than virtually any other product produced by the human brain. This is because software can be viewed as a work of authorship, a commercial product and a part of a machine. As we'll discuss briefly in this chapter, there are four separate bodies of law that may be used to protect software. These are:

- trade secret law
- copyright law
- patent law, and
- trademark law.

Each of these bodies of law may be used to protect different aspects of computer software, although there is a great deal of overlap. In most cases, both copyright and trade secret law can and should be used together to protect the same piece of software. Patent law is used much more rarely than copyright or trade secrecy to protect software; but, when it is used, it can provide the most powerful protection of all. State and federal trademark laws are used to protect product names, logos, slogans, packaging and other symbols used to market software and distinguish it from the competition.

Let's take a brief look at each type of intellectual property law. (All four types of protection are covered in more detail in later chapters.)

1. Trade Secret Law

A trade secret is information or know-how that is not generally known in the business community and that provides its owner with a competitive advantage in the market-place. The information can be an idea, written words, formula, process or proce-

dure, technical design, list, marketing plan or any other secret that gives the owner an economic advantage.

If a trade secret owner takes reasonable steps to keep the confidential information or know-how secret, the courts will protect the owner from unauthorized disclosures of the secret to others by:

- the owner's employees,
- other persons with a duty not to make such disclosures,
- industrial spies, and
- competitors who wrongfully acquire the information.

This means that the trade secret owner may be able to sue the person who stole or disclosed the secret and obtain an injunction (a court order preventing someone from doing something, like stealing or disclosing trade secrets) and damages. However, the trade secret owner must truly take steps to preserve the trade secret; the more widely known a trade secret is, the less willing the courts are to protect it.

> EXAMPLE: AcmeSoft, a small software developer, decides to create a revolutionary new virtual reality program for the World Wide Web. AcmeSoft knows that several of its competitors are working on similar programs, but its star programmer has given AcmeSoft a substantial lead.
>
> AcmeSoft doesn't want its competitors to know about its program, so it keeps this information as a closely guarded trade secret. It requires its employees to

sign employment agreements in which they promise not to disclose valuable information to outsiders without Acme-Soft's permission. AcmeSoft also implements other trade secrecy measures (discussed in detail in Chapter 7), such as marking documents that contain sensitive information "confidential." These and other measures are designed to:

- prevent outsiders from learning about AcmeSoft's development activities; and
- give AcmeSoft legal grounds to stop the information from being used by a competitor if the competitor learns about them illegally (by hiring away or bribing an AcmeSoft employee).

By relying on trade secrecy principles, AcmeSoft gets a leg-up on its competition, all of whom are pursuing different, less original and imaginative designs for their own virtual reality programs. Trade secrecy is more difficult to maintain once the program is distributed, however. AcmeSoft will have to use license agreements with end users and make sure not to make its source code publicly available. "Source code" is computer code written by programmers in high-level programming languages such as C+ and Java. Any programmer can read source code and discern the trade secrets contained in a program.

Trade secrecy is increasingly being seen as the most important form of protection for most software, in part because of the limitations on copyright protection (discussed briefly below).

(For a detailed discussion of trade secrets, see Chapter 6.)

2. Copyright Law

Virtually all software qualifies for protection under the federal copyright law, at least to some extent. The copyright law protects original works of authorship. Computer software is considered to be a work of authorship, as are all types of written works (books, articles, etc.), music, artwork, photos, films and videos.

A copyright costs nothing, is obtained automatically and lasts a very long time—at least 50 years and usually much longer. But copyright protection for software is relatively weak. Here's why. The owner of a copyright has the exclusive right to copy and distribute the protected work, and to create derivative works based upon it (updated versions, for example). However, this copyright protection extends only to the particular way the ideas, systems and processes necessarily embodied in software are expressed by a given program. Copyright never protects an idea, system or process itself. In other words, copyright protects against the unauthorized duplication or use of computer code and, to some extent, a program's structure and user interface, but copyright never protects the underlying functions, methods, ideas, systems or algorithms used in software.

In contrast, the ideas, processes and systems embodied in software can be protected as trade secrets if reasonable steps are taken to keep the information confidential—for example, by keeping a tight rein on the source code and making sure that anyone who obtains a copy of the source code signs a license respecting the owner's trade secret rights.

> EXAMPLE: AcmeSoft's virtual reality program is automatically protected by copyright as soon as it's written. This means no one may make or sell copies of the program without AcmeSoft's permission.
>
> In addition, it is illegal for anyone to create new software very similar to AcmeSoft's using a substantial amount of AcmeSoft's program. Nonetheless, AcmeSoft's competitors are free to independently create a new program accomplishing the same purpose.
>
> Because of the complexity of the law and confusion in the courts, the extent of copyright protection for such aspects of AcmeSoft's program as its structure and interface is not entirely clear.

(For a detailed discussion of copyright law, see Chapter 3.)

3. Patent Law

The federal patent laws protect inventions. By filing for and obtaining a patent from the U.S. Patent and Trademark Office, an inventor is granted a monopoly on the use and commercial exploitation of an invention for up to 20 years. A patent may protect the functional features of a machine, process, manufactured item or composition of matter, the ornamental design of a non-functional feature, or asexually reproduced plants

To qualify for a patent, the invention must be:

- novel—that is, unique in one or more of its elements when compared to previous technology, and
- nonobvious—that is, surprising to a person with ordinary skills in the relevant technology.

Most software is not sufficiently novel and/or nonobvious to qualify for a patent. When a patent is appropriate, obtaining it can be a difficult, expensive and time-consuming process. It usually takes about two to three years.

As mentioned above, a computer program can be viewed as part of a machine or process as well as a work of authorship, and computer programs may be patented if they meet the underlying requirements. A patent provides broad protection for the ideas, inventive functions, methods, systems and algorithms that, taken together, constitute the invention, not just the computer code used to express or implement them. In effect, patent protection gives the patent holder an absolute monopoly over the use of its invention as described in the patent. Where available, patent protection is so strong that it takes the place of both copyright and trade secret protection.

> **EXAMPLE:** Certain features of AcmeSoft's virtual reality program are quite revolutionary and have never been used before. If AcmeSoft applies for and obtains a patent on these features, it will have a monopoly on their use in widget manufacturing for up to 20 years. In other words, no one else may use the patented features of AcmeSoft's program in a virtual reality program without AcmeSoft's permission. If they do, AcmeSoft could successfully sue for patent infringement.

(See Chapter 8 for a detailed discussion of software patents.)

4. Trademark Law

Trade secret, copyright and patent laws do not protect names, titles or short phrases. This is where trademark protection comes in. Under both federal and state laws, a manufacturer, merchant group or individual associated with a product or service can obtain protection for a word, phrase, logo or other symbol used to distinguish that product or service from others. If a competitor uses a protected trademark, the trademark holder can obtain a court injunction (a court order preventing the infringement) and money damages.

> **EXAMPLE:** AcmeSoft markets its program under the name "Virtualoso" and registers this trademark with the U.S. Patent and Trademark Office. None of AcmeSoft's competitors can use its name on a virtual reality program without AcmeSoft's consent. If they do, AcmeSoft could get a court to order them to stop and sue for damages. And because AcmeSoft registered the name, any competitor who began using the name after the registration date will be considered a willful infringer and be subject to treble damages and possibly the trademark owner's attorneys fees.

(See Chapter 9 for a detailed discussion of trademarks.)

C. Implementing an Intellectual Property Plan

Every software developer, no matter what the size, needs to create and implement an intellectual property plan. This consists primarily of using forms and procedures to identify, establish ownership of and protect the developer's intellectual property.

1. Using the Intellectual Property Forms in This Book

Following are the basic forms any software developer should have. Samples are included in this book.

a. Employment agreement

Every employee engaged in the creation of software and other intellectual property, or who may be exposed to company trade secrets, should sign an employment agreement. Ideally, each employee should sign the agreement no later than the first day of work on the project. The agreement should assign (transfer) to the employer ownership of all software and other work-related intellectual property the employee creates within the scope of employment. The agreement should also include nondisclosure provisions designed to make clear to the employee that she has a duty to protect the company's trade secrets. Existing employees who have not signed such agreements should be asked to do so. (See Chapter 14 for a detailed discussion and sample agreements.)

b. Consulting agreement

Every independent contractor—that is, each nonemployee who performs work for the company—you hire to work on software should sign an independent contractor agreement, ideally no later than the start of work. This agreement includes trade secrecy provisions and provisions designed to make it clear that the worker is an independent contractor, not an employee. Most importantly, the agreement should assign ownership of the contractor's work product to the company. This is absolutely vital. Without such a provision, the company may not end up owning the copyright in the contractor's work product, even though it paid for it.

If you work as a consultant for others, you should have the client sign your own consulting agreement.

(See Chapter 15 for a detailed discussion and sample agreements.)

c. Nondisclosure agreements

No software developer should ever reveal its trade secrets to an outsider unless he or she signs a nondisclosure agreement promising to keep them confidential. "Outsiders" can include potential customers, beta testers and even office visitors. (See Chapter 7 for a detailed discussion and sample agreements.)

d. Software license agreements

It's generally advisable to license your software to end users rather than sell it outright. This way, you can maximize your legal protection. Individual licenses can be negotiated and signed for limited distribution software. Shrink-wrap and click-wrap licenses may be used for mass-marketed software. (See Chapter 16 for a detailed discussion and sample license agreements.)

e. Custom software development agreements

It is in the best interests of both a software developer and its clients that a detailed development agreement be negotiated and signed before custom software is developed. This agreement should, among other things, describe the software to be developed, contain payment provisions, state who will own the software when it is completed and contain any desired warranties. (See

Chapter 17 for a detailed discussion and sample agreements.)

2. Taking Trade Secrecy Measures

In addition to using the form agreements outlined above, certain physical security measures should be taken to prevent outsiders from obtaining access to company trade secrets—for example, marking documents containing trade secrets confidential. Just how many such measures you need to take depends on the size of your company. If you're running a one-person operation, you'll need fewer secrecy measures than a large company. (See Chapter 7.)

3. Exploring Patenting

Most software cannot be patented. However, if a program contains a truly innovative approach to a problem that is a significant advance in the field or that has long stymied other programmers, it may qualify for a patent. Chapter 8 provides a brief introduction to software patents. But if you're really serious about obtaining one, you'll need to spend some serious time getting up to speed with Nolo's *Patent it Yourself* by David Pressman or contact a patent attorney.

4. Copyrighting Software

Relatively little has to be done to preserve copyright protection—it begins automatically the moment a protectible work is created. However, it is highly advisable—but not mandatory—to register the copyright in all software with the Copyright Office in Washington, D.C. For maximum protection, this must be done no later than three months after the software is published. A copyright notice should also be placed on all copies of published software and documentation. (See Chapter 4 for a detailed discussion.)

5. Using and Protecting Business and Product Names As Trademarks

The company should conduct a trademark search before adopting a trademark to see if the same or similar trademarks are already in use on competing or related products or services. This is done by checking state and federal trademark registration records and other sources of trade name listings, such as industry directories.

Although trademark ownership arises from use, additional valuable rights may be obtained by registering the trademark with the U.S. Patent and trademark Office. (See Chapter 9 for a detailed discussion.) ■

Chapter 3

Copyright Basics

This chapter is an introduction to basic copyright concepts and vocabulary. Copyright law provides one of the two major vehicles by which most software is protected, the other being trade secrecy. The importance of copyright law in the software industry cannot be overemphasized. Copyright law is used to allocate contractual rights and responsibilities—who will own the program code, who has the right to develop and market the product and so forth. To protect the rights of everyone involved, these commercial relationships should be carefully described in any agreement dealing with software development and distribution.

The copyright law will also usually serve as your first line of defense against software pirates. However, as discussed in Chapter 5, there are significant limitations on the scope of copyright protection for software. As a result, in most cases software owners need to supplement their copyright protection with the stronger protection afforded by trade secrecy. (See Chapter 6.)

A. Why Have a Copyright Law?

The Founding Fathers recognized that everyone would benefit if creative people were encouraged to create new intellectual and artistic works. When the United States Constitution was written in 1787, the framers took care to include a Copyright Clause (Article I, Section 8) stating that "The Congress shall have Power ... To promote the Progress of Science and useful Arts, by securing for limited times to Authors ... the exclusive Right to their ... writings."

The primary purpose of copyright, then, is not to enrich authors; rather, it is to promote the progress of science and the useful arts—that is, human knowledge. To pursue this goal, copyright encourages authors in their creative efforts by giving them a mini-monopoly over their works—termed a copyright. But this monopoly is limited when it appears to conflict with the overriding public interest in encouraging creation of new intellectual and artistic works generally.

Although the constitution only mentions copyright protection for writings, over the past 200 years the scope of the copyright laws has been expanded to cover all forms of creative expression, including computer software.

B. What is a Copyright?

A copyright is a legal device that provides the creator of a work of authorship the right to control how the work is used. The Copyright Act of 1976 (17 U.S.C. 101 et seq.) —the federal law providing for copyright protection—grants creators (called "authors") a bundle of intangible, exclusive rights over their work. These rights include the:

- reproduction right—the right to make copies of a protected work
- distribution right—the right to initially sell, rent, lease or lend copies to the public (but this right is limited by the "first sale" doctrine, which permits the owner of a particular copy of a work

to sell, lend or otherwise dispose of the copy without the copyright owner's permission—for example, libraries may lend the books they purchase without getting permission)

- right to create adaptations (or "derivative works")—the right to prepare new works based on a protected work
- public display right—the right to show a copy of a work at a public place or transmit it to the public, and
- public performance right—the right to perform a protected work in public.

An author's copyright rights may be exercised only by the author or by a person or entity to whom the author has transferred all or part of his or her rights. (See Chapter 5.) If someone wrongfully uses the material covered by the copyright, the copyright owner can sue and obtain compensation for any losses suffered as well as an injunction (court order) requiring the copyright infringer to stop the infringing activity.

In this sense, a copyright is a type of intangible property—it belongs to its owner and the courts can be asked to intervene if anyone uses it without permission. And, like other forms of property, a copyright may be sold by its owner, or otherwise exploited for his or her economic benefit.

C. What Can Be Protected by Copyright?

Copyright protects all kinds of original works of authorship. This includes, but is not limited to:

- literary works—this comprises any work "expressed in words, numbers, or other verbal or numerical symbols or indicia" (17 U.S.C. 101), including novels, plays, screenplays, nonfiction prose, newspapers and magazines, manuals, catalogs, text advertisements and compilations such as some business directories
- motion pictures, videos and other audiovisual works—this includes movies, documentaries, training films and videos, television shows, television ads, and interactive multimedia works
- photographs, graphic works and sculpture—this includes maps, posters, paintings, drawings, graphic art, display ads, cartoon strips, statues and works of fine art
- music—this includes all types of songs, instrumental works and advertising jingles
- sound recordings—this includes recordings of music, sounds or words
- pantomimes and choreographic works—this includes ballets, modern dance, and mime works, and
- architectural works—this includes building designs, whether in the form of architectural drawings or blueprints, or the design of actual buildings.

1. Copyright Protection for Computer Software

The Copyright Act specifically classifies computer programs as "literary works" and affords them full copyright protection. The Copyright Act defines computer programs as "sets of statements or instructions to be used directly or indirectly in a computer to bring about a certain result." (17 U.S.C. 101.) However, all experts agree that many aspects of software—in addition to computer programs—are protected by copyright. Copyright not only protects all forms of software code, but may extend to:

- program design documents—that is, schematic or other representations such as flowcharts or detailed specifications that describe a program's structure, sequence and organization
- supporting materials such as users' manuals, software documentation and instructions
- at least to some extent, the way a program itself is structured, sequenced and organized, and
- at least to some extent, a program's user interface. That is, the way it presents itself to and interacts with the user; this is often called "look and feel," and may include the design of computer screen displays as well as how the user actually operates the program.

As discussed in detail in Chapter 5, these additional elements of software (particularly the user interface and program structure and organization) may in fact receive little or even no copyright protection because of various copyright doctrines. In any event, what all this means is that the owner of the copyright in software as defined here (including computer code, documentation, and, to some extent, user interface and structure, sequence and organization) has the five exclusive rights outlined in Section B above.

EXAMPLE: AcmeSoft, a small software developer, has its employees create a software package called AcmeMap— Website mapping software that allows a Webmaster to see a graphical description of all the pages in a Website. The package consists of the AcmeMap program itself and an extensive manual. AcmeSoft is the sole copyright owner of every element of the AcmeMap package that is protected by copyright. This may include the program's source code and object code; the structure, sequence and organization of the program modules, routines and subroutines; the user interface; and the program's online and written documentation.

As the owner of the copyright in AcmeMap, AcmeSoft has the exclusive right to copy it, to distribute it to the public, to create derivative works based upon it (new or enhanced versions, for example), and to perform and display it in public—for example, over the Internet. Subject to some exceptions discussed below, no one else can exercise AcmeSoft's copyright rights without its permission. If they do, AcmeSoft is entitled to sue them in federal court for copyright infringement to make them stop the infringing activity and to obtain damages.

Can Computer Languages Be Copyrighted?

No court has ruled on whether high-level computer languages like C++ or Java can themselves be protected by copyright. However, the Copyright Office apparently believes they cannot be protected since it refuses to register a work consisting solely of a computer language. The Copyright Office's view is supported by decades-old copyright cases involving telegraphic codes and stenographic systems. The courts in these cases held that the component elements of shorthand systems and telegraphic codes—that is, the individual coined words or symbols that form the vocabulary of the system—are not protected by copyright. But a particular arrangement of such symbols is protected if it meets the originality, fixation and minimal creativity requirements discussed for copyright protection. (*Hartfield v. Peterson*, 91 F.2d 998 (2d Cir. 1937).) It seems likely, therefore, that anyone is free to write any program in any computer language. Although the language itself is not protected, a particular program written in that language is, just as the English language itself is not protected, but a poem written in English is.

2. Screen Displays Protectible As Audiovisual Works

The copyright law defines audiovisual works as "works that consist of a series of related images" intended to be shown through the use of a machine or device. (17 U.S.C. 112.) Computer screen displays may constitute an audiovisual work that is separate and distinct from the "literary work" comprising the actual computer code. For example, several early software copyright cases held that the computer screen displays contained in video games such as Pac-Man were protectible as audiovisual works. In more recent years, audiovisual copyrights have been claimed, with varying degrees of success, in the "look and feel" of computer programs such as Lotus 1-2-3 and in the Apple Macintosh graphical user interface. (See Chapter 5.)

3. Software Distributed Online

Today, much software is distributed online over the Internet, commercial online services such as America Online and CompuServe and BBS's. Software distributed online is entitled to exactly the same copyright protection as software that is sold by mail order or in stores. That is, it is illegal to download or otherwise use the software without the copyright owner's consent. Of course, due to the ease of copying works in the online environment, huge amounts of software are illegally copied from and to the online world every day.

D. Three Prerequisites for Copyright Protection

Not every work of authorship is necessarily protected by copyright. None of the works of authorship described above, including software, will be protected unless they satisfy the following three fundamental prerequisites for copyright protection.

1. Fixation

The first requirement for copyright protection is that the work must be fixed in a tangible medium of expression. Any stable medium from which the work can be read back or heard, either directly or with the aid of a machine or device, is acceptable. For example, a work is protected when it is written or drawn on a piece of paper, typed on a typewriter or recorded on tape.

Copyright does not protect a work that exists in your mind but that you have not fixed in a tangible medium. Trade secrecy must be used to protect such unfixed works. (See Chapter 6.)

Copyright protection begins the instant you fix your work. There is no waiting period and it is not necessary to register with the Copyright Office; but important benefits are obtained by doing so (see Chapter 4). Copyright protects both completed and unfinished works, and works that are widely distributed to the public or never distributed at all.

When software is sufficiently "fixed" to qualify for copyright protection has been the subject of great controversy. It's clear that software satisfies the fixation requirement the moment it is stored on magnetic media such as disks or tapes; imprinted on devices such as ROMs, chips and circuit boards; or, of course, written down on paper.

But does fixation also occur when a program is loaded into computer RAM (volatile random access memory) or transmitted over the Internet? This is not so clear. Several courts have held that fixation does occur when a program is loaded from a permanent storage device into computer RAM. (*MAI v. Peak*, 991 F.2d. 511 (9th Cir. 1993).)

However, these cases involved situations where a program was retained in RAM for several minutes or even longer. It remains unclear whether transmitting a program or other material over the Internet counts as fixation. Such transmissions involve making several temporary copies of portions of the work ("data packets") and sending them over computer networks.

If such transmissions constitute fixation, simply browsing on the Internet could constitute a violation of copyright owners' exclusive rights to make copies of their protected online material. But many experts believe the copying involved in Internet transmissions is too temporary and ephemeral in nature to count as "copying" for copyright purposes. This issue has been the subject of international treaty negotiation, and may be the subject of legislation in the near future.

2. Originality

A work is protected by copyright only if, and to the extent, it is original. But this does not mean that it must be novel—that is, new to the world—to be protected. For copyright purposes, a work is original if it—or at least a part of it—owes its origin to the author. Many works consist of some elements that are original and others that are copied. In this event, only the original elements will be protected (but, of course, the copied elements might be protected under someone else's copyright).

3. Minimal Creativity

Finally, a minimal amount of creativity over and above the originality requirement is necessary for copyright protection. Works completely lacking creativity are denied copyright protection even if they have been independently created. For example, one court held that a programmer's minute variations on a standard communications protocol for fax machines were not suffi-ciently creative to be copyrightable. (*Secure Servs. Technology v. Time & Space Process-ing, Inc.* 722 F.Supp. 1354 (E.D. Va. 1989).)

In addition, there are some types of works that are usually deemed to contain no creativity at all. For example, telephone directory white pages are deemed to lack even minimal creativity and are therefore not protected by copyright. Other alpha-betical or numerical listings of data in computer databases may also completely lack creativity. (See Chapter 12.)

Technically speaking, the amount of creativity required for copyright protection is very slight. However, as a practical matter, the more creative a work, the more copy-right protection it will receive. This may be particularly true for software. Programs con-sisting primarily of standard programming techniques may receive little or no protection even if they are original, because the code will be judged to merge with the underlying ideas rather than qualify as protectible expression. In contrast, highly creative programs—programs unlike anything created before—receive full protection. (See Chapter 5 for detailed discussion.)

Copyright Does Not Protect Hard Work

In the past, some courts held that copyright protection extended to works lacking originality and/or creativity if a substantial amount of work had been involved in their creation. For example, these courts might have protected a telephone directory or similar alphabetical database if the author had personally verified every entry. However, the Supreme Court has outlawed this sweat of the brow theory in *Feist Publications, Inc. v. Rural Telephone Service Co.*, 111 S.Ct. 1282 (1991). It is now clear that the amount of work expended to create a program or other work of authorship has absolutely no bearing on the degree of copyright protection it will receive. Copyright only protects fixed, original, minimally creative expressions, not hard work.

E. Limitations on Copyright Protection

The purpose of copyright is to encourage intellectual creation. Paradoxically, giving authors too much copyright protection could inhibit rather than enhance creative growth. To avoid this, some important limitations on copyright protection can be found in the federal copyright laws and the federal court cases that interpret them.

1. Fair Use

Copyright protection also is limited by the fair use doctrine. To foster the advancement of the arts and sciences, there must be a free flow of information and ideas. If no one could make any use at all of a protected work without the copyright owner's permission—which could be withheld or given only upon payment of a permission fee—the free flow of ideas would be greatly impeded. To avoid this, Congress created a special fair use exception to copyright owners' rights. Under this exception, as a general rule, you are free to copy from a protected work for purposes such as research and editorial comment so long as the value of the copyrighted work is not diminished. (See Chapter 5.)

2. Material in the Public Domain

An intellectual creation that is not legally protected is said to be in the public domain. Public domain material belongs to the world, and anyone is free to use it in any way she wishes. For copyright purposes, a creative work enters the public domain when the term of the copyright expires (see Section G below). This means that the work can be used without obtaining permission from the copyright owner. (See Chapter 13 for detailed discussion.)

However, even if a work—or some aspect of the work—is not protected by copyright, it still may not be in the public domain in the sense that you are definitely free to use it without having to get anyone's permission. This is because there are many different ways to legally protect software. Software may be protected not only by copyright, but by patent, trademark and trade secret laws as well. (See Chapters 6, 8 and 9.)

The fact that all or part of a software product may not be protected by copyright doesn't necessarily mean it isn't protected by one or more of these other laws. For example, although the ideas, discoveries, methods, procedures, processes, systems, concepts, principles, algorithms and facts embodied in software (or any other work) are not protected by copyright, all these things possibly could be protected by patent law or trade secrecy.

If you're not sure whether an item you want to use is in the public domain, seek legal assistance or get permission to use it from its owner.

F. Copyright Ownership and Transfer of Ownership

The exclusive rights outlined in Section B above initially belong to a work's author. However, for copyright purposes, the author of a work is not necessarily the person who created it; it can be that person's employer—a corporation, for example. There are four ways a person or business may become an author:

- An individual may independently author the work.
- An employer (whether a person or business entity such as a corporation or partnership) may pay an employee to author the work, in which case the employer is the author under the work made for hire rule. (See Chapter 11.)
- A person or business entity may specially commission an independent contractor to author the work under a written work made for hire contract, in which case the commissioning party becomes the author. (See Chapter 11.)
- Two or more individuals or entities may collaborate to become joint authors. (See Chapter 11.)

The initial copyright owner of a work is free to transfer some or all of his, her or its copyright rights to other people or businesses, who will then be entitled to exercise the rights transferred. (See Chapter 16.) For example, a software copyright owner may license its software to end users.

The majority of software is created by employees or independent contractors who transfer their copyright rights to the hiring firms. As a result, most software is owned by businesses, not by the people who actually create it.

G. Copyright Duration

One of the advantages of copyright protection is that it starts immediately when software or any other work of authorship is created and lasts a very long time—far longer than the vast majority of software copyright owners will ever need.

1. Software Created After 1977

The copyright in a program or other protectible work created after 1977 by an individual creator lasts for the life of the creator plus an additional 50 years. If there is more than one creator, the life plus 50 term is measured from the year-date the last creator dies.

The copyright in works created by employees for their employers (probably the majority of software) lasts for the earlier of:

- 75 years from the date of publication, or
- 100 years from the date of creation.

This term also applies to works created by individuals under a work made for hire contract, and individuals who choose to remain anonymous or use a pseudonym (pen name) when they publish their work.

Copyright protection lasts so long that it is highly likely that any software you create will have long been obsolete by the time the copyright expires.

2. Pre-1978 Published Works

Software and other works published before 1978 have a different copyright term. Soft-

ware published before 1978, but after 1964, has a 75-year copyright term from the date of publication. Software published before 1964 had an initial 28-year copyright term and an additional 47-year renewal term if a renewal application was filed with the Copyright Office during the 28th year after publication. (See *The Copyright Handbook: How to Protect and Use Written Works*, by Stephen Fishman (Nolo Press), for a detailed discussion of pre-1978 copyrights.)

HOW IMPORTANT ARE THE DATES OF PUBLICATION?

THEY'RE "OF THE ESSENCE" DARLING - "OF THE ESSENCE."

H. Copyright Infringement

Copyright infringement occurs when a person other than the copyright owner exploits one or more of the copyright owner's exclusive rights without the owner's permission. Infringement of software usually involves the unauthorized exercise of a copyright owner's exclusive rights to reproduce and distribute the work or prepare derivative works based on it. In plain English, this means that someone incorporates your protected expression into their work without your permission. Here are some examples of infringement:

> EXAMPLE: Tush, Rose, a large accounting firm, buys one copy of TaxEze, a tax preparation software package, and makes 100 copies for its employees without the copyright owner's permission. The purchaser of a computer program may legally make only one copy of the program for archival purposes without the copyright owner's permission. (See the sidebar below.) Thus, the making of the 100 unauthorized copies constitutes infringement on the copyright owner's exclusive right to reproduce and distribute TaxEze.

> EXAMPLE: Without authorization, Larry creates a Mac version of a popular PC video game and sells copies over the Internet. Larry has infringed on the video game owner's right to create derivative works from its game—that is, the right to create new works based upon or derived from the PC game.

> EXAMPLE: BigTech, Inc., creates a plug-in program for a popular Web browser that brings high quality speech audio to Web pages. In doing so, it obtains a copy of the source code for a preexisting, similar program owned by Audiodata, Inc., from a former Audiodata employee. BigTech copies hundreds of lines of code from Audiodata's program. BigTech has infringed Audiodata's exclusive right to reproduce (copy) the code in its program.

The Copyright Act doesn't prevent copyright infringement from occurring, just as the laws against auto theft do not prevent cars from being stolen. However, the Copyright Act does give copyright owners a legal remedy to use after an infringement has occurred—they may sue the infringer in federal court.

A copyright owner who wins an infringement suit can stop any further infringement, get infringing software destroyed, obtain damages from the infringer—often the amount of any profits obtained from the infringement—and recover other monetary losses. This means, in effect, that a copyright owner can make a copyright pirate restore the author to the same economic position she would have been in had the infringement never occurred. And, in some cases, the copyright owner may even be able to obtain monetary penalties that may far exceed his or her actual losses. (See Chapter 5.)

Software Purchasers' Limited Right to Make Copies and Adaptations

Earlier we said that a software copyright owner has the exclusive right to reproduce his work and create adaptations (derivative works) from it. However, there is an important exception to this rule. A person who purchases a computer program has the right to copy or adapt the program if the copy or adaptation is either:

1. "an essential step in the utilization of the computer program in conjunction with a machine and that it is used in no other manner"—in other words, the purchaser has to adapt the program to get it to work on his computer; or

2. the copy or adaptation is for archival purposes only (a single back-up copy) and is made and kept only by the person who owns the legally purchased copy. (17 U.S.C. 117)

This limited right to make a back-up or archival copy is not really very generous. Since the copy is for back-up purposes only, it cannot be used on a second computer. This means, for example, that if you own a desktop computer and a laptop, and want to use your word processor on both, legally you must buy two copies. In an effort to make their customers happy, some large software publishers are now including provisions in their license agreements permitting their customers to use a program on two different computers. For example, Microsoft permits purchasers of many of its programs to use them on both office and home computers. (See Chapter 16.)

I. Copyright Formalities

There are certain simple technical formalities that must be attended to in order to obtain maximum copyright protection.

1. Copyright Notice

Before 1989, all published works had to contain a copyright notice (the © symbol followed by the publication date and copyright owner's name) to be protected by copyright. This is no longer true. Use of copyright notices is now optional. Even so, it is always a good idea to include a copyright notice on all works distributed to the public so that potential infringers will be informed of the underlying claim to copyright ownership.

Besides deterring potential infringers, inclusion of a copyright notice makes it impossible for an infringer to claim he or she didn't know the software was copyrighted; this may enable the copyright owner to obtain greater damages if a copyright infringement suit is brought.

It has never been necessary to include a copyright notice on unpublished works. A work is published for copyright purposes when copies are sold, rented, lent, given away or otherwise distributed to the public on an unrestricted basis. Software that is distributed to the public without a signed license agreement is normally considered published. Software that is under development or licensed to a limited number of users under a signed license agreement is usually considered unpublished. However, since unpublished copies of your work may receive limited distribution—to beta testers for example—it is a good idea to include a notice on them as well. (See Chapter 4.)

2. Registration

Copyright registration is a legal formality by which a copyright owner makes a public record in the U.S. Copyright Office in Washington, D.C., of some basic information about a copyrighted work, such as the title of the work, who wrote it and when, and who owns the copyright. When people speak of copyrighting a work, they usually mean registering it with the Copyright Office.

Contrary to what many people think, it is not necessary to register a work to create or establish a copyright in it. Copyright protection begins automatically the moment an original work of authorship is fixed in a tangible medium of expression. However, registration is required before a copyright owner may file a lawsuit to enforce his or her rights. In addition, timely registration in the U.S. Copyright Office—within three months of publication or before the infringement begins—makes a copyright a matter of public record and provides some very important advantages if it is ever necessary to go to court to enforce the copyright—for example, the court can order the infringer to pay your attorney fees. (See Chapter 4.)

J. Masks Used to Manufacture Computer Chips

Until 1985, a burning (and economically important) question was whether the intricate designs imposed on a computer chip in the form of masks were protectible as intellectual property—as an expression subject to the copyright laws or as a physical invention covered by the patent laws. Congress stepped in and passed the Semiconductor Chip Protection Act, a law that extends a type of copyright protection for a ten-year period to these designs (masks) and the three-dimensional templates (mask works) that are used to create them. To qualify for this protection, the mask or mask work must be truly original and independently created, and the owner of the mask or mask work must be:

- a U.S. national or resident on the date the work is registered with the U.S. Copyright Office or first commercially exploited anywhere in the world;
- a national or resident of a country that is a signatory to a mask work treaty;
- the owner of a mask or mask work that is commercially exploited in the U.S.; or
- an owner who is made subject to protection through presidential proclamation.

Because the creation of the mask works and masks used to manufacture integrated circuits involves a process costing many millions of dollars, it's likely that the creators have ample access to lawyers who specialize in this area. Accordingly, this book doesn't go further into this subject. If you want more information on protection of mask works and masks, short of visiting a lawyer, call the Copyright Office at 202-707-3000 for more information. ∎

Chapter 4

Copyright Registration and Notice

Part I. Copyright Registration

Part II. Software Copyright Notice

One of the great things about copyright protection is that it is free and begins automatically the moment you create a software product or other work of authorship. There is no need to go through a lengthy and expensive application process as is required for patent protection, or set up an elaborate regimen to establish and maintain trade secrecy.

However, there are two relatively simple and inexpensive copyright formalities that you can and should follow: registering your copyright with the Copyright Office and using a copyright notice on your published software. Both procedures are optional (although you must register before filing a copyright infringement lawsuit). But by adopting them you will obtain the maximum copyright protection available—that is, you will be in the strongest legal position you can be if you need to sue a pirate for copyright infringement. If your software is at all valuable, both formalities are well worth the minimal effort they involve.

Part I. Copyright Registration

Part I covers copyright registration—a legal formality by which a copyright owner makes a public record in the U.S. Copyright Office in Washington, D.C., of some basic information about a copyrighted work.

Where to Get Help

If you have difficulty understanding any aspect of the registration process, you can get help by calling the Copyright Office at 202-707-3000 between 8:30 a.m. and 5:00 p.m. eastern time, Monday through Friday. An Information Specialist will be available to give you advice on selecting the proper form, filling it out and making the required deposit. Copyright Office Information Specialists are very knowledgeable and helpful; however, they are not allowed to give legal advice. If you have a particularly complex problem that calls for interpretation of the copyright laws, consult a copyright attorney. (See Chapter 18.)

A. What is Copyright Registration?

When people speak of copyrighting software or other works, they usually mean registering them with the Copyright Office. To register, you fill out the appropriate pre-printed application form, which requires you to provide various information about your work, including:

- the title of the work
- who created the work and when, and
- who owns the copyright.

You then mail the completed application form and a small application fee to the

Copyright Office along with (depending on the type of work) one or two copies of all or part of the work. The Copyright Office reviews your application and then issues you a certificate of registration.

Contrary to what many people think, it is not necessary to register a work to create or establish a copyright in it. This is because an author's copyright comes into existence automatically the moment a work is fixed in tangible form. (See Chapter 3.) However, as discussed below, it is a good idea to register any work that may have commercial value.

B. Why Register?

Although registration is not required, there are several excellent reasons to register any valuable work.

1. Registration Is a Prerequisite to Filing an Infringement Suit

If you're an American citizen or legal resident and your software or other copyrighted work is first published in the United States (or simultaneously in the U.S. and another country), you may not file a copyright infringement suit in this country unless your work has been registered with the Copyright Office.

It's as simple as that. You legally own a copyright, whether you register or not, but you may not use the legal process to enforce your rights unless you've first followed the legal procedure for registration. This doesn't mean that infringers of unregistered copyrights can never be sued—you can register your copyright at any time and then sue.

You may be thinking, "Big deal, I'll register if and when someone infringes on my software and I need to file a lawsuit." If you adopt this strategy and someone infringes on your work, you'll probably end up having to register in a hurry so you can file suit quickly. You'll have to pay an extra $330 for such expedited registration. (See Section K.) Moreover, if there are problems completing and sending in the application or getting it approved by the Copyright Office, there could be a substantial delay before you can file your suit.

Works First Published Outside the United States

Copyright owners who are not U.S. citizens or legal residents and whose work is first published in foreign countries that are members of the Berne International Copyright Convention need not register to sue for infringement in the U.S. (See Chapter 10.) But, if they do register, noncitizens and nonresidents will obtain the important benefits discussed in this section.

2. Registration Protects Your Copyright by Making it a Public Record

When you register your copyright, it becomes a matter of official public record. In practical terms, this means:

- you're the presumed owner of the copyright in the material deposited with the registration, and
- the information contained in your copyright registration form is presumed to be true.

These legal presumptions are applied if you become involved in a court dispute. This does not mean that if you register you automatically win a copyright infringement case. Registration only causes the court to make these presumptions in the absence of proof to the contrary. In other words, if another author claims original authorship in a work that's identical or similar to yours, everything you state on your registration form, including the date you created your work, will be taken by the court as true unless the other author proves differently. However, you will still have to prove the other elements necessary to win a copyright infringement case—access to your work and substantial similarity—described in Chapter 5.

 Potential Problems Arising From Copyright Registration. Let's assume you're convinced that registration is wise. Before you register, you should know about a possible downside to making your work a public record by registering it with the U.S. Copyright Office: Your copyright application and at least some part of your work become available for public inspection when you register. Others will have the opportunity to examine your work. They can view everything you send to the Copyright Office, although they cannot normally make copies.

If making your material public in this way concerns you, make sure to read Section I. It addresses this concern in detail and suggests several practical ways to alleviate it. In most situations, the danger that copyright registration will leak your work to the public is usually more fanciful than real, assuming you take several routine self-protection steps described in Section I.

3. Timely Registration Makes it Easier to Win Money in Court

The benefits discussed in Section 2 above are available whenever you register. However, if you register either before an infringement of your work begins or within three months of publishing the work, you'll become entitled to two additional benefits if you sue an infringer and prevail in the case:

- the court can order the other side to pay your attorney fees and court costs, and
- you may elect to have the court award statutory damages (special damages of up to $100,000 per infringement) without having to establish what damage you actually suffered.

Details on how to fulfill the time limit requirements for registering a work are discussed in detail in Section C, below.

As a practical matter, the potential to recover attorney fees can determine whether you can afford to sue. In many copyright infringement cases, attorney fees exceed the potential benefits of winning the lawsuit. However, if your case is a strong one, the infringer has the apparent ability to pay and attorney fees can be collected because you promptly registered, a lawyer may well take your case for little or no money down and hope to collect from your opponent.

The ability to collect statutory damages is also a hugely important benefit. Proving a specific monetary loss can often be far more difficult than establishing that infringement occurred. With statutory damages, you don't need to prove the infringement caused you any monetary loss. If you've promptly registered your work, a judge may award from $250 to $100,000 in statutory damages, depending on the circumstances of the case. (See Chapter 5.) Either way, the possibility of statutory damages is a real incentive to register early.

EXAMPLE: AcmeSoft publishes a program called AcmeHTML, A full-featured, easy-to-use HTML editor. A former AcmeSoft programmer uses some of the code from AcmeSoft's program to help create a competing program published by ShadyWare. AcmeSoft easily proves in court that ShadyWare's program contains code copied from AcmeHTML. But when it comes to damages, AcmeSoft cannot show any direct losses caused by the copyright infringement. Sales of AcmeHTML remained about the same after the infringing program was published. For this reason, AcmeSoft elects to ask the judge to award it statutory damages. The judge decides to award $25,000, since she decides ShadyWare's copying was willful—that is, it knew the copying was wrong but did it anyway.

It may seem that all the benefits of prompt registration relate to litigation. You're also probably aware that the overwhelming majority of copyrights are never involved in a lawsuit. Why, then, should you go to the trouble of registering? The answer is that registration is a very inexpensive type of insurance. As with other forms of insurance, you buy protection against fairly unlikely occurrences, but occurrences that are so potentially devastating that you're willing to plan in advance to cushion their impact.

Timely registration may actually help keep you out of court because an infringer may be more willing to negotiate and settle your claim if he or she knows that you could recover substantial statutory damages in court. For example, ShadyWare in the example above might have elected to pay AcmeSoft a substantial sum to settle the case rather than facing a potentially hefty statutory damages award.

Since registration is very easy to accomplish, currently costs only $20 per work registered and provides significant benefits, it's one of the great insurance deals of all time.

Of course, no insurance, whether it consists of copyright registration or a more conventional variety, makes sense if what you're protecting has little or no value. Some published instruction materials, promotion copy and, occasionally even a program may have no realistic value to anyone but you. In this situation, placing a copyright notice on the material and not bothering to register may be a wise choice. You'll have to decide that question. However, in most situations, if your work is valuable enough to publish, it's valuable enough to register.

C. When to Register

A work may be registered at any time. However, to receive the benefit of statutory damages and attorney fees in infringement suits, copyright owners must register their works within the time periods prescribed by the Copyright Act. The time periods differ for published and unpublished works.

1. When to Register Published Works

The copyright owner of a published work is entitled to statutory damages and attorney fees only if the work is registered:

- within three months of the date of the first publication, or

- before the date the copyright infringement began.

A work is published for copyright purposes when copies are made available to the public on an unrestricted basis. Obviously, a software product is published when it is made available to the public in stores or by mail order. It's not entirely clear whether software distributed online is considered published. But, to be on the safe side, you should assume that it is. (See Chapter 3 for detailed discussion of what constitutes publication.)

It's important to get your work registered within the three-month postpublication period because many infringements begin shortly after publication.

2. When to Register Unpublished Works

If an unpublished program or other work is infringed upon, its author or other copyright owner is entitled to obtain statutory damages and attorney fees from the infringer only if the work was registered before the infringement occurred.

You cannot get around this requirement by publishing the work after the infringement has begun and then registering it within three months of the publication date. The three-month rule discussed in Section C1 just above, only applies to published works.

D. Who May Register

Any person or entity, such as a corporation or partnership, that owns all or part of the rights that make up a work's copyright may register that work, as can that owner's authorized agent (representative). This means registration may be accomplished by:

- the author or authors of a work
- anyone who has acquired one or more of an author's exclusive copyright rights, or
- the authorized agent of any of the above.

Ownership of copyrights is discussed in detail in Chapter 11. The following discussion briefly describes ownership solely for registration purposes.

1. Registration by a Work's Authors

Unless a work is a work made for hire (see Section b, below) the copyright initially belongs to whoever created it.

a. Individually authored works

The copyright in a work created by a single individual is owned by that individual (unless it was a work made for hire as discussed below). An individually authored work can be registered by the author or his or her authorized agent—that is, someone the author asks to register for him or her.

b. Works made for hire

A work created by an employee as part of his or her job is a work made for hire. For registration purposes, the author of a work made for hire is the creator's employer or other person for whom the work was prepared. The employer normally registers a work made for hire, not the employee-programmer.

> **EXAMPLE:** Bruno, Hilda, Eric, Hans, Gertrude and Heinrich are programmers employed by BigTech, Inc. Their latest project was creating an English-German translation program. The program is a work made for hire and should be registered by BigTech, their employer.

Certain types of works created by independent contractors—that is, nonemployees—can also be works made for hire. But this is so only if the contractor signs a work made for hire contract before the work is created and the work falls into one of the work made for hire categories enumerated in the Copyright Act. These categories include contributions to a collective work (a work created by more than one author), instructional texts, parts of an audiovisual work, translations and compilations.

> **EXAMPLE:** Heidi, a self-employed technical writer-translator, is hired by BigTech on a freelance basis to translate a computer manual into German. Before undertaking the work, she signs an agreement stating that her translation shall be a work made for hire owned by BigTech. The resulting manual is a work made for hire and should be registered by BigTech, the hiring party.

However, it is unclear whether software—that is, computer code itself—falls within any of the work made for hire categories. For this reason, persons who hire independent contractors to work on software should never rely on the work made for hire rule. Instead, they should have the independent contractor assign all copyright rights that the independent contractor might own to the hiring party. (See Chapter 11.) The hiring party can then register the software as a transferee as discussed in Section 2 below.

c. Joint works

If two or more persons jointly create a program or other protectible work with the intent that their contributions be combined into a single work, the work is called a joint work. A joint work is co-owned by its creators (unless it's a work made for hire), and can be registered by one, some or all of the authors or by their authorized agent.

(Again, for a detailed discussion of these categories, see Chapter 11.)

2. Registration by Publishers and Other Transferees

As discussed in Chapter 3, an author's copyright is really a bundle of separate exclusive rights. These exclusive rights include the right to reproduce, distribute and adapt a work. A copyright owner can sell or otherwise transfer all or part of his or her exclusive copyright rights. Indeed, this is usually how an author benefits economically from his or her work.

Persons or entities who obtain copyright rights from software authors (transferees) need to be concerned about the timing of the registration. If the work is not timely registered, (accomplished before an infringement begins or within three months of publication), they will not be entitled to obtain statutory damages and attorney fees if they successfully sue someone who infringes on the copyright.

Fortunately, transferees do not have to rely on authors to register. Anyone who obtains any of an author's exclusive rights is entitled to register the author's work. For example, if the exclusive right to publish a program were divided geographically and licensed to distributors in 18 states, there would be at least 18 persons or entities that could register the work.

Although a number of people may be entitled to register a work, normally only one registration is allowed for each version of a published work. It makes absolutely no difference who gets the job done. The single registration protects every copyright owner. It behooves a transferee to register a work immediately if the author has not already done so.

As a practical matter, registration is almost always accomplished by a work's creator or publisher. The publisher usually has a right to register either as an owner of all or some exclusive rights or as the creator's authorized agent.

In the software publishing business, it is common practice for authors to sign over all copyright rights to their publishers by contract. When this occurs, the publisher usually registers the copyright on its own behalf as the owner of these rights. Remember, however, that except for work made for hire situations, the author always has the original power to register, and should do so unless a publisher is already in the picture who will accomplish this.

Works Created by Independent Contractors

The copyright in a computer program created by an independent contractor generally is owned by the contractor, not the hiring party, unless the contractor transfers his or her ownership rights in the program to the hiring party. (See Chapter 11.) Absent such a transfer agreement, only the contractor would be entitled to register the program.

Other types of works created by independent contractors—for example, translations, contributions to collective works, audiovisual works, indexes—may be works made for hire if the contractor signs an agreement to that effect before the work is created. In these cases, the hiring party is deemed the author for registration (and all other) purposes and should register the work.

E. Registering All the Elements of a Single Software Package

Computer software is a multifaceted product that usually consists of several different works of authorship, including:

- computer code,
- documentation, and
- screen displays and other elements of the user interface.

Moreover, software is rarely one giant program, but is usually a system of modules, including screens, overlays, drivers, help files, config files and so forth. Many or even all of these modules and files may be able to stand on their own as independent works of authorship.

The question naturally arises: "Do I register each type of authorship separately or everything together at the same time?" Fortunately, the answer is that you usually register every element of a software package together on one application form for one fee, saving you both time and money.

A Copyright Office decision provides that "all copyrightable expression owned by the same claimant and embodied in a computer program, including computer screen displays, is considered a single work and should be registered on a single application form." (53 Fed.Reg. 21817 (June 10, 1988).)

In other words, you may register any number of separate works of authorship together on one registration application if:

- the copyright claimant is the same for all elements of the work for which copyright registration is sought, and

- all such elements are either unpublished or are published together as a single unit—that is, sold together in a single package.

1. The Copyright Claimant

Because the copyright claimant must be the same for all elements of the work being registered, you'll need to know who this is.

a. The creator

When a work is first created, it is owned by the original author—the creator or the original owner of a work made for hire. If the work is registered at this point, the author is the claimant.

> **EXAMPLE:** FrancoSoft publishes a French language instruction software package called Lingua Franca. All the elements of the software package—code, documentation, screens—were created by FrancoSoft employees or independent contractors who assigned all their copyright rights in the work to FrancoSoft. FrancoSoft is considered the author of this work made for hire. As such, it initially owns all the copyright rights in every element of Lingua Franca and is the copyright claimant for registration purposes. Assuming all the elements are sold together, the entire package can be registered by Franco-Soft on a single application.

b. Creator's transferee

However, authors are free to transfer all or part of their exclusive copyright rights to others. These exclusive rights are the right to copy, distribute, display, perform or create derivative works from an original work. When a software author transfers all of his or her exclusive copyright rights in one bundle to a single person or entity (the transferee), the transferee becomes the copyright claimant for registration purposes. Such a transferee must have a written transfer document from the author—for example, a software publishing agreement transferring the original author's "entire right, title and interest" in the software. (See Chapter 11.)

> **EXAMPLE:** AcmeSoft purchases all the copyright rights in a flowcharting program from DataDo. Since the program has not been registered by DataDo, AcmeSoft decides to register it. The entire software package can be registered on one application with AcmeSoft listed as the copyright claimant (owner of all the rights in the work).

c. Multiple claimants

Often an author transfers some of his or her copyright rights and retains others, or transfers some rights to one person or entity and others to another person or entity. This may occur where an author transfers fewer than all exclusive rights to a publisher, or where a person or entity that acquired all the author's rights transfers some, but not all, of the rights to a third party. In this event, nobody will own all the copyright rights. If the work hasn't been registered already, any person or entity that owns one or more exclusive rights in the work may register. (See Section D2 for a detailed discussion.) The original author is listed as the claimant on the application, even if someone else is registering the work. In effect, this means that the authors will always be listed as the copyright claimant unless somebody else ends up owning all the exclusive copyright rights before registration occurs.

> **EXAMPLE:** Assume that AcmeSoft purchases from DataDo in the above example only the exclusive right to distribute the flowcharting program on the Macintosh platform. AcmeSoft may still register the entire software package on one application (or DataDo may do so, it makes no difference who does; see Section D2 above). DataDo, the initial author of this work made for hire, would be listed as the claimant, since no single person or entity now owns all the rights in the program.

d. Works made for hire

In the case of a work made for hire, the author is the creator's employer, or person or entity for whom the work was created. This means the copyright claimant is either (1) the employer or hiring party; or (2) the person or entity to whom the employer or hiring party has transferred all of its exclusive rights in the work.

2. Registering Computer Screen Displays

Computer screen displays—the way a program looks on the computer screen— form an important part of a program's user interface, and as such are a very valuable component of any software package. Whether and to what extent user interfaces are protected by copyright has been the subject of much litigation and is still an unsettled question. (See Chapter 5.)

As discussed earlier in this section, it normally is not necessary to separately register computer screens. A single registration of the entire program will extend to the screen displays. The only exception is where the copyright claimant in the underlying program is different than the claimant for the displays —that is, where the code and displays are owned by different parties. In this event, separate registrations by each claimant are required. (See Section 1, above, for a discussion of identifying copyright claimants.)

Indeed, the Copyright Office takes the position that screen displays cannot be registered separately from a program itself where the displays and program are owned by the same copyright claimant.

Nevertheless, because computer screen displays are so valuable, some software publishers have sought to separately register them. Doubtless the primary motivation for this was to make it clear to the world that the displays were protected by copyright and thereby deter potential copiers and make it easier to win an infringement case. One well-known software publisher, the video game maker Atari, sued the Copyright Office when it refused to register the displays for a video game called Breakout as a separate audiovisual work. The court held that the game displays were copyrightable and should be registered by the Copyright Office. (*Atari Games Corp. v. Oman,* 979 F.2d 242 (D.C. Cir. 1992).)

However, it's rarely worth the trouble to separately register screen displays. If you want to make it clear your displays have been registered, simply mention the displays in the nature of authorship space on your one basic registration application. Also, include photos or other identifying material for them with your deposit as discussed in Section 15. This is not required, but will make it abundantly clear that your displays have been registered. Be aware, however, that this will probably delay approval of your application, because the copyright examiner will have to examine your identifying material to determine whether your computer screens are copyrightable.

3. Registering Documentation

Where documentation—such as manuals, user guides and tutorials—is sold along with a program as a single unit, the documentation can and should be registered along with the program on a single application. The only exception to this rule would be the unusual situation where the copy-right owner of the documentation is different from the copyright owner of the program.

Documentation published or distributed separately from the program it describes or supplements must be registered separately.

4. Registering Complex Computer Systems

Most modern sophisticated software packages consist of numerous subsystems or modules that can be considered independent works of authorship in their own right and that might be independently worth stealing. For example, a software package for designing Websites might, among other things, consist of an HTML editor, a Web graphics editing tool and a collection of Java applets.

Again, the Copyright Office's rule is that, if the various modules making up a computer system are all published for the first time in a single software package as an integrated unit, they should be registered together on one application form. The only exceptions are where:

- there are different copyright claimants for the various modules, or
- one or more of the modules have been previously published.

If any modules or subsystems of a program that is registered on one application are subsequently published or otherwise marketed independently, they can and should be separately registered.

5. How Many Times to Register

Subject to the exceptions noted below, a software package constituting a single integrated unit of publication (that is, all elements of the package are sold together) need be and can be registered only once.

a. Reregistering published works

A second registration may be made if the prior registration was unauthorized or legally invalid—for instance, where registration was effected by someone other than the author, owner of exclusive rights or an authorized representative.

If the facts stated in the registration application change after the work has been registered—for instance, the work's title is changed—corrections should be made on an application for supplemental registration filed with the Copyright Office. (See Section O.)

b. Unpublished works

A work originally registered as unpublished may be registered again after publication, even if the published and unpublished versions are identical. If they are identical, it is still a good idea to register the published version of a previously registered unpublished work. If you ever become involved in an infringement suit, it may be helpful to have the published version of the software on deposit with the Copyright Office—the deposit shows exactly what was published and the second registration establishes the date of publication, which may later aid you in proving that an infringer had access to your work. (See Chapter 5.)

F. Registering New Versions and Other Derivative Works

A derivative work is a work based upon or recast from preexisting material. (See Chapter 5.) To qualify for registration, the new material in a derivative work must be significant enough to constitute copyrightable authorship.

If you own the preexisting material and your alterations don't have independent value, there's no pressing reason to register. If, however, the derivative work involves a significant new and creative effort, as is often the case, registration is recommended.

> **EXAMPLE:** AcmeSoft first published a small business accounting program for the Macintosh in 1995. The program, called Bean Counter, was not a success and AcmeSoft withdrew it from the market in 1996. In 1998, AcmeSoft creates a new accounting program called AccountHelp using a substantial amount of Bean Counter in addition to much valuable new code. AccountHelp should be registered as a derivative work.

1. Registering New Versions of a Work

Computer software is never really finished; it is constantly being updated and otherwise revised and modified. A new version of a preexisting program is one type of derivative work.

Once you've registered a version of a software program, all material contained in that version is covered, regardless of how many new versions are produced. New material contained in new versions, however, is not covered.

If the changes are minor, or merely correct routine errors, registration is probably not necessary—and will not be allowed. This is particularly true where the changes are sprinkled here and there and do not make sense standing alone.

If, on the other hand, your changes are significant (say you issue a new release of your work containing literally hundreds of changes, because the old one is out-of-date or simply not up to speed), then you'll want to register the new release as a new version of the original. Examples of software modifications that can and should be registered include situations where:

- substantial new program code is added to a previously published program to enable it to accomplish new functions
- a previously published program is translated from one computer language to another
- a previously published program is adapted to run on a different model or brand of computer (as long as the changes are not functionally predetermined—that is, the basic software that is being changed was specifically designed to accommodate such changes).

Where modifications such as these are registered, the registration covers only the new material added to the preexisting software. Note carefully that under Copyright Office rules, registering a later version of the same software will not constitute registration of any earlier versions.

> **EXAMPLE:** MicroArt, Inc., creates a new computer graphics program called Draw All. MicroArt publishes versions 1.0 and 2.0 of the program without registering them with the Copyright Office. MicroArt then registers version 3.0. This registration covers only the copyrightable materials added to the program since the last published version of the work (version 2.0). Obviously, MicroArt needs to separately register versions 1.0 and 2.0 as well as 3.0.

2. Registering Software Under Development

You may, if you wish, register your unfinished software as it undergoes various stages of development. This may be useful if you're worried about others claiming you've copied from them. When you register your software, you deposit a copy of the work with the Copyright Office. (See Section I.) The deposit can help you show that your software was independently created, not copied from others.

G. Selecting the Appropriate Registration Form

The Copyright Office has developed several different preprinted registration forms used to register various types of works. But don't worry if you're not sure which form to use. The forms are virtually identical and the Copyright Office will accept your registration on either form.

1. Form TX

Software is usually registered on Form TX, the form used to register all types of writings and other literary works Software is classified as a literary work for registration purposes.

2. Form PA

Where pictorial or graphic authorship predominates, registration may be made on Form PA as an audiovisual work. If your registration consists primarily of display screens or other audiovisual elements, rather than computer code and documentation, you should use Form PA. An arcade game is a good example of a software work that would be registered on Form PA. Form PA is also normally used to register multimedia programs. (See Chapter 13.).

3. Short Forms TX and PA

The Copyright Office has created simplified versions of Forms TX and PA called Short Form TX and Short Form PA. These forms are only one page instead of two and are easier to complete than the regular Forms TX and PA. However, these forms may only be used if:

- there is only one author *and* copyright owner of the work
- the work was not made for hire—that is, was not created by employees or freelance programmers under a work for hire agreement (see Chapter 11), and
- the work is completely new—that is, does not contain a substantial amount of material that has been previously published or registered, or is in the public domain.

In addition, the short forms must be signed by the author personally—no one can sign on his or her behalf. This means, for example, that a software publisher may not sign the form on behalf of an author.

It's likely that relatively few computer programs will be eligible to be registered on the new short forms. Most software today is created by more than one person and is created by employees and freelancers. Such software does not qualify.

Short Forms TX and PA will most likely be used by hobbyists and others registering programs they've created themselves. Keep in mind, however, that the form may only be used for the first version of a work, not a revised or updated version.

4. Other Forms Not Used for Software

The Copyright Office has several other registration forms not used for software itself, but which may be used for software-related items. These include:

- **Form VA.** This form is used for pictorial, graphic and sculptural works, including photographs, maps, diagrams and technical diagrams. Form VA would be used, for example, to register a work consisting primarily of graphics-based flowcharts. Similarly, the owner of photos or other graphic elements licensed for use in a multimedia program would separately register them on Form VA. (See Chapter 13.)

- **Form SR.** This is the correct form to register phonograph records, tapes, CDs and other recorded music or sounds. Form SR should be used to separately register the sounds contained in a software program or to register a software instructional tape. If sounds are owned by the same copyright claimant as the computer program itself, a single registration on Form TX will register the sounds.

- **Form SE series.** There are several different Form SEs, which are used to register all types of serial publications, including magazines, newspapers, newsletters, journals and the like. One of the SE forms would be used to register a computer magazine, journal or newsletter. They are also be used to register a magazine, newsletter or similar publication distributed online.

For a detailed discussion of how to register all types of writings (other than software) refer to *The Copyright Handbook: How to Protect and Use Written Works*, by Stephen Fishman (Nolo Press).

5. Where to Obtain the Forms

Electronic copies of the Copyright Office application forms are contained on the CD-ROM disk under the following file names:

- **Form TX**: formtxi.pdf
- **Form PA:** formpai.pdf
- **Short Form TX:** formtxs.pdf
- **Short Form PA:** formpas.pdf
- **Form VA:** formvai.pdf
- **Short Form VA:** formvas.pdf
- **Form ___/CON:** formcon.pdf

You must print the forms out and then complete them by hand or typewriter. The forms are in Adobe Acrobat PDF format. You must have the Adobe Acrobat Reader installed on your computer to view and print the forms. A copy of the appropriate reader is included on the CD-ROM. (See Chapter 1.)

Electronic copies of the forms can also be downloaded from the Copyright Office's Internet site at http://lcweb.loc.gov/copyright.

You can obtain hardcopies of the forms by calling the Copyright Office. Call 202-707-9100 24 hours a day (you may have an easier time getting through at night). Leave your name, mailing address and identify the type of forms you need according to the class or title—for example, "Form TX." The Copyright Office will send up to ten copies of each form; specify how many you want.

The forms can also be obtained by writing to the Copyright Office at the following address:

Information and Publication Section
  LM-455
Copyright Office
Library of Congress
Washington, DC 20559

H. How to Fill Out Forms TX and PA

Forms TX and PA are virtually identical, except that Form TX has one additional space to be filled out. Step-by-step instructions are provided on how to fill out both forms. Each form consists of several numbered blank spaces calling for specific information.

Type your application form or use only black ink. When filling out the form, remember that it could end up being submitted in court to help prove your infringement case. If any part of it is inaccurate, your case could suffer—perhaps greatly. Moreover, a person who intentionally lies on a copyright registration application may be fined up to $2,500.

Space 1: Title Information

You must provide information about your work's title in Space 1.

Title of This Work

The Copyright Office uses the title for indexing and identifying your software. If your software has a title, fill in that wording. This should be the same title that appears on your deposit. (See Section O, below.) If your work is untitled, either state "untitled" or make a title up.

If the title includes a version number (such as, AccountHelper, Version 1.0) list it along with the title. Note carefully that under Copyright Office rules registering a later version of the same software will not constitute registration of any earlier versions.

> **EXAMPLE:** Microstuff, Inc., creates a small business accounting program called AccountHelper. Microstuff publishes versions 1.0 and 2.0 of the program without registering them with the Copyright Office. Microstuff then registers version 3.0. This registration covers only the copyrightable materials added to the program since the last published version of the work (version 2.0). Obviously, Microstuff also needs to separately register versions 1.0 and 2.0 as well.

Copyright Tip. Titles and other identifying phrases cannot be copyrighted. This means that registration will not prevent anyone from using the title to your work. You may, however, be able to protect titles under the trademark laws. (See Chapter 9.)

Previous or Alternative Titles

Provide additional titles under which someone searching for the registration might be likely to look, if any. You don't need to include additional titles known only to you or a few others, such as working titles.

If you're registering a new version of software under a new title that contains substantial new material, you don't need to list the old title here.

Space 2: Author Information

Here you must provide information about the work's author or authors. Space 2 is divided into three identical subspaces: "a," "b" and "c." Subspaces b and c are filled out only if there is more than one author.

Name of Author

Following is a brief review of who the author is for registration purposes. If you need still more information, reread Section D.

- **Works not made for hire:** Unless the work was made for hire, the person or people who created the work are the authors. Give the full name—full first, middle and last name—of the first (or only) author. (For use of anonymous or pseudonymous names, see below.)
- **Works made for hire:** Works made for hire were briefly defined in Section D1b. If the work to be registered is a work made for hire, the author for registration purposes is the employer or other person or entity for whom the work was prepared. The full legal name of the employer or commissioning party must be provided as the "Name of Author" instead of the name of the person who actually created the work.

> **EXAMPLE 1:** MicroJohnny, Inc., publishes a jury trial simulation game called Litigator. The program was created by

FORM TX

For a Literary Work
UNITED STATES COPYRIGHT OFFICE

REGISTRATION NUMBER

_____

TX _____ TXU _____
EFFECTIVE DATE OF REGISTRATION

_____

Month _____ Day _____ Year _____

DO NOT WRITE ABOVE THIS LINE. IF YOU NEED MORE SPACE, USE A SEPARATE CONTINUATION SHEET.

1

TITLE OF THIS WORK ▼

_____

PREVIOUS OR ALTERNATIVE TITLES ▼

_____

PUBLICATION AS A CONTRIBUTION If this work was published as a contribution to a periodical, serial, or collection, give information about the collective work in which the contribution appeared.   **Title of Collective Work ▼**

If published in a periodical or serial give: **Volume ▼**   **Number ▼**   **Issue Date ▼**   **On Pages ▼**

2   a

NAME OF AUTHOR ▼

DATES OF BIRTH AND DEATH
Year Born ▼   Year Died ▼

Was this contribution to the work a "work made for hire"?
☐ Yes
☐ No

AUTHOR'S NATIONALITY OR DOMICILE
Name of Country
OR { Citizen of ▶ _____
     { Domiciled in ▶ _____

WAS THIS AUTHOR'S CONTRIBUTION TO THE WORK
Anonymous?   ☐ Yes ☐ No
Pseudonymous?   ☐ Yes ☐ No
If the answer to either of these questions is "Yes," see detailed instructions.

NATURE OF AUTHORSHIP Briefly describe nature of material created by this author in which copyright is claimed. ▼

NOTE

Under the law, the "author" of a "work made for hire" is generally the employer, not the employee (see instructions). For any part of this work that was "made for hire" check "Yes" in the space provided, give the employer (or other person for whom the work was prepared) as "Author" of that part, and leave the space for dates of birth and death blank.

b

NAME OF AUTHOR ▼

DATES OF BIRTH AND DEATH
Year Born ▼   Year Died ▼

Was this contribution to the work a "work made for hire"?
☐ Yes
☐ No

AUTHOR'S NATIONALITY OR DOMICILE
Name of Country
OR { Citizen of ▶ _____
     { Domiciled in ▶ _____

WAS THIS AUTHOR'S CONTRIBUTION TO THE WORK
Anonymous?   ☐ Yes ☐ No
Pseudonymous?   ☐ Yes ☐ No
If the answer to either of these questions is "Yes," see detailed instructions.

NATURE OF AUTHORSHIP Briefly describe nature of material created by this author in which copyright is claimed. ▼

c

NAME OF AUTHOR ▼

DATES OF BIRTH AND DEATH
Year Born ▼   Year Died ▼

Was this contribution to the work a "work made for hire"?
☐ Yes
☐ No

AUTHOR'S NATIONALITY OR DOMICILE
Name of Country
OR { Citizen of ▶ _____
     { Domiciled in ▶ _____

WAS THIS AUTHOR'S CONTRIBUTION TO THE WORK
Anonymous?   ☐ Yes ☐ No
Pseudonymous?   ☐ Yes ☐ No
If the answer to either of these questions is "Yes," see detailed instructions.

NATURE OF AUTHORSHIP Briefly describe nature of material created by this author in which copyright is claimed. ▼

3   a

YEAR IN WHICH CREATION OF THIS WORK WAS COMPLETED   This information must be given in all cases.   ◀ Year

b
DATE AND NATION OF FIRST PUBLICATION OF THIS PARTICULAR WORK
Complete this information ONLY if this work has been published.
Month ▶ _____ Day ▶ _____ Year ▶ _____   ◀ Nation

4

COPYRIGHT CLAIMANT(S) Name and address must be given even if the claimant is the same as the author given in space 2. ▼

See instructions before completing this space.

TRANSFER If the claimant(s) named here in space 4 is (are) different from the author(s) named in space 2, give a brief statement of how the claimant(s) obtained ownership of the copyright. ▼

DO NOT WRITE HERE
OFFICE USE ONLY

APPLICATION RECEIVED

ONE DEPOSIT RECEIVED

TWO DEPOSITS RECEIVED

FUNDS RECEIVED

MORE ON BACK ▶   • Complete all applicable spaces (numbers 5-11) on the reverse side of this page.
• See detailed instructions.   • Sign the form at line 10.

DO NOT WRITE HERE

Page 1 of _____ pages

MicroJohnny employees within the scope of their employment. Micro-Johnny, Inc., should be listed in the "Name of Author" space.

EXAMPLE 2: Assume instead that MicroJohnny purchased all the copyright rights in Litigator from its creator, a self-employed programmer named Jane Milsap. Jane Milsap should be listed as the program's author, since it was not a work made for hire.

EXAMPLE 3: Assume instead that when Jane Milsap created Litigator she was employed by MicroGames, Inc., and that the game was originally a work made for hire owned by MicroGames. Micro-Johnny purchases all the rights in the game from MicroGames. Who should be listed as the author? MicroGames. The employer is the author of a work made for hire for copyright purposes. But a person or company that buys all the copyright rights in such a work for hire from the employer does not become the author (the new owner should just be listed as the copyright claimant in Space 4 below).

While not required, the name of the employee(s) who created a work made for hire may also be included if you want to make this part of the public record—for example: "MicroJohnny, Incorporated, employer for hire of Ken Grant, Jack Aubrey, Mona Wildman and Jane Kendall."

Copyright Tip. Don't guess about the full legal name of a corporation, partnership or other entity. Find out the organization's full legal name and use it. For example, do not state "ASC, Inc." when the full legal name is Acme Software Company, Incorporated. The full legal name may be found on the entity's organizing document, such as the articles of incorporation, partnership agreement or registration certificate filed with the appropriate state filing office (often called the Secretary of State).

Anonymous or Pseudonymous Authors

A work is anonymous if the author or authors are not identified on the published copies of the work. A work is pseudonymous if the author is identified under a fictitious name (pen name).

If the work is published as an anonymous work, you may:
- leave the Name of Author line blank (or state "N/A" for not applicable),
- state "anonymous" on the line, or
- reveal the author's identity.

If the work is pseudonymous, you may:
- leave the line blank,
- give the pseudonym and identify it as such—for instance, "Nick Danger, pseudonym," or
- reveal the author's name, making it clear which is the real name and which is the pseudonym—for example, "Harold Lipshitz, whose pseudonym is Nick Danger."

Of course, if the author's identity is revealed on the application, it will be a simple matter for others to discover it, because the application becomes a public document available for inspection at the Copyright Office.

Dates of Birth and Death

If the author is a human being, his or her year of birth may be provided here, but this is not required (the birth year is used for identification purposes). However, if the author has died, the year of death must be listed unless the author was anonymous or pseudonymous. This date will determine when the copyright expires (50 years after the author's death).

Leave this space blank if the author is a corporation, partnership or other organization. Corporations, partnerships and other business entities do not "die" for copyright purposes, even if they dissolve.

Was this contribution to the work a "work made for hire"?

Check the "Yes" box if the author is the owner of a work made for hire. Always check this box where the author is a corporation, partnership or other organization.

Author's Nationality or Domicile

This information must always be provided, even if the author is a business, is anonymous or used a pseudonym.

If the work is a work made for hire and the author is a corporation, partnership or other entity, state the country where the business has its principal office or headquarters. If this is anywhere in the U.S., simply state "U.S.A."

If the author is a person, his citizenship (nationality) and domicile could be different. An author's domicile generally is the country where she maintains her principal residence and where she intends to remain indefinitely. An author is a citizen of the country in which she was born or moved to and became a citizen of by complying with its naturalization requirements.

> **EXAMPLE:** Evelyn is a Canadian citizen, but she has permanent resident status and has lived year-round in Boston since 1990 and intends to remain there for the indefinite future. She is domiciled in the United States. She can state "Canada" in the citizenship blank or "U.S.A." in the domicile blank.

Was This Author's Contribution to the Work Anonymous or Pseudonymous?

Check the "Yes" box if the author is anonymous or used a pseudonym as described above. Check the "No" boxes if the author is identified by her correct name. Don't check either box if the work was made for hire.

Nature of Authorship

You must give a brief general description of the nature of the author's contribution to the work. This is the most important box on the registration form. What you put in this box will determine whether your registration sails through without incident or whether you're in for a round of correspondence. The Copyright Office primarily relies on this box to determine whether your work is deserving of registration under the copyright laws.

The Copyright Office maintains a manual for use by its examiners containing specific words and phrases that are, and are not, acceptable to describe the nature of the authorship. The main idea underlying these guidelines is that some descriptions adequately describe a work as something subject to copyright protection while others don't. The advice below is based on these internal Copyright Office guidelines

What you put on the Nature of Authorship line will vary most depending on whether this is:

- your first registration for an original work (discussed under "How to Describe Original Works," just below), or
- a registration for a new version of a previously published work or a derivative work (discussed below under "How to Describe New Versions and Other Derivative Works").

How to Describe Original Works

Most computer programs or code can be described using general descriptive terms such as "entire text of computer program." The Copyright Office takes the view that this simple phrase registers every aspect of the program that is within the scope of copyright protection, including screen displays.

Other terms the Copyright Office will accept include:

- "program listing"
- "computer program code"
- "program text and screen displays"
- "program text"
- "computer software"
- "routine"
- "entire program"
- "entire program code"
- "software"
- "entire text"
- "subroutine"
- "entire work"
- "module"
- "text of program"
- "program instructions"
- "wrote program."

If documentation is included with the program registration (which is only appropriate if all items are published as one unit—see Section E) you should add:

- "with users' manual," or
- "entire text of computer program with accompanying documentation."

Pick a term that accurately describes your work. If your deposit doesn't match the descriptive term you choose, you'll get a letter asking for clarification and your registration will accordingly be delayed.

Unacceptable Terms. Here is a listing of terms that will cause the Copyright Office to bounce your registration back for another try:

- "algorithm"
- "analysis"

- "cassette"
- "chip"
- "computer game"
- "disk"
- "encrypting"
- "eprom"
- "firmware"
- "format"
- "formatting"
- "functions"
- "language"
- "logic"
- "menu screen"
- "mnemonics"
- "printout"
- "programmer"
- "prom"
- "rom"

- "software methodology"
- "structure"
- "sequence"
- "organization"
- "system"
- "system design"
- "text of algorithm."

Should you mention computer display screens in the nature of authorship statement? As noted above, a simple statement in the nature of authorship space like "entire text of computer program" or "entire work" will cover any copyrightable computer screen displays included in the work. It is not necessary to separately mention the displays; however, it is permissible to do so. But if you do, there are two consequences:

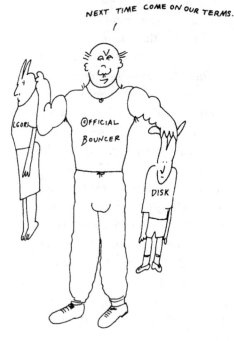

A BUNCH OF UNACCEPTABLE TERMS

- You will have to deposit identifying materials for the screen displays with your application (that is, photos, drawings or printouts clearly revealing the screens; see Section I5).
- The Copyright Office examiner will look at the identifying material to see if it is copyrightable (which will probably delay approval of your application).

If the examiner determines that the displays are not copyrightable, a letter to this effect will be sent to you and placed in the file for your application. The existence of such a letter could have a deleterious effect on any subsequent copyright infringement suit regarding the displays.

Clearly, then, you should never mention screen displays in the nature of authorship space if your displays are essentially not copyrightable. The Copyright Office has expressed the view that menu screens and similar functional interfaces consisting of words or brief phrases in a particular format generally are not registrable. (See Chapter 5.)

On the other hand, if you are certain that your computer screens are copyrightable and you are really want to protect the look and feel of your screen design, you may wish to indicate that screen displays are part of your authorship and deposit identifying material for the screens with your program code. Although this is not required, it will make it clear that both you and the Copyright Office thought your screens were copyrighted. This could deter a potential infringer and might help in any infringement litigation.

In this event, you should state "entire text of computer program and screen displays" in the Nature of Authorship space; or, if you are also registering documentation, state "entire text of computer program and screen displays with user documentation."

Another approach is to include identifying material for your screen displays but *not* to mention them in your nature of authorship statement. Instead, simply say "entire work," "computer program" or "all." When you do this, the copyright examiner will not examine the displays to see if they are copyrightable. The screens will ride along with the code without comment by the Copyright Office. This has the advantage of avoiding having approval of your application delayed. The disadvantage, however, is that you won't get a determination by the Copyright Office that your screens are copyrightable. But at least they will remain on record with the Copyright Office as part of your deposit.

How to Describe New Versions and Other Derivative Works

If you're registering a new version or other derivative work (see Section F), you have more to consider in explaining your "Nature of Authorship" under Space 2.

To be eligible for separate registration, a work based on a prior work must involve enough changes in the prior work to be separately copyrightable. The Copyright Office uses the term *de minimis* to describe works (or changes in existing works) that aren't significant enough to warrant a separate copyright registration. This concept applies whether or not the whole work is registered as a derivative work or the changes are registered separately, as might be the case if whole new sections of code added to an existing program are able to stand on their own.

If the new material you wish to register consists of changes in or revisions to a prior program, you must use very precise language. Your registration should sail through if you describe the nature of the new material as:

- "editorial revisions"
- "revised revisions of [name of program]"
- "computer program"
- "text of program"
- "programming text"
- "program listing"
- "program instructions"
- "text of computer game"
- "module"
- "routine"
- "subroutine"
- "additional program text and extensively modified text"
- "wrote program."

EXAMPLE: MicroJohnny, Inc., issues a new release of its Litigator game program, which it originally registered as one package. MicroJohnny adds three new programs and modifies four others substantially. In the Nature of Authorship box, it states "additional program text and extensively modified text." MicroJohnny's registration is quickly approved.

 Functionally Predetermined Changes Are Not Registrable. If you state "error corrections," "debugging," "patching," "features," or "enhancements" in the Nature of Authorship box you'll receive a letter from the Copyright Office requesting that you either submit a new application with a better statement of authorship, or abandon your registration by notifying them that the changes are too minor or "functionally predetermined" to warrant registration as an original work of authorship.

Functionally predetermined means the basic software that is being changed has been specifically designed to accommodate such changes. For example, many operating systems and applications software are deliberately made to easily accept preplanned changes (patches) that will permit them to compatibly operate with a number of different central processors (i.e., boards or chips). When such patches are made, they're considered functionally predetermined and ordinarily don't either alter the work or stand by themselves sufficiently to warrant a new registration.

Translation Note

Programs that are significantly adapted or translated to another computer language are usually considered to be a derivative work and registrable as such. In this situation, to correctly describe what is going on in the Nature of Authorship box, you need to include the name of the language into which the work has been translated. Thus "translation to C++" is deemed sufficient, while "translation" by itself is not. If, however, it appears to the Copyright Office that your translation really only enables the preexisting program to operate on a different machine without the need for a different language, your registration may or may not be approved as a new version, depending on the magnitude of the changes.

For example, if you simply change some of the initial commands to the computer and make a few minor format changes to enable an already registered program to run on different hardware, the Copyright Office will usually consider this to be de minimis, and thus not registrable. (This would also be an example of a functionally predefined modification described in the sidebar above.)

Information for Additional Authors

If there are two or three authors, go back now and fill in subspaces 2b and 2c for each of them using the above discussion as a guide. Space 2 only has enough subspaces for three authors. If the work you're registering has more than three authors, provide the required information for all the additional authors on a Copyright Office "Continuation Sheet" and clip (do not tape or staple) it to your application.

 A copy of a Continuation Sheet can be found on the CD-ROM forms disk under the file name formcon.pdf. See Chapter 1 for guidance about how to use the disk.

Space 3: Relevant Dates

Year in Which Creation of This Work Was Completed

Fill in the year in which the work you're registering first became fixed in its final form, disregarding minor changes. This year has nothing to do with publication, which may occur long after creation. Deciding what constitutes the year of creation may prove difficult if the work was created over a long period of time. Give the year in which the author(s) completed the particular version of the work for which registration is now being sought, even if other versions exist or further changes or additions are planned.

Date and Nation of First Publication of This Particular Work

Leave this blank if an unpublished work is being registered. Publication occurs for copyright purposes when a work is made widely available to the public. (See Chapter 3.) Give only one date, listing the month, day, year and country where publication first occurred. If you're not sure of the exact publication date, state your best guess and make clear it is approximate—for example, "November, 15, 199X (approx.)." If publication took place simultaneously in the United States and one or more foreign countries, you can just state "U.S.A." Make sure the publication date you list is for the version of the software being registered, not for some previous version.

If the software is being distributed online, it's up to you to decide whether it is published or not. The Copyright Office will not second-guess you on this.

The nation of publication for a work distributed online is either the nation from which the work is uploaded or the nation containing the server where the work is located. Use the name of a real country such as U.S.A. or Canada. Don't use non-specific terms such as "global," "worldwide" or "Internet" in the nation of publication space.

Space 4: Information About Copyright Claimants

Copyright Claimants

Provide the name and address of each copyright claimant, which must be:

- the author or authors of the work (including the owner of a work made for hire, if applicable), or
- persons or organizations that have, on or before the date the application is filed, obtained in writing ownership of all the exclusive United States copyright rights that initially belonged to the author, or
- persons or organizations that the author or owner of all U.S. copyright rights has authorized by contract to act as the claimant for copyright registration (there is no legal requirement that such contract be in writing, but it's not a bad idea). (37 C.F.R. 202.3(a)(3) (1984).)

(See Section E1 above for a detailed discussion of who qualifies as the copyright claimant.)

A copyright claimant must be listed even for anonymous or pseudonymous works. You can provide the claimant's real name alone, the real name and the pseudonym, the pseudonym alone if the claimant is generally known by it or, if the claimant wishes to remain anonymous, the name of the claimant's authorized agent.

Copyright Tip. When the name listed for the claimant is different than the name of the author given in space 2, but the two names identify one person, explain the relationship between the two names.

EXAMPLE: John Smith is the author of the work he is registering, but all of the copyright rights have been transferred to his corporation, Smith Software Publishing Company, Inc., of which Smith is the sole owner. Smith should not just state Smith Software Publishing Company, Inc. Rather, he needs to explain the relationship between himself and his company claimant—for example, "Smith Software Publishing Company, Inc., solely owned by John Smith."

Transfers

If the copyright claimant named just above is not the author or authors named in Space 2, give a brief general description of how ownership of the copyright was obtained. However, do not attach any transfer documents to the application. If there is not enough space to list all the claimants on Form TX, you can list additional claimants on the reverse side of Form/CON.

This statement must indicate that all the author's United States copyright rights have been transferred by a written agreement or by operation of law. Examples of acceptable transfer statements include: "By written contract," "Transfer of all rights by author," "By will," "By inheritance," "Assignment," "By gift agreement."

 Copyright Tip. Note that the transfers space is used only to inform the Copyright Office about transfers that occurred *before* registration. If a copyright is transferred after registration, there is no need to reregister (indeed, it is not permitted). However, although not required, it is a good idea to record (send) a copy of the post-registration transfer document to the Copyright Office. (See Chapter 11.)

If the author or owner of all rights has authorized another person or organization to act as the claimant, this should be indicated by including language like the following: "Pursuant to the contractual right from [author or owner of all U.S. copyright rights] to claim legal title to the copyright in an application for copyright registration."

Space 5: Previous Registration

If none of the material in the work you're registering has been registered before, check the "No" box and skip ahead to Space 6.

If all or part of the work has been previously registered, check the "Yes" box. Then, you need to check one or more of the next three boxes to explain why a new registration is being sought:

- Check the first box if you are now registering a work you previously registered when it was unpublished.
- Check the second box if someone other than the author was listed as the copyright claimant in Space 4 in the prior registration, and the author is now registering the work in her own name. For example, where an anonymous or pseudonymous author previously listed an authorized agent in Space 4 and now wishes to re-register in her own name.
- Check the third box if the previously registered work has been changed, and you are registering the changed version or new edition to protect the additions or revisions.

EXAMINED BY	FORM TX
CHECKED BY	
☐ CORRESPONDENCE Yes	FOR COPYRIGHT OFFICE USE ONLY

DO NOT WRITE ABOVE THIS LINE. IF YOU NEED MORE SPACE, USE A SEPARATE CONTINUATION SHEET.

PREVIOUS REGISTRATION Has registration for this work, or for an earlier version of this work, already been made in the Copyright Office?

☐ Yes ☐ No If your answer is "Yes," why is another registration being sought? (Check appropriate box) ▼

a. ☐ This is the first published edition of a work previously registered in unpublished form.

b. ☐ This is the first application submitted by this author as copyright claimant.

c. ☐ This is a changed version of the work, as shown by space 6 on this application.

If your answer is "Yes," give: **Previous Registration Number** ▼   **Year of Registration** ▼

5

DERIVATIVE WORK OR COMPILATION Complete both space 6a and 6b for a derivative work; complete only 6b for a compilation.
a. **Preexisting Material** Identify any preexisting work or works that this work is based on or incorporates. ▼

b. **Material Added to This Work** Give a brief, general statement of the material that has been added to this work and in which copyright is claimed. ▼

6

See instructions
before completing
this space.

—space deleted—

7

REPRODUCTION FOR USE OF BLIND OR PHYSICALLY HANDICAPPED INDIVIDUALS A signature on this form at space 10 and a check in one of the boxes here in space 8 constitutes a non-exclusive grant of permission to the Library of Congress to reproduce and distribute solely for the blind and physically handicapped and under the conditions and limitations prescribed by the regulations of the Copyright Office: (1) copies of the work identified in space 1 of this application in Braille (or similar tactile symbols); or (2) phonorecords embodying a fixation of a reading of that work; or (3) both.

a ☐ Copies and Phonorecords   b ☐ Copies Only   c ☐ Phonorecords Only

8

See instructions.

DEPOSIT ACCOUNT If the registration fee is to be charged to a Deposit Account established in the Copyright Office, give name and number of Account.
Name ▼   **Account Number** ▼

9

CORRESPONDENCE Give name and address to which correspondence about this application should be sent.   Name/Address/Apt/City/State/ZIP ▼

Area Code and Telephone Number ▶

Be sure to
give your
daytime phone
◀ number

CERTIFICATION* I, the undersigned, hereby certify that I am the

Check only one ▶ {
☐ author
☐ other copyright claimant
☐ owner of exclusive right(s)
☐ authorized agent of _____

of the work identified in this application and that the statements made
by me in this application are correct to the best of my knowledge.

Name of author or other copyright claimant, or owner of exclusive right(s) ▲

10

Typed or printed name and date ▼ If this application gives a date of publication in space 3, do not sign and submit it before that date.

Date ▶ _____

☞ Handwritten signature (X) ▼

MAIL CERTIFI- CATE TO	Name ▼	YOU MUST: • Complete all necessary spaces • Sign your application in space 10

	Number/Street/Apt ▼	SEND ALL 3 ELEMENTS
		IN THE SAME PACKAGE:
		1. Application form
		2. Nonrefundable $20 filing fee
		   in check or money order
		   payable to *Register of Copyrights*
		3. Deposit material

Certificate will be mailed in window envelope	City/State/ZIP ▼	MAIL TO: Register of Copyrights Library of Congress Washington, D.C. 20559-6000

11

*17 U.S.C. § 506(e): Any person who knowingly makes a false representation of a material fact in the application for copyright registration provided for by section 409, or in any written statement filed in connection with the application, shall be fined not more than $2,500.

May 1995—300,000

✩U.S. COPYRIGHT OFFICE WWW FORM: 1995

Then provide the registration number and year of previous registration in the blanks indicated. The registration number can be found stamped on the certificate of registration. It is usually a multi-digit number preceded by the two-letter prefix of the application form used—for example: TX 012345. The Copyright Office places a small "u" following the prefix if the registered work is unpublished—for example: TXu 567890. If you made more than one prior registration for the work, you only need to give the latest registration number and year.

Space 6: Description of Derivative Works or Compilations

You'll usually need to complete Space 6 if your software is:

- a derivative work—that is, a work based upon or derived from one or more preexisting works
- a changed version of another work (this is really just one type of derivative work), or
- a compilation of preexisting works— that is, a work created by selecting, arranging and coordinating preexisting materials into a new work of authorship.

(Derivative works are discussed in detail in Chapter 5. Compilations are discussed in Chapter 12.)

You'll need to complete Space 6 only if the software or other work being registered contains a substantial amount of material (such as subroutines, modules or textual images) that was:

- previously published,
- previously registered, or
- in the public domain.

Preexisting Material (6a):

If your software is a derivative work and the preexisting material was substantial, you must generally describe the preexisting material here. You can simply state "previous version"; you need not provide any more detail. If the derivative work was based on a series of preexisting works, it is not necessary to list every one.

Don't fill out Space 6a if the software is a compilation.

Material Added to This Work (6b): Describe the new "protectible" material you are registering.

Typical examples of descriptions of new material for derivative works in Space 6b include "revised computer program," "editorial revisions," and "revisions and additional text of computer program." Often, you can simply repeat what you stated in the Nature of Authorship line in Space 2.

EXAMPLE: AcmeSoft created and registered version 1.0 of a database program in 1997. AcmeSoft later thoroughly revises the software, adding many new features and redesigning the user interface. This new version 2.0 is published in 1998. AcmeSoft should state "revised computer program" in Space 6b when it registers version 2.0.

As mentioned earlier, you shouldn't use words such as "enhancements," "error corrections," "patches," "features," or "debugging." This is because the Copyright Office tends to rule that these types of changes aren't significant enough to warrant another registration.

If the work is a compilation, the statement should describe both the compilation itself and the material that has been compiled.

> EXAMPLE: Internet Magazine compiles a number of previously published and public domain Java applets onto a disk. It should state in Space 6b: "Compilation of Java applets and text."

If your software is both a derivative work and compilation, you may state "Compilation and additional new material."

> EXAMPLE: Internet Magazine in the example above not only compiles pre-existing Java applets, but has its staff create a number of new applets as well. It could state in Space 6b: "Compilation and additional new material (programming and text)."

If the preexisting material in your work is not substantial or was not published, registered or in the public domain, put "N/A" in Space 6.

> EXAMPLE 1: You would not need to complete Space 6 for a computer program entitled "X-103 Program, Version 3," incorporating material from two earlier developmental versions that were unpublished and unregistered.

> EXAMPLE 2: You would not be required to complete Space 6 for a program containing a total of 5,000 lines of program text, only 50 of which were previously published.

There are two situations where you should provide an explanatory cover letter to the Copyright Office if you don't complete Space 6:

- the title of your work contains a version number other than 1 or 1.0, or
- the deposit for the software has a copyright notice containing multiple year dates.

In either case, the examiner will question (by letter or phone) whether the program is a revised or derivative version if Space 6 has not been completed.

If the software is not a derivative work and the version number or multiple year dates in the copyright notice on the deposit refer to internal revisions or the history of development of the program, put that information in a cover letter to the Copyright Office to help speedup processing.

> EXAMPLE: PubSoft developed a desktop publishing program called Practical Publisher over a number of years. It produced several versions of the program that it used for internal testing and development only. The final published

version of the program PubSoft registers in 1998 has a copyright notice that says "Copyright © 1996, 1997, 1998 by PubSoft, Inc." Although it was not required (see Section R2), PubSoft included the multiple year dates in the notice to make clear the copyright covers the earlier versions. PubSoft should include a letter such as the following with its registration application:

Register of Copyrights
Library of Congress
Washington, DC 20559

Dear Register:

Enclosed is a copyright registration application for Practical Publisher 1.0 submitted by PubSoft, Inc.

Please note that the deposit material for the program contains a copyright notice with multiple-year dates.

Practical Publisher 1.0 is not a derivative work or revised version for registration purposes. The multiple-year dates in the copyright notice refer to internal revisions that have not been published or registered.

I certify that the statements made in this letter are true.

Very truly yours,

Keith Stoke

Software Development Manager

Space 7 on Form TX

If you're filling out Form TX, skip this space. If you're filling out Form PA, skip to the instructions for Space 9, below.

Space 8 on Form TX: License for Handicapped

If you're using Form PA, instructions for Space 8 are covered below under Space 10.

The Library of Congress produces and distributes braille editions and recorded readings of registered works for the exclusive use of the blind and physically handicapped. Of course, this license doesn't apply to computer programs or any other machine-readable work, only printed text such as computer manuals and other written works.

If you wish to grant the library a license to copy and/or record your work for this purpose, check one of the boxes: a, for copies and phonorecords; b, for copies only; or c, for phonorecords. Most applicants give the blind and disabled a break and check one of these boxes.

Only a person who owns the right to reproduce and publish the work being registered can grant this license to the Library of Congress. If you're a transferee of one or more exclusive rights, but you don't own the right to reproduce and publish the work, skip this item completely.

The license is entirely voluntary and nonexclusive. You can terminate the license at any time by sending a written notice to the National Library Service for the Blind and Physically Handicapped (NLS), Library of

Congress, 1291 Taylor Street NW, Washington. DC 20542.

Space 9 on Form TX (Space 7 on Form PA): Deposit Account and Correspondence

Deposit Account.

If you plan to have 12 or more transactions per year with the Copyright Office, you may establish a money deposit account to which you make advance money deposits and charge your copyright fees against the account instead of sending a separate check each time. You must deposit at least $250 to open an account. For an application, obtain Circular R5 from the Copyright Office by calling 202-707-9100 or by downloading it from the Copyright Office Website at http://lcweb.loc.gov/copyright.

If you already have a deposit account and wish to charge the registration fee to the account, state the account name and number.

Correspondence

Provide the name, address, area code and telephone number of the person the Copyright Office should contact if it has questions about your application. If the registration is being made by a corporation or other entity, list the name of the person in the organization who should be contacted. The Copyright Office makes calls between 8:00 a.m. and 5:00 p.m. eastern time; so give the number or numbers where the contact person can be reached at these times.

If you have a fax number, include that along with your regular phone number (remember to specify which is a fax). The Copyright Office may soon start corresponding by fax.

Space 10 on Form TX (Space 8 on Form PA): Certification

Check the appropriate box indicating your capacity as the person registering the work:

- Check the Author box if you are the person (or one of several people) named in Space 2. If there are several authors, only one need sign.
- Check the Other Copyright Claimant box if you are not named in Space 2 as the author, but have acquired all the author's rights.
- Check the Owner of Exclusive Right(s) box if you only own one or more—but not all—of the exclusive rights making up the entire copyright.
- Check the Authorized Agent of box if you are not signing for yourself as an individual, but as the authorized representative of the author, the copyright claimant who owns all the copyright rights or the owner of some exclusive rights. State the name of the person or organization on whose behalf you're signing on the dotted line following the box.

Copyright Tip. Check the Authorized Agent box if you, as an individual, are signing on behalf of a corporation, partnership or other organization that is the author, copyright claimant or holder of exclusive rights.

Type or print your name and date in the appropriate blanks, then sign your name on the line following "Handwritten signature."

⚠ **Watch Your Dates.** If you are registering a published work, the Copyright Office will not accept your application if the date listed in the certification space is earlier than the date of publication shown in Space 3.

Space 11 on Form TX (Space 9 on Form PA): Return Mailing Address

Fill in your name and the return mailing address for your copyright registration certificate in the last box on the form. Make sure the address is legible, since the certificate will be returned to you in a window envelope.

Now that you've completed the form, you'll need to prepare your deposit, covered in Section I, just below.

I. Complying With Copyright Deposit Requirements

To register your work with the U.S. Copyright Office, you're required to submit (deposit) one or two copies of the work itself. When it comes to the registration of long programs, Copyright Office rules usually allow you to send a portion of the work instead of the whole thing.

Deposit requirements serve three primary functions:

- Deposits show the Copyright Office that your work is eligible for copyright protection (that it is an original work of authorship).
- Deposits show the Copyright Office that your work is adequately described on your application form.
- Deposits serve as an identifier for your work in the event a dispute arises involving your copyright.

Except where the software is embodied on a CD-ROM disk (see Section 4 below), you may not deposit floppy disks or other magnetic media (or computer chips in the case of firmware). Rather, the Copyright Office wants a hard-copy printout of all or part of your code. There are four alternative types of deposits for you to choose from:

- a printout of all or part of your software source code (Section 1, below)
- a copy of part of the source code with any trade secrets blacked out so no one can read them (Section 2, below)
- a combination of source code and object code (Section 2, below), or
- object code only (Section 3, below).

These requirements are the same however software is distributed—whether in stores, by mail order or online over the Internet, commercial online services or BBS's. However, there are special requirements when software is contained on a CD-ROM.

Please read this entire section through at least once before making a decision as to what you wish to deposit. This material is potentially confusing, and you may well find yourself changing your mind several times.

1. Depositing Straight Source Code

Your first alternative is to deposit all or part of your program source code—that is, the computer program instructional code that the programmer writes using a particular programming language such as C++ or Java.

This is what most people do and what the Copyright Office prefers. The advantage to depositing source code is that it better identifies the nature of your original work of authorship than does object code.

Should you end up in litigation over your copyright, you'll want the best possible proof of the exact code you have copyrighted. A source code deposit may make it easier to prove copyright infringement.

Depositing your source code serves to register your object code as well even though the object code is not deposited. (*CGA Corp. v. Chance,* 217 U.S.P.Q. 718 (N.D. CA 1982).)

Under Copyright Office regulations (37 C.F.R. 202.70), you generally don't have to deposit your entire program source code. This is fortunate, both from your standpoint and the Copyright Office's, since programs are often lengthy.

To satisfy the deposit requirement for program source code, you must deposit either:

- the entire program source code if the source code is no more than 50 pages, or
- if the source code is longer than 50 printed-out pages, the first and last 25 pages.

A page isn't precisely defined, but in practice, standard 8½-inch by 11-inch paper is most often used.

There are no requirements as to the format or spacing of the code—that is, it may be single- or double-spaced.

As an alternative to a printout, you may deposit a microfiche of the identifying material. If you do this, deposit the entire program code or, if it's longer than 50 pages, microfiche the first and last 25 pages.

If the code contains a copyright notice, you must include the page or equivalent unit containing the notice. A photograph or drawing showing the form and location of the notice is acceptable. Whatever you do, it's always a good idea to sprinkle many copyright notices throughout the code.

If the deposit material does not give a printed title and/or version indicator, add the title and any indicia that can be used to identify the particular program.

Deposits and Trade Secrets

If you deposit the first and last 25 pages of your source code, you may wish to arrange the source code modules so that the most innovative and/or secret portions of the code do not appear in the first or last 25 pages. Copyright Office rules do not prevent this. You may also take out any comment statements that might help an infringer. The downside to this is that your deposit may not provide the best possible evidence of your work to prove copyright infringement. So there is a trade-off involved.

a. Revised programs

If the program you're registering is a revision of a previously registered program, and the revisions are uniformly (more or less) spread throughout the program, deposit the first and last 25 pages as indicated above and the page containing the copyright notice, if any.

If, on the other hand, the revisions are concentrated in a part of the program that isn't fairly represented by the first and last 25 pages requirement, you may deposit any 50 pages that are representative of the revised material in the new program together with the page containing the copyright notice.

b. Programs created in scripted language

For programs created in scripted language such as Hypercard, Supercard and Java-Script, the script is considered the equivalent of source code. Thus, the same number of pages of script are required as are required for source code.

2. Depositing Source Code with Trade Secrets Blacked Out or Depositing Source Code and Object Code

As discussed in Chapter 6, trade secret protection can be used in conjunction with copyright protection to protect the ideas, concepts and algorithms embodied in software. Source code is usually a software developer's or publisher's most closely guarded trade secret. Software is normally distributed in object code form only. The source code is usually kept locked away and shown only to employees and others who have agreed to keep it secret.

If you plan to keep your source code a trade secret, there's a danger that you'll compromise this status by using the source code as a registration deposit. Your deposit becomes a public record on file at the Copyright Office in Washington, DC, and if you deposit source code, it could conceivably be studied by a competitor or pirate, and reproduced in an infringing program. This is not supposed to happen, but it has.

In one well-known case, an attorney employed by Atari Games Corporation gained access to, and made a copy of, source code that Nintendo of America had deposited. The attorney accomplished this feat by falsely claiming the code was involved in litigation. Using this information, Atari was able to create a key to open the ROM-based lock that controlled access to the Nintendo game system. Nintendo brought a copyright infringement suit against Atari for making the unauthorized copy of the code and won. (*Atari Games Corp. v. Nintendo of America, Inc.*, 980 F.2d 857 (Fed.Cir. 1992).) No one can say how many other times this has occurred.

To avoid revealing trade secrets in your deposit, Copyright Office rules permit you to deposit source code with any trade secrets blacked out, or a combination of source code and object code. Under these rules, you have the option of depositing:

- the first and last 25 pages of source code with up to 49% of the source code blacked out (in other words, you deposit 50 pages with only 26 being readable; this obviously helps you to protect source code against infringement), or
- the first and last ten pages of source code with no blacked out portions (this smaller deposit may, depending on the length of the program, or program package, pretty well frustrate pirates), or

- the first and last 25 pages of object code, plus any ten or more consecutive pages of source code with no blacked out portions (because object code is unreadable by humans, this should frustrate potential infringers), or
- for programs consisting of less than 50 pages, the entire source code with up to 49% of the code blacked out.

In all cases, the visible portion of the code must represent an "appreciable amount" of computer code.

If the code contains a copyright notice, you must include the page or equivalent unit containing the notice. A photograph or drawing showing the form and location of the notice is acceptable.

If the deposit material does not give a printed title or version indicator, add the title and any indicia that can be used to identify the particular program.

If you're depositing a revised program with the revisions contained in the first and last 25 pages, you may select any of the four options described just above.

If the revisions are not contained in the first and last 25 pages of code, your deposit must consist of either:

- 20 pages of source code containing the revisions with no blacked out portions, or
- any 50 pages of source code containing the revisions with up to 49% of the code blacked out.

3. Depositing Object Code Only

If you do not want to deposit any source code (even with portions blacked out), you may deposit object code only—that is, the machine language version of the program which the computer executes. Because object code is unreadable by most mortals, a deposit in this form won't likely be examined for ideas and code by a competitor. Also, if you're treating your work as a trade secret, an object code deposit doesn't reveal it.

However, depositing object code only has a down side. Because Copyright Office personnel can't read object code to determine whether it constitutes an original work of authorship, the Copyright Office registration will be made under the Office's "rule of doubt" and you'll receive a warning letter to that effect. The rule of doubt means the Copyright Office is unable to independently verify that your deposit is a work of original authorship.

Having your registration issued under the rule of doubt results in loss of one of the benefits of registration: the presumption that your copyright is valid. (*Freedman v. Select Information Sys.*, 221 U.S.P.Q. 848 (1984) (N.D. Ca. 1983).) This means that if you end up suing someone for copyright infringement, you will have to prove to the court that your software is an original work of authorship and otherwise qualifies for copyright protection. (See Chapter 3). Usually this is not too difficult, but it will complicate matters. Loss of this presumption may be particularly damaging if you wish to obtain a quick pretrial injunction forcing an alleged infringer to stop distributing a pirated work.

Programs Not Compiled Into Object Code

When you compile a program written in C or most other languages, the compiler translates the source code into machine code or processor instructions—this is what the Copyright Office terms object code. However, not all programs are compiled into object code. For example, programs written in the Java programming language are compiled into bytecode instead of machine code. The bytecode is then executed by a program called a bytecode interpreter. For programs such as Java, you may deposit the bytecode or similar intermediate code instead of your source code.

---

a. What to deposit

Deposit the same amount of object code as is required when depositing straight source code as described in Section 1, above. In other words, you must deposit either:

- The entire program in object code, or
- If the object code is longer than 50 printed-out pages, the first and last 25 pages.

Make sure you deposit 50 pages of object code, and not the equivalent of 50 pages of source code translated into object code form.

If the code contains a copyright notice, you must include the page or equivalent unit containing the notice. A photograph or drawing showing the form and location of the notice is acceptable. Where the copyright notice is encoded within the object code so that its presence and content are not easily readable, the notice should be underlined or highlighted and its contents decoded.

If the deposit material does not give a printed title or version indicator, add the title and any indicia that can be used to identify the particular program.

b. Letter to Copyright Office

All deposits consisting solely of object code must be accompanied by an assurance to the Copyright Office that the work contains copyrightable authorship. If you fail to include this assurance with your deposit, the Copyright Office will write you and state that since they can neither read your deposit nor verify that its subject material is copyrightable, you must either send human-readable source code or a letter assuring the Copyright Office that your deposit contains copyrightable material. Obviously, it makes sense to anticipate this request.

A letter such as the following will provide the needed assurance if you deposit object code.

Sample Letter Declaring Your Work Is Copyrightable

April 1, 1998

Register of Copyrights
Library of Congress
Washington, DC 20559

Dear Register:

Enclosed is a copyright registration application for Website Maker submitted by Julia Youngster.

Julia Youngster is submitting the deposit in object code form in order to protect trade secrets that are contained in the computer code.

Website Maker as deposited in object code form contains copyrightable authorship.

I certify that the statements made in this letter are true.

Very truly yours,

Julia Youngster

4. Special Deposit Requirements for Software Embodied on CD-ROMs

The Library of Congress wants to establish a collection of CD-ROMs, so a regulation was enacted in 1991 requiring applicants of works embodied on CD-ROMs to deposit the CD-ROM disk along with a printout of the program code.

CD-ROMs are often used for multimedia works—that is, works containing text, audiovisual elements like photos and video, and music or other sounds, in addition to software (usually operating software or software that produces screen displays).

A single copyright registration and deposit can cover all these elements—that is, the software plus the "content." These types of multimedia registrations and deposit requirements are discussed in detail in Chapter 13.

However, a separate registration and deposit for the software used for a multimedia work embodied on a CD-ROM is required when the software:

- was previously published or was previously registered as an unpublished work, or
- was, or will be, sold or otherwise distributed separately.

When you make a separate registration for only the software on a CD-ROM, you need to make clear in your application that this is all you're registering—that is, that you're not registering the content or other elements on the CD-ROM. Otherwise, the copyright examiner will ask you whether you want to register these other elements. To avoid this, include a letter with your application stating that you wish to register the software only.

You must deposit one copy of the entire CD-ROM package. Everything that is marketed or distributed together must be deposited, whether or not you're the copyright claimant for each element. This includes:

- the CD-ROM disk(s)
- instructional manual(s), and
- any printed version of the work that is sold with the CD-ROM package—for example, where a book accompanies a CD-ROM.

In addition, you must deposit a printout of all or part of the source code or object code for the software you're registering as described in Sections 1,2 and 3 above.

5. Deposit Requirements for Computer Output Screens

You don't have to deposit identifying material for your screens unless you make specific reference to them in Space 2 (Nature of Authorship) of your registration form. (See Section H.) If you specifically mention the screens, you must deposit them. Doing so will likely delay approval of your application, because the copyright examiner will have to examine the identifying material to see if the screens are copyrightable.

To deposit application software screens, use a printout, photograph or drawing of the screens. These reproductions should be no smaller than 3" by 3" and no larger than 9" by 12". The Copyright Office will also accept a manual accompanying the program as a deposit for the computer output screens if it contains clear reproductions of the screens.

Where the authorship on the screens is predominantly audiovisual (for example, an arcade game), a ½-inch VHS format videotape that clearly shows the copyrightable expression should be deposited. In the case of arcade games, you should deposit your "attract" and "play" modes together as part of a single registration in videotape form. For game screens, you should include any sound component, either as part of the videotape recording or separately on a cassette. Don't neglect this. The uniqueness of the sound that accompanies game programs has been helpful in establishing ownership of these types of works in several court decisions.

Even if you think your screen authorship is predominately audiovisual, don't deposit a videotape if the computer screens simply show the functioning of the program. Instead, deposit printouts, photos or drawings as described above.

As part of this type of registration, you should also explain your deposit in a letter.

Sample Letter

June 11, 1998

Dear Chief Examiner:

Please find enclosed my deposit consisting of identifying material related to my computer program Celestial Tease. The material consists of videotape and photographs. These represent the output screens and accompanying sound from the above-mentioned program. I request you accept this material as a deposit accompanying my copyright registration.

Sincerely,

Crystal Star

Senior Programmer

When you submit identifying material for screen displays, the Copyright Office will examine them for copyrightability. To be copyrightable, a screen display must contain original authorship. (See Chapter 5.) The Copyright Office has expressed the view that menu screens and similar functional interfaces consisting of words or brief phrases in a particular format generally are not registrable.

If the Copyright Office determines that all the displays are uncopyrightable, a new application omitting reference to the displays will be requested. Where some or most of the screen displays are uncopyrightable, a warning letter to that effect will be sent by the Copyright Office.

6. Deposit Requirements for Documentation

Documentation includes user manuals, training manuals, instruction sheets, textual flowcharts, film, slide shows and all other works that are used to support a program in some way. Written documentation can be anything from two pages stapled together to a bound, full-color 500-page book.

If you register your documentation separately (see Section E3), you must deposit two copies of your entire work if it's in written, sound recording or graphic form.

If your documentation isn't registered separately and you include a reference to it on your registration form, you must deposit one copy of the documentation. If you don't refer specifically to the documentation, the deposit is optional.

Be sure any documentation you deposit contains the proper copyright notice. (See Section P.)

7. Full Term Retention of Deposit Option

Ordinarily, deposits are destroyed by the Copyright Office after five years, with the Copyright Office first making a copy of unpublished works that have been deposited.

If you wish, you may request full term retention of your deposit. Full term retention means that the Copyright Office will retain one copy of your deposit for 75 years from the date of publication. You must request full term retention in writing and pay a $220 fee.

Given the pace of developments in the software industry, most software won't have much value more than five years after it's registered. So, in most cases, there is no reason to seek full term retention of a software deposit.

Full term retention may be requested only by the person who made the deposit, the copyright owner or an authorized representative. You can make this request when you register the work or any time thereafter. There is no form for this purpose. Simply send a letter to the Chief, Information and Reference Division, Copyright Office, Library of Congress, Washington, DC 20559, stating that you desire full term retention of your deposit. Identify the deposit by title, author and, if you have already registered, Copyright Office registration number.

If you request full term retention of your deposit when you make your initial registration, include this request in a letter with your application along with the increased fee. You must also send the Copyright Office one additional copy of the entire deposit.

J. Mailing Your Application to the Copyright Office

By now, you have completed your application form and have your deposit ready to go. Make a photocopy of your application form and retain it in your records along with an exact copy of your deposit.

1. Application Fee

You must submit a check or money order for the nonrefundable application fee payable to the Register of Copyrights. Clip—don't staple—your check or money order to the application.

At this writing, the registration fee is $20. Application fees change from time to time, however, so call the Copyright Office at 202-707-3000 to double-check the current fees before mailing your application. Also, check the Nolo Press Website at www.nolo. com or read the *Nolo News* for updates on fee changes. (See back of the book for information about requesting a *Nolo News* subscription.)

2. Mail Single Package to Copyright Office

Put your application, deposit and check or money order for the appropriate application fee in a single package. If you send them separately, all the packages will be returned by the Copyright Office. But, if you send a deposit of a published work separately, the Copyright Office will turn it over to the Library of Congress rather than return it to you, so you'll get the application and fee back, but not the deposit.

If you're registering a published work, your application must be received by the Copyright Office after the publication date listed in Space 3 of your application. (See Section H, above.).

Reason: A published work cannot be registered prior to the date of publication.

Mail your single package to:
Register of Copyrights
Copyright Office
Library of Congress
Washington, DC 20559

How to Make Sure the Copyright Office Received Your Application

The Copyright Office will not send an acknowledgment when it has received an application. The best way to know for sure that they got it is to send the application by certified or registered mail, return receipt requested. Allow three weeks for the receipt to be returned by the post office. The receipt will show exactly when the Copyright Office received the application. (If time is an important factor, See Section K, below, on expedited registration.)

3. Registration Effective When the Application Is Received

Your registration is effective on the date the Copyright Office receives all three elements: application, deposit and application fee in acceptable form. This means you don't need to worry about how long it takes the Copyright Office to process the application

and send you a certificate of registration. You'll be eligible to obtain statutory damages or attorney fees from anyone who copies your work while your application is being processed. (You can obtain such fees and damages only if the work was registered before the infringement occurred or within three months of publication; see Section C.)

K. Expedited Registration

In a few special circumstances, you may request that your application be given special handling by the Copyright Office. Special handling applications are processed in five to ten days, rather than the normal three to six months or more. Special handling is available only if needed:

- for copyright litigation; under current law, a work must be registered before a copyright infringement suit may be filed; you'll need to have a certified copy of your registration certificate to show the court
- to meet a contractual or publishing deadline, or
- for some other urgent need.

You must pay an additional $330 fee for special handling. To request special handling, send a letter along with your application containing the following information:

- why there is an urgent need for special handling—for example, because of litigation or to meet contractual or publishing deadlines

- if special handling is needed for litigation, whether the case has been filed already or is pending, who the parties to the litigation are or will be and in what court the action has been or will be filed
- a certification that your statements are true to the best of your knowledge.

To request special handling for a submission that is already in the Copyright Office, the cover letter should also include as much identifying information as possible about the pending claim. Include the date of the original submission and how it was delivered to the Copyright Office (in person, by courier, or by mail). If sent by mail, indicate the date of the mailing and the type of mailing (registered, certified, first class, etc.). Include a full description of the copies sent and a photocopy of the application form if available. Processing for such cases will not begin until the material already in the Copyright Office is located.

Sample Request for Special Handling

Library of Congress
Box 100
Washington, DC 20540

Dear Information Specialist:

I am requesting that my enclosed copyright registration application be given special handling. There is an urgent need for special handling because of prospective litigation.

I plan to file a copyright infringement lawsuit in the Federal District Court in Indianapolis, IN. I will be the plaintiff and Scrivener & Sons Publishing Co. will be the defendant.

I certify that the statements made above are correct to the best of my knowledge.

_____/s/_____
Sam Smucker
111 Main St.
Muncie, IN 34939
555-555-5555

If you're registering for litigation purposes, you'll need a certified copy of your registration certificate to submit to the court; so enclose an additional $8 fee and request that the Copyright Office provide you with a certified copy.

Mail the special handling form or letter, your application and deposit, and a certified check or money order payable to the Register of Copyrights for $358 (the $20 application fee, plus the $330 special handling fee, plus the $8 certification fee) all in one package to:

Library of Congress
Department 100
Washington, DC 20540

Write the words "Special Handling" on the outside of the envelope. But don't put the words "Copyright Office" on the envelope.

L. Dealing with the Copyright Office

The Copyright Office has an enormous workload: they handle over 600,000 applications per year. As this book went to press in late 1997, the Copyright Office was seriously understaffed and had a backlog of tens of thousands of applications. It can take anywhere from three to six months or even longer for your application to be processed.

Be patient and remember that the registration is effective on the date it is received by the Copyright Office (assuming the forms were filled out properly), not the date you actually receive your registration certificate.

The Copyright Office will eventually respond to your application in one of three ways:

- If your application is acceptable, the Copyright Office will send you a registration certificate, which is merely a copy of your application with the official Copyright Office seal, registra-

tion date and number stamped on it. Be sure to retain it for your records.

- If your application contained errors or omissions the Copyright Office believes are correctable, a copyright examiner may phone you for further information. Or he may return the application or deposit with a letter explaining what corrections to make.

- If the Copyright Office determines that your work cannot be registered, it will send you a letter explaining why. Neither your deposit nor fee will be returned.

1. If You Don't Hear From the Copyright Office

If you don't hear anything from the Copyright Office within four to six months after your application should have been received, you may wish to write them to find out the status of your application. They may have lost the application, it may have never been received or—most likely—they may be very far behind in their work. In your letter, identify yourself, the author and the copyright owner; give the date of your application and the form you used; and describe the work briefly. If the Copyright Office cashed your check, you'll know that they did receive the application. Include a copy of the canceled check with your letter. It will contain a number that will help the Copyright Office trace your application.

Copyright Tip. You'll have to pay the Copyright Office a fee if you want to find out about the status of an application fewer than 16 weeks after the Copyright Office received it. Call the Copyright Office at 202-707-3000 to ask about this.

2. Extent of Copyright Examiner's Review of Your Application

The Copyright Examiner will examine your deposit to see whether it constitutes copyrightable subject matter and review your application to determine whether the other legal and formal requirements for registration have been met.

a. The rule of doubt

As a matter of policy, the Copyright Office will usually register a work even if it has a reasonable doubt as to whether the work is copyrightable or whether the other requirements have been met. This is called the rule of doubt. The Copyright Office takes the view that determining a copyright's validity in such cases is a task for the courts. For example, the office would ordinarily register a new version of a previously registered software package under the rule of doubt, even though it had a reasonable doubt whether the new version contained enough new expression to be registerable.

When registration is made under the rule of doubt, the Copyright Office will ordinarily send the applicant a letter cautioning that the claim may not be valid and stating the reason.

b. Clearly unregisterable material

However, the Copyright Office will refuse to register a work that is definitely unprotectible. For example, the Copyright Office will not register a title, since titles are not copyrightable.

c. Presence of errors or omissions

The Copyright Office will not issue a certificate if the application contains errors or omissions or is internally inconsistent or ambiguous. Here are some of the more common errors:

- the application is not signed
- the application fee is incorrect or unpaid
- the nature of authorship is not adequately described
- the work's title is not contained on the deposit
- deposit does not match description of nature of authorship
- the publication date is not provided
- the Work Made for Hire box is checked, but the employer is not listed as the copyright claimant
- there is no statement as to how ownership was transferred where the copyright claimant is not the same as the author
- the date the application is signed is before the publication date in the application.

The Copyright Office will ordinarily call you or send a letter asking you to fix technical errors such as these. Reread the discussion about how to complete the application form in Section H to help you make your corrections. Send your corrected application and any new deposit back to the Copyright Office in one package.

Be sure you respond within 120 days to any correspondence from the Copyright Office concerning your application. Otherwise, your file will be closed, your fee will not be returned to you, and you'll have to reapply by sending in a new application, deposit and fee.

3. Review of Copyright Office's Refusal to Register Application

If you think the Copyright Examiner has wrongfully refused to register your work, you may submit a written objection and request that the Copyright Office reconsider its action. The appeal letter should be addressed to the appropriate section of the Examining Division, Copyright Office, Washington, DC 20559. The first request for reconsideration must be received in the Copyright Office within 120 days of the date of the Office's first refusal to register, and the envelope containing the request should be clearly marked: FIRST APPEAL/ EXAMINING DIVISION.

If the claim is refused after reconsideration, the head of the appropriate Examining Division section will send you written notice of the reasons for the refusal. After this, you

may again request reconsideration in writing. This second appeal must be received in the Copyright Office within 120 days of the date of the Office's refusal of the first appeal, and be directed to the Board of Appeals at the following address: Copyright GC/I&R, P.O. Box 70400, Southwest Station, Washington, DC 20024.

The second appeal is handled by the Copyright Office Board of Appeals, which consists of the Register of Copyrights, the General Counsel and the Chief of the Examining Division. The Chair of the Board of Appeals will send you a letter setting out the reasons for acceptance or denial of your claim. The Appeals Board's decision constitutes the Copyright Office's final action. You may then bring a legal action to have a court review the Copyright Office's decision. In addition, you can bring a copyright infringement action notwithstanding the Copyright Office's refusal to register your

work. You'll need to see a lawyer about this. (See Chapter 18.)

M. What the Copyright Office Does With Deposits

Whether or not your registration application is accepted, your deposit becomes the property of the U.S. government and will never be returned to you. The Library of Congress has the option of adding the deposit to its own collection. If the library chooses not to do so, (which is usually the case), and your application is accepted, the Copyright Office will retain the deposit in its own storage facilities for five years. Due to a lack of storage space, the Copyright Office normally destroys all deposits of published works after five years. However, the Copyright Office may not destroy a deposit of an unpublished work without first making a copy of it.

1. Examining Deposits From Copyright Office Files

The Copyright Office is located in Washington, DC, so anyone who wants to look at any records must go there. Direct copying from Copyright Office files by nonagency employees is prohibited by law. Because the Copyright Office stores great masses of information, it normally takes from one to five days to even get access to a particular deposit.

To look at any specific deposit, a person normally needs:

- the registration number or the exact name of the work and author, and
- a signed, written statement as to why access is needed.

This written statement is placed in a file associated with the copyright deposit and is available to the copyright owner for examination.

When a deposit is retrieved, a Copyright Office employee is assigned to stay with the deposit at all times and to prevent the requester from taking notes or copying the deposit in any way. As a practical matter, this means that it's unlikely that your code will be directly copied from Copyright Office files. However, it won't stop an intelligent pirate from getting a pretty good overview of your approach.

If you suspect that your deposit has been copied, you may well want to have the Copyright Office conduct a search of your file for evidence of an examination of your deposit. The Copyright Office charges $20 an hour to conduct searches. Call the Copyright Office at 202-287-8700, explain that you want a search of your file to see whether it has been examined by anyone else, and ask what the charge will be. Then, mail this amount and a written request to have your file examined to:

Reference and Bibliography Section, LM-451
Copyright Office
Library of Congress
Washington, DC 20559

2. Obtaining Copies of Deposits From the Copyright Office

It's possible to obtain copies of deposits from the Copyright Office if any one of the following three conditions is met:

- Written authorization is received from the copyright claimant, the claimant's authorized agent or the owner of any of the exclusive rights. The owner of an exclusive right must also provide written documentation to support the exclusivity claim.
- A written request is received from an attorney representing either the plaintiff or defendant in pending or anticipated litigation involving the work. This request must be accompanied by an overall description of the dispute, a description of all parties involved in the dispute, the name of the court, a factual recounting of the case and an assurance that the reproduced deposit will only be used in connection with the specified litigation.
- A court order in pending litigation requires production of the work for submission as evidence.

If one of these conditions is met, and you also provide the other information necessary to locate the requested deposit, a reproduction of the deposit will be released from the Copyright Office for a fee to be determined on a case-by-case basis.

N. Library of Congress Deposit Requirement

Subject to various exceptions, the Copyright Act requires the copyright owner of any work published in the United States to deposit two copies of the best edition of the work with the Library of Congress in Washington, D.C., within three months after publication. Computer software that is published only in the form of machine-readable copies is specifically exempted from this deposit rule. However, the law apparently requires software publishers to deposit copies of their published documentation.

When you register with the U.S. Copyright Office, your Library of Congress obligations are fulfilled at the same time. It's only if you don't register with the Copyright Office that you might run afoul of this extra deposit rule. You need do nothing unless you receive a letter requiring you to deposit your published work for the Library of Congress archives. If you get such a letter, it will tell you how to comply with the deposit requirements and will include a telephone number to which you may direct inquiries.

The Library of Congress deposit requirement is seldom enforced and failure to comply with this requirement will in no way affect the validity or protectability of your copyright. However, you can be required to pay a $250 fine if you ignore the request (and an additional $2,500 fine can be imposed if you willfully or repeatedly fail to comply).

Donating Public Domain Software to the Library of Congress

Some software authors decide that they don't want their software to be protected by copyright. Instead, they dedicate it to the public domain, meaning anyone is free to use the software without the author's permission. Such software is sometimes called freeware. You cannot register such public domain software with the Copyright Office, but you may donate a copy to the Library of Congress for the benefit of its Machine-Readable Collections Reading Room. Doing so ensures that a copy of your work will be preserved for posterity and enables members of the public who use the reading room to become aware of your work.

To be eligible for donation, the software must contain an explicit disclaimer of copyright protection from the copyright owner. Send your computer disks along with any documentation. If the documentation is on disk, you need to send a printout of the documentation. If the software is distributed in a box or other packaging, send the entire package. Along with this material, include a letter explaining that you're making a donation. Send donations to:

Gift Section, Exchange & Gift Division
Library of Congress
Washington, DC 20540

O. Corrections and Changes After Registration Is Completed (Supplemental Registration)

The same published work normally can only be registered once with the Copyright Office (see Section E5). However, a second supplemental registration may be necessary to augment your original basic registration if you later discover that you forgot something important, supplied the Copyright Office with the wrong information or important facts have changed. A special form, Form CA, is used for this purpose.

If you ever become involved in copyright litigation, your registration certificate (which is simply a copy of your basic registration application form stamped and returned to you by the Copyright Office) will be submitted into evidence to prove the existence of your copyright. It could prove embarrassing, and possibly harmful to your case, if the certificate is found to contain substantial errors, is unclear or ambiguous or if important facts have changed since you registered. For this reason, you should file a supplemental registration to correct significant errors in your certificate or to reflect important factual changes.

Also, remember that your registration is a public record. By keeping your registration accurate and up-to-date you will make it easier for those searching the Copyright Office records to discover your work and locate you or your company. This may result in new marketing opportunities and help to prevent an infringement.

1. Corrections

A supplemental registration should be filed to correct significant errors that occurred at the time the basic registration was made, and that were overlooked by the Copyright Office. This includes:

- identifying someone incorrectly as the author or copyright claimant of the work
- registering an unpublished work as published (or vice versa), or
- inaccurately stating the extent of the copyright claim.

Errors in these important facts could cast doubt upon the validity and duration of your copyright and could needlessly confuse and complicate copyright litigation. They will also confuse anyone searching the Copyright Office records. Correct them as soon as you discover them.

DEAR COPYRIGHT OFFICER:
I AM WRITING REGARDING.

Supplemental Registration Not Needed to Correct Obvious Errors

It is not necessary to file a formal supplemental registration to correct obvious errors the Copyright Office should have caught when it reviewed your application. This includes, for example, the omission of necessary information, such as the names of the author or claimant, and obvious mistakes (like a publication date of 1098.) If, when you receive your registration certificate, you discover that such errors have been overlooked by the copyright examiner, simply notify the Copyright Office and the mistake will be corrected with no need for a supplemental registration and additional fee.

2. Changes and Amplifications

You should file a supplemental registration to:

- reflect important changes in facts that have occurred since the basic registration was made,
- provide additional significant information that could have been provided in the original application but was not, or
- clarify or explain information in the basic registration.

a. If you have changed your address

It's an excellent idea, although not legally necessary, for you to keep your address current in the Copyright Office's records. By doing so, you will make it easy for people who want to use your work to locate you and arrange for permission and compensation. The harder you are to locate, the more likely it is that your copyright will be infringed if someone else wants to use your work. You may file a supplemental registration to change your address.

b. If an author or copyright claimant was omitted

All the authors and copyright claimants must be listed in the registration (unless they are anonymous or pseudonymous; see Section H). This means a supplemental registration should be filed if an author or copyright claimant's name was omitted.

c. Change in claimant's name

A supplemental registration should be made where the name of the copyright claimant has changed for reasons other than a transfer of ownership.

d. Change in title of the registered work

File a supplemental registration if you changed the title of the registered work without changing its content. However, if the content of the work is changed, a new registration will have to be made.

3. When Supplemental Registration Cannot Be Used

Certain kinds of errors should not be corrected by supplemental registration. In addition, supplemental registration may not be used to reflect some kinds of factual changes.

a. Changes in copyright ownership

Supplemental registration cannot be used to notify the Copyright Office of post-registration changes in ownership of a copyright, whether by license, inheritance or other form of transfer. A special recordation procedure is used for this. (See Chapter 11.)

b. Errors or changes in content of registered work

A supplemental registration cannot be filed to reflect changes or corrections to the content of a registered work. Where such changes are so substantial as to make the new work a new version, it must be registered separately with a new deposit. If the content changes are minor, there is no need to file a new registration, since the original registration will provide adequate protection. (See Section F.)

c. Failure to mention computer screens

A single registration for a computer program covers all the copyrightable content of the program, including screen displays. (See Section E2.) It is not necessary, although permissible, to specifically mention screen displays in the application or to deposit identifying material for them. (See Section H.) Once you have registered your software, however, you cannot seek a supplementary registration to allow a separate claim in the screen displays.

4. How to File a Supplemental Registration

Complete the Copyright Office's official Form CA to file a supplemental registration. Make a copy of the completed Form CA for your records. Attach the registration fee ($20 as of the date of this writing), either a check or money order payable to the Register of Copyrights, to the Form CA. No deposit is necessary for a supplemental registration. Send the form and payment to:

Register of Copyrights
Library of Congress
Washington, DC 20559

 A Copy of Form CA is contained on the CD-ROM at the end of this book under the file name formca.pdf. See Chapter 1 for instructions on how to use the forms disk.

5. Effect of Supplemental Registration

If your supplemental registration application was completed correctly, the Copyright Office will assign you a new registration number and issue a certificate of supplementary registration under that number. The certificate is simply a copy of your Form CA with the new registration number, date and certification stamped on it. Be sure to keep it in your records.

The information in a supplementary registration augments, but does not supersede, that contained in the original basic registration. The basic registration is not expunged or canceled. However, if the person who filed the supplementary registration was the copyright claimant for the original registration (or his heir or transferee), the Copyright Office will place a note referring to the supplementary registration on its records of the basic registration. This way, anyone needing information regarding the registration will know there is a supplemental registration on file if an inquiry is made regarding the work.

Part II. Software Copyright Notice

Part II is about copyright notice—the "c" in a circle—©—followed by a publication date and name, usually seen on published works. The purpose of such a notice is to inform the public that a work is copyrighted, when it was published and who owns the copyright. A copyright notice is not required as a condition of obtaining or keeping a copyright. Nevertheless, it's a very good idea to include a notice anyway on all your published software and other copyrightable works.

P. Why Use a Copyright Notice?

Contrary to what many people believe, a copyright notice is not required to establish or maintain a copyright in the United States or most foreign countries. Nor is a notice necessary to register a work with the Copyright Office. However, notice was required for software and other copyrightable works published in the U.S. before March 1, 1989.)

So if a notice is not mandatory, why bother to include one on your published software and other copyrightable works? There are several excellent reasons.

1. Notice Helps Makes Infringement Suits Economically Feasible

Authors and other copyright owners are able to enforce their copyright rights only because they can sue those who violate them. Unfortunately, copyright infringement litigation is expensive (copyright attorneys charge at least $150 an hour and often much more). As a result, copyright infringement lawsuits may be economically feasible only if the author can obtain substantial damages (money) from the infringer and use some of this money to pay the attorney.

The easiest way to get substantial damages is to prove that the infringement was willful—that is, that the infringer knew that he or she was breaking the law but did so anyway. Courts usually award far more damages where the infringement was willful than where the infringer didn't realize what he or she was doing was wrong. (See Chapter 5.)

Proving "willfulness" can be difficult if a published work lacks a valid copyright notice. The reason for this is what's known as the innocent infringement defense. If a person infringes upon a published work

that does not contain a copyright notice, the infringer can claim in court that the infringement was innocent—that is, he or she didn't know the work was protected by copyright. If the judge or jury believes this, the infringer may still be liable for infringement, but the damages (monetary compensation) the infringer is required to pay may be drastically reduced from what they otherwise would have been. On the other hand, if there is a valid copyright notice on the work, the infringer cannot claim innocence and will be treated as a willful infringer.

EXAMPLE 1: Art self-publishes a collection of Java applets. He sells the programs by mail order and through his own Website. He fails to place any copyright notice in the program itself or the floppy disks he sells. Suzy, a programmer employed by NastySoft, obtains a copy of the program, decompiles it and incorporates much of the code in a program she creates for NastySoft. Art finds out about the copying and sues Suzy and NastySoft for copyright infringement. Suzy, while admitting that she copied Art's work, claims that she thought the code was in the public domain because it lacked a copyright notice. The judge buys Suzy's story, and as a result awards Art only $1,000 in damages. The judge tells Art that had his program contained a copyright notice he would have awarded substantially more statutory damages because Suzy's copying clearly would have been willful.

EXAMPLE 2: Assume instead that Art included a valid copyright notice in his program. He sues Suzy and NastySoft for copyright infringement. Since his program contained a valid notice, Suzy cannot claim that she did not realize the work was protected by copyright. As a result, the judge awards Art $20,000 in damages.

Note that the innocent infringement rule applies only to published software. Theoretically, an alleged infringer of an unpublished work can raise the innocent infringement defense whether or not the work contains a notice. However, it does not seem likely that an alleged infringer could convince a judge or jury that his or her infringement of an unpublished work was innocent if the work contained a copyright notice.

2. Copyright Notice May Deter Potential Infringers

Another important reason to place a copyright notice on all copies of your published software is that it may help deter copyright infringement. The notice lets users know that the work is protected by copyright and may not be copied without the owner's permission. Moreover, since copyright notices appear on the vast majority of published software and other copyrighted works, a

user of software not containing a notice might mistakenly assume that it is not protected by copyright, and feel free to copy it or otherwise infringe upon your copyright.

3. Notice Informs the World Who the Copyright Owner Is

A copyright notice contains the name of the copyright owner(s) of the work. This information will help third parties—who might want to obtain permission to use or purchase the work—to identify and locate the owner.

4. Notice Protects Your Work in Countries Not Adhering to the Berne Convention

Finally, some foreign countries (notably, Russia and South Korea) do not afford copyright protection to works unless they contain valid copyright notices. (See Chapter 10.) Providing a copyright notice on your work will enable your work to be protected in these countries.

Q. When to Place a Copyright Notice on Software

Many people are confused about exactly when to place a copyright notice on their software or other copyrighted works. Should you use a copyright notice from the day you write the first line of code, when you test the first module, or only when you first market your software to the public?

The best practice is to put a modified informal copyright notice on your work (described in Section R4 below) even before it is published, and put a formal copyright notice on your work when it is published.

1. Copyright Notices for Published Software

A full-blown formal copyright notice of the type described in Section R below should be used for all published software and other published works. A work is published for copyright purposes when copies are sold, licensed, rented, lent, given away or otherwise distributed to the public. Selling copies to the public through retail outlets or by mail order, publishing code in a magazine, selling a program at a widely attended computer show and allowing a number of educational institutions to use your program without restriction are all examples of publication.

However, publication occurs only when software is made available to the general public on an unrestricted basis. Distributing copies of software to a restricted group of users does not constitute publication. For example, sending copies to a few friends or beta testers would not constitute a publication. Similarly, a court held that software used by a company's salespeople solely for sales presentations for customers was not published. (*Gates Rubber, Inc. v. Bando American*, 798 F.Supp. 1499 (D. Colo. 1992).)

In addition, software licensed to a select group of end users who sign license agreements imposing confidentiality requirements probably is not published for notice purposes. However, one court has held that software distributed to automobile and recreational vehicle dealers throughout the country was published even though signed licenses were obtained. The court reasoned that all the auto dealers in the United States did not constitute a select group. (*D.C.I. Computer Systems, Inc. v. Pardini*, 1992 Copr.L.Dec. 27,005 (9th Cir. 1992).)

Finally, a publication does not occur for copyright notice purposes when software is made available only for use on a time-shared computer system or simply displayed on a computer terminal (for example, in an on-line library catalog). But even in these situations, it is wise to use a copyright notice.

Software Distributed Online. It is common to distribute software by uploading it to sites on the Internet, commercial online services such as America Online and CompuServe and computer bulletin boards. It's not entirely clear whether making a program available online constitutes publication. However, you should assume it does. Accordingly, all such programs should carry a proper copyright notice to achieve maximum copyright protection.

If you're not sure whether your software has been published for copyright notice purposes, the best course is to assume that it has been published and include a copyright notice.

2. Copyright Notices for Unpublished Software

Placing a copyright notice on unpublished software provides all the benefits discussed in Section P above, except that technically it will not prevent an infringer from raising the innocent infringement defense discussed above. For these reasons, it is sensible to place a copyright notice on unpublished software before sending it to beta testers, potential publishers, product reviewers and other third parties.

R. Form of Notice

There are strict technical requirements as to what a copyright notice must contain if it is to serve its purpose of preventing an innocent infringer defense. A valid copyright notice contains three elements:

- the copyright symbol or the words "Copyright" or "Copr.,"
- if the software or other work is published, the year of publication, and
- the name of the copyright owner.

It is not required that these elements appear in any particular order in the notice, but most notices are written in the order set forth above.

⚠ Errors in Copyright Notice. If you discover an error in the copyright notice for your published software, it's wise

ANOTHER "NOT-GETTING-IT-RIGHT-COPYRIGHT-FRIGHT" NIGHT.

to have it corrected when subsequent copies are produced. However, it is not necessary to recall any copies already distributed.

1. Copyright Symbol or the Words "Copyright" or "Copr."

In the United States either the © symbol or the words "Copyright" or "Copr." may be used. Or you can use the © symbol and the words Copyright or Copr. (This will help make it clear to even the dullest minds that your work is copyrighted.)

However, in those 20 or so foreign countries that require that a copyright notice appear on a published work for it to be protected by copyright at all, you must use the © symbol (you can also use the words Copyright or Copr. if you wish). So if your work might be distributed outside the U.S., be sure to always use the © symbol.

Virtually all word processing programs come with alternate character sets which include the c in a circle. However, if, for some reason, your computer is unable to make a © symbol, the word Copyright or abbreviation Copr. should be used along with a c in parentheses—like this: (c). This will be a valid notice in the U.S., but there might be problems in some foreign countries. So if your work has particular international application, use a © symbol.

A different copyright symbol is used for sound recordings. A capital P in a circle (℗)—is used instead of the © symbol.

2. Year of Publication

The copyright notice must also state the year the work was published. For initial versions of software, this is easy.

As discussed in the preceding section, a publication date should not be provided in a notice for unpublished software.

a   Software updates

Of course, many publicly distributed software programs are continually revised and updated. The copyright notice doesn't have to be changed if an update consists only of minor revisions.

However, if an update contains a substantial amount of new material, it is considered to be a separate work of authorship in its own right. The notice for such a derivative work should contain the date the new work was published. The notice need not contain the date or dates of the prior version or versions; however, it is common practice to include such dates in the copyright notice. One reason is to let the user know when the earlier versions were created. Another reason to do this is that it is not always easy to tell if a work qualifies as a derivative work under copyright office rules. (See Chapter 5.)

> **EXAMPLE:** AcmeSoft, Inc., published version 1.0 of a VRML authoring tool in 1997. The copyright notice read "Copyright © 1997 by AcmeSoft, Inc." The software was revised and republished as a new 2.0 version in 1998. If the 2.0

version qualifies as a new derivative work, the notice need only state "Copyright © 1998 by AcmeSoft, Inc." However, AcmeSoft is not sure whether the changes it made were substantial enough to make the 2.0 version a new derivative work. AcmeSoft decides to err on the side of caution and writes the notice like this: "Copyright © 1997, 1998 by AcmeSoft, Inc."

If AcmeSoft revises the program again in 1999, it may write the copyright notice like this: "Copyright © 1997–1999 by AcmeSoft, Inc."

b. Form of date

The date is usually written in Arabic numerals—for instance, "1998." But you can also use:

- abbreviations of Arabic numerals—for instance, "'98";
- Roman numerals—for instance, "MCMXCVIII"; or
- spelled out words instead of numerals —for instance, "Nineteen Hundred Ninety-Eight."

3. Copyright Owner's Name

The name of the copyright owner must also be included in the notice. Briefly, the owner is one of the following:

- the person or persons who created the work
- the legal owner of a work made for hire, or

- the person or entity (partnership or corporation) to whom all the author's exclusive copyright rights have been transferred.

a. Person or persons who created the work

Unless a work is made for hire (see below), the original creators initially own all the copyright rights. Where all these rights are retained, the creator's name should appear in the copyright notice.

> **EXAMPLE:** Eli Yale creates a database program for churches. He distributes the program though religious bookstores and the Internet. Eli is the sole copyright owner of the program. The copyright notice should state: "Copyright © 1998 by Eli Yale."

If there are multiple creators, they should all be listed in the copyright notice. The names can appear in any order.

b. Works made for hire

A work made for hire is a work made by an employee as part of his or her job, or a work specially ordered or commissioned under a written work for hire contract. (See Chapter 11.) The creator's employer or other person for whom the work was prepared is considered the author of such a work for copyright purposes and that person's (or entity's) name should appear in the copyright notice as owner unless the copyright has been assigned to someone else. The creator-employee's name should not be included in the notice.

EXAMPLE: A team of systems analysts, software designers and programmers employed by Datavue Publications, Inc., create a multimedia scripting and presentation software package. The software is a work made for hire created by Datavue's employees as part of their job. Datavue is considered the author, and thus the owner, and only Datavue's name should appear in the copyright notice: "Copyright © 1998 by Datavue Publications."

c. Transferees

If all of the copyright rights owned by a software author or authors (whether the author is the actual creator or the owner of a work made for hire) are transferred to another person or entity, that name should appear in the copyright notice on all copies produced and distributed after the transfer. However, any copies produced before the transfer occurred may be distributed without updating the notice.

EXAMPLE 1: Assume that Datavue Publications published its presentation package in the example above in 1998. In 1999 Datavue, a small closely held corporation, is purchased by Behemoth Software Inc. As part of the purchase, Behemoth acquires all the copyright rights in the presentation package. Behemoth can go ahead and distribute all unsold copies of the presentation software without updating the copyright notice they contain, even though

the notice states that Datavue is the copyright owner. But if Behemoth produces and distributes any new copies, its name alone should appear in the copyright notice.

EXAMPLE 2: Cheapskate Software hires over a dozen freelance programmers to create a new equation-writing program. All the programmers signed independent contractor agreements transferring all their copyright rights in their work to Cheapskate. Cheapskate's name alone should appear in the copyright notice.

d. Name on notice where rights are transferred to different people or entities

A copyright is completely divisible—that is, the owner may transfer all or part of her exclusive copyright rights to whomever and however she wishes. For example, a copyright owner can transfer less than all of his or her rights and retain the others, or transfer some rights to one person or entity and all the others to other transferees. (See Chapter 11.)

Because copyrights are divisible, it can be confusing to determine just who the owner of copyright is for purposes of the copyright notice. The general rule is that unless the author—whether it is the actual creator or the owner of a work made for hire—transfers all of his or her copyright rights to a single person or entity, the author's name should appear in the notice.

EXAMPLE: Dick and Jane create an educational computer game for young children. They sell to Moppet Publishing Co. the right to publish the game in North America. Dick and Jane sell the right to publish the game outside North America to Foreign Press, Inc. They sell TV, video and film rights based on the game to Repulsive Pictures. Dick and Jane's names alone should appear in the copyright notice in all published versions of the game. In contrast, had Dick and Jane sold all their rights to Moppet, its name should appear alone in the notice.

The one exception to this general rule is where a collective or derivative work is created from preexisting material (see Section S, below).

e. Form of name

Usually, the owner's full legal name is used. However, it is permissible to use an abbreviation of the owner's name, a last name alone, a trade name, nickname, fictitious name, pseudonym, initials or some other designation as long as the copyright owner is generally known by the name or other words or letters used in the notice. For example, International Business Machines Corporation may use the abbreviation IBM. Remember, however, that the point of a notice is to notify, so don't be cryptic or cute.

If You Want to Remain Anonymous

The word "anonymous" should not be used in a copyright notice because an author is obviously not generally known by that name. Likewise, it is not advisable to use a pseudonym by which you are not generally known. You can avoid revealing your name in a copyright notice, and still ensure the notice's validity, by transferring all of your copyright rights to a publisher. This way, the publisher's name may appear in the notice. Another approach would be to form a corporation, transfer your entire copyright to it, and then use the corporation's name in the notice.

If the copyright owner is a corporation, it is not necessary to include the word "Inc." in the name, even if this is part of the corporation's full legal name. Nor is it necessary for the word "by" to precede the copyright owner's name, although it is commonly used—for example, a notice can be written as "Copyright © 1998 by AcmeSoft" or "Copyright © 1998 AcmeSoft."

4. Form of Notice for Unpublished Works

All the rules discussed above should be followed for notices on unpublished software, with the exception that you can't include a publication date in the copyright notice. Instead, the notice should indicate the work's unpublished status. A copyright notice for an unpublished work should be in one of the following forms:

- Copyright © AcmeSoft, Inc. (This work is unpublished.)
- Copyright © AcmeSoft, Inc. (Work in progress.)

S. Notice on Compilations and Derivative Works

Compilations and adaptations are formed all or in part from preexisting material. Nevertheless, it is usually not necessary that the copyright notice for this type of work refer to the preexisting material.

1. Compilations

A compilation may be a collective work—that is, a work that consists of separate and independent works assembled into a collective whole. A good example in the software realm is a computerized encyclopedia. Hard copy or digital versions of serial publications, such as periodicals, magazines and newspapers, are also collective work compilations. A compilation may also be a work in which preexisting materials—usually data of various types—are selected, coordinated and arranged so that a new work is created — for example, a catalog. (See Chapter 12 for detailed discussion.)

Unless the person or entity who creates a compilation uses material in the public domain, he or she must either own the preexisting material used in the work or obtain the permission of those who do own it. If the creator of a compilation does not own the preexisting material, all he or she owns is the copyright in the compilation as a whole—that is, the copyright in the creative work involved in selecting, combining and assembling the material into a whole work. Nevertheless, a compilation need only contain one copyright notice in the name of that copyright owner. That notice will extend, for the purposes of defeating the innocent infringer rule, to the individual components of the compilation.

> **EXAMPLE:** Hardsell, Inc., compiles and publishes a CD-ROM containing the 100 best new Java applets. The copyright owners of each program gave Hardsell permission to publish them on the CD-ROM, but still retain all their copyright rights. The CD-ROM need contain only one copyright notice in Hardsell's name: "Copyright © 1998 by Hardsell, Inc." Separate copyright notices need not be provided for the 100 Java programs.

Although an individual contribution to a compilation does not have to have its own copyright notice, a notice is permissible where the copyright in the contribution is owned by someone other than the owner of the compilation as a whole. This may help deter a potential infringer and make clear that the owner of the copyright in the compilation does not own that particular contribution. It will also make it clear to end users whom to contact for permission to use the particular contribution.

> EXAMPLE: The owner of a Java applet program included in Hardsell's CD-ROM above could include a copyright notice on the user's computer screen upon start-up of the program and/or continuously on-screen (for example, in a status line). A notice could also be provided in a written manual or other documentation accompanying the CD-ROM.

a. Publication date for compilations

The copyright notice for a compilation need only list the year the compilation itself is published, not the date or dates the preexisting material was published.

> EXAMPLE: The publication date for the notice on Hardsell's CD-ROM would be 1998, the year the CD-ROM was published.

b. Advertisements

The rule that a single notice for a compilation as a whole covers all the material in the work does not apply to advertisements. Advertisements in serial publications such as periodicals, magazines and newspapers must carry their own copyright notice. However, an advertisement inserted in a compilation on behalf of the copyright owner of the compilation need not contain its own notice—for example, an ad inserted in *PC Magazine* by its owners urging readers to subscribe would not need its own notice.

2. Derivative Works

A derivative work is a work that is created by recasting, transforming or adapting a previously existing work into a new work of authorship. Examples in the software world include revised versions of preexisting programs. "Porting" a program from one type of hardware to another—from a Mac to a PC, for example—is another type of derivative work.

Unless the preexisting material used by a derivative work is in the public domain or owned by the creator of the derivative work, the creator must obtain the copyright owner's permission to use it.

As with compilations, the copyright notice for a derivative work need only contain the name of the owner of the copyright of the derivative work itself, not the owner of the preexisting material upon which the derivative work was based.

> EXAMPLE: Inumeracy Software published a mathematical equation-writing program for the Macintosh in 1997. Oxymoron Software, Inc., obtains permission to create an updated and revised PC version of the program. The PC program is a derivative work based upon the preexisting Macintosh program. However, only Oxymoron's name need

appear on the copyright notice for its program, since Oxymoron is the owner of the copyright in the derivative work.

As with collective works, the publication date in the notice for a derivative work should be the year the derivative work was published, not the year or years the pre-existing material was published.

3. Work Containing Previously Copyrighted Material

If your software is not a derivative work but nevertheless includes code or other material that was previously published by another copyright owner, you needn't include a separate copyright notice for the work unless this is required by the other copyright owner. Your single copyright notice protects the entire work as a whole. However, if the copyright owner of the earlier work you use wishes his or her copyright to be specifically noted, you would do it like this:

- © Copyright 1997 Sid Simm
- © Copyright 1996 Mary Michaels

4. Works Containing United States Government Materials

The rule that a single general notice is sufficient for a compilation or derivative work does not always apply to publications incorporating United States government works.

United States government publications are in the public domain—that is, they are not copyrighted and anyone can use them without asking the federal government's permission. However, if a work consists preponderantly of one or more works by the U.S. government, the copyright notice must affirmatively or negatively identify those portions of the work in which copyright is claimed—that is, that part of the work not consisting of U.S. government materials. This enables readers of such works to know which portions of the work are government materials in the public domain.

It's up to you to decide if your work consists preponderantly of U.S. government materials. Certainly, if more than half of your product consists of federal government materials, your notice should enable readers to determine which portions of the work are copyrighted and which are in the public domain.

EXAMPLE: Databest Inc. publishes a CD-ROM containing analyses of U.S. census data and including several appendices containing U.S. Census Bureau material. The CD-ROM is a collective work in which independently created contributions have been combined to form a collective whole. The appendices amount to over half the CD-ROM. The copyright notice for the work could state: "Copyright © 1998 by Databest Inc. No protection is claimed in works of the United States Government as set forth in Appendices 1, 2, 3, 4, 6."

Alternatively, the notice could affirmatively identify those portions of the work in which copyright is claimed—that is, those portions not containing government materials. In this event, the notice might look like this: "Copyright © 1998 by Databest Inc. Copyright claimed in Sections 1 through 10."

Failure to follow this rule will result in the copyright notice being found invalid. This means that an infringer of the material in which you claim a copyright would be allowed to raise the innocent infringement defense at trial. (See Section P1 above.)

T. Where to Place Copyright Notice

Although it's not strictly required by law, you should place your copyright notice in lots of different places to ensure that it serves its intended purposes—to be seen and give notice of your copyright to the world. Indeed, every component of a published software package should contain a copyright notice. This includes:

- the package or box the software comes in, if any
- the manual and other written documentation
- the computer disks or other media containing the software, and
- the appropriate computer screens

1. Packaging

Most published software that is not distributed online is sold in some sort of box or

other package. A copyright notice should appear somewhere on the box. It is often placed on the back of the box, but you can also place it on the front or sides. The notice will apply to your cover art and graphics as well as to the software and other materials inside the box or package.

2. Computer Diskettes, CD-ROMs

A copyright notice should also be printed on a label permanently affixed to the computer diskettes, CD-ROM disks or other magnetic media containing the software.

3. Computer Code

If you license or otherwise distribute your source code, at a minimum include a copyright notice on the first and last page. Even better, include a notice on every page.

Also, place a copyright notice on the first page and liberally sprinkle notices throughout the remainder of the code. This way, anyone who prints out the code will see that you claim copyright in it.

In addition, use a confidentiality legend in conjunction with your copyright notice. (See Section U1.)

4. Computer Screens

According to Copyright Office regulations, providing a copyright notice on the box or disk containing published software is sufficient. But it shouldn't be sufficient for you. Remember, you want to make sure that users do really see your notice. It should appear somewhere on the computer screen when the software is used. This can be done in one or more of the following ways:

- by printing the notice in or near the title of the program or at the end of the program
- displaying the notice when the program is first activated (on the opening screen or in an about or credit box), or
- displaying the notice continuously while the program is being used (for example, in a status bar).

A good rule is to display it on the screen at the beginning and end of a program, as well as every time the program title is displayed. Also include a notice in any "read me" files.

Certain programs have more than one mode or version when they are running or performing their task. For example, many complicated programs have a training mode, separate from the program itself. Each mode should have a correct copyright notice.

5. Software Documentation and Other Materials in Book or Pamphlet Form

Documentation includes everything that accompanies, explains, illustrates or otherwise complements your program. Many manuals, such as user manuals, programmer reference manuals, and training manuals, look more or less like books. Short manuals and program documentation often take the form of a pamphlet. The rules for placing your copyright notice are the same for both, as long as the pamphlet consists of at least two pages.

The copyright notice for a manual or other similar written work may be placed in any of the following locations:

- the title page
- the page immediately following the title page (this is the most commonly used location for books)
- either side of the front cover
- if there is no front cover, either side of the back leaf of the copies—that is, the hinged piece of paper at the end of a book or pamphlet consisting of at least two pages
- the first or last page of the main body of the work.

6. Pictorial, Graphic and Sculptural Works

This category includes computer-generated art, charts, graphs, etc. Notice must be affixed directly or by label that is sewn, cemented or otherwise durably attached to two- or three-dimensional copies. The notice must be attached to the front or back of copies, to any backing, mounting, base, matting, framing or any permanent housing. Again, the idea is to give notice, not bury it, so be sure your notice can be seen easily.

U. Other Information Near Notice

Certain other information in addition to the copyright notice itself is commonly included on the same page as the notice.

1. Trade Secret Notices

Most software qualifies for trade secret protection as well as copyright protection. For this reason, it's a good idea to include a trade secret notice along with a copyright notice. (See Chapter 6.)

a. Unpublished programs

A confidentiality notice such as the following can be used for unpublished programs and other unpublished materials:

THIS IS AN UNPUBLISHED WORK CONTAINING *[your or your company name]* CONFIDENTIAL AND PROPRIETARY INFORMATION. DISCLOSURE, USE OR REPRODUCTION WITHOUT AUTHORIZATION OF *[your or your company name]* IS PROHIBITED.

b. Published programs

When you publish a program—for example, mass-market it in computer stores or over the Internet—include a combined confidentiality notice such as the following in the program itself and on any diskettes, manuals and other documentation:

THIS *[choose one: program, document, material]* IS CONFIDENTIAL AND PROPRIETARY TO *[your company name]* AND MAY NOT BE REPRODUCED, PUBLISHED OR DISCLOSED TO OTHERS WITHOUT COMPANY AUTHORIZATION.

2. All Rights Reserved

Until recent years, some Central and Latin American countries required that the words "All rights reserved" be used along with a copyright notice. This is no longer true. Nevertheless, out of force of habit, you sometimes see the words "All rights reserved" accompanying a copyright notice

FIRST THE WORD COPYRIGHT OR THE © SYMBOL OR COPR. THEN THE DATE, THEN YOUR NAME, THEN ALL RIGHTS RESERVED.

on published works. These words are unnecessary, but do no harm if they are used.

3. Warning Statements

Since many people do not really understand what a copyright notice means, many copyright owners include various types of warning or explanatory statements near the copyright notice. The purpose is to make clear to users that the work is copyrighted and may not be reproduced without the copyright owner's permission. It does not cost anything to place this type of statement near the copyright notice, and it may help deter copyright infringement. But remember, such statements do not take the place of a valid copyright notice as described earlier in this chapter.

a. Statements used in software

Here's a simple warning statement that could be used near a copyright notice contained in software itself—both on diskette labels and on the computer screen when the program is activated (for example, it could be placed inside an about or credit box or near the program's title):

This software is copyrighted. The software may not be copied, reproduced, translated or reduced to any electronic medium or machine-readable form without the prior written consent of *[Name of Copyright Owner]* except that you may make one copy of the program disks solely for back-up purposes.

b. Statements commonly used in manuals

Here is an example of the type of warning statements that are commonly used in software manuals:

This manual, and the software described in this manual, are copyrighted. No part of this manual or the described software may be copied, reproduced, translated or reduced to any electronic medium or machine-readable form without the prior written consent of *[Name of Copyright Owner]* except that you may make one copy of the program disks solely for back-up purposes.

Friendly Copyright Statements

A growing number of software publishers are departing from negative sounding statements like those above. Rather, they employ friendly language that is positive and inviting. The reasoning behind this approach is that appealing to an end-user's sense of fair play will get better results than attempting to scare him. Here's an example of such language:

We have worked very hard to create a quality product and wish to realize the fair fruits of our labor. We therefore insist that you honor our copyright. However we want to encourage the use of our product in all possible circumstances and will work very hard to meet your needs if you will call and ask us for permission.

1. Unpublished computer program created by a single author; not a work made for hire

---

FORM TX
For a Literary Work
UNITED STATES COPYRIGHT OFFICE

REGISTRATION NUMBER

_____

TX _____ TXU _____
EFFECTIVE DATE OF REGISTRATION

_____

Month _____ Day _____ Year _____

DO NOT WRITE ABOVE THIS LINE. IF YOU NEED MORE SPACE, USE A SEPARATE CONTINUATION SHEET.

1 TITLE OF THIS WORK ▼

Birdbrain

PREVIOUS OR ALTERNATIVE TITLES ▼

PUBLICATION AS A CONTRIBUTION If this work was published as a contribution to a periodical, serial, or collection, give information about the collective work in which the contribution appeared. **Title of Collective Work ▼**

If published in a periodical or serial give: Volume ▼ _____ Number ▼ _____ Issue Date ▼ _____ On Pages ▼ _____

2 **a** NAME OF AUTHOR ▼
Basilio Chan

DATES OF BIRTH AND DEATH
Year Born ▼ 1960 Year Died ▼

Was this contribution to the work a "work made for hire"?
☐ Yes
☒ No

AUTHOR'S NATIONALITY OR DOMICILE
Name of Country
OR { Citizen of ▶ U.S.A.
Domiciled in ▶ U.S.A.

WAS THIS AUTHOR'S CONTRIBUTION TO THE WORK
Anonymous? ☐ Yes ☒ No
Pseudonymous? ☐ Yes ☒ No
If the answer to either of these questions is "Yes," see detailed instructions.

NATURE OF AUTHORSHIP Briefly describe nature of material created by this author in which copyright is claimed. ▼
Entire text of computer program

NOTE
Under the law, the "author" of a "work made for hire" is generally the employer, not the employee (see instructions). For any part of this work that was "made for hire" check "Yes" in the space provided, give the employer (or other person for whom the work was prepared) as "Author" of that part, and leave the space for dates of birth and death blank.

b NAME OF AUTHOR ▼

DATES OF BIRTH AND DEATH
Year Born ▼ Year Died ▼

Was this contribution to the work a "work made for hire"?
☐ Yes
☐ No

AUTHOR'S NATIONALITY OR DOMICILE
Name of Country
OR { Citizen of ▶
Domiciled in ▶

WAS THIS AUTHOR'S CONTRIBUTION TO THE WORK
Anonymous? ☐ Yes ☐ No
Pseudonymous? ☐ Yes ☐ No
If the answer to either of these questions is "Yes," see detailed instructions.

NATURE OF AUTHORSHIP Briefly describe nature of material created by this author in which copyright is claimed. ▼

c NAME OF AUTHOR ▼

DATES OF BIRTH AND DEATH
Year Born ▼ Year Died ▼

Was this contribution to the work a "work made for hire"?
☐ Yes
☐ No

AUTHOR'S NATIONALITY OR DOMICILE
Name of Country
OR { Citizen of ▶
Domiciled in ▶

WAS THIS AUTHOR'S CONTRIBUTION TO THE WORK
Anonymous? ☐ Yes ☐ No
Pseudonymous? ☐ Yes ☐ No
If the answer to either of these questions is "Yes," see detailed instructions.

NATURE OF AUTHORSHIP Briefly describe nature of material created by this author in which copyright is claimed. ▼

3 **a** YEAR IN WHICH CREATION OF THIS WORK WAS COMPLETED This information must be given
199X ◀ Year in all cases.

b DATE AND NATION OF FIRST PUBLICATION OF THIS PARTICULAR WORK
Complete this information Month ▶ _____ Day ▶ _____ Year ▶ _____
ONLY if this work has been published. ◀ Nation

4 COPYRIGHT CLAIMANT(S) Name and address must be given even if the claimant is the same as the author given in space 2. ▼
Basilio Chan
123 1st St.
Berkeley, CA 94700

See instructions before completing this space.

TRANSFER If the claimant(s) named here in space 4 is (are) different from the author(s) named in space 2, give a brief statement of how the claimant(s) obtained ownership of the copyright. ▼

APPLICATION RECEIVED

ONE DEPOSIT RECEIVED

TWO DEPOSITS RECEIVED

FUNDS RECEIVED

DO NOT WRITE HERE OFFICE USE ONLY

MORE ON BACK ▶ • Complete all applicable spaces (numbers 5-11) on the reverse side of this page.
• See detailed instructions. • Sign the form at line 10.

DO NOT WRITE HERE
Page 1 of _____ pages

1. Unpublished computer program created by a single author; not a work made for hire (back)

EXAMINED BY	FORM TX
CHECKED BY	
CORRESPONDENCE ☐ Yes	FOR COPYRIGHT OFFICE USE ONLY

DO NOT WRITE ABOVE THIS LINE. IF YOU NEED MORE SPACE, USE A SEPARATE CONTINUATION SHEET.

PREVIOUS REGISTRATION Has registration for this work, or for an earlier version of this work, already been made in the Copyright Office?
☐ Yes ☒ No If your answer is "Yes," why is another registration being sought? (Check appropriate box) ▼
a. ☐ This is the first published edition of a work previously registered in unpublished form.
b. ☐ This is the first application submitted by this author as copyright claimant.
c. ☐ This is a changed version of the work, as shown by space 6 on this application.
If your answer is "Yes," give: **Previous Registration Number** ▼   **Year of Registration** ▼

5

DERIVATIVE WORK OR COMPILATION Complete both space 6a and 6b for a derivative work; complete only 6b for a compilation.
a. **Preexisting Material** Identify any preexisting work or works that this work is based on or incorporates. ▼

b. **Material Added to This Work** Give a brief, general statement of the material that has been added to this work and in which copyright is claimed. ▼

6
See instructions before completing this space.

—space deleted—

7

REPRODUCTION FOR USE OF BLIND OR PHYSICALLY HANDICAPPED INDIVIDUALS A signature on this form at space 10 and a check in one of the boxes here in space 8 constitutes a non-exclusive grant of permission to the Library of Congress to reproduce and distribute solely for the blind and physically handicapped and under the conditions and limitations prescribed by the regulations of the Copyright Office: (1) copies of the work identified in space 1 of this application in Braille (or similar tactile symbols); or (2) phonorecords embodying a fixation of a reading of that work; or (3) both.

a ☒ Copies and Phonorecords   b ☐ Copies Only   c ☐ Phonorecords Only

8
See instructions.

DEPOSIT ACCOUNT If the registration fee is to be charged to a Deposit Account established in the Copyright Office, give name and number of Account.
Name ▼   Account Number ▼

9

CORRESPONDENCE Give name and address to which correspondence about this application should be sent.   Name/Address/Apt/City/State/ZIP ▼

Basilio Chan
123 1st St.
Berkeley, CA 94700
Area Code and Telephone Number ▶ 510-555-1234

Be sure to give your daytime phone number ◀

CERTIFICATION* I, the undersigned, hereby certify that I am the
Check only one ▶
☒ author
☐ other copyright claimant
☐ owner of exclusive right(s)
☐ authorized agent of _____
of the work identified in this application and that the statements made
by me in this application are correct to the best of my knowledge.   Name of author or other copyright claimant, or owner of exclusive right(s) ▲

Typed or printed name and date ▼ If this application gives a date of publication in space 3, do not sign and submit it before that date.
Basilio Chan   Date ▶ 1/2/9X

☞ Handwritten signature (X) ▼
Basilio Chan

10

MAIL CERTIFI-CATE TO	Name ▼ Basilio Chan	YOU MUST: • Complete all necessary spaces • Sign your application in space 10
Certificate will be mailed in window envelope	Number/Street/Apt ▼ 123 1st St.	SEND ALL 3 ELEMENTS IN THE SAME PACKAGE: 1. Application form 2. Nonrefundable $20 filing fee in check or money order payable to *Register of Copyrights* 3. Deposit material
	City/State/ZIP ▼ Berkeley, CA 94700	MAIL TO: Register of Copyrights Library of Congress Washington, D.C. 20559-6000

11

*17 U.S.C. § 506(e): Any person who knowingly makes a false representation of a material fact in the application for copyright registration provided for by section 409, or in any written statement filed in connection with the application, shall be fined not more than $2,500.
May 1995—300,000   ☼U.S. COPYRIGHT OFFICE WWW FORM: 1995

2. Published work made for hire; computer program and documents registered together

---

FORM TX

For a Literary Work
UNITED STATES COPYRIGHT OFFICE

REGISTRATION NUMBER

_____

TX _____ TXU _____
EFFECTIVE DATE OF REGISTRATION

_____
Month   Day   Year

DO NOT WRITE ABOVE THIS LINE. IF YOU NEED MORE SPACE, USE A SEPARATE CONTINUATION SHEET.

1

TITLE OF THIS WORK ▼

Orchid 1-2-3
_____
PREVIOUS OR ALTERNATIVE TITLES ▼

PUBLICATION AS A CONTRIBUTION If this work was published as a contribution to a periodical, serial, or collection, give information about the collective work in which the contribution appeared.   **Title of Collective Work ▼**

If published in a periodical or serial give: **Volume ▼**   **Number ▼**   **Issue Date ▼**   **On Pages ▼**

2

a **NAME OF AUTHOR ▼**
Micro Wierd, Inc.

DATES OF BIRTH AND DEATH
Year Born ▼   Year Died ▼
1960

Was this contribution to the work a "work made for hire"?
☒ Yes
☐ No

AUTHOR'S NATIONALITY OR DOMICILE
Name of Country
OR { Citizen of ▶ U.S.A.
      Domiciled in ▶

WAS THIS AUTHOR'S CONTRIBUTION TO THE WORK
Anonymous? ☐ Yes ☒ No
Pseudonymous? ☐ Yes ☒ No
If the answer to either of these questions is "Yes," see detailed instructions.

NATURE OF AUTHORSHIP Briefly describe nature of material created by this author in which copyright is claimed. ▼
Entire text of computer program with accompanying documentation

NOTE

Under the law, the "author" of a "work made for hire" is generally the employer, not the employee (see instructions). For any part of this work that was "made for hire" check "Yes" in the space provided, give the employer (or other person for whom the work was prepared) as "Author" of that part, and leave the space for dates of birth and death blank.

b **NAME OF AUTHOR ▼**

DATES OF BIRTH AND DEATH
Year Born ▼   Year Died ▼

Was this contribution to the work a "work made for hire"?
☐ Yes
☐ No

AUTHOR'S NATIONALITY OR DOMICILE
Name of Country
OR { Citizen of ▶
      Domiciled in ▶

WAS THIS AUTHOR'S CONTRIBUTION TO THE WORK
Anonymous? ☐ Yes ☐ No
Pseudonymous? ☐ Yes ☐ No
If the answer to either of these questions is "Yes," see detailed instructions.

NATURE OF AUTHORSHIP Briefly describe nature of material created by this author in which copyright is claimed. ▼

c **NAME OF AUTHOR ▼**

DATES OF BIRTH AND DEATH
Year Born ▼   Year Died ▼

Was this contribution to the work a "work made for hire"?
☐ Yes
☐ No

AUTHOR'S NATIONALITY OR DOMICILE
Name of Country
OR { Citizen of ▶
      Domiciled in ▶

WAS THIS AUTHOR'S CONTRIBUTION TO THE WORK
Anonymous? ☐ Yes ☐ No
Pseudonymous? ☐ Yes ☐ No
If the answer to either of these questions is "Yes," see detailed instructions.

NATURE OF AUTHORSHIP Briefly describe nature of material created by this author in which copyright is claimed. ▼

3

a **YEAR IN WHICH CREATION OF THIS WORK WAS COMPLETED** This information must be given in all cases.
199X ◀ Year

b **DATE AND NATION OF FIRST PUBLICATION OF THIS PARTICULAR WORK** Complete this information ONLY if this work has been published.
Month ▶ 4 Day ▶ 1 Year ▶ 199X
U.S.A. ◀ Nation

4

See instructions before completing this space.

COPYRIGHT CLAIMANT(S) Name and address must be given even if the claimant is the same as the author given in space 2. ▼
Micro Wierd, Inc.
666 Dreary Lane
Marred Vista, CA 90000

TRANSFER If the claimant(s) named here in space 4 is (are) different from the author(s) named in space 2, give a brief statement of how the claimant(s) obtained ownership of the copyright. ▼

DO NOT WRITE HERE
OFFICE USE ONLY

APPLICATION RECEIVED

ONE DEPOSIT RECEIVED

TWO DEPOSITS RECEIVED

FUNDS RECEIVED

MORE ON BACK ▶ • Complete all applicable spaces (numbers 5-11) on the reverse side of this page.
• See detailed instructions.   • Sign the form at line 10.

DO NOT WRITE HERE
Page 1 of _____ pages

2. Published work made for hire; computer program and documents registered together (back)

EXAMINED BY	FORM TX
CHECKED BY	
CORRESPONDENCE ☐ Yes	FOR COPYRIGHT OFFICE USE ONLY

DO NOT WRITE ABOVE THIS LINE. IF YOU NEED MORE SPACE, USE A SEPARATE CONTINUATION SHEET.

PREVIOUS REGISTRATION Has registration for this work, or for an earlier version of this work, already been made in the Copyright Office?
☐ Yes ☒ No If your answer is "Yes," why is another registration being sought? (Check appropriate box) ▼
a. ☐ This is the first published edition of a work previously registered in unpublished form.
b. ☐ This is the first application submitted by this author as copyright claimant.
c. ☐ This is a changed version of the work, as shown by space 6 on this application.
If your answer is "Yes," give: **Previous Registration Number** ▼   **Year of Registration** ▼

5

DERIVATIVE WORK OR COMPILATION Complete both space 6a and 6b for a derivative work; complete only 6b for a compilation.
a. **Preexisting Material** Identify any preexisting work or works that this work is based on or incorporates. ▼

b. **Material Added to This Work** Give a brief, general statement of the material that has been added to this work and in which copyright is claimed. ▼

6

See instructions before completing this space.

—space deleted—

7

REPRODUCTION FOR USE OF BLIND OR PHYSICALLY HANDICAPPED INDIVIDUALS A signature on this form at space 10 and a check in one of the boxes here in space 8 constitutes a non-exclusive grant of permission to the Library of Congress to reproduce and distribute solely for the blind and physically handicapped and under the conditions and limitations prescribed by the regulations of the Copyright Office: (1) copies of the work identified in space 1 of this application in Braille (or similar tactile symbols); or (2) phonorecords embodying a fixation of a reading of that work; or (3) both.

a ☒ Copies and Phonorecords   b ☐ Copies Only   c ☐ Phonorecords Only

8

See instructions.

DEPOSIT ACCOUNT If the registration fee is to be charged to a Deposit Account established in the Copyright Office, give name and number of Account.
Name ▼   Account Number ▼

9

CORRESPONDENCE Give name and address to which correspondence about this application should be sent.   Name/Address/Apt/City/State/ZIP ▼
Micro Wierd, Inc.
666 Dreary Lane
Marred Vista, CA 90000
Area Code and Telephone Number ▶   818-555-1212

Be sure to give your daytime phone number ◀

CERTIFICATION* I, the undersigned, hereby certify that I am the
Check only one ▶
☒ author
☐ other copyright claimant
☐ owner of exclusive right(s)
☐ authorized agent of
of the work identified in this application and that the statements made
by me in this application are correct to the best of my knowledge.

Name of author or other copyright claimant, or owner of exclusive right(s) ▲

10

Typed or printed name and date ▼ If this application gives a date of publication in space 3, do not sign and submit it before that date.
Leslie Howard   Date ▶ 4/1/9X

Handwritten signature (X) ▼
Leslie Howard

MAIL CERTIFI-CATE TO
Name ▼
Micro Wierd, Inc.
Number/Street/Apt ▼
666 Dreary Lane.
City/State/ZIP ▼
Marred Vista, CA 90000

Certificate will be mailed in window envelope

YOU MUST:
· Complete all necessary spaces
· Sign your application in space 10
SEND ALL 3 ELEMENTS IN THE SAME PACKAGE:
1. Application form
2. Nonrefundable $20 filing fee in check or money order payable to *Register of Copyrights*
3. Deposit material
MAIL TO:
Register of Copyrights
Library of Congress
Washington, D.C. 20559-6000

11

*17 U.S.C. § 506(e): Any person who knowingly makes a false representation of a material fact in the application for copyright registration provided for by section 409, or in any written statement filed in connection with the application, shall be fined not more than $2,500.

May 1995—300,000   ☉U.S. COPYRIGHT OFFICE WWW FORM: 1995

3. Published computer game created by joint authors; all rights transferred to publisher; screen displays listed in Nature of Authorship statement

FORM TX
For a Literary Work
UNITED STATES COPYRIGHT OFFICE

REGISTRATION NUMBER

_____

TX _____ TXU _____

EFFECTIVE DATE OF REGISTRATION

_____

Month   Day   Year

DO NOT WRITE ABOVE THIS LINE. IF YOU NEED MORE SPACE, USE A SEPARATE CONTINUATION SHEET.

1

TITLE OF THIS WORK ▼

You Are What You Eat

PREVIOUS OR ALTERNATIVE TITLES ▼

PUBLICATION AS A CONTRIBUTION If this work was published as a contribution to a periodical, serial, or collection, give information about the collective work in which the contribution appeared.   **Title of Collective Work ▼**

If published in a periodical or serial give: Volume ▼   Number ▼   Issue Date ▼   On Pages ▼

2

a NAME OF AUTHOR ▼

Ron Claiborne

DATES OF BIRTH AND DEATH
Year Born ▼   Year Died ▼
1950

Was this contribution to the work a "work made for hire"?
☐ Yes
☒ No

AUTHOR'S NATIONALITY OR DOMICILE
Name of Country
OR { Citizen of ▶ U.S.A.
Domiciled in ▶

WAS THIS AUTHOR'S CONTRIBUTION TO THE WORK
Anonymous?   ☐ Yes ☒ No
Pseudonymous? ☐ Yes ☒ No
If the answer to either of these questions is "Yes," see detailed instructions.

NATURE OF AUTHORSHIP Briefly describe nature of material created by this author in which copyright is claimed. ▼
Entire text of computer program and screen display with user documentation

NOTE

Under the law, the "author" of a "work made for hire" is generally the employer, not the employee (see instructions). For any part of this work that was "made for hire" check "Yes" in the space provided, give the employer (or other person for whom the work was prepared) as "Author" of that part, and leave the space for dates of birth and death blank.

b NAME OF AUTHOR ▼

Sue Sweet

DATES OF BIRTH AND DEATH
Year Born ▼   Year Died ▼
1960

Was this contribution to the work a "work made for hire"?
☐ Yes
☒ No

AUTHOR'S NATIONALITY OR DOMICILE
Name of Country
OR { Citizen of ▶ U.S.A.
Domiciled in ▶

WAS THIS AUTHOR'S CONTRIBUTION TO THE WORK
Anonymous?   ☐ Yes ☒ No
Pseudonymous? ☐ Yes ☒ No
If the answer to either of these questions is "Yes," see detailed instructions.

NATURE OF AUTHORSHIP Briefly describe nature of material created by this author in which copyright is claimed. ▼
Entire text of computer program and screen display with user documentation

c NAME OF AUTHOR ▼

Jessie Quicksilver

DATES OF BIRTH AND DEATH
Year Born ▼   Year Died ▼
1970

Was this contribution to the work a "work made for hire"?
☐ Yes
☒ No

AUTHOR'S NATIONALITY OR DOMICILE
Name of Country
OR { Citizen of ▶ U.S.A.
Domiciled in ▶

WAS THIS AUTHOR'S CONTRIBUTION TO THE WORK
Anonymous?   ☐ Yes ☒ No
Pseudonymous? ☐ Yes ☒ No
If the answer to either of these questions is "Yes," see detailed instructions.

NATURE OF AUTHORSHIP Briefly describe nature of material created by this author in which copyright is claimed. ▼
Entire text of computer program and screen display with user documentation

3

a YEAR IN WHICH CREATION OF THIS WORK WAS COMPLETED   This information must be given in all cases.
199X ◀ Year

b DATE AND NATION OF FIRST PUBLICATION OF THIS PARTICULAR WORK
Complete this information ONLY if this work has been published.
Month ▶ 6   Day ▶ 1   Year ▶ 199X
U.S.A. ◀ Nation

4

COPYRIGHT CLAIMANT(S) Name and address must be given even if the claimant is the same as the author given in space 2. ▼

Micro Games, Inc.
100 Commerce Way
Cambridge, WA 01234

See instructions before completing this space.

TRANSFER If the claimant(s) named here in space 4 is (are) different from the author(s) named in space 2, give a brief statement of how the claimant(s) obtained ownership of the copyright. ▼

APPLICATION RECEIVED

ONE DEPOSIT RECEIVED

TWO DEPOSITS RECEIVED

FUNDS RECEIVED

DO NOT WRITE HERE
OFFICE USE ONLY

MORE ON BACK ▶ • Complete all applicable spaces (numbers 5-11) on the reverse side of this page.
• See detailed instructions.   • Sign the form at line 10.

DO NOT WRITE HERE
Page 1 of _____ pages

3. Published computer game created by joint authors; all rights transferred to publisher; screen displays listed in Nature of Authorship statement (back)

EXAMINED BY	FORM TX
CHECKED BY	
CORRESPONDENCE ☐ Yes	FOR COPYRIGHT OFFICE USE ONLY

DO NOT WRITE ABOVE THIS LINE. IF YOU NEED MORE SPACE, USE A SEPARATE CONTINUATION SHEET.

PREVIOUS REGISTRATION Has registration for this work, or for an earlier version of this work, already been made in the Copyright Office?
☐ Yes ☒ No If your answer is "Yes," why is another registration being sought? (Check appropriate box) ▼

5

a. ☐ This is the first published edition of a work previously registered in unpublished form.
b. ☐ This is the first application submitted by this author as copyright claimant.
c. ☐ This is a changed version of the work, as shown by space 6 on this application.
If your answer is "Yes," give: **Previous Registration Number ▼**   **Year of Registration ▼**

DERIVATIVE WORK OR COMPILATION Complete both space 6a and 6b for a derivative work; complete only 6b for a compilation.
a. **Preexisting Material** Identify any preexisting work or works that this work is based on or incorporates. ▼

6

b. **Material Added to This Work** Give a brief, general statement of the material that has been added to this work and in which copyright is claimed. ▼

See instructions before completing this space.

—space deleted—

7

REPRODUCTION FOR USE OF BLIND OR PHYSICALLY HANDICAPPED INDIVIDUALS A signature on this form at space 10 and a check in one of the boxes here in space 8 constitutes a non-exclusive grant of permission to the Library of Congress to reproduce and distribute solely for the blind and physically handicapped and under the conditions and limitations prescribed by the regulations of the Copyright Office: (1) copies of the work identified in space 1 of this application in Braille (or similar tactile symbols); or (2) phonorecords embodying a fixation of a reading of that work; or (3) both.

8

a ☒ Copies and Phonorecords   b ☐ Copies Only   c ☐ Phonorecords Only   See instructions.

DEPOSIT ACCOUNT If the registration fee is to be charged to a Deposit Account established in the Copyright Office, give name and number of Account.
Name ▼   **Account Number ▼**

9

Micro Games, Inc.

CORRESPONDENCE Give name and address to which correspondence about this application should be sent.   Name/Address/Apt/City/State/ZIP ▼

Micro Games, Inc.
100 Commerce Way
Cambridge, WA 01234

Area Code and Telephone Number ▶ 012-555-5555

Be sure to give your daytime phone ◀ number

CERTIFICATION* I, the undersigned, hereby certify that I am the
Check only one ▶
☐ author
☐ other copyright claimant
☐ owner of exclusive right(s)
☒ authorized agent of Micro Games, Inc.

10

of the work identified in this application and that the statements made by me in this application are correct to the best of my knowledge.

Name of author or other copyright claimant, or owner of exclusive right(s) ▲

Typed or printed name and date ▼ If this application gives a date of publication in space 3, do not sign and submit it before that date.

Art Atlas   Date ▶ 5/15/9X

Handwritten signature (X) ▼
Art Atlas

MAIL CERTIFI-CATE TO		**11**
Name ▼	Micro Games, Inc.	
Number/Street/Apt ▼	100 Commerce Way	
Certificate will be mailed in window envelope	City/State/ZIP ▼ Cambridge, WA 01234	

YOU MUST:
• Complete all necessary spaces
• Sign your application in space 10
SEND ALL 3 ELEMENTS IN THE SAME PACKAGE:
1. Application form
2. Nonrefundable $20 filing fee in check or money order payable to *Register of Copyrights*
3. Deposit material
MAIL TO:
Register of Copyrights
Library of Congress
Washington, D.C. 20559-6000

May 1995—300,000

◦U.S. COPYRIGHT OFFICE WWW FORM: 1995

4. Published derivative work made for hire; a new version of previously published program

---

FORM TX
For a Literary Work
UNITED STATES COPYRIGHT OFFICE

REGISTRATION NUMBER

TX	TXU

EFFECTIVE DATE OF REGISTRATION

_____ _____ _____
Month   Day   Year

DO NOT WRITE ABOVE THIS LINE. IF YOU NEED MORE SPACE, USE A SEPARATE CONTINUATION SHEET.

1

TITLE OF THIS WORK ▼

Account Handler 2.0

PREVIOUS OR ALTERNATIVE TITLES ▼

PUBLICATION AS A CONTRIBUTION If this work was published as a contribution to a periodical, serial, or collection, give information about the collective work in which the contribution appeared.   **Title of Collective Work** ▼

If published in a periodical or serial give: **Volume** ▼   **Number** ▼   **Issue Date** ▼   **On Pages** ▼

2

a

NAME OF AUTHOR ▼

CPA Software

DATES OF BIRTH AND DEATH
Year Born ▼   Year Died ▼

Was this contribution to the work a "work made for hire"?
☒ Yes
☐ No

AUTHOR'S NATIONALITY OR DOMICILE
Name of Country
OR { Citizen of ▶ U.S.A.
{ Domiciled in▶

WAS THIS AUTHOR'S CONTRIBUTION TO THE WORK
Anonymous?   ☐ Yes ☒ No
Pseudonymous? ☐ Yes ☒ No
If the answer to either of these questions is "Yes," see detailed instructions.

NATURE OF AUTHORSHIP Briefly describe nature of material created by this author in which copyright is claimed. ▼
Entire text of computer program

NOTE

Under the law, the "author" of a "work made for hire" is generally the employer, not the employee (see instructions). For any part of this work that was "made for hire" check "Yes" in the space provided, give the employer (or other person for whom the work was prepared) as "Author" of that part, and leave the space for dates of birth and death blank.

b

NAME OF AUTHOR ▼

DATES OF BIRTH AND DEATH
Year Born ▼   Year Died ▼

Was this contribution to the work a "work made for hire"?
☐ Yes
☐ No

AUTHOR'S NATIONALITY OR DOMICILE
Name of Country
OR { Citizen of ▶
{ Domiciled in▶

WAS THIS AUTHOR'S CONTRIBUTION TO THE WORK
Anonymous?   ☐ Yes ☐ No
Pseudonymous? ☐ Yes ☐ No
If the answer to either of these questions is "Yes," see detailed instructions.

NATURE OF AUTHORSHIP Briefly describe nature of material created by this author in which copyright is claimed. ▼

c

NAME OF AUTHOR ▼

DATES OF BIRTH AND DEATH
Year Born ▼   Year Died ▼

Was this contribution to the work a "work made for hire"?
☐ Yes
☐ No

AUTHOR'S NATIONALITY OR DOMICILE
Name of Country
OR { Citizen of ▶
{ Domiciled in▶

WAS THIS AUTHOR'S CONTRIBUTION TO THE WORK
Anonymous?   ☐ Yes ☐ No
Pseudonymous? ☐ Yes ☐ No
If the answer to either of these questions is "Yes," see detailed instructions.

NATURE OF AUTHORSHIP Briefly describe nature of material created by this author in which copyright is claimed. ▼

3

a

YEAR IN WHICH CREATION OF THIS WORK WAS COMPLETED This information must be given in all cases.
199X ◀ Year

b

DATE AND NATION OF FIRST PUBLICATION OF THIS PARTICULAR WORK Complete this information ONLY if this work has been published.
Month ▶ 11   Day ▶ 1   Year ▶ 199X
U.S.A. ◀ Nation

4

See instructions before completing this space.

COPYRIGHT CLAIMANT(S) Name and address must be given even if the claimant is the same as the author given in space 2. ▼

CPA Software, Inc.
240 5th Ave.
New York, NY 12345

TRANSFER If the claimant(s) named here in space 4 is (are) different from the author(s) named in space 2, give a brief statement of how the claimant(s) obtained ownership of the copyright. ▼

DO NOT WRITE HERE
OFFICE USE ONLY

APPLICATION RECEIVED

ONE DEPOSIT RECEIVED

TWO DEPOSITS RECEIVED

FUNDS RECEIVED

MORE ON BACK ▶ • Complete all applicable spaces (numbers 5-11) on the reverse side of this page.
• See detailed instructions.   • Sign the form at line 10.

DO NOT WRITE HERE

Page 1 of _____ pages

4. Published derivative work made for hire; a new version of previously published program (back)

EXAMINED BY	FORM TX
CHECKED BY	
CORRESPONDENCE ☐ Yes	FOR COPYRIGHT OFFICE USE ONLY

DO NOT WRITE ABOVE THIS LINE. IF YOU NEED MORE SPACE, USE A SEPARATE CONTINUATION SHEET.

PREVIOUS REGISTRATION Has registration for this work, or for an earlier version of this work, already been made in the Copyright Office?
☒ Yes   ☐ No   If your answer is "Yes," why is another registration being sought? (Check appropriate box) ▼
a.☐ This is the first published edition of a work previously registered in unpublished form.
b.☐ This is the first application submitted by this author as copyright claimant.
c.☒ This is a changed version of the work, as shown by space 6 on this application.
If your answer is "Yes," give: **Previous Registration Number** ▼   **Year of Registration** ▼
TX123456   1994

5

DERIVATIVE WORK OR COMPILATION Complete both space 6a and 6b for a derivative work; complete only 6b for a compilation.
a. **Preexisting Material** Identify any preexisting work or works that this work is based on or incorporates. ▼
previous version

b. **Material Added to This Work** Give a brief, general statement of the material that has been added to this work and in which copyright is claimed. ▼
revised computer program

See instructions before completing this space.

6

—space deleted—

7

REPRODUCTION FOR USE OF BLIND OR PHYSICALLY HANDICAPPED INDIVIDUALS A signature on this form at space 10 and a check in one of the boxes here in space 8 constitutes a non-exclusive grant of permission to the Library of Congress to reproduce and distribute solely for the blind and physically handicapped and under the conditions and limitations prescribed by the regulations of the Copyright Office: (1) copies of the work identified in space 1 of this application in Braille (or similar tactile symbols); or (2) phonorecords embodying a fixation of a reading of that work; or (3) both.

a ☒ Copies and Phonorecords   b ☐ Copies Only   c ☐ Phonorecords Only

See instructions.

8

DEPOSIT ACCOUNT If the registration fee is to be charged to a Deposit Account established in the Copyright Office, give name and number of Account.
Name ▼   Account Number ▼

9

CORRESPONDENCE Give name and address to which correspondence about this application should be sent.   Name/Address/Apt/City/State/ZIP ▼
CPA Software, Inc.
240 5th Ave.
New York, NY 12345
Area Code and Telephone Number ▶   212-555-5555

Be sure to give your daytime phone ◀ number

CERTIFICATION* I, the undersigned, hereby certify that I am the
Check only one ▶
☐ author
☐ other copyright claimant
☐ owner of exclusive right(s)
☒ authorized agent of CPA Software, Inc.
of the work identified in this application and that the statements made by me in this application are correct to the best of my knowledge.
Name of author or other copyright claimant, or owner of exclusive right(s) ▲

Typed or printed name and date ▼ If this application gives a date of publication in space 3, do not sign and submit it before that date.
Sid Shuster   Date ▶ 8/15/9X

Handwritten signature (X) ▼
Sid Shuster

10

MAIL CERTIFICATE TO

Name ▼
CPA Software, Inc.
Number/Street/Apt ▼
240 5th Ave.
City/State/ZIP ▼
New York, NY 12345

Certificate will be mailed in window envelope

YOU MUST:
· Complete all necessary spaces
· Sign your application in space 10
SEND ALL 3 ELEMENTS IN THE SAME PACKAGE:
1. Application form
2. Nonrefundable $20 filing fee in check or money order payable to *Register of Copyrights*
3. Deposit material
MAIL TO:
Register of Copyrights
Library of Congress
Washington, D.C. 20559-6000

11

*17 U.S.C. § 506(e): Any person who knowingly makes a false representation of a material fact in the application for copyright registration provided for by section 409, or in any written statement filed in connection with the application, shall be fined not more than $2,500.
May 1995—300,000

☼U.S. COPYRIGHT OFFICE WWW FORM: 1995

5. Documentation registered separately from computer program

FORM TX
For a Literary Work
UNITED STATES COPYRIGHT OFFICE

REGISTRATION NUMBER

_____

TX _____ TXU _____
EFFECTIVE DATE OF REGISTRATION

_____

Month   Day   Year

DO NOT WRITE ABOVE THIS LINE. IF YOU NEED MORE SPACE, USE A SEPARATE CONTINUATION SHEET.

1

TITLE OF THIS WORK ▼

Acme Word Users' Manual

PREVIOUS OR ALTERNATIVE TITLES ▼

PUBLICATION AS A CONTRIBUTION If this work was published as a contribution to a periodical, serial, or collection, give information about the collective work in which the contribution appeared.   **Title of Collective Work ▼**

If published in a periodical or serial give: **Volume ▼**   **Number ▼**   **Issue Date ▼**   **On Pages ▼**

2

a

NAME OF AUTHOR ▼

Acme Soft

DATES OF BIRTH AND DEATH
Year Born ▼   Year Died ▼

Was this contribution to the work a "work made for hire"?
☒ Yes
☐ No

AUTHOR'S NATIONALITY OR DOMICILE
Name of Country
OR { Citizen of ▶ U.S.A.
     { Domiciled in ▶

WAS THIS AUTHOR'S CONTRIBUTION TO THE WORK
Anonymous?   ☐ Yes ☒ No
Pseudonymous? ☐ Yes ☒ No
If the answer to either of these questions is "Yes," see detailed instructions.

NATURE OF AUTHORSHIP Briefly describe nature of material created by this author in which copyright is claimed. ▼
Entire text

NOTE

Under the law, the "author" of a "work made for hire" is generally the employer, not the employee (see instructions). For any part of this work that was "made for hire" check "Yes" in the space provided, give the employer (or other person for whom the work was prepared) as "Author" of that part, and leave the space for dates of birth and death blank.

b

NAME OF AUTHOR ▼

DATES OF BIRTH AND DEATH
Year Born ▼   Year Died ▼

Was this contribution to the work a "work made for hire"?
☐ Yes
☐ No

AUTHOR'S NATIONALITY OR DOMICILE
Name of Country
OR { Citizen of ▶
     { Domiciled in ▶

WAS THIS AUTHOR'S CONTRIBUTION TO THE WORK
Anonymous?   ☐ Yes ☐ No
Pseudonymous? ☐ Yes ☐ No
If the answer to either of these questions is "Yes," see detailed instructions.

NATURE OF AUTHORSHIP Briefly describe nature of material created by this author in which copyright is claimed. ▼

c

NAME OF AUTHOR ▼

DATES OF BIRTH AND DEATH
Year Born ▼   Year Died ▼

Was this contribution to the work a "work made for hire"?
☐ Yes
☐ No

AUTHOR'S NATIONALITY OR DOMICILE
Name of Country
OR { Citizen of ▶
     { Domiciled in ▶

WAS THIS AUTHOR'S CONTRIBUTION TO THE WORK
Anonymous?   ☐ Yes ☐ No
Pseudonymous? ☐ Yes ☐ No
If the answer to either of these questions is "Yes," see detailed instructions.

NATURE OF AUTHORSHIP Briefly describe nature of material created by this author in which copyright is claimed. ▼

3

a

YEAR IN WHICH CREATION OF THIS WORK WAS COMPLETED This information must be given in all cases.
199X ◀ Year

b

DATE AND NATION OF FIRST PUBLICATION OF THIS PARTICULAR WORK
Complete this information ONLY if this work has been published.
Month ▶ 12   Day ▶ 1   Year ▶ 199X
U.S.A. ◀ Nation

4

See instructions before completing this space.

COPYRIGHT CLAIMANT(S) Name and address must be given even if the claimant is the same as the author given in space 2. ▼

Acme Soft, Inc.
123 Computer Rd.
Silicon Valley, OR 80500

TRANSFER If the claimant(s) named here in space 4 is (are) different from the author(s) named in space 2, give a brief statement of how the claimant(s) obtained ownership of the copyright. ▼

DO NOT WRITE HERE
OFFICE USE ONLY

APPLICATION RECEIVED

ONE DEPOSIT RECEIVED

TWO DEPOSITS RECEIVED

FUNDS RECEIVED

MORE ON BACK ▶ • Complete all applicable spaces (numbers 5-11) on the reverse side of this page.
• See detailed instructions.   • Sign the form at line 10.

DO NOT WRITE HERE
Page 1 of _____ pages

5. Documentation registered separately from computer program (back)

EXAMINED BY	FORM TX
CHECKED BY	
☐ CORRESPONDENCE Yes	FOR COPYRIGHT OFFICE USE ONLY

DO NOT WRITE ABOVE THIS LINE. IF YOU NEED MORE SPACE, USE A SEPARATE CONTINUATION SHEET.

PREVIOUS REGISTRATION Has registration for this work, or for an earlier version of this work, already been made in the Copyright Office?
☐ Yes ☒ No If your answer is "Yes," why is another registration being sought? (Check appropriate box) ▼
a.☐ This is the first published edition of a work previously registered in unpublished form.
b.☐ This is the first application submitted by this author as copyright claimant.
c.☒ This is a changed version of the work, as shown by space 6 on this application.
If your answer is "Yes," give: **Previous Registration Number** ▼   **Year of Registration** ▼

5

DERIVATIVE WORK OR COMPILATION Complete both space 6a and 6b for a derivative work; complete only 6b for a compilation.
a. **Preexisting Material** Identify any preexisting work or works that this work is based on or incorporates. ▼

b. **Material Added to This Work** Give a brief, general statement of the material that has been added to this work and in which copyright is claimed. ▼

6

See instructions
before completing
this space.

—space deleted—

7

REPRODUCTION FOR USE OF BLIND OR PHYSICALLY HANDICAPPED INDIVIDUALS A signature on this form at space 10 and a check in one of the boxes here in space 8 constitutes a non-exclusive grant of permission to the Library of Congress to reproduce and distribute solely for the blind and physically handicapped and under the conditions and limitations prescribed by the regulations of the Copyright Office: (1) copies of the work identified in space 1 of this application in Braille (or similar tactile symbols); or (2) phonorecords embodying a fixation of a reading of that work; or (3) both.

a ☒ Copies and Phonorecords   b ☐ Copies Only   c ☐ Phonorecords Only

8

See instructions.

DEPOSIT ACCOUNT If the registration fee is to be charged to a Deposit Account established in the Copyright Office, give name and number of Account.
Name ▼   **Account Number** ▼

9

CORRESPONDENCE Give name and address to which correspondence about this application should be sent.   Name/Address/Apt/City/State/ZIP ▼
Acme Soft, Inc., Attn. George Apley
123 Computer Rd.
Silicon Valley, OR 80500
          Area Code and Telephone Number ▶   012-555-5555

Be sure to
give your
daytime phone
◀ number

CERTIFICATION* I, the undersigned, hereby certify that I am the
Check only one ▶
☐ author
☐ other copyright claimant
☐ owner of exclusive right(s)
☒ authorized agent of   Acme Soft, Inc.
of the work identified in this application and that the statements made
by me in this application are correct to the best of my knowledge.
          Name of author or other copyright claimant, or owner of exclusive right(s) ▲

Typed or printed name and date ▼ If this application gives a date of publication in space 3, do not sign and submit it before that date.
George Apley   Date ▶ 12/15/9X

☞   Handwritten signature (X) ▼
    George Apley

10

MAIL CERTIFICATE TO
Name ▼
Acme Soft, Inc.
Number/Street/Apt ▼
123 Computer Rd.
City/State/ZIP ▼
Silicon Valley, OR 80500

Certificate will be mailed in window envelope

YOU MUST:
• Complete all necessary spaces
• Sign your application in space 10
SEND ALL 3 ELEMENTS IN THE SAME PACKAGE:
1. Application form
2. Nonrefundable $20 filing fee in check or money order payable to *Register of Copyrights*
3. Deposit material
MAIL TO:
Register of Copyrights
Library of Congress
Washington, D.C. 20559-6000

11

May 1995—300,000   ☐U.S. COPYRIGHT OFFICE WWW FORM: 1995

6. Computer game

FORM TX
For a Literary Work
UNITED STATES COPYRIGHT OFFICE

REGISTRATION NUMBER

_____

TX _____ TXU _____
EFFECTIVE DATE OF REGISTRATION

_____

Month _____ Day _____ Year _____

DO NOT WRITE ABOVE THIS LINE. IF YOU NEED MORE SPACE, USE A SEPARATE CONTINUATION SHEET.

1

TITLE OF THIS WORK ▼

Kill or Die

PREVIOUS OR ALTERNATIVE TITLES ▼

PUBLICATION AS A CONTRIBUTION If this work was published as a contribution to a periodical, serial, or collection, give information about the collective work in which the contribution appeared. **Title of Collective Work ▼**

If published in a periodical or serial give: **Volume ▼**   **Number ▼**   **Issue Date ▼**   **On Pages ▼**

2

a

NAME OF AUTHOR ▼

Game Soft, Inc.

DATES OF BIRTH AND DEATH
Year Born ▼   Year Died ▼

Was this contribution to the work a "work made for hire"?
☒ Yes
☐ No

AUTHOR'S NATIONALITY OR DOMICILE
Name of Country
OR { Citizen of ▶ U.S.A.
Domiciled in▶

WAS THIS AUTHOR'S CONTRIBUTION TO THE WORK
Anonymous?   ☐ Yes ☒ No
Pseudonymous?   ☐ Yes ☒ No
If the answer to either of these questions is "Yes," see detailed instructions.

NATURE OF AUTHORSHIP Briefly describe nature of material created by this author in which copyright is claimed. ▼
Text of program, game screens and sounds.

NOTE

Under the law, the "author" of a "work made for hire" is generally the employer, not the employee (see instructions). For any part of this work that was "made for hire" check "Yes" in the space provided, give the employer (or other person for whom the work was prepared) as "Author" of that part, and leave the space for dates of birth and death blank.

b

NAME OF AUTHOR ▼

DATES OF BIRTH AND DEATH
Year Born ▼   Year Died ▼

Was this contribution to the work a "work made for hire"?
☐ Yes
☐ No

AUTHOR'S NATIONALITY OR DOMICILE
Name of Country
OR { Citizen of ▶
Domiciled in▶

WAS THIS AUTHOR'S CONTRIBUTION TO THE WORK
Anonymous?   ☐ Yes ☐ No
Pseudonymous?   ☐ Yes ☐ No
If the answer to either of these questions is "Yes," see detailed instructions.

NATURE OF AUTHORSHIP Briefly describe nature of material created by this author in which copyright is claimed. ▼

c

NAME OF AUTHOR ▼

DATES OF BIRTH AND DEATH
Year Born ▼   Year Died ▼

Was this contribution to the work a "work made for hire"?
☐ Yes
☐ No

AUTHOR'S NATIONALITY OR DOMICILE
Name of Country
OR { Citizen of ▶
Domiciled in▶

WAS THIS AUTHOR'S CONTRIBUTION TO THE WORK
Anonymous?   ☐ Yes ☐ No
Pseudonymous?   ☐ Yes ☐ No
If the answer to either of these questions is "Yes," see detailed instructions.

NATURE OF AUTHORSHIP Briefly describe nature of material created by this author in which copyright is claimed. ▼

3

a YEAR IN WHICH CREATION OF THIS WORK WAS COMPLETED This information must be given ◀Year in all cases.
199X

b DATE AND NATION OF FIRST PUBLICATION OF THIS PARTICULAR WORK
Complete this information ONLY if this work has been published.
Month ▶ 4   Day ▶ 1   Year ▶ 199X
U.S.A. ◀ Nation

4

See instructions before completing this space.

COPYRIGHT CLAIMANT(S) Name and address must be given even if the claimant is the same as the author given in space 2. ▼
Game Soft, Inc.
1000 3rd St.
Miami, FL 40600

TRANSFER If the claimant(s) named here in space 4 is (are) different from the author(s) named in space 2, give a brief statement of how the claimant(s) obtained ownership of the copyright. ▼

DO NOT WRITE HERE
OFFICE USE ONLY

APPLICATION RECEIVED

ONE DEPOSIT RECEIVED

TWO DEPOSITS RECEIVED

FUNDS RECEIVED

MORE ON BACK ▶ • Complete all applicable spaces (numbers 5-11) on the reverse side of this page.
• See detailed instructions.   • Sign the form at line 10.

DO NOT WRITE HERE
Page 1 of _____ pages

6. Computer game (back)

<table>
<tr><td>EXAMINED BY</td><td>FORM TX</td></tr>
<tr><td>CHECKED BY</td><td></td></tr>
<tr><td>☐ CORRESPONDENCE
Yes</td><td>FOR
COPYRIGHT
OFFICE
USE
ONLY</td></tr>
</table>

DO NOT WRITE ABOVE THIS LINE. IF YOU NEED MORE SPACE, USE A SEPARATE CONTINUATION SHEET.

PREVIOUS REGISTRATION Has registration for this work, or for an earlier version of this work, already been made in the Copyright Office?
☐ Yes ☒ No If your answer is "Yes," why is another registration being sought? (Check appropriate box) ▼
a.☐ This is the first published edition of a work previously registered in unpublished form.
b.☐ This is the first application submitted by this author as copyright claimant.
c.☐ This is a changed version of the work, as shown by space 6 on this application.
If your answer is "Yes," give: **Previous Registration Number** ▼   **Year of Registration** ▼

5

DERIVATIVE WORK OR COMPILATION Complete both space 6a and 6b for a derivative work; complete only 6b for a compilation.
a. Preexisting Material Identify any preexisting work or works that this work is based on or incorporates. ▼

b. Material Added to This Work Give a brief, general statement of the material that has been added to this work and in which copyright is claimed. ▼

6

See instructions
before completing
this space.

7

—space deleted—

REPRODUCTION FOR USE OF BLIND OR PHYSICALLY HANDICAPPED INDIVIDUALS A signature on this form at space 10 and a check in one of the boxes here in space 8 constitutes a non-exclusive grant of permission to the Library of Congress to reproduce and distribute solely for the blind and physically handicapped and under the conditions and limitations prescribed by the regulations of the Copyright Office: (1) copies of the work identified in space 1 of this application in Braille (or similar tactile symbols); or (2) phonorecords embodying a fixation of a reading of that work; or (3) both.

a ☒ Copies and Phonorecords   **b** ☐ Copies Only   **c** ☐ Phonorecords Only

8

See instructions.

DEPOSIT ACCOUNT If the registration fee is to be charged to a Deposit Account established in the Copyright Office, give name and number of Account.
Name ▼   **Account Number** ▼

9

CORRESPONDENCE Give name and address to which correspondence about this application should be sent.   Name/Address/Apt/City/State/ZIP ▼

Game Soft, Inc.
1000 3rd St.
Miami, FL 40600

Area Code and Telephone Number ▶   123-459-7890

Be sure to
give your
daytime phone
◀ number

CERTIFICATION* I, the undersigned, hereby certify that I am the
Check only one ▶
☐ author
☐ other copyright claimant
☐ owner of exclusive right(s)
☒ authorized agent of Game Soft, Inc.
of the work identified in this application and that the statements made
by me in this application are correct to the best of my knowledge.
Name of author or other copyright claimant, or owner of exclusive right(s) ▲

10

Typed or printed name and date ▼ If this application gives a date of publication in space 3, do not sign and submit it before that date.
Andrea Andrews   Date ▶ 4/15/9X
Handwritten signature (X) ▼
Andrea Andrews

MAIL CERTIFI-CATE TO
Name ▼
Game Soft, Inc.
Number/Street/Apt ▼
1000 3rd St.
City/State/ZIP ▼
Miami, FL 40600

Certificate will be mailed in window envelope

YOU MUST:
• Complete all necessary spaces
• Sign your application in space 10
SEND ALL 3 ELEMENTS IN THE SAME PACKAGE:
1. Application form
2. Nonrefundable $20 filing fee in check or money order payable to *Register of Copyrights*
3. Deposit material
MAIL TO:
Register of Copyrights
Library of Congress
Washington, D.C. 20559-6000

11

*17 U.S.C. § 506(e): Any person who knowingly makes a false representation of a material fact in the application for copyright registration provided for by section 409, or in any written statement filed in connection with the application, shall be fined not more than $2,500.

May 1995—300,000   ☐U.S. COPYRIGHT OFFICE WWW FORM: 1995

7. Published multimedia program; work made for hire

FORM PA
For a Work of the Performing Arts
UNITED STATES COPYRIGHT OFFICE

REGISTRATION NUMBER

PA _____ PAU

EFFECTIVE DATE OF REGISTRATION

_____ _____ _____
Month   Day   Year

DO NOT WRITE ABOVE THIS LINE. IF YOU NEED MORE SPACE, USE A SEPARATE CONTINUATION SHEET.

1

TITLE OF THIS WORK ▼

History of Art

PREVIOUS OR ALTERNATIVE TITLES ▼

NATURE OF THIS WORK ▼ See instructions

Audiovisual work

2

a

NAME OF AUTHOR ▼

Acme Soft, Inc.

DATES OF BIRTH AND DEATH
Year Born ▼   Year Died ▼

Was this contribution to the work a "work made for hire"?
☒ Yes
☐ No

AUTHOR'S NATIONALITY OR DOMICILE
Name of Country
OR { Citizen of ▶ U.S.A.
    Domiciled in▶

WAS THIS AUTHOR'S CONTRIBUTION TO THE WORK
Anonymous? ☐ Yes ☒ No
Pseudonymous? ☐ Yes ☒ No
If the answer to either of these questions is "Yes," see detailed instructions.

NATURE OF AUTHORSHIP Briefly describe nature of material created by this author in which copyright is claimed. ▼
Audiovisual work, artwork on computer screens and text of computer program.

NOTE

Under the law, the "author" of a "work made for hire" is generally the employer, not the employee (see instructions). For any part of this work that was "made for hire" check "Yes" in the space provided, give the employer (or other person for whom the work was prepared) as "Author" of that part, and leave the space for dates of birth and death blank.

b

NAME OF AUTHOR ▼

DATES OF BIRTH AND DEATH
Year Born ▼   Year Died ▼

Was this contribution to the work a "work made for hire"?
☐ Yes
☐ No

AUTHOR'S NATIONALITY OR DOMICILE
Name of Country
OR { Citizen of ▶
    Domiciled in▶

WAS THIS AUTHOR'S CONTRIBUTION TO THE WORK
Anonymous? ☐ Yes ☐ No
Pseudonymous? ☐ Yes ☐ No
If the answer to either of these questions is "Yes," see detailed instructions.

NATURE OF AUTHORSHIP Briefly describe nature of material created by this author in which copyright is claimed. ▼

c

NAME OF AUTHOR ▼

DATES OF BIRTH AND DEATH
Year Born ▼   Year Died ▼

Was this contribution to the work a "work made for hire"?
☐ Yes
☐ No

AUTHOR'S NATIONALITY OR DOMICILE
Name of Country
OR { Citizen of ▶
    Domiciled in▶

WAS THIS AUTHOR'S CONTRIBUTION TO THE WORK
Anonymous? ☐ Yes ☐ No
Pseudonymous? ☐ Yes ☐ No
If the answer to either of these questions is "Yes," see detailed instructions.

NATURE OF AUTHORSHIP Briefly describe nature of material created by this author in which copyright is claimed. ▼

3

a YEAR IN WHICH CREATION OF THIS WORK WAS COMPLETED This information must be given
199X ◀Year in all cases.

b DATE AND NATION OF FIRST PUBLICATION OF THIS PARTICULAR WORK
Complete this information ONLY if this work has been published.
Month▶ 11 Day▶ 1 Year▶ 199X
U.S.A. ◀Nation

4

See instructions before completing this space.

a COPYRIGHT CLAIMANT(S) Name and address must be given even if the claimant is the same as the author given in space 2. ▼
Acme Soft, Inc.
100 Broadway
Chicago, IL 12345

b TRANSFER If the claimant(s) named here in space 4 is (are) different from the author(s) named in space 2, give a brief statement of how the claimant(s) obtained ownership of the copyright. ▼

APPLICATION RECEIVED

ONE DEPOSIT RECEIVED

TWO DEPOSITS RECEIVED

FUNDS RECEIVED

DO NOT WRITE HERE OFFICE USE ONLY

MORE ON BACK ▶
• Complete all applicable spaces (numbers 5-9) on the reverse side of this page.
• See detailed instructions.   • Sign the form at line 8.

DO NOT WRITE HERE
Page 1 of _____ pages

7. Published multimedia program; work made for hire (back)

EXAMINED BY	FORM PA
CHECKED BY	
CORRESPONDENCE ☐ Yes	FOR COPYRIGHT OFFICE USE ONLY

DO NOT WRITE ABOVE THIS LINE. IF YOU NEED MORE SPACE, USE A SEPARATE CONTINUATION SHEET.

PREVIOUS REGISTRATION Has registration for this work, or for an earlier version of this work, already been made in the Copyright Office?
☐ Yes ☒ No If your answer is "Yes," why is another registration being sought? (Check appropriate box) ▼
a. ☐ This is the first published edition of a work previously registered in unpublished form.
b. ☐ This is the first application submitted by this author as copyright claimant.
c. ☐ This is a changed version of the work, as shown by space 6 on this application.
If your answer is "Yes," give: **Previous Registration Number** ▼   **Year of Registration** ▼

5

DERIVATIVE WORK OR COMPILATION Complete both space 6a and 6b for a derivative work; complete only 6b for a compilation.
a. Preexisting Material Identify any preexisting work or works that this work is based on or incorporates. ▼

Previously published text, photos, artwork, video footage and music.

b. Material Added to This Work Give a brief, general statement of the material that has been added to this work and in which copyright is claimed. ▼

Compilation and editing of preexisting text, photos, video clips and music plus new original text

6

See instructions before completing this space.

DEPOSIT ACCOUNT If the registration fee is to be charged to a Deposit Account established in the Copyright Office, give name and number of Account.
Name ▼   **Account Number** ▼

a

7

CORRESPONDENCE Give name and address to which correspondence about this application should be sent.   Name/Address/Apt/City/State/ZIP ▼

b
Acme Soft, Inc.
100 Broadway
Chicago, IL 12345

Area Code and Daytime Telephone Number ▶ 123-456-7890   Fax Number ▶ 123-555-6666

CERTIFICATION* I, the undersigned, hereby certify that I am the
Check only one ▼
☐ author
☐ other copyright claimant
☐ owner of exclusive right(s)
☒ authorized agent of ___Acme Soft___
      Name of author or other copyright claimant, or owner of exclusive right(s) ▲

of the work identified in this application and that the statements made
by me in this application are correct to the best of my knowledge.

8

Typed or printed name and date ▼ If this application gives a date of publication in space 3, do not sign and submit it before that date.
Sue Smitters   Date ▶ 12/10/9X

Handwritten signature (X) ▼
Sue Smitters

Mail certificate to:
Name ▼
Acme Soft, Inc.
Number/Street/Apt ▼
100 Broadway
City/State/ZIP ▼
Chicago, IL 12345

Certificate will be mailed in window envelope

YOU MUST:
• Complete all necessary spaces
• Sign your application in space 8
SEND ALL 3 ELEMENTS IN THE SAME PACKAGE:
1. Application form
2. Nonrefundable $20 filing fee in check or money order payable to *Register of Copyrights*
3. Deposit material
MAIL TO:
Register of Copyrights
Library of Congress
Washington, D.C. 20559-6000

9

*17 U.S.C. § 506(e): Any person who knowingly makes a false representation of a material fact in the application for copyright registration provided for by section 409, or in any written statement filed in connection with the application, shall be fined not more than $2,500.

September 1995—400,000   ♻ PRINTED ON RECYCLED PAPER   ☆U.S. GOVERNMENT PRINTING OFFICE: 1995-387-237/20,024

8. Computer database; group registration for patent database updated weekly

FORM TX
For a Literary Work
UNITED STATES COPYRIGHT OFFICE

REGISTRATION NUMBER

TX   TXU

EFFECTIVE DATE OF REGISTRATION

Month   Day   Year

DO NOT WRITE ABOVE THIS LINE. IF YOU NEED MORE SPACE, USE A SEPARATE CONTINUATION SHEET.

1 TITLE OF THIS WORK ▼

Group registration for automated database titled U.S. Patent
Database: published updates from 2/1/97 thru 5/1/97

PREVIOUS OR ALTERNATIVE TITLES ▼

PUBLICATION AS A CONTRIBUTION If this work was published as a contribution to a periodical, serial, or collection, give information about the collective work in which the contribution appeared. **Title of Collective Work ▼**

2/1/97 updated weekly

If published in a periodical or serial give: Volume ▼   Number ▼   Issue Date ▼   On Pages ▼

2 a NAME OF AUTHOR ▼

Patent Soft, Inc.

DATES OF BIRTH AND DEATH
Year Born ▼   Year Died ▼

Was this contribution to the work a "work made for hire"? ☒ Yes ☐ No

AUTHOR'S NATIONALITY OR DOMICILE Name of Country
OR Citizen of ▶ U.S.A.
Domiciled in ▶

WAS THIS AUTHOR'S CONTRIBUTION TO THE WORK
Anonymous? ☐ Yes ☒ No
Pseudonymous? ☐ Yes ☒ No
If the answer to either of these questions is "Yes," see detailed instructions.

NATURE OF AUTHORSHIP Briefly describe nature of material created by this author in which copyright is claimed. ▼
Entire text of computer program

NOTE
Under the law, the "author" of a "work made for hire" is generally the employer, not the employee (see instructions). For any part of this work that was "made for hire" check "Yes" in the space provided, give the employer (or other person for whom the work was prepared) as "Author" of that part, and leave the space for dates of birth and death blank.

b NAME OF AUTHOR ▼

DATES OF BIRTH AND DEATH
Year Born ▼   Year Died ▼

Was this contribution to the work a "work made for hire"? ☐ Yes ☐ No

AUTHOR'S NATIONALITY OR DOMICILE Name of Country
OR Citizen of ▶
Domiciled in ▶

WAS THIS AUTHOR'S CONTRIBUTION TO THE WORK
Anonymous? ☐ Yes ☐ No
Pseudonymous? ☐ Yes ☐ No

NATURE OF AUTHORSHIP Briefly describe nature of material created by this author in which copyright is claimed. ▼

c NAME OF AUTHOR ▼

DATES OF BIRTH AND DEATH
Year Born ▼   Year Died ▼

Was this contribution to the work a "work made for hire"? ☐ Yes ☐ No

AUTHOR'S NATIONALITY OR DOMICILE Name of Country
OR Citizen of ▶
Domiciled in ▶

WAS THIS AUTHOR'S CONTRIBUTION TO THE WORK
Anonymous? ☐ Yes ☐ No
Pseudonymous? ☐ Yes ☐ No

NATURE OF AUTHORSHIP Briefly describe nature of material created by this author in which copyright is claimed. ▼

3 a YEAR IN WHICH CREATION OF THIS WORK WAS COMPLETED This information must be given Year in all cases.
199X

b DATE AND NATION OF FIRST PUBLICATION OF THIS PARTICULAR WORK Complete this information ONLY if this work has been published.
Month ▶ 5 Day ▶ 1 Year ▶ 199X
U.S.A. ◀ Nation

4 COPYRIGHT CLAIMANT(S) Name and address must be given even if the claimant is the same as the author given in space 2. ▼

Patent Soft, Inc.
950 2nd St.
Washington, D.C. 10100

TRANSFER If the claimant(s) named here in space 4 is (are) different from the author(s) named in space 2, give a brief statement of how the claimant(s) obtained ownership of the copyright. ▼

APPLICATION RECEIVED
ONE DEPOSIT RECEIVED
TWO DEPOSITS RECEIVED
FUNDS RECEIVED
DO NOT WRITE HERE OFFICE USE ONLY

MORE ON BACK ▶ • Complete all applicable spaces (numbers 5-11) on the reverse side of this page.
• See detailed instructions. • Sign the form at line 10.
DO NOT WRITE HERE
Page 1 of _____ pages

8. Computer database; group registration for patent database updated weekly (back)

EXAMINED BY	FORM TX
CHECKED BY	
☐ CORRESPONDENCE Yes	FOR COPYRIGHT OFFICE USE ONLY

DO NOT WRITE ABOVE THIS LINE. IF YOU NEED MORE SPACE, USE A SEPARATE CONTINUATION SHEET.

PREVIOUS REGISTRATION Has registration for this work, or for an earlier version of this work, already been made in the Copyright Office?
☒ Yes ☐ No If your answer is "Yes," why is another registration being sought? (Check appropriate box) ▼
a. ☐ This is the first published edition of a work previously registered in unpublished form.
b. ☐ This is the first application submitted by this author as copyright claimant.
c. ☒ This is a changed version of the work, as shown by space 6 on this application.
If your answer is "Yes," give: **Previous Registration Number** ▼   **Year of Registration** ▼
TX18742   1997

5

DERIVATIVE WORK OR COMPILATION Complete both space 6a and 6b for a derivative work; complete only 6b for a compilation.
a. **Preexisting Material** Identify any preexisting work or works that this work is based on or incorporates. ▼
public domain data

b. **Material Added to This Work** Give a brief, general statement of the material that has been added to this work and in which copyright is claimed. ▼
weekly updates

6

See instructions before completing this space.

—space deleted—

7

REPRODUCTION FOR USE OF BLIND OR PHYSICALLY HANDICAPPED INDIVIDUALS A signature on this form at space 10 and a check in one of the boxes here in space 8 constitutes a non-exclusive grant of permission to the Library of Congress to reproduce and distribute solely for the blind and physically handicapped and under the conditions and limitations prescribed by the regulations of the Copyright Office: (1) copies of the work identified in space 1 of this application in Braille (or similar tactile symbols); or (2) phonorecords embodying a fixation of a reading of that work; or (3) both.

a ☒ Copies and Phonorecords   b ☐ Copies Only   c ☐ Phonorecords Only

8

See instructions.

DEPOSIT ACCOUNT If the registration fee is to be charged to a Deposit Account established in the Copyright Office, give name and number of Account.
Name ▼   Account Number ▼

9

CORRESPONDENCE Give name and address to which correspondence about this application should be sent.   Name/Address/Apt/City/State/ZIP ▼
Patent Soft, Inc.
950 2nd St.
Washington, D.C. 10000
Area Code and Telephone Number ▶   212-555-1115

Be sure to give your daytime phone ◀ number

CERTIFICATION* I, the undersigned, hereby certify that I am the
Check only one ▶
☐ author
☐ other copyright claimant
☐ owner of exclusive right(s)
☒ authorized agent of Patent Soft, Inc.
of the work identified in this application and that the statements made
by me in this application are correct to the best of my knowledge.
Name of author or other copyright claimant, or owner of exclusive right(s) ▲

10

Typed or printed name and date ▼ If this application gives a date of publication in space 3, do not sign and submit it before that date.
David Edison   Date ▶ 5/1/9X

Handwritten signature (X) ▼
☞ *David Edison*

MAIL CERTIFI-CATE TO

Name ▼
Patent Soft, Inc.
Number/Street/Apt ▼
950 2nd St.
City/State/ZIP ▼
Washington, D.C. 10000

Certificate will be mailed in window envelope

YOU MUST:
• Complete all necessary spaces
• Sign your application in space 10
SEND ALL 3 ELEMENTS IN THE SAME PACKAGE:
1. Application form
2. Nonrefundable $20 filing fee in check or money order payable to *Register of Copyrights*
3. Deposit material
MAIL TO:
Register of Copyrights
Library of Congress
Washington, D.C. 20559-6000

11

*17 U.S.C. § 506(e): Any person who knowingly makes a false representation of a material fact in the application for copyright registration provided for by section 409, or in any written statement filed in connection with the application, shall be fined not more than $2,500.
May 1995—300,000   ⊙U.S. COPYRIGHT OFFICE WWW FORM: 1995

Chapter 5

Software Copyright Infringement

Part I. Avoiding Copyright Infringement

Part II. Suing Others for Copyright Infringement

Previous chapters have provided an overview of copyright law and have discussed the steps a software copyright owner must take to give his or her work maximum protection under the copyright laws. This chapter explores how these protections are enforced. This subject is referred to as copyright infringement.

Copyright infringement is where the rubber hits the road in the copyright law. It concerns how authors and other copyright owners enforce their legal rights. However, the right to bring copyright infringement suits is a two-edged sword: you may have the right to sue others, but others may also have the right to sue you. Consequently, this chapter is divided into two parts. Part I discusses how to avoid being sued for copyright infringement. Part II provides an overview of infringement lawsuits from the plaintiff's point of view.

Part I. Avoiding Copyright Infringement

Many software developers have been sued for copyright infringement or threatened with such suits. Others are fearful of being sued. This fear is understandable. Unfortunately, in the litigation-happy United States the answer to the question "Can I be sued"? is always yes. You can be sued by anyone at any time for anything. The only way a developer can be absolutely sure he or she will never be accused of copyright infringement is to never develop and sell any new software.

Even if you don't copy other people's software you can still end up getting sued if, because of factors like coincidence and external constraints, your software turns out to be similar to someone else's. So if you want to stay in the software business, being sued one day is a risk you'll have to take. Obviously, however, the less you copy from others the less risk there will be.

A. Things You Should Never Do

The clearest cases of software copyright infringement involve direct copying of computer code, particularly where you copy all or most of a program. If you're caught doing these types of copying you likely won't have a legal leg to stand on should the copyright owner elect to sue you for infringement. Indeed, your best course would probably be to seek the settle the case as cheaply as possible without going to court.

Creating derivative works without permission and going beyond the restrictions contained in software license agreements also usually present clear cases of copyright infringement.

It goes without saying that you should never become involved in these types of copyright infringement. The risks will usually be greater than the rewards. See Section I for a detailed discussion of the many unpleasant legal consequences of copyright infringement.

1. Wholesale Unauthorized Copying of Computer Code

A simpler caption for this section would be software piracy. It means copying all or most of a program's code without permission. Subject to important limitations discussed in Section B1 below, copyright protects source code (code written in high-level computer languages consisting of English-like words and symbols readable by humans, such as C++, and Java), object code (the series of binary ones and zeros read by the computer itself to execute a program, but not readable by ordinary humans), microcode (instructions that tell a microprocessor chip how to work) and other forms of computer code such as Java bytecode.

Copyright protects both applications programs (programs that perform a specific task for the user, such as word processing, will and trust writing, accessing the World Wide Web, bookkeeping or playing a video game) and operating systems and utility programs (programs that manage a computer's internal functions and facilitate use of applications programs).

Wholesale copying or software piracy takes a variety of forms, including:

- **Creating "new" Software from old.**
  Creating a "new" program by copying a substantial amount of the protected expression in a preexisting program, is a classic example of software piracy.
- **End user piracy by companies and individuals.**

EXAMPLE: AcmeSoft, Inc., a large software developer, makes 100 unauthorized copies of a well known HTML editor program and distributes them to its employees.

- **Counterfeiting published software.**

EXAMPLE: Fly By Night Software, Inc., a software distributor, makes 50,000 unauthorized copies of the popular

computer arcade game, *Kill or Die*, and distributes them throughout the world.

- **Online piracy.** This includes uploading and downloading computer programs to and from the Internet and computer BBSs without the copyright owners' permission.

What About Copying Only a Small Amount of Code?

Copying only a small portion of a program's code could constitute copyright infringement. Then again, it might not. Because of the various factors discussed in Section B1 below, a particular routine or subroutine or other piece of code may enjoy little or no copyright protection. In this event, copying it wouldn't be an infringement. On the other hand, if the code is protected, copying only a small amount could be an infringement, particularly if it is a highly creative or important example of the programmer's art. Copyright infringement has been found to exist where only 14 lines of source code out of a total of 186,000 lines were copied verbatim. (*SAS Inst., Inc. v. S&H Computer Sys., Inc.*, 605 F.Supp. 816 (M.D.Tenn. 1985).) You'll usually be better off not copying other people's code.

---

2. Creating Unauthorized Derivative Works

Copyright infringement is not limited to the crude wholesale copying described in the previous section. It can take a more subtle form—creating "new" software from old, for example, by transferring a chunk of code to the new program and subsequently modifying it. If such a "new" program contains a substantial amount of copyrighted material from an existing program, it may constitute a derivative work. You need to obtain permission to create a derivative work from someone else's software.

a. What is a derivative work?

A derivative work is "a work based upon one or more preexisting works." It includes any "form in which a work may be recast, transformed, or adapted." (17 USC Sec. 101.) To be derivative, a work must incorporate in some form a portion of the protected expression of a preexisting copyrighted work.

A derivative work stands on its own for copyright purposes and is entitled to its own copyright protection independent of the original work it was derived from.

A good example of a derivative work is a screenplay based upon a novel. The screenwriter would have to incorporate a substantial portion of the novel's plot, characters and dialog into the screenplay. But the screenwriter would also have to contribute original copyrightable work of his or her own, including organizing the material into cinematic scenes, editing the story down to film length, adding new dialog and camera directions. The end result would be a new work of authorship separately protected by copyright: a screenplay that is clearly different from original novel, yet clearly based upon or derived from it.

Other examples of derivative works would be an abridgment, condensation, sound recording, translation or any other form in which a novel was recast, transformed or adapted.

Of course, all works are derivative to some extent. Authorship, whether of a novel or a computer program, is more often than not a process of translation and recombination of previously existing elements—ideas, facts, discoveries, procedures, concepts, principles, systems and so forth. Rarely, if ever, does an author create a work that is entirely new. For example, writers of fiction often draw bits and pieces of their characters and plots from other fictional works they have read. The same is true of software authors. For example, it's likely that any spreadsheet program could be said be derived to some extent from VisiCalc, the first computer spreadsheet.

However, a work is derivative for copyright purposes only if its author has taken a previously existing work's protected expression. As discussed in Section B1a below, copyright only protects an author's expression of his or her ideas, facts, systems and discoveries, not the ideas, facts, systems and discoveries themselves. Thus, a new computer spreadsheet would not be deriva-

tive of VisiCalc or Lotus 1-2-3 unless its creators copied substantial portions of the protected expression in those programs.

A substantial amount of expression must be copied to make a work derivative. How much is substantial? Enough so that the average intended user of the work would conclude that it had been adapted from or based upon the previously existing work. Enough so that, absent consent to use the material from the preexisting work, the second work would constitute an infringement on the copyright in the first work. This is, of course, a judgment call and in close cases opinions may differ as to whether one work is derivative of another.

Some derivative works can only be created by copying all or most of a program's code. Such an unauthorized work would violate both the copyright owner's exclusive rights to copy and create derivative works from his or her program. Other derivative works can be created by copying no code at all. Examples of derivative works in the software field include:

- **Updates and New Versions.** An updated or new version of an existing program is perhaps the most common example of a derivative work in the software field. Only the person who owns the derivative work's rights in a program may create an updated or new version or permit others to do so.
- **Translations.** A translation of a work from one language to another— whether a human or computer language—is a very common type of

derivative work. It is usually necessary, therefore, to obtain permission from the copyright owner to translate a program into a new source code language.

- **Transferring Software From One Medium to Another.** "Medium" refers to whatever physically holds or carries computer code or output, such as the tape, disk, screen, printout or ROM on which software is housed. Changing the medium in which an original work is fixed normally creates a derivative work consisting of the expression as fixed in the new medium. And, regardless of what new medium is used, a copyright infringement occurs if you don't first obtain permission from the owner.
- **Software Based on Other Underlying Works.** Some software is based on or derived from other works. Computer games are a good example. A computer game based on a movie, television show, board game or other underlying work is a derivative work. Naturally, you need permission from the owner of the derivative work's rights in the underlying work to create a program based upon it.

b. Why you need permission to create derivative works

One of the five exclusive copyright rights that automatically come into existence the moment an original work of authorship is fixed in a tangible form is the exclusive right to prepare and distribute derivative works based on the work's protected expression. This is why, subject to the important exceptions discussed in Section B below, you cannot create and distribute a derivative work by using someone else's protected expression without obtaining their permission. If you do, you violate that person's copyright and would be subject to a copyright infringement suit.

Permission must be obtained from the owner of the exclusive right to prepare derivative works based upon the underlying work. Usually the owner is the author or publisher but not always. If you intend to create a derivative work from someone else's copyright work, be sure to get permission before you go to the time and trouble of adapting it into a new work.

A derivative work created without the necessary permission exists in a kind of legal limbo. The author of the derivative work cannot distribute it without infringing on the copyright in the preexisting material. But nobody else can use the derivative work without its creator's permission. Absent such permission, the derivative work is essentially worthless.

3. Going Beyond Software License Restrictions

Yet another form of copyright infringement is going beyond the restrictions in software license agreements. Today, most software is licensed rather than sold outright. License agreements typically contain many restrictions on what a licensee may do with his or her copy. (See Chapter 16.) For example, software licensees are typically barred from using the software on a local area network (LAN). You must obtain a special license for this sort of use. Using a program on a LAN in violation of a license agreement constitutes copyright infringement.

One of the most hotly contested disputes involving software license restrictions concerns the use of computer manufacturers' licensed software by competing third-party computer maintenance firms (often called independent service organizations or ISOs). In the best known case of its kind, a computer manufacturer called MAI Systems licensed its operating system and diagnostic software to its customers. The license agreements provided that only the purchasers could use the software. MAI sued an ISO called Peak Computer, Inc., for copyright infringement when it used MAI software to perform routine maintenance on MAI computers. MAI claimed that illegal copying beyond the bounds of its license agreements took place when Peak Computer loaded MAI's operating software into computer RAM.

The court agreed, holding that a licensee cannot load licensed software into computer RAM unless permitted by the license. This meant that the licensee could not permit a third party ISO to service its computers because doing so required that the licensed operating system be loaded into RAM by the ISO. (*MAI Systems Corporation v. Peak Computer Inc.*, 991 F.2d 511 (9th Cir. 1993).)

This issue has been the source of much litigation over the past five years, with most, but not all, courts agreeing with *MAI Systems*. A bill submitted in Congress to overturn the decision failed to pass. If you're an ISO, it's advisable to review your customers' license agreements and seek permission before using a computer manufacturer's licensed software.

B. Things You May Be Able to Do

You may be surprised to learn that many copyright protections for computer software are limited in scope. You may be free to copy or otherwise use those software elements that are unprotected by copyright. (See Section B1.) Additionally, copying of protected material may be permissible under the fair use doctrine. (See Section B3.) Finally, the copyright laws never prevent you from independently creating new software, even if it's similar to software already in existence. (See Section B2.)

⚠ Be Careful. The following discussion provides an overview of a complex area of law subject to varying interpretations. Even if you and the author of this book believe that a particular software element is unprotected by copyright, the copyright owner might disagree and take legal action against you if you copy it. Before you do any serious copying of someone else's work, it's advisable to seek advice from an experienced computer lawyer. (See Chapter 18.)

1. Using Software Elements Unprotected by Copyright

Software is a multifaceted product consisting of many elements. These include not only the computer code that tells the computer what to do, but the way a program is organized and structured, the way it looks on the computer screen and how it interacts with the user. These non-code elements are often called non-literal elements.

Software publishers, trade groups such as the Software Publisher's Association and other powers-that-be in the software industry would like you to believe that the copyright laws always protect both computer code and all the non-literal elements of software. However, this is not the case. Copyright protection is limited in scope. This is because the copyright laws are intended to promote the advancement of knowledge, not to enable copyright owners to maximize their profits. Too much copyright protection for works of authorship would end up retarding, not promoting, this purpose.

All works of authorship—particularly functional works such as computer programs —contain some elements that are protected by copyright and other elements that are not. Anyone is free to use the unprotected elements without obtaining permission from the copyright owner. Unfortunately, there is no system available to an interested party to precisely identify which aspects of a given work are protected by copyright. The Copyright Office makes no such determination when software is registered. The only time we ever obtain a definitive answer as to how much any particular program (or other work of authorship) is protected is when it becomes the subject of a copyright infringement lawsuit. In this event, a judge or jury determines the question. Of course, such litigation is usually very expensive and time consuming.

Since the late 1970s, federal courts all across the country have been deciding an ever-increasing number of software copyright infringement disputes. Their legal opinions are the only concrete guidance available on how and how much software is protected by the copyright law. Studying these opinions is the only means available, short of filing a lawsuit, to determine the extent to which a given work is protected.

This is a difficult and complex area of the law subject to varying interpretations. Courts in different parts of the country sometimes disagree with each other on the extent of copyright protection for software. However, a growing consensus has been developing in recent years that many of the most important elements of software should receive little or no copyright protection.

The following software elements are never protected by copyright and may be freely copied by anyone unless they are protected by another form of intellectual property such as trade secrecy (see Chapter 6), patent law (see Chapter 8) or trademark law (see Chapter 9).

a. Ideas embodied in software

Copyright only protects a creative person's particular expression of an idea, system or process, *not the idea, system or process itself.* Ideas, procedures, processes, systems, mathematical principles, formulas or algorithms, methods of operation, concepts, facts and discoveries are not protected by copyright. (17 U.S.C. 102(b).) Copyright is designed to aid the advancement of knowledge. If the copyright law gave a person a legal monopoly over his or her ideas, the progress of knowledge would be impeded rather than helped.

> **EXAMPLE:** Grace writes a book about gardening that describes a revolutionary new method of growing vegetables with minimal amounts of water. The literal way in which Grace sets forth her ideas—that is, her actual words—are protected by copyright—no one can copy and publish them without her permission. But the ideas, facts, processes and methods contained in Grace's book are not protected. This means that any one is free to read Grace's book and employ her method for low-water gardening. In addition, anyone else is free to write his own book describing Grace's system—so long as he doesn't copy the literal expression contained in Grace's book.

This idea-expression dichotomy also applies to software. Consider the following real-life example:

EXAMPLE: While a student at the Harvard business school in the late 1970s, Daniel Bricklin conceived the idea of an electronic spreadsheet—a "magic blackboard" that recalculated numbers automatically as changes were made in other parts of the spreadsheet. Eventually, aided by others, he transformed his idea into VisiCalc, the first commercial electronic spreadsheet. The program, designed for use on the Apple II, sold like hotcakes and helped spark the personal computer revolution.

Of course VisiCalc was protected by copyright. Nevertheless, others were free to write their own original programs accomplishing the same purpose as VisiCalc. The copyright law did not give Bricklin et al. any ownership rights over the idea of an electronic spreadsheet, even though it was a revolutionary advance in computer programming. The copyright in VisiCalc extended only to the particular way VisiCalc expressed this idea.

Very soon, many competing programs were introduced. The most successful of these was Lotus 1-2-3, originally created by Mitchell Kapor and Jonathan Sachs. Building on Bricklin's revolutionary idea, Kapor and Sachs expressed that idea in a different, more powerful way. Designed for the IBM PC, Lotus 1-2-3 took advantage of that computer's more expansive memory and more versatile screen display capabilities and keyboard. In short, Lotus 1-2-3 did all that VisiCalc did, only better. VisiCalc sales plunged and the program was eventually discontinued.

Of course, it's easy to say that copyright does not protect ideas, only expression. But what does this mean in the real world? Almost all computer programs embody systems or processes. When does the unprotectible system end and the protectible expression begin? In point of fact it can be very difficult to tell the difference between an unprotected idea, system or process and its protected expression.

Legal Protection for Ideas, Processes and Systems

What if Bricklin in the above example had wanted to protect his idea or system of an electronic spreadsheet itself, not just Visicalc? He would have had to look to laws other than copyright. If the electronic spreadsheet had qualified as a patentable invention, it could have been protected under the federal patent law. In this event, Bricklin would have had a 17-year monopoly on its use. Anyone else seeking to write a program implementing the spreadsheet idea would have had to obtain Bricklin's permission or been liable for patent infringement. Bricklin did not apply for a patent, and it is far from clear whether, at the time, he could have obtained one had he done so. (See Chapter 8.)

---

b. When an idea and its expression merge

Part of the essence of original authorship is the making of choices. Any work of authorship is the end result of a whole series of choices made by its creator. For example, the author of a novel expressing the idea of love must choose the novel's plot, characters, locale and the actual words used to express the story. The author of such a novel has a nearly limitless array of choices available.

However, the choices available to the creators of many works of authorship are severely limited. In these cases, the idea or ideas underlying the work and the way they are expressed by the author are deemed to "merge." The result is that the author's expression is either treated as if it were in the public domain (given no protection at all) or protected only against virtually verbatim or "slavish" copying. If this were not so, the copyright law would end up discouraging authorship of new works and thereby retard the progress of knowledge.

The range of choices available to creators of functional works such as computer programs are often especially constrained, resulting in especially limited copyright protection.

EXAMPLE: Data East USA created a video game called Karate Champ for the Commodore computer. Data East sued the creator of a competing karate video game called World Karate Champ for copyright infringement. Data East claimed that World Karate Champ had impermissibly copied the audiovisual elements of Karate Champ. Data East lost because of the merger doctrine.

The court found that the similarities between the two games—similar game procedures, common karate moves, a time element, a referee, computer graphics and bonus points—necessarily followed from the idea of creating a martial arts karate combat game: they were "inseparable from, or indispensable to … the idea of the karate sport." In other words, there were only a limited number of ways to express the idea of a karate video game for the Commodore computer. Anyone who wanted to create such a game would have no choice but to include these elements in the game.

As a result, the idea of a karate video game for the Commodore computer and its expression by Data East were deemed to merge, and Data East's game received very limited copyright protection. If this were not so, no one other than Data East could ever create a karate video game. (*Data East USA, Inc. v. Epyx, Inc.*, 862 F.2d 204 (9th Cir. 1988).)

The result of the merger doctrine is that the fewer choices a programmer has when setting out to create a given element of a piece of software, the less copyright protection that element will receive. Or, to put it another way: *The scope of copyright protection is proportional to the range of expression available to articulate the underlying ideas communicated by the program.*

In recent years, courts have been finding that more and more elements of computer programs are not protectible because of the merger doctrine. The seminal court decision of *Computer Associates Int'l v. Altai, Inc.* 982 F.2d 693, (2d Cir. 1992), identified the following constraints on the range of software expression (this list is not exclusive):

- elements dictated by efficiency
- elements dictated by external factors, and
- standard programming techniques and program features.

c. Elements dictated by efficiency

Programmers usually strive to create programs that meet the user's needs as efficiently as possible. The desire for maximum efficiency may operate to restrict the range of choices available to a programmer. For example, there may only be one or two efficient ways to express the idea embodied in a given program, module, routine or subroutine. If a programmer's choices regarding a particular program's structure, interface or even source code are necessary to efficiently implement the program's function, then those choices will not be protected by copyright. In other words, no programmer may have a monopoly on the most efficient way to write any program. Paradoxically, this means that the better job a programmer does—the more closely the program approximates the ideal of efficiency—the less copyright protection the program will receive.

EXAMPLE 1: A court held that Lotus 1-2-3's basic spreadsheet screen display resembling a rotated "L" was not protected by copyright because there are only a few ways to make a computer screen resemble a spreadsheet; nor was the use of "+," "-," "*," and "/" for their corresponding mathematical functions; or use of the enter key to place keystroke entries into cells. The use of such keys was the most efficient means to implement these mathematical functions. (*Lotus Dev. Corp. v. Borland Int'l, Inc.* 799 F.Supp. 203 (D.Mass. 1992).)

EXAMPLE 2: Another court held that a cost-estimating program's method of allowing users to navigate within screen displays (by using the space bar to move the cursor down a list, the backspace key to move up, the return key to choose a function and a number selection to edit an entry) was not protectible. The court noted that there were only a limited number of ways to enable a user to navigate through a screen display on the hardware in question while facilitating user comfort. The court also found that the program's use of alphabetical and numerical columns in its screen displays was not protectible. The constraints of uniformity of format and limited page space

(requiring either a horizontal or vertical orientation) permitted only a very narrow range of choices. (*Manufacturers Technologies, Inc. v. Cams*, 706 F.Supp. 984 (D.Conn. 1989).)

d. Elements dictated by external factors

A programmer's freedom of design choice is often limited by external factors such as:

- the mechanical specifications of the computer on which the program is intended to run
- compatibility requirements of other programs which the program is designed to operate in conjunction with
- computer manufacturers' design standards, and
- the demands of the industry being serviced.

EXAMPLE 1: Intel Corp. charged that NEC Corp. had unlawfully copied the microcode to Intel Corp.'s 8086/88 microprocessor chip to create compatible microprocessor chips of its own. (Microcode is a series of instructions that tells a microprocessor chip how to work.) NEC sued Intel to obtain a judicial declaration that it did not infringe on Intel's microcode. The court held that NEC had not committed infringement. Although some of the simpler microroutines in NEC's microcode were substantially similar to Intel's, the court held that machine constraints were largely responsible for the similarities; that is, NEC's programmers had very limited choices in designing their microcode to operate a chip compatible with Intel's 8086/88. Given these constraints, Intel's microcode was protected only against "virtually identical copying." (*NEC Corp. v. Intel Corp.* 10 U.S.P.Q.2d 1177 (N.D. Cal 1989).)

EXAMPLE 2: A cotton cooperative developed a program for mainframe computers called Telcot that provided users with cotton prices and information, accounting services and the ability to consummate cotton sales transactions. Former employee-programmers of the cooperative created a PC version of the cotton exchange program. The two programs were similar in their sequence and organization. The cooperative sued for infringement and lost. The court held that many of the similarities between the two programs were dictated by the externalities of the cotton market. The programs were designed to present the same information as contained in a cotton recap sheet, and there were not many different ways to accomplish this. (*Plains Cotton Cooperative Assoc. v. Goodpasture Computer Service, Inc.* 807 F.2d 1256 (5th Cir. 1987).)

EXAMPLE 3: Q-Co Industries created a program to operate a TelePrompTer. The program was written in BASIC and Atari to run on an Atari 800-XL. Hoffman created a program accomplishing the same purpose, written in another programming language and designed to run on the IBM PC. All four modules of Hoffman's program corresponded closely to four of the 12 modules contained in Q-Co's program. Q-Co sued for copyright infringement. The court held there was no infringement because "the same modules would be an inherent part of any prompting program." In other words, any programmer wishing to create a TelePrompTer program would have no choice but to include the four modules. (*Q-Co Industries, Inc. v. Hoffman*, 625 F.Supp. 608 (S.D.N.Y. 1985).)

e. Standard programming techniques and software features

Certain programming techniques and software features are so widely used as to be standard in the software industry. To create a competitive program, a software developer may have no choice other than to employ such techniques and features because users expect them. Courts treat such material as being in the public domain—it is free for the taking and cannot be owned by any single software author even though it is included in an otherwise copyrightable work.

EXAMPLE 1: A court held that the following basic elements of the Macintosh user interface were unprotectible because they were common to all graphical user interfaces and were standard in the industry:

- overlapping windows to display multiple images on a computer screen

- iconic representations of familiar objects from the office environment, such as file folders, documents and a trash can
- opening and closing of objects in order to retrieve, transfer or store information
- menus used to store information or control computer functions, and
- manipulation of icons to convey instructions and to control operation of the computer. (See *Apple Computer v. Microsoft Corp.*, 779 F.Supp. 133 (N.D.Ca. 1992).)

EXAMPLE 2: The owner of an outlining program called PC-Outline sued the owner of a competing program called Grandview for copyright infringement. Grandview had nine pull-down menus functionally similar to those of PC-Outline. Nevertheless, the court held that Grandview did not infringe on PC-Outline. The court reasoned that use of a pull-down menu was commonplace in the software industry. The court declared that a copyright owner cannot claim "copyright protection of an ... expression that is, if not standard, then commonplace in the computer software industry." (*Brown Bag Software v. Symantec Corp.*, 960 F.2d 1465 (9th Cir. 1990).)

f. Copying user interfaces

The user interface of a computer program is the way a program presents itself to and interacts with the user. It consists principally of the sequence, flow and content of the display screens that appear on a computer's monitor (permitting the user to select various options and/or input data in a pre-scribed format) and the use of specific keys on the computer keyboard to perform particular functions. The look and feel of a program's interface can be very important to the user (a well-designed interface makes a program much easier to use) and therefore very valuable to the program's owner. It's possible to copy the way a user interface looks and works without copying any computer code.

After years of litigation involving some of the most famous software interfaces in the world it seems clear that copyright provides very little protection for most of the elements of a user interface. Anything less than slavish copying of an entire interface is likely not an infringement. As a result, developers need not go to the trouble of devising different words to convey simple menu commands and may use commands that are familiar to users of competing works.

The two most important cases involve the Macintosh interface and the Lotus 1-2-3 computer spreadsheet program.

Apple sued Microsoft, claiming that the user interface of Microsoft's Windows system violated Apple's copyright in the Macintosh user interface. Ultimately, all of Apple's claims were dismissed and the case was upheld on appeal. The trial court held that the "desktop metaphor" underlying the Macintosh user interface—suggesting an office with familiar office objects such as file folders, documents and a trash can—was an unprotectible idea. The court also ruled that most of the individual elements of the user interface at issue in the case were not protectible, either because Apple had licensed them to Microsoft, because they were not original or because of the factors discussed in Sections B1c, d and e above. However, the court also held the Macintosh interface might be protected as a whole, at least from virtually identical copying, even though its individual elements were not protected. In other words, although many of the individual elements of the interface were not protectible standing alone, they still formed part of a larger arrangement, selection or layout that was protected expression. (*Apple Computer, Inc. v. Microsoft Corp.*, 35 F.3d.1435 (9th Cir. 1994).)

Lotus Development Corp. sued Borland International, Inc., claiming that its Lotus 1-2-3 spreadsheet program had been infringed by Borland's Quattro and Quattro Pro spreadsheet programs. In order to enable users familiar with Lotus 1-2-3 to switch to Quattro without having to learn new commands or rewrite their Lotus macros, Borland included in its programs an alternate command menu structure that was a virtually identical copy of the Lotus 1-2-3 menu command hierarchy. Borland did not copy any of Lotus's code. It copied only the words and structure of Lotus's menu commands. After losing at trial, Borland finally won on appeal. The Court of Appeal held that 1-2-3's command hierarchy was a method of operation that was not protected by copyright. The court stated that a software developer should be able to create a program that users can operate in exactly the same way as a competing program. (*Lotus Development Corp. v, Borland International, Inc.*, 49 F.3d 807 (1st Cir. 1995).) In the words of one copyright expert, this decision "safeguards interoperability between computer programs and allows users to port macros, which they themselves have composed, to competitive environments." (*Nimmer On Copyright*, Section 13.03[F][3][e].)

Other Ways to Protect User Interfaces

Since copyright may not be an effective means to protect user interfaces, software developers may seek protection under other intellectual property laws. It may be possible to obtain patent protection for user interface elements. (See Chapter 8.)

Another way interfaces might be protected is under the state and federal trademark laws. These laws protect a product's "trade dress"—that is, the image and overall appearance of a product—and also provide some protection against activity that misleads consumers about the origins of a product. However, as of this writing, the trademark laws have not provided the basis for any decision regarding the copying of a computer interface. (See Chapter 9.)

g. Copying elements in the public domain

There are some categories of works that copyright can never protect. Unless they are protected by some body of law other than copyright (patent or trademark law, for example), they are in the public domain freely available to anyone. These include:

- **Purely functional items.** Copyright only protects works of authorship. Things that have a purely functional or utilitarian purpose are not considered to be works of authorship and are not copyrightable. For example, there is no copyright protection for the purely functional aspects of machinery, refrigerators, lamps or automobiles. However, if the design of a useful article incorporates artistic features that are independent of the article's functional aspects, such features are protectible. For example, the decorative hood ornament on a Jaguar automobile is an artistic feature that is separable from any functional aspects of a Jaguar; therefore it is protectible.

  Those elements of a computer program that are purely functional may also be denied copyright protection. For example, certain aspects of the Apple Macintosh graphical user interface were found by the court to be purely functional, the same as the dials, knobs and remote control devices of a television or VCR, or the button and clocks of a stove. These functional aspects included the ability to move a window partially off the screen, and the presence of menu items allowing a user to create a new folder within an existing folder.

- **Words, names, titles, slogans, and other short phrases.** No matter how highly creative, novel or distinctive they may be, individual words and short phrases are not protected by copyright, and will not be registered by the Copyright Office (37 C.F.R. 202.1(a)). For this reason, the use of words and short phrases in the menus and icons of the Macintosh user interface—"Get Info" and "Trash," for example—were found not to be protectible.

The words and short phrases rule may be applied to source code, as well as to words. For example, a court has stated that a security code used with the Genesis video game system was "of such de minimis [minimal] length that it is probably unprotected under the words and short phrases doctrine." (*Sega Enterprises, Ltd. v. Accolade, Inc.*, No. 92-15655 (9th Cir. 1993).)

Names (whether of individuals, products or business organizations or groups), titles and slogans are also not copyrightable. However, these items may be protectible under the trademark laws. (See Chapter 9.)

- **Blank forms designed solely to record information.** In addition, blank forms designed solely to record information are not protected by copyright. The Copyright Office will not register such items. (37 C.F.R. 202.1(c).) According to the Copyright Office, this includes such items as time cards, graph paper, account books, bank checks, scorecards, address books, diaries, report forms and order forms.

This rule may also apply to computer screen templates designed to fit with electronic spreadsheets or database programs. If such templates are designed solely to record information, and do not convey information, they should not be protected.

However, it can be difficult in many cases to determine if a form is designed solely to record information. Even true blank forms—that is, forms consisting mainly of blank space to be filled in—may convey valuable information. For example, the columns or headings on a blank form may be interlaced with highly informative verbiage. Moreover, the configuration of columns, headings and lines itself may convey information.

- **Typeface designs.** The Copyright Office and courts have concluded that typeface designs—whether digital or analog—are industrial designs and are therefore not protected by copyright. The reasoning for this is that typeface styles or fonts are purely utilitarian. The Copyright Office, therefore, will not register a work consisting solely of a typeface design. However, copyright can protect typeface software (computer programs designed to produce fonts). In addition, some typefaces have been protected by design patents, including ITC Stone, Adobe Garamond and Adobe Minion.

- **Works for which copyright has expired.** As discussed in Chapter 3, copyright protection does not last forever. When it expires the work enters the public domain. In effect, public domain works belong to everybody. Anyone is free to use them but no one can ever own them. However, copyright protection lasts so long—at least 50 years—that by the time the vast majority of software enters the public domain it will be worthless because of changes in technology.

The only software now in the public domain because of expiration of the copyright is software published before 1964 for which no renewal registration was filed with the Copyright Office during the 28th year after publication. Such software entered the public domain at the start of the 29th year after publication. For example, a program published in 1960 which was not renewed during 1988 entered the public domain on January 1, 1989. Of course, not much software was published before 1964, and what there was probably has little or no value today.

Note that this rule applies only to published software. Copyright protection for all unpublished software, whenever written, lasts at least 50 years from the time it was written and usually longer. (See Chapter 3.)

• **Works dedicated to the public domain.** The author of a computer program or other copyrightable work is free to decide that he or she doesn't want it protected by copyright and may dedicate it instead to the public domain. By doing so, the author gives up all ownership rights in the work and permits anyone to copy or otherwise use the work without permission. There are no official forms to file to do this. The author merely needs to state clearly somewhere on the work that no copyright is claimed in the work. The Copyright Office will not register a work for which copyright has been expressly disclaimed. Without such registration, a copyright infringement suit cannot be filed.

Huge amounts of software has been dedicated to the public domain. For example, computer programming texts often contain code dedicated to the public domain that programmers are encouraged to copy. Much public domain software can also be found on the Internet and BBSs.

Freeware and Shareware Are Not In the Public Domain

Freeware is software that is made available to the public for free. Although it's free, freeware is not the same as public domain software because the author retains his or her copyright rights and can place restrictions on how the program is used. In contrast, authors who dedicate software to the public domain give up all their copyright rights. This means you can use their software any way you wish without restriction.

Shareware refers to a method of marketing software by making trial copies available to users for free. If the user wishes to keep the software, he or she is supposed to pay the shareware owner a fee. Shareware is fully protected by copyright and may be used only in the manner and to the extent permitted by the owner.

2. Creating Similar Works Independently

So long as a program or other work is independently created, it is entitled to copyright protection even if other similar works already exist. This means that if a programmer can prove he or she independently created the program, he or she cannot be guilty of infringing on a preexisting program, even if it is very similar to that program.

Of course, proving that a program was independently created can be difficult. The creators of the program must be able to show they did not have access to the preexisting program; or, even if they could have had access to it, they never saw it. One approach taken by some software developers who wish to create programs similar to and/or compatible with preexisting software is the use of clean room procedures to establish independent creation. Clean room procedures are used to isolate the persons who actually develop the software. In some cases such persons are denied access to any information about the preexisting software. In other cases they may be given only information about the preexisting program's purpose or functions.

The important decision *Computer Associates v. Altai*, 982 F.2d 693 (2d Cir. 1992) shows that clean room procedures can really work and serve as a good defense to copyright infringement claims. Here's what happened in that case: Altai hired a programmer formerly employed by CAI to create a job scheduling program. Unbe-

knownst to Altai, the programmer used substantial chunks of CAI code to create Altai's software. When Altai learned what happened, it decided to create a clean version of its scheduling program. Altai hired eight new programmers to create the new version. They were denied access to the infringing version of the software and forbidden to talk to the programmer who created that version. The new programmers were only provided with a specification developed from an earlier noninfringing version of the software. It took about six months to create the new program. It accomplished everything the prior version did, but used none of CAI's code. Altai was sued for copyright infringement by CAI, but the court held that this version of the program did not infringe on CAI's copyright.

For clean room procedures to be effective, great care must be taken not to give the clean room personnel information protected by copyright. For example, an overly specific description for a user interface might contain protected expression which, if used, could taint the clean room. Before implementing a clean room procedure of your own, you should consult with a knowledgeable software attorney.

3. Copying Within the Bounds of Fair Use

The Copyright Act contains several exceptions to the general rule that copyright rights are exclusive to their owners. These exceptions are generally referred to as fair use.

If a particular use of a copyrighted item comes within the legal definition of fair use, the copyright owner's permission isn't necessary, nor is the user required to pay the owner compensation for the use. Often, whether a particular act is or isn't fair use is a major issue in a copyright infringement case, with the defendant claiming, "I didn't infringe your copyright, I only made fair use of it."

The Copyright Act contains several broad categories of what constitutes fair use. A more specific description is found in the congressional committee report that accompanied the act as it was being considered by Congress. According to this report, examples of when unauthorized copying of a copyrighted work is considered fair use include:

- quotations or excerpts in a review or criticism for purposes of illustration or comment
- quotation of a short passage in a scholarly or technical work for illustration or clarification of the author's observation
- use in a parody of some of the content of the work parodied
- summary of an address or article, with brief quotations, in a news report
- reproduction by a library of a portion of a work to replace part of a damaged copy
- reproduction by a teacher or student of a small part of a work to illustrate a lesson

- reproduction of a work in legislative or judicial proceedings or reports, and
- incidental and fortuitous reproduction, in a newsreel or broadcast, of a work located at the scene of an event being reported.

As you may glean from these examples, fair use has historically been used to allow the media broad latitude in reporting on items of public interest, even if they're otherwise subject to copyright protection. Fair use has also been important to educational, scientific and political pursuits. Note also that, with the exception of uses by the for-profit press and mass media, most of these examples involve nonprofit uses of copyrighted material. Authors of works created primarily for financial gain usually have had a difficult time successfully invoking the fair use privilege. This seemed to mean that the fair use doctrine had relatively limited application to the commercial software industry.

However, fair use law underwent a major change with the Supreme Court's highly publicized decision in the so-called Pretty Woman case. In that case the Court held that a parody of the song "Pretty Woman" by the rap group 2 Live Crew was a fair use. (*Campbell v. Acuff-Rose Music, Inc.* 114 S.Ct. 1164 (1994).) But the decision has broad implications for creators of all types of works, not just song parodies. Perhaps the most important aspect of the decision is the Supreme Court's ruling that a commercial use of copyrighted material may be a fair use if the new work is more than a mere duplication of the original, what the court terms a transformative use (see Section a, below). This may mean that the fair use privilege can apply to at least some for-profit commercially motivated software. All the ramifications of the Supreme Court's decision are unclear, and will have to be resolved by the lower courts.

a. Four factors considered in fair use analysis

Four primary factors are considered to determine whether an unauthorized use is a fair use, rather than copyright infringement:

- **The character and purpose of the use.** The test here is to see whether the subsequent work merely serves as a substitute for the original or "instead adds something new, with a further purpose or different character, altering the first with new expression, meaning, or message." (*Campbell v. Acuff-Rose Music, Inc.*, 114 S.Ct. 1164 (1994).) The Supreme Court calls such a new work transformative. This is the most significant fair use factor. The more transformative a work, the less important are the other fair use factors, such as commercialism, that may weigh against a finding of fair use. Why should this be? It is because the goal of copyright to promote human knowledge is furthered by the creation of transformative works. "Such works thus lie at the heart of the fair use doctrine's guarantee of a breathing space within the confines of copyright." (*Campbell v. Acuff-Rose Music, Inc.*)

- **The nature of the copyrighted work.** Legal, scientific, historical and other factual works are more often subject to the fair use defense than fanciful works like novels or movies.

- **The amount and substantiality of the portion of the copyrighted work used in relation to the entire work.** Using a small part of a large work is more likely to be considered fair use than if most of the work is used. Similarly, a part of a work that is somewhat tangential to the whole will qualify as fair use more easily than a portion of core importance.

- **The effect of the use on the potential market for the copyrighted work, and/ or the work's value.** The fact that the use actually competes with the copyrighted work (for example, creating a competing program) weighs against fair use. However, the more transformative the subsequent work, the less important this factor is. In other words, if a software author borrows some copyrighted material to create a new and better work, the fact that it may harm the market for the previous work will not necessarily bar a finding of fair use.

b. Making archival copies is a fair use

Congress has specifically authorized two fair uses that relate to computer programs. A person who purchases a computer program has the right to copy or adapt the program if the copy or adaptation is either:

1. "An essential step in the utilization of the computer program in conjunction with a machine and that it is used in no other manner"—in other words, the purchaser has to copy the program from a floppy disk to his hard disk or adapt the program to get it to work on his computer; or

2. The copy or adaptation is for archival purposes only (a single back-up copy) and is made and kept only by the person who owns the legally purchased copy. (17 U.S.C. 117.)

This limited right to make a back-up or archival copy is not really very generous. Since the copy is for back-up purposes only, it cannot be used on a second computer. This means, for example, that if you own a desktop computer and a laptop, and want to use your word processor on both, legally you must buy two copies. In an effort to make their customers happy, some large software publishers are now including provisions in their license agreements permitting their customers to use a program on two different computers.

c. Reverse engineering as a fair use

Reverse engineering is the process of taking a product or device apart and reducing it to its constituent parts or concepts to see how it works. Reverse engineering has long been used by manufacturers of all types of products to help them create new products. Reverse engineering is perfectly legal so long as it doesn't violate another's patent or copyright rights.

Computer hardware may be reverse engineered by unscrewing the box and looking inside. The best way to reverse engineer a computer program is usually to read the source code. To prevent competitors from reading their valuable source code, software owners normally distribute their programs in object code form only while the source code is kept locked away. However, it is possible, though often difficult, to reverse engineer object code by translating it into human-readable assembly language which programmers then read to understand the object code. This process is called decompilation or disassembly.

The information gained by reverse engineering can be put to a variety of uses, each with a different economic effect on the owner of the original program. For example, the information can be used to develop a competitive product. In other cases, decompilation can be used to create a program that is functionally compatible—a clone program. Decompilation can also be used to help develop a program that is not competitive, but complementary to the original program—for example, creating a video game cartridge to run on a video game system like Nintendo or Genesis.

Decompilation and disassembly involve the making of at least a partial reproduction or derivative work of the object code. Typically, a copy of the original program is made on a disk, decompiler software is then used to load the program into computer memory; the copy is then transformed into human-readable form, which is then fixed on disk and/or paper.

Both source and object code may be protected by copyright and a copyright owner has the exclusive right to copy and create derivative works from his protected material. Does this mean that decompilation and disassembly constitute copyright infringement? In 1992, two courts said "no," and apparently gave the green light to decompilation, at least under certain circumstances.

The most important of these cases involved Sega Enterprises, manufacturer of the Genesis video game system. (*Sega Enterprises, Ltd. v. Accolade, Inc.,* 977 F.2d 1510 (9th Cir. 1992).) Accolade, Inc., wanted to manufacture a video game cartridge to be used with the Genesis system. Rather than pay Sega for a license to do so, Accolade reversed engineered the Genesis system. It disassembled the object code stored in commercially available read-only memory (ROM) chips in Sega's games to learn the requirements for creation of a Genesis-compatible game cartridge. This process required that Accolade make unauthorized copies of Sega's code for study and analysis (called intermediate copies). Sega sued Accolade for copyright infringement, claiming that Accolade's copying violated its copyright. Sega lost.

The federal appeals court held that disassembly of object code is a fair use if:

1. it is the *only* means available to obtain access to the unprotected elements of a computer program—ideas, functional

principles and so forth (see Section B1), and

2. the copier has a legitimate reason for seeking such access.

In applying the fair use factors discussed above, the court found "the purpose and character of the use" to be noncommercial, despite the fact that the copying was being done to create competing game cartridges. The court reasoned that the interim copies were not themselves sold. The court also said that the copying would not harm the market for Sega's video games because consumers might easily purchase both Sega-made and Accolade-made game cartridges. The court also stressed that, if disassembly like Accolade's were prohibited, Sega would in effect enjoy a monopoly over the unprotected ideas and functional principles contained in its code, since the only way to obtain access to those ideas was through disassembly.

d. Limitations on decompilation as a fair use

The Sega case did not create a blanket rule permitting all decompilation. Rather it demonstrated that decompilation may be a permissible fair use when necessary to develop compatible or complementary programs that do not cause the copyright owner economic harm. If a copyright owner can establish that decompilation of its object code has or will cause it economic harm, a court should conclude that the decompilation was not a fair use.

Furthermore, decompilation can be a fair use only when it is the *only* available means to study the unprotected elements of a program. Often, there are means available other than decompilation to study such elements—simply studying the screen display will reveal the ideas and concepts of many programs. The Sega court stated that the need for disassembly "arises, if at all, only in connection with operations systems, system interface procedures, and other programs that are not visible to the user when operating."

The fair use factors discussed above are subject to varying interpretations and it is often difficult to predict the outcome of any particular case. This fact is illustrated by another court decision on fair use, involving decompilation of security system source code for the Nintendo video game system by Atari Games. (*Atari Games Corp. v. Nintendo of America, Inc.*, 980 F.2d 857 (Fed.Cir. 1992).) The court reached the same legal conclusion as the Sega decision— decompilation can be a fair use in the proper circumstances. But the court held that Atari's decompilation was not a fair use because it obtained the Nintendo source code from the Copyright Offices under false pretenses. Atari's bad faith and lack of fair dealing obviated a finding of fair use.

The question of whether a use qualifies as a fair use must always be decided on a case-by-case basis. For these reasons, anyone wishing to reverse engineer any program to create a new product should first consult with a qualified software attorney.

C. Protecting Against Infringement Claims

To protect yourself against infringement claims, you must not only avoid committing copyright infringement yourself, but guard against infringement by your employees, independent contractors and other people you deal with.

1. When You Can Be Held Liable for Infringement

Unfortunately, you don't have to commit copyright infringement yourself to be held liable. You can be held legally responsible for infringements carried out by your employees, consultants and others you deal with.

a. Employers Liable for Infringement by Employees

A copyright infringer's employer (whether a corporation, partnership or individual) will be held liable for any infringing acts by employees within the scope of employment. This is based on the general legal principle that an employer has the right to supervise and control employees' activities and is therefore responsible for their wrongful acts. Because an employer has the right to control the work-related activities of an employee, it will be held liable for an employee's infringement even though it didn't actually know about or condone it at the time. Indeed, liability may be imposed even if the employer instructed the employee not to commit the infringement. The reasoning behind this is that the employer should have used its right of control to prevent the infringement.

b. Hirers of independent contractors

You don't have to be an employer of someone to be held liable for their infringement. The hirer of an independent contractor may be liable for the contractor's infringement if the hirer actively participated in, materially contributed to or furthered the hired party's infringing acts.

Liability may also be imposed if a contractor had a direct financial interest in the infringing activities and the right to supervise the contractor or at least police his or her conduct.

c. Corporate officers and partners

The president and other officers of a corporation may be held personally liable for infringement by the corporation if the officer caused the infringement, participated in it or benefited financially from it.

Partners in a partnership may also be held personally liable for infringement by their fellow partners if they participated in it, benefited from it or arranged it.

d. Employee Liability

An employee who commits infringement on his or her own initiative will be held liable. However, liability usually will not be imposed where an employee is ordered to commit an infringement by the employer. But the employer would of course be liable.

e. Anyone who induces an infringement

In addition, any person who induces, causes or helps another to commit copyright infringement may be held liable as a contributory infringer and subjected to the same penalties as the person who actually committed the infringement.

Owners of online services and BBSs can be held liable for contributory infringement when users use their systems to commit copyright infringement, even if the owners didn't know about or authorize it. Similar cases have been brought against Internet access providers.

> EXAMPLE: Users of a BBS uploaded and downloaded copies of copyrighted Sega computer video games. Sega sued the BBS's sysops (systems operators) for copyright infringement and won. The court held that although there was no evidence the sysops were themselves posting the Sega games on the board, they knew the games were there, knew they were being uploaded and downloaded, and encouraged the process. They were therefore liable as contributory copyright infringers. (*Sega Enterprises v. Maphia*, 30 U.S.P.Q.2d 1921 (N.D. Ca. 1994).)

2. Preventing Illegal Copying in the Development Process

As we discussed in detail in the previous Section, many elements of computer software are not protected by copyright and can therefore be copied at will unless they are protected by some other body of law, such as the federal patent law. But exactly what these uncopyrightable elements are in any given instance can be very hard to know because the legal decisions in this area are not always clear or consistent. So before you do this type of copying, you may want to consult with a computer law attorney.

a. Keep good records

It is also very important for software developers to keep meticulous records of the entire development process, from the initial idea stage to coding, debugging and testing. This includes copies of storyboards and prototypes, interim versions, flowcharts and internal memoranda documenting the many decisions that must be made in the course of software development. Documentation

like this will help prove that your work was original and not copied from others, which is an absolute defense to all copyright infringement claims.

b. Registering software under development

If you're especially concerned about being sued for copyright infringement, you may wish to register your software with the Copyright Office while it's still under development. The advantage of this is that you deposit a copy of the software with the Copyright Office as part of the registration process. This copy is kept on file at the Copyright Office. The existence of this registered copy can serve as proof that you didn't copy from someone else. If your software was deposited before the software you are alleged to have copied was created, then you couldn't have copied it.

c. Don't indemnify clients for infringement claims

Another thing a developer can do to help reduce his or her exposure is to refuse to indemnify customers for infringement claims. Indemnification means the developer promises to defend the customer in court if it is sued for infringement and to pay any damages awarded. Indemnification provisions have been commonly included in software development agreements in the past; but, in light of the risks involved, more and more developers are refusing to agree to them or insist on limiting their exposure. (See Chapter 17.)

Insurance Coverage for Infringement Claims

Your business may be insured for intellectual property infringement claims and not even know it. The Comprehensive General Liability Insurance (CGL) policies typically obtained by businesses may provide such coverage. Several courts have held that the advertising injury provision included in many CGL policies covers infringement claims. However, not all CGL policies provide such coverage, particularly those written after 1986. You should ask your insurance broker whether your policy provides this coverage. If the broker doesn't know, you may need to consult with an insurance attorney who represents policyholders. If your CGL policy doesn't cover infringement claims, you may be able to obtain such coverage by purchasing a rider to your policy that covers such claims.

3. Preventing Illegal Copying in the Workplace

The Business Software Alliance, a software publishers' trade organization, estimates that 30% of all software used in the U.S. is pirated. Much of this copying occurs in the workplace. For the past several years a vigorous and effective campaign against workplace software piracy has been waged by the two largest software industry trade groups: the Software Publishers Association (SPA) and Business Software Alliance (BSA).

SPA and BSA investigators are actively seeking out companies that routinely make illegal copies and both organizations maintain toll-free hotlines to which people can report violations (this is often done by disgruntled employees or ex-employees).

Once evidence of illegal copying is obtained, the SPA or BSA will send the company a cease and desist letter asking the company to voluntarily destroy the illegally copied software and buy legal copies. The SPA or BSA will also often seek permission to have its investigators conduct an audit of the company's computers. If illegally copied software is found during an audit, they ask the company to pay twice—once for the illegal copies, which are destroyed, and a second time to buy legal replacement copies.

If a company does not cooperate voluntarily with the SPA or BSA, they or the company whose software has been copied will take the violator to court or even seek to have it criminally prosecuted by the government. In one case, a $500,000 criminal fine was imposed. Initially, the SPA only went after large Fortune 500 companies; but in recent years it has focused on smaller companies as well.

Since it can be held liable for copyright infringement engaged in by its employees, any company that uses software should have an established policy forbidding employees from making unauthorized copies of software or otherwise committing copyright infringement on the job. Here are some of the steps the SPA advises a company to take to ensure that illegal copying is not taking place:

- First, the company should designate someone to serve as a software manager. This person will be responsible for implementing the company's software policy and maintaining records.
- Conduct an inventory of all the software the company is using. Illegal copies should be destroyed and legal copies purchased.
- Establish clear procedures for purchasing and registering new software.
- Maintain a software log listing each software package the company owns and the computer it runs on.
- Conduct periodic audits of the company computers to ensure they contain no illegal software. Software is commercially available that can scan hard drives on networked computers to see what applications they are running. The SPA also can provide a free inventory program called SPAudit. You can download a copy from the SPA's Web page at www.spa.org; or obtain a copy by calling 202-452-1600.
- Establish an employee education program stressing that copyright infringement will not be tolerated.
- Maintain a library of the company's software licenses.

A wealth of information on these issues can be obtained from the SPA's Website at www.spa.org/piracy/info.htm. The SPA can also be contacted at 800-388-7478.

D. What to Do if You're Accused of Copyright Infringement

What should you do if you're accused of copyright infringement? First, see how serious the claim is. If it's minor—for example, a photographer claims you used one of her pictures in your latest multimedia work without permission—the matter can usually be settled very quickly for a small amount of money. This kind of thing happens all the time. There is no need to see a lawyer (who'll probably charge you at least $150 per hour) to deal with this type of minor annoyance. Have the copyright owner sign a letter releasing you from liability in return for your payment. (See Section G4 for an example of a settlement letter.).

On the other hand, if you receive a letter from a copyright owner or owner's attorney alleging a substantial claim—for example, that your popular spreadsheet program is an unauthorized derivative work and its sale should be halted immediately—it's probably time to find a copyright lawyer. If, even worse, you are served with a court Complaint (a document initiating a lawsuit), you must act quickly because you may have as little as 20 days to file an answer (response) in court. If you don't respond in time, a judgment can be entered against you. Finding a lawyer is discussed in Chapter 18.

Even if the case is serious, don't despair. The fact is, many infringement suits are won by the defendant, either because the plaintiff did not have a valid claim to begin with or because the defendant had a good defense. This chapter is not a substitute for a consultation with an experienced attorney; rather, it is designed to give you an idea of some of the things you need to discuss when you see an attorney.

If a substantial claim is involved, the decision whether to settle the case or fight it out in court should only be made after consulting with an attorney who is familiar with the facts of your particular case. However, in making this decision you need to carefully weigh the following factors:

- how likely is it that the plaintiff will prevail
- how much the plaintiff is likely to collect if the plaintiff does win
- the costs of contesting the case, not only in terms of money, but also in terms of the time it will take, and the embarrassment and adverse publicity it will generate, and
- how much the plaintiff may be willing to settle for.

Typically, a copyright infringement plaintiff will seek a preliminary injunction (a court order) soon after the lawsuit is filed stopping you from continuing the infringing activity. A hearing will be held at which the judge must determine whether it's likely the plaintiff would prevail at trial and would be irreparably harmed if an injunction doesn't issue. Most often, infringement cases are settled on the basis of such a hearing's outcome. That is, if the plaintiff obtains an injunction, the defendant will usually agree to settle the case on terms favorable to the plaintiff. If an injunction doesn't issue, the plaintiff may drop the case entirely or accept a settlement favorable to the defendant.

In cases where a settlement can't be reached, you may be able to have his suit dismissed very quickly by filing what's called a summary judgment motion. Under this procedure the judge examines the plaintiff's claims and decides whether there is any possibility he could prevail if a trial were held. If not, the judge will dismiss the case. Of course, you must pay a lawyer to file a summary judgment motion, but, if successful, it will cost far less than taking the case to trial. Summary judgment motions are frequently used—and are frequently successful—against plaintiffs who bring patently frivolous infringement suits. Moreover, if the plaintiff's claim was clearly frivolous or brought in bad faith, the judge might order the plaintiff to pay all or part of your attorney fees.

On the other hand, if the plaintiff does have a valid claim, paying an attorney to fight a losing battle will only compound your problems. Valid claims should be settled whenever possible. If the plaintiff was able to obtain a preliminary injunction from a federal judge, he or she probably has a valid claim.

given very limited protection. (See Section B1.) Most courts require that these elements be eliminated from consideration when the plaintiff's software is compared with the allegedly infringing software to determine whether they are substantially similar. This means that if you've only copied or paraphrased these unprotected elements, you won't be found to have committed copyright infringement.

1. Defenses to Copyright Infringement

Even if there are substantial similarities between the plaintiff's work and your work, you will not necessarily be found guilty of infringement. The similarities may simply be the result of coincidence; in this event there is no liability. But, even direct copying from the plaintiff's work may be excused if it constitutes a fair use or there is another valid defense.

Possible defenses to an infringement action include many general legal defenses that often involve where, when and how the lawsuit was brought, who was sued, and so on. We obviously can't cover all of this here. This section is limited to outlining the major defenses that are specific to copyright infringement actions. Again, if you find yourself defending a serious copyright infringement action, retain a qualified attorney.

a. Material copied was not protected by copyright

Many elements of computer programs are not protected by copyright at all or are

b. The use was authorized

In some cases, you may not be an infringer at all, but a legal transferee. For example:

- You might legitimately claim to have received a license to use the plaintiff's work, and that the work the plaintiff claims to infringe on his copyright falls within that license. For instance, Programmer A orally tells Programmer B he can copy his work, then later claims never to have granted the permission.

- Conflicting or confusing licenses or sublicenses are granted and you claim to be the rightful owner of the right(s) in question.

- You received a transfer from the plaintiff and weren't restricted in making further transfers, and transferred the copyright to individuals unknown to the original owner.

Several examples of lawful transfers are presented in Chapter 11. If any of these transferees were sued they would have a good defense—that is, that their use was lawful.

c. Statute of Limitations

A plaintiff can't wait forever to file an infringement suit. As discussed in Section H3, the statute of limitations is three years from the time the infringement should reasonably have been discovered (but applying this rule can be extremely tricky). If the plaintiff waited too long, you may be able to have the case dismissed.

d. Other Defenses

Some of the other possible defenses to copyright infringement include such things as:

- the notion that if the plaintiff is guilty of some serious wrongdoing himself or herself—for example, falsifying evidence—he or she cannot complain about your alleged wrongs
- the notion that the plaintiff waited so long to file suit that it would be unfair to find the defendant guilty of infringement—"it is inequitable for the owner of a copyright, with full notice of an intended infringement, to stand inactive while the proposed infringer spends large sums of money on its exploitation, and to intervene only when his speculation has proved a success. Delay under such circumstances allows the owner to speculate without risk with the other's money; he cannot possibly lose, and he may win." (*Hass v. Leo Feist, Inc.*, 234 Fed. 105 (S.D.N.Y. 1916).)
- The idea that the copyright owner knew of your acts and expressly or impliedly consented to them.

2. Collecting Your Attorney Fees If You Prevail

If the plaintiff (the person who sues you for infringement) loses his or her suit, the court has discretion to award you all or part of your attorney fees. In the past, many courts would award such fees to a defendant only if they found that the plaintiff's suit was frivolous or brought in bad faith. But these courts would not use this criterion when making fees awards to plaintiffs. In 1994 the Supreme Court held that this approach was incorrect and that attorney fees must be awarded to plaintiffs and defendants in an evenhanded manner. In other words, the same criteria must be applied to both plaintiffs and defendants. (*Fogerty v. Fantasy, Inc.*, 114 S.Ct. 1023 (1994).)

What this means is that if you defeat your accuser in court, you have a good chance of getting an award against him or her for some or all of your attorney fees. The actual amount you'll be awarded, if any, is up to the judge. However, such an award will be useless unless the plaintiff has the money or insurance to pay it.

Part II. Suing Others for Copyright Infringement

The other side of the copyright infringement equation involves suing others for infringing on your protected work. When a copyright dispute arises, there are often several self-help steps a copyright owner can take.

These generally amount to telling the infringer to stop the infringing activity and/or pay for the infringement. When push comes to shove, however, there is only one remedy with teeth in it: to ask a federal court to order the infringing activity halted and to award a judgment for damages. Because this type of litigation is procedurally complex, an attorney skilled in copyright litigation is required. (See Chapter 18.)

This discussion is not intended as a substitute for a good copyright attorney. Rather, its aim is to:

- help you recognize when copyright infringement has occurred
- suggest some steps you—as a software author or other copyright owner— might take on your own to deal effectively with infringement without resorting to lawyers and the courts
- tell you what to expect in the event of a court action, and
- help you estimate what damages and other types of court relief are potentially available to you in an infringement suit.

E. What is Software Copyright Infringement?

In Chapter 3, a copyright was described as a bundle of five exclusive rights. These include the right to reproduce, distribute, prepare derivative works based upon, perform and display a protected work. Subject to important exceptions discussed in Section

B, these rights cannot be exercised by anybody but the copyright owner unless the owner's permission is obtained. If copyright rights are exercised without the owner's permission, the copyright is said to be infringed.

Software copyright infringement usually involves the unauthorized exercise of a copyright owner's exclusive rights to reproduce and/or distribute the work and/or prepare derivative works based on it. However, the display and performance rights can be violated as well. For example, simply using a program might violate a copyright owner's display rights.

Courts generally use the word copying as shorthand for violation of any of these exclusive copyright rights (not just the reproduction right). Thus, a copyright owner must prove copying by the defendant to win an infringement suit.

F. How to Know Whether You Have a Valid Infringement Claim

When a civil copyright infringement action is filed, the person bringing the action (called the plaintiff) must prove certain facts in order to prevail. This is called the burden of proof. While a detailed discussion of court procedure is beyond the scope of this book, here are the major things you must establish to prove infringement:

- you are the lawful owner of all or part of a work protected by a valid copyright

- one or more of the copyright rights you own has been infringed, and
- the person, partnership or corporation being sued has actually done the infringing act or contributed to it (called a contributory infringer).

Once you've proven infringement, the next step is to establish what remedies you're entitled to. If you can show that the infringer profited from the infringement, or negatively affected your profits, you may be able to recover these profits (what the infringer gained or what you lost) from the infringer, subject, of course, to any defenses the infringer may have (discussed in Section D1). Or you may be eligible to elect to receive statutory damages instead of your actual damages caused by the infringement (see Section I2b). In addition, the judge has discretion to award you attorney's fees (see Section I4). Finally, you can have the court order the infringer to stop future infringement and destroy all existing copies.

Let's look at these proof requirements one at a time:

1. Ownership of a Work Protected by Copyright

The question of infringement does not even arise unless the work allegedly infringed is protected by copyright. This means that the work must meet the three prerequisites for copyright protection discussed in detail in Chapter 3; that is, the work must be:

- **Fixed in a tangible medium of expression.** A work is sufficiently fixed if it exists on paper, on disk, or even just in computer RAM.
- **Independently created.** You cannot sue someone for copying software or other materials that you copied from others.
- **Minimally creative.** The work you believe has been infringed upon must have been the product of a minimal amount of creativity. The vast majority of software easily satisfies this requirement; but some databases may not.

Timely Registration Creates Presumption of Validity of Copyright and Ownership

As long as your work is registered within five years of the date of first publication, it is presumed to be protected by a valid copyright and the persons named in the registration certificate are presumed to be the lawful copyright owners. This is one of the greatest benefits of copyright registration. It means that you do not have to go to the time and trouble of proving that your work is original (which can be very hard to prove) or that you actually created it. Rather, it's up to the alleged infringer to try to prove that the work was not original or that your copyright is invalid for some other reason, or that you are not really the owner of the copyright.

2. Infringement of Your Copyright Rights

As a practical matter, most cases of software copyright infringement involve a violation of the owner's exclusive right to make copies. That is, someone copies all or part of somebody else's program without the owner's permission. For purposes of illustration, this discussion assumes that is the case here. Although the focus here is on the right to make copies, the principles discussed relative to copying also apply to all copyright rights that make up the entire bundle of rights (such as the exclusive right to display the work or create derivative works based on it).

To prevail in an infringement lawsuit, the plaintiff must prove that an infringement actually occurred. If someone is caught with an exact copy of a copyrighted work, or is seen copying it, the plaintiff has what is aptly called a smoking gun. The infringing villain has been caught red-handed.

Unfortunately, this type of evidence usually isn't available. Most infringers are smart enough to attempt to disguise their copying. Where source code is involved, for example, it is easy for an infringer to use a text editor to disguise its origin by rearranging lines or blocks of code, changing variable names or altering certain sequences of operations. Moreover, there are rarely any witnesses to copyright infringement. Infringement usually happens behind closed doors and the participants rarely admit their involvement.

This means that in most cases you must prove two things to establish infringement:

- that the claimed infringer had access to your work, and
- that the infringing work is *substantially similar* to your work.

If these are proven, copying is *inferred* because there is no other reasonable explanation for the similarities. However the defendant can rebut (defeat) the inference by proving independent creation—that is, that his or her work was created without copying your work. Let's take a closer look at these two infringement criteria.

a. Access

To prove access, you must show that the alleged infringer had the opportunity to view and copy your software. This requirement is easy to show if the work is mass-marketed. It may be more difficult if the work has only been accessible to a very few people or the source code has been protected as a trade secret. Problems can develop, for example, when software that is very narrowly distributed under a license agreement is pirated. In one legal decision, access was established when a marketing firm changed clients and showed a copy of the former client's product to the new clients, resulting in copyright infringement. (*Synercom Technology, Inc. v. University Computing Company*, 462 F.Supp. 1003 (1978).)

Salting Code to Prove Copying

The best evidence of infringement is to produce a smoking gun in the hands of the infringer. In the software business, this usually means catching the pirate with a program that is somehow instantly identifiable as being the plaintiff's. Since even the most stupid pirate will probably be smart enough to remove the plaintiff's copyright notice if one is used, the wary programmer should bury nonfunctional and idiosyncratic symbols somewhere in the code or salt it with intentional non-harmful errors or unnecessary codings. The idea is to subtly brand the program so it can easily be identified in the event it is copied by someone else.

b. Substantial similarity

Proving substantial similarity is usually the crux of any copyright infringement case. Assuming the alleged infringer had access to your work, the similarities between your work and his must be compared to see if copying may reasonably be inferred. The similarities must be such that they can only be explained by copying, not by factors such as coincidence, independent creation or the existence of a prior common source for both programs.

Today, the first step most courts take is to filter out the unprotectible elements of the plaintiff's program before comparing it with the allegedly infringing program. Under this filtration test, those elements of the plaintiff's program that are not protected by copyright are identified and eliminated from consider-

ation. This includes, for example, ideas, elements dictated by efficiency or external factors or taken from the public domain. (See Section B1.) After this filtration process is completed, there may or may not be any protected program elements left. If there are, this core of protected expression is compared with the allegedly infringing program of the defendant to see if there has been impermissible copying. (*Computer Associates International, Inc. v. Altai, Inc.* 982 F.2d 692 (2d Cir. 1992); *Gates Rubber Co. v. Bando Ltd.*, 9 F.3d 823 (10th Cir. 1993).)

The defendants in most software copyright infringement actions will doubtless claim that any alleged similarities relate only to elements of the plaintiff's program that should be filtered out as unprotectible. This filtration test can make it very difficult for plaintiffs to win infringement cases. Indeed, it makes it difficult for plaintiffs and their attorneys to know whether they have a good infringement case in the first place, since opinions can and will naturally differ as to what elements should and should not be filtered from the infringement analysis.

The clearest cases of copyright infringement involve wholesale copying of your computer code as described in Section A1 above. You'll likely have far more difficulty proving infringement when you allege that nonliteral elements of your program have been copied—that is, things other than computer code such as the user interface. (See Section B.)

The bottom line is that it is virtually impossible for even the most experienced software attorney to predict with confidence whether a nonliteral infringement claim will succeed. In effect, plaintiffs who bring these cases enter a crap shoot: You pay your money and take your chance.

Good Records May Help Win Infringement Cases

Good records of the development process may be crucial for success by infringement plaintiffs where the filtration test discussed above is used. Software developers should get in the habit of keeping meticulous records from the initial idea stage of development, through coding, debugging, testing and the revision process. This should include copies of storyboards and prototypes, interim versions, flowcharts and internal memoranda documenting the many decisions that must be made in the course of software development. Documentation like this may prove very useful if the defendant claims that important elements of your work should be filtered out of the infringement analysis because they were in the public domain, dictated by external factors or efficiency and so forth. If your documentation shows that the disputed elements were the result of creative thinking and problem-solving on your part, not merely the result of standard programming techniques, they should not be filtered out.

G. Self-Help Remedies for Copyright Infringement

If you suspect your copyright has been infringed, you should discuss your problem with a copyright attorney, even if you plan to try to settle or compromise with the infringer without court action. A preliminary conference shouldn't be expensive. However, whether you see an attorney at this stage or not, there are some preliminary things you can safely do on your own.

1. Determine Scope of the Problem

Your first step is to make a common sense assessment of how large the problem is. Who is the infringer? What are the infringer's motives? How much infringement is occurring?

If you believe your copyright has been infringed by an ex-employee who created a program substantially similar to your own without authorization, the possible ways of dealing with the infringement are different than if you're dealing either with an unauthorized posting on the Internet or with an international pirate based in Taiwan. In one situation (the Internet), a cease and desist letter (Section G3) might be sufficient, whereas in another (the international pirate), nothing short of a large scale lawsuit will probably work. And something in between may be the correct approach for the infringement by the ex-employee.

2. Collect Information About Your Copyright Registration

It is a good idea to make sure your copyright records are complete in the event a visit to a lawyer is necessary to stop the infringer. Hopefully, you've registered your copyright and have retained copies of all filed documents and correspondence with the Copyright Office. You should also have retained copies of all copyright transfers you've made.

Because you're human, however, one or more of these documents may have slipped through your fingers. If so, you'll need to obtain a copy of the missing documents from the Copyright Office. Fortunately, Copyright Office records are public records. This means that any member of the public can obtain copies of the information, application, deposit, other documents relating to registration or ownership. However, you must provide the Copyright Office with specific information, including:

- The type of record you're interested in (for instance, the correspondence between the Copyright Office and the copyright owner, a copy of the deposit, a certificate of registration).
- Whether you require certified or uncertified copies (you would want certified copies in case you need to introduce them in a lawsuit).
- Complete identification of the record, such as the type of work (program, novel, manual, etc.), the complete

registration number, the year or approximate year of registration, the complete title of the work as it appears on the application, the author, including any pseudonym by which the author may be known, the claimants, and the volume and page number where the document is recorded if you're seeking a copy of an assignment, any exclusive license, or other recorded contract.

- Any additional information that may be required for the specific record you want. For instance, obtaining copies of deposits requires that you comply with some additional conditions.
- $4 for each certification requested and $4 for additional copies of the application. The fees for all other requests will be added up by the Copyright Office on a case-by-case basis.
- Your telephone number and address, so the Copyright Office can contact you for additional information.

If you don't provide the year or the title of the work, a search of the records may be required for verification of your request. The fee for this search is $20 per hour.

Mail your request to:

Certification and Documents Section
 LM-402
Copyright Office
Library of Congress
Washington DC 20559

3. Cease and Desist Letter

Once you've mailed your request for any missing copyright records, you may want to send the alleged infringer a cease and desist letter. This sort of letter serves several functions:

- First, it lets the infringer know that you believe she is infringing your copyright.
- Second, it dates your discovery of the infringing activity, should more serious action be warranted later. This is important for purposes of the statute of limitations on copyright infringement lawsuits discussed below.
- Third, it tells the infringer that you have every intention of stopping her.
- Fourth, and perhaps most important, it gives the infringer a chance to explain her conduct and perhaps offer a satisfactory compromise, before you've spent a lot of money initiating a lawsuit. Even if you're sure you're right, it doesn't hurt to listen to the other person's story. In addition, by giving the infringer a chance to respond, you may find out a lot about how he or she plans to defend a court action.

Here is what is normally covered in a cease and desist letter:

- who you are, including your business address and telephone number, or, if you want to protect your privacy, some way to contact you—such as a P.O. Box

- the name of your work, date of first publication, and the copyright registration certificate number, if your work is registered
- the nature of the activity you believe to be an infringement of your copyright
- a demand that the infringer cease and desist from the activity, and
- a request for a response within a stated period of time.

Your letter can threaten legal action, but you're probably wiser not to at this stage. The specter of courts and lawyers usually does little but make the other person paranoid, defensive and unwilling to cooperate.

If you act as if your lawsuit is only hours away, the answer to your letter is likely to come from the infringer's lawyer. Once two lawyers are involved, the chances of any compromise settlement is greatly reduced, as lawyers, by the very nature of their profession, usually get paid more to fight than to compromise.

When you draft your letter, remember that you may end up wanting to use it in court. Accordingly, avoid being cute, nasty, tentative or overly dramatic. The following example contains about the right tone and level of information.

Sample Cease and Desist Letter

January 1, 199X

Ms. Oleo Oboe, President
Oboe, Inc.
567 Symphony Drive
Anywhere, USA 11111

Dear Ms. Oboe:

I recently became aware of your manufacture and sale of a CD-ROM called *100 Best Java Applets*. I am the owner of the copyright in a Java Applet entitled *Java 1-2-3*, copyright registration No. 22222222. I believe that your CD-ROM contains a copy (or a substantial copy) of *Java 1-2-3*. Since I have not authorized you or your company to make or sell copies of *Java 1-2-3,*, it follows that you're infringing my copyright by doing so.

This letter is to demand that you and Oboe, Inc., immediately cease and desist from the manufacture and sale of *Java 1-2-3*, on the CD-ROM *100 Best Java Applets* or by any other means. In addition, I request reasonable compensation for the copies you have already sold and your remaining inventory.

Please respond to this letter by January 15, 199X.

Sincerely,

Carl Jones
123 Action Street
Hollywood, CA

Cease and desist letters should be sent by certified mail, return receipt requested. If the infringer refuses to accept your letter, arrange to have it delivered personally, by someone who isn't involved in the dispute and who'll be available to testify that the letter was delivered to the party, if that should become necessary.

What you do next depends on the response you receive, as well as the nature of the infringer and the infringing conduct. Reasonable and routine solutions to many infringements include:

- payment for profits previously made on the infringing work
- making the infringement legal through a license under which you're paid an agreed-upon fee for all future copies, and
- getting the infringer to agree to stop future infringements.

Mediation as an Alternative to Litigation

One low-cost alternative to filing a lawsuit is getting the other party to agree to mediation. In mediation, the parties to a dispute work with a mediator to attempt to reach an amicable settlement. Mediation is informal. Typically, the mediator either sits the parties down together and tries to provide an objective view of their disputes, or shuttles between the parties as a cool conduit of what may be red-hot opinions. A good mediator may be able to lead the parties to a mutually satisfactory resolution that will obviate time-consuming and expensive litigation. Mediation is nonbinding—that is, either side can still file a lawsuit if it wants to. The mediator can be a lawyer, but doesn't have to be. Many organizations provide mediation services, including the American Arbitration Association, which has offices in most major cities. In most cases, however, mediation is a realistic alternative only where the parties are located near each other. It's not likely that either party would want to incur substantial travel expenses to take part in such an informal, nonbinding procedure. For further information on mediation, refer to *Mediate Your Dispute,* by Peter Lovenheim (Nolo Press).

4. Settlement Letter

Any compromise settlement should be in writing, and signed by all parties. At this point, you should definitely get the help of a lawyer with experience in the area.

Here is a sample of the way the *Java 1-2-3* dispute might be settled:

Sample Settlement Letter

Ms. Oleo Oboe, President
Oboe, Inc.
567 Symphony Drive
Anywhere, USA 11111

Dear Ms. Oboe:

This letter embodies the terms and conditions to settle all outstanding disputes between Oboe, Inc., and Carl Jones and to authorize Oboe, Inc., to market the computer program, *Java 1-2-3*.

Carl Jones and Oboe, Inc., hereby agree:

1. Oboe, Inc., will pay Carl Jones the sum of $10,000 for copies of *Java 1-2-3* sold up to the date of our agreement, January 20, 199X.

2. Oboe, Inc., will place the following copyright notice on all copies of *Java 1-2-3* sold from January 20, 199X, until termination of our Standard Resellers Agreement: © copyright Carl Jones 199X

3. Oboe, Inc., will execute and be bound by the terms of our Standard Resellers Agreement attached hereto.

4. Carl Jones agrees that this agreement completely settles the matter in dispute between Carl Jones and Oboe, Inc., and releases Oboe, Inc., from any further liability for the sale of *Java 1-2-3* prior to January 20, 199X.

Carl Jones
123 Acton Street
Hollywood, CA

H. Nuts and Bolts of Infringement Lawsuits

If you can't satisfactorily resolve the matter yourself (perhaps through mediation and/or with a short consultation with a copyright lawyer), you have two alternatives: forget about it, or hire a lawyer and bring an infringement suit in federal court. The following is an overview of the nuts and bolts of a copyright infringement suit. It is intended to give you a general idea of what you can expect from copyright litigation, not as a substitute for further research or a consultation with an experienced copyright attorney. See Chapter 18, for a guide to further research and ways to find a copyright attorney.

1. Who Can Sue

A person or entity who files an infringement suit is called the plaintiff. The plaintiff must be someone who owns the copyright rights at issue, or holds an exclusive license to them. This will typically be the creator of the software or a person or entity to whom the creator has transferred ownership—for example, a software publisher.

> **EXAMPLE:** DynoSoft, Inc., a software publisher, purchases the exclusive right to publish in the United States a computer game called *Life or Death*. DynoSoft discovers that a pirated version of the game is being sold in the U.S. by CopySoft, Inc. DynoSoft is entitled to sue CopySoft for copyright infringement.

a. Copyright registration prerequisite to suit

A civil lawsuit based on a claim of copyright infringement of a U.S. copyright cannot be brought unless and until the copyright has been registered with the U.S. Copyright Office. Registration can occur after an infringing act and you can still sue for that infringement. However, if you registered prior to the infringement (or within three months of publication), you're eligible for special statutory damages, attorney fees and certain other procedural benefits that are not available if you waited to register until after the infringement began. (See Chapter 4.)

Registration is not required where a resident of a foreign country that has signed the Berne copyright convention files an infringement suit in the U.S. See Chapter 10 for a list of Berne signatory countries.)

Copyright registration can take anywhere from three to six months or even longer. However, if you need to register immediately so that you can sue, there is an expedited procedure by which registration can be accomplished in a much shorter period. You must pay an extra fee and follow the procedure set out in Chapter 4, Section K.

Criminal Prosecutions for Copyright Infringement

Willful copyright infringement is a federal crime (17 U.S.C. 506). Accordingly, the United States Attorney General has the power to prosecute infringers. Any person criminally convicted for copyright infringement can be imprisoned for up to one year and/or fined up to $25,000, and the infringing software will be destroyed. In addition, a person who is convicted of piracy of at least ten copies of a computer program with a retail value of more than $2,500 can be imprisoned for up to five years and required to pay a fine up to $250,000. Such a conviction constitutes a felony. In the case of a second or subsequent offense, jail time can be increased to ten years. (17 U.S.C. 2319(b).)

In recent years the Department of Justice, U.S. Attorney's Office and FBI have begun to take copyright infringement seriously and vigorously enforce the copyright laws. In the best known case of its kind, the U.S. Attorney attempted to prosecute for wire fraud a student who set up a BBS to dispense copyrighted software to subscribers for free. The case was ultimately dismissed. (*United States v. LaMacchia*, 871 F.Supp. 535 (D.Mass. 1994).) The Department of Justice responded to this defeat by seeking to have Congress enact even tougher penalties for copyright infringement.

In addition, the FBI has established a computer crime squad headquartered in San Francisco. In early 1997, it raided homes and offices in eight cities seizing computers it alleged were being used in nationwide software piracy rings that made use of the Internet and BBSs.

If you wish to have someone criminally prosecuted for copyright infringement, contact the local U.S. Attorney's office. See Chapter 6, Section C4, for a discussion of the pros and cons of seeking criminal prosecutions for intellectual property infringement.

2. Who Is Liable for Infringement

Although a primary goal may be simply to stop an infringer from distributing any more copies of an infringing software, you are also entitled to collect damages from those liable for the infringement. You may also be able to receive special statutory damages, which is an important right when your actual damages are very small or difficult to prove, and attorney fees as well. (See Section I below for a detailed discussion of damages.)

Who may be liable for such damages and fees? Quite simply, *everybody* who participates in or contributes to copyright infringement.

3. How Much Time You Have to Sue: Statute of Limitations

There are strict time limits on when copyright infringement suits may be filed. If you fail to file in time, the infringer may be able to have your suit dismissed, even though you have a strong case.

The general rule is that an infringement suit must be filed within three years after the date the copyright owner should reasonably have discovered the infringing act occurred. This is usually plenty of time. However, in some cases, it can reasonably take the copyright owner a long time to discover that the infringement took place, especially where the infringer attempted to conceal the act of infringement. For this reason, if more than three years have passed since the infringing work was first published, don't jump to the conclusion that your suit is barred by the statute of limitations. Again, see a copyright attorney.

Seek Legal Help. In cases where you have not discovered the infringement fairly promptly after it has occurred, statute of limitations questions can be tricky. It's wise to see a knowledgeable copyright lawyer about the proper application of the limitations period to your particular case.

I. What You Can Get If You Win: Remedies for Copyright Infringement

Once you've proven the elements of infringement discussed in Section F above, the next step is to establish what remedies you're entitled to. The potential remedies include:

- **Injunctive relief.** This typically consists of a court order requiring the infringer (the defendant) to stop the infringing activity and destroy all remaining copies of the infringing work.
- **Actual damages and infringer's profits.** The plaintiff is entitled to be compensated for the value of lost sales (often difficult to prove) and for other monetary losses resulting directly from the infringement. The plaintiff is also entitled to collect the amount of the

defendant's profits from the infringement.

- **Statutory damages.** If the plaintiff's work was timely registered and she so chooses, she is entitled to receive special statutory damages provided in the copyright law (statute) instead of actual damages and other economic damages.
- **Attorney fees.** A copyright owner may also be awarded attorney fees by the judge.

We'll examine each remedy in turn. Again, this isn't a complete description of the legal procedures involved, but is designed to give you an overview of the available remedies.

1. Injunctive Relief

An injunction is a court order telling someone to stop doing something. In a copyright infringement action, the order usually is simply for the defendant to stop the infringing activity. This is commonly a quick, effective remedy because, in many cases, it is possible to get positive action from the court long before the actual trial is held to decide who wins.

Indeed, it is possible to get a temporary restraining order (TRO) almost immediately with very short notice to the defendant. A TRO may last ten days at most. A hearing must then be held on whether the judge should issue a preliminary injunction. A preliminary injunction operates between the time it is issued and the final judgment in the case. This interim court order is available when it appears likely to a federal judge, on the basis of written documentation and a relatively brief hearing at which the lawyers for each side present their view of the dispute, that (1) the plaintiff will most likely win the suit when the trial is held, and (2) the plaintiff will suffer irreparable injury if the preliminary injunction isn't granted. Ordinarily, irreparable injury is presumed to exist where someone infringes upon a copyright owner's exclusive rights. (*Apple Computer, Inc. v. Franklin Computer Corp.,* 714 F.2d 1240 (3rd Cir. 1983).)

If the judge grants the preliminary injunction, the plaintiff must post a bond in an amount determined by the judge. If the injunction is later found to have been wrongfully granted, the defendant can collect from the bond the damages and costs he incurred due to the injunction.

Once a preliminary injunction is granted, it remains in effect pending a further determination of whether infringement occurred at the formal trial. In theory, a trial will probably be held one or two years later. In fact, the parties often fashion a settlement based on the results of the preliminary injunction hearing.

If a settlement is not reached and a full-scale trial occurs, the same issues raised in the preliminary injunction hearing (and possibly additional issues) will be litigated in more detail. If the plaintiff again prevails, the preliminary injunction will be converted into a permanent one, either including the same terms and orders or different ones, depending on what the plaintiff proves at trial. If the plaintiff loses, the preliminary injunction (if one was granted) will be dissolved and the defendant can go back to doing what it was doing before, plus be compensated for the consequences of the lawsuit by the issuer of the bond that was required for the preliminary injunction.

2. Damages

If you win a copyright infringement suit, you usually have the right to collect money (called damages) from the infringer.

a. Actual damages and infringer's profits

Actual damages are the lost profits and/or other losses sustained as a result of the copyright infringement. In other words, actual damages are the amount of money that the plaintiff would have made but for the infringement. This may include compensation for injury to plaintiff's reputation due to the infringement and for lost business opportunities (often difficult to prove). To obtain actual damages, the plaintiff must prove in court that the alleged losses actually occurred. This may not be too difficult where the plaintiff can prove (through witnesses, software audits, business records or other means) that the defendant has committed software piracy. It should be easy to show how much each unauthorized copy cost the plaintiff.

Proving damages may be much more difficult where the defendant has copied from the plaintiff's work to create a competing product. How does the plaintiff prove that its sales have been hurt by the competition? Evidence that sales of plaintiff's software immediately went down when the defendant's infringing competing product was introduced to the market might be the best means to establish damages in this situation.

As stated above, the plaintiff is also entitled to recover the amount of the defendant's profits from the infringement to the extent they exceed the plaintiff's recovery for her lost profits.

> **EXAMPLE:** Plaintiff is awarded $10,000 for lost sales due to defendant's infringement. The defendant earned $15,000 in profits from the infringement. Plaintiff is entitled to $5,000 of defendant's profits.

To establish the defendant's profits, the plaintiff is required only to prove the defendant's gross revenue from the infringing work. The defendant's business records (obtained by the plaintiff through formal "discovery" procedures) would usually be presented for this purpose. The defendant must then prove what its actual net profit from the infringement was—that is, the defendant must produce records or witnesses to show the amount of expenses deductible from the infringing work's gross revenues (such as production and distribution costs in the case of published infringing software) and the amount of profit, if any, attributable to the noninfringing material in the defendant's work (often difficult to prove).

b. Statutory damages

Statutory damages are set by the copyright law and require no proof of how much the loss was in monetary terms. However, statutory damages are only available if the work was timely registered—that is, before the infringement began or within three months of publication. Statutory damages are awarded at the judge's discretion and don't depend on having to prove a loss in any specific amount due to the infringement. You have to decide whether you want statutory damages or your actual damages and the defendant's profits. You can't collect both.

Statutory damages fall within the following range:

- Absent a finding that the infringer acted either willfully or innocently, between $500 and $20,000 for all the infringements by a single infringer of a single work, no matter how many infringing acts there were. If multiple separate and independent works were infringed, statutory damages may be awarded for each work.
- If the court finds that the infringer acted willfully—that is, knew he or she had no legal right to the material he used, but took it anyway—it may increase the amount of statutory damages up to $100,000.

- But if the court finds that the infringer acted innocently—that is, he or she used the copyrighted material sincerely believing he had the right to do so—the judge has discretion to award as little as $200. However, if the work to which the infringer had access contained a valid copyright notice, the infringer may not claim to have acted innocently. This is why it is always a good idea to include a valid copyright notice on your software (even though a notice is not legally required for works published after March 1, 1989). (See Chapter 4.)

3. Seizing the Infringing Software

Another civil remedy for copyright infringement consists of an impound and destroy order from the court. This tells the federal marshal to go to the infringer's place of business (or wherever the infringing material is located) and impound any infringing works. If the plaintiff wins, the court may order the sheriff to destroy the infringing material. To obtain such an order, however, the plaintiff must post a bond at a value at least twice the reasonable value of the infringing software.

Seizure can happen at any time after the suit has been filed. It's usually done as soon as a complaint is filed, but before the defendant is served with a copy of the suit. This way, the defendant learns he or she has been sued only when the marshal comes to the defendant's premises to impound the infringing software.

This is an extremely effective remedy because it deprives the defendant of the infringing software . The defendant can only get it back if the plaintiff is defeated at trial.

4. Attorney Fees and Costs

If your suit is successful and you timely registered your copyright, the court may also order the defendant to pay your attorney fees and other costs of going to court, such as filing fees. However, this is not required. It's up to the judge to decide whether to make such an award and how much it should be (the amount must be reasonable). The criteria some courts use to decide whether to award attorney fees include whether the defendant acted in bad faith, unreasonably or was otherwise blameworthy. Many courts will be especially likely to award fees to a plaintiff whose actions helped to advance the copyright law or defend or establish important legal principles.

The cost of bringing an infringement suit can be very high, easily tens of thousands of dollars. If for no other reason than to have the opportunity of recovering your attorney fees should you have to bring an infringement suit, you should always timely register your work with the Copyright Office.

If the plaintiff loses his or her suit, the court has discretion to award the defendant all or part of his attorney fees. In the past, many courts would award such fees to a defendant only if they found that the plaintiff's suit was frivolous or brought in bad faith. But these courts would not use this criterion when making fees awards to plaintiffs. In 1994 the Supreme Court held that this approach was incorrect and that attorney fees must be awarded to plaintiffs and defendants in an evenhanded manner. In other words, the same criteria must be applied to both plaintiffs and defendants. (*Fogerty v. Fantasy, Inc.*, 114 S.Ct. 1023 (1994).)

⚠ Plaintiffs Should Only File Legitimate Infringement Cases. You should never file a copyright infringement case in order to get even with somebody even though you know you don't have a good case. Likewise, don't file clearly frivolous claims in the hope the defendant will pay you something merely to get you off his or her back and avoid having to pay for expensive litigation. In either instance, you will not only lose your case, but the judge will likely order you to pay all or part of the defendant's attorney fees. ■

Chapter 6

Trade Secret Basics

Trade secrecy is basically a do-it-yourself form of intellectual property protection. It is based on this simple idea: By keeping valuable information secret, one can prevent competitors from learning about and using it and thereby enjoy a competitive advantage in the marketplace. Trade secrecy is by far the oldest form of intellectual property, dating back at least to ancient Rome. It is as useful now as it was then.

Trade secrecy should be an integral part of any software developer's intellectual property protection program. The fundamentals of trade secret protection are introduced in this chapter. How to establish your own trade secret protection program is covered in Chapter 7.

A. What is a Trade Secret?

A trade secret is any formula, pattern, physical device, idea, process, compilation of information or virtually any other information that 1) is not generally known or readily ascertainable by a company's (or individual's) competitors, 2) offers a business an actual or potential economic advantage over others, and 3) is treated in a way that can reasonably be expected to prevent the public or competitors from learning about it, absent improper acquisition or theft.

Trade secrecy may be used to:

- protect ideas that offer a business a competitive advantage, thereby enabling a software developer to get a head start on the competition
- keep competitors from knowing that a program is under development and from learning its functional attributes
- protect source code, software development tools, design definitions and specifications, manuals and other documentation, flow diagrams and flow charts, data structures, data compilations, formulas and algorithms embodied in software
- protect valuable business information such as marketing plans, cost and price information and customer lists
- protect "negative know-how"—that is, information you've learned during the course of research and development on what not to do or what does not work optimally, and
- protect any other information that has some value and is not generally known by your competitors.

Unlike copyrights and patents, whose existence is provided and governed by federal law that applies in all 50 states, trade secrecy is not codified in any federal statute (although theft of trade secrets can be a federal crime; see Section C4a). Instead, it is made up of individual state laws.

Nevertheless, the protection afforded to trade secrets is similar in every state. This is largely because some 42 states have based their trade secrecy laws on the Uniform Trade Secrecy Act (UTSA), a model trade secrecy law designed by legal scholars. (For a text of the UTSA and a list of those states adopting it, refer to volume 14 of the *Uniform Laws Annotated,* published by West Publishing Co.)

Trade Secrets Compared With Copyright Protection

Trade secrecy can provide much broader protection for software than can the copyright law. Copyright only protects a programmer's expression of the ideas embodied in a program, not the ideas themselves. Copyright does not protect ideas, systems, facts, methods, discoveries or algorithms. There are no such limitations on trade secrets. That is, an idea or algorithm can be a protected trade secret. Moreover, copyright only protects works that are fixed in a tangible medium of expression (written down, saved on disk, etc.). A trade secret need not be written down or otherwise fixed. Stated simply, trade secrecy can protect everything copyright can protect and everything copyright cannot protect (provided the requirements discussed in this section are satisfied).

You may be wondering why you should bother with copyrights at all if trade secrecy is available. There are several important reasons why copyright remains useful:

- Trade secrecy only protects against misappropriation by people in a confidential relationship with the trade secret owner or who acquire a trade secret through improper means (see Section B). In contrast, copyright protection is effective against the entire universe of people who have access to a copyrighted work.
- Trade secret protection is lost when the information becomes available to the public. This is not the case with copyright protection—that is, copyright protects both published and unpublished works.
- Copyright protection is more readily available in many foreign countries than is trade secret protection (see Chapter 10), and
- In some instances courts hold that the copyright law preempts (supersedes) trade secrecy and must be relied on exclusively. When this occurs is not always clear or predictable.

1. No Protection for Generally Known Information

Information that is public knowledge or generally known in the software industry cannot be a trade secret. Things that everybody knows cannot provide anyone with a competitive advantage. However, information constituting a trade secret need not be novel or unique. All that is required is that the information not be generally known by people who could profit from its disclosure and use.

Most software qualifies as a trade secret. Computer programs usually contain at least some elements or combination of elements that are different from other programs and are not generally known in the software industry. Thus, for example, trade secret protection has been extended to accounts receivable programs, database management software, time-sharing systems and communications programs, even though similar software already existed.

2. Ownership of Trade Secrets

Only the person or entity that owns a trade secret has the right to seek relief in court if someone else improperly acquires or discloses the trade secret. Also, only the trade secret owner may grant others a license to use the secret.

As a general rule, any trade secrets developed by an employee in the course of employment belong to the employer. However, trade secrets developed by an employee on her own time and with her own equipment can sometimes belong to the employee. To avoid possible disputes, it is very good idea for employers to have all employees who may develop new technology sign an employment agreement. The agreement should assign in advance all trade secrets developed by the employee during her employment. Courts generally will enforce such agreements. (See Chapter 7 for a detailed discussion.)

3. Multiple Trade Secrets for the Same Information

Because trade secrets are by definition kept secret, a software developer cannot know what trade secrets are already possessed by others. The result is that, without even knowing it, a software developer may create trade secrets identical to trade secrets currently possessed by others. This has no effect on trade secret protection. So long as a trade secret provides its owner with a competitive advantage, it can be identical to other existing trade secrets if it was independently conceived and not generally known by others in the relevant industry.

EXAMPLE: SoftWays devises a new method of coordinate tracking for a graphics program it's developing. Unbeknownst to SoftWays, DataTek, Inc., has already devised the same method for its own graphics program, and has kept it secret. Both SoftWays and DataTek are entitled to trade secret protection for their coordinate tracking techniques, so long as they are not generally known in the software industry.

4. Reasonable Secrecy Must Be Maintained

Software or other information qualifies as a trade secret only if precautions are taken to keep it secret. Absolute secrecy is not required—it is not necessary to turn your office into an armed camp. A trade secret owner's secrecy precautions need only be *reasonable under the circumstances.* What precautions are "reasonable" will vary from case to case, depending on the size of the company, the nature and value of the information and other factors. After reading Chapter 7, you should have a pretty good idea of how to judge what is reasonable secrecy under your particular circumstances.

5. How Trade Secrets Are Lost

A trade secret is lost if either of these conditions is met:
- the product in which it is embodied is made widely available to the public through sales and displays on an *unrestricted* basis, or
- the secret can be discovered by reverse engineering (see Section D1) or inspection.

This means that trade secrecy will be lost if a program's source code is made available to the public on an unrestricted basis through such means as a Copyright Office deposit, listing in a computer magazine or Website, or distribution on a floppy disk or other medium. For this reason software is normally distributed only in object code form, which is difficult to reverse engineer. All object code can be reverse engineered, but because of the difficulty, the code can still qualify as a trade secret unless it actually is reverse engineered.

This is also the reason why limited distribution software is normally licensed rather than sold outright—that is, purchasers and other end users are required to sign license agreements in which they promise not to use or disclose the trade secrets embodied in the program without permission. Publishers of mass-marketed software often seek to impose the same restrictions on consumers by including "shrink-wrap licenses" with their products. (See Chapter 16.)

6. Duration of Trade Secrets

Trade secrets have no definite term. A trade secret continues to exist as long as the requirements for trade secret protection remain in effect. In other words, as long as secrecy is maintained, the secret does not become generally known in the industry and the secret continues to provide a competitive advantage, it will be protected. Some trade secrets have lasted for a very long time indeed. For example, the formula for Coca-Cola has been maintained as a trade secret by the Coca-Cola Company for over 100 years.

B. Trade Secret Owner's Rights

A trade secret owner has the legal right to prevent the following four groups of people from copying, using and benefiting from its trade secrets or disclosing them to others without the owner's permission:

- people who are bound by a *duty of confidentiality* not to disclose or use the information
- people who acquire the trade secret through *improper means* such as theft, industrial espionage or bribery
- people who knowingly obtain trade secrets from others—that is, third parties—who acquired them through improper means or were bound by a duty of confidentiality not to disclose them, and
- people who learn about a trade secret by accident or mistake but had reason to know that the information was a protected trade secret.

For example, if a software developer's employee signs an agreement establishing a duty of confidentiality (see below) but later discloses the developer's trade secrets to a competitor without the developer's permission, the developer will be able to sue both the employee and competitor for damages and may be entitled to obtain a court order

preventing the competitor from using the information. The employee would have breached his or her duty of confidentiality to the developer. At the same time the competitor would have acquired the trade secret from a person who had a duty not to disclose it.

1. Duty of Confidentiality

Persons who learn about a trade secret through a confidential relationship with its owner may not use or disclose the trade secret without permission. A duty of confidentiality may be deemed by the courts to arise automatically (is "implied in law") from many types of relationships, including those between employers and employees who routinely receive trade secrets as part of their jobs. (See the sidebar below.) But by far the best way for a trade secret owner to establish a duty of confidentiality is to have each person to whom trade secrets are disclosed agree in writing to preserve their confidentiality. This type of agreement is called a confidentiality agreement or non-disclosure agreement.

a. Employees

The cornerstone of any trade secret protection program is to have all employees who are exposed to trade secrets read and sign nondisclosure agreements. Such an agreement should require the employee to treat as confidential any trade secrets he or she learns in the course of employment. If the employer later tries to prevent the employee from using information considered to be a trade secret, the existence of a signed non-disclosure agreement will establish that the employee knew that he owed a duty of confidentiality toward his or her employer.

Many courts consider the use of employee nondisclosure agreements the single most important reasonable precaution an employer can take to establish and maintain the secrecy of confidential information. In other words, confidential information may be deemed not to be a trade secret where an employer fails to use such written agreements. (Nondisclosure agreements are discussed in detail in Chapter 7.)

However, there are limitations on the effectiveness of nondisclosure agreements with employees. In particular, the general knowledge, skills and experience an employee acquires during her term of employment are *not* trade secrets and therefore are not covered by a nondisclosure agreement. Difficult and costly disputes can develop as to whether information constitutes a trade secret or merely an employee's general knowledge. For this reason, some employers utilize noncompetition agreements with their employees in addition to nondisclosure agreements. (See Chapter 14.) Some employers also use other methods to help ensure their employees' loyalty, such as stock-options or other benefits that fully vest only if the employee stays with the company for several years.

Employees Have a Duty of Confidentiality Imposed by Law

All is not lost if an employer fails to have an employee sign a nondisclosure agreement. Even if an employee has never signed such an agreement, he or she will usually be deemed by the courts to have a confidential relationship with the employer if the employee routinely comes into contact with the employer's trade secrets as part of the employee's job. Such an employee is duty bound not to disclose or use, without the employer's permission, information that:

- the employer tells the employee is confidential (preferably in writing), or
- the employee knew or should have known was confidential because of the context in which it was disclosed, the measures the employer took to keep the information secret and/or the fact that the information was of a type customarily considered confidential in the industry.

However, an employer's failure to use nondisclosure agreements will tend to show that the employer was not protecting any trade secrets and will surely not impress a judge if the company goes to court to enforce its claimed trade secret rights. Employers have won trade secret cases against employees in the absence of nondisclosure agreements, but it is much easier to do so with them.

b. Independent contractors and consultants

People who perform services for a trade secret owner but who are not employees—freelance programmers, technical writers or beta testers, for example—may have a duty of confidentiality implied by law just as employees may (see the sidebar above). However, as is the case with employees, independent contractors should always sign nondisclosure agreements. (See the detailed discussion in Chapter 15.)

c. End users and other third parties

A trade secret owner can protect his or her trade secrets from unauthorized disclosure and/or use by end users and other third parties by having them agree not to disclose or use the information without permission. Such nondisclosure agreements are legally enforceable contracts. This is accomplished in the typical software transaction by licensing the software to the user, rather than selling it outright. The license gives the user permission to use the software under the terms of the license, which includes a nondisclosure provision. Nondisclosure agreements work best for programs that are distributed to a specialized market where licenses can be negotiated and signed with each individual end user.

> EXAMPLE: AcmeSoft develops and markets a highly specialized program used to automate the manufacture of widgets. AcmeSoft negotiates and signs license agreements with all the purchasers of the program (about 50 in all). Each license includes a nondisclosure provision stating that the existence and attributes of the program are not to be disclosed to persons other than those employees of the manufacturer that use the program. The widget manufacturers do not have a confidential relationship with AcmeSoft, but are contractually bound by the license agreements.

Let's assume that there are only about 200 widget manufacturers in the whole country, so it was easy for AcmeSoft to have all the manufacturers who purchased its widget manufacturing program sign license agreements. But what about mass-marketed software? A software publisher cannot negotiate and sign a nondisclosure agreement with every end user of a widely distributed program.

In an attempt to get around this problem, mass marketed programs often contain "shrink-wrap licenses." These are license agreements that are usually printed on or inside the mass-marketed software package. Such licenses attempt to convert what would appear to the average person to be a simple purchase of a piece of software into a licensing transaction. The shrink-wrap license typically provides that, by opening the package and using the program, the purchaser agrees to possess the software under the terms of the license. Agreement to the license's terms is also often elicited from the user on screen when the program is first used. Among other things, a shrink-wrap license usually prohibits the purchaser from disclosing any trade secrets learned from the program and contains various limitations on the seller's liability.

Although a recent court decision upheld the validity of shrink-wrap licenses. there are still questions as to whether they are enforceable in court. (See Chapter 16.) Distributors of mass-marketed software should not rely exclusively on such licenses. They should also distribute the software in a form that makes reverse engineering difficult (compiled code), use copyright protection and, where available, obtain software patents. Of course, up to the time a program is made available to the public, it can and should be protected by an effective internal trade secrecy program.

2. Obtaining Trade Secrets by "Improper Means"

Even in the absence of a confidential relationship (whether implied by law or created by contract), a trade secret owner is protected from persons who discover a trade secret by "improper means." This includes anyone who:

- obtains trade secrets through theft, bribery, fraud or misrepresentations or industrial espionage
- knowingly obtains or uses trade secrets that have been improperly disclosed by a breach of a nondisclosure agreement or breach of a confidential relationship, or
- obtains trade secrets by inducing someone (an employee, for example)

to breach an express or implied agreement not to disclose them.

The prohibition on a third party's knowingly obtaining or using trade secrets that have been improperly disclosed is of particular importance in the software industry, where there is a high degree of job mobility. It means that if an employee who has had access to trade secrets goes to work for a competitor, the new employer cannot obtain or use the employee's trade secrets if it knows that doing so would breach the employee's confidentiality obligation to the prior employer. One way to ensure that the new employer is on notice is to inform it in writing that the new employee has knowledge of the former employer's trade secrets and is duty bound not to disclose them to the new employer. (See detailed discussion in Chapter 7.) If the new employer obtains trade secrets from the former employee, the old employer may sue and be able to obtain an injunction prohibiting their use and enacting other legal remedies. (See Section C2.) It might even be possible to have a court bar the ex-employee from working for the competitor. (See Section C3.)

C. Enforcement of Trade Secrets

A trade secret owner may enforce his or her rights by bringing a trade secret infringement action in court. Such suits may be used to:

- prevent another person or business from using the trade secret without proper authorization, and

- collect damages for the economic injury suffered as a result of the trade secret's improper acquisition and use.

All persons responsible for the improper acquisition, and all those who have benefited from the acquisition, are typically named as defendants in trade secret infringement actions.

The most common situations that give rise to infringement actions include:

- An employee having knowledge of a trade secret changes employment and discloses the secret to his or her new employer in violation of her duty of confidentiality.
- Improper use or disclosure of trade secrets is made in violation of a non-disclosure agreement—for example, by an independent contractor or licensee.
- A theft of trade secrets occurs through industrial espionage.

To prevail in a trade secret infringement suit, the plaintiff (person bringing the suit) must show that the information alleged to be secret is actually a trade secret. (See the discussion in Section A, above.) In addition, the plaintiff must show that the information was either improperly acquired by the defendant (if accused of making commercial use of the secret) or improperly disclosed—or likely to be so—by the defendant (if accused of leaking the information).

1. Preliminary Relief for Threatened Trade Secret Infringement

Once a trade secret is improperly disclosed to others, the harm done may be impossible to adequately remedy. For this reason, it is not necessary to wait until a competitor actually learns a trade secret through an improper disclosure and/or uses it before filing suit. Rather, where there is an imminent threatened unauthorized disclosure or use of a trade secret, the trade secret owner may file suit before the disclosure actually occurs. The owner may obtain a temporary court order preventing the defendant from disclosing or using the trade secret.

Courts are authorized to issue immediate court orders (temporary restraining orders and preliminary injunctions) prohibiting the defendants in a trade secret infringement action from disclosing or using a trade secret without permission. This allows an injured business to obtain immediate and continuous protection pending a final court determination of the case. To obtain a preliminary injunction, the plaintiff must demonstrate to the court that:

- there is a substantial imminent likelihood that plaintiff's trade secrets will be disclosed or used without its permission
- irreparable injury will occur unless a preliminary injunction is issued (usually easy to show in trade secret infringement cases), and
- the plaintiff will probably prevail in the end.

These preliminary orders are often viewed by the parties as harbingers of the case's final outcome, and accordingly lead to settlement in advance of trial in the majority of trade secret cases.

The most difficult task the trade secret owner faces in obtaining an injunction is convincing the court that there is a real imminent threat of an unauthorized disclosure or use. Mere suspicions not backed up by any facts are not sufficient. An imminent threat of disclosure can be shown by direct evidence—for example, where a departing employee tells his ex-employer he can say good-bye to his trade secrets as he walks out the door. But, more often, a threat of disclosure is shown by circumstantial evidence—facts from which it can be reasonably inferred that an unauthorized disclosure or use is imminent.

EXAMPLE: AcmeSoft has spent one year developing software allowing for the sending of secure credit card information from Web servers to credit card clearinghouses. AcmeSoft has been in a race with its chief competitor, Universal Systems, Inc., which has been working around the clock to build a similar system. Having solved most of the bugs in the system, AcmeSoft plans to make a product announcement in about a month.

Universal Systems hires Fred, AcmeSoft's chief engineer, at twice what AcmeSoft paid him. Before Fred leaves, AcmeSoft's personnel officer conducts an exit interview with him in which he asks him to sign a statement acknowledging his obligation not to disclose AcmeSoft's trade secrets. Fred refuses to sign.

After Fred leaves, AcmeSoft discovers that a number of confidential documents dealing with the software are missing from his old office. AcmeSoft is convinced that Universal hired Fred and agreed to pay him such a high salary because he will disclose AcmeSoft's trade secrets. AcmeSoft immediately files a trade secret infringement action against Universal and Fred and asks the court to first grant a temporary restraining order and then a preliminary injunction preventing Fred from disclosing any confidential information about AcmeSoft's system to Universal.

The court concludes that, based on this circumstantial evidence, there is an imminent threat that Fred will disclose AcmeSoft's trade secrets to Universal and immediately issues a 14-day restraining order. The court later holds a hearing on whether to grant a preliminary injunction to last until the case is tried. The judge then decides to issue a preliminary injunction because it is necessary to preserve AcmeSoft's trade secrets and because, when the case is tried, AcmeSoft probably will win.

2. Permanent Relief for Trade Secret Infringement

If the plaintiff is able to establish that a trade secret was or will be improperly used, disclosed or acquired by the defendant, the court can enjoin its disclosure or use. Such injunctions can last forever. More commonly, the courts will employ the "head start rule." This gives the rightful owner of the trade secret a "head start" in commercially exploiting it by prohibiting its disclosure or use by the competitor for as long as it would have taken the competitor to independently develop the information.

> **EXAMPLE:** AcmeSoft wins its case against Universal and Fred. The court grants AcmeSoft an injunction prohibiting Fred from disclosing any confidential information about AcmeSoft's Web commerce software to Universal for one year—the time in which Universal could perfect its own software independently.

In addition to injunctive relief, a court may award damages to a plaintiff who wins

at trial. Damages can consist of lost profits resulting from the sales by the trade secret infringer, profits realized by the infringer from the wrongfully acquired trade secret, and, occasionally, substantial punitive damages designed to punish and make an example of the defendant in particularly egregious cases. The availability and amount of punitive damages differs from state to state.

3. Court Orders Preventing Ex-Employees From Working for Competitors

Misappropriation of trade secrets by ex-employees is the hottest trade secret issue in the software industry where job mobility is high. As discussed above, a trade secret owner may obtain a court order preventing a former employee from divulging trade secrets to a competitor. However, some courts will go even farther and bar an ex-employee from working at all for a competitor for a period of time.

Under what is termed the "inevitable disclosure doctrine," a company may obtain a court order preventing an ex-employee from working for a competitor if:

- the former employer and new employer are competitors
- the employee's new position is comparable to his or her former position, and
- the steps taken by the new employer to prevent misappropriation of trade secrets are inadequate.

EXAMPLE: William Redmond, PepsiCo's general manager for new age and sports drinks, quit his job and accepted a position as vice president with Quaker Oat's Gatorade and Snapple division. PepsiCo filed suit seeking a court order stopping Redmond from taking his new job. PepsiCo had no evidence that Redmond had actually stolen or used any of its trade secrets. Instead, PepsiCo argued that he would inevitably use its trade secrets because of his extensive knowledge of PepsiCo's marketing plans. The court agreed and issued an order barring Redmond from working for Quaker Oats for six months and, once he took his new job, from disclosing or using any of PepsiCo's trade secrets. The court found that "unless Redmond possessed an uncanny ability to compartmentalize information, he would necessarily be making decisions about Snapple by relying on PepsiCo's trade secrets." (*PepsiCo, Inc. v. Redmond*, 54 F.3d 1262 (1995).)

Not all courts will issue an order preventing a person from taking a job, viewing it as too harsh a remedy. You may be able to obtain the same result with less fuss by requiring an employee to sign a covenant not to compete—that is, promise to refrain from taking a job with a competitor for a certain period of time after leaving your company. However, covenants not to compete are not legally enforceable in all states, most notably California. (See Chapter 7.)

4. Criminal Penalties for Trade Secret Infringement

Intentional theft of trade secrets can constitute a crime under a variety of federal and state laws.

a. Federal criminal laws

Trade secret misappropriation may violate the federal National Stolen Property Act, which prohibits transferring or transporting stolen goods worth more than $5,000 in interstate commerce (18 U.S.C. 2314). Where the phone or mails are used, trade secret infringement may constitute wire fraud or mail fraud.

However, by far the most significant federal law dealing with trade secret theft is the Economic Espionage Act of 1996 (18 U.S.C. Sections 1831-1839). The Act gives the U.S. Attorney General sweeping powers to prosecute any person or company involved in trade secret misappropriation.

The Act punishes intentionally stealing, copying or receiving trade secrets "related to or included in a product that is produced for or placed in interstate commerce." (18 U.S.C. 1832.) This includes virtually all software. Penalties for violations are severe: Individuals may be fined up to $500,000 and corporations up to $5 million. Prison terms up to ten years may also be imposed. If the theft is performed on behalf of a foreign government or agent, the corporate fines can double and jail time increase to 15 years. (18 U.S.C. 1831.) In addition, the property used and proceeds derived from the theft can be seized and sold by the government. (18 U.S.C. 1831, 1834.)

The Act applies not only to thefts that occur within the United States, but also to conduct outside the U.S. if the thief is a U.S. citizen or corporation or if any act in furtherance of the offense occurred in the U.S. (18 U.S.C. 1838.)

As the Act is worded, it could apply not only to important cases of trade secret misappropriation—for example, where there are substantial monetary losses or a foreign government is involved—but also to common "garden-variety" trade secret cases that traditionally have been dealt with solely by the parties themselves in the civil courts. However, the U.S. Attorney General has promised that the Act would not be used to criminalize such disputes. To ensure this, no filings will be made under the Act without review and approval by the head of the Criminal Branch of the Department of Justice.

b. State criminal laws

Several states have also enacted laws making trade secret infringement a crime. For example, in California it is a crime to acquire, disclose or use trade secrets without authorization. Trade secrets include computer programs or information stored in a computer. Violators may be fined up to $5,000, sentenced to up to one year in jail, or both. (Cal. Penal Code Section 499c.)

c. Initiating a criminal prosecution

Criminal prosecutions are initiated and handled by the government, not private individuals. On the state level, criminal cases are handled by your State Attorney General and local District Attorneys. Prosecutions involving federal crimes are dealt with by the United States Attorney's office, which is part of the Department of Justice.

State and federal prosecutors pick and choose which cases to prosecute. Since they have limited budgets and staffs, they'll usually prosecute a trade secret misappropriation case only if there is strong evidence and the monetary amount involved is very substantial, the trade secret somehow relates to national defense or a foreign power is involved.

If you feel you have a case that merits criminal prosecution, it's advisable to contact an attorney with experience in trade secret matters. You'll need to provide the attorney with all the evidence you have that trade secret violations have occurred, a list of any witnesses you know of and any information you have about the defendants. Your attorney will contact the appropriate federal or local prosecutor and provide them with your evidence.

The fact that a trade secret violator is criminally prosecuted or even convicted does not bar you from suing him or her in court yourself and seeking civil damages and other remedies. However, once the criminal action begins, the defendant can usually have your civil case stayed (halted) until the criminal case is over. Even if the case isn't stayed, you may be unable to go forward because key witnesses may refuse to testify on the ground that it could incriminate them in the pending criminal case.

Pros and Cons of Seeking Criminal Prosecutions

Criminal prosecutions for trade secret misappropriation have both good and bad points for the trade secret owner.

Pros:

- Many people will give back your trade secrets when they're contacted by the authorities in the hope it will end the criminal investigation.
- The government pays the cost of investigating and prosecuting the case.
- Criminal cases are usually resolved much more quickly than civil cases.
- The person who stole your trade secrets can be heavily fined or even required to serve jail time.

Cons:

- The government controls the criminal case, you don't.
- Your trade secrets might be publicly exposed during the course of the case, although legal procedures are available to prevent this.
- If the trade secret violator is convicted, his or her liability insurance may be canceled. This means there may be no money to pay any civil judgment you obtain against the violator.

D. Limitations on Trade Secret Protection

There are two important limits on trade secret protection: It does not prevent others from discovering a trade secret through "reverse engineering"; nor does it apply to persons who independently create or discover the same information.

1. Reverse Engineering

One of the most significant limitations on trade secret protection is that it does not protect against "reverse engineering." This is the process of taking a product or device apart and reducing it to its constituent parts or concepts to see how it works and to learn any trade secrets it contains. Any information learned through reverse engineering is considered to be in the public domain and no longer protectible as a trade secret. Reverse engineering is an accepted business practice and is perfectly legal so long as it does not violate anybody's copyright or patent rights. (See Chapter 5, Section B3c, for a discussion of whether reverse engineering constitutes copyright infringement.)

Any trained person who has access to a program's source code can readily learn any trade secrets it contains. "Source code" consists of the specific instructions written by a programmer to tell a computer what to do. It is usually written in a computer language such as C++, Java or BASIC, consisting of English words and common mathematical notations. It is easily read and understood by properly trained humans.

For this reason, computer programs are normally distributed in "object code" form only, while the source code is kept locked away. Object code, or machine language, is the code actually read and executed by the computer. The computer creates object code by translating (compiling or interpreting) the source code into a series of binary ones and zeros. Object code cannot be understood by even the most experienced programmers. However, it is possible, though often difficult, to reverse engineer object code. The object code may be translated back into source code, often by using a decompiler. It can also be possible to deduce a program's trade secrets simply by running it on a computer and seeing how it interacts with the computer, the data and the user.

To prevent end users from reverse engineering object code, software licenses often contain a provision prohibiting the practice. For example, the standard IBM license agreement states that the "customer shall not reverse assemble or reverse compile the licensed programs in whole or in part." Some view such restrictions as invalid because they attempt to preempt (replace) the federal copyright and patent laws. For example, one court has held invalid on ground of federal preemption a Louisiana state law providing that restrictions on reverse engineering contained in "shrink-wrap licenses" were enforceable (*Vault*

Corp. v. Quaid Software Ltd., 847 F.2d 255 (5th Cir. 1988)). However, another court has held that shrink-wrap licenses can be legally enforced. *ProCD, Inc. v. Zeidenberg*, 86 F.3d 1447 (7th Cir. 1996). (See Chapter 16.)

Even if enforceable, it is unclear how effective such provisions are. They may not be binding on anyone who has not signed the license agreement—for example, a freelance programmer invited to work on the licensee's premises who obtains access to the object code program.

2. Independent Creation

The other significant limitation on trade secrecy is that it does not protect against independent creation. A trade secret owner has no rights against a person who independently discovers or develops his or her trade secret. Moreover, if such person makes the information generally available to the public, it will lose its trade secret status.

EXAMPLE: New Ideas, Inc., develops a new method of translating existing forms into HTML code. New Ideas, Inc., markets its NewConversion program to the public, but keeps the conversion method as a trade secret. Dave, a freelance programmer, independently develops the conversion technique and writes an article describing it in a computer programming journal. New Ideas, Inc., has no claim against Dave. In addition, its conversion method is no longer a trade secret because it is now generally known in the software industry.

One legal expert has described trade secret protection as a leaky sieve because over time many of the most valuable trade secrets are lost when others independently discover them. Few people have or develop information that is incapable of being independently discovered by others.

E. Using Trade Secrets With Other IP Protections

Trade secrecy is a vitally important protection for software, but, because of the limitations discussed in Section D, above, it should be used in conjunction with copyright and, in some cases, patent protection.

1. Trade Secrets and Copyrights

Trade secrecy and copyright are not incompatible. To the contrary, they are typically used in tandem to provide the maximum legal protection available for most programs. (Patents provide far greater protection than either trade secrets or copyright, but are available only for a small minority of software; see Chapter 8.)

a. Development phase

Typically, trade secrecy is most important during a software product's development phase. As discussed in Chapter 3, the copyright laws grant a copyright owner the exclusive right to copy, distribute, adapt or display protected expression, but not ideas. The moment a program or other information is fixed in a tangible medium of expression (saved on disk or other media, written down, etc.) it is protected by the federal copyright laws to the extent it is original (independently created). Provided that secrecy is maintained, trade secret protection can still continue.

Because an item is automatically protected by copyright upon its fixation, rather than when it is first published, there usually is a substantial time period during which both trade secret and copyright protection apply. This is because a program is usually tested and modified for some time after it is first "fixed," but before it is distributed. As long as it is maintained as a trade secret during this period, the program enjoys both trade secret and copyright protection.

b. Distribution phase

Once a program is distributed, it will lose trade secret status unless steps are taken to preserve secrecy. Such steps may include distributing the program only in object code form and having each person who receives the work sign a license restricting disclosure of the secrets it contains. Of course, it is impossible to have the purchasers of mass-marketed programs all sign licenses. Pre-printed shrink-wrap licenses must be relied upon to establish a duty of nondisclosure for mass-marketed software. (See Chapter 16.)

2. Trade Secrets and Patents

The federal patent laws provide the owner of a patentable invention with far greater protection than that available under trade secrecy or copyright laws—in effect, a total 17- to 19- year monopoly (20 years from the filing date) on the use of the invention as described in the patent. To obtain a patent, the inventor must file a lengthy application with the U.S. Patent Office, fully disclosing the ideas underlying the invention.

Trade secret protection is not lost when a U.S. patent is applied for. The Patent Office keeps patent applications secret unless or until a patent is granted—a process that usually takes two to three years. However, once a patent is granted and an issue fee paid, the patent becomes a public record. Then all the information disclosed in the patent application is no longer a trade secret. This is so even if the patent is later challenged in court and invalidated.

However, in many cases a software patent applies only to certain isolated elements of a computer program. The remainder of the program need not and should not be disclosed in the patent and can remain a trade secret.

F. Avoiding Trade Secret Misappropriation Claims

There are several relatively simple steps you can take to avoid trade secret misappropriation claims.

1. Hiring New Employees

Software companies have frequently been sued for trade secrecy violations when they hire competitors' employees. For example, Borland filed such a suit against Microsoft in early 1997 when it hired several Borland employees.

This is particularly likely to occur where a company hires a large number of employees from a single competitor to obtain a competitive advantage (a practice known as "raiding"). Of course it is improper to hire anyone for the purpose of gaining access to anther's trade secrets.

To prevent or defeat trade secrecy claims, it's important to hire employees in a way that shows that you did not hire any particular person for the purpose of obtaining access to trade secrets. In other words, you want to be able to show that all your employees were hired because of their qualifications and expertise, not because they knew competitors' trade secrets.

Here are some simple steps a company should take when hiring its employees:

- Spread your hiring around—avoid targeting a specific company.
- Place advertisements for new employees that list the required qualifications and expertise; consider using a professional recruiter for particularly sensitive positions.
- Make all job applicants complete an employment application and present a resume.
- Interview all job applicants, even if you already know them.

- Maintain thorough records of your hiring program.
- If you hire someone who has been exposed to a competitor's especially sensitive information, consider placing him or her in a position where that information will not be used for a period of time—this helps show that you did not hire the person to steal trade secrets.
- Require all employees to sign employment agreements containing a promise that they will not use or disclose their prior employer's confidential information (the employment agreements in this book contain such a clause).
- Make sure new employees don't bring any confidential records or other materials from their old job.
- Require the employee to document all work done in the new employment.

2. Educate Employees About Trade Secrets

You should also make clear to your employees that they should not engage in trade secret misappropriation. Make clear both orally and in writing that they should not use or disclose any trade secrets of former employers or colleagues in other companies or engage in industrial espionage or trade secret theft. Emphasize that the potential civil and criminal liabilities are too great to engage in this kind of behavior. Every employee should be required to sign an employment agreement barring him or her from misappropriating trade secrets. (See Chapter 14 for sample agreements.)

3. Be Careful About Signing Confidentiality Agreements

Software developers not only hire employees, they also work for clients who are concerned about protecting their own trade secrets. Many software developers' or computer consultants' clients routinely include confidentiality provisions in their development agreements. It's not unreasonable for a client to want you to keep its secrets away from the eyes and ears of competitors. Unfortunately, however, many of these provisions are worded so broadly that they can make it difficult for you to work for other clients without fear of violating your duty of confidentiality.

If, like many developers or consultants, you make your living by performing similar services for many firms in the same industry, insist on a confidentiality provision that is reasonable in scope and defines precisely what information you must keep confidential. Such a provision should last for only a limited time—five years at the most.

a. Unreasonable provision

A general provision barring you from making any unauthorized disclosure or using any technical, financial or business information you obtain directly or indirectly from the client is unreasonable. Such broad restrictions can make it very difficult for you to do similar work for other clients without fear of violating the duty of confidentiality clause. Here's an example:

Developer may be given access to Client's proprietary or confidential information while working for Client. Developer agrees not to use or disclose such information except as directed by Client.

Such a provision doesn't make clear what information is and is not the client's confidential trade secrets, so you never know for sure what information you must keep confidential and what you can disclose when working for others.

Also, since this provision bars you from later using *any* of the client's confidential information to which you have access, it could prevent you from using information you already knew before working with the client. It could also bar you from using information that becomes available to the public. You would then be in the absurd position of not being allowed to use information that the whole world, including other developers, knows about. Always attempt to delete or rewrite such a provision.

b. Reasonable provision

A reasonable nondisclosure provision makes clear that, while you may not re-use confidential information the client provides, you have the right to freely use *any* information you obtain from other sources or that the public learns later.

Specifically, do not sign a contract requiring you to keep confidential any information:

- you knew about before working with the client
- you learn from a third person who has no duty to keep it confidential
- you develop independently even though the client later provides you with similar or identical information, or
- that becomes publicly known though no fault of your own—for example, you wouldn't have to keep a client's manufacturing technique confidential after it is disclosed to the public in an article in a trade journal written by someone other than you.

4. Document Development Efforts

As discussed above, trade secrecy does not protect against independent creation or reverse engineering. Carefully document your attempts at independent development or reverse engineering by keeping meticulous records of the entire development process, from the initial idea stage to coding, debugging and testing. This includes copies of storyboards and prototypes, interim versions, flowcharts and internal memoranda documenting the many decisions that must be made in the course of software development. ■

Chapter 7

Establishing a Trade Secret Protection Program

Trade secret protection is based on the common sense notion that keeping information close to the chest can provide a competitive advantage in the marketplace. But simply saying that a computer program or other information is a trade secret will not make it so. You must affirmatively behave in a way that manifests your desire to keep the information secret. This chapter shows you how to establish and maintain an adequate trade secret protection program.

A. Can You Keep a Secret?

Some companies go to extreme lengths to keep their trade secrets secret. For example, the formula for Coca-Cola (perhaps the world's most famous trade secret) is kept locked in a bank vault in Atlanta, which can be opened only by a resolution of the Coca-Cola Company's board of directors. Only two Coca-Cola employees ever know the formula at the same time; their identities are never disclosed to the public and they are not allowed to fly on the same airplane.

Fortunately, such extraordinary secrecy measures are seldom necessary. You don't have to turn your office into an armed camp to protect your trade secrets, but you must take *reasonable* precautions to prevent people who are not subject to confidentiality restrictions from learning them.

How much secrecy is "reasonable"? This depends largely on two factors:

- the physical and financial size of your company, and

- the value of your trade secrets.

A small start-up company need not implement the same type of trade secrecy program as a Microsoft or IBM. A trade secret's value also affects how much secrecy will be deemed reasonable by the courts. For example, more care should be taken to protect extremely valuable source code than relatively unimportant personnel information.

Someone needs to be in charge of a company's secrecy program. In some companies, management devises a security plan and then designates someone to serve as the company's security officer to manage and enforce it. Another approach taken by some hi-tech firms is to have the employees involved with each new project devise and enforce their own security plan. Either approach can work. The key to any trade secret protection program is to devise a secrecy plan you and your employees can live with—and then stick to it.

B. Identifying Your Trade Secrets

The first step in any trade secret protection program is to identify exactly what information and material is a company trade secret. As discussed in Chapter 6, a trade secret can be any information used by the company that gives it an advantage over competitors who do not know or use the information. For a software company, trade secrets typically include:

- unpublished computer code—both source code and object code

- design definitions and specifications

- flow diagrams and flowcharts
- storyboards and concept outlines
- technical notes, memoranda and correspondence relating to the design and development of computer code
- software development tools
- formulas and algorithms embodied in software
- system and user documentation
- data structures and data compilations,
- product development agreements and other related agreements
- business plans
- marketing plans
- sales data
- unpublished promotional material
- cost and pricing information
- customer lists, and
- pending patent applications.

It makes no difference in what form a trade secret is embodied. Trade secrets may be stored on computer hard disks or floppies, written down, or kept only in employees' memories.

Not Everything Is a Trade Secret.
Some companies make the mistake of assuming that virtually all information about the company and its products is a trade secret that must be protected from disclosure to outsiders. They then find that attempting to protect such a morass of information is very expensive and burdensome, and they may end up abandoning their protection program. Use your common sense in deciding whether disclosure of a particular item of information to a competitor would really harm the company.

C. Basic Trade Secret Protection Program

Trade secrecy measures take time, cost money, can result in aggravation and in some cases lower employee morale and productivity. Don't adopt an overly ambitious security program that you'll be unable or unwilling to follow. It is much better to have a modest security program that you and your employees will stick to rather than an extravagant program that will be ignored or resented.

Presented below are the absolute minimum safeguards a software company should take to protect its trade secrets. Such a basic secrecy program is adequate for small companies, particularly start-ups. In other words, if you file suit in court to prevent unauthorized disclosure or misappropriation of your trade secrets, a judge would likely conclude that you took the minimum reasonable precautions to prevent the public or competitors from learning about your secrets absent improper acquisition or theft. (See Chapter 6.)

As your company grows, you'll want to implement some or all of the advanced secrecy measures discussed in Section D, below.

1. Maintaining Physical Security

Although trade secrets are most often misappropriated by employees or ex-employees, not industrial spies, courts usually require that a company take at least some steps to ensure the physical security of its trade secrets. At a minimum, a software company should implement a "clean desk" and "locked file cabinets and desk drawers" policy. Documents containing trade secrets—such as hard copy printouts of source code—should not be left hanging about on desks when not in use; rather, they should be locked in desk drawers or filing cabinets. Your office should also be securely locked at the end of the day. Also, consider making periodic copies of valuable source code and place them in an office safe or bank safety deposit box for security and back-up purposes.

2. Computer Security

Your computer system likely not only contains the software you develop, but other sensitive information as well such as financial records. It's vital to take reasonable measures to prevent unauthorized people from gaining access to your computer system. Here's a list of some of the security measures that can be employed; you can probably think of others. Some of these measures may be too much of a hassle, particularly for small companies. By no means are all required. But the more you employ, the safer your trade secrets will be.

- Use secret passwords, access procedures and firewalls to prevent trade secret theft from your company's file server. The passwords should be periodically changed, especially when an employee who knows the current passwords quits or is fired.
- Place computers, terminals and other peripherals in a physically secure location to which access is restricted.
- Put "fuses" into software to detect unauthorized access and to stop or erase the program if unauthorized access occurs.
- Program your computers not to duplicate or reproduce software unless special programming instructions are input.
- Keep software in coded or encrypted form so it can't be read by outsiders.
- Include secret codes in software identifying the employees who created it.
- Consider using separate computer systems, without modem access, for your most sensitive information.

Take Care With E-Mail

Make certain that both you and your employees take care not to inadvertently disclose trade secrets in e-mail. Always keep in mind that an e-mail recipient can easily forward copies of a message to any number of others without any change in the information or protection of its source. Given the enormous volume of e-mail sent over the Internet and online services—over 100 billion messages are sent each year—it's unlikely that anyone will intercept a specific e-mail message. However, just to be on the safe side, it's wise to encrypt any e-mail that contains any particularly sensitive information. Inexpensive encryption programs such as PGP (Pretty Good Privacy) are readily available.

3. Using Confidentiality Legends

Documents, software and other materials containing trade secrets should always contain a confidentiality legend. This is the best way to alert employees and others that a document contains trade secrets. Moreover, nondisclosure agreements—including those in this book—often require that trade secret documents be so marked.

Following is a legend that can be used on any type of trade secret material:

THIS *[choose one: program, document, database]* IS CONFIDENTIAL AND PROPRIETARY TO *[your company name]* AND MAY NOT BE REPRODUCED, PUBLISHED OR DISCLOSED TO OTHERS WITHOUT COMPANY AUTHORIZATION.

You should also obtain a rubber stamp reading CONFIDENTIAL and use it to mark documents for which it is inconvenient to use the longer legend above.

Don't Mark Everything Confidential. Workers should be admonished not to go overboard and mark everything in sight confidential. If virtually everything is marked "confidential," including public information, a court may conclude that nothing was really confidential. Indeed, it is better not to mark anything than to mark everything.

a. Computer code

It's wise to combine a confidentiality legend with a copyright notice.

Be sure to mark all copies of source code (including disks and disk jackets), with a confidentiality notice. Also, when you create source code, flowcharts or data compilations on your computer, include the confidentiality notice at the beginning and end of the program and a few places in between.

THIS PROGRAM IS CONFIDENTIAL AND PROPRIETARY TO *[your company name]* AND MAY NOT BE REPRODUCED, PUBLISHED OR DISCLOSED TO OTHERS WITHOUT COMPANY AUTHORIZATION.

COPYRIGHT © [year] BY [your company name]

THIS PROGRAM IS CONFIDENTIAL AND PROPRIETARY TO [your company name] AND MAY NOT BE REPRODUCED, PUBLISHED OR DISCLOSED TO OTHERS WITHOUT COMPANY AUTHORIZATION.

COPYRIGHT © [your company name] THIS WORK IS UNPUBLISHED.

b. Faxes and e-mail

Try to keep faxing and e-mailing of trade secrets to a minimum. But if you do fax or e-mail trade secrets, be sure to include a confidentiality legend such as the following:

> The messages and documents transmitted with this notice contain confidential information belonging to the sender.
>
> If you are not the intended recipient of this information, you are hereby notified that any disclosure, copying, distribution or use of the information is strictly prohibited. If you have received this transmission in error, please notify the sender immediately.

This legend can be placed on a fax cover sheet or at the beginning of an e-mail message.

4. Using Nondisclosure Agreements

A nondisclosure agreement is a document in which a person who is given access to trade secrets promises not to disclose them to others without permission from the trade secret owner. Before you give *any* person

access to your trade secrets, make sure that he or she has signed a nondisclosure agreement. This includes people both inside and outside your company.

Don't neglect the important step of preparing nondisclosure agreements. Using nondisclosure agreements consistently is the single most important element of any trade secret protection program.

Using a nondisclosure agreement accomplishes these basic purposes:

- It conclusively establishes that the parties have a confidential relationship. As discussed in detail in Chapter 6, only persons who are in a confidential relationship with a trade secret owner have a legal duty not to disclose the owner's trade secrets without permission.
- Signing such an agreement makes clear to a person who receives a trade secret that it is to be kept in confidence. It impresses on him or her that the company is serious about maintaining its trade secrets.
- If it's ever necessary to file a lawsuit, a signed nondisclosure agreement precludes a court from concluding that the company didn't bother to use nondisclosure agreements because it really didn't have any trade secrets.

a. Employees

All employees who may have access to trade secrets should be required to sign nondisclosure agreements before they begin work, or on their very first day of work. If you have employees who have not signed nondisclosure agreements, you should ask them to do so if they are given access to any trade secrets. A nondisclosure agreement may be part of an employment agreement, which covers all aspects of employment, including confidentiality issues. Chapter 14 contains sample employment agreements including nondisclosure provisions.

Top management should sign nondisclosure agreements as well. Although such individuals owe a duty of loyalty to their company, which includes a duty not to disclose information that would harm the business, it's prudent to put it in writing. Potential customers or investors may wish to have the extra safeguard of a signed nondisclosure agreement before buying your product or investing in your company. If your business is a partnership, all partners should sign a partnership agreement containing a nondisclosure provision.

b. Independent contractors (consultants)

The consultant you hire today may end up working for a competitor tomorrow. Never expose a non-employee consultant to trade secrets without having a signed nondisclosure agreement on file. The nondisclosure agreement may be contained in an independent contractor agreement, which covers all aspects of the work relationship. This is discussed in detail in Chapter 15; sample forms are included.

The sample agreements in Chapter 15 limit the consultant's confidentiality obligation to information in writing that is marked

Noncompetition Agreements With Employees

In addition to having employees exposed to trade secrets sign nondisclosure agreements, many employers have them agree to noncompetition restrictions (also called "covenants not to compete"). A covenant not to compete is used to prevent an employee with access to confidential information from directly competing with his employer within a given geographic area for a limited time period after he quits or is fired.

A covenant not to compete is usually much easier to enforce than a confidentiality agreement because the ex-employer need only show that the ex-employee went to work for a competitor or started his own business in violation of the agreement's terms. Moreover, an employee who can't work for a competitor or start his own competitive business will have no incentive or opportunity to use or disclose his ex-employer's trade secrets. However, there are many restrictions on noncompete agreements; they are unenforceable in California, for example. (See Chapter 14 for a detailed discussion.)

confidential, or information orally disclosed that is later reduced to writing and appropriately marked. This is a reasonable limitation because it enables the consultant to know exactly what is and is not a trade secret. However, it means that whenever trade secrets are orally disclosed to a consultant, a follow-up letter must be sent stating that the information is confidential. If you're an employer, make sure that your employees understand this policy and confirm all oral disclosures to outside consultants in writing.

c. Licensees and purchasers

Nondisclosure provisions are routinely included in software license and sale agreements. However, the enforceability of such provisions is questionable when they are included in "shrink-wrap" licenses for mass-marketed software. (See Chapter 16.)

d. Other outsiders

Have any other outsider who may be exposed to your trade secrets sign a nondisclosure agreement as well. This may include people interviewing for jobs with your company, suppliers, outside beta testers, product reviewers, potential investors, bankers, accountants and outside auditors, as well as people who visit your company.

5. Preparing Nondisclosure Agreements

Following are instructions and samples of five nondisclosure agreements:

- General Nondisclosure Agreement;
- Nondisclosure Agreement With Prospective Licensees;
- Beta Tester's Nondisclosure Agreement
- Visitor's Nondisclosure Agreement, and
- Prospective Employee's Nondisclosure Agreement.

For nondisclosure agreements to be used with employees, use the employment agreements in Chapter 14. For independent contractors, use the consulting agreements in Chapter 15.

a. General nondisclosure agreement

The General Nondisclosure Agreement can be used with any outside individual or company to whom you grant access to your trade secrets.

In some cases, both parties may agree to disclose confidential information to each other. This may occur, for example, where the parties are considering a joint development project or a merger. In this event, two General Nondisclosure Agreements can be used, with the parties switching roles as Discloser and Recipient.

The full text of the General Nondisclosure Agreement is on the CD-ROM forms disk under NONDISC1. See Chapter 1 for instructions on using the forms disk.

The General Nondisclosure Agreement is self-explanatory, with the following clarifications.

Introductory Paragraph

Fill in the date. Next, fill in the disclosing company's name (the "Discloser"). Finally, fill in the name of the outside individual or company being granted access to your trade secrets (the "Recipient"). Remember to have everyone who will have access to your trade secrets sign a nondisclosure agreement.

Trade Secrets

Select either Alternative 1 or 2 (the full text of both alternatives is on disk), and delete the alternative you are not using. Here's how to choose:

Alternative 1. It's best to specifically identify the trade secrets covered by the agreement; use this clause if you can individually list the material being provided. However, be careful that your description is not so narrowly worded that it may leave out important information you wish to have covered by the agreement.

Alternative 2. Use this clause if it's not possible to specifically identify the trade secrets—for example, if the information to be disclosed does not exist when the agreement is signed. This clause contains a general description of the types of information covered.

Purpose of Disclosure

Describe the reason for disclosing trade secrets. For example, this may be to evaluate software for use, to explore joint marketing possibilities or to further the parties' business relationship.

Return of Materials

In this clause, the Recipient promises to return original materials you've provided, as well as copies, notes and documents pertaining to the trade secrets. The form gives Recipient 30 days to return the materials, but you can change this time period if you wish.

Term of Agreement

The forms disk includes two alternative provisions dealing with the agreement's term. Select the clause that best suits your needs and delete the other:

Alternative 1. This provision has no definite time limit—in other words, the recipient's obligation of confidentiality lasts until the trade secret information ceases to be a trade secret. This may occur when the information becomes generally known, is disclosed to the public by the disclosing party or ceases being a trade secret for some other reason.

Alternative 2. Some recipients don't want to be subject to open-ended confidentiality obligations. Use this clause if the Recipient requires that the agreement state a definite date in which the agreement, and the Recipient's confidentiality obligations, expires.

Applicable Law

Fill in the state in which the Discloser has its principal office.

Signature

The parties don't have to be in the same room when they sign the agreement. It's

General Nondisclosure Agreement

This is an agreement, effective June 11, 199X, between The Accountant's Own Software Company (the "Discloser") and Sandra Miller (the "Recipient"), in which Discloser agrees to disclose, and Recipient agrees to receive, certain trade secrets of Discloser on the following terms and conditions:

1. Trade Secrets: Recipient understands and acknowledges that Discloser's trade secrets consist of information and materials that are valuable and not generally known by Discloser's competitors. Discloser's trade secrets include:

(a) Any and all information concerning Discloser's current, future or proposed products, including, but not limited to, unpublished computer code (both source code and object code), drawings, specifications, notebook entries, technical notes and graphs, computer printouts, technical memoranda and correspondence, product development agreements and related agreements.

(b) Information and materials relating to Discloser's purchasing, accounting and marketing, including, but not limited to, marketing plans, sales data, unpublished promotional material, cost and pricing information and customer lists.

(c) Information of the type described above which Discloser obtained from another party and which Discloser treats as confidential, whether or not owned or developed by Discloser.

2. Purpose of Disclosure: Recipient shall make use of Discloser's trade secrets only for the purpose of evaluating Discloser's software for use in Recipient's business.

3. Nondisclosure: In consideration of Discloser's disclosure of its trade secrets to Recipient, Recipient agrees that it will treat Discloser's trade secrets with the same degree of care and safeguards that it takes with its own trade secrets, but in no event less than a reasonable degree of care. Recipient agrees that, without Discloser's prior written consent, Recipient will not:

(a) disclose Discloser's trade secrets to any third party,

(b) make or permit to be made copies or other reproductions of Discloser's trade secrets, or

(c) make any commercial use of the trade secrets.

Recipient will not disclose Discloser's trade secrets to Recipient's employees, agents and consultants unless: (1) they have a need to know the information in connection with their employment or consultant duties; and (2) they personally agree in writing to be bound by the terms of this Agreement.

4. Return of Materials: Upon Discloser's request, Recipient shall promptly (within 30 days) return all original materials provided by Discloser and any copies, notes or other documents in Recipient's possession pertaining to Discloser's trade secrets.

5. Exclusions: This agreement does not apply to any information which:

(a) was in Recipient's possession or was known to Recipient, without an obligation to keep it confidential, before such information was disclosed to Recipient by Discloser;

(b) is or becomes public knowledge through a source other than Recipient and through no fault of Recipient;

(c) is independently developed by or for Recipient;

(d) is or becomes lawfully available to Recipient from a source other than Discloser; or

(e) is disclosed by Recipient with Discloser's prior written approval.

6. Term of Agreement: This Agreement and Recipient's duty to hold Discloser's trade secrets in confidence shall remain in effect until the above-described trade secrets are no longer trade secrets or until Discloser sends Recipient written notice releasing Recipient from this Agreement, whichever occurs first.

7. No Rights Granted: Recipient understands and agrees that this Agreement does not constitute a grant or an intention or commitment to grant any right, title or interest in Discloser's trade secrets to Recipient.

8. Warranty: Discloser warrants that it has the right to make the disclosures under this Agreement. NO OTHER WARRANTIES ARE MADE BY DISCLOSER UNDER THIS AGREEMENT. ANY INFORMATION DISCLOSED UNDER THIS AGREEMENT IS PROVIDED "AS IS."

9. Injunctive Relief: Recipient recognizes and acknowledges that any breach or threatened breach of this Agreement by Recipient may cause Discloser irreparable harm for which monetary damages may be inadequate. Recipient agrees, therefore, that Discloser shall be entitled to an injunction to restrain Recipient from such breach or threatened breach. Nothing in this Agreement shall be construed as preventing Discloser from pursuing any remedy at law or in equity for any breach or threatened breach of this Agreement.

10. Attorney Fees: If any legal action arises relating to this Agreement, the prevailing party shall be entitled to recover all court costs, expenses and reasonable attorney fees.

11. Modifications: All additions or modifications to this Agreement must be made in writing and must be signed by both parties to be effective.

12. No Agency: This Agreement does not create any agency or partnership relationship between the parties.

13. Applicable Law: This Agreement is made under, and shall be construed according to, the laws of the State of Nevada.

Discloser: The Accountant's Own Software Company

By: _____
(signature)

_____
(typed or printed name)

Title: _____   Date: _____

Recipient: Sandra Miller

By: _____
(signature)

_____
(typed or printed name)

Title: _____   Date: _____

even fine if the dates are a few days apart. Each party should sign at least two copies, and keep at least one. This way, both parties have an original signed agreement. (Instructions on preparing and signing documents are covered in Chapter 1.)

b. Nondisclosure Agreement With Prospective Licensee

The following nondisclosure agreement is specially designed to be used when a software company provides a copy of a finished software product to a prospective licensee or other customer for evaluation.

 The full text of the following agreement is on the CD-ROM forms disk under the file name NONDISC2. See Chapter 1 for instructions on using the forms disk.

The Nondisclosure Agreement (Prospective Customer) is self-explanatory, with the following clarifications.

Introductory Paragraph

Fill in the date. Next, fill in the disclosing company's name. Finally, fill in the name of the outside individual or company being granted access to your trade secrets (the "Customer"). Remember to have everyone who will have access to your trade secrets sign a nondisclosure agreement.

Purpose of Agreement

Describe the software or other information disclosed or provide its name.

Nonexclusive License

Fill in the number of days you are allowing the Customer to use the software for evaluation purposes.

Term of Agreement

Again, fill in the number of days you are allowing the Customer to use the software for evaluation purposes. This must be identical to the time period you listed in the Nonexclusive License clause, above.

Applicable Law

Fill in the state in which the Company has its principal office.

Signature

The parties don't have to be in the same room when they sign the agreement. It's even fine if the dates are a few days apart. Each party should sign at least two copies, and keep at least one. This way, both parties have an original signed agreement. (Instructions on preparing and signing documents are covered in Chapter 1.)

Nondisclosure Agreement
(Prospective Licensee)

This is an agreement, effective March 22, 199X, between EfficientSoft (the "Company") and Mazes, Inc. (the "Customer").

1. Purpose of Agreement: This Agreement is entered into for the purpose of authorizing Customer to receive from Company and evaluate certain proprietary computer software and documentation known as EfficientWork, hereafter referred to as "the Software."

2. Nonexclusive License: Company hereby grants Customer a nonexclusive license to install the Software on its computer system and use the Software for a period of 30 days from the date of delivery only for the purpose of evaluating the performance of the Software and not for a productive purpose. Customer shall acquire no other intellectual property rights under this Agreement.

3. Software a Trade Secret: Customer acknowledges that the Software is proprietary to, and a valuable trade secret of, the Company and is entrusted to Customer only for the purposes set forth in this Agreement.

4. Nondisclosure: In consideration of the Company's disclosure of the Software to Customer, Customer shall treat the Software with the same degree of care and safeguards that it takes with Customer's own trade secrets, but in no event less than a reasonable degree of care. Customer agrees that it will not, without the Company's prior written consent:

(a) reverse engineer, decompile or disassemble the Software or any portion of it;

(b) copy any portion of the Software;

(c) download the Software in a retrieval system or computer system of any kind except as authorized by this Agreement; or

(d) disclose any portion of the Software to any third party.

Customer shall limit use of the Software to those employees, agents and consultants of Customer who are performing the evaluation for Customer.

The restrictions and obligations contained in this clause shall survive the expiration, termination or cancellation of this Agreement, and shall continue to bind Customer, its successors, heirs and assigns.

5. Term of Agreement: This Agreement shall last for a term of 30 days from the date the Software is delivered to Customer, or until the Software is returned by Customer to the Company, whichever occurs first. Further, the Company may terminate this Agreement immediately upon written notice to Customer.

6. Return of Software and Materials: Customer shall promptly return the Software and all related materials to the Company and erase all copies and portions thereof from computer memory upon:

(a) termination of this Agreement;

(b) the Company's request; or

(c) the Customer's decision not to purchase or license the Software.

7. Limitation of Liability: Customer understands and acknowledges that the Software is being provided to Customer only for the purpose of evaluating the performance of the Software and not for any productive purpose. Accordingly, the Company shall not be responsible for any loss or damage to Customer or any third parties caused by Customer's use of the Software.

THE COMPANY SHALL NOT BE LIABLE FOR ANY DIRECT, INDIRECT, SPECIAL, INCIDENTAL OR CONSEQUENTIAL DAMAGES, WHETHER BASED ON CONTRACT OR TORT OR ANY OTHER LEGAL THEORY, ARISING OUT OF ANY USE OF THE SOFTWARE OR ANY PERFORMANCE OF THIS AGREEMENT.

8. Injunctive Relief: Customer recognizes and acknowledges that any breach or threatened breach of this Agreement by Customer may cause the Company irreparable harm for which monetary damages may be inadequate. Customer agrees, therefore, that the Company shall be entitled to an injunction to restrain Customer from such breach or threatened breach. Nothing in this Agreement shall be construed as preventing the Company from pursuing any remedy at law or in equity for any breach or threatened breach of this Agreement.

9. Attorney Fees: If any legal action arises relating to this Agreement, the prevailing party shall be entitled to recover all court costs, expenses and reasonable attorney fees.

10. Entire Agreement: This Agreement contains the entire understanding and agreement of the parties relating to the subject matter hereof. Any representation, promise, or condition not explicitly set forth in this Agreement shall not be binding on either party.

11. Modifications: All additions or modifications to this Agreement must be made in writing and must be signed by both parties to be effective.

12. Applicable Law: This Agreement is made under, and shall be construed according to, the laws of the State of Massachusetts.

Discloser: EfficientSoft

By: _____
                           (signature)

_____
            (typed or printed name)

Title: _____   Date:_____

Customer: Mazes, Inc.

By: _____
                           (signature)

_____
            (typed or printed name)

Title: _____   Date:_____

c. Beta Tester's Nondisclosure Agreement

Here is a nondisclosure agreement to be used with all outside persons or companies that beta test software that is under development.

 The full text of the following agreement is on the CD-ROM forms disk under NONDISC3. See Chapter 1 for instructions on using the forms disk.

The Nondisclosure Agreement (Beta Tester) is self-explanatory, with the following clarifications.

Introductory Paragraph

Fill in the date. Next, fill in the disclosing company's name. Fill in the name of the outside individual or company that is beta testing your software (the "Tester"). Finally, fill in the name of the software being tested.

Company's Obligations

Typically, a beta tester is given a free copy of the software as payment. That is what this agreement provides, although some other payment provision can be agreed to—for example, hourly payment or a fixed fee.

Term of Agreement

Fill in the time frame during which you are allowing the beta tester to test the software.

Applicable Law

Fill in the state in which the Company has its principal office.

Signature

The parties don't have to be in the same room when they sign the agreement. It's even fine if the dates are a few days apart. Each party should sign at least two copies, and keep at least one. This way, both parties have an original signed agreement. (Instructions on preparing and signing documents are covered in Chapter 1.)

Nondisclosure Agreement
(Beta Tester)

This is an agreement, effective November 12, 199X, between Earth Dreams (the "Company") and Lewis Industries (the "Tester"), in which Tester agrees to test a software program known as Heavenly Power (the "Software") and keep the Company aware of the test results.

1. Company's Obligations: The Company shall provide Tester with a copy of the Software and any necessary documentation and instruct Tester on how to use it and the desired test data to be gained. Upon satisfactory completion of the testing, the Company shall furnish Tester with one free copy of the production version of the Software, contingent upon the Company's decision to proceed with production of the Software. Tester shall be entitled to the same benefits to which regular purchasers of the Software will be entitled.

2. Tester's Obligations: Tester shall test the Software under normally expected operating conditions in Tester's environment during the test period. Tester shall gather and report test data as mutually agreed upon with the Company. Tester shall allow the Company access to the Software during normal working hours for inspection, modifications and maintenance.

3. Software a Trade Secret: Tester acknowledges that the Software is proprietary to, and a valuable trade secret of, the Company and is entrusted to Tester only for the purpose set forth in this Agreement. Tester shall treat the Software in the strictest confidence. Tester agrees that it will not, without the Company's prior written consent:

(a) disclose any information about the Software, its design and performance specifications, its code, and the existence of the beta test and its results to anyone other than Tester's employees who are performing the testing;

(b) copy any portion of the Software or documentation, except to the extent necessary to perform the beta testing; or

(c) reverse engineer, decompile or disassemble the Software or any portion of it.

4. Security Precautions: Tester shall take reasonable security precautions to prevent the Software from being seen by unauthorized individuals. This includes locking all copies of the Software and associated documentation in a desk or file cabinet when not in use.

5. Term of Agreement: The test period shall last from November 12, 199X, until December 12, 199X. This Agreement shall terminate at the end of the test period or when the Company asks Tester to return the Software, whichever occurs first. The restrictions and obligations contained in Clauses 3, 6, 7, 8 and 9 shall survive the expiration, termination or cancellation of this Agreement, and shall continue to bind Tester, its successors, heirs and assigns.

6. Return of Software and Materials: Upon the conclusion of the testing period or at the Company's request, Tester shall promptly (within 10 days) return the original and all copies of the Software and all related materials to the Company and erase all portions thereof from computer memory.

7. Disclaimer of Warranty: Tester understands and acknowledges that the Software is a test product and its accuracy and reliability are not guaranteed. Owing to its experimental nature, Tester is advised not to rely exclusively on the Software for any reason. Tester waives any and all claims it may have against the Company arising out of the performance or nonperformance of the Software.

THE SOFTWARE IS PROVIDED AS IS, AND THE COMPANY DISCLAIMS ANY AND ALL REPRESENTATIONS OR WARRANTIES OF ANY KIND, WHETHER EXPRESS OR IMPLIED, WITH RESPECT TO IT, INCLUDING ANY IMPLIED WARRANTIES OF MERCHANTABILITY OR FITNESS FOR A PARTICULAR PURPOSE.

8. Limitation of Liability: The Company shall not be responsible for any loss or damage to Tester or any third parties caused by the Software or by the Company's performance of this Agreement.

THE COMPANY SHALL NOT BE LIABLE FOR ANY DIRECT, INDIRECT, SPECIAL, INCIDENTAL OR CONSEQUENTIAL DAMAGE, WHETHER BASED ON CONTRACT OR TORT OR ANY OTHER LEGAL THEORY, ARISING OUT OF ANY USE OF THE SOFTWARE OR ANY PERFORMANCE OF THIS AGREEMENT.

9. No Rights Granted: Tester understands and acknowledges that the Software is provided for its own use for testing purposes only. This Agreement does not constitute a grant or an intention or commitment to grant any right, title or interest in the Software or the Company's trade secrets to Tester. Tester may not sell or transfer any portion of the Software to any third party or use the Software in any manner to produce, market or support its own products. Tester shall clearly identify the Software as the Company's property.

10. No Assignments: This Agreement is personal to Tester. Tester shall not assign or otherwise transfer any rights or obligations under this Agreement.

11. Entire Agreement: This Agreement contains the entire understanding and agreement of the parties relating to the subject matter hereof. Any representation, promise or condition not explicitly set forth in this Agreement shall not be binding on either party. All additions or modifications to this Agreement must be made in writing and must be signed by both parties to be effective.

12. Applicable Law: This Agreement is made under, and shall be construed according to, the laws of the State of Illinois.

The Company: Earth Dreams

By: _____
                          (signature)

_____
                    (typed or printed name)

d. Visitor's Nondisclosure Agreement

This is a nondisclosure agreement that can be used with visitors to your office who might have access to company trade secrets

 The text of the following agreement is on the CD-ROM forms disk under the file name NONDISC4. See Chapter 1 for instructions on using the forms disk.

The Visitor's Nondisclosure Agreement is self-explanatory, with the following clarifications.

Introductory Paragraph

Visitor's Name. Fill in the name of the outside individual who is visiting your company. Remember to have everyone who visits your company and may have access to your trade secrets sign a nondisclosure agreement.

Affiliation. Fill in the name of the company or organization the individual represents.

Place Visited. Fill in your company's name and address.

Date Visited. Fill in the date or dates of the visit.

Clause 1. Fill in your company's name.

Signature. Each visitor should sign and date the agreement, preferably before he or she is exposed to trade secrets. (Instructions on preparing and signing documents are covered in Chapter 1.)

Visitor's Nondisclosure Agreement

Visitor's Name (print): _____

Affiliation: _____

Place Visited: _____

Date(s) Visited: _____

1. I understand that I may be given access to confidential information belonging to _____
_____ (the "Company") through my relationship with the
Company or as a result of my access to the Company's premises.

2. I understand and acknowledge that the Company's trade secrets consist of information and
materials that are valuable and not generally known by the Company's competitors. The Company's
trade secrets include:

(a) Any and all information concerning the Company's current, future or proposed products,
including, but not limited to, unpublished computer code (both source code and object code),
drawings, specifications, notebook entries, technical notes and graphs, computer printouts, technical
memoranda and correspondence, product development agreements and related agreements.

(b) Information and materials relating to the Company's purchasing, accounting and marketing;
including, but not limited to, marketing plans, sales data, unpublished promotional material, cost
and pricing information and customer lists.

(c) Information of the type described above which the Company obtained from another party and
which the Company treats as confidential, whether or not owned or developed by the Company.

(d) Other: _____

3. In consideration of being admitted to the Company's facilities, I agree to hold in the strictest
confidence any trade secrets or confidential information which is disclosed to me. I agree not to
remove any document, equipment or other materials from the premises without the Company's
written permission. I will not photograph or otherwise record any information to which I may have
access during my visit.

4. This Agreement is binding on me, my heirs, executors, administrators and assigns; and inures to
the benefit of the Company, its successors and assigns.

5. This Agreement constitutes the entire understanding between the Company and me with respect
to its subject matter. It supersedes all earlier representations and understandings, whether oral or
written.

Visitor:

_____
                         (Signature)

Date: _____

e. Prospective employee's nondisclosure agreement

You may end up divulging trade secrets when interviewing prospective employees, especially for sensitive jobs. Any person you hire should be required to sign an employment agreement containing a non-disclosure provision. But, of course, those interviewees you don't hire won't be signing an employment agreement. For this reason, have all prospective employees sign a simple nondisclosure agreement at the beginning of a job interview.

 The full text of the following agreement is on the CD-ROM forms disk under the file name NONDISC5. See Chapter 1 for instructions on using the forms disk.

The Interview Confidential Disclosure Agreement is self-explanatory, with the following clarifications.

First paragraph

Fill in your company's name and the name of the job applicant.

Signature

Each visitor should sign and date the agreement, preferably before he or she is exposed to trade secrets. (Instructions on preparing and signing documents are covered in Chapter 1.)

D. Advanced Trade Secret Protection Program

Presented below are some additional security precautions that will help ensure the safety of your trade secrets. As your company grows and you develop increasingly valuable trade secrets, you'll want to consider making some or all of these precautions a part of your security plan.

1. Limiting Employee Access to Trade Secrets

Obviously, the fewer people who know a trade secret, the less likely it will leak out. In very small companies, particularly start-ups, it may not be possible or desirable to limit access to trade secrets, since everyone is involved in every facet of the company's operation. However, as a company grows larger, it's a good idea to restrict access to trade secrets only to those employees who really need to know them.

One way to control employees' access to trade secrets is to use project logs. Start by making a list of which employees need to have access to confidential materials for each of your company's ongoing projects. Create a log for each project and have every employee sign in and out each time they use confidential materials. The log should contain room for the date, the employee's name, the time in, the time out and perhaps additional information,

Interview Confidential Disclosure Agreement

Earth Dreams, Inc. (the "Company") and J. Alfred Prufrock (the "Applicant") agree as follow:

1. Company is interviewing Applicant for the position of Website developer and to work on the following projects: developing Company's new Website.

2. Applicant understands that Company's trade secrets may be disclosed during the interview process or as a result of Applicant's access to Company's premises.

3. Applicant understands and acknowledges that Company's trade secrets consist of information and materials that are valuable and not generally known by the Company's competitors. The Company's trade secrets include:

(a) Any and all information concerning the Company's current, future or proposed products, including, but not limited to, unpublished computer code (both source code and object code), drawings, specifications, notebook entries, technical notes and graphs, computer printouts, technical memoranda and correspondence, product development agreements and related agreements.

(b) Information and materials relating to the Company's purchasing, accounting and marketing; including, but not limited to, marketing plans, sales data, unpublished promotional material, cost and pricing information and customer lists.

(c) Information of the type described above which the Company obtained from another party and which the Company treats as confidential, whether or not owned or developed by the Company.

(d) Other: Information regarding Company's Website development plans.

4. At all times during and after the interview, Applicant will keep confidential and will not make use of or disclose to any third party any of Company's trade secrets.

5. Applicant will not use, disclose to company, or cause Company to use any trade secret or confidential information of any other person or entity.

The Accountant's Own Software Company

By: _____
(signature)

_____
(typed or printed name)

Title: _____ Date: _____

Applicant: Sandra Miller

By: _____
(signature)

_____
(typed or printed name)

Date: _____

depending on the project. The log can be maintained manually or via computer. Consistent use of logs will help ensure that unauthorized employees don't get their hands on company trade secrets.

2. Additional Physical Security

In larger companies, additional security precautions can be taken. Company trade secrets can be kept in a specified protected location or even in geographically separate facilities. Access to these areas can then be restricted.

3. Not Writing Down Trade Secrets

Perhaps the best way to maintain a trade secret is not to write it down at all. Particularly in small companies, a good deal of sensitive information—marketing plans, for example—can be transmitted orally to those who need to know.

4. Restricting Photocopying

If trade secrets are written down, one of the principal means by which they can be lost is through unauthorized photocopying. Try to restrict access to photocopiers, particularly at night. Keep a logbook next to the copier and require anyone who copies a document marked "confidential" to record the following information: the date, name

of person making the copy, name of the person for whom the copy is made, number of copies, and the subject matter and name of the document. In addition, a record should be kept of anyone who receives confidential copies—for example, the names could be written on a cover transmittal sheet. As always, those people should sign nondisclosure agreements.

5. Shredding Documents

Security experts warn that wastepaper awaiting pickup often contains valuable trade secrets. It's not wise to leave such papers lying around. Companies have been known to hire investigators to engage in dumpster diving at their competitors' premises. Obtain a shredding machine to effectively dispose of any documents containing trade secrets.

6. Noncompetition Agreements With Employees and Consultants

We've already discussed above that all employees and consultants should be required to sign nondisclosure agreements before being exposed to trade secrets. However, nondisclosure agreements are not a panacea. It can be very difficult for an employer to know whether an ex-employee has disclosed trade secrets to a competitor. Moreover, even if the employer is sure trade secrets have been disclosed, it can be difficult to obtain court relief for violations of a nondisclosure agreement. The ex-employer must prove that the employee actually disclosed confidential information. This can be an onerous task, especially where the ex-employee claims that the information allegedly disclosed didn't qualify as a trade secret.

One way to avoid these problems is to have employees and consultants sign noncompetition agreements. These are agreements by which an employee or independent contractor promises not to compete with the employer's business for a stated time period (usually no more than two years).

It's usually easy to discover whether an ex-employee has gone to work for a competitor. To enforce a noncompetition agreement in court, the ex-employer need only show that the ex-employee went to work for a competitor in violation of the agreement's terms. But, the best part about a noncompetition agreement from an employer's point of view is that it will deter both the employee from seeking employment with a competitor and the competitor from hiring him or her. This significantly reduces an employee's incentive and opportunity to divulge trade secrets.

From the company's point of view, this all sounds great, but there is a down side. Noncompetition agreements are very unpopular with many employees and consultants, and some will refuse to sign them. You could lose an outstanding prospective employee or consultant by insisting on it. Moreover, they are unenforceable in a number of states, including California. Even in those states where such agreements are enforceable, they must be carefully drafted to withstand judicial scrutiny. (For a detailed discussion and sample forms, see Chapters 14 and 15.)

7. Screening Employee Publications and Presentations

A trade secret is lost if it is disclosed to the public on an unrestricted basis. For example, the trade secret status of valuable source code will be lost if it is published in a computer magazine. Trade secrets also may be lost through disclosures in speeches and presentations at trade shows and professional conferences. Trade secrets can even be lost through advertising—for example, a software company that lists its clients in an advertising brochure cannot claim later that its customer list is a trade secret.

Companies with advanced trade secret programs screen all papers, articles and advance texts of speeches and presentations. This screening process can be done by a formal screening committee consisting of members who, taken together, are familiar with all the company's products and trade secrets, or by individuals who may specialize in a particular area. Special care must be taken to avoid disclosing patentable inventions in articles or other publications. Patent protection in some foreign countries can be lost through such inadvertent disclosures, and disclosure in all countries starts running the one year period during which a patent application must be filed or the right to do so is lost forever. (See Chapter 8.)

8. Controlling Visitors

Visitors to your company should not be allowed to wander unsupervised in areas where confidential materials are kept. Larger software companies should require all visitors to sign a log book, including the visitor's name, address, affiliation, reason for visit, person being seen at the company and times of entering and leaving. Visitors who might be exposed to trade secrets should be asked to sign a nondisclosure agreement before leaving the reception area. (See Section C5d, above, for a sample visitor's nondisclosure agreement.)

9. Dealing With Departing Employees

The primary source of trade secret leaks are former employees. Thus, it's important to take special precautions when an employee decides to leave or is fired.

a. Exit interviews and acknowledgment of obligations form

Before an employee leaves, the company's security officer or other person in charge of the trade secrecy program should conduct an exit interview. This opportunity should be used to remind the employee of his or her obligation not to disclose the company's trade secrets to others, particularly the new employer. Wherever possible, prepare a list generally describing the specific trade secrets the employee was exposed to during his or her employment. Review this list with the employee and give him or her a copy. Also, make sure the employee understands that he or she must return all company documents and materials before leaving. If the employee wants to take a work sample with him or her, make sure it contains no confidential information. Finally, try to find out as much as possible about the worker's new employer and what the worker's job responsibilities will be. This will help you determine whether the employee might be tempted to reveal trade secrets to his or her new employer. If so, you may want to send the new employer the letter in Section 9B, below.

Give the employee a copy of the employment agreement signed when the employee started work. (See Chapter 14.) Go over the confidentiality and, if applicable, the non-competition restrictions. Make sure the employee understands the provisions and appreciates that the company is serious about protecting its trade secrets. Finally, ask the employee to sign an acknowledgment of obligations (a sample form is shown below). If the employee refuses to sign, be sure to note that in her personnel file. The refusal may be helpful if you later attempt to obtain an injunction to prevent the employee from disclosing company trade secrets.

The full text of the Acknowledgment of Obligations agreement is on the forms disk under ACKOBLIG. See Chapter 1 for instructions on using the forms disk.

Acknowledgment of Obligations

1. I understand and acknowledge that during my employment with Mystery Software, Inc. (the "Company") I have received or been exposed to trade secrets of the Company including, but not limited to, the following: those listed on Exhibit A to this Agreement.

2. I acknowledge that I have read, signed and been furnished with a copy of my Employment Agreement with the Company. I certify that I have complied with and will continue to comply with all of the provisions of the Employment Agreement, including my obligation to preserve as confidential all of the Company's trade secrets.

3. I certify that I do not have in my possession, I have not retained copies of, nor have I failed to return: any system documentation, user manuals, modification reports, training instructions, formulas, compilers, data structures, algorithms, computer source code, notebooks, notes, drawings, proposals or other documents or materials (or extracts thereof), or equipment or other property belonging to the Company.

4. During my employment I contributed to the development of the Company's trade secrets. I acknowledge that, as provided in my Employment Agreement, all right, title and interest in and to any programming conceived or developed by me, whether in whole or in part, during the course of my employment by the Company belongs to the Company.

_____/s/_____

Jennifer Jones

Date: 2/15/9___

b. Informing new employer about nondisclosure agreement

If, as a result of your exit interview or otherwise, you're concerned that a departing employee may reveal company trade secrets to his or her new employer, send a letter to the new employer to let it know that your ex-employee has signed a nondisclosure agreement and that you are serious about enforcing it. Your letter serves two purposes:

1. It may help deter both the employee and new employer from breaching the nondisclosure agreement.

2. If a breach does occur, it will establish that the new employer knew that the employee possessed your trade secrets and had a duty not to acquire them without your permission. This will make the new employer liable for the unauthorized disclosure along with your ex-employee. It also will enable you to obtain a court order barring the new employer from using any of your trade secrets if the ex-employee makes an unauthorized disclosure. (See Chapter 6.)

Be careful how you write this letter. Avoid unnecessary accusations or personal inferences; just stick to the facts. Otherwise, if your ex-employee loses his new job as a result of your letter, he or she might sue your company for defamation or slander. Also, don't describe the trade secrets involved in detail; a general description of the subject matter is sufficient.

The full text of this sample letter is on the forms disk under LTRSECRT. See Chapter 1 for instructions on using the forms disk.

Send this letter by certified mail, return receipt requested. A copy should also be sent to the former employee.

Letter to New Employer

July 12, 199X

To Whom It May Concern:

We understand that Olivia Williams has decided to join your company. We would like to inform you of the following facts:

1. During her employment by us, Olivia Williams had access to our trade secrets including, but not limited to, advanced information about robotic visual scanning algorithms.

2. In connection with her employment, Olivia Williams signed an Employment Agreement in which she promised not to disclose or utilize any of our trade secrets without our permission. The Agreement remains in full force and effect.

3. At the time Olivia Williams left our company, she was informed of her continuing obligations under the Employment Agreement and she signed an acknowledgment of such obligations, a copy of which is enclosed.

We are confident that Olivia Williams intends to comply with her obligations and respect our trade secrets. We also trust that your company will not assign her to a position which might risk disclosure of our trade secrets.

If you have any questions regarding these matters, we will be happy to clarify them for you. In addition, if at any time you wish to know whether information provided you by Olivia Williams is a trade secret owned by us, we will be happy to work out a procedure for providing you with this information.

Very truly yours,

Jane Matthews

cc: Olivia Williams

Chapter 8

Software Patents

This chapter provides the briefest possible overview of the subject of software patents. This is an extremely complex area of the law. If you're serious about obtaining a patent, it's highly advisable to seek the assistance of a patent lawyer. But reading this chapter first will help you decide whether to apply for a patent and, if you do, communicate intelligently with your lawyer.

A. Patent Basics

Following is a brief overview of patent law. For a detailed discussion of all these topics, refer to *Patent It Yourself*, by David Pressman (Nolo Press).

1. What Is a Patent?

A patent is a document issued by the U.S. Patent and Trademark Office (PTO) that grants a monopoly for a limited period of time on the use and development of an invention which the PTO finds to qualify for patent protection. This right lasts between 14 and 20 years, depending on the type of invention. The monopoly right conferred by a patent extends throughout the United States and its territories and possessions. It's also possible to obtain patents in most foreign countries. (See Chapter 10.)

The U.S. Patent and Trademark Office (PTO) issues three different kinds of patents: utility patents, design patents and plant patents.

- Utility patents are inventions that have some type of usefulness—this includes virtually all software patents.
- Design patents protect a device's ornamental characteristics—some design patents have been obtained to protect computer screen icons.
- Plant patents protect certain types of plants and obviously have no bearing on software.

2. Patents Compared With Copyright, Trade Secrets and Trademarks

Although this chapter is about software patents, it is important to remember that there are other ways to protect products of the intellect. The main ways are:

- **Copyright laws.** These protect the expressive aspects of intellectual property and are discussed in Chapter 3.
- **Trade secret laws.** These protect information that both is maintained as a proprietary secret and that provides its owner with a competitive advantage in the marketplace. Trade secret law is discussed in Chapter 6.
- **Trademark laws**. These laws protect original names, symbols and slogans that are used to identify the source of and distinguish goods and services in the marketplace. Trademark law is discussed in Chapter 9.

Each of these protection schemes has its limitations when it comes to protecting pure ideas.

Copyright does not protect ideas per se, but only the way ideas are expressed. If there are only one or two ways in which a particular idea can be expressed, then the idea and the expression are said to "merge" and no copyright protection is allowed. Also, copyright only protects against copying. If someone else independently produces an expression that is very similar to yours, but didn't result from copying, there is nothing you can do about it. Also, copyright does not protect procedures, processes, systems or methods of operation—all items that may be protectible in a patent.

Unlike copyright, trade secret law does protect ideas, but only as long as they are kept secret. If the ideas are legally accessible to the public, either because they are obvious from the innovation itself or because someone discovers the ideas by reverse engineering or decompiling the innovation, protection ends. But it is possible to preserve trade secrets in software that is selectively distributed on a one-on-one basis to large customers—rather than sold in the mass market. This is done by requiring the purchaser to sign an agreement binding the purchaser to keep confidential any secrets that are discovered while using the software.

Trademark law protects marketing ideas that are reduced to symbolic form (words, logos, slogans, etc.), but does not protect either the ideas or the expression in the software innovation itself. Although branding software (for Example, Lotus 1-2-3) can be an effective marketing technique in the short run, if a competitor introduces a similar or better product at a lower cost, branding doesn't provide much in the way of long term protection.

In contrast to these other software protection schemes, utility patents do the best job in that the patent owner can keep others from using the idea covered by the patent for the life of the patent. But utility patents for most software innovations are hard won, and even where a patent is possible, the application process can be costly and the enforcement process can be difficult.

3. Types of Inventions That Can Be Patented

Most inventions must pass several basic tests to qualify for a patent:

- The invention must fall within one or more of five statutory classes of inventions (that is, it must be "statutory subject matter").
- The invention must have some utility, no matter how trivial.
- The invention must be novel (this means that it must have one or more new main elements).
- The invention must be nonobvious (a significant development) to somebody positioned to understand the technical field of the invention.

Unpatentable Inventions

Some types of inventions do not qualify for a patent, no matter how interesting or important they are. For instance, mathematical formulas, laws of nature, newly discovered substances that occur naturally in the world, and purely theoretical phenomena (for instance a scientific principle like superconductivity without regard to its use in the real world) have long been considered unpatentable. But the law in this area can be subtle and tricky. For instance, some computer software heavily based on mathematical formulas may nevertheless qualify for a patent if the patent application limits the software to specific uses on specific machines. This is because the patent laws may not be used to create a monopoly on an idea per se, but can be used to create a monopoly on a specific application of an idea. For example, no patent may issue on the complex mathematical formulae that are used in space navigation, but a patent is certainly appropriate for the software and machines that translate those equations and make the space shuttle go where it's supposed to go.

a. Statutory subject matter

To qualify for a utility patent an invention must be:

- a process or method of getting something useful done (such as a genetic engineering procedure, a manufacturing technique or computer software)
- a machine (usually something with moving parts or circuitry, such as a cigarette lighter, sewage treatment system, laser or photocopier)
- an article of manufacture (such as an eraser, tire, transistor or hand tool)
- a composition of matter (such as a chemical composition, drug, soap or genetically altered life form), or
- an improvement of an invention that fits within one of the first four categories.

Often, an invention will fall into more than one category. Computer software can usually be described both as a process (the steps that it takes to make the computer do something) and as a machine (a device that takes information from an input device and moves it to an output device). Regardless of the number of categories a particular invention falls under, only one utility patent may be issued on it.

b. Utility

Patents may issue on inventions that have some type of usefulness (utility), even if the use is humorous, such as a musical condom or a motorized spaghetti fork. However, the invention must work—at least in theory. For this reason, no patent has ever issued on a perpetual motion machine (a device that does more work than the energy supplied to it).

c. Novelty

In the context of a patent application, an invention is considered to be novel when it is different from all previous inventions (called "prior art") in one or more of its basic elements. When deciding whether an invention is novel for purposes of issuing a patent, the PTO will consider all prior art that existed as of the date the inventor files a patent application on the invention, or if necessary, as of the date the inventor can prove he or she first built and tested the invention, or conceived the invention and then followed up with diligence by building and testing it or filing a patent application. (It may be necessary to look to one of these earlier dates when two or more inventors are fighting over who's entitled to a patent, because U.S. patents are awarded to the first inventor.) An invention will flunk the novelty test if it was described in a published document or put to public use more than one year prior to the date the patent application was filed (this is known as the one-year rule).

d. Nonobviousness

In addition to being novel, an invention must be nonobvious to qualify for a patent. An invention is considered nonobvious if someone who is skilled in the particular field of the invention would view it as an unexpected or surprising development. In deciding whether an invention is non-obvious, the PTO may consider all previous developments in the field (called "prior art") that existed when the invention was conceived. As a general rule, an invention is considered nonobvious when it does one of the following:

- solves a problem that people in the field have been trying to solve for some time
- does something significantly faster than was previously possible, or
- performs a function that could not be performed before.

EXAMPLE: In August 1996, Future Enterprises invents a portable high quality virtual reality system. A virtual reality engineer would most likely find this invention to be truly surprising and unexpected. Even though increased portability of a computer-based technology is always expected in the broad sense, the specific way in which the portability is accomplished by this invention would be a breakthrough in the field and thus nonobvious.

Predicting whether an invention will be considered nonobvious by the PTO is difficult because it is such a subjective exercise —what one patent examiner may consider surprising, another may not. In addition, the examiner will usually be asked to make the nonobviousness determination well after the date of the invention, because of delays inherent in the patent process. The danger of this type of retroactive assessment is that the examiner may unconsciously be affected by the intervening technical improvements. To avoid this, the examiner generally relies only on the prior-art references that existed as of the date of invention.

EXAMPLE: In 1999, Future Enterprises' application for a patent on the 1996 invention is being examined in the Patent and Trademark Office. Assume further that by 1999, portable virtual reality units are to be found in every consumer electronics store for $200. The patent examiner will have to go back to the time of the invention to fully appreciate how surprising and unexpected it was when it was first conceived, and ignore the fact that in 1999 the technology of the invention is very common.

4. How to Obtain a Patent

There is no such thing as an automatic patent through creation or usage of an invention. To obtain patent protection, an inventor must file an application (with the appropriate filing fees) and be issued a patent. To apply for a U.S. patent, the inventor must file an application with a branch of the U.S. Department of Commerce, known as the U.S. Patent and Trademark Office (PTO). A U.S. patent application typically consists of:

- an explanation of why the invention is different from all previous and similar developments (the "prior art")
- a detailed description of the structure and operation of the invention (called a patent specification) that teaches how to build and use the invention
- a precise description of the aspects of the invention to be covered by the patent (called the patent claims)
- all drawings that are necessary to fully explain the specification and claims
- a statement under oath that the information in the application is true, and
- the filing fee.

In addition, small inventors often include a declaration asking for a reduction in the filing fee.

Provisional Patent Applications

Often inventors want to have a patent application on file when they go out to show their invention to prospective manufacturers because it will discourage rip-offs. Also, inventors like to get their invention on record as early as possible in case someone else comes up with the same invention. To accomplish both these goals an inventor may file what is known as a Provisional Patent Application (PPA). The PPA need only contain a complete description of the structure and operation of an invention and any drawings that are necessary to understand it—it need not contain claims, formal drawings, a Patent Application Declaration (a statement under penalty of perjury that everything in the application is true) or an Information Disclosure Statement (a statement of all prior art known to the applicant). The PPA isn't examined when filed. Instead, it sits in a PTO file and is examined only if the inventor files a regular patent application on the same invention within a one-year period and the applicant wishes to claim the earlier filing date. (An inventor would need to claim the earlier date only if prior art surfaced after the PPA's filing date but before the filing date of the regular application, or if a patent application for the same invention was filed by another inventor and the PTO had to decide which applicant should get the patent.)

a. Patent examinations

When the PTO receives an application, a patent examiner is assigned to it. Because a patent grants the inventor a monopoly on the invention for a relatively long period of time (between 14 and 17–19 years depending upon the invention), patent applications are rigorously examined. Typically the application process takes between one and three years.

The examiner is responsible for deciding whether the application meets all technical requirements, whether the invention qualifies for a patent and, assuming it does, what the scope of the patent should be. Typically, a patent application travels back and forth between the applicant and the patent examiner until an agreement is reached. Then, the applicant pays a patent issue fee and receives an official copy of the patent, and the PTO issues a patent deed.

To keep a patent in effect, three additional fees must be paid over the life of the patent. At present, the total patent fee for a small inventor, from application to issue to expiration, is well over $3,000. For large corporations, it is twice this amount.

b. Multiple applications for the same invention

If the patent examiner discovers that another pending application involves the same invention, and that both inventions appear to qualify for a patent, the patent examiner will declare that a conflict (called an interference) exists between the two applications. In that event, a hearing is held to determine who is entitled to the patent.

Who gets the patent depends on such variables as who first conceived of the invention and worked on it diligently, who first built and tested the invention and who filed the first provisional or regular patent application. Because of the possibility of a patent interference, it is wise to document all invention-related activities in a signed and witnessed inventor's notebook, so that you can later prove the date the invention was conceived and the efforts taken to build and test the invention or quickly file a patent application.

5. Enforcing a Patent

Should you receive a software-based patent, your program and its unique, novel approach cannot be used by others without your permission. In other words, independent creation, which is sufficient to beat a claim that a copyright or trade secret has been infringed, isn't good enough to defend against a charge of patent infringement. As long as you patent it first, it's yours and yours alone for up to 20 years.

However, patents are not self-enforcing; and the U.S. government will not help you enforce yours. Patents are a little like hunting licenses. If someone uses your invention as described in your patent without your permission you have the right to sue them in federal court. Patent suits are among the most expensive of all forms of litigation.

However, the potential rewards can be enormous if a patent suit is successful (treble damages may be recovered in the case of willful infringement).

It is very common for a company or person accused of patent infringement to agree to license (pay for the use of) the invention rather than face the uncertainties and expenses of litigation. However, some accused infringers elect to fight and seek to have the patent overturned in court. Many software experts believe that the Patent Office has issued a number of software-related patents that should have been rejected on grounds of failure to satisfy the nonobviousness test. Such patents are particularly likely to be subject to court challenge.

6. Patent Duration and Expiration

Patent protection usually ends when the patent expires. For utility patents, the statutory period is 20 years after the date of the regular patent application. Thus, for Example, if it takes two years to obtain a patent after the application is filed, you would have 18 years of effective patent protection.

For design patents, the statutory period is 14 years from date of issuance. For patents filed before June 8, 1995, the patent term is 20 years from date of filing, or 17 years from date of issuance, whichever period is longer.

A patent may expire if its owner fails to pay required maintenance fees. Usually this occurs because attempts to commercially exploit the underlying invention have failed and the patent owner chooses to not throw good money after bad.

Finally, patent protection will end if a patent is found to be invalid. This may happen if someone shows that the patent application was insufficient, that the applicant committed fraud on the PTO (usually by lying about or failing to disclose the applicant's knowledge about prior art that would legally preclude issuance of the patent), or that the inventor engaged in illegal conduct when using the patent—such as conspiring with a patent licensee to exclude other companies from competing with them.

Once a patent has expired for any reason, the invention described by the patent falls into the public domain: it can be used by anyone without permission from the owner of the expired patent. The basic technologies underlying television and personal computers are good Examples of valuable inventions that are no longer covered by in-force patents.

The fact that an invention is in the public domain does not mean that subsequent developments based on the original invention are also in the public domain. Rather, new inventions that improve public domain technology are constantly being conceived and patented. For instance, televisions and personal computers that roll off today's assembly lines employ many recent inventions that are covered by in-force patents.

B. Patents for Software

Ten or 15 years ago there was no apparent reason for a software developer to worry about software patents. Only a tiny number of highly specialized patents had ever been issued on software innovations. The general legal view was that software innovations weren't patentable, because software technology itself did not appear to fit comfortably within any of the patentable subject matter groups discussed in Section A3 above. All this has changed. Thousands of software and software-related patents have now been issued and thousands more are in the application stage.

1. Brief History of Software Patents

When first faced with applications for patents on software-based inventions in the 1950s, the United States Patent and Trademark Office (PTO) routinely rejected the applications on the grounds that software consists of mathematical algorithms (that is, a series of mathematical relationships, like differential equations). Mathematical algorithms were considered a law of nature, or "pure thought." Patents cannot be granted for a law of nature or mental process. For Example, no one can legally have a patent on the use of "1 + 1 = 2" because it would create too huge (and fundamental) a monopoly. Thus, software by itself was considered to be non-patentable.

However, in 1981 the Supreme Court held that an algorithm may be patentable if it works in connection with a specific apparatus—that is, a physical structure of some type—and is described that way in the patent claims (the precise statements in the patent application that describe the parameters of the invention). *Diamond v. Diehr*, 450 U.S. 171 (1981).

The *Diamond v. Diehr* decision cleared the way for patentability of software-based inventions. Nevertheless, there continued to be great controversy and uncertainty about when software could be patented. The PTO in particular, was opposed to software patents and adopted a restrictive view of what software was patentable. Several applicants who were denied software-related patents by the PTO appealed to the federal courts and won reversals of the PTO's rejections. As a result, the PTO has changed its practices. In early 1996, it adopted a detailed set of "Examination Guidelines for Computer Related Inventions," designed to give guidance both to applicants and patent examiners about when software is patentable and how to obtain such patents. Some think the guidelines are still too restrictive and will be challenged in court. But at least it is far clearer now than it has ever been when a software patent is obtainable.

A copy of the PTO Software Guidelines may be downloaded from the PTO's Website at www.uspto.gov/web/offices/com/hearings/software/analysis/computer/html.

2. When Software Is Patentable

Software itself—that is, computer code by itself—is not considered statutory subject matter. In other words, it's not patentable. For this reason, patents don't issue on software itself; rather, they issue on inventions that use software to produce a useful result —that is, "software-based" inventions. The term "software patent" is somewhat confusingly used to describe these software-based inventions.

Under the PTO's Software Guidelines, software-based inventions that require activity outside the computer most easily qualify for patent protection. These inventions often involve software connected to and running hardware components. The essence of these inventions is found in the functional combination of their software and hardware.

> **EXAMPLE:** A software program calculates the time needed to cure a certain type of rubber in a certain type of mold, and then directs the mold to open when the curing is completed.

Patents are also obtainable for software-based inventions that involve feeding information into a computer and acting on that information so as to transform it into instructions that produce a specific action by the computer—or by a machine linked to the computer—that in turn produces a useful result.

EXAMPLE: Raw information from a heart monitoring device is fed into a computer. The software program analyzes the information according to a set of principles and causes the results of this analysis to be displayed in a format that shows whether the person is at risk for a heart attack.

Following are several examples of software-based inventions that have received patents.

The invention:

- operates a system of manufacturing plants (Deutch); controls and optimizes the operation of a system of multi-unit plants (oil refineries) at different geographic locations, where each plant has a different, unique cost function in producing the product,
- controls a computerized method and apparatus for curing molded rubber— (Diehr),
- translates between natural languages— #4,502,128 (Toma),
- determines boundaries of graphic regions on a computer screen— #4,788,438,
- governs removable menu windows on a computer screen— #4,931,783,

- generates and overlays graphic windows for multiple active program storage areas in the computer— #4,555,775,
- qualifies and sorts file record data in a computer— #4,510,567,
- compresses and manipulates images in a computer— #4,622,545,
- handles the data structure and search method for a database management system— #4,468,728,
- automates spelling error corrections— #4,355,471—as in some form of a spell-checker system,
- sets up a securities brokerage–cash management system— #4,346,442,
- evaluates geological formations traversed by a borehole— #4338,664,
- operates a system that valuates stocks, bonds and other securities— #4334,270,
- automatically makes a two-dimensional portrayal of a three-dimensional object (Bernhart); specifically, it transforms a 2-D drawing of an object into a computer-presentable 3-D drawing—in the simplest case, a box would be transformed into a cube,
- sets up an information storage and retrieval system— #4,068,298—system allows information to be stored on a hard drive and retrieved by multiple users at different locations,
- measures the performance of a general purpose digital computer— #3,644,936, and
- analyzes electrocardiographic signals in order to determine certain characteristics of heart function— #4,422,459.

Design Patents

In some instances, software inventors can apply for what is known as a design patent. A design patent provides a 14-year monopoly to industrial designs that have no functional use. That is, contrary to the usefulness rule discussed just above, designs covered by design patents must be purely ornamental. The further anomaly of design patents is that while the design itself must be primarily ornamental, as opposed to primarily functional, it must at the same time be embodied in something people-made. For example, you can't get a design patent on rock dug up from the ground. In patent terms, the design has to be embodied in an "article of manufacture." This "article" can, however, be something non-functional, like a doll or a decorative water fountain. Design patents have also been obtained for computer interface icons—for example, in 1988 Xerox Corporation obtained 22 design patents for various icons including an icon for a virtual floppy disk.

3. Should You Apply for a Software Patent?

The fact that your software-based innovation may qualify for a patent doesn't necessarily mean that you should apply for one. There are several reasons to hesitate.

a. Most software is not patentable

As discussed above, an invention must be both novel and nonobvious to qualify for a patent. Nonobviousness means it would have been surprising or unexpected to someone who is familiar with the field of the invention. It's likely that the great majority of software lacks any elements that can pass this test.

Although it may seem simplistic, it will help if you ask yourself whether seeing your program would cause other knowledgeable computer programmers or software developers familiar with your field to ooh and aah. If the answer isn't a resounding yes, your code is probably not sufficiently innovative and therefore not patentable.

b. By the time you get a patent your invention may be worthless

It generally takes two to three years to obtain a software-based patent. Given the incredible pace of change in the software industry, your software-based invention may be obsolete and worthless by the time you receive your patent. For a patent to add real value to your business, you need to feel confident that the invention you are patenting will not soon be out-dated by newer technology.

c. Patents on software-based inventions are suspect

Because the United States Patent and Trademark Office (PTO) has had problems deciding what kinds of software really are patentable, patents on software-based inventions are suspect. The fact that the PTO issues a patent doesn't mean the patent is valid. It only means that a particular examiner has decided that a patent should issue on your invention. If you should later go to court to enforce the patent, the infringer may be able to successfully prove that the patent never should have issued in the first place. In other words, a judge can (and often does) second guess the patent examiner and—assuming your adversary appeals—an appellate judge can second guess the first judge.

This second-guessing routine, which is potentially a problem for all patents, is especially troublesome for patents on software-based innovations. This is primarily because the PTO lacks both sufficient personnel who are qualified to examine software-related applications and comprehensive information about previous software developments (the prior art in this particular field).

Simply, it's well known that many software patents have been and continue to be improperly issued. The fact that you get a patent on your software may be little more than an invitation to spend piles of money on lawyers and courts in an unsuccessful effort to enforce it against attacks on its validity.

On a more positive note, however, the issuance of the PTO's Software Guidelines should lead to more consistency in PTO practices. Also, if your patent ends up in court, it is presumed to be valid until your adversary proves the opposite—a bit like a person accused of a crime being presumed innocent.

d. Only the powerful (or very determined) can play the patent game

Seeking and then enforcing a patent can cost a bundle. Therefore you will want to make a cost-benefit analysis, weighing the costs of obtaining and maintaining the patent over its up to 17–19-year life (several thousand dollars) against the probability that you really will be able to commercially profit from it.

As a general rule, seeking a software patent is unwise unless you are reasonably sure that your invention deserves a patent and at least one of the following is true:

- You are economically strong enough to fund patent litigation should the need for it arise (patent litigation is hellishly expensive because you must hire lawyers—commonly in excess of $100,000).
- You are stubborn and savvy enough to take time to understand how the patent system works and willing to do some or all of your own legal work (a good-sized hill to climb, but others have done it, with huge rewards).
- The innovation is sufficiently important to another company to cause it to come to terms with you if you have the patent (by purchasing your patent rights or paying you for a license to use the innovation).
- You own a lot of patents and are a big enough player in the industry to wheel and deal with other patent holders by trading them the right to use your patents in exchange for your being able to use theirs.

- You know your idea will change the course of a particular field, and without a patent on it you risk forfeiting the credit and profit from the idea to others, who may then obtain their own patent and freeze you out.
- You think the patent will impress prospective financial backers that your business really is special (venture capitalists have been known to tell start-ups to come back and see them after they have obtained a patent).
- You are looking ahead to possibly selling your business and want to increase its value.

4. What to Do if You Want to Apply for a Software Patent

As the above discussion illustrates, the subject of software patents is an exceedingly complex one, beyond the competence of most lawyers, let alone lay people. There are two things you should do if you're really serious about obtaining a software-based patent:

- Obtain a copy of *Patent It Yourself,* by David Pressman (Nolo Press), and read it. This will give you an excellent grounding in the entire patent process and help you deal with your patent attorney.
- Seek out a patent attorney who has not only applied for software-based patents, but has actually obtained them. Most patent attorneys have no experience with software—make sure

you find one who does. Your attorney will prepare the patent application and deal with the PTO examiner. An experienced patent lawyer is particularly helpful when it comes to drafting your patent claims—that is, the legal definition of your invention. This is an arcane art that can be particularly difficult when it comes to software. If you don't think your software-based invention is valuable enough to pay several thousand dollars in fees to a patent attorney, forget about obtaining a software-based patent.

Beware of the One-Year Rule. Under what is called the one-year rule, an invention must be filed within one year of the time it is first offered for sale or commercially or publicly used or described. Otherwise, the invention will be considered no longer novel at the time the application is filed and therefore unpatentable. File your patent application as soon as possible but in any event no later than one year after the invention has become known to the public in some way. As a general rule, the limited testing of software by the public in a structured beta test program should not start the one-year period running. But the year period might start running if the beta test release were widespread enough, or if one of the testers posted it on a widely accessed bulletin board or website and as a result it became well known. In any event, you are always better off to assume the worst and get your patent application in as soon as possible. ■

Chapter 9

Trademarks and Software

Trademarks help a software company carve out a distinct and recognizable identity in the highly competitive and rapidly changing software industry. Trademarks like *Lotus* and *WordPerfect* have become well-established in the public's mind and help the companies that own them continually dominate their markets despite the introduction of competing products. A well-known trademark can be just as valuable as a copyright or patent, if not more so.

This chapter provides a brief overview of what you need to know about trademarks and Internet domain names—which often double as trademarks. But for step-by-step guidance on all important aspects of selecting and protecting a trademark, turn to *Trademark: How to Name a Business and Product*, by Kate McGrath & Stephen Elias (Nolo Press).

A. What Are Trademarks and Service Marks?

A trademark is a distinctive word, phrase, logo, graphic symbol or other device that is used to identify the source of a product and to distinguish a manufacturer's or merchant's products from anyone else's. Some examples are IBM computers and Microsoft software.

A service mark fulfills the same function as a trademark, but for a company's services rather than a particular product. For example, America Online provides a service and AOL is therefore a service mark. The same law applies to both service marks and trademarks, and in this chapter we use the term trademark to refer to both types of marks.

In the trademark context, "distinctive" means unique enough to reasonably serve as an identifier of an underlying product or service in the marketplace. The more distinctive a trademark is, the more legal protection it will receive from the courts and the better job it will do of identifying the goods or services it's being used for.

A trademark can be more than just a brand name or logo. It can include other non-functional but distinctive aspects of a product or service that tends to promote and distinguish it in the marketplace, such as shapes, letters, numbers, sounds, smells or colors.

The word "trademark" is also a generic term used to describe the entire broad body of state and federal law that covers how businesses distinguish their products and services from the competition. Each state has it own set of laws establishing when and how trademarks can be protected. There is also a federal trademark law called the Lanham Act (15 U.S.C. 1050 et seq.), which applies in all 50 states. Generally, state trademark laws are relied upon for marks used only within one particular state, while the Lanham Act is used to protect marks for products that are sold in more than one state or across territorial or national borders. As commerce grows on the Web, so does the number of trademarks that are national in scope and therefore subject to the Lanham Act.

1. Trade Names

A trade name is the formal name of a business or other organization. For example, Apple Computer Inc. and Lotus Development Corp. are trade names. A trade name is used to identify a business for such purposes as opening bank accounts, paying taxes, ordering supplies, filing lawsuits and so on. However, a trade name may become a trademark when it is used to identify individual products (or services) sold in the marketplace. Businesses often use shortened versions of their trade names as all or part of a trademark; a good example is the trademark *Lotus 1-2-3*.

Trade names, whether the name of a corporation, partnership or sole proprietorship, must be registered with appropriate state or local authorities. Each state has its own business license requirements requiring that trade names be registered with city, county or state offices. (For more information, see *Trademark: How to Name a Business and Product*, by Kate McGrath & Stephen Elias (Nolo Press), Chapter 3.)

2. Trademarks Compared With Copyrights and Patents

Trademarks coexist with copyrights and patents and may protect different aspects of the same work.

a. Copyright law

Copyright law provides software programmers and other creators of expressive works such as writers, artists, photographers and musicians the exclusive right to control how their works are used. Copyright protects any type of work of authorship including software of all types, writings, music, artwork, photos, movies and videos.

Copyright does not, however protect names, titles or short phrases; these are covered by trademark law. Copyright law and trademark law most commonly intersect in advertising copy. The trademark laws protect the product or service name or logo, any distinctive slogans used in the advertising, and the distinctive features associated with the name or logo, such as its color or lettering style. The copyright laws protect any additional literal expression that the ad contains, such as the artwork and overall composition of the ad.

Copyright law and trademark law also meet on occasion in regard to graphic designs used as logos. Trademark law protects the aspect of the logo that is used as a trademark, while copyright law protects the creativity in the design. This means that a similar design can't be used as a trademark by anyone else when customer confusion would result (trademark law) and even absent customer confusion the identical design can't be used without the design owner's permission (copyright law). See Chapter 3 for a more detailed discussion of copyright law.

b. Patent law

By filing for and obtaining a patent from the U.S. Patent and Trademark Office, an inventor is granted a monopoly on the use and commercial exploitation of his or her invention for a limited time. A patent may protect the functional features of a machine, process, manufactured item, composition of matter, ornamental design or asexually reproduced plants. A patent also protects new uses for any such items. However, to obtain a patent, the invention must be novel and nonobvious.

Trademarks or service marks consisting of words, logos or slogans are not patentable no matter how creative they are. However, it is sometimes possible to get a design patent on the ornamental aspects of a functional device as long as the ornamental aspects are merged with—that is, inseparable from—the device itself. In some situations the feature that is covered by the design patent may also be protected as trade dress (see Section H). See Chapter 8 for a detailed discussion of patents.

B. Trademark Ownership

For most purposes, the "owner" of a trademark doesn't have a total monopoly on the use of the mark. Rather, the owner has the legal right to prevent others from using the mark in such a way as to cause confusion about the products or services the owner provides, or about their origins. (See Section G.) However, if the trademark is famous enough, the owner can prevent other uses even if no customer confusion would result. (See Section G1.)

As a general rule, the first user of a trademark owns it. There are two ways to qualify as a first user:

- by being the first to actually use the trademark on products or to market a service
- by applying to register the trademark on the federal principal trademark register (See Section D4) on the grounds that you intend to use it in the future (if you do actually use it later, your date of first use will be considered to be the date of your application).

The fact that a mark is not registered or that a registration is canceled or not renewed does not affect the basic ownership of the mark, which is primarily based on use. However, additional remedies provided by federal registration will not be available to the owner if an infringement occurs. (See Section D1.)

There is no outside time limit on how long trademark ownership can last. However, ownership rights end if a mark is abandoned. Abandonment commonly occurs when:

- a mark is not used over an extended period of time
- a mark's owner fails to protest the unauthorized use of the mark by others, or
- a mark's owner authorizes others use of the mark without adequate supervision of how it is used.

In each of these instances, the connection between the mark and the product or service it was originally intended to identify may become so weak that the mark no longer is entitled to protection.

Ownership of a mark also ceases if the mark becomes generic—that is, the mark becomes so widely used as a synonym for the underlying product or service that it no longer is able to distinguish one product or service from another. (See Section C1c.)

C. Selecting a Trademark

Not all trademarks are treated equally by the law. As mentioned, the best trademarks are "distinctive"—that is, they stand out in a customer's mind because they are inherently memorable. The more distinctive a trademark is, the "stronger" it will be and the more legal protection it will receive. Less distinctive marks are "weak" and may be entitled to little or no legal protection. Obviously, it is much better to have a strong trademark than a weak one.

For some reason, software companies often do a very poor job in selecting their trademarks and end up using weak marks that will be difficult or impossible to enforce. Companies that use weak trademarks often throw away the chance to develop a very valuable asset. Examples of poorly chosen marks include:

- personal names, including nicknames, first names, surnames and initials
- marks that describe the attributes of the product or service or its geographic locations—for example, marks such as *Quick Mail* and *Spreadsheet 2000* are initially legally weak and not exten-

sively protectible until they have been in use long enough to be easily recognized by customers, and

- names with bad translations, unfortunate homonyms (sound-alikes) or unintended connotations—for example, the French soft drink called *Pschitt* had to be renamed by the U.S. market.

Generally, selecting a mark begins with brainstorming for general ideas (possibly with the aid of a professional name consultant or a name-generating computer program). After several possible marks have been selected, the next step is often to use formal or informal market research techniques to see how the potential marks will be accepted by consumers. Next, a "trademark search" is conducted. This means that an attempt is made to discover whether the same or similar marks are already in use. (See Section F.)

An excellent book to aid you in the process of coming up with strong trademarks is *The Name's the Thing*, by Henri Charmasson, published by Dow Jones-Irwin, Homewood, Ill. 60430. It's a thorough and beautifully written analysis of the art and science of creating effective commercial names.

Some computer software programs may also be helpful when brainstorming possible business, product or service names, although they may cost too much for a one-time naming process. A few are listed below. Call the companies for the current price and other details.

The NameStormers
4347 W. N.W. Highway
Suite 1040
Dallas, TX 75220-3864

They provide a comprehensive name consultation service, called NameStorming, and sell two name-generating computer programs that help you name products, services or corporations in a variety of ways. *Namer*® (DOS platform) costs $195 and *NamePro* (Windows) costs $495. The service, which is individually tailored, costs $5,500.

IdeaFisher Systems Inc.
2222 Martin St., #110
Irvine, CA 92715
800-289-4332

This software company produces *Idea Fisher*, a "concept thesaurus" in a database that can generate ideas, associations or connotations for use in naming businesses, marketing products and any other creative activity that uses free-associated ideas. You can follow an initial concept through a hierarchy of linked ideas and images to arrive at a list of related names. It also allows you to walk through a set of questions and answers that deal specifically with naming businesses, products or services. The product costs between $39.95 and $89.95, depending on your needs and the type or size of business.

1. What is a Distinctive Trademark?

Certain types of marks are deemed to be inherently distinctive and are automatically entitled to maximum protection. Others are viewed as not inherently distinctive and can be protected only if they acquire "secondary meaning" through use.

a. Inherently distinctive marks

Arbitrary, fanciful or coined marks are deemed to be inherently distinctive and are therefore very strong marks. These are words and/or symbols that have absolutely no meaning in the particular trade or industry prior to their adoption by a particular manufacturer for use with its goods or services. After use and promotion, these marks are instantly identified with a particular company and product, and the exclusive right to use the mark is easily asserted against potential infringers.

Fanciful or arbitrary marks consist of common words used in an unexpected or arbitrary way so that their normal meaning has nothing to do with the nature of the product or service they identify. For example, the trademark *Lotus 1-2-3* in no way describes any aspect of a computer spreadsheet program. Other examples of arbitrary/fanciful marks include *Peachtree Software* and *Apple Computer*. Coined words are words made up solely to serve as trademarks. Examples in the computer field include the marks *Zeos*, *Intel* and *Zilog*.

Suggestive marks are also inherently distinctive. A suggestive mark indirectly describes the product it identifies but stays away from literal descriptiveness. That is, the consumer must engage in a mental process, to associate the mark with the product it identifies. For example, the trademark *WordPerfect* indirectly suggests word processing, as does *Word*. *PageMaker* indirectly suggests desktop publishing. *CrossTalk* suggests communication between different computers.

b. Descriptive marks

Descriptive marks are not considered to be inherently distinctive. They are generally viewed by the courts as weak and thus not deserving of much, if any, judicial protection unless they acquire a "secondary meaning" —that is, become associated with a product in the public's mind through long and continuous use.

There are three basic types of descriptive marks:

- Marks that directly describe the nature or characteristics of the product they identify—for example, the mark *Quick Mail* used for an electronic mail program, *Calendar Creator* for a calendar program, or *ChessMaster* for a computer chess game.
- Marks that describe the geographic location from which the product emanates—for example, *Oregon Software*.
- Marks consisting primarily of a person's last name—for example, *Norton Utilities*.

A mark that is in continuous and exclusive use by its owner for a five-year period is presumed to have acquired secondary meaning and qualifies for registration as a distinctive mark.

> EXAMPLE 1: Pinnacle Software, Inc., develops and markets a desktop publishing program called "Self-Publisher." This name is clearly descriptive of the nature of the product. However, over time, and with the help of an advertising campaign the name loses its sole

meaning as a description and instead becomes associated with the Pinnacle program.

EXAMPLE 2: *Norton Utilities*, which started out descriptive, by now has acquired a secondary meaning and is distinctive for that reason.

c. Generic marks

A generic mark is a word or symbol that is commonly used to describe an entire category or class of products or services, rather than to distinguish one product or service from another. Generic marks are in the public domain and cannot be registered or enforced under the trademark laws. Words and phrases that are inherently generic in the software field undoubtedly include: "software," "computer," "mouse," "crt," "cpu," "floppy disk," "hard disk," "modem," "ROM," "RAM," "dot matrix," "menu," "pull-down menu," "footprint," "laptop" and "icon."

D. Federal Trademark Registration

A trademark is federally registered by filing an application with the United States Patent and Trademark Office (PTO) in Washington, D.C. The PTO keeps two lists of registered trademarks along with their owners, dates of registration and other information. These lists are called the principal register and the supplemental register.

Registration is not mandatory; under both federal and state law, a company may obtain trademark rights in the parts of the country in which the mark is actually used. However, placement of a mark on the federal register (especially the principal register) provides important protections that make registration worthwhile. It is placement on this register that is usually meant by the phrase "federally registered."

1. Advantages of Registration

Placement of a mark on the principal register provides many important benefits. These include:

- The mark's owner is presumed to have the exclusive right to use the mark nationwide.
- Everyone in the country is presumed to know that the mark is already taken (even if they haven't actually heard of it).
- The trademark owner obtains the right to put an "®" after the mark (see Section E).
- Anyone who begins using a confusingly similar mark after the mark has been registered will be deemed a willful infringer. This means that the trademark owner can collect large damages and thus afford to file an infringement lawsuit.
- The trademark owner obtains the right to make the mark "incontestable" by keeping it in continuous use for five years. This substantially reduces others' ability to legally challenge the mark on

grounds it's insufficiently distinctive to warrant protection.

2. Marks Qualifying for Registration on the Principal Register

To qualify for registration on the principal register, a mark must actually be used in commerce (but not solely within one state's borders) and be sufficiently distinctive to reasonably operate as a product identifier.

However, a mark will not qualify for registration on the principal register if it is:

- confusingly similar to an existing federally registered trademark
- consists primarily of a surname or geographical name, unless the mark has become well known over time or unless the geographical name is used in an arbitrary or evocative way
- the name of a living person without his or her consent, the U.S. flag or other government insignias.

3. How to Register

The registration process involves filling out a simple application, paying an application fee ($245, current in October 1997) and being willing to work with an official of the PTO to correct any errors that he or she finds in the application.

Once the PTO receives a trademark registration application, it determines the answers to these questions:

- Does the application have to be amended (because of errors) before it can be examined?
- Is the mark the same as or similar to an existing mark used on similar or related goods or services?
- Is the mark on a list of prohibited or reserved names?
- Is the mark generic—that is, does the mark describe the product or service itself rather than its source?
- Is the mark descriptive—that is, does it consist of words or images that are ordinary or that literally describe one or more aspects of the underlying goods or services?

When the PTO can answer all of these questions in the negative, it will publish the mark in the Official Gazette (a publication of the U.S. Patent and Trademark Office) as being a candidate for registration. Existing trademark and service mark owners may object to the registration by filing an opposition. If this occurs, the PTO will schedule a hearing to resolve the dispute. Even if existing owners don't challenge the registration of the mark at this stage, they may later attack the registration in court if they believe the registered mark infringes one they already own.

If there is no opposition the PTO will place the mark on the list of trademarks known as the principal register.

If a mark consists of ordinary or descriptive terms (that is, it isn't considered distinctive), it may be placed on a different list of trademarks and service marks known as the supplemental register. Placement of a mark on the supplemental register produces significantly fewer benefits than those offered by the principal register, but still provides notice of ownership and allows you to use the ® symbol, itself a powerful deterrent against use of the mark by others. Also, if the mark remains on the supplemental register for five years—that is, the registration isn't canceled for some reason—and also remains in use during that time, it may then be placed on the principal register under the secondary meaning rule (secondary meaning will be presumed).

4. Intent to Use Registration

If you seriously intend to use a trademark on a product in the near future, you can reserve the right to use the mark by filing an intent to use registration. If the mark is approved, you have six months to actually use the mark on a product sold to the public and file papers with the PTO describing the use (with an accompanying $100 fee). If necessary, this period may be increased by five additional six-month periods if you have a good explanation for each extension

The ownership vests (becomes effective) when the mark is put in use and the application process is complete, but ownership will be deemed to have begun on the date the ITU application was filed.

You should promptly file an intent to use registration as soon as you have definitely selected a trademark for a forthcoming product. Your competitors are also trying to come up with good trademarks, and they

may be considering using a mark similar to the one you want.

 For step-by-step guidance on how to register a trademark, refer to *Trademark: How to Name a Business and Product*, by Kate McGrath & Stephen Elias (Nolo Press), Chapter 8.

E. Trademark Notice

The owner of a trademark that has been placed on either the principal register or supplemental register of the U.S. Patent and Trademark Office (PTO) is entitled to use a special symbol along with the trademark. This symbol notifies the world of the fact of registration. Use of trademark notices is not mandatory, but makes it much easier for the trademark owner to collect meaningful damages in case of infringement. It is also a powerful deterrent against use of the mark by others.

The most commonly used notice for trademarks registered with the PTO is an "R" in a circle—®—but "Reg. U.S. Pat. & T.M. Off." may also be used. The "TM" superscript—™—may be used to denote marks that have been registered on a state basis only or marks that are in use but which have not yet officially been registered by the PTO.

Although only marks that are federally registered can use the "®" symbol, any business that uses a mark can place the "™" symbol after it to publicly claim ownership of the mark. The "™" mark has no legal significance other than to notify the public that the mark owner views the words, design and/or symbol as a protectible trademark. It also may serve as evidence against a claim of innocent infringement by a junior user and thus enhance the possibility of collecting damages.

F. Trademark Searches

A mark you think will be good for your product could already be in use by someone else. If your mark is confusingly similar to one already in use, its owner may be able to sue you for trademark infringement and get you to change it and even pay damages. (See Section G.) Obviously, you do not want to spend time and money marketing and advertising a new mark, only to discover that it infringes on another preexisting mark and must be changed. To avoid this you should do a trademark search or hire someone to do a search for you.

A trademark search is a systematic hunt for the existence of any registered or unregistered trademark or service mark that:

- is the same or similar to a mark proposed for use by the business initiating the search
- is being used anywhere in the country (or world if the proposed mark is to be used internationally), and
- is being used in a context that would likely result in customer confusion if the proposed mark is also put into use.

1. Types of Trademark Searches

Whether you decide to do your own trademark search or hire some one to do it for you, you will immediately encounter trademark lingo that describes several different kinds of searches. Some are more thorough and expensive than others. Here is what you need to know:

- **A direct hit federal trademark register search.** This search compares your mark with identical or very similar federally registered (and pending) marks in one or more of the classes set up by the U.S. Patent and Trademark Office. This type of search is the quickest, cheapest and most minimal ("shallowest" in trademark speak) search you can do.
- **An analytical search of federal and state registered and pending marks.** This type of search compares your mark with all registered and pending marks (both federal and state) that sound or look like your mark, plus all marks that mean the same or in some other way might lead to customer confusion between them and your mark. This type of search is more thorough, or "deeper," than a direct hit search, and consequently more expensive and time-consuming.
- **A common law search.** This search examines white and Yellow Pages, trade directories, corporate and business databases and so forth for all commercial uses of similar names in

specified geographical areas. This type of search, in addition to the other searches, is appropriate when you want to make sure that your proposed mark doesn't conflict with an unregistered mark.

- **A comprehensive trademark search.** This type of search hunts for all possibly relevant unregistered marks (the common law search) as well as for federal and state registered (and pending) trademarks.

Resources Examined in a Trademark Search

A trademark search may involve looking for similar marks on some or all of these resources, depending on the scope of the search:

- **The federal trademark register:** a list of all trademarks and service marks that have been authorized for federal trademark registration.
- **Pending trademark applications:** a list of all trademarks and service marks for which a federal registration application has been filed.
- **State trademark registrations:** a list of all trademarks and service marks that have been registered at the state level (usually with a state's Secretary of State).
- **Publications containing relevant product and service names:** Trade magazines, print directories of commercial names, Yellow Pages and electronic databases containing product and service names that are in use in the U.S. generally, or in respect to specific fields such as computers, biotechnology and bicycles.
- **The Internet:** domain names, World Wide Websites and goods and services being offered on the World Wide Web.

2. Hiring a Search Firm

Traditionally, most trademark searches were conducted by specialized trademark search firms at the behest of trademark attorneys who were handling the trademark registration process. Even today, some of the largest trademark search firms refuse to conduct searches for anyone but a lawyer. But most search firms aren't so choosy and will conduct a search for anyone willing to pay them.

The Role of Attorneys in Trademark Searches

If you decide to hire a trademark attorney to advise you on the choice and registration of a trademark or service mark, the attorney will be able to arrange for the trademark search. Some attorneys do it themselves, but most farm the search out to a search firm, the same as they've always done. Once the report comes back from the search firm, the attorney will interpret it for you and advise you on whether to go ahead with your proposed mark. Although you are getting considerably more in this attorney package than you'll get from a search service, it will cost you.

The services provided by various trademark search firms, and the fees they charge for different types of searches, vary considerably. Often the cost of the service will depend on how much massaging of the information is done before it is delivered to you. Generally, the more raw the data you receive, the cheaper it will be. Only attorneys are allowed to offer opinions about potential trademark conflicts, and as a result, trademark search services offered by attorneys tend to cost the most because they come with legal advice.

Next to hiring a trademark attorney, paying a trademark search firm is the most expensive means of clearing your mark. However, except for a direct hit search—which you can reliably do yourself—a search service is likely to provide more reliable results than you will produce on your own. There are several reasons for this. Most importantly, analytical and common law searches come with a considerable learning curve, regardless of which database or resources are being used. Searching for possible conflicts is a kind of art form that involves a lot more than typing in a word or phrase and asking whether it appears on the source being searched.

Firms that search (but do not give legal advice) generally charge as follows:

- direct hit search (for identical marks)—from $30 to $100 per mark searched.
- analytical federally registered trademark search (for similar or related marks)—from $85 to $300 per trademark.

- common law search only—from $100 to $200 per mark searched.
- comprehensive search (combining analytical federal, state and common law)—between $185 and $500 per mark searched.

The difference in rates may reflect variations in the coverage of the search, the sort of report you get, the experience of the searchers or simply economies of scale. On the other hand, some firms may advertise an unusually low price to draw in customers, but then add on charges that end up exceeding another firm's total price (a professional version of bait-and-switch). For example, does one fee cover the whole cost, or is there also a per-page charge for the report? Obviously, to sensibly shop you need to know the total cost of each service.

You can find a trademark search firm by:

- looking in the Yellow Pages under trademark consultants or information brokers
- consulting a legal journal or magazine, which will usually contain ads for search firms, or
- doing an Internet search.

3. Doing a Search Yourself

Many resources are available to enable you to do all or part of a trademark search yourself. However, if you only want to search for one mark, it may be that the cost in terms of time alone will favor using a trademark search service.

a. Using a Patent and Trademark Depository Library (PTDL)

There are 80 Patent and Trademark Depository Libraries (PTDLs) throughout the country, mostly located at major public or academic libraries. The U.S. Patent and Trademark Office publishes a federal trademark database called *Cassis* (on CD-ROM), available to the public for free at most PTDLs. The *Cassis* trademark list is a good way to search for a direct hit. It is also possible to use *Cassis* to do an analytical trademark search.

If you are computer-challenged, or the wait to use the PTDL *Cassis* work station is too long for comfort, every PTDL has print materials that also let you search the federal registered trademark database.

Using a Patent and Trademark Depository Library (PTDL) to do your own federal trademark search involves the least cash outlay, but will cost you in time and transportation expenses unless you live or work close to one.

A list of PTDLs is contained on the CD-ROM forms disk at the end of this book under the file name PTDLLIST. See Chapter 1 for instructions on how to use the forms disk.

b. Using the internet to do your own trademark search

The Internet now offers access to a database derived from *Cassis* for a reasonable fee. Owned by a company called

Micropatent [www.micropatent.com], this database offers unlimited online searching of the federal trademark register for a 24-hour period for $20. If you are adequately prepared, you can get an awful lot accomplished in 24 hours. This is potentially the cheapest way to search, especially if you wish to conduct a direct hit search for two or more prospective marks. You can best prepare by downloading the help file and studying it before starting your search. Micropatent's online help tells you how to save the help file and your search results to your hard disk.

The Micropatent database contains all active trademark registrations and pending applications filed with the United States Patent and Trademark Office, as well as inactive registrations and applications for recent years. The database is updated weekly.

The Micropatent interface is very user-friendly and the help is written in plain English. You should be up to speed in less than 15 minutes, a small bite out of your 24 -hour window of opportunity.

You may also use the Internet to search for unregistered marks. You can use a variety of search engines to find out whether your proposed mark appears anywhere on the Internet and if so in what context. Probably the best way to get started is to use the Alta Vista [www.altavista.digital.com] or Excite [www.excite.com] search engines. Run your mark through the Yellow Pages and through the general purpose search boxes that these services provide. If the list

you get back is too long, pare it down by adding some additional search terms to limit the search.

Another useful Internet search tool is the Commercial Sites Index, a central index for Websites representing commercial businesses. You may access this index by typing http://www.directory.net. Simply enter the name of the product or service that you're looking for and you will obtain a list of sites that have such products or services. This may give you an indication of some names or marks in use that are the same or similar to the one you propose to use.

If you are interested in finding out whether your proposed mark is already in use as an Internet domain name, you can access the InterNIC Directory, which, as explained in Section I4, is the site where domain names are determined. If you are using a Web browser, type http://www.internic.net. The InterNIC directory can be used to find domain names (which may assist in searching for trade names or common law service marks). From the home page, select the link to Network Solutions, Inc., Registration Services. In the search field, enter the trade name (usually followed by ".com") such as sony.com.

Finally, The Thomas Register of goods and services is now available on the Internet at http://www.thomasregister.com.

c. Online subscription services

Two private subscription-based companies, Dialog and CompuServe, offer access to the TrademarkScan database (owned by

Thompson & Thompson) that lists federal and state and some international trademarks (including Canada, the U.K. and Japan). These are available through subscription to the service and can be accessed through a computer and modem.

Using the TrademarkScan database can produce a reliable analytical search of registered trademarks, assuming you conquer the trademark search learning curve. However, the cost of doing your own search on CompuServe or Dialog is likely to be higher than the lowest cost trademark search services

d. Purchasing CD-ROMs to search

The PTO offers two CD-ROMs good for trademark searching: one for pending applications and one for registered marks. These are the same CD-ROMs as are available in the PTDLs described in Section 3a. Each costs $300, which includes bi-monthly updates for one year. If you have a fair amount of trademark searching to do, it may be worth your while to purchase these products. For more information on how to order them, call 1-800-PTO-9199.

The TrademarkScan database of federal and state trademarks is also available on CD-ROMs from the Thompson & Thompson company. A subscriber to a CD-ROM service receives periodic updates to the database. There are two disadvantages to using CD-ROMs. Unless you are doing large numbers of searches, the cost is prohibitive. Second, the discs are not updated as regularly as the online services. The advantage of using a CD-ROM is that there is no cost per search.

Only if you are doing large numbers of federal trademark searches, should you acquire CD-ROMs.

For more on trademark searches, refer to *Trademark: How to Name a Business and Product,* by Kate McGrath & Stephen Elias (Nolo Press), Chapters 5 and 6.

G. Enforcing Trademark Rights

Depending on the strength of the mark and whether and where it has been registered, a trademark owner may be able to bring a court action to prevent others from using the same or similar marks on competing or related products.

Trademark infringement occurs when an alleged infringer uses a mark that is likely to cause consumers to confuse the infringer's products with the trademark owner's products. A mark need not be identical to one already in use to infringe upon the owner's rights. If the proposed mark is similar enough to the earlier mark to risk confusing the average consumer, its use will constitute infringement.

Determining whether an average consumer might be confused is the key to deciding whether infringement exists. The determination depends primarily on whether the products or services involved are related (that is, sold through the same marketing channels), and, if so, whether the marks are sufficiently similar to create a likelihood of consumer confusion.

If a trademark owner is able to convince a court that infringement has occurred, he or she may be able to get the court to order the infringer to stop using the infringing mark and to pay monetary damages. Depending on whether the mark was registered, such damages may consist of the amount of the trademark owner's losses caused by the infringement or the infringer's profits. In cases of willful infringement (infringement occurring where the infringer is aware of the existence of the infringed mark—which is presumed if the infringed mark was on the federal principal trademark register), the courts may double or triple the damages award.

> **EXAMPLE:** AcmeSoft develops a computer program designed to automate the manufacture of widgets. AcmeSoft markets the program under the name "Widgeteer." AcmeSoft registers this descriptive mark with the U.S. Patent & Trademark Office. One year later, Badd Software, Inc., markets a widget manufacturing program under the name "Widgeter." AcmeSoft sues Badd for using a mark confusingly similar to its own on a similar product. AcmeSoft is able to convince a judge that a substantial number of consumers are being confused by Badd's use of the "Widgeter" mark. The judge orders Badd to stop using the mark on its widget manufacturing programs and awards AcmeSoft damages for willful infringement.

A trademark owner must be assertive in enforcing its exclusive rights. Each time a mark is infringed upon it loses strength and distinctiveness and may eventually become so common as to lose its protection. (See Section C1c, above.)

1. Trademark Dilution

Dilution means the lessening of the capacity of a famous mark to identify and distinguish goods or services, regardless of the presence or absence of:

- competition between the owner of the famous mark and other parties, or
- likelihood of confusion, mistake or deception.

Dilution is therefore different than trademark infringement because trademark infringement always involves a probability of customer confusion whereas dilution can occur even if customers wouldn't be misled. For example, if Fred starts selling a line of sex aids named "Microsoft," no consumer is likely to associate Fred's products with the original Microsoft. However, because *Microsoft* has become such a strong and famous mark, the use of the word on sex aids would definitely trivialize the original *Microsoft* mark (dilute its strength by tarnishing its reputation for quality or blurring its distinctiveness).

Until 1996 there was no federal law against trademark dilution. And only about half the states provided some recourse— usually an injunction against further use of the mark. In January 1996, however, the Federal Trademark Dilution Act of 1995 was signed into law. (15 USC §1125(c).) As with the state statutes, this new federal law applies only to famous marks, and provides primarily for injunctive relief (a court order requiring the infringing party to stop using the mark). However, if the famous mark's owner can prove the infringer "willfully intended to trade on the owner's reputation or to cause dilution of the famous mark," the court has discretion to award the owner attorney's fees and defendant's profits as well as actual damages.

While it is still possible to sue for dilution under a state statute, it is expected that most actions to stop dilution will now be brought under the new federal law. One possible exception to this may be if the use of the famous mark also tarnishes its reputation. For example, in the *Microsoft* sex aid example, the association of "Microsoft" with sex aids may fairly be said to detract from the dignity of the *Microsoft* mark (there is little room for humor in the commercial world). Under state statutes, an action may be brought for tarnishment as well as dilution whereas the federal act does not speak to tarnishment at all, although many observers believe that the courts will interpret the statute to include it as a basis for relief.

H. Trade Dress Protection

The overall appearance and image of a product or its packaging is known as its "trade dress." Trade dress may include product shapes, designs, colors, advertising and graphics, and, under the law, may be treated in the same manner as a more traditional trademark.

As with other types of trademarks, trade dress can be registered with the PTO, and receive protection from the federal courts. To receive protection:

- the trade dress must be inherently distinctive, unless it has acquired secondary meaning (becomes associated with a product in the public's mind through long and continuous use), and
- the subsequent use of the trade dress by another person or entity (called the junior user) must cause a likelihood of consumer confusion.

For trade dress to be considered inherently distinctive, one court has required that it "must be unusual and memorable, conceptually separable from the product and likely to serve primarily as a designator of origin of the product." (*Duraco Products Inc. v. Joy Plastic Enterprises Ltd.*, 40 F.3d 1431 (3d Cir. 1994).)

Functional aspects of trade dress cannot be protected under trademark law. Only designs, shapes or other aspects of the product that were created strictly to promote the product or service are protectible trade dress.

Trade dress protection can be important to software developers and publishers in three ways:

- It can be used to protect the distinctive design of the packaging used to sell software.

- Some trademark experts believe that trade dress protection may be available for graphical user interfaces (GUIs). As discussed in Chapter 5, little or no copyright protection is available for GUIs, so trade dress may be the only way to protect them. However, no court has yet ruled that such protection is available.
- Trade dress protection may also be available to protect the nonfunctional and distinctive design of Web pages.

This is a very complex area of trademark law. If you wish to seek trade dress protection for a GUI, you should obtain guidance from an experienced trademark lawyer.

I. Trademarks and the Internet

As you probably know, the Internet is a computer network that allows near-instantaneous communication between computers anywhere in the world. Unlike the telephone, or fax, the Internet allows the transmission of digital files which can be read by computers to produce software, text, photographs, graphics, sounds, videos and movies. The World Wide Web adds to the Internet by providing an appealing graphical interface which makes it much easier to get around and that, for businesses and consumers, has become a powerful new type of "Yellow Pages" extending to all parts of the country and many parts of the world.

Today, virtually all software publishers have a presence on the World Wide Web.

Consumers can download demo versions of software, pay for and download entire software packages and download updates and bug fixes. By all accounts the Web will be the software marketing channel of the future, and anyone who wants to do business will have to join up and create their own Web pages.

The first trademark issue to arise when you create a Web page has to do with the name you give your Website—called an Internet domain name. If you choose a domain name that is the same or similar to a business name that is already in use as a trademark anywhere in the country (in physical or virtual space), you are courting a trademark infringement dispute and possible lawsuit.

An excellent resource for keeping abreast of the legal developments associated with conflicts between domain names and trademarks is an article prepared by attorneys Sally M. Abel and Marilyn Tiki Dare titled *Trademark Issues in Cyberspace*. The authors have posted this article on the Fenwick and West Website at www.fenwick. com, and periodically update it to account for new developments. Other articles about this issue can be found through the online trademark resources described in Chapter 18.

1. What is a Domain Name?

Every business on the Web has what's called a domain name—a unique "address" that computers understand. Most World Wide Web business addresses consist of two main sections. Consider this Web address: http://www.nolo.com. The first section (http://www) tells the computer that it is looking for a site on the World Wide Web. You will find this section in virtually every Web address, although increasingly the "www" is omitted. The second section (nolo.com) is the domain name. The domain name itself consists of two parts. The ".com" portion is termed a top level domain name (TLD) while the "nolo" section is termed a second level domain name (SLD).

The reason the .com part is called a top level domain is that the World Wide Web has been organized, for the purpose of U.S. participants, into five broad categories:

- com (for commercial groups)
- edu (for educational institutions)
- gov (for governmental institutions)
- org (for nonprofit organizations), and
- net (for interactive discussion groups).

The reason the nolo part is called a second level domain is that the name denotes one of the approximately 600,000 unique identifiers that is part of the .com top level domain. The fact that all businesses in the U.S. who want to do business on the Web have had to operate under one domain, the .com domain, has given rise to enormous trademark-related problems. To reduce the pressure placed on existing top level domain names, an International Ad Hoc Committee created by the Internet Society has come up with a plan to add seven new TLDs:

.firm, for businesses or firms;

.store, for businesses selling goods;

.web, for entities emphasizing activities involving the World Wide Web;

.arts, for entities emphasizing cultural and entertainment activities;

.rec, for entities emphasizing recreational entertainment;

.info, for sites offering information services; and

.nom, for sites supported by individuals.

These new top level domain names are expected to be available for assignment by the end of 1997.

2. Domain Names as Trademarks

As a general rule, domain names can qualify as trademarks if they are being used to market underlying products or services being offered on the Internet site. Domain names probably will be treated like any other mark in that they will be considered an infringement of an existing mark if:

- they conflict with the mark in way that creates the likelihood of customer confusion, or
- the existing mark is famous and the use of the domain name can be said to dilute its strength.

3. Clearing a Domain Name

Because each domain name must be unique—so that all the computers attached to the Internet can find it—it is impossible for two different businesses to have the same domain name. If somebody is already using a name you want, you won't be able to use it subject to some important exceptions discussed in Section 15a.

There are two ways to find out whether you will be able to use your proposed mark as a domain name. One is to buy a domain name search from Thompson & Thompson [http://ttdomino.thomson-thomson.com/]. The other is to do it yourself by visiting Tabnet on the World Wide Web [www. tabnet.com]. Tabnet not only lets you search to see whether your name is available, but also provides information about the registrant if it turns out that someone got there ahead of you. Selling domain names is a cottage industry; they go for about $2,000. So if you are set on a particular name but find that you are blocked, you may want to try to negotiate a sale.

4. Registering a Domain Name

Domain names are reserved for your use alone by registering the name with a domain name clearinghouse organization called Network Solutions, Inc. (NSI). Once a domain name is registered with NSI, no one else can use it for the same purpose.

Domain names are like trade names in that they identify business entities. And like trade names, they can also function as trademarks or service marks by identifying the source of goods or products. Like trade names, domain names are registered. And, like trade names, a domain name registration does not guarantee trademark status. For instance, even if you are first to register the domain name Ixas (as in Ixas.com), which gives you the exclusive right to that domain name on the Internet, you can't necessarily use it as a trademark or service mark, either on or off the Internet. That will depend on a different set of principles and facts—basically, whether someone else has used Ixas first as a mark and whether your use of that term as a mark in reference to your products or services would likely create customer confusion.

There are two ways to register your name:
- use Tabnet (www.tabnet.com) to do it for you (for $50 plus the registration fees),
- get help from your Internet service provider, or
- do it yourself.

If you choose to do it yourself, the first step to registering a domain name is to acquire "operational name service." This is usually done by signing on with an Internet service provider (ISP). These providers are companies that connect to the Internet and can be located in the Yellow Pages or in computer magazines. An Internet provider can also help with the registration of your domain name with the NSI.

The domain name application can be obtained electronically. However, you will have to be familiar with the Internet in order to connect and locate it at ftp://rs. internic.net. You will find the application file (domain-template.txt) located in the template library. The file includes instructions on completing the application. Registration used to be free, but the explosive volume of domain registrations has resulted in a registration fee of $100. This charge covers the $50 maintenance fee for two (2) years. After the two-year period, an invoice will be sent on an annual basis.

The NSI application requires you to certify that:

- the information you provide in the application is true
- you intend to use the domain name, and
- your use of your domain name will not infringe an existing trademark or violate any other law.

The NSI makes it clear that registering a domain name does not confer any legal rights to that name and any disputes between parties over the rights to use a particular name are to be settled between the contending parties using normal legal methods. Equally important, the applicant agrees to be bound by the terms of NSI's current domain name policy ("Policy Statement") which is at ftp://rs.internic.net/policy/internic/internic-domain-1.txt.

NSI's Days Are Numbered

The contract between NSI and the National Science Foundation expired in 1997. A major reorganization of how domain names get registered was in the works when this book went to press, but details of the changes had not yet emerged. Most likely, however, NSI will no longer be the sole registrar of domain names in the U.S., but rather will be one of many registries. Also expected is a new administrative procedure under which domain name disputes can be resolved without the need to file a lawsuit.

---

5. Disputes Involving Domain Names

The entity responsible for assigning domain names (NSI) does not check to see if a requested domain name violates an existing trademark. It is only concerned with whether the name is already taken as a domain name. In short, whether or not you are assigned the domain name you request says nothing about whether it will conflict with an existing trademark—that is, whether it is the same or similar to a famous mark or is likely to cause customers to confuse your site with the business or products carrying the existing mark.

If you do pick a domain name that creates a trademark conflict, several outcomes are possible:

- If your domain name prevents the owner of a registered trademark from using its mark as its domain name, the owner of the registered mark may be able to cause your domain name to be deregistered (you can't use it anymore).

- If your domain name is the same or similar to an existing famous mark, the mark's owner may file a lawsuit preventing any further use of your domain name, even if customers wouldn't likely be confused by its use.

- If your domain name conflicts with any existing mark that is being used in a way that would likely lead to customer confusion between your business or products and those offered by the mark's owner, you may be forced to stop using the name and possibly be liable for large damages if your infringement is judged to be willful.

a. The role of NSI in domain name conflicts

Much of the flak about domain name conflicts has been directed at Network Solutions, Inc. (NSI), the organization that—under a contract with the National Science Foundation—is responsible for handling domain name registrations.

NSI registers domain names on a first come first served basis. If and when a business decides to do business on the Web and discovers that it can't because its name is already being used as a second level domain name, it typically files a complaint with NSI demanding that NSI reassign the domain name to it, the name's rightful owner.

In response to these demands, NSI has developed a policy that is periodically updated and that basically works this way (as of November 1997):

- A business may challenge a domain name registration by showing that it (the challenging business) owns a registered U.S. or foreign trademark or service mark in the identical second level domain name.

- NSI then allows the domain name registrant to show either that 1) its domain name registration has priority over the trademark registration or 2) the domain name registrant has its own federal or foreign trademark registration.

- If the registrant can establish priority, it will be allowed to continue using the disputed domain name. If the registrant can't establish the earlier date, it will be required to come up with a different name. In the meantime, NSI will place the disputed name onto a "hold" status, where it is not available to anyone, until the outcome of the dispute has been settled. ■

Chapter 10

International Software Protection

According to the Business Software Alliance (an industry trade association), U.S. publishers hold 75% of the global market for prepackaged software and about 60% of the market for custom software and software-related services. Obviously, American software developers and publishers need to be concerned about protecting their products abroad.

Most foreign countries provide at least some legal protection for software; and, because of recently enacted international trade agreements discussed below, the level of international copyright protection for software is growing. This doesn't mean that international software piracy isn't a major problem, far from it. But the overall picture is improving.

The topic of international software protection is an exceedingly complex one. This chapter probably won't answer all your questions, but it should help you when you see a computer attorney for specific legal assistance.

A. Copyright Protection

There is no single body of international copyright law. Each country has its own copyright law that applies within its own borders. Thus, the protection afforded to software and other copyrighted works by the U.S. copyright laws ends at the United States borders. However, through a series of international treaties and trade agreements, almost all nations have agreed to give each other's citizens at least the same copyright protection they afford to their own citizens and to provide certain minimum protections for copyrighted works in general and software in particular.

As a result, whenever you create any software that is entitled to copyright protection in the U.S. you automatically receive copyright protection for the software in almost all the countries of the world. There is no need to file an application to obtain copyright protection in a foreign country—unlike the requirement for foreign filings to obtain patent and trademark protection in other countries. International copyright protection is automatic, free and essentially painless.

This section first discusses the five major international copyright and trade treaties providing for international copyright protection and then covers copyright protection for software in Western Europe, Canada and Japan.

The following chart show which of the world's nations are members of the most important of these treaties.

Members of Berne Convention, U.C.C. and GATT

Country	Berne Convention	U.C.C.	GATT	Country	Berne Convention	U.C.C.	GATT
Albania	✔			Cyprus	✔	✔	✔
Algeria		✔		Czech Republic	✔	✔	✔
Andorra		✔		Denmark	✔	✔	✔
Argentina	✔	✔	✔	Dominican Republic	✔	✔	✔
Armenia		✔		Ecuador	✔	✔	
Australia	✔	✔	✔	Egypt	✔		✔
Austria	✔	✔	✔	El Salvador	✔	✔	✔
Azerbaijan		✔		Fiji	✔	✔	✔
Bahamas	✔	✔		Finland	✔	✔	✔
Bahrain			✔	France	✔	✔	✔
Bangladesh		✔	✔	Gabon	✔		✔
Barbados	✔	✔	✔	Gambia	✔		✔
Belarus		✔		Germany	✔	✔	✔
Belize		✔	✔	Ghana	✔	✔	✔
Benin (Dahomey)	✔			Greece	✔	✔	✔
Bolivia	✔	✔	✔	Guatemala		✔	✔
Bosnia	✔	✔		Guinea-Bissau	✔		
Botswana			✔	Haiti		✔	✔
Brazil	✔	✔	✔	Honduras	✔		✔
Burkina Faso	✔		✔	Hungary	✔	✔	✔
Bulgaria	✔	✔		Iceland	✔	✔	✔
Burundi			✔	India	✔	✔	✔
Cambodia		✔		Indonesia			✔
Cameroon	✔	✔	✔	Ireland	✔	✔	✔
Canada	✔	✔	✔	Israel	✔	✔	✔
Central African Republic	✔		✔	Italy	✔	✔	✔
Chad	✔		✔	Jamaica	✔		✔
Chile	✔	✔	✔	Japan	✔	✔	✔
China	✔	✔	✔	Jordan	✔	✔	
Colombia	✔	✔	✔	Kazakhstan		✔	
Costa Rica	✔	✔	✔	Kenya	✔	✔	✔
Côte d'Ivoire	✔		✔	Korea (South)			✔
Croatia	✔	✔		Kuwait			✔
Cuba		✔	✔	Laos		✔	

Members of Berne Convention, U.C.C. and GATT (continued)

Country	Berne Convention	U.C.C.	GATT	Country	Berne Convention	U.C.C.	GATT
Lebanon	✔	✔		Portugal	✔	✔	✔
Lesotho	✔			Romania	✔		✔
Liberia	✔	✔		Russia	✔	✔	
Libya	✔			Rwanda	✔	✔	✔
Liechtenstein	✔	✔		Senegal	✔	✔	✔
Lithuania	✔			Singapore			✔
Luxembourg	✔	✔	✔	Slovakia	✔	✔	
Madagascar	✔		✔	Slovenia	✔	✔	✔
Malawi	✔		✔	South Africa	✔		✔
Malaysia		✔	✔	Spain	✔	✔	✔
Maldives			✔	Sri Lanka	✔	✔	✔
Mali	✔		✔	Suriname	✔		✔
Malta	✔	✔	✔	Sweden	✔	✔	✔
Mauritania	✔		✔	Switzerland	✔	✔	✔
Mauritius	✔		✔	Tanzania			✔
Mexico	✔	✔	✔	Thailand	✔		✔
Moldova		✔		Tobago	✔	✔	✔
Monaco	✔	✔		Togo	✔		✔
Morocco	✔	✔	✔	Tunisia	✔	✔	✔
Mozambique			✔	Turkey	✔		✔
Namibia	✔		✔	Turkmenistan		✔	
Netherlands	✔	✔	✔	Uganda			✔
New Zealand	✔	✔	✔	Ukraine		✔	
Nicaragua		✔	✔	United Kingdom	✔	✔	✔
Niger	✔	✔	✔	United States	✔	✔	✔
Nigeria	✔	✔	✔	Uruguay	✔	✔	✔
Norway	✔	✔	✔	Uzbekistan		✔	
Pakistan	✔	✔	✔	Vatican City	✔	✔	
Panama		✔		Venezuela	✔	✔	✔
Paraguay	✔	✔	✔	Yugoslavia	✔	✔	
Peru	✔	✔	✔	Zambia	✔	✔	✔
Philippines	✔		✔	Zimbabwe	✔		✔
Poland	✔	✔	✔				

1. The Berne Convention

The world's first major international copyright convention was held in Berne, Switzerland, in 1886. The resulting agreement was called the Berne Convention for the Protection of Literary and Artistic Works, or the Berne Convention for short. One hundred countries have signed the Berne Convention, including almost all major industrialized countries. These countries include the United States (as of March 1, 1989), most of western Europe, Japan, Canada, Mexico and Australia. (See the chart above for a complete list of Berne member countries.)

The basic protections for literary, artistic and scientific works under the Berne convention are discussed below.

a. Principle of national treatment

Every country that has signed the Berne Convention must give citizens or permanent residents of other Berne countries at least the same copyright protections that it affords its own nationals; this is known as national treatment. As a U.S. citizen or permanent resident, any protectible work you create or publish after March 1, 1989 (the date the U.S. joined the Berne Convention), is entitled to national treatment in every country that has signed the Berne Convention.

EXAMPLE: AmeriSoft, a U.S. software developer, creates a German-English translation program. AmeriSoft publishes the program both in the U.S. and Germany. AmeriSoft subsequently discovers that unauthorized copies of the program are being made and sold by a small German publisher. Since the U.S. and Germany have both signed the Berne Convention, if AmeriSoft sues the German publisher for copyright infringement in the German courts, it will be entitled to the same treatment as any German citizen who brought such a suit.

b. No formalities

No formalities, such as notice and registration, may be required by a Berne country for basic copyright protection. However, some Berne countries offer greater copyright protection if a copyright is registered or carries a particular type of notice. For example, in Japan and Canada (as well as in the U.S.), registration provides a means of making your work a public record and may thus be helpful in case of an infringement action (see discussion in Sections 7 and 8 below). Other countries have certain procedural requirements that must be followed before foreign works may be distributed within their borders, such as customs rules, censorship requirements or other regulations. Compliance with these types of formalities should be taken care of by a foreign attorney or agent hired by a software publisher.

c. Minimal protections required

Every Berne country is required to offer a minimum standard of copyright protection in their own country to works first published or created by nationals of other Berne countries. This protection must include:

- Copyright duration of at least the author's life plus 50 years
- Authorization for governmental seizure of infringing goods as a remedy for copyright infringement
- Granting authors the following exclusive rights in their works:
  - translation,
  - performance in public,
  - broadcasting their works,
  - reproducing their works,
  - motion pictures, and
  - creating adaptations and arrangements from a protected work
- The granting of moral rights to authors. Moral rights are rights an author can never transfer to a third party because they are considered an extension of his or her being. Briefly, they consist of the right to:
  - claim authorship,
  - disclaim authorship of copies,
  - prevent or call back distribution under certain conditions, and
  - object to any distortion, mutilation or other modifications of the author's work injurious to her reputation

    The right to prevent colorization of black and white films is an example of a moral right. Moral rights are generally of most concern to visual artists and, despite the Berne Convention requirement, are not recognized in the U.S. except for artists.

- Some provision allowing for fair dealing or free use of copyrighted works. This includes material used in quotations for educational purposes, for reporting current events, and so forth. (In the United States, this is called fair use, and is discussed in detail in Chapter 5.)

The Berne Convention and Works Created Before March 1, 1989

As mentioned earlier, the United States was a latecomer to the Berne Convention. It did not join until March 1, 1989. The Berne Convention does not apply to a work first published in the U.S. before that date unless the work was also published in a Berne country at the same time (that is, within 30 days of each other). This is called simultaneous publication. Before 1989, American book publishers (and some software publishers) often had their works published simultaneously in the U.S. and Canada and/or Great Britain (both Berne countries) so that they could receive the protection of the Berne Convention. This fact was usually indicated on the same page as the work's copyright notice.

2. The Universal Copyright Convention

Another important international copyright treaty is the Universal Copyright Convention (U.C.C.). The United States joined the U.C.C. on September 16, 1955; it applies to all works created or originally published in the U.S. after that date. Where a country has signed both the U.C.C. and Berne Conventions, the Berne Convention has priority over the U.C.C. Since the U.S. has joined the Berne Convention, the U.C.C. is relevant to works by American nationals only (1) in countries that have signed the U.C.C. but not the Berne Convention (about 20 countries in all, most notably Russia and South Korea); and (2) to works first published in the U.S. before March 1, 1989, that were not simultaneously published in a Berne country.

The U.C.C. is very similar to the Berne Convention. It requires member countries to afford foreign authors and other copyright owners national treatment. The U.C.C. also requires that each signatory country provide adequate and effective protection of the rights of foreign authors and other foreign copyright owners of literary, scientific and artistic works.

Unlike the Berne Convention, the U.C.C. does not require member countries to dispense with formalities as a prerequisite to copyright protection. But an author or copyright owner of a work first published in one U.C.C. country can avoid complying with another U.C.C. country's formalities (registration, deposit, payment of fees, etc.) simply by placing the following copyright notice on all published copies of the work: © [Your name] [Date of first publication]. Compliance with the U.S. requirements for a valid copyright notice discussed in Chapter 4 also constitutes compliance with the U.C.C. notice requirement. This is one very good reason to always affix a valid copyright notice to your published work.

3. The WIPO Copyright Treaty

The Berne Convention was last revised in 1971, and neither it nor the U.C.C. specifically provided for copyright protection for software or digital technologies. A copyright convention discussing protection for such technologies was held in 1996 by the World Intellectual Property Organization (WIPO), a United Nations agency headquartered in Geneva, Switzerland, that is responsible for administering the various international intellectual property treaties.

In late 1996 the U.S. and several other countries signed the WIPO Copyright Treaty (WCT). The WCT has yet to be ratified by the U.S. Senate and has not yet taken effect. However, approval seems likely. The treaty requires no significant changes in U.S. copyright law.

The WCT has also been signed by Belgium, Bolivia, Burkina Faso, Chile, Finland, Germany, Ghana, Greece, Hungary, Indonesia, Israel, Italy, Kazakhstan, Kenya, Luxembourg, Monaco, Mongolia, Namibia, Nigeria, Spain, Togo, the United Kingdom, Uruguay and Venezuela.

a. Protection for digital works

As written, existing international copyright agreements protect authors by giving them the right to control the production and distribution of physical copies. But, of course, there are no physical copies on the Internet and digital networks. By far the most significant aspect of the WCT is that it requires member countries to give copyright protection to works in digital form. This means, for example, that unauthorized copying of a program posted on a Website can constitute copyright infringement.

b. Software protections

The WCT provisions concerning software are very similar to those already enacted as part of the GATT trade agreement. (See Section 4.) Specifically, the WCT provides that:

- Computer programs are protected by copyright as literary works within the meaning of the Berne Convention. (See Section A1.) Such protection applies to computer programs "whatever may be the mode or form of their expression." This means that both source code and object code are protected as literary works.
- In addition, the WCT gives software owners the right to prohibit the commercial rental of their works to others. However, this does not apply "where the program itself is not the essential object of the rental"—for example, one may rent a car that includes a computer program.

- The WCT also requires member countries to provide effective legal remedies against anyone who removes or alters electronic Rights Management Information (RMI) from copyrighted digital works—that is, electronically stored information regarding who owns the copyright in a digital work.

4. International Trade Agreements: GATT and NAFTA

The Berne Convention, U.C.C. and WIPO Copyright Treaty all sound good on paper. The problem with them, however, is they have few enforcement teeth. Because of this serious inadequacy, important protections for intellectual property, particularly software, were included in two international trade agreements: the GATT and NAFTA.

a. GATT and intellectual property rights

The General Agreement on Tariffs and Trade is called GATT for short. GATT is a multinational treaty signed by 117 nations dealing with tariffs and other international trade matters. It is, quite simply, the most important international trade agreement in history. Most of the world's trading nations are parties to GATT, including the U.S. GATT was ratified by the U.S. Senate in 1994.

For our purposes, what is most important about GATT is that it includes a special agreement on intellectual property called

Trade Related Aspects of Intellectual Property Rights (TRIPS for short). TRIPS requires each member country to agree, as a minimum, to enact national copyright laws giving effect to the substantive provisions of the Berne Convention discussed above. However, moral rights, which are generally not recognized in the U.S., were expressly left out of TRIPS. This means that the U.S. cannot be subject to GATT dispute settlement procedures over the scope of moral rights.

Specifically with respect to software, TRIPS:

- provides that computer programs (whether object code or source code) are literary works within the meaning of the Berne Convention and are therefore entitled to full copyright protection and national treatment in all Berne countries, and

- requires GATT member countries to grant software owners the right to prohibit commercial rental of their computer programs (except if the program is not an essential object of the rental—for example, the copyright owner of the computerized electronic system that controls many automobile functions could not prohibit car rentals because the car, not the computer program, is the object of the rental).

But, perhaps most important of all, TRIPS requires all GATT member countries to provide significant penalties for copyright infringement. These must include injunctive relief (including preliminary injunctions that can be obtained to stop infringing activities before trial) and adequate monetary damages. In addition, member countries must adopt procedures for excluding infringing software and other goods at their borders upon application by U.S. or other copyright owners to their customs services.

GATT also includes mechanisms for enforcement of country-to-country disputes regarding implementation of these requirements. The entity responsible for handling disputes under GATT is the World Trade Organization, a new international agency based in Geneva—similar to the World Bank. Special GATT remedies (for example, withdrawal of tariff concessions) may be imposed for violation of GATT rules.

The only bad thing about the GATT/TRIPS agreement from software publishers' point of view is that it will not take effect immediately in many countries. Developing countries and countries in transition from centrally planned to market economies (primarily countries that were part of the former Soviet Union or Warsaw Pact members) will not have to comply until the year 2000. What are termed "least developed countries," need not comply until 2006.

b. NAFTA

The North American Free Trade Agreement (NAFTA for short) was approved by Congress in November 1993 and became effective on January 1, 1994. As the name implies, NAFTA is a treaty between Canada, Mexico and the U.S. Its primary purpose is to eliminate tariffs and other trade barriers between the three countries. However, NAFTA also contains important provisions regarding intellectual property protection for software. These provisions are very similar to those of the GATT/TRIPS agreement above.

First, NAFTA provides that all types of computer programs are literary works within the meaning of the Berne Convention above, and requires each country to protect them as such. NAFTA provides for the unrestricted transfer of copyright rights by contract and protects licensees' rights.

Like the GATT/TRIPS agreement, NAFTA requires that adequate damages and injunctive relief be provided for copyright infringement. NAFTA also provides for criminal penalties in cases of willful software piracy on a commercial scale, including fines, imprisonment and seizure and/or destruction of infringing goods. (NAFTA Article 1717.)

Perhaps most importantly, member countries are required to enforce the rights granted under NAFTA at the border—that is, prevent the importation or export of infringing goods.

5. Protections in Countries Not Covered by Treaties

There are some countries that have not signed any of the copyright treaties discussed above and that are not a party to trade agreements such as GATT. These include some countries in which copyright piracy is widespread, such as Taiwan. The United States has entered into bilateral

(country-to-country) copyright treaties with some of these countries, including Taiwan, Indonesia and Singapore. Under these treaties, works by U.S. citizens are afforded copyright protection in the country involved. In addition, many countries afford foreign authors and their works copyright protection if the foreign author's country of origin provides similar treatment. This means it is possible for your work to be protected in a country that has not signed any of the multinational conventions or entered into a bilateral copyright treaty with the U.S.

However, some countries have no copyright relations with the U.S. and provide no protection for U.S. authors' works. These include Afghanistan, Bahrain, Bhutan, Ethiopia, Iran, Iraq, Mongolia, Nepal, Oman, Qatar, San Marino, Saudi Arabia, Sierra Leone, Tonga, United Arab Emirates and Yemen.

6. Software Protection in the European Community (EC)

The European Community (EC for short) comprises most of the nations of Western Europe, including Belgium, Denmark, France, Germany, Greece, Ireland, Italy, Luxembourg, the Netherlands, Portugal, Spain and the United Kingdom. The EC is in the process of being transformed into a single integrated market without internal frontiers in which the free movement of goods, services, people and capital will be ensured. The EC is the largest trading block in the world, with over 340 million consumers, and the largest market for software outside the U.S.

All EC countries are also members of the Berne Convention and GATT. U.S. software copyright owners are therefore entitled to the same copyright protection in an EC country as citizens of that country.

The EC is much like a supranational government, with its own parliament, courts and executive body. The EC passes and implements various types of legislation. In 1991, the EC adopted the Council Directive on the Legal Protection of Computer Programs (often referred to as the EC Software Directive). The purpose of the directive was to harmonize legal protection for software throughout the EC and provide computer software with a level of copyright protection comparable to that provided for such works as books, films and music recordings.

The EC Software Directive generally mirrors U.S. software copyright law; but there are a few differences which are noted below.

a. What is protected?

The directive mirrors U.S. law regarding what software is protected. It requires that all computer programs be protected as literary works within the meaning of the Berne Convention. So long as it is original—that is, the author's own intellectual creation—any program will be protected by copyright. Both source and object code are protected, as well as software embodied in semiconductor chips. Preparatory design materials—for example, specifications and flowcharts—are also protected. (EC Software Directive Art. 1(1).)

b. Scope of protection

As under U.S. law, protection applies only to the expression and not to the "ideas and principles which underlie any element of a computer program, including those which underlie its interfaces." (EC Software Directive Art. 1(2).) Whether, and to what extent, a program's look and feel and/or sequence, structure and flow will be protected is up to each EC country's courts.

c. Exclusive copyright rights

As under U.S. law, the owner of the copyright in a computer program has the exclusive right to:

- reproduce the program by any means
- translate, adapt, arrange or otherwise alter the program, and
- distribute the program to the public in any form. (EC Software Directive Art. 4.)

As under U.S. law, once a copy of a program is sold, the copyright owner loses all control over further distribution of that copy, except that the owner's permission must be obtained to rent or lease the program copy to the public.

Furthermore, in the absence of an express prohibition in a software license or other contract, a lawful owner of a program or a program copy may reproduce, translate or otherwise alter the program if necessary to use the program for its intended purpose or to correct program errors. For example, the user may load the program onto computer RAM for use in his computer. (EC Software Directive Art. 5(1).)

It is also permissible for a lawful user of a program to make a back-up copy of the program. (EC Software Directive Art. 5(2).)

d. Copyright ownership

Software copyright ownership under the directive mirrors U.S. law. The exclusive copyright rights in programs created by an employee "in the execution of his duties or following the instructions given by his employer" are owned by the employer unless otherwise provided by contract. (EC Software Directive Art. 2(3).)

Programs created by a number of individuals are jointly owned. (EC Software Directive Art. 2(2).)

The drafters of the directive omitted a provision which provided that the rights to a commissioned work automatically vest in the commissioning party. This means that a person or company that hires an independent contractor—that is, a nonemployee—to create software must enter into an agreement with the contractor to acquire his copyright rights. This is generally the same as under U.S. law.

e. Formalities

Unlike in the U.S., there is no system of copyright registration in the EC. It is not necessary for a copyright owner to comply with any formalities (copyright notice or registration) to obtain or maintain copyright protection within the EC. However, it is advisable to include a copyright notice on any published work distributed in the EC. Including a notice on your work ensures that it will be protected if it finds its way to a country that belongs to the U.C.C. but not the Berne Convention. There are about 20 such countries, most notably Russia.

f. Reverse engineering

Reverse engineering is the process of examining or taking apart a product to see how it works. This is permitted under U.S. copyright law and under the EC Software Directive. The directive seeks to aid standardization and interoperability of software, particularly computer interfaces. Therefore, the directive provides that a person having a right to use a copy of a computer program is entitled to "observe, study or test the functioning of the program" to understand its underlying principles and ideas. Such observation, study or testing is limited to the acts of normal use of the program— that is, it may be done while loading, displaying, running or storing the program. This provision does not permit any alteration or decompilation of the program. (EC Software Directive Art.5(3).) But see Section g just below.

g. Decompilation

Where reverse engineering alone does not provide sufficient information to "achieve the interoperability of an independently created computer program with other programs," the user may decompile the program under certain limited circumstances. Decompilation means using a decompiler to translate an object code copy of a program (which is unreadable by humans) into human-readable assembly language.

The question whether decompilation of software should be allowed was the most hotly debated issue during the deliberations over the directive. As enacted, the directive permits decompilation for the purposes of ascertaining sufficient information to permit the interoperability of hardware and software, but not to permit creation of competitive products.

Decompilation is allowed only if the following three conditions are met:

- First, decompilation of the code must be indispensable to obtain the interface information necessary to make software interoperable with the decompiled program. Therefore, such interface information must not have been readily available to the person wishing to make an interoperable program.
- Second, decompilation may be performed only by a person who has a license or some other right to use the software or a person acting on his behalf.
- Finally, decompilation is restricted to those parts of the original program necessary to achieve interoperability. This means that only the interface may be decompiled, not the entire program. (EC Software Directive Art. 6(1).)

The directive specifically bars information obtained from decompilation from being used for the development of competing substantially similar programs. Furthermore, such information cannot be given to others except when necessary for the inter-operability of an independently created program. (EC Software Directive Art. 6(2)(c).)

U.S. copyright law does not contain any counterpart to the EC Software Directive's limited decompilation right. However, U.S. courts have held that decompilation may be a fair use of a copyrighted program where it is necessary to gain access to elements of a program that are not protected by copyright—that is, ideas and other unprotected expression. (See Chapter 5.)

The upshot of all this is that U.S. companies that import software into the EC may find other companies decompiling their programs to create interoperable programs.

7. Software Copyright Protection in Japan

Japan accounts for about 20% of the worldwide computer market. It is a member of the Berne Convention and GATT. U.S. software copyright owners are therefore entitled to the same copyright protection in Japan as Japanese citizens.

a. Protection for software

Computer programs that are original or creative are expressly protected by the Japanese copyright law. Protection begins automatically upon creation. However, protection does not extend to programming languages, rules (an interface or protocol permitting one computer to interact with another), or algorithms. Both source code and object code are protected. (Japanese Revised Copyright Law, Arts. 2, 10.)

b. Exclusive rights

Under Japanese law a copyright owner has the exclusive right to reproduce, translate, adapt, perform or publicly exhibit the copyrighted work. The owner also has the exclusive right to rent copies of the work—that is, third parties cannot rent copies without getting the owner's permission. (Japanese Revised Copyright Law, Arts. 21-27.)

In addition, copyright owners are granted certain moral rights, these include the:

- right to make a work public—that is, to publish an unpublished work
- right to claim authorship—that is, the right to be recognized as author of a work and to determine the way the author's name should be used on a work or not to disclose the name
- right to integrity of one's work—that is, the right to prevent a work from being distorted, mutilated, or otherwise modified against the author's will. (Japanese Revised Copyright Law, Arts. 18-20.)

c. Exceptions to exclusive rights

Japanese law recognizes that the possessor of a copy of a computer program will often have to modify the program to get it to work on his computer. The owner of a copy of a program may make copies or adaptations of the program if and to the extent necessary for using use the program or protecting against its destruction. However, the owner must dispose of such copies if he transfers possession of the original copy of the program. (Japanese Revised Copyright Law, Arts. 20(2), 47.)

d. Software ownership

A work created by a single author is initially owned by that author. Works created by two or more authors are jointly owned. No single joint author may exercise the copyright rights in the joint work or transfer his ownership interest without the other joint authors' consent (which cannot be unreasonably withheld). (Japanese Revised Copyright Law, Art.65.)

A program created by an employee at the employer's instruction and within the scope of employment, is a work made for hire to which the employer owns the entire copyright, including any moral rights. (Japanese Revised Copyright Law, Art. 15.)

However, the Japanese work made for hire rule does not extend to works created by independent contractors. The copyright in a program created by an independent contractor is owned by the contractor unless the contractor transfers her rights to the hiring party. For this reason, companies hiring independent contractors in Japan to do programming should obtain an assignment of their copyright rights. Such an assignment should be in writing and contain a specific assignment of the rights to prepare and control derivative works (such rights are not transferred unless specifically indicated).

An independent contractor's moral rights, including the rights of integrity and authorship discussed above, may not be transferred or assigned to others. This means, for example, that an independent contractor-programmer could conceivably prevent a hiring firm from modifying software the contractor created for the firm, developing derivative works based upon it, or distributing it without identifying the contractor as the author, because such acts would violate his moral rights. To avoid this problem, hiring firms should obtain a contractor's affirmative consent in writing to carry out these and any other acts that might otherwise be barred by moral rights.

e. Formalities—copyright notice and registration

Since Japan is a Berne Convention signatory, it is not legally necessary to comply with any formalities to obtain or maintain a copyright. However, as in the United States, copyright notices are generally used on published works. Although not mandatory, a copyright notice prevents a defendant in an infringement suit from seeking to limit damages by arguing that the infringement was innocent.

Japan also has a nonmandatory copyright registration procedure. A special registry called the Program Register was established in 1986 for registration of computer programs. A foundation called the Software Information Center administers the Program Register. Registration provides certain evidentiary benefits in the event a copyright infringement suit is filed; for example, it establishes the date of creation and publication of the work. However, these benefits have rarely proved important in practice.

Copyright transfers may also be registered with the Copyright Register administered by the Director General of the Cultural Affairs Agency. It is important to register any assignment or transfer of copyright, since it will not be enforceable against any third party (that is, any person not covered by the transfer) unless it is registered. (Japanese Revised Copyright Law, Art. 77.)

f. Copyright infringement

A person who exercises any of an author's exclusive rights without the author's consent is guilty of copyright infringement. Japanese law specifically provides that a person who uses a pirated copy of a computer program is liable for copyright infringement if he or she was aware the copy was pirated. (Japanese Revised Copyright Law, Art. 113(2).)

Civil remedies for infringement include monetary damages, injunctions, seizure and destruction of infringing goods. Criminal penalties including imprisonment and fines may also be imposed on infringers.

8. Software Copyright Protection in Canada

Canada is a member of the Berne Convention, GATT and NAFTA. U.S. software copyright owners are therefore entitled to the same copyright protection in Canada as Canadian citizens.

a. Protection for software

Computer programs are protected as literary works so long as they are original and "expressed, fixed, embodied or stored in any manner." (Canadian Copyright Act, Sec. 2.) As under U.S. law, a minimum amount of creativity must have been required to create the software, but it need not be novel or inventive. It makes no difference whether a program is expressed as object or source code, or is embodied on computer chips, disks or any other form. Both application and operating system programs are protected.

b. Exclusive rights

A copyright owner has the exclusive right to reproduce, publish, adapt, translate or perform a protected work. (Canadian Copyright Act, Sec. 3(1).) In addition, Canadian law grants software authors certain "moral rights." These include the:

- right of integrity (permitting the software author to prevent modifications to software by the owner of a copy under certain circumstances), and
- right of paternity (the right to be recognized as author of the software). (Canadian Copyright Act, Sec. 5.)

c. Exceptions to exclusive rights

There are two important exceptions to a software copyright owner's exclusive rights:

- the owner of a copy of a program may alter or adapt it to the extent necessary for personal use, and
- the owner of a copy may make one copy of the program to serve as a back-up. (Canadian Copyright Act, Sec. 27(2).) Such copies must be destroyed if the copier ceases to be the lawful owner of the original program.

d. Software ownership

A work's author is its initial copyright owner. A work created by two or more authors is jointly owned by all of them. However, to qualify as a joint author, a person must contribute actual expression, not mere ideas. (Canadian Copyright Act, Sec. 13(1).)

Works created by employees within the course of employment are works made for hire to which the employer is considered the author and initial copyright owner. (Canadian Copyright Act, Sec. 13(3).)

However, the copyright in works created by independent contractors is owned by the contractor, not the hiring party. (*Goldner v. C.B.C.*, (1971) 7 C.P.R.(2d) 158 (Fed.Ct.).) This means that when a software consultant creates a program to a client's order, the consultant retains the copyright in the work and may recreate it and use it for other clients unless copyright is later transferred to the first client or such later use would violate any duty of confidentiality toward the client. As in the U.S., then, it is necessary for persons hiring Canadian independent contractors to create software to have them sign a written agreement transferring their copyright rights to the hiring party.

e. Copyright notice

Since Canada is a member of the Berne Convention, no formalities need be complied with to obtain copyright protection. It is not necessary to place a copyright notice. However, as discussed in Chapter 4, it is wise to do so anyway to obtain copyright protection in those countries that have signed only the U.C.C. copyright convention (notably, Russia and South Korea).

f. Copyright registration

Copyright registration is completely optional. Unlike in the U.S., it is not necessary to register to file a copyright infringement suit in Canada. The benefits of registration are much more limited than in the U.S. A person who registers a work in Canada receives a registration certificate from the Canadian Copyright Office. The certificate serves as evidence that your work is protected by copyright and that you—the person registered—are the owner. This means that in the event of a legal dispute, you do not have to prove ownership; the burden is on your opponent to disprove it. This will prove modestly beneficial if you ever sue someone for copyright infringement in Canada. It may be particularly helpful if you need to obtain a quick court injunction against a copyright pirate to stop an infringing activity.

To register, a completed application form and fee must be sent to the Canadian Copyright Office, which is part of the Department of Consumer and Corporate Affairs in Ottawa. It is not necessary to send a copy of the work being registered. You may obtain a copy of the application form by contacting the Canadian Copyright Office at:

> Canadian Intellectual Property Office (CIPO)
>
> Industry Canada
>
> 50 Victoria Street
>
> Place du Portage, Phase I
>
> Hull, Quebec
>
> K1A 0C9
>
> 819-997-1936

The fee for registration is $35 in Canadian dollars. U.S. and other foreign applicants should pay by money order payable in Canadian funds. Registration is valid for as long as the copyright for the work exists. Once you register your copyright, you do not have to pay any additional fees to maintain or renew it.

Documents transferring copyright rights may also be registered with the Copyright Office upon production of the original document, a certified copy and payment of a fee. Registration is not mandatory, but gives a transfer certain priority rights over unregistered transfers.

g. Software infringement

A software copyright is infringed under Canadian law whenever a person exercises any of a software copyright owner's exclusive rights without receiving authorization. (Canadian Copyright Act, Sec. 27(1).)

Copyright infringement occurs where a substantial part of a protected work (in terms of quality) is taken or copied. However, as in the U.S., a Canadian copyright only protects the form or expression of a work, not the underlying ideas it contains. Thus, copyright does not protect a program's algorithm, only the particular way a program is written to express or implement an algorithm. (*Systems informatises Solartronix v. College d'enseignement general et professional de Jonquiere,* (1990) 38 C.P.R. (3d) 143 (Que. S.C.).)

Canada has a wide range of penalties for copyright infringement, including monetary penalties, injunctions, destruction of infringing copies and criminal penalties.

h. Fair use

Canadian law recognizes the concept of fair use (called fair dealing): "any fair dealing with any work for the purposes of private study, research, criticism, review, or newspaper summary" is not a copyright infringement. (Canadian Copyright Act, Sec. 27(2)(a).) However, this provision is narrowly construed by Canadian courts.

9. Suing Foreign Copyright Infringers

Generally, suing foreign copyright infringers is not economically feasible for a single software company. However, in some cases of large-scale piracy it may be worthwhile, particularly if you can get other software publishers to join you to help pay the cost.

The first thing to do is consult with an experienced American copyright attorney. Even if the infringement occurred in another country, you may be able to sue the infringer in the United States. In this event, an American court would apply the copyright law of the foreign country, not American law. If you have to file suit abroad, you'll need to hire a copyright attorney in the foreign country involved to represent you. Your American copyright attorney should be able to refer you to an experienced copyright lawyer in the country involved.

Before you go to the expense of filing suit, however, be sure to have your attorney explain to you what remedies (for instance, monetary damages, injunctions) you will be entitled to if the suit is successful. Remember, you'll only be entitled to the same treatment that a citizen of the country involved would receive.

Some (particularly developing) countries still do not impose meaningful penalties on copyright infringers. This means it is not economically worthwhile to bring infringement suits against infringers in some countries.

10. Protection in the United States for Foreign Nationals' Software

This section examines software copyright protection in the United States from the point of view of non-U.S. citizens.

a. Protection for nationals of berne countries

If you're a citizen or permanent resident (that is, a national) of a country that is a member of the Berne Convention (see list of Berne countries above), you are entitled to full copyright protection in the U.S. so long as your work was first created or published on or after March 1, 1989 (the date the U.S. joined the Berne Convention). This is true regardless of where the work was first created or published.

EXAMPLE 1: Pierre, a French citizen and resident creates a computer program in 1998. Since France joined the Berne Convention in 1887, the work is entitled to protection in the U.S. pursuant to the Berne Convention.

EXAMPLE 2: Assume that Pierre had published another program way back in 1988. Since this was before the U.S. joined the Berne Convention, the program could not be protected in the U.S. under that convention. Pierre would have to look to the U.C.C. for protection (see below).

b. Protection under the U.C.C.

What if your work does not qualify for protection under the Berne Convention because it was first created or published before March 1, 1989, or because you are a citizen or permanent resident of a country that is not a member of the Berne Convention? Your published or unpublished work will still be entitled to full protection in the U.S. if your country is a member of the Universal Copyright Convention and the work is published with the proper copyright notice (see Section A2, above). This is true regardless of where the work was first created or published.

EXAMPLE: Pierre, the French citizen in Example 2 above, who was not entitled to copyright protection in the U.S. for a program published in 1988, is entitled to full U.S. protection under the U.C.C.

(to which France belongs) provided that his program was published with the proper copyright notice.

c. First publication rule

Regardless what country you are a citizen of or permanently reside in, if your work is first (or simultaneously) published on or after March 1, 1989, in any country that is a member of the Berne Convention, you are entitled to full copyright protection in the United States under the Berne Convention. Similarly, if your work was first published with a valid copyright notice prior to March 1, 1989, in a country that is a member of the U.C.C., you are entitled to full copyright protection in the U.S. pursuant to the U.C.C.

**d. Compliance with U.S.
   copyright formalities**

Neither U.S. citizens nor noncitizens need place a copyright notice on their published work for it to be protected by copyright. However, it is a good idea to use a copyright notice anyway on all software published in the U.S. See Chapter 4, for detailed discussion.

Unlike the case with U.S. citizens, a non-U.S. citizen need not register her work before filing suit in the U.S. for copyright infringement. However, as discussed in Chapter 4, important advantages are gained under U.S. copyright law if a published or unpublished work is registered with the Copyright Office. Therefore, registration is advised for all foreign authors of software and other protectible works.

B. Trade Secret Protection

Most foreign countries enforce reasonable contractual restrictions on the use and disclosure of trade secrets—for example, those contained in distribution or license agreements. Such agreements should be carefully drafted with the help of an attorney versed in the law of the foreign nation involved.

In addition, both the GATT and NAFTA treaties discussed above require that trade secrets be legally protected. Many countries have adopted trade secret laws similar to those of the United States (see Chapter 6) that provide for enforcement of trade secrecy against people who have not signed written agreements but who nonetheless misappropriate trade secrets.

1. GATT and NAFTA

GATT, a trade treaty signed by 117 nations, includes an agreement on intellectual property called Trade Related Aspects of Intellectual Property Rights (TRIPS for short). This agreement requires that signatory nations provide minimum legal protections for all forms of intellectual property. (See Section A4.)

The GATT TRIPS Agreement requires legal protection be given to information that:

- is not generally known or readily accessible to "persons within the circles that normally deal with the kinds of information in question"
- has commercial value because it is kept secret, and
- reasonable measures are taken to keep the information secret.

TRIPS requires all GATT member countries to provide effective penalties for trade secret misappropriation. These must include injunctive relief (including preliminary injunctions that can be obtained to stop misappropriation before trial) and adequate monetary damages.

NAFTA, a trade agreement between the United States, Canada and Mexico, requires trade secret protections similar to those mandated by GATT.

2. Trade Secret Protection in Selected Countries

As the following discussion shows, foreign countries don't always use the same terminology as the U.S. In many countries, trade secret misappropriation is called "breach of confidence." In other countries, trade secrets are called "industrial and business secrets." But, whatever the nomenclature, most foreign trade secret laws provide both damages and injunctive relief to those whose confidential information has been stolen or used or disclosed to others without permission.

In addition to the countries mentioned below, trade secret laws of some kind have been adopted in Argentina, Armenia, Austria, Australia, Belgium, Brazil, Chile, Columbia, Czech Republic, Denmark,

Ecuador, Estonia, France, Germany, Georgia, Hungary, India, Ireland, Israel, Italy, Kazakhstan, Malaysia, the Netherlands, New Zealand, Peru, Philippines, Singapore, Slovak Republic, South Africa, Spain, Sweden, Taiwan, Thailand and Ukraine.

a. Canada

Each Canadian province—ten in all—has it's own trade secret law. Trade secret misappropriation claims are called "breach of confidence" claims in Canada. Trade secret owners may obtain damages and injunctive relief if they can prove that:

- they had proprietary information that was kept confidential
- such information was shared under an obligation of confidence
- the person with whom the information was shared made use of it without the owner's consent, and
- the unauthorized use of the information caused the trade secret owner damages or other injuries.

b. China

China adopted its first trade secrets law in 1993. The law gives trade secret protection to "business secrets"—that is, technical or business information that is not publicly known, provides economic benefits to the owner, has practical application and for which measures have been taken to preserve confidentiality. Remedies for unauthorized use or disclosure of business secrets include damages, disgorgment of profits and injunctive-type relief.

c. Japan

Japan enacted a national trade secrets law in 1993. (Japanese Unfair Competition Prevention Law, Law No. 47, May 19, 1993.) Trade secrets include any "manufacturing method, marketing method or other technical or business information" that has commercial value, is not publicly known and which has been "administered" as a trade secret. An injured party may obtain injunctive relief and damages.

d. United Kingdom

The United Kingdom (Great Britain and Northern Ireland) has no specific trade secrets law. Rather, protection is defined by court decisions. As in Canada, trade secret misappropriation claims are called "breach of confidence" claims. Such claims may be brought whenever there is an unauthorized use or dissemination of confidential information.

C. Patent Protection

The U.S. patent law applies only in the U.S.—that is, a U.S. patent is not automatically recognized outside the U.S. If you want patent protection in a foreign country, you must apply for a patent under its patent laws. Several international treaties (including the Patent Cooperation Treaty and the Paris Convention) allow U.S. inventors to obtain patent protection in these other countries if they take certain required steps, such as filing a patent application in the countries on a timely basis and paying required patent fees.

For a detailed discussion of how to obtain foreign patents, refer to *Patent It Yourself,* by David Pressman (Nolo Press), Chapter 12. If you decide to file for a foreign patent, you'll need the help of an experienced patent attorney. (See Chapter 18.)

There are several different international patent treaties that provide varying methods of obtaining a foreign patent.

1. Paris Convention

The U.S. and over 100 other countries are members of the Convention for the Protection of Industrial Property, sometimes known as the Paris Convention. Under this international treaty, U.S. inventors are entitled to the same treatment under the patent laws of member countries as are citizens of the foreign country—for example, a U.S. inventor is entitled to the same patent rights as a British subject. To obtain a patent, you must file an application in the foreign country where patent protection is desired, within one year of the date that an application is first filed in any other member country. For example, if a U.S. patent application has a filing date of February 5, 1998, all additional Convention filings in other countries must be made by February 5, 1999.

2. Patent Cooperation Treaty (PCT)

The U.S. and over 50 countries are also members of the Patent Cooperation Treaty (PCT). This international agreement provides streamlined procedures for obtaining uniform patent protection in its member countries. The PCT is administered by the World Intellectual Property Organization (WIPO) in Geneva, Switzerland. A U.S. inventor applying for PCT patent protection can file a single application with the U.S. Patent and Trademark Office, which has been designated a receiving office, with the effect of filing in every member country where the inventor desires protection.

3. European Patent Convention

This treaty covers patent law relationships primarily among the members of the European Community and a few other countries. Under the EPC, an inventor need only make one filing and undergo one examination procedure to obtain patent protection in all member countries. Filings and examinations are conducted by the European Patent Office in Munich, Germany, and The Hague, Netherlands. To date, the EPO has issued over 11,000 patents for software-related inventions and has rejected only 100 applications.

File Within One Year of U.S. Application. It's highly desirable to file a foreign application under any of the conventions discussed above within one year after you filed your U.S. patent application. This way, your foreign patent application date relates back to the date your U.S. patent application was filed. This may give you priority over others attempting to patent similar inventions. If you want a foreign patent, it's advisable to take action two or three months before the end of the one-year period.

D. Trademark Protection

Trademark rights in each country depend solely on the trademark laws of that country; there is no set of international laws. Mark owners must start anew to establish rights to a mark in every new country they enter for commercial purposes, a concept known as "territoriality." In other words, previous use or registration in other countries is generally irrelevant.

In the U.S., first use often decides who owns a mark. Most other countries, however, award ownership to whoever is the first to register a mark (although use on the same or related goods usually must follow within a reasonable time). As a result, if the seller of a computer program under the mark "Sueno" wants to expand to a first-to-register country, it will have to pick a new mark if "Sueno" is already registered in that country. This is true even if the U.S. seller was first to use the mark and even if the company that registered that mark in the other country does not currently make

related goods. This "registration" system often allows people to anticipate international marketing trends, and to register the rights to valuable marks before another company thinks to do so.

1. Paris Convention

The primary treaty regulating trademark relations between the U.S. and other countries is called the Paris Convention. The Paris Convention provides that each signatory country will give members of other signatory countries the same protections regarding marks and unfair competition that it affords its own nationals. In the U.S., the Lanham Act allows nationals of the Paris Convention countries to register their marks in the U.S. based on registration in their native country without alleging use here first (if they allege a bona fide intention to use the mark in the U.S. within a reasonable time).

2. Madrid Agreement

Another important trademark treaty is called the Madrid Arrangement on International Registration of Trademarks and the Madrid Protocol. Trademark owners in member nations may submit their national trademark registrations to the International Bureau of the World Intellectual Property Organization (WIPO) for registration. The mark may then be protected in all member countries on the same basis as a national trademark. The U.S. is not a member of the Madrid treaties.

However, each country still can accept or reject any mark registered with WIPO, so the fact that a mark is registered with WIPO does not mean that it will be given protection by any particular country. Rather, the list is primarily for informational purposes. Each member country has one year from the date of international registration to reject the mark for coverage in that country. If the year passes without such rejection, however, and the mark is used for five years after the international registration, it is valid for an additional 15 years, and longer if it is renewed on a timely basis.

The U.S. has not signed the Madrid treaties, but all members of the European Community have, plus 16 other countries.

For detailed guidance on international protection of trademarks, refer to *Trademark: How to Protect a Business & Product*, by Kate McGrath and Stephen Elias (Nolo Press).

E. Strategies to Prevent International Software Piracy

Software piracy is not limited to the United States; it occurs around the world. The Software Publishers Association estimates that in one recent year the software publishing and distribution industries lost more than $12.8 billion due to software theft. The dollar loss was largest in the United States ($2.25 billion) with an estimated piracy rate of 35%. But the software piracy rate is thought to be much greater in most foreign countries: an estimated 80% in Japan, for example. The rates of piracy are even greater in less developed nations. According to the SPA, 99% of the software used in Pakistan, Thailand and Indonesia is pirated; 94% in China; 83% in Brazil; and 84% in Taiwan.

International copyright and trade agreements, and foreign copyright laws, may look good on paper but, of course, they don't prevent software piracy unless they are enforced. U.S. software owners can't rely on foreign governments to protect their rights for them. Indeed, some (particularly developing) countries look on piracy as a cheap and easy way to gain access to new technology. Following are some steps an American software owner can take to prevent, or at least reduce, piracy abroad.

1. Join a Software Trade Association

It is usually not economically feasible for an American software company to take direct action on its own to enforce its copyrights outside the U.S. Litigation costs are too high, the prospects of success are too dim and it's too difficult to find the pirates in the first place.

Realizing that some sort of joint action was required, the software industry has formed two trade associations that are waging an effective war against software piracy both in the U.S. and abroad. These are the:

- Software Publishers Association, 1730 M Street, NW, Suite 700, Washington, DC 20037, 202-452-1600; www.spa.org.
- Business Software Alliance, 2001 L Street NW, Suite 400, Washington, DC 20036, 202-872-5500.

These organizations have substantial budgets to fight software piracy worldwide. Any company that sells software abroad should seriously consider joining either or both.

The Software Publishers Association (SPA), the older and larger software trade association, was originally formed to fight piracy in the United States. However, it has recently begun an international anti-piracy campaign, specifically targeting Singapore, Korea, Taiwan, France, Mexico, Brazil, Australia and Italy. Membership in the SPA is open to any software publisher. Members range from game manufacturers to mainframe manufacturers. Costs of membership are based on the size and revenue of the company.

The Business Software Alliance is active in the U.S. and 55 other countries and has brought hundreds of lawsuits since 1988. Full membership in the Alliance is very expensive and is usually limited to large software publishers. However, smaller companies are allowed to become regional members at a lesser cost. For example, if a company has a piracy problem in Europe, it can get a European membership.

2. Consider Technical Solutions

Technical solutions to software piracy such as copy protection devices have proved to be so unpopular in the United States that they have been abandoned by most software publishers. However, consumers in many foreign countries do not object to copy protection schemes.

Other technical approaches to prevent piracy include:

- placing a unique serial number on every software copy; this costs almost nothing and makes it easy to prove piracy has occurred—that is, if multiple software copies used by a company all have the same serial number, illegal copying must have occurred
- building things into software packaging that are difficult for counterfeiters to reproduce—for example, holograms
- employing hardware locks that tie software to a particular piece of hardware, and
- including network limiting features in software that prevent a user from using more than one copy of a program with the same serial number on a network.

3. Preventing Infringing Software From Entering the United States

It is against U.S. law for anyone to import pirated software into the United States. (17 U.S.C. 602.) The U.S. Customs Service is supposed to prohibit infringing goods from entering the country. However, as a practical matter, customs officials cannot carefully scrutinize every work of authorship being imported to see whether it does or doesn't infringe an existing U.S. work. Indeed, even if they had the time, it would be impossible to determine whether a particular imported software infringed protected copyright.

Accordingly, the burden of enforcing the prohibition against infringing works falls squarely on the shoulders of the copyright owner. There are two ways to do this:

a. Recordation with Customs Service

Under the U.S. Customs Act, a copyright owner may record her work with the U.S. Customs Service. (19 C.F.R. Part 133 Subpart (D).) Once this is done, any imports that are either pure copies or are highly similar to yours may be held up until you have a chance to go into court and obtain a court order preventing importation. Unfortunately, the chances of the infringing work being spotted and you being notified are relatively slim. However, the procedure for registering is relatively easy and you've nothing to lose.

b. Initiating an International Trade Commission complaint

Under the Customs Act, it's possible to seek an order having a work excluded from the U.S. on the ground its importation would be an unfair act or would constitute an unfair method of competition. (19 U.S.C. 1337.) Copyright infringement meets this test.

Finally, to get a work excluded you must also prove that:

- it's produced in another country
- it has a tendency to destroy an industry existing in the U.S. (in practice, this qualification is much easier than it looks), and
- the industry being destroyed must be efficiently and economically operated (also almost always found to be the case).

For the most part, any major importation of works that are clearly piratical or that substantially infringe a domestic U.S. work will qualify for exclusion under this law. One well-known example of this happening is when Apple Computers, Inc., prevented the importation of Pineapple Computers. (*Apple Computers, Inc. v. Formula International, Inc.*, 725 F.2d 521 (1983).)

To utilize this law, the copyright owner must file a formal complaint with the United States International Trade Commission. The case is heard by an Administrative Law Judge who's empowered to grant immediate relief and, ultimately, to either ban the works entirely or only a portion. As with infringement cases, it would be unwise to attempt this procedure without the assistance of a skilled attorney. ■

Chapter 11

Software Ownership

This chapter is about software ownership—that is, who owns the intellectual property rights in software created by individuals, people working together, employees and independent contractors. It also covers transferring software ownership and use rights.

A. Copyright Ownership

Software, documentation and works of authorship that satisfy the criteria for copyright protection discussed in Chapter 3, are protected automatically upon creation and fixation in a tangible medium. At that same moment, the author or authors of the work become the initial owners of the copyright in the work. This Section is about determining who these authors—and initial owners—are.

There are several basic ways to author software and thereby become its initial owner.

- An individual may independently author the software.
- An employer may pay an employee to author the software, in which case the employer is the author under the work made for hire rule.
- A person or company may hire an independent contractor (not an employee) to create software on its behalf, in which case the hiring party is the author, assuming the independent contractor signs a written agreement to this effect.

- Two or more individuals or entities may collaborate to become joint authors.

We discuss each of these types of authorship (and initial ownership) in turn.

1. Independent Authorship by an Individual

Software created by a single self-employed individual is initially owned by that individual.

> EXAMPLE: Lucy is a self-employed freelance programmer. She writes a program that helps investors analyze stock market data. Lucy created the program on her own time—that is, not on anyone's behalf. Lucy owns all the copyright rights in the program.

Individual copyright owners may exercise any of their copyright rights themselves. For example, they may reproduce and sell their work themselves, or authorize others to do so. They may also transfer their ownership in whole or in part to others. (See Section C.) Individual copyright owners can do whatever they want with their copyright; they are accountable to no one.

2. Ownership of Works Created by Employees (Works Made for Hire)

Today, the majority of software is created by employees, not self-employed programmers working on their own behalf. Copyrightable works created by an employee *within the scope of employment* are owned by the employer. Such works are called works made for hire. Not only is the employer the owner of the copyright in a work made for hire, it is considered to be the work's author for copyright purposes. This is so whether the owner is a human being or a business entity, such as a partnership or corporation. As the author, the employer is entitled to register the work with the Copyright Office, exercise its copyright rights in the work such as distributing it to the public, permit others to exercise these rights or sell all or part of its rights. The employee—the actual creator of the work—has no copyright rights at all. All he or she receives is whatever compensation the employer gives him or her.

This result is considered to be an obvious and natural consequence of the employer-employee relationship. It's assumed that an employee understands and agrees to this when he or she takes a job. Thus, an employer doesn't have to tell an employee that it will own copyrightable works she creates on the employer's behalf; the employee is supposed to know this without being told. Likewise, the employer need not have the employee sign an agreement relinquishing his copyright rights—he or she doesn't have any to relinquish.

EXAMPLE: John is hired to work as a programmer for AcmeSoft, Inc. John is AcmeSoft's employee. He is assigned to a project to develop a new database program. All of John's work on the program will be work made for hire to which AcmeSoft owns all the copyright rights. AcmeSoft need not tell John this or have him sign a copyright transfer agreement.

At first glance, this all sounds very straight-forward. It would seem that both the hiring firm and the worker should always know who owns any copyrightable works created by the worker. However, things are not always so simple. In fact, it can be very difficult to know for sure who owns software created by workers for hiring firms. This is because there are problems in determining:

- just who is an employee, for copyright ownership purposes, and
- when a work is created within the scope of employment.

a. Problem 1: Who is an employee?

A person is an employee for copyright ownership purposes if the person or entity on whose behalf the work is done has the right to control the manner and means by which the work is created. If the hiring firm does not have the right to control the worker, he or she is not an employee for copyright purposes; rather, the worker is an independent contractor and a whole other set of ownership rules apply, as discussed in Section A3 below.

The requisite right of control is present, and the worker will be considered an employee, where the hiring firm has the right to direct the way the worker performs, including the details of when, where and how the work is done.

It makes no difference what the parties call themselves or how they characterize their relationship. If the person or entity on whose behalf the work is done has the right of control, the person hired is an employee and any protectible work he creates within the scope of his employment is a work made for hire. It also makes no difference whether the control is actually exercised. All that matters is that the hiring firm has the *right* to exercise such control. (*CCNV v. Reid*, 109 S.Ct. 2166 (1989).)

When a legal dispute arises as to whether the creator of a protectible work is an employee, the courts are supposed to examine a variety of factors to determine if the hiring firm has the right to control the worker. The rules are ambiguous and given to highly subjective interpretation. Thus, if a dispute later arises, it is always possible that a judge could decide the programmer an employer thought was an employee was actually an independent contractor. The consequences could be disastrous for the employer and quite surprising for the worker. (See Section A5 below.)

However, legal decisions in recent years make clear that two of the factors listed in the sidebar titled Factors Considered in Determining Employee Status are of prime importance in determining whether a worker is an employee for copyright owner-ship purposes:

- whether the hiring firm pays the worker's Social Security taxes, and
- whether the hiring firm provides the worker with employee benefits.

Obviously, if a company (or individual) hires someone and pays their Social Security taxes and gives him or her employee benefits, the company (and worker) must believe that the worker is an employee. Why else would the hiring firm incur these expenses? A hiring firm that pays such expenses for a worker will almost always treat him or her like an employee and have the right to control his or her work.

In one important decision, the court held that a part-time programmer employed by a swimming pool retailer was not the com-pany's employee for copyright purposes and the programmer was therefore entitled to ownership of a program he wrote for the company. The court stated that the com-pany's failure to provide the programmer with health, unemployment or life insurance benefits, or to withhold Social Security, federal or state taxes from his pay was a "virtual admission" that the programmer was an independent contractor. These factors were so important they outweighed other factors that indicated a right of con-trol by the pool company, such as the fact that the company could assign the program-mer additional projects. (*Aymes v. Bonelli*, 980 F.2d. 857 (2d Cir. 1992).)

Another reason the tax treatment of the worker is so important is fairness. It is manifestly unfair for a hiring firm to treat a worker like an independent contractor for tax purposes (and thereby avoid paying payroll taxes and employee benefits) and then turn around and claim he or she is an employee for copyright ownership purposes

Factors Considered in Determining Employee Status

Here is a list of some of the factors the Supreme Court has said judges might consider in determining if a hiring firm has the right to control a worker. As stated above, if the right to control is present, the worker is an employee; if not, he is an independent contractor. This is not an exclusive list, and no single factor is determinative:

- the skill required to do the work (highly skilled workers are less likely to perform their work under a hirer's direct control)
- the source of tools and materials used to create the work (workers who supply their own equipment are less likely to be under a hirer's control)
- the duration of the relationship (long-term relationships indicate control by the hiring firm and employee status)
- whether the person who pays for the work has the right to assign additional projects to the creative party
- who determines when and how long the creative party works
- the method of payment (paying by the hour indicates an employment status, payment by the job indicates the worker is an independent contractor)
- who decides what assistants will be hired, and who pays them
- whether the work is in the ordinary line of business of the person who pays for the work (if yes, the hiring party will more likely control the worker)
- whether the creative party is in business for herself
- whether the creative party receives employee benefits from the person who pays for the work
- the tax treatment of the creative party.

(and thereby claim that his or her copyrightable creations are works made for hire). Simply as a matter of fairness, a worker must be treated consistently for both tax and copyright purposes.

All the other courts that have considered this question have reached the same result as *Aymes v. Bonelli*. No court has allowed a hiring firm to treat a worker as an independent contractor for tax purposes and an employee for copyright purposes

The moral for hiring firms: If a hiring firm doesn't pay a worker's Social Security taxes or provide him or her with benefits available to other employees, the firm should assume the worker is an independent contractor for copyright ownership purposes. See the following section for a discussion of what this means in practical terms.

Given the track record of the courts, a hiring firm can probably safely assume that a formal salaried employee for whom the firm pays Social Security taxes and provides employee benefits would be considered an employee for copyright purposes. When anything short of a formal, salaried employment relationship is involved, there is always the risk it will not be deemed an employment relationship for copyright purposes. See Section A2c below for what hiring firms should do in this event.

Results May be Different for IRS and State Purposes. Not paying a worker's Social Security taxes will likely make him or her an independent contractor for copyright ownership purposes, but this does not necessarily mean he or she will be an independent contractor for IRS or state law purposes such as workers' compensation and state unemployment insurance. The IRS and state agencies look at a variety of factors to determine whether a worker is an employee or independent contractor. Whether Social Security taxes are paid for a worker is just one of these factors and is not determinative in and of itself. For a detailed discussion, refer to *Hiring Independent Contractors*, by Stephen Fishman (Nolo Press).

What Should Software Workers Do?

A worker should always clarify his or her employment status before beginning any job. If you're supposed to be an employee, you should be put on the hiring firm's payroll and classified and treated as an employee for tax, salary, job benefit and all other purposes. If you're going to be an independent contractor, you should have the firm sign a written independent contractor agreement that states what it is you're supposed to do, how and how much you will be paid and who will own the copyright in your work. If you are going to transfer ownership of your work to the hiring firm, try to make the transfer contingent on payment as provided under the agreement. (See Chapter 15 for sample independent contractor agreements.)

b. Problem 2: When is a work created within the scope of employment?

Even when it is clear that an employment relationship exists, serious disputes can arise as to whether an employee who creates a copyrightable work did so within the scope of employment. For example, many people employed in the software industry are moonlighters—they create software or other copyrightable works on their own time, using their own equipment, alone or with others. If such work is closely related to an employee's job duties, the employer may claim an ownership interest in it, while the employee insists that he is the sole owner.

Where such a dispute arises, the courts look to the common law of agency relationships to determine whether a work was created within the scope of employment. Under these rules, an employee's work is created within the scope of employment if it:

- is the kind of work the employee is paid to perform
- occurs substantially within work hours at the work place, and
- is performed, at least in part, to serve the employer. (*Miller v. CP Chemicals, Inc.*, 808 F.Supp. 1238 (D.S.C. 1992).)

These rules are ambiguous and given to highly subjective and inconsistent interpretations. Consider these real-life examples where opposite results were reached in cases involving similar fact situations:

EXAMPLE 1: Miller was a supervisor who worked at CP Chemical's quality control lab. He created a program for making mathematical computations needed for in-process adjustments to one of CP's products. Miller was paid by the hour and created the program primarily at home on his own computer during off hours, and without any overtime pay. Nevertheless, the court held that the program was created within the scope of Miller's employment and was therefore owned by CP Chemicals, not Miller. The court held that the first and third factors listed above favored CP Chemicals, while only the second favored Miller. The court reasoned that "the ultimate purpose of the development of the computer program was to benefit CP by maximizing the efficiency of the operation of the quality control lab." (*Miller v. CP Chemicals, Inc.*, 808 F.Supp. 1238 (D.S.C. 1992).)

EXAMPLE 2: While employed by Avtec Systems, Pfeiffer created a computer program for managing and presenting satellite data. The court held that the program was not created within the scope of Pfeiffer's employment, and was therefore not a work for hire owned by Avtec. This was so even though the program performed many of the same functions found in other programs used by Avtec and by Pfeiffer during his employment by Avtec. The court found that the majority of Pfeiffer's work on the program was done on his own time and his own computer in furtherance of a personal hobby, and not to satisfy any specific work obligations for Avtec. (*Avtec Systems, Inc. v. Pfeiffer,* 805 F.Supp. 1312 (E.D.Va. 1992).)

The result of all this is that an employee (or ex-employee) might be able to legitimately claim that he or she should own the copyright in his contribution to a software project because he was not hired or paid to create that work. As you might expect, such disputes can get messy and very expensive, particularly if the software involved is quite valuable.

c. What employers should do

The best policy for companies and individuals who employ others to create software or any other copyrightable works is to have all creative (or potentially creative) employees sign employment agreements. Such an agreement should:

- make clear that the employee's job duties include creating, or contributing to the creation of, software and other copyrightable works
- provide that any software or copyrightable works the employee creates as part of his job are works made for hire to which the company owns all the copyright rights, and
- provide that if for some reason such works are determined not to be works made for hire, the employee assigns in advance (transfers) to the employer all his copyright rights in such works.

A signed document like this will help convince a court that creating software or

other copyrightable works was part of the employee's job. And the assignment provision will serve as a back-up in case a court determines the work made for hire rule does not apply.

Not only should new employees assign their copyright rights to their employers, but existing employees should do so as well if they haven't already. (See Chapter 14 for a detailed discussion and sample employment agreements.)

d. Copyright concerns for moonlighting employees

Employees of software companies who create software or other copyrightable works on their own time need to be very

careful. As discussed above, an employer owns the intellectual property rights in software created by an employee within the scope of her employment. Moreover, an employer may even have certain rights over works created outside the scope of employment if the employee used the employer's resources (for example, did a substantial amount of the work during business hours or used the employer's equipment). If an employee creates a valuable work on his or her own time, an unscrupulous employer might try to assert ownership over it by claiming that the work was within the scope of employment or the employee used its resources.

To avoid potential problems, if you plan to do software-related work on your own, make sure you inform your employer and obtain written acknowledgment that the employer will not have an ownership interest in such work. For obvious reasons, it's a lot easier to get that acknowledgment before you do the work than after.

EXAMPLE: Art Acres is hired by Acme-Soft to help develop communications software. On his own time, Art decides to develop a computer game. Art's work on the game is in no way connected with his work for AcmeSoft, nor could the game be competitive with any of AcmeSoft's products. However, just to make sure there will be no problems, Art informs his boss about his plans and gets AcmeSoft to sign the following letter of agreement:

March 1, 199_

Bill Fates
President
AcmeSoft, Inc.
1000 Main St.
Seattle, WA 90002

Dear Bill:

This letter is to confirm the understanding we've reached regarding ownership of my computer game program, tentatively titled *You Are What You Eat.*

You acknowledge that my program will be written on my own time and shall not be written within the scope of my employment with AcmeSoft, Inc.

It is expressly agreed that I shall be the owner of all rights in the program, including the copyright. Furthermore, AcmeSoft, Inc., will sign all papers necessary for me to perfect my ownership of the entire copyright in the work.

If this agreement meets with your approval, please sign below to make this a binding contract between us. Please sign both copies and return one to me. The other signed copy is for your records.

Sincerely,
Art Acres
Art Acres

I agree with the above understanding and represent that I have authority to make this agreement and to sign this letter on behalf of AcmeSoft, Inc.

Bill Fates
Bill Fates

Date: March 2, 199_

3. Ownership of Works Created by Independent Contractors

Subject to the important exceptions discussed in Section A3a below, works created by independent contractors (nonemployees) are not works made for hire, that is, the independent contractor, *not the hiring firm,* owns the copyright in what he or she creates. This means that the hiring firm must *always* require independent contractors to sign written agreements assigning their copyright ownership to the hiring firm. To ensure that such an agreement will be effective, it should be signed *before* the independent contractor begins work on the project. (See Chapter 15 for sample independent contractor agreements.)

> EXAMPLE 1: AcmeSoft hires Dana, a freelance programmer, to help code a new version of an accounting program. Dana is not AcmeSoft's employee. AcmeSoft has Dana sign an independent contractor agreement before commencing work. The agreement contains a provision whereby Dana assigns to AcmeSoft all his ownership rights in the work he will perform on the accounting program. Dana completes his work and his relationship with AcmeSoft ends. Because of the signed agreement, AcmeSoft owns all the copyright in Dana's work.

> EXAMPLE 2: Assume instead that AcmeSoft hires Dana, but fails to have him sign an independent contractor agreement transferring his ownership rights. When Dana completes his work he, not AcmeSoft, will own the copyright in the code he created for AcmeSoft. This is so even though AcmeSoft paid for it! However, AcmeSoft would be at least entitled to use the work. (See Section A5 below for detailed discussion.)

a. When works created by independent contractors are works made for hire

Certain types of works created by independent contractors are considered to be works made for hire to which the hiring party automatically owns all the copyright rights —provided that:

- the hiring party and independent contractor both sign an agreement before the work is created stating that the work shall be a work made for hire, and
- the work falls within one of the following work for hire categories:
  - a contribution to a collective work (a work created by more than one author such as an anthology)
  - a part of an audiovisual work
  - a translation
  - "supplementary works" such as forewords, afterwords, supplemental pictorial illustrations, maps, charts, editorial notes, bibliographies, appendixes and indexes
  - a compilation
  - an instructional text

- a test and test answer materials
- an atlas.

User manuals and other software documentation (whether printed or online) written by independent contractor technical writers would probably fall within the instructional text, supplementary work and/or collective work categories. This means that such works can be works made for hire if the independent contractor signs an agreement to that effect before starting work.

EXAMPLE: AcmeSoft, Inc., hires Alberta, a freelance technical writer, to write the user manual for its new small business accounting software. AcmeSoft has Alberta sign an agreement before she commences work stating that her work on the manual shall be a work made for hire. When Alberta finishes her work, the manual will be considered a work made for hire to which AcmeSoft owns all the copyright rights. Indeed, AcmeSoft will be considered the author for copyright purposes. Alberta will have no copyright ownership interest whatsoever in the manual.

b. Does software fall within a work made for hire category?

Unfortunately for software companies, most of the work made for hire categories set out above don't seem to have much application to computer programs themselves (but merely to their written documentation). A computer program might arguably constitute a collective work, compilation or even an audiovisual work, but no court has so ruled. Moreover, Copyright Office officials have stated that in their opinion none of the work made for hire categories applied to software. For this reason, until the question is conclusively resolved by court or congressional action, persons who hire independent contractors to create, or contribute to the creation of, computer programs should never rely on the work made for hire rule but rather should obtain an assignment of rights as discussed in Section C2.

⚠ Work For Hire Agreements May Be Ineffective. Many software companies have independent contractors who work on software projects sign agreements stating that their work "shall be a work made for hire." Such an agreement will not make the contractor's work a work made for hire unless it falls within one of the categories listed above. (See the discussion in Section A3.)

4. Jointly Authored Works

Given the time and expense involved in creating new software, joint authorship has become common in the software industry. Two or more companies or individuals (or combinations of companies and individuals) will agree to jointly contribute to the creation of new software. When such a work is completed, it is normally jointly owned by its creators—that is, each contributing author shares in the ownership of the entire work.

Special Rules for California

California law provides that a person or business entity such as a corporation, partnership or limited liability company that commissions a work made for hire is considered to be the employer of the creator of the work for purposes of the workers' compensation, unemployment insurance and unemployment disability insurance laws. (Cal. Labor Code Section 3351.5(c); Cal. Unemployment Insurance Code Sections 621, 686.) No one is entirely sure what impact this has on persons or entities who commission works made for hire. Neither the California courts nor state agencies have addressed the question. However, it may mean that the commissioning party has to obtain workers' compensation coverage for the creative party and might be liable for any injuries he or she sustains in the course of her work. It might also mean that special penalties could be assessed against a commissioning party who willfully fails to pay the creative party any monies due him or her after he or she is discharged or resigns.

These potential requirements and liabilities are one reason why it might be desirable for those commissioning work in California not to enter into work made for hire agreements, and instead have the creator assign the desired copyright rights to the commissioning party in advance. One theoretical disadvantage of using an assignment of rights as opposed to a work made for hire agreement is that an assignment can be terminated by the author or her heirs 35 to 40 years after it is made. However, this disadvantage is essentially meaningless because little or no software can be expected to have a useful economic life of more than 35 years. (See Section 3.)

A joint author's life is not as simple as that of an individual copyright owner. There may be restrictions on what each joint author can do with its ownership share, and joint authors must account to each other for any profits they receive from commercial exploitation of the joint work.

A work is jointly authored automatically upon its creation if (1) two or more authors contributed material to the work; and (2) each of the authors prepared his or her contribution with the intention that it would be combined with the contributions of the other authors as part of a single unitary work. We'll refer to such works as "joint works."

The key to determining whether a work is a joint work is the authors' intent at the time the work is created. If the authors intended that their work be absorbed or combined with other contributions into an integrated unit, the work that results is a joint work. It is not necessary that the authors work together or work at the same time. Indeed, it is not even necessary that they know each other when they create their respective contributions.

EXAMPLE: Peter and Mary agree to create a new computer game. Peter designs the game and Mary does the actual computer coding. When the game is completed, it will be jointly owned by Peter and Mary because they intended that their respective contributions be combined to form one integrated work—a new computer game.

a. How much material must a person contribute to be a joint author?

The respective contributions made to a joint work by its authors need not be equal in terms of quantity or quality. But to be considered a joint author, a person must contribute more than a minimal amount of work to the finished product.

Most courts require that a person's contribution be separately copyrightable in its own right for him or her to be considered a joint author. A person who merely contributes ideas or other unprotectible items is not entitled to an ownership interest in the work's copyright unless the parties expressly agree to it, preferably in writing.

As the following real-life example illustrates, simply describing to a programmer what a program should do is not sufficient to become a joint author. Such a description will be viewed as a mere idea, not copyrightable expression.

EXAMPLE: Ross and Wigginton decided to collaborate to develop a computer spreadsheet program. They agreed that Ross would write the computational component of the program (the engine) and Wigginton design the user interface. Ross provided Wigginton with a handwritten list of potential commands that should be incorporated in the user interface. The two later went their own ways and Wigginton's interface was combined with another engine component and marketed by Ashton-Tate. Ross filed suit, claiming that Wigginton's interface was a joint work. The court held that the interface was not a joint work because Ross's list of commands was not separately copyrightable. The court stated that the list was merely an unprotectible idea, telling Wigginton what tasks Ross believed the spreadsheet interface should perform. *(Ashton-Tate Corp. v. Ross*, 916 F.2d 516 (9th Cir. 1990).)

Copyright Tip. It is always a good idea for collaborators to have a written agreement setting forth their respective interests in the work to be written. This way, if one contributor is found not to be a joint owner of the work because he did not contribute protectible expression to it, he or she would still be entitled (as a matter of contract law) to the ownership interest stated in the collaboration agreement. (See Section A4d below.)

b. Employees are not joint authors

An employee who contributes copyrightable work to a joint work is not a joint author. As discussed above, copyrightable works created by employees within the scope of employment are owned by the employer, indeed the employer is deemed author of such a work made for hire. Thus, the employer would be the joint author, not the employee.

EXAMPLE: Simon and Sally agree to jointly create a shareware program. Simon hires Suzy, a skilled programmer, to aid him in coding the program. The code Suzy creates is a work made for hire owned by Simon, Suzy's employer. Suzy is not a joint author of the game, only Simon and Sally are.

c. Joint authors need not be human beings

A joint author doesn't have to be a human being. A corporation, partnership or other business entity can also be a joint author. For example, two software companies can agree to jointly develop new software. This type of strategic partnering is now common.

EXAMPLE: Sunnydale Software, Inc., and AcmeSoft, Inc., agree to jointly develop a new software package designed to enable dairy farmers to automate milk production. Sunnydale and AcmeSoft employees work together to design, code and test the new software. The software package, called *Milkrun*, is a joint work that is also a work made for hire. The joint authors are Sunnydale and AcmeSoft.

d. Joint authors' agreement

A written agreement is not legally required to create a joint work; an oral agreement is sufficient. However, as Samuel Goldwyn supposedly once said, "An oral agreement isn't worth the paper it's printed on." It is vital that joint authors draft and sign a written agreement spelling out their rights and responsibilities. This avoids innumerable headaches later on.

If you're collaborating with one or more people or companies to create and market software, you're entering into a partnership or joint venture. You're in a partnership if you intend the collaboration to be open-ended—that is, to involve more than one software project. If you intend to collaborate only on a single project, you're in a joint venture. Joint ventures are governed by the same laws as partnerships. The only legal difference between partnerships and joint ventures is that the latter are for a limited purpose.

You and your collaborators should sign a written partnership or joint venture agreement setting forth each person's ownership interests, rights and duties. *The Partnership Book,* by Denis Clifford and Ralph Warner (Nolo Press), contains a form partnership/joint venture agreement that may fill your needs.

e. Joint author's rights and duties in the absence of an agreement

The drafters of the Copyright Act realized that not all joint authors would be prudent enough to enter into a written (or even oral) agreement setting forth their ownership interests, rights and duties. To avoid chaos, they made sure that the act contained provisions governing the most important aspects of the legal relationship between joint authors who fail to agree among themselves how their relationship should operate. You might think of these provisions as similar to a computer program's "default settings" that control the program when the user fails to make his own settings.

- **Ownership interests.** Unless they agree otherwise, joint authors each have an undivided interest in the entire work. This is basically the same as joint ownership of a house or other real estate. When a husband and wife jointly own their home they normally each own a 50% interest in the entire house; that is, they each have an undivided one-half interest. Similarly, joint authors share ownership of all five exclusive rights that make up the joint work's copyright.

- **Right to exploit copyright.** Unless they agree otherwise, each joint author has the right to exercise any or all of the five copyright rights inherent in the joint work: any of the authors may reproduce and distribute the work or prepare derivative works based upon it (or display or perform it). Each author may do so without the other joint authors' consent.

- **Right to license joint work.** Unless they agree otherwise, each joint author may grant third parties permission to exploit the work—on a nonexclusive basis—without the other joint authors' consent. This means that different authors may grant nonexclusive licenses of the same right to different persons!

Copyright Tip. Anyone who wishes to purchase an exclusive right in a joint work should require signatures by all the authors to ensure that they all agree to the transfer.

- **Right to transfer ownership.** Unless they agree otherwise, each author of a joint work may transfer her entire ownership interest to another person without the other joint authors' consent. Such person then co-owns the work with the remaining authors. But a joint author can only transfer her particular interest, not that of any other author.

- **Duty to account for profits.** Along with these rights, each joint author has the duty to account to the other joint authors for any profits received from his use or license of the joint work. All the joint authors are entitled to share in these profits. Unless they agree otherwise, the profits must be divided among the authors according to their proportionate interests in the joint work. (Note, however, that such profits do not include what one author gets for selling his or her share of the copyright.)

  It may not seem fair that a joint author—who goes to the time and trouble of exploiting the copyright in the joint work by getting it published or creating derivative works based upon it—is required to share his profits equally with the other joint authors, who did nothing. This is still another reason why it's wise to enter into a written agreement.

- **When joint authors die.** When a joint author dies, his or her share in the joint work goes to the author's heirs. If the author wrote a will, the share would go to whomever the will directs. If the author died without a will, the share would go to whomever state inheritance laws require—normally the author's closest living relatives. The other joint authors do not acquire a deceased owner's share unless, of course, the deceased author willed it to them, or the author died without a will and another joint author was related to her and inherited her interest under the state inheritance laws. However, joint authors can change this result by entering into a joint tenancy with right of survivorship agreement. Under such an agreement, a deceased joint author's share would automatically go to the remaining joint author(s).

5. What If a Hiring Firm Fails to Obtain Ownership of Works It Pays For?

The discussion above should make clear that it's quite possible for a company or person to hire another person to create or contribute to the creation of software, pay for the work, and yet end up not owning the copyright in that person's work product. This can happen in a variety of ways:

- a worker the hiring firm thought was an employee turns out to be an independent contractor
- the work performed by the employee was outside his or her scope of employment
- the hiring firm fails to obtain a written assignment of copyright rights in advance from an independent contractor, or
- the hiring firm has an independent contractor sign a work for hire agreement, but the work does not fall within one of the work for hire categories enumerated in Section A3 above.

Whenever any of these things happen there are three possible consequences:

- the creator of the work will be considered the sole copyright owner
- the creator and hiring party will be considered to be joint authors and share ownership, or
- the hiring party will be considered the sole copyright owner.

a. The creator of the work owns the copyright

First of all, unless the hiring firm can obtain an ownership interest by claiming joint authorship or by virtue of some written document (see below), the worker will solely own all of the copyright rights in her work product.

EXAMPLE 1: The law firm of Dewey, Cheatum and Howe hires Sally, a freelance systems analyst and programmer, to design and code custom case management software for the firm. Sally is not Dewey's employee and signs no document transferring her ownership rights in her work to Dewey. Sally completes the program and is paid in full. Sally is also the sole copyright owner of the case management software. This means that Sally may sell the software to others, reproduce it, create derivative works from it or otherwise exercise her copyright rights in the software.

However, all will not be lost for the hiring firm. At the very least, a company or person who pays an author to create a protectible work has a nonexclusive license to use it as intended. (*Avtec Systems, Inc. v. Pfeiffer*, 805 F.Supp. 1312 (E.D.Va 1992).) This seems only fair, considering that the hiring party paid for the work. A person with a nonexclusive license in a work may use the work, but may not prevent others from using it as well. Nonexclusive licenses may be implied from the circumstances; no express agreement is required.

EXAMPLE 2: Since Dewey in Example 1 paid Sally to create the case management software, it would have a nonexclusive license to use the software. But this would not prevent Sally from allowing others to use the software as well.

b. Joint work created

The best thing that could happen from the hiring firm's point of view, would be for it to be considered a joint author of the work. This way, it would share ownership with the other creators. However, as discussed in Section A4a above, for a person or company to be considered a joint author, it must contribute actual copyrightable expression to the finished work. Simply describing how a program should function or contributing other ideas or suggestions is not sufficient.

> **EXAMPLE 3:** Assume that Sally in the examples above was aided by Dewey's employees. The employees contributed not only ideas, but actually helped design the program; contributing work that was separately copyrightable in its own right (flowcharts, for example). In this event, the software would probably constitute a joint work and would be jointly owned by Sally and Dewey. (See Section A4 above for a detailed discussion of joint works.)

c. Hiring party is sole copyright owner under work made for hire contract

As discussed in Section A3 above, many companies use form agreements with independent contractors that state that the contractor's work will be a work made for hire. But such an agreement will be effective only if the contractor's work falls within one of the work for hire categories enumerated in Section A3a above. Software may not fall into any of these categories. This means that the contractor's work will not be deemed a work made for hire even though he signed the agreement.

> **EXAMPLE 4:** Assume that Dewey in the example above had Sally sign a contract stating that the case management software would be a work made for hire. Unfortunately for Dewey, such software does not come within one of the nine categories of specially commissioned works. This means that regardless of what the contract said, the work is not a work made for hire and Sally is the author and initial owner of the copyright.

However, it is possible that a court would interpret the work made for hire contract as a transfer by Sally to Dewey of all her copyright rights in his work. Sally would still be the initial owner and author, but Dewey would still end up owning all the copyright rights in the work—that is, Dewey would have the exclusive right to use and reproduce it, create derivative works based upon it, and so on. But it's also possible that a judge would rule the contract unenforceable and simply award Dewey a nonexclusive license.

6. Marriage, Divorce and Software Copyright Ownership

This section is for individuals who already own software copyrights, or who may own software copyrights in the future because of software they will create. Like everybody else, individuals who own software copyrights get married and get divorced. A copyright is an item of personal property that must be given to one spouse or the other, or somehow shared, upon divorce. Every state has a set of laws about how property acquired or created by married persons is owned and divided upon divorce. These laws vary greatly from state to state. This section highlights some basic principles. You'll need to consult an attorney to answer specific questions about how the laws of your state operate.

a. Copyrights as community property

Nine states have community property laws: Arizona, California, Idaho, Louisiana, Nevada, New Mexico, Texas, Washington and Wisconsin (in all but name). Under these state laws, unless they agree otherwise, a husband and wife automatically become joint owners of most types of property they acquire during their marriage. Property acquired before or after marriage is separately owned.

A court in the most populous community property state—California—has held that a copyright acquired by one spouse during marriage is community property jointly owned by both spouses. (*Marriage of Worth*, 195 Cal.App.3d 768, 241 Cal. Rptr. 135 (1987).) This means that if you are married and reside in California (or later move there), any work you have created or will create automatically would be owned jointly by you and your spouse unless you agree otherwise in writing (see below).

EXAMPLE: Emily and Robert are married and live in California. Emily writes a computer program. Under the federal Copyright Act, Emily becomes the sole owner of the program the moment it's created. But at that same moment, under California's community property law, Robert automatically acquires an undivided one-half interest in the copyright (unless they agree otherwise).

Courts in the eight other community property states have yet to consider whether copyrights are community property. No one knows whether they will follow California's lead. If you're married and reside in Arizona, Idaho, Louisiana, Nevada, New Mexico, Texas, Washington or Wisconsin, the most prudent approach is to assume that the copyright in any protectible work you create during marriage is community property. However, check with a family law or copyright lawyer familiar with the laws of your state before taking any action such as entering into a prenuptial agreement dividing your and your spouse's property in advance in the event you later divorce.

The following discussion briefly highlights the effect of according copyrights community property status in California.

b. Right to control copyrights

Normally, either spouse is entitled to sell community personal property (which would include a copyright) without the other's consent. But the profits from such a sale would themselves be community property (that is, jointly owned). The rule is different, however, as to gifts: neither spouse can give away community property without the other's consent. However, a special provision of California law (Civil Code Section 5125(d)) provides that a spouse who operates a business has the primary management and control of that business and its assets. In most cases, a married freelance programmer or software engineer would probably be considered to be operating a business and would therefore have primary management and control over any work he or she creates (the business's assets).

This means that a married freelance programmer may transfer all or part of the copyright in a work he or she creates during marriage without his or her spouse's consent and/or signature on any contract. However, the programmer is legally required to give his or her spouse prior written notice of such transfers (but failure to do so only results in giving the nonauthor spouse the right to demand an accounting of the profits from the transfer).

c. When a spouse dies

Under California law (Probate Code Section 201.5) each spouse may will a one-half interest in their community property to whomever they choose; this would include, of course, their interest in any community property copyright. If a spouse dies without a will, the surviving spouse acquires all the deceased spouse's community property.

d. Division of copyrights at divorce

When a California couple gets divorced, they are legally entitled to arrange their own property settlement, jointly dividing their property as they wish. If, however, they can't reach an agreement and submit the dispute to the court, a judge will divide the community property equally. A judge would have many options as to how to divide community property copyrights—for instance, he or she could award all the copyrights to one spouse and give the other cash or other community property of equal value; if there were say ten copyrights of equal value, she could give five to one spouse and five to the other; or the judge could permit each spouse to separately administer their one-half interest in all the copyrights.

e. Changing marital ownership of copyrights by contract

Property acquired during marriage by California residents does not have to be community property. Spouses are free to agree either before or during marriage that all or part of their property will be separately owned. Such an agreement must be in writing and signed by the spouse giving up their community property interest. In some cases, it is desirable for the spouse giving up their community property interest to first consult a lawyer. This is something a husband and wife or engaged couple must discuss and decide on their own.

f. Equitable distribution states

All states other than the nine community property states listed above and Mississippi employ a doctrine known as equitable distribution when dividing property at divorce. Under the equitable distribution doctrine, assets (including copyrights) acquired during marriage are divided equitably (fairly) at divorce. In theory, equitable means equal, or nearly so. In some equitable distribution states, however, if a spouse is shown to be at fault in making the marriage fail, that spouse may receive less than an equal share of the marital property. Check with a family law attorney in your state for details.

B. Trade Secret and Patent Ownership

The rules for determining ownership of trade secrets and patentable inventions are essentially the same. Unless one of the very important exceptions discussed below applies, a patent or trade secret is initially owned by the person who creates or invents it. If there are more than one creators/inventors, they each jointly own their creation or invention.

1. Trade Secrets and Inventions Developed by Employees and Independent Contractors

Unlike copyright ownership, the basic rule for patents and trade secrets is that if you pay someone to invent or develop something, you own any patents or trade secrets developed in the course of the work.

a Employees and independent contractors hired to invent specific items

When an employee or independent contractor is hired to develop or invent a specific product, device or procedure, the employer owns the patent and trade secret rights to that item. In this situation, the employee or independent contractor is deemed to have sold whatever rights he may have had in the invention or trade secret to the employer in advance, in return for his salary or other compensation.

> **EXAMPLE:** Abe, a programmer, is hired by TopSoft to develop an Internet security program. TopSoft owns the rights to any patentable inventions and trade secrets developed by Abe in the course of his assigned task.

b. Generally inventive employees or independent contractors

If, instead of being hired to invent or develop a specific item, the employee or independent contractor is hired to do research in a general area and/or is generally employed to design something, the employer will own the rights to any patentable inventions and trade secrets developed by the worker so long as they were created:

- during working hours, and
- within the scope of employment.

> **EXAMPLE:** Assume that instead of being hired specifically to invent an Internet security program, Abe in the example above is hired by TopSoft simply to create new and useful programs. Abe decides to develop the security program and designs it during working hours. TopSoft owns the rights to any patents and trade secrets created by Abe in developing the program.

An employee who is not hired to invent or develop new products or technology owns the rights to any patentable inventions or trade secrets she creates. However, the employer will be entitled use the invention and include it in the products it sells without the employee's permission and without paying the employee for the use if:

- the employee used the employer's resources in creating the invention (for example, did a substantial amount of the work during business hours or used the employer's equipment), or
- the employee allowed the employer to promote the invention with a reasonable expectation of royalty-free use by the employer.

This type of license is called a "shop right." It is nonexclusive (it does not prevent an employee-inventor from transferring her patent rights to others) and nontransferable by the employer.

EXAMPLE 1: Ada is employed by Phoenix Developers as an accountant. Her job duties do not include developing new software. Ada develops a tax accounting program containing patentable features and other features that she maintains as a trade secret. Ada owns these patent and trade secret rights because she is a non-inventive employee—she was hired by Phoenix solely to do accounting work.

EXAMPLE 2: Assume that Ada developed her program during working hours on a Phoenix computer. Ada still owns the patentable inventions and trade secrets she developed, but Phoenix is entitled to use the program for free—it has a "shop right" in the program. But Phoenix cannot sell the program or use rights to others.

EXAMPLE 3: Assume that Ada develops her program at home and then shows it to a Phoenix programmer. She permits him to use a portion of the program in a new tax accounting package he's developing for Phoenix. Ada does not ask to be compensated for the use. Phoenix subsequently sells the package to the public. Phoenix has a shop right in the code Ada let Phoenix use for free. By failing to ask for compensation, Ada led Phoenix reasonably to believe that they could use the code without paying her.

2. Contracts Assigning Patentable Inventions and Trade Secrets to Hiring Party

Unless someone is clearly hired to develop a specific product, bitter and costly disputes can develop as to the ownership of patentable inventions and/or trade secrets developed by employees and independent contractors. The way virtually all high-technology companies avoid these types of disputes is to have all employees and independent contractors sign agreements transferring their ownership rights in advance to the hiring firm.

Most states permit a hiring firm to use employment contracts providing for the transfer of all inventions created by the employee or independent contractor in exchange for his or her salary or other compensation. However, seven states, notably including California, have statutory restrictions on invention assignments in employment contracts. Employment contracts are discussed in detail in Chapter 14. Contracts with independent contractors are discussed in Chapter 15.

C. Transferring Software Ownership and Use Rights

Like other forms of property, intellectual property can be sold or otherwise transferred to another party. There are two basic types of intellectual property transfers: exclusive licenses and assignments. Although these terms are often used interchangeably, there are some differences.

1. Licenses

A license is a grant of permission to do something. For example, when you get a driver's license the government gives you permission to drive a car. A copyright, patent, trade secret or trademark owner can give others permission to exercise one or more of the owner's exclusive rights, while retaining overall ownership. Such a permission is usually called a license.

Today, most software is licensed to end users rather than sold outright. Software licenses are discussed in detail in Chapter 16.

2. Assignments

The word "assignment" means a transfer of all the rights a person owns in a piece of property. So whenever a person or entity transfers all the intellectual property rights it owns in a work of authorship, the transaction is usually called an "assignment" or sometimes an "all rights transfer." An assignment of a copyright or patent must be in writing to be valid.

Trade secrets are usually not assigned to others except when a business is being sold, they are licensed instead. A written agreement is not required for assignments of trade secrets, but it is always a good idea to use one anyway.

When such an assignment transaction is completed, the original intellectual property owner no longer has any ownership rights at all. The new owner—the assignee—has all the rights the transferor formerly held .

Unless software involved has been patented (a rare situation), you'll normally use a copyright assignment to transfer ownership to others or obtain ownership of others' software. Such an assignment need not be a lengthy or complex document. Following is an example of a simple copyright assignment.

Copyright Assignment

_____ [name of copyright owner], for value received, grants to _____ [name of person or entity receiving assignment] all right, title and interest in the work described as follows:

_____

[list work's title and copyright registration number, if any].

[Name of Copyright Owner]

By: _____

_____

Typed name

Date: _____

Address: _____

_____

_____

[Name of Person or Entity Receiving Assignment]

By: _____

_____

Typed name

Date: _____

Address: _____

_____

_____

The text of this Copyright Assignment is on the CD-ROM forms disk at the end of this book under the file name ASSIGN. See Chapter 1 for guidance on how to use the forms disk.

3. Recording Copyright Transfers With the Copyright Office

The Copyright Office does not make or in any way participate in transfers of copyright ownership. But the office does record transfer documents after they have been signed by the parties. When a transfer document is recorded, a copy is placed in the Copyright Office files, indexed and made available for public inspection. This is similar to what happens when a deed to a house or other real estate is recorded with a county recorder's office. Recordation of transfer documents is not mandatory, but it results in so many valuable benefits that it is almost always a good idea.

Right to Terminate Copyright Transfers After 35 Years

There are many sad stories about authors or artists who sold their work for a pittance when they were young and/or unknown, only to have it become extremely valuable later in their lives or after their death. In an effort to protect copyright owners and their families from unfair exploitation, the Copyright Act gives individual authors or their heirs the right to terminate any transfer of their copyright rights 35 to 40 years after it was made. This special statutory termination right may be exercised only by individual authors or their heirs, and only as to transfers made after 1977. This termination right can never be waived or contracted away by an author. The owner of a work made for hire, whether an individual or a business entity such as a corporation or partnership, has no statutory termination rights.

EXAMPLE: Art, a teenaged video game enthusiast, creates a new and exciting computer arcade game in 1980. He sells all his rights in the game to Fun & Gameware for $500 the same year. The game becomes a best-seller and earns Fun & Gameware millions. Art is entitled to none of these monies, but he or his heirs can terminate the transfer to Fun & Gameware in the year 2015 and get back all rights in the game without paying Fun & Gameware anything.

This statutory termination right may be important to visual artists (painters and sculptors, for example), but, the fanciful example above aside, it probably doesn't mean much in the software world. Given the pace of development in the software industry, it is likely that little or no software will have any economic value 35 years after its creation.

There are no similar termination rights for patents or trademarks.

The Difference Between Recordation and Registration

As described in detail in Chapter 4, copyright registration is a legal formality by which an author or other copyright owner fills out a registration application for a published or unpublished work and submits it to the Copyright Office along with one or two copies of the work. If the copyright examiner is satisfied that the work contains protected expression and the application is completed correctly, the work is registered—that is, assigned a registration number, indexed and filed in the Copyright Office's records and the copies retained for five years.

Recordation does not involve submitting copies of a work. Recordation simply means that the Copyright Office files a document so that it is available for public inspection. As mentioned above, this can be any document relating to copyright. It can be for a work that is published, unpublished, or even not yet created. A good way to distinguish the two procedures is to remember that computer programs themselves are registered, while contracts or other documents relating to the copyright in a program are recorded.

a. Why record a copyright transfer?

Because a copyright is intangible and can be transferred simply by signing a piece of paper, it is possible for dishonest copyright owners to rip off copyright purchasers.

EXAMPLE: AcmeSoft signs a contract transferring the exclusive right to publish and distribute a new database program to Scrivener & Sons. Scrivener fails to record the transfer with the U.S. Copyright Office. Two months later, AcmeSoft sells the same rights in the program to MegaSoft. MegaSoft had no idea that AcmeSoft had already sold the same rights to Scrivener. AcmeSoft has sold the same property twice! As a result, if Scrivener and MegaSoft both publish the program, they'll be competing against each other (and they'll both probably be able to sue AcmeSoft for breach of contract, fraud and other causes of action).

Recordation of transfer documents protects copyright transferees from these and other abuses by establishing the legal priorities between copyright transferees if the transferor makes overlapping or confusing grants. Recordation also establishes a public record of the contents of transfer documents. This enables prospective purchasers of copyright rights to search the Copyright Office's transfer records to make sure that the copyright seller really owns what she's selling. (This is similar to the title search that a home buyer conducts before purchasing a house.) Finally, recordation of a transfer document for a registered work gives the entire world constructive notice of the transfer; constructive notice means everyone is deemed to know about the transfer, whether or not they really do.

Things would be much better for Scrivener & Sons in our example above if it had recorded the copyright transfer from Acme-Soft. In that event, the transfer to Scrivener would have priority over MegaSoft and would be deemed the only valid transfer. This would mean that as the sole copyright owner, only Scrivener would have the right to distribute the computer program.

b. What can be recorded?

Any document pertaining to a copyright can be recorded with the Copyright Office. Of course, this includes any document transferring all or part of a copyright—whether it be an exclusive license or assignment. It also includes nonexclusive licenses, wills, powers of attorney in which authors or other copyright owners give others the power to act for them and other contracts dealing with a copyrighted work.

You can record a document without registering the underlying work it pertains to, but important benefits are obtained if the work is registered. You can even record a document for a work that doesn't exist because it has yet to be written, such as, a publishing contract.

It's a very good idea to record any document that affects a transfer of copyright ownership. Also record any document that contains information you want the world at large to be aware of—for example, a change of the copyright owner's name.

Documents pledging a copyright as collateral or security for a loan should also be recorded.

c. How to record transfer documents

To record a document with the Copyright Office, you must complete and sign the Copyright Office Document Cover Sheet form and send it to the Copyright Office along with the document and recordation fee.

If the work involved hasn't already been registered with the Copyright Office, it should be at the same time the document is recorded. It's possible to record without registering, but important priority rights are obtained if the work is registered. (Of course, you can't register if the work is not yet in existence.)

Step 1: Complete the Document Cover Sheet

First, complete and sign the Document Cover Sheet.

 An electronic copy of the Document Cover Sheet is included in the CD-ROM disk at the end of this book under the file name formdoc.pdf. You must print the form out and then complete it by hand or typewriter. The forms is in Adobe Acrobat PDF format. You must have the Adobe Acrobat Reader installed on your computer to view and print the form. A copy of the appropriate reader is included on the CD-ROM. For detailed guidance on using the forms disk, see Chapter 1.

Space 1: Name of Parties to Document

In Space 1, you must name all the parties to the document you are recording. The document will be indexed under their names. Under "Party 1," list the name of the assignor or grantor—that is, the name of the person making a transfer of copyright rights (a work's author, for example). Under "Party 2," list the name of the assignee or grantee—that is, the name of the person receiving the transfer of copyright rights (a publisher, for example). If you don't have enough space to list all the parties involved, use a white 8½- inch by 11- inch sheet of paper to list them.

Space 2: Description of Document

Check the box that best describes the document you're recording. This will usually be the first box, "Transfer of Copyright."

Space 3: Title(s) of Work(s)

List here the titles, registration numbers (if any) and authors of all the works covered by the document being recorded. Use additional white sheets if you can't fit them all in on the form.

Space 4: Completeness of Document

A document being recorded with the Copyright Office should be complete on its own terms. At a minimum, it should contain (1) the names and addresses of the copyright owner(s) and person(s) or entity acquiring the copyright right(s); and (2) a description of the rights that are being transferred. The transfer document must also be signed by the transferor.

The Copyright Office will not examine your document to see if it meets these requirements. It will be recorded whether it does or not. However, if it doesn't, it may not be legally effective to establish a priority in case of conflicting transfers.

If your document meets these requirements, check the first box in Space 4. If not, and you want it recorded anyway, check the second box instructing the Copyright Office to record it as is.

Space 5: Number of Titles in Document

List in Space 5 the number of titles covered by the document. This will determine the recordation fee.

Space 6: Fee

State the amount of the recordation fee in Space 6. The Copyright Office charges a $20 fee to record a transfer document covering one to ten titles. For additional titles, there is an added charge of $10 for each group of up to ten titles—for example, it would cost $30 to record 11–20 titles, $40 to record 21–30 titles and so forth.

Space 7: Deposit Account

If you have a deposit account with the Copyright Office and want the fee charged to it, give the account number and name in Space 7.

Space 8: Date of Execution

State in Space 8 the date the document being recorded (not the Cover Sheet) was signed or became effective.

DOCUMENT COVER SHEET

For Recordation of Documents
UNITED STATES COPYRIGHT OFFICE

DATE OF RECORDATION
(Assigned by Copyright Office)

Month _____ Day _____ Year _____

—————————————Do not write above this line.—————————————

Volume _____ Page _____

Before you complete this form, please read the instructions on the reverse side. If additional space is needed, use white 8 ½ x 11 inch paper.

Volume _____ Page _____

Attachments to Cover Sheet? Yes ❏ No ❏ If so, how many?_____

REMITTANCE _____

To the Register of Copyrights:
Please record the accompanying original document or copy thereof.

FUNDS RECEIVED ⌐ _____

1 Name of the Party or Parties to the Document Spelled as They Appear in the Document.

Party 1: (assignor, grantor, etc.)_____   Party 2: (assignee, grantee, etc.)_____

2 Description of the Document:
❏ Transfer of Copyright
❏ Security Interest
❏ Change of Name of Owner

❏ Termination of Transfer(s) [Section 304]
❏ Shareware
❏ Life, Identity, Death Statement [Section 302]

❏ Transfer of Mask Works
❏ Other _____

3 Title(s) of Work(s), Author(s), Registration Number(s), and Other Information to Identify Work.

Title	Author(s)	Registration Number	Registration Date/Year

4 ❏ Document is complete by its own terms.
❏ Document is not complete. Record "as is."

5 Number of titles in Document: _____

6 Amount of fee enclosed or authorized to be charged to a Deposit Account _____ .

7 Deposit account number _____

Deposit account name _____

8 Date of execution and/or effective date of accompanying document _____ .
(Month)   (Day)   (Year)

9 Affirmation:* I hereby affirm to the Copyright Office that the information given on this form is a true and correct representation of the accompanying document. This affirmation will not suffice as a certification of a photocopy signature on the document. (Affirmation *must* be signed.)

10 Certification:* Complete this certification in addition to the Affirmation if a photocopy of the original signed document is submitted in lieu of a document bearing the actual signature.
I certify under penalty of perjury under the laws of the United States of America that the accompanying document is a true copy of the original document.

Signature _____

Date _____

Phone Number _____   Fax Number _____

Signature _____

Duly Authorized Agent of: _____

Date _____

MAIL RECORDA-TION TO

Name▼ _____

Number/Street/Apt▼ _____

City/State/ZIP▼ _____

YOU MUST:
• Complete all necessary spaces
• Sign your cover sheet in Space 9

SEND ALL 3 ELEMENTS IN THE SAME PACKAGE:
1. Two copies of the Document Cover Sheet
2. Fee in check or money order payable to *Register of Copyrights*
3. Document

MAIL TO:
Documents Unit, Cataloging Division
Copyright Office, Library of Congress
Washington, D.C. 20559-6000

*Knowingly and willfully falsifying material facts on this form may result in criminal liability. 18 U.S.C.§1001.

September 1996

☆ U.S. COPYRIGHT OFFICE WWW FORM: 1997

Space 9: Affirmation

The person submitting the document being recorded or her representative must sign where indicated in Space 9.

Space 10: Certification

You are supposed to submit one copy of the original transfer document signed by the transferor. If this is not possible, and you need to record a photocopy of the original document instead, Space 10 must be completed. Leave it blank if you submit the original.

To submit a photocopy in lieu of the original document, one of the parties to the document or his or her authorized representative must sign and date Space 10. By doing so, the signer certifies under penalty of perjury that the copy is a true copy of the original document.

Address

Finally, include at the bottom of the form the address where the Copyright Office should send the Certificate of Recordation.

Step 2: Send Your Recordation Package to the Copyright Office

You need to send all the following to the Copyright Office in one package:

- the original signed Document Cover Sheet and one copy,
- the proper recordation fee in a check or money order payable to the Register of Copyrights (unless you have a deposit account), and
- the document to be recorded.

Send your package to:

Documents Unit, LM-462
Cataloging Division
Copyright Office
Library of Congress
Washington, DC 20559

Within six to eight weeks you should receive a Certificate of Recordation from the Copyright Office showing that your transfer document (or nonexclusive license) has been recorded. The original signed transfer document (or nonexclusive license) will be returned with the certificate. ■

Chapter 12

Computer Databases

A computer database (or "automated database" in Copyright Office parlance) is a body of facts, data or other information assembled into an organized format suitable for use in a computer. For a computer database to be constructed, a computer must be told (programmed) where the information placed in it is stored and how that information can be retrieved upon request. Accordingly, when a database is actually constructed, it consists of:

- the data, and
- the database software—that is, the unique set of instructions that defines the way the data is to be organized, stored and retrieved.

This chapter discusses legal protection for the data in computer databases. The database software is protected in the same manner and to the same extent as any other computer software. Accordingly, protection for database software is covered throughout the rest of the book.

A. Types of Computer Databases

The variety of information contained on computer databases is nearly endless and growing rapidly. However, for our purposes they can be classified into two types: published databases and unpublished databases.

1. Published Databases

Published databases are those that are made available to the general public. These include databases that are available online—that is, the database is housed on a computer in a remote location and end users retrieve information from the database via telephone lines or computer networks. Examples include large commercial online information services such as America Online, Nexis and Dialog. Online services such as these are actually collections of many databases provided by a variety of

publishers and other sources. The services negotiate contracts with the owners of the databases for the right to distribute them, and pay royalties based primarily on how much the database is used. Costs to use such services are usually based on a subscription fee plus usage charges for actual use of particular databases.

Untold thousands of computer databases are also maintained by universities, research institutions, government agencies companies and individuals. Many of these can be accessed via the Internet—a global network of networks linking together tens of thousands of regional, state, federal, academic and corporate computer networks.

Still other published computer databases are available on CD-ROM disks or other magnetic storage media. For example, a CD-ROM database containing over 2 million patents issued by the United States Patent and Trademark Office has recently been published. The user purchases or licenses such databases directly from the publisher and uses them directly on her own computer, rather than accessing them via an online service or computer network. This allows the database publisher to bypass the online service and market its product directly to end users.

2. Unpublished Databases

As the name implies, unpublished databases are those not available to the general public. These include all types of computer databases created and maintained by businesses—for example, a database containing customer ordering and payment information, or a computerized list of auto parts used by an auto parts store. Many individuals also have their own private databases; for example, containing tax information, or a list of personal property for identification and valuation purposes in the event of fire or theft.

B. Copyright Protection for Computer Databases

Copyright law is the primary vehicle for legally protecting databases. However, not all databases are protected by copyright, and even those that are may enjoy very limited protection.

1. Databases Are Compilations or Collective Works

First, a little copyright law background. The individual bits of data contained in many databases are not entitled to copyright protection on their own. For example, names and addresses or numerical data may not qualify for copyright in their own right. But the way the database creator selected and arranged all these bits of data may constitute an original work of authorship protected by copyright (see below). In other words, the individual materials contained in a database may not be entitled to copyright protection, but the selection and arrangement of the entire database may be. This type of database is called a fact compilation.

However, many databases contain items that qualify for copyright protection on their own—for example, a database containing the full text of copyrighted articles. This type of database is a collective work. A collective work is a special type of compilation. It is a work created by selecting and arranging into a single whole work preexisting materials that are separate and independent works entitled to copyright protection in their own right. Also, as with fact compilations, there may be copyright protection for the selection and arrangement of the materials making up a collective work.

Of course, some databases contain both protectible and unprotectible material, and are therefore both fact compilations and collective works.

2. Database Selection and Arrangement Constitutes Protected Expression

You may be wondering why any compilation should be protected by copyright. The author of a compilation does not really create anything new, he merely selects and arranges preexisting material; so what is there to protect? For example, say that you compile a computer database listing the 1,000 baseball cards you consider most desirable for collectors listed in order of desirability. What makes such a database protectible is the creativity and judgment you would have to employ in deciding which of the thousands of baseball cards in existence belong on your list of the 1,000 most desirable cards and in deciding what order the names should appear on the list. It is this selection and arrangement of the material comprising a compilation that constitutes protected expression.

The copyright in a protectible fact compilation or collective work as a whole extends only to this protected expression—that is, only to the compiler's selection and arrangement of the preexisting material, not to the preexisting material itself. Of course, the individual items in a collective work may be copyrightable themselves.

3. Minimal Creativity Required for Protection

A work must be the product of a minimal amount of creativity to be protected by copyright. This requirement applies to fact compilations as well as all other works. The data contained in a factual compilation need not be presented in an innovative or surprising way, but the selection or arrangement cannot be so mechanical or routine as to require no creativity whatsoever. If no creativity was employed in selecting or arranging the data, the compilation will not receive copyright protection.

In a landmark decision on fact compilations, the U.S. Supreme Court held that the selection and arrangement of white pages in a typical telephone directory fails to satisfy the creativity requirement and is therefore not protected by copyright. (*Feist Publications, Inc. v. Rural Telephone Service Co.*, 111 S.Ct. 1282 (1991).) There are doubtless many other types of compilations that are unprotectible for the same reason.

Copyright Does Not Protect Hard Work

In the past, some courts held that copyright protected databases and other works that lacked originality and/or creativity if a substantial amount of work was involved in their creation. These courts might have protected a telephone directory, for example, if the authors had personally verified every entry. However, the Supreme Court outlawed this "sweat of the brow" theory in the Feist decision. It is now clear that the amount of work done to create a database or other work has absolutely no bearing on the degree of copyright protection it will receive. As discussed in detail in Chapter 3, copyright protects original expression, not hard work.

The *Feist* decision caused great concern in the database industry because many databases would appear to involve no more creativity in their compiling than telephone book white pages. Does this mean they are not entitled to copyright protection? The answer is not entirely clear. However, database publishers should take heart from the Supreme Court statement in *Feist* that only a very minimal degree of creativity is required for copyright protection and that the vast majority of compilations should make the grade.

Nevertheless, for a database to be protected by copyright (and registrable by the Copyright Office), the selection, arrangement and/or coordination involved in its creation must rise to the level of original authorship.

Arguably, the *arrangement* of the data in databases is never minimally creative because it is the database software that arranges the data into the form requested by the searcher, not the compiler of the database. (But, of course, the software is entitled to separate copyright protection.) However, the *selection* of the data to be included in a database may pass the minimal creativity test, at least where less than all of the available information on a particular topic is included. For example, a database containing the titles of every article written on toxic waste disposal in the United States since 1980 would likely not qualify for protection. No creativity would be required to select the data in such a database. On the other hand, a database consisting of what the database's compilers consider to be the most useful and important articles on toxic waste would likely be entitled to protection. Creativity and judgment would have to be employed to select which articles to include in such a database.

Databases whose creation was dictated solely by mechanical or functional considerations will likely not be protectible. Examples of databases that likely lack copyright protection include:

- exhaustive lists or collections of all the data on a given topic—for example, an alphabetical list of all the parts contained in Ford automobiles.
- databases whose selection, arrangement and/or coordination was determined by external guidelines or rules—for example, a database containing the names and addresses of contributors to the Republican Party under 50 years of age who voted for Pat Buchanan in the 1996 presidential primaries and for Ross Perot in the general election and who subscribe to *Penthouse* magazine.
- databases that are so commonplace in their parameters that a great possibility exists that someone else would arrive at the same selection—for example, a database of physicians' phone numbers, names and addresses arranged according to their medical specialties.

One of the first post-*Feist* cases dealing with computer databases illustrates that the more "value-added" features a database publisher adds to the raw facts contained in a database, the more likely it is that the database will be copyrightable. The case involved a computerized database of state trademarks. The state trademark records were themselves in the public domain. However, the publisher added to each trademark record a code indicating the type of mark, modified the state records' description of the mark to conform to standard descriptions, divided the data into separate search fields, and added search indices to facilitate computer searches of the records. The court held that the publisher's "selection, coordination, arrangement, enhancement, and programming of the state trademark data" satisfied the originality and creativity requirements set forth in the *Feist* decision. (*Corsearch, Inc. v. Thomson & Thomson,* Guide to Computer L. (CCH) 46,645 (S.D.N.Y. 1992).) In other words, the database qualified for copyright protection.

4. Using Raw Data From Protected Fact Compilation Databases

As discussed above, the copyright in a fact compilation extends only to the selection, coordination and arrangement of the data contained in the compilation and to any new expression the database author adds—for instance, instructions on how to use the database. The raw data itself is not protected. This is sometimes called a thin copyright.

Since the copyright in a fact compilation extends only to the compiler's selection and arrangement of the facts, the raw facts or data themselves are not protected by copyright. The Supreme Court has stated that the raw facts may be copied at will and that a compiler is even free to use the facts contained in another's compilation to aid in preparing a competing compilation. (*Feist*

Publications, Inc. v. Rural Telephone Service Co., 111 S.Ct. 1282 (1991).) But the competing work may not feature the exact same selection and arrangement as the earlier compilation—provided that this selection and arrangement passes the minimal creativity test as described in the previous section.

This means that a database user may extract the individual bits of data from a fact compilation database without incurring liability for copyright infringement, but may not copy the entire database, since this would involve copying the copyright owner's protected expression—that is, selection and arrangement. Thus, for example, the court held that the copyright in the state trademark database discussed above extended only to the publisher's "internally generated information and to its particular enhancements" to the state trademark records. The state trademark records themselves were not protected. Anyone could extract those records from the database and select and arrange them to create her own database without violating the publisher's copyright.

Copyright protection is greater where a database is a collective work—a work consisting of materials entitled to their own copyright protection. In this event, the database owner holds a thin copyright in the selection and arrangement of the entire database, and the items contained in the database may be protected individually. For example, each article contained in a full-text bibliographic database may be protected by copyright, as well as the selection and arrangement of the database as a whole.

Increased Protection for Databases in Europe: The EC Database Directive

The European Community (EC), which comprises most of the nations of Western Europe, enacted a final directive on the legal protection of commercial databases in early 1996. It is expected to be implemented by legislation in EC member states by early 1998. The Directive requires greater protection for databases than is available under U.S. law.

The Directive establishes two new sui generis (unique) rights for the makers of databases. It gives them the right to:
- prevent unauthorized extraction of all or a substantial part of the data from a database for commercial purposes, and
- prevent unauthorized re-utilization of all or part of the contents of a database for commercial purposes.

In other words, even if the data in a database lack sufficient creativity to qualify for copyright protection, the database maker can still prevent unauthorized extraction (copying) or use of the data. However, if the data in a database cannot be independently created, collected or obtained from other sources, the database maker may be required to grant licenses to those who wish to extract or use it.

These rights are to be available whenever a database maker has made a substantial investment in obtaining, verifying

---

The EC Database Directive (cont'd)

or presenting the contents of a database. They are to last for 15 years. However, if substantial changes are made to the content of a database, it receives a new 15-year term of protection.

Protection under the Directive is to be available only to nationals of members of the EC. Other countries will obtain such protection only if they offer comparable protection to databases of European nationals and if a bilateral agreement is reached. Current U.S. law does not provide comparable protection for databases, so U.S. residents will not enjoy the protection afforded by the Directive.

What all this means is that it may be illegal for you to extract the data from a database located in Europe, but perfectly legal to copy the same data from a database located in the U.S. However, legislation is being considered to amend U.S. law along the lines of the Directive.

---

5. Registering Contents of Computer Databases

If a computer database is protected by copyright, it should be registered with the Copyright Office for all the reasons discussed in Chapter 4. Since most databases are frequently updated or revised, the Copyright Office has instituted a special group registration procedure whereby a database and all the updates or other revisions made within any three-month period may be registered in one application. This way, a database need only be registered a maximum of four times per year, rather than each time it is updated or revised.

Database Software Must Also Be Registered

The discussion below is only about how to register the selection and arrangement of the contents of a computer automated database. It does not cover registration of computer software designed to be used with databases to facilitate retrieval of the data. (See Chapter 4.)

---

a. Databases qualifying for group registration

To qualify for group registration, a database must meet all of the following conditions:

- all of the updates or revisions must be fixed or published only in machine-readable copies
- all of the updates or revisions must have been created or published within a three-month period, all within the same calendar year
- all of the updates or revisions must be owned by the same copyright claimant (see Chapter 4, Section E1, for more on copyright claimants)

- all of the updates or revisions must have the same general title, and
- the updates or revisions must be organized in a similar way.

b. Completing Form TX

Form TX must be submitted for a group database registration. Here's how to fill it out:

Space 1: Title

At the Title of this Work line, insert the following statement: "Group registration for automated database titled _____; published/unpublished (choose one) updates from _____ to _____." Give the earliest and latest dates for the updates included in the group registration. Remember, this time period must be three months or less, all within the same calendar year.

Use the Publication as a Contribution line to give the following information: The date (day, month, year) that is represented by the marked portions of the identifying material submitted as a deposit (see Space 3 below). Also indicate the frequency with which revisions are made—for example, "daily," "weekly," "monthly."

Space 2: Author(s)

You need to give the requested information about every author who contributed any appreciable amount of protectible material to the version of the work being registered. We're talking about the compilation/collective work authorship here, not the authorship of the individual articles or other works in the database. After the words "Nature of Authorship," give a brief general statement of the nature of the particular author's contribution to the work. Examples: "updates," "revisions," "revised compilation," "revised and updated text."

Space 3: Creation and Publication

Give the year in which the author(s) completed the group of updates or revisions being registered.

If the updates or revisions have been published, you must give the date (month, day, year) and nation of publication. This should be the last date on which revisions were added during the three-month period covered by the application. When is a database published? This is not exactly clear. For copyright purposes, "publication" means distributing or offering to distribute copies of a work to the public on an unrestricted basis. It is unclear whether online availability with or without printers for the user constitutes publication. The Copyright Office leaves it up to the copyright owners to determine whether their database has been published.

Space 4: Claimants

Follow the instructions in Chapter 4, Section H, on how to complete this space.

Space 5: Previous Registration

If the database has been previously registered, check the last box and give the previous registration number and date. If more than one previous registration has been made for the database, give the number and date of any one previous registration.

Space 6: Derivative Work or Compilation

Space 6 must be completed if the updates or the database and its updates contain a substantial amount of previously published, registered or public domain material. Leave Space 6 blank if the material contained in the database and its updates is entirely new and never before registered or published.

Preexisting Material (Space 6a): State "previously registered material," "previously published material" or "public domain data" for a new database that has not been previously registered or published, but that contains an appreciable amount of previously registered, published or public domain material.

For a previously published or registered database that has not been revised or updated periodically, describe the preexisting material as "previously published database" or "previously registered database," or "database prior to (earliest date represented in the present group of updates)."

Material Added to This Work (Space 6b): Describe the updates or revisions or new database being registered for the first time and specify the frequency of these updates or revisions—for example, "weekly updates," "daily revisions" or "revised compilation updated monthly."

Spaces 7 and 8

Leave these spaces blank. They're not applicable to computer databases.

Spaces 9, 10, 11: Fee, Correspondence, Certification, Return Address

Follow the instructions in Chapter 4, Section H on how to complete these spaces.

c. Deposit requirements for group registration

You must submit the following deposit with your registration application:

- Identifying material: Samples meeting the following requirements:
  - 50 representative pages of printout (or equivalent units if reproduced in microfilm) from a single-file database; or
  - 50 representative complete data records (not pages) from each updated data file in a multiple-file database.

The printout or data records must be marked to show the copyrightable revisions or updates from:

- one representative publication date (if the database is published), or
- one representative creation date (if the database is unpublished)

within the three-month period covered by the registration.

Alternatively, you may deposit a copy of the actual updates or revisions made on a representative date.

- Descriptive statement: In addition, you must submit a brief, typed descriptive statement providing the following information:
  - the title of the database

- the name and address of the copyright claimant
- the name and content of each separate file in a multiple-file database, including its subject, origin(s) of the data, and the approximate number of data records it contains
- information about the nature, location and frequency of the changes within the database or within the separate data files in multiple-file databases, and
- information about the copyright notice, if one is used, as follows:
- for a machine-readable notice, transcribe the contents of the notice and indicate the manner and frequency with which it's displayed—for example, at user's terminal only, at sign-on, continuously on terminal display or on printouts.
- for a visually perceptible notice on any copies of the work (or on tape reels or containers), include a photocopy or other sample of the notice.

d. Non-group registration

If your database doesn't qualify for group registration, or for some reason you do not wish to use that procedure, simply complete Form TX in the same manner as for any other compilation. You should deposit the first and last 25 pages of a single-file database. If the database consists of separate and distinct data files, deposit one copy of 50 complete data records (not pages) from each file, or the entire file, whichever is less. You must also include a descriptive statement for a multiple-file database containing the same information described in Section B5c just above.

If the database is fixed in a CD-ROM, deposit one complete copy of the CD-ROM package, any instructional manual, and a printed version of the work which is fixed on the CD-ROM if such an exact print version exists. The deposit must also include any software that is included as part of the package. A print-out of the first and last 25 pages of the software source code is acceptable. If the software contains trade secrets, other deposit arrangements can be made. See the discussion in Chapter 4, Section I.

C. Using Contracts to Protect Databases

Given the limitations on copyright protection for computer databases, and the fact that some databases are probably not even entitled to these protections, the database industry has been placing increasing reliance on the use of contracts to prevent unauthorized use of databases. These include form contracts as well as negotiated agreements tailored for individuals or institutions. They may appear in traditional print, in shrink-wrap form, on a computer screen as part of software or online or in a combination of these formats.

Samples of numerous database agreements can be found in *Contracts in the Information Industry III*, published by the Information Industry Association; 202-986-0280; www.infoindustry.org.

1. Terms of Use

Though terms vary from company to company and from product to product, database contracts typically contain provisions restricting access and specifying conditions of use. These agreements limit users' ability to use the contents of databases in ways that the law would otherwise allow.

> EXAMPLE: A Dun & Bradstreet online license for its database provides: "You are granted a nonexclusive, nontransferable limited license to access and use for research purposes the Online Services and Materials from time to time made available to you ... are prohibited from downloading, storing, reproducing, transmitting, displaying, copying, distributing, or using Materials retrieved from the Online Services. You may not print or download Materials without using the printing or downloading commands of the Online Services."

Other agreements used for databases in CD-ROM format make explicit reference to fair use. For example, a Lexis-Nexis contract for CD-ROMs allows users to "create a print-out of an insubstantial portion of material retrieved from the Licensed Databases," and reproduce them "to the extent permitted under the fair use provisions of the Copyright Act."

Terms may be more restrictive for particularly valuable or sensitive information. Dun & Bradstreet, for example, has strict practices for its sensitive information, such as information relating to bankruptcy filings. For these products, it restricts third party distribution and exercises extreme caution in its licensing practices. By keeping direct control over distribution, the company is always in a position to recall or expand earlier data. It also conducts thorough background checks on potential patrons and extends licenses only to those who are creditworthy and risk-free.

2. Limitations on Contracts

Despite their usefulness, there are important practical limitations on the effectiveness of database contract restrictions. Most significant is the privity requirement for enforcing a contract—that is, a contract may only be enforced against a person who has agreed to it. A contract is not enforceable against third persons who never agreed to it. For example, the contract accompanying a CD-ROM database product binds only the initial contracting parties; it would not bind third parties who come into possession of the CD-ROM. Once such a CD-ROM leaves a database owner's possession, it has no practical way of preventing third party's from obtaining it. ■

Chapter 13

Multimedia Programs

This Chapter is for anyone who is developing or thinking about developing a multimedia program. Sections A though E discuss the special copyright problems faced by multimedia developers. Section F covers publicity and privacy concerns. Section G contain a multi-media license agreement and Section H discusses copyright registration and notice for multimedia programs.

A. Introduction

Multimedia programs—software that com-bines text, graphics and sounds, have become ubiquitous in the software world. However, before you or your company jump on the multimedia bandwagon, you need to be aware that multimedia projects can present difficult and expensive legal problems. These fall into two main categories:

- **The copyright permissions problem.** You may need to obtain permission to use materials protected by copyright, whether it be text, photos, video and film clips, software or music. Obtain-ing permissions for a project can involve tracking down many different copyright owners and negotiating licenses to use their material. (This is discussed in detail in Section B, below.)
- **Publicity/privacy problems.** Use of photos, film or video footage or audio recordings can constitute a breach of the privacy and/or publicity rights of

the people whose likenesses are used. You'll need to consider whether you must obtain privacy releases from persons whose images or voices are used. (This is discussed in detail in Section F, below.)

Obtaining copyright permission and publicity privacy releases can be a weighty task.

EXAMPLE: MultiSolutions Software, a small software developer, decides to create an interactive multimedia CD-ROM package about Columbus's "discovery" of America. MultiSolutions wants its package to contain operating system software, programming soft-ware, and many other third party appli-cation software programs to support graphics, sound and animation. Multi-Solutions also wants to incorporate into the program a variety of preexisting materials about Columbus, including:

- text from various articles and books
- photos from books, magazines and other sources
- video clips from several television programs
- film clips from two theatrical movies about Columbus
- music to be used as background to the images and text, and
- excerpts from a Broadway musical and Italian opera based on Columbus's life.

All in all, MultiSolutions intends to incorporate hundreds of separate items into its software package. This sounds like a fine idea for a multimedia product. However, MultiSolutions needs to address and resolve the copyright permissions problem and publicity/privacy problems before it can legally distribute its Columbus CD-ROM.

Clearly, MultiSolutions has its work cut out for it. The more third party material it uses, the more time and money it must spend to obtain the necessary permissions and releases.

Some developers have discovered that certain multimedia projects are not economically feasible in today's marketplace because the legal and licensing costs are too high. For example, one developer abandoned a project to copy baseball cards on CD-ROM disks when it discovered that to obtain the necessary rights, it would have to go through separate negotiations with more than 500 individual players (or their lawyers). The developer concluded that the profits that could reasonably be expected from the sales of the CD-ROM would be far too small to justify such an undertaking.

Other Intellectual Property Concerns

A multimedia developer's main concerns are with copyright and publicity/privacy problems. However, other intellectual property laws may come into play as well. For example:

- Third party software may be patented; photographic special effects may also be protected by patents. A license must be obtained to use any material protected by a patent.

- The federal and state trademark laws may protect character names, physical appearance and costumes; some titles; as well as product names, logos, slogans and packaging. A developer may have to obtain permission to use a trademark in a multimedia work. (See Chapter 9 for an overview of trademarks.)

- Finally, trade secret problems may occur whenever a multimedia developer uses or is exposed to any material or information (even a mere idea) that is covered by a confidentiality agreement. A developer must be particularly vigilant about avoiding use of confidential information any employee obtained from a prior employer. (See Chapter 6 for a detailed discussion of trade secrets.)

There are ways to get around, or at least alleviate, permissions problems. First we'll discuss when a software developer does and does not need to obtain permissions, and second, where and how to get them if they are needed. We'll then review the privacy and publicity issues that arise in multimedia projects.

The legal problems associated with multimedia projects are varied and complex. This chapter doesn't discuss all of them in detail. For further information refer to:

- *Multimedia Law and Business Handbook,* by J. Dianne Brinson and Mark F. Radcliffe, published by Ladera Press; 3130 Alpine Road, Suite 9002-200, Menlo Park, Calif. 94025, 800-523-3721.
- *The Software Publishers Association Legal Guide to Multimedia*, by Thomas J. Smedinghoff, published by Addison-Wesley Publishing Co.

It is not necessary that you handle all the legal problems associated with multimedia programs yourself. You can hire an outside company or individual to deal with them for you. For example:

- Professional copyright search firms can determine if a work is in the public domain; see Section C1b for a list of such firms.
- Copyright clearance firms will find out who owns the rights you need and negotiate them for you. See Section E1e for a list of such firms.

If you intend to hire such professional help, it's not absolutely necessary for you to read this entire chapter. You can skip Sections E and G. However, the more of this chapter you read, the better able you'll be to communicate with a multimedia professional.

B. When to Obtain Permission to Use Material in a Multimedia Project

Whether or not a software developer needs permission to include any given item in a multimedia project depends on:

- whether the item is protected by copyright or is in the public domain
- whether or not the material is created especially for the multimedia project
- who created it (employee, independent contractor or third party), and
- the extent and nature of the intended use.

1. New Material Created for a Multimedia Project

No copyright permissions problems are normally presented when material is created especially for a multimedia project, whether by the developer's employees or independent contractors. For this reason, many multimedia programs today consist primarily of original material.

Under the copyright laws, a developer will automatically own the copyright in materials created in-house by its own employees. (See Chapter 11 for a detailed discussion of copyright ownership.) As a result, the developer need not obtain permission from its employees to use copyrighted works—the developer already owns those rights. For example, MultiSolutions Software would not need to obtain permission to use drawings created by a staff artist in its multimedia program on Columbus. It is wise, however, to have creative employees sign employment agreements transferring whatever ownership rights they might conceivably have to the developer. (See Chapter 14 for a detailed discussion and sample forms.)

When a developer hires an independent contractor to contribute to a multimedia project, it should require the contractor to assign copyright rights to the developer. For example, if MultiSolutions hires a freelance artist to create drawings for its Columbus project, it should have the artist, before commencing work, sign an independent contractor agreement assigning her rights in the drawings to MultiSolutions. (See Chapter 15 for a detailed discussion and sample forms.)

2. Preexisting Materials

The permissions problem raises its ugly head when a developer wishes to use preexisting materials—that is, materials previously created by non-employees (or created by employees before they became employees). You can figure out whether permission is required by answering the following two questions:

- Is the material in the public domain?
- Does your intended use of the material constitute a "fair use?"

If your answer to both questions is "no," you need permission; otherwise you don't. To help you answer these questions, Section C discusses what is in the public domain and Section D examines the fair use rule.

3. Using Copyrighted Material Without Permission

You might be tempted to use copyrighted material without permission if you are unable to locate the copyright owner or simply don't have the time, money or staff to obtain numerous permissions. If the copyright owner later discovers what you've done, at the very least you will be liable for the reasonable value of the use. If the material is not terribly valuable, this won't amount to much, and the owner will probably accept a small permission fee.

EXAMPLE: MultiSolutions Software wants to quote two pages from an old magazine article about Columbus. The magazine is out of business and neither the author nor her heirs can be located. MultiSolutions decides to use the quotation anyway. One year later, Multi-Solutions is contacted by the article's copyright owner. The owner agrees to accept $250 from MultiSolutions for retroactive permission to use the quotation.

On the other hand, if the material is valuable, you could find yourself in big trouble. At the very least, you'll be liable for a substantial permission fee, perhaps more than you'd be able or willing to pay. Instead of settling for a permission fee, the copyright owner might sue you for copyright infringement. In this event, you could face substantial damages. The copyright owner you've stolen from could ask the court for the reasonable value of the use and the amount of any economic loss caused by your theft; or, if the material has been registered with the U.S. Copyright Office, the copyright owner could ask for special statutory damages, which can range up to $100,000 (it's up to the judge to decide how much). In some cases, you could even be subject to criminal prosecution. And don't forget, you'll be paying your attorney handsomely, regardless of how the case turns out.

EXAMPLE: MultiSolutions Software "borrows" several minutes from the video version of a recent theatrical movie about Columbus and uses it in its multimedia program. The film's copyright owners discover the theft and sue MultiSolutions for copyright infringement. They obtain an injunction prohibiting MultiSolutions from distributing the program with the pirated footage and ultimately obtain a court judgment against MultiSolutions. They ask the judge to award statutory damages, and, because the judge finds that the infringement was willful and blatant, she awards $50,000 in damages against MultiSolutions.

(See Chapter 5 for a detailed discussion of copyright infringement.)

C. Works That Are in the Public Domain

The general nature of copyright protection is discussed in Chapter 3. If you haven't read that material, do so now. Copyright protects all original works of authorship. This includes, but is not limited to, writings of all kinds, music, sound recordings, paintings, sculptures and other works of art, photographs, film and video. Of course, computer software is protected as well.

Luckily for multimedia developers, however, not every work of authorship ever created is currently protected by copyright—not by a long shot. A work that is not protected by copyright is said to be in the "public domain"; in effect, it belongs to everybody. Anyone is free to use it without asking permission, but no one can ever own the work again. By using public domain materials, a multimedia software developer can avoid going through the time, trouble and expense involved in getting permission to use copyrighted materials.

There are two main reasons why a work or other item may be in the public domain:

- the copyright in the work has expired, or
- the work was never protected by copyright in the first place.

> ⚠️ **Foreign distribution.** This discussion only covers works in the public domain in the United States. A work in the public domain in the United States may still be protected by the copyright laws of foreign countries. One reason is that, before 1978, most foreign countries granted a longer period of copyright protection than did the United States. If you intend to distribute a multimedia work outside the United States, seek expert advice as to whether any public domain material included in the work must be licensed for use abroad.

1. Works in Which Copyright Protection Has Expired

Copyright protection does not last forever. When a work's copyright protection expires, it automatically enters the public domain. The copyright has expired on a vast body of literature, art, music, photographs and even early films. Two categories of works are now in the public domain because the copyright has expired:

- works published at least 75 years ago, and

- works published before 1964 that weren't copyright renewed.

a. Works published more than 75 years ago

All works *first published* in the United States (see sidebar below) more than 75 years before January 1 of the current year are in the public domain because the copyright has expired.

All copyright durations run until the end of the calendar year in which they would otherwise expire. For example, the copyright in a work that was first published in 1900 expired on December 31, 1975, regardless of what month and day during 1900 it was published. To determine whether a book or other work was first published more than 75 years ago, simply look at the year-date in the work's copyright notice. This should show the year of first publication.

What Constitutes Publication

A work is "published" for copyright purposes when copies are sold, rented, lent, given away or otherwise distributed to the public by the copyright owner or by others acting with the owner's permission—for example, a publisher. It is not necessary to sell thousands of copies of a work for it to be "published." So long as copies of a work are made available to the public, the work is published for copyright purposes, even if no copies are actually sold or otherwise distributed.

A work of art is published if it is offered for sale to the public or if copies —photographs, for example—are publicly distributed. Simply displaying artwork in a gallery or museum does not constitute publication.

b. Works published before 1964 that were not timely renewed

Many works that were first published before 1964, but less than 75 years ago, have also entered the public domain. This is because a work published before 1964 had an initial copyright term of 28 years and an additional 47-year renewal term if a renewal application was filed with the Copyright Office during the 28th year. This means that pre-1964 works that were renewed in time are protected by copyright for a total of 75 years (28 + 47 = 75). All pre-1964 works that were not renewed during the 28th year entered the pubic domain on the 29th year after publication.

EXAMPLE: Lisa, an outdoor photographer, published a book of photographs in 1960. The work had an initial copyright term of 28 years. For some reason, Lisa and her publisher failed to renew the copyright in the book by filing a renewal application with the Copyright Office during 1988, the 28th year after publication. As a result, the work entered the public domain on January 1, 1989. Had a renewal been filed, the book would have received an additional renewal term of 47 years. But once the work entered the public domain, there was no way for Lisa to get it back. The book is freely available for anyone to use.

It is estimated that only about 15% of all pre-1964 works had their copyrights renewed. This means that 85% of all works published before 1964, but less than 75 years ago, have entered the public domain. The 15% that were renewed, however, probably include many of the works that are still valuable today. Nevertheless, mistakes occasionally were made and some noteworthy works were never renewed.

When a book or other written work is reprinted after renewal, the copyright notice usually provides this information. Otherwise you'll probably need to research the Copyright Office's records to find out if a renewal was filed in time. (See the sidebar below.)

⚠ Copyright in many public domain foreign works has been restored The GATT agreement (an international trade agreement that contains important provisions regarding intellectual property), has automatically restored the copyright in certain works that were originally published outside the United States and that entered the public domain in the U.S. because they weren't timely renewed, were published without notice or published in a country with which the U.S. had no copyright relations. The restoration took effect January 1, 1996, and applies to all works:

- originally published in a country that is a member of the Berne Convention or GATT (which includes most of the nations of the world; see Chapter 10)
- authored by at least one person who was not a U.S. citizen or resident
- with copyright protection which has not expired under the copyright laws of the foreign country—in most foreign countries, copyright protection lasts for the life of the author plus 50 years; in western Europe the copyright term is life plus 70 years.

EXAMPLE: The novel *The Far Side of Paradise* was originally published in Great Britain in 1933 and republished in the United States in 1935. No copyright renewal was filed for the work during 1963, the 28th year after the U.S.

publication, so it entered the public domain in the U.S. on January 1, 1964. However, because of GATT, copyright in the work was automatically restored on January 1, 1996. The work will remain under copyright until the end of 2008 (75 years from the year of initial U.S. publication).

Some of the most noteworthy works for which copyright has been restored are musical compositions by modern composers such as Prokofiev and Shostakovich who lived and worked in the former Soviet Union. Their works, originally published in the Soviet Union in the 1920s through the 1960s, were not protected by copyright in the United States because the Soviet Union was not a member of any of international copyright treaty and had no copyright relations with the U.S. The Soviet Union did not join a copyright treaty until it signed the Universal Copyright Convention in 1973. Copyright in most of these pre-1973 works has now been restored under GATT.

Because of GATT, you can basically forget about using without permission any foreign works published less than 75 years ago. Most are now protected by copyright, even if they were never renewed or were published without a valid copyright notice. For a more detailed discussion, see *The Copyright Handbook: How to Protect and Use Written Works,* by Stephen Fishman (Nolo Press). A list of some of the works for which copyright has been restored can be found at the Copyright Office's Website at http://lcweb.loc.gov/copyright/gatt.html.

How to Research Copyright Renewals

There are three ways to find out if a renewal was filed in time for a work:

1. **Have the Copyright Office search its records for you.** They charge $20 an hour for this service. Call the Reference & Bibliography Section at 202-707-6850 and ask for an estimate of how long they think your particular search will take. Then, complete and send in the Copyright Office's Search Request form. Be sure to include your name, address and phone number and indicate if you want to receive the results of the search by phone. The request form should be sent to:

   Reference & Bibliography Section,
      LM-451
   Copyright Office
   Library of Congress
   Washington, DC 20559

   A copy of the Copyright Office Search Request form is contained on the CD-ROM forms disk at the end of this book under the file name SEARCH. See Chapter 1 for instructions on how to use the forms disk.

2. **Have a professional search firm conduct the search for you.** This will probably cost much more than having the Copyright Office do the search (fees start at about $100), but you will get much faster service. Search firms usually report back in two to ten working days, while it often takes the Copyright Office one or two months to conduct a search. There are several copyright search firms, located primarily in the Washington, D.C. area:

Government Liaison Services, Inc.
3030 Clarendon Blvd., Ste. 209
Arlington, VA 22201
800-642-6564 or 703-524-8200

Robert G. Roomian
P.O. Box 7111
Alexandria, VA 22307
703-690-6451

Thomson & Thomson
1750 K St., NW, Ste. 200
Washington, DC 20006
800-356-8630
(This is the largest and best-known search firm.)

XL Corporate Services
Attn.: Mark Moel
62 White St.
New York, NY 10013
800-221-2972

3. **Search the Copyright Office records yourself.** This entails looking up the work in the *Catalog of Copyright Entries* (CCE). The CCE is a monumental series of annual catalogs listing and cross-referencing every work registered and

How to Research Copyright Renewals (continued)

renewed by the Copyright Office. The CCE is available to the public at the Copyright Office, located in the James Madison Memorial Building, 101 Independence Ave. S.E., Washington, DC. The Office is open from 8:30 a.m. to 5:00 p.m., Monday through Friday. Alternatively, the CCE can be found in government depository libraries throughout the country.

Renewal records made during or after 1978 are available online at the Copyright Office's Website. However, these records are only useful for determining whether works published between 1960 and 1963 have been renewed. The URL is http://lcweb.loc.gov/copyright.

Before researching a copyright renewal yourself, obtain a copy of *Researching Copyright Renewal,* by Iris J. Wildman and Rhonda Carlson (Fred B. Rothman & Co., 10368 West Centennial Rd., Littleton, CO 80127, 800-457-1986). This 85-page paperback, written by two law librarians, clearly explains exactly how to go about determining whether a renewal was timely filed, including how to decipher the often cryptic entries in the CCE.

2. Pre-1989 Works Published Without a Valid Copyright Notice

There is one more class of works less than 75 years old that are in the public domain. These are works that were published before March 1, 1989, without a valid copyright notice. For written and most other works, that's the "c" in a circle—©—followed by a publication date (the date isn't mandatory on pictorial, graphic and sculptural works) and the copyright owner's name. A "p" in a circle (℗) is used for sound recordings.

Prior to 1989, all published works had to have a valid copyright notice to be protected by copyright. This is not the law anymore; copyright notices are now optional.

Few valuable works have been published without a copyright notice. But on rare occasions, mistakes have been made. Moreover, works not considered valuable when originally published may have lacked a copyright notice. Such works may be useful today—for example, old postcards.

Any work published before 1978 (the date the current copyright law took effect) without a valid notice is now in the public domain, unless the notice was inadvertently left off a mere handful of copies. That may not be the case with unnoticed works published between January 1, 1978, and March 1, 1989, however. Such works did not enter the public domain if the copyright owner cured the omission by registering the work and making a reasonable effort to add a copyright notice to all copies distributed after the omission was discovered. If you want to use a work published between 1978 and March 1, 1989, without a copyright notice, contact the copyright owner to see if it cured the omission.

Note that individual contributions to a collective work, like a magazine or anthology, don't need to have their own copyright notice; a single notice at the front of the work is sufficient. Also, bear in mind that a notice is only required for published works. Unpublished works have never had to have a copyright notice to be protected; they have automatic copyright protection. (See Chapter 4 for a detailed discussion of copyright notices.)

Special Rules for Pre-1972 Sound Recordings

None of the rules covered in this discussion of the public domain apply to sound recordings made before 1972. That's because recordings—phonograph records, for example—were not protected by the federal copyright laws until February 15, 1972. The underlying musical composition was protected by copyright, but not the recording itself. Before 1972, sound recordings were protected by state anti-piracy laws and common law (judge-made law). You probably won't find any copyright notice on a pre-1972 recording, but this does not mean it is not legally protected. These state law protections will not all expire until 2047.

3. Post-1963 Works Are Protected by Copyright Far Into the 21st Century

All works first published after 1963 will be protected by copyright until well into the 21st Century. Works published during the years 1964 through 1977 will be under copyright for 75 years after publication.

In 1978, the current copyright law took effect, and new copyright terms apply. Individually authored works created after 1977 usually are protected for the life of the author plus 50 years. Post-1977 works made for hire are protected for 75 years after publication or 100 years from date of creation, whichever date expires first.

You don't have to memorize all these rules. Just remember that any work published after 1963 will be under copyright for many decades to come. Permission must be obtained to use such works in a multimedia project unless the use constitutes a fair used as discussed in Section D, below.

4. Unpublished Works

An unpublished manuscript, artwork or other work of authorship created by an individual author is under copyright for the life of the author plus 50 years. An unpublished work for hire is protected for 100 years after creation.

A special rule applies to unpublished works created by individual authors who have been dead over 50 years and unpublished works for hire created over 100 years ago. Under the rules outlined above, such works should now be in the public domain —but they're not. A special provision of the copyright law protects such works through December 31, 2002. But if such works are published before 2003, they will remain under copyright until the end of 2027.

Again, you don't have to memorize all of these rules. Just remember that, at least until 2003 (and far longer in most cases), you'll need permission to use any unpublished work.

5. Derivative Works

Special problems often arise determining the copyright status of derivative works—that is, works created by transforming or adapting preexisting works. Examples of derivative works include translations of foreign language works into English and transformation of a work into a new medium, such as a photograph of a painting or sculpture.

A derivative work is considered to be a brand new work for copyright purposes and is entitled to its own term of copyright protection, independent of the protection given to the underlying work. This means that many works you might think are in the public domain really aren't. Consider these examples:

- The original Greek version of Homer's *Iliad* is in the public domain, but a 1980 English translation of Iliad is a derivative work protected by copyright until well into the next century.

- Shakespeare's *Hamlet* is in the public domain, but a 1960 film of Hamlet is a protected derivative work. Likewise, a 1980 printed student edition of Hamlet is in the public domain, but footnotes and other explanatory material included in the edition are protected by copyright.
- Gainsborough's famous 18th century painting Blueboy is in the public domain, but a 1970 photograph of Blueboy is a copyrighted derivative work.
- The traditional song *Greensleeves* is in the public domain, but a 1950 arrangement of the song is protected by copyright.
- Beethoven's Fifth Symphony is in the public domain, but a 1990 recording of it by the New York Philharmonic is under copyright.

A multimedia developer must obtain permission to use the derivative works described above, or, alternatively, must go back to the original public domain source for the derivative work and use that instead. For example, a developer that didn't want to pay for permission to use the New York Philharmonic's recording of Beethoven's Fifth could hire musicians to make its own recording without getting permission from anybody.

It can be difficult to determine which parts of a derivative work are in the public domain and which are protected by copyright. You may wish to retain the services of a copyright search firm to investigate the work's copyright status. By searching Copyright Office and other records, these firms can tell you when each element of a work was created and/or published. (See the sidebar in Section C1b, above, for a list of search firms.)

6. Things That Are Never Protected by Copyright

Certain works of authorship and other items are never protected by copyright. These consist of:

- **Ideas and facts.** Because copyright only protects an author's expression, ideas and facts themselves are not protected. (See Chapter 3 for a detailed discussion.)
- **Words, names, titles, slogans and other short phrases.** Individual words are always in the public domain, even if they are invented by a particular person. Names (whether of individuals, products or business organizations or groups), titles, slogans and other short phrases are also not copyrightable. However, these items may be protected under state and federal trademark laws if they are used to identify a product or service. (See Chapter 9.)
- **United States government works.** All works created by U.S. government employees as part of their jobs are in the public domain. This includes, for example, everything printed by the U.S. Printing Office, NASA photo-

graphs, the President's speeches and publications and other works by federal agencies. But this rule does not apply to U.S. postage stamps, which are protected by copyright. Also, this rule does not apply to works by state and local government employees; those works may be protected by copyright.

Works created for the federal government by independent contractors—that is, persons who are neither U.S. government officers nor employees—can be protected by copyright. However, the government may require these persons to sign "work made for hire" agreements as a condition to receiving federal money. In this event, the U.S. government, not the individual who actually created the work, would be considered the "author" of the work; this would mean that the work would be in the public domain.

7. Works Dedicated to the Public Domain

The owners of some works have decided they don't want them to be protected by copyright and dedicate them to the public domain. For example, some software has been dedicated to the public domain. There are no formal procedures for dedicating a work to the public domain. The author just has to indicate on the work that no copyright is claimed. The Copyright Office will not register such a work.

8. Public Domain Works Are Not Always Freely Available

The fact that a work is in the public domain does not necessarily mean that it is freely available for use by a multimedia developer. Although the copyright in a work may have expired, the work itself may still be owned by someone, who may restrict or charge for access to it.

This is usually not a problem for written works, which can be found in bookstores and libraries, but it is a problem for other types of works. For example, all works of art published over 75 years old are in the public domain, but recent photographs of them are not. Museums and individual collectors usually control access to valuable works of art that are in the public domain and often own all available photographs of such works. Getting permission to use such photographs or to take new ones can be difficult and expensive. Some large software developers, such as Microsoft, have purchased the exclusive right to use the photographs of many important artworks in multimedia programs.

Fees may also have to be paid to obtain access to and make use of public domain

WHAT'S HE SO SMUG ABOUT?

I HEAR HE JUST ENTERED THE PUBLIC DOMAIN.

photographs, film and music from collectors, private archives and other sources. (See Section E, below.)

D. The "Fair Use" Exception to Copyrighted Works

Even if the material you want to use is protected by copyright, you will not need permission if your intended use constitutes a "fair use." Under the fair use rule, an author is permitted to make limited use of preexisting protected works without asking permission. All copyright owners are deemed to give their automatic consent to the fair use of their work by others. The fair use rule is an important exception to a copyright owner's exclusive rights.

The fair use rule is designed to aid the advancement of knowledge, which is the reason for having a copyright law in the first place. If scholars, educators and others were required to obtain permission every time they quoted or otherwise used brief portions of other authors' works, the progress of knowledge would be greatly impeded.

Determining whether the fair use privilege applies in any given situation is not an exact scientific process. Rather, it requires a delicate balancing of all the factors discussed below. Probably the best rule for fair use is the following variant of the Golden Rule: "Take not from others to such an extent and in such a manner that you would be resentful if they so took from

you." (McDonald, "Non-infringing Uses," 9 *Bull. Copyright Society* 466 (1962).)

The following four factors must be considered to determine whether an intended use of an item constitutes a fair use:

- the purpose and character of the use
- the nature of the copyrighted work
- the effect of the use upon the potential market for or value of the copyrighted work, and
- the amount and substantiality of the portion used in relation to the copyrighted work as a whole (17 U.S.C. 107).

Not all these factors are equally important in every case, but all are considered by the courts in deciding whether a use is "fair." You should consider them all in making your own fair use analysis.

⚠️ If you're not sure whether an intended use is a fair use, seek legal advice or get permission.

1. The Purpose and Character of the Use

First, the purpose and character of your intended use must be considered in determining whether it is a fair use. The test here is to see whether the subsequent work merely serves as a substitute for the original or "instead adds something new, with a further purpose or different character, altering the first with new expression, meaning, or message." *Campbell v. Acuff-Rose Music,*

Inc., 114 S.Ct. 1164 (1994). The Supreme Court calls such a new work "transformative."

This is a very significant factor. The more transformative a work, the less important are the other fair use factors, such as commercialism, that may weigh against a finding of fair use. Why should this be? It is because the goal of copyright to promote human knowledge is furthered by the creation of transformative works. "Such works thus lie at the heart of the fair use doctrine's guarantee of a breathing space within the confines of copyright." *Campbell v. Acuff-Rose Music, Inc.*

Following are very typical examples of "transformative" uses where preexisting expression is used to help create new and different works. These types of uses are most likely to be fair uses:

- **Criticism and comment**—for example, quoting or excerpting a work in a review or criticism for purposes of illustration or comment.
- **News reporting**—for example, summarizing an address or article, with quotations, in a news report.
- **Research and scholarship**—for example, quoting a passage in a scholarly, scientific or technical work for illustration or clarification of the author's observations.

Although not really "transformative," photocopying by teachers for classroom use may also be a fair use, since teaching also furthers the knowledge-enriching goals of the copyright laws.

Note that the uses listed above, with the possible exception of news reporting, are primarily for nonprofit educational purposes. Although some money may be earned from writing a review or scholarly work, financial gain is not usually the primary motivation—disseminating information or otherwise advancing human knowledge is. The fact that a work is published primarily for private commercial gain weighs against a finding of fair use.

2. The Nature of the Copyrighted Work

Since the purpose of the fair use privilege is to advance knowledge, you have more leeway in taking material from factual works (for example, scientific treatises, histories, newspapers) than you do from original creative works like novels, plays, artworks or musical compositions.

a. Unpublished Works

As a general rule, you need to get permission to use an unpublished work—that is, a work that has not been made available to the public on an unrestricted basis. Publishing someone's work before she has authorized it infringes upon the creator's right to decide when and whether her work will be made public.

> **EXAMPLE:** MultiSolutions Software discovers an unpublished Ph.D. thesis on Columbus. It would probably not be

a fair use for MultiSolutions to publish portions of the thesis in its multimedia program. The work's author should have the right to decide when and how to first publish her work. For example, she may want to incorporate it into a book.

3. Effect of Use on Market for Work

You must also consider the effect of the use upon the potential market for or value of the copyrighted work. You must contemplate not only the harm caused by your act of copying, but whether similar copying by others would have a substantial adverse impact on the potential market for the original work.

Since fair use is an affirmative defense to copyright infringement, it is up to the defendant—the copier—in an infringement case to show there is no harm to the potential market for the original work. This can be difficult. The more "transformative" the subsequent work—the more it differs from the original and is aimed at a different market—the less likely will it be deemed to adversely affect the potential market for the original.

But, if you want to use an author's protected expression in a work of your own that is similar to the prior work and aimed at the same market, your intended use will probably be deemed to adversely affect the potential market for the prior work. This weighs against a finding of fair use.

For example, it would likely not be a fair use for MultiSolutions Software to take material from a competitor's multimedia work about Columbus, since this could impair the market for the competitor's program.

Giving Credit Does Not Make a Use "Fair"

Some people have the mistaken idea that they can use any amount of material so long as they give the creator or copyright owner credit. This is simply not true. Providing credit will not in and of itself make a use "fair." Nevertheless, attribution should always be provided for any material obtained or copied from third parties. Passing yourself off as the creator of other people's work is a good way to get sued for copyright infringement, and is likely to make a judge or jury angry if you are sued. Quoting with attribution is a very good hedge against getting sued, or losing big if you are sued. Thus, you should always provide a credit line for any material you make fair use of.

4. The Amount of Material Used

The more material you take, the more likely it is that your use will adversely affect the ability of the copyright owner to commercially exploit the work, which in turn makes it less likely that the use can be a fair use. There are no set limits on how much material can be taken under the fair use doctrine; it is not always "okay" to take one paragraph or fewer than 200 words of a written work. For instance, copying 12 words from a 14-word haiku poem wouldn't be a fair use. Nor would copying 200 words from a work of 300 words likely qualify as a fair use. However, copying 2,000 words from a work of 500,000 words might be "fair."

The quality of the material you want to use must be considered as well as the quantity. The more important the material is to the original work, the less likely is your use a fair use. For example, in one famous case, *The Nation* magazine obtained a copy of Gerald Ford's memoirs prior to their publication. The magazine published an article about the memoirs in which only 300 words from Ford's 200,000-word manuscript were quoted verbatim. The Supreme Court held that this was not a fair use because the material quoted, dealing with the Nixon pardon, was the "heart of the book ... the most interesting and moving parts of the entire manuscript." (*Harper & Row Publishers, Inc. v. Nation Enterprises*, 471 U.S. 539 (1985).)

E. Obtaining Permission to Use Copyrighted Materials

If you want to use material that is not in the public domain and your use doesn't qualify as a fair use, you need to get permission.

With the notable exception of the music industry, which has had a system of rights collectives in place for many decades, obtaining permission to use copyrighted materials in a multimedia project can be a difficult, time-consuming and often chaotic process.

Obtaining multimedia permissions can be especially hard because, for a variety of reasons, many copyright owners are reluctant to grant any multimedia permissions. Many owners have decided not to grant multimedia permissions for the time being because they're unsure how much such rights are worth. Others are reluctant to permit their work to be reduced to digitized form for fear they will lose control over unauthorized copying. Still others intend to launch their own multimedia ventures and don't want to help potential competitors. Some owners will grant permission, but only for exorbitant amounts of money (there are generally no standard rates for such permissions).

Securing a multimedia permission, then, can require a good deal of persistence, salesmanship and creative negotiating on a developer's part. You should follow a two-step process:

Step 1: Find out who owns the rights you need permission to exercise (license).

Step 2: Negotiate and have the rights owner sign a written Multimedia Publicity/ Privacy Release or Multimedia License Agreement (see Sections F and G, below, for further information and sample forms).

We'll first provide an overview of copyright rights and ownership and then take a look at how to go about obtaining permission to use text, images, music and third-party software.

1. Who Owns the Rights You Need to License?

Finding out who owns the multimedia rights to the material you want to use can be your biggest headache of all. Let's first look at the different type of copyright rights then examine how to find out who owns the rights you need to license.

a. Which rights you may need to license

When a copyrightable work is created, the creator or his or her employer or hirer automatically becomes the owner of a bundle of the following exclusive rights:

- **Reproduction rights.** The right to make copies of a protected work
- **Distribution rights.** The right to sell or otherwise distribute copies to the public
- **Rights to create adaptations (or "derivative works").** The right to prepare new works based on the protected work, and
- **Performance and display rights.** The right to perform or display in public a protected literary, musical, dramatic, choreographic, pantomime, motion picture or audiovisual work, whether in person or by means of a device like a television.

Which rights do you need to license? You'll always need permission to exercise the reproduction and distribution rights. If you plan to alter the original work in any way, you'll also need to license the right to creative adaptations (usually called "derivative works").

Performance and display rights will also be needed if the multimedia work will be performed or displayed to the public or at any place where a substantial number of persons outside the normal circle of a family and its social acquaintances are gathered. For example, performance rights would have to be licensed to use a clip from a motion picture in a multimedia sales presentation for a sales convention or in bars. Performance and display rights are not needed where a multimedia work is intended for personal use in the home or office.

b. Unitary vs. multiple ownership of copyright rights

Each of the copyright rights a work contains may be separately sold or licensed to others. For example, the author of a novel can grant the right to publish (reproduce and distribute) it to a publisher and sell the right to create adaptions (movies, for example) to another person or entity. Things don't stop there, however. Each copyright right may be subdivided and sold or licensed in an almost infinite number of ways; a copyright is infinitely divisible. For example, a book author may divide his or her reproduction and distribution rights by territory, time, and/or type of publication (an author may grant a publisher the right to publish her work in book form, but retain the right to use it in an electronic publication). Moreover, any of these rights can be granted on an exclusive or non-exclusive basis.

In many cases, a single person or entity will own all the rights in a work. In this event, it is clear who has the multimedia rights, and you need only have the copyright owner sign a single license agreement.

But where the rights in a work have been transferred to multiple people or entities (or where an author has transferred some rights and retained others), you may need to obtain permission from several sources. Some investigation will often be necessary to determine who has the rights you need to license.

c. Investigating the copyright status of a work

It is always a good idea to investigate a work's copyright status to make sure that you obtain permission from all the people or entities who control the rights you need. All transfer agreements (publishing and licensing agreements) should be reviewed and Copyright Office records searched. You can do a copyright search yourself at the Copyright Office in Washington, D.C., have the Copyright Office to do it or hire a search firm. The last option is often the best, even though it is the most expensive. Copyright search firms such as Thomson & Thomson Copyright Research Group (the best known search firm) can search not only the Copyright Office records to see if a work's copyright rights have been transferred or assigned, but can look through the extensive databases they maintain as well. Thomson & Thomson can research the status of an individual work, as well as all works by a given author. Depending on the extent of the search you request, search firms charge anywhere between $250–$500 or more. (See the sidebar, "How to Research Copyright Renewals," in Section C1b, above, for a list of these firms and the address of the Copyright Office.)

d. Obtaining warranties and indemnifications from the copyright owner

It will not always be economically feasible to do a copyright search for every item to be included in a multimedia work. In addition, even if a search is done, it may not always be conclusive. This means there will often be some uncertainty as to whether the person or entity you're dealing with really has the rights you need. For this reason, you should try to get the person you think is the copyright owner of the rights you need to warrant (guarantee) that your use of the work will not infringe upon the proprietary rights of any third party and agree to indemnify you (pay any attorney fees and damages) if a third party later claims that your use of the material violates her ownership rights. (See Section G1g, below, for detailed discussion.)

e. Insurance coverage for copyright, publicity and privacy disputes

If a developer makes a mistake and fails to get the necessary permissions and/or releases to use a work, it can become embroiled in expensive litigation. The costs of defending lawsuits and perhaps paying damages could conceivably bankrupt a multimedia developer. It is possible—and often advisable—to obtain insurance to cover potential claims arising from alleged copyright infringement, invasions of privacy, violation of publicity rights and defamation. This kind of insurance is called "Errors and Omissions" coverage or "E&O" insurance. Producers of theatrical film and television shows commonly obtain this type of insurance; it is available for multimedia products as well. E&O insurance is expensive, however, and deductibles are often high. Also, an E&O insurer will demand that you make a diligent effort to obtain all necessary licenses and releases for the material you use, as well as conduct copyright searches. E&O policies typically exclude coverage for any work for which you failed to obtain the necessary licenses and releases. In other words, you can't use a work without permission just because you have E&O insurance.

Lenders and venture capitalists may require that you obtain such insurance. Some copyright owners may demand that you do so as well and name them as an additional insured on the policy. E&O coverage is offered by several companies; rates vary, so it pays to shop around. Contact an insurance broker familiar with these types of policies for help.

Clearance Firms

If you need to obtain many permissions, or simply don't want to bother getting them yourself, there are private companies and individuals who obtain permissions on an author or publisher's behalf. These permission specialists may have contacts with some publishers that enable them to get better and faster results than you can yourself. Clearance firms usually charge by the hour.

Some of the best known clearance firms are:

- Jill Alofs, Total Clearance, P.O. Box 836, Mill Valley, CA 94942, 415-389-1531
- BZ Rights and Permissions, Inc., 125 West 72nd St., New York, NY 10023, 212-580-0615, Fax: 212-769-9224
- Clearing House, Ltd., 6605 Hollywood Blvd., Hollywood, CA 90028 213-469-3186, Fax: 213-469-1213
- The Content Company, C/O Richard Curtis Associates, Inc., 171 E. 74th Street, 2nd Floor, New York, NY 10021, 212 772-7363
- DeForest Research, 8899 Beverly Blvd., Ste. 500, Los Angeles, CA 90048, 310-273-2900.
- Betsy Strode, 1109 Southdown Rd., Hillsborough, CA 94010, 415-340-1370
- Suzy Vaughn Clip Clearance Services, 2029 Century Park East, #420, Los Angeles, CA 90067, 310-566-1409, Fax: 310-556-1861

Others are listed in the *Literary Market Place* (LMP), a directory for the publishing business, under "Permissions." The LMP can be found in the reference section of many libraries.

2. Written Materials (Text)

Obtaining permission to use any type of copyrighted written materials—excerpts from books, magazines, journals and so forth—can be merely difficult or simply impossible. There is no single, centralized group or organization granting such permissions and there are no standard fees. You— or someone you hire—must track down the copyright owner of the material you want to use, or his or her representative (usually publisher or agent), and cut your own deal.

a. Contact the publisher

Your first step should be to contact the "permissions department" of the publisher of the material you want to use. The publisher may own the right to reproduce the material as part of a multimedia program or may have been given authority by the author or other copyright owner to grant permissions. If not, the publisher may forward your request to the author or other copyright owner.

If the publisher proves uncooperative, is out of business or can't be located, you'll need to contact the work's author or other copyright owner directly. A search of the Copyright Office's records will yield an address for the author or other copyright owner, which may or may not be current. (See discussion in Section C1b, above.)

Use the Multimedia License Agreement Form set forth in Section G2, below, and be prepared to wait. It can take weeks or months for a publisher to process your request; some may never respond.

b. Verify ownership of multimedia rights

When an author sells a book to a publisher, the publishing contract will define which rights the publisher gets and which the author keeps, if any. Normally, the publisher will acquire the exclusive right to publish the book in the U.S.; this is sometimes called the "primary right." All the other rights are called "subsidiary rights." These include, for example, film, television, radio and live-stage adaptation rights, as well as the right to create and distribute nondramatic audio recordings. The right to license a work for use in a multimedia program or other electronic publication is also a subsidiary right.

Typically a book author will transfer some or all of her subsidiary rights to the publisher and the publisher will agree to give the author a percentage of any monies it makes from them. (A 50-50 split is common.) Established authors with agents who can sell their subsidiary rights for them typically insist on retaining many of their more valuable subsidiary rights—film rights, for example. Such authors often retain the electronic rights to their work. Authors who do not have agents typically transfer all their subsidiary rights to their publisher.

When you're dealing with a publisher or agent, it will normally review the publishing contract to determine whether it has the rights you're seeking. If you're dealing directly with the author or other individual, you should ask for a copy of the publishing agreement and review it to see whether the author actually has the rights you need.

What should you look for? Newer publishing agreements usually contain provisions regarding ownership of "electronic rights," "motion picture and audiovisual rights" and/or "videocassette rights." Unfortunately, there are no standard definitions of these terms. Thus, in some contracts the holder of the electronic rights may have the multimedia rights, while in others they may belong to the owner of the motion picture and audiovisual rights. Older publishing contracts will not have any provisions directly mentioning computer software or electronic rights. Such contracts often contain a provision granting the publisher the right to sell all or part of the work for "mechanical reproduction and transmission" by any then known or later devised method for information storage, reproduction and retrieval. This may include multimedia rights, but it's not entirely clear.

Authors who are employees. Determining ownership of multimedia rights is usually straightforward for works created by authors employed by the publisher—for example, articles written by magazine or newspaper staff writers. These are works made for hire to which the publisher owns all the rights.

3. Photographs

If you need photographs, several sources are available:

- you can obtain images from the Internet
- you can use commercially available clipmedia
- you can try to get the rights to use photos that have appeared in magazines, books and other publications
- you can directly contact photographers and try to get permission to use their work
- you can deal with stock photo agencies.

a. Internet resources

There are many sites on the World Wide Web that offer images for free or a small charge. You can copy these with your Web browser and download them to your hard drive for later use. For example, the NASA JSC Digital Image Collection contains over 250,000 images of spaceflight that are in the public domain and freely available. The URL is http://images.jsc.nasa.gov/html/home.htm.

Several other government agencies have sites with free images such as the Library of Congress and National Archives. A good way to find these sites is by using an Internet directory such as Yahoo or doing an Internet search with a search engine such as Alta Vista. Try using the key words "free photos."

Of course, using a Web browser, it's possible to download images from almost any Website without permission. Using such images in a commercial product without the copyright owner's constitutes copyright infringement and is not recommended.

Before downloading images from Websites, be sure to check if there are any restrictions on their use. For example, you may be required to give credit to the source of the image and be barred from using it in such a way that implies an endorsement for a product or service. For example, you may not use a photo with the NASA logo if it would lead the public to believe NASA is endorsing a product or service.

b. Clipmedia

A wide variety of photographs (as well as drawings and other graphics and sounds) is commercially available in the form of clipmedia. These materials are typically published on CD-ROM disks specifically for users to incorporate into multimedia and other works. Clipmedia is usually owned by someone, although some is in the public domain. Before you buy any clipmedia, review the license agreement that comes with the clipmedia to make sure you can

publicly distribute the material for commercial purposes. Some clipmedia is available for personal use only or may be used only for a specific number of copies.

c. Photos in magazines, books and newspapers

Start by contacting the publication's permissions department. As with text, there may be difficulty determining who owns the right to reproduce a photo. Photos taken by employee-photographers (staff photographers for newspapers and magazines) are works made for hire, to which the employer owns all rights. However, photos taken by freelance photographers may or may not be owned by the publication in which they appear.

Some publications acquire all the copyright rights to the photos they publish, but this is generally not the case. This means the contract between the photographer and publication in which the photo first appeared must be tracked down and reviewed.

Simply locating the contract can be difficult and time-consuming. If it is found, you should read the contract yourself to make sure you're getting what you pay for. The contract may not directly address reuse in a multimedia product, so it can be hard to tell who has the right to permit such use. In addition, some contracts may require that an additional fee be paid to the photographer when a photo is reused, and may even impose restrictions on how it may be used.

d. Stock photo agencies

Stock photo agencies are companies that acquire the rights to thousands or, in some cases, millions, of photos and license them over and over again to magazines, advertising agencies, book publishers and others. Some stock houses specialize in particular types of photographs—for example, sports photos or historical pictures. Stock houses typically charge a flat fee for each photo, usually at least $100–$200. However, it may be possible for a software developer to obtain a "blanket license" to use any of the photos in a stock agency's collection at a reduced rate.

There are hundreds of stock photo agencies in the U.S. Below is a list of directories that list stock photo agencies. No one directory lists all of them.

The ASMP Stock Photo Handbook
ASMP—National
419 Park Avenue S., #1407E
New York, NY 10016

ASPP—Member Directory
P.O. Box 594
Church Street Station
New York, NY 10008

Photo Marketing Handbook
Images Press
22 East 17th Street, 4th Floor
New York, NY 10003

Photographer's Market
Writer's Digest Books
1507 Dana Avenue
Cincinnati, OH 45207

Picture Sources
Special Libraries Association
1700 Eighteenth St. NW, Ste. 5
Washington, DC 20009

Stock Photo Deskbook
The Photographic Arts Center
163 Amsterdam Ave., #201
New York, NY 10023

Many stock photo agencies have their own Websites. Some even include all or part of their catalogs online and permit online ordering. You can find a list of over 250 of photo agencies in the Yahoo Internet directory at http://www.yahoo.com/Business_and_Economy/Companies/Photography/Stock_Photography/.

4. Film and Video

A variety of film and video footage is available from stock houses—companies that acquire the right to license films and videos. Available footage may include historical and newsreel footage, commercials, documentaries and other material. Normally a flat fee is charged, depending on the number of seconds or frames of film being used and the nature of the use. Stock footage typically costs about $1,000 per minute, but you may be able to find some footage for much less.

An excellent directory of stock photo, film and video houses, which is available either in book form or CD-ROM is:

Footage 91: Film and Video Sources
Prelinger Associates, Inc.
430 W. 14th St., Rm. 403
New York, NY 10014
800-243-2252

A directory that may be more easily found in libraries is:
Video Sourcebook, by Furtaw (R.R. Bowker).

Other excellent sources of information about video footage are these video trade magazines:

AV Video
Montage Publishing
25550 Hawthorne Blvd., Ste. 314
Torrance, CA 90505

Videography
United Business Publications
475 Park Ave. South
New York, NY 10016

Obtaining clips from theatrical films and TV shows is difficult and extremely expensive. In addition to obtaining the rights you need from the work's copyright owner, you may need permission from the work's creators—actors, writers, directors, choreographers and musicians. Re-use fees may have to be paid to some or all of these, pursuant to entertainment union contracts.

If you want to use theatrical film or TV footage, it's advisable to hire a professional clearance firm or entertainment lawyer to negotiate the rights for you.

Image Sampling

With modern digital technology, it is very easy for a multimedia developer to take a photo or film or video footage and alter it to such an extent that it is no longer recognizable by its original creator. Is this copyright infringement? If the end result is not recognizable as coming from the original, it may not be. In the words of one court, "copying ... so disguised as to be unrecognizable is not copying" (*See v. Durang*, 711 F.2d 141 (9th Cir. 1983)). However, before the final result is reached, it may be necessary to create intermediate copies of the original work that are clearly recognizable. It is unclear whether this would constitute copyright infringement. The conservative approach is to obtain permission before using any copyrighted photo or footage.

5. Drawings and Other Artwork

Many drawings and other artwork can be obtained in the form of clipmedia and from the Internet. Permission to use and reproduce other drawings, paintings and other works of art must be obtained from the owner, or sometimes the artist. Artists sometimes retain the reproduction rights to a particular piece while selling the piece itself and the right to display it. The person or entity controlling the reproduction rights must be tracked down—whether a museum, individual collector, artist or artist's estate. Fees and terms for such rights vary widely.

a. Artists' moral rights

In many countries, creative people are granted "moral rights" in addition to and separate from their copyright rights in their creations. Briefly, moral rights consist of the right to proper credit or attribution whenever a work is published, to disclaim authorship of unauthorized copies, to prevent or call back distribution of a work if it no longer represents the author's views, and to object to any distortion, mutilation or other modification of the creator's work injurious to her reputation. The right to prevent colorization of a black and white film or photograph is one example of a "moral right."

In many countries, an author retains her moral rights even after she transfers her copyright rights in a work. In some countries, moral rights may be waived by contract; in others, they cannot. This means that an artist or author may have moral rights in some countries even after she has contractually granted a multimedia developer the right to edit or otherwise alter her work. Moral rights are particularly strong in France and other countries that follow the French civil law tradition.

Historically, moral rights have not been recognized in the United States. However, in 1991 Congress enacted the Visual Artists Rights Act ("VARA"; 17 U.S.C. 106A) to extend some of the moral rights discussed above to visual artists. The VARA covers only works of fine art: paintings, drawings, sculptures and photographs produced for exhibition in a limited signed edition of no more than 200 copies. The VARA does not apply to motion pictures or other audiovisual works, electronic publications, works made for hire or applied artwork such as advertisements or technical drawings.

The VARA gives artists the rights of attribution (the right to be named as author of the work) and integrity (the right to prevent the intentional destruction or modification of the work in a way that harms the artist's reputation). This means that an artist might be able to object if she believes a multimedia developer has distorted or mutilated her work for inclusion in a multimedia product.

An artist's rights under VARA can be waived by contract. It is a good idea to obtain such a waiver whenever possible. Our sample multimedia license agreement contains such a waiver (see Section G1e, below). Such a waiver will also be effective in some, but not all, foreign countries.

6. Cartoons

The rights to cartoons are usually handled by distribution syndicates or agents. A flat fee is customarily charged for a limited time use. You should be able to find out who to contact for permission by calling the publication in which the cartoon appeared.

7. Music

The music industry is the only branch of the copyright industry that has in place a standardized process for obtaining permissions. For this reason, obtaining multimedia rights to music is far easier than for any other form of third party material.

 This discussion just scratches the surface of music licensing. For a superb detailed explanation of all the issues involved in music licensing, including a special chapter on multimedia, refer to *The Art of Music Licensing*, by Al and Bob Kohn (Prentice Hall Law & Business, 270 Sylvan Ave, Englewood Cliffs, NJ 07632; 800-223-0231). This book is expensive—about $80—but it's well worth it.

a. Music copyrights

As noted in Section E1b, above, a copyright is infinitely divisible. A given piece of music will usually be sold or licensed in a number of different ways. For example, here are some (but not all) of the different licenses a songwriter can grant for the same song:

- a print license authorizing someone to print the song as sheet music
- a mechanical license permitting the licensee to reproduce the song in a record, CD, tape, etc.
- a synchronization license permitting the song to be used in a film, video or other audiovisual work, and
- a performance license authorizing the song to be performed publicly.

Things are made even more complicated by the fact that there are two completely separate copyrights involved in a musical recording:

- **The copyright in the song or other musical composition itself.** The copyright in a song is usually owned solely by a music publisher or co-owned by the publisher and songwriter. Copyrights in songs themselves are sometimes called "publishing rights."
- **The copyright in the recording company's sound recording.** When a song or other musical composition is recorded by a recording company, a new work (a "derivative" work) is created. The recording company usually owns the copyright in a sound recording. Unless the song is in the public domain, the recording company must obtain permission from the copyright owner of the song to record it.

This means that to make a new recording of a song for inclusion in a multimedia work, a developer must obtain permission from the music publisher and perhaps the songwriter. But to use an existing recording, permission must be obtained from the music publisher, perhaps the songwriter and the recording company. As outlined below, it's far easier to do the first than the second.

Music Sampling

With modern digital audio technology, anyone with access to a digital synthesizer can capture all or part of a previous recording and reuse bits and pieces in new recordings. The unauthorized sampling of even a few seconds of a sound recording can constitute copyright infringement of both the sound recording from which the sample is taken and the underlying song. Particularly if the recording is well known, there is a real risk of being sued for illegal copying and having to pay substantial damages. This risk is reduced if the sampled sounds are so altered that their original source is not recognizable. But if the source of sampled music is recognizable, permission for the use should be obtained as outlined in this section. A good general rule is, "If you can name the tune, get permission." (For a detailed discussion of sampling, see *The Art of Music Licensing*, by Al and Bob Kohn (Prentice Hall Law & Business).)

b. Making new recordings of existing music

The music industry has developed a highly efficient process for obtaining permission to make a new recording of existing copyrighted music and reproducing it in a multimedia program. The Harry Fox Agency—a subsidiary of the National Music Publishers' Association—issues licenses and collects and distributes royalties on behalf of music publishers who have entered into agreements with Fox for this service. About 80% of all music publishers utilize the Harry Fox Agency.

A software developer need only tell the Harry Fox Agency what music it would like to license. Fox will determine who owns the rights and contact them for a price quotation. There are no set rates for the use of music in multimedia programs. Most music publishers will demand a royalty for the use of their music rather than charge a fixed fee up-front. Currently, the average royalty is 12 cents per unit manufactured and distributed. Thus, if a software developer used eight songs at this rate, it would have to pay 96 cents to the Harry Fox Agency for each program it distributed. However, keep in mind that the 12-cent rate is only an average. Some publishers may demand more, some less. This is a matter for negotiation.

The Harry Fox Agency will help with negotiations. It has developed a multimedia recording license for music, called an MMERL License, for the parties to sign. The agency can be contacted at:

The Harry Fox Agency
711 Third Ave., 8th Floor
New York, NY 10017
212-370-5330 Fax: 212-489-5699

The Harry Fox Agency handles what are known as mechanical and synchronization licenses—licenses to record a song or other musical composition and use it in conjunction with still or moving images. This is sufficient for personal use of a multimedia program. However, if a multimedia product containing a musical composition is to be performed publicly, a public performance license must be obtained from the copyright owner as well. Under the Copyright Act, a public performance occurs when a work is performed "at a place open to the public or at any place where a substantial number of persons outside the normal circle of a family and its social acquaintances is gathered" (17 U.S.C. 101). Thus, for example, the developer of a multimedia program designed to be used for sales presentations at conventions, in bars, nightclubs, rock concerts or other public places would need to obtain a performance license for any songs it wanted to include in the work.

Almost all U.S. music publishers and composers use one of three performing rights societies to serve as their agents for the licensing of performance rights. These are (in order of size):

ASCAP (American Society of Composers, Authors & Publishers)
One Lincoln Plaza
New York, NY 10023
212-595-3050

BMI (Broadcast Music, Inc.)
320 W. 57th St.
New York, NY 10019
800-326-4264

SESAC (Society of European State Authors and Composers)
421 W. 54th St.
New York, NY 10019
212-586-3450

Contact ASCAP first. If it does not serve as agent for the music publisher or composer involved, contact BMI. Together, ASCAP and BMI represent 99% of all U.S. music publishers and composers.

c. Using existing recordings

Obtaining permission to use an existing recording can be more difficult and expensive than making a new one. First, it is necessary to obtain the mechanical and synchronization rights to the music itself through the Harry Fox Agency, as outlined above. If the multimedia product is to be performed in public, a performance license must also be obtained through the appropriate performing rights society. Permission must also be obtained to use the recording itself (termed "master recording rights") from the owner of the copyright in the recording.

The "special markets division" of the appropriate recording company must be contacted to obtain master recording rights. The recording contract must be examined to see who has the right to grant permission to re-use the recording. This may be the record company or the artist. Recording companies are generally reluctant to permit their recordings to be reused, particularly if a well-known song is performed by a well-known artist. Where obtainable, permission to do so is usually very expensive. Musician union agreements may also require that re-use fees be paid to the musicians, vocalists and others who worked on the recording.

Music Clearance Firms

Developers who do not wish to go to the time and trouble of obtaining music permissions themselves can retain the services of music clearance firms. For a fee, these companies will request, negotiate and process music permissions. Using such firms will usually be cheaper than retaining a music attorney, and they are often more effective. These firms are located primarily in New York, Los Angeles and Nashville, the centers of the music business. Two of the best known firms are:

BZ Rights and Permissions, Inc.
125 West 72nd St.
New York, NY 10023
212-580-0615
Fax: 212-769-9224

Clearing House, Ltd.
6605 Hollywood Blvd.
Hollywood, CA 90028
213-469-3186
Fax: 213-469-1213

---

d. Music libraries

Probably the cheapest and easiest way to obtain the rights to "generic" music is to license it from music libraries (also called Production Music Libraries or "PMLs"). Original music by lesser known artists and sound effects are available from music libraries. Several libraries are listed in the publication *Songwriter's Market* (Writer's Digest Books). Make sure the library controls all the rights you need. Some grant only limited licenses to use their music.

8. Software

Multimedia programs often include third party software—software "engines"— that drive the program and application software programs to support graphics, sound and animation. A license from the copyright owner must be obtained to distribute third party software with a multimedia program. To obtain such a license, contact the software publisher.

F. Privacy and Publicity Problems

Privacy and publicity problems arise when a multimedia work uses photographs, video, film or other images of an individual's likeness or recordings of a person's voice. This is a complex area of the law and privacy publicity rights vary from state to state. The following is a brief overview.

The definitive work on these issues is *The Rights of Publicity and Privacy*, by J. Thomas McCarthy (Clark Boardman Callaghan).

1. Right to Privacy

The right to privacy is simply the right to be left alone. The law protects a person from humiliation, embarrassment, loss of self-esteem or other injury to his or her sensibilities caused by the following types of activities:

- using a person's name, likeness or voice for commercial purposes, without authorization—for example, in an advertisement
- entering or observing a private or secluded area without consent—for example, spying on a person's home or office without permission to take photographs
- publicly displaying an image which shows or implies something embarrassing and untrue about someone—for example, using a picture of an uninfected person in a work about sexually transmitted diseases in a way that implies that the person has such a disease, or
- publicly disclosing true, but private and embarrassing facts about a person that are of no legitimate public concern—for example, displaying film footage of a person hugging someone other than his or her spouse.

These privacy rights belong primarily to private individuals. Public officials (persons who hold important elective or appointed offices) and "public figures" have little or no right of privacy for acts relating to their public life. Determining if someone qualifies as a public figure can be difficult. Persons who are extremely influential and powerful, frequently appear in the media, or are in the forefront of public controversies all qualify as "public figures." This includes not only people we normally think of as "celebrities"—film and TV stars, rock stars, sports heroes, famous business tycoons, and so forth—but lesser known individuals involved in public affairs—for example, the heads of the ACLU and NRA.

A person's privacy rights cease when he or she dies. Thus, there are no privacy issues presented in using old photos or archival or newsreel footage of people who are dead.

2. Right of Publicity

The right of publicity is the right to control when and how one's name, voice or likeness may be used for purposes of advertising or trade—for example, to advertise or sell a product or service. Public figures—famous athletes or film stars, for example—can earn substantial sums by endorsing products and appearing in commercials. No one would pay for an endorsement if the right of publicity were not legally protected. Only human beings have a right of publicity; corporations, firms and institutions do not.

Unlike the privacy rights discussed above, the right to publicity continues in some states for many years after a celebrity's death. For example, in California, the right to publicity lasts for 50 years after a person's death; in Oklahoma, 100 years. This means, for example, that it is illegal to use a photo of Marilyn Monroe or Elvis Presley for commercial purposes in California or Oklahoma without the consent of their estates. Because most multimedia programs are nationally distributed, permission must be obtained to use a deceased celebrity's name, likeness or voice for commercial purposes. That is, a developer normally cannot restrict distribution only to those states not providing privacy rights after a person dies.

3. First Amendment Limitations on Privacy/Publicity Rights

The rights to privacy and publicity are not absolute. The First Amendment to the U.S. Constitution guarantees freedom of speech and of the press. The First Amendment gives priority to the public's right to know about newsworthy events of public significance. Courts have held that a person's name or likeness may be used without consent where it is done for educational or informational purposes. This enables the news media to publicly disclose a person's name, likeness or other characteristics without permission for newsworthy and editorial purposes.

The First Amendment applies to software developers as well as to the news media. Under the First Amendment, a multimedia developer has broad latitude to use a person's image, voice or name for educational, cultural and artistic purposes. This is particularly true where public figures are involved. But, if your purpose is primarily to sell a product or service, the First Amendment will not protect the use. For example, film footage of General Norman Schwartzkopf could be used in a CD-ROM history of the Persian Gulf War without violating the General's privacy or publicity rights. Such a work has an educational purpose, even though it may be sold for a profit. However, the General's right to publicity would likely be violated if the same footage was used in a multimedia sales presentation at an arms dealer's convention.

4. Releases of Privacy/Publicity Claims

A release is simply a contract by which a person consents to the use of his or her name, likeness or other element of his persona for the purposes specified in the release. A release should be obtained from any individual whose likeness, voice, name or other identifiable characteristics are used in recognizable form in a multimedia work that has a purely commercial purpose. It may be difficult to determine whether a multimedia work is just commercial in nature or has an educational, artistic or cultural purpose so as to be protected under the First Amendment (as discussed in Section F3, above). In this event, the conservative approach is to obtain privacy/publicity releases.

In most cases, you'll have to obtain any necessary releases yourself. Unless they happen to already have releases, it's unlikely that most copyright owners will be willing to get them for you. Stock photo and stock footage houses customarily do not provide releases, although some will do so for an additional fee.

Commercial photographers customarily obtain releases from their models, so you might be able to obtain releases from them when you deal directly with a photographer. If a photographer or other copyright owner has obtained a release for the material you wish to use, make sure to ask for a copy and review it. Here's what to look for:

- Make sure the release covers the material you want to use.

- The release should specify that the photographer may sell or assign the right to use the photos or other materials to third parties.
- If you intend to alter or otherwise change or distort the image, make sure the release allows this.
- A release should always be in writing. If the subject is a minor (under 18 years old), the release should be signed by his or her parent or legal guardian.
- Finally, the release should specify that it is irrevocable—otherwise the release could be terminated by the person giving it at any time.

If these requirements are not met, a new release must be obtained.

Below is a sample of a self-explanatory valid Multimedia Publicity/Privacy Release, which may be used in connection with any kind of material.

I SEE MANY MEDIUMS IN YOUR FUTURE.

Multimedia Publicity/Privacy Release

In consideration of MultiSolutions Software, Inc.'s ("Developer") agreement to incorporate some or all of the Materials identified below (the "Materials") in one or more of its multimedia works (the "Works"), and other good and valuable consideration, the receipt and sufficiency of which is hereby acknowledged, I hereby grant Developer permission to use, adapt, modify, reproduce, distribute, publicly perform and display, in any form now known or later developed, the Materials specified in this release (as indicated by my initials) throughout the world, by incorporating them into one or more Works and related advertising and promotional materials.

This release is for the following Materials: (*initial appropriate lines*):

_____ Name

_____ Voice

_____ Visual likeness (on photographs, video, film, etc.)

_____ Photographs, graphics or other artwork as specified:

_____ Film, videotape or other audiovisual materials as specified:

_____ Music or sound recordings as specified:

_____ Other:

I warrant and represent that the Materials identified above are either owned by me, are original to me or that I have full authority from the owner of the Materials to grant this release.

I release Developer, its agents, employees, licensees and assigns from any and all claims I may have now or in the future for invasion of privacy, right of publicity, copyright infringement, defamation or any other cause of action arising out of the use, reproduction, adaptation, distribution, broadcast, performance or display of the Works.

I waive any right to inspect or approve any Works that may be created containing the Materials.

I understand and agree that Developer is and shall be the exclusive owner of all right, title and interest, including copyright, in the Works, and any advertising or promotional materials containing the Materials, except as to preexisting rights in any of the Materials released under this agreement.

I am of full legal age and have read this release and am fully familiar with its contents.

By: _____
(signature)

_____
(typed or printed name)

Date: _____

The full text of this release is on the CD-ROM forms disk under the file name MULTIREL. See Chapter 1 for instructions on using the forms disk.

G. Multimedia License Agreements

Permission to use all or part of a copyrighted work in a multimedia program should always be obtained in writing. Many of the copyright owners you'll be dealing with—publishers, record companies, and stock photo houses, for example—will likely have their own permission forms or license agreements for you to sign. In that case, there may not be much room for you to negotiate changes.

1. Negotiating a Multimedia License Agreement

Following are the most important things you should be aware of when negotiating a multimedia license agreement. A sample Multimedia License Agreement that covers all of these issues is provided in Section H2, below.

a. Definition: territory

The agreement should state what territory the license covers. A license may be limited to a particular geographical area—the United States or North America, for example—or it may be worldwide. A worldwide license is best for the developer.

Care must be taken that the territory is the same for every license negotiated for a single multimedia work. This is because the license with the narrowest territory will govern the entire project. For example, if MultiSolutions in our example above negotiated 99 worldwide licenses for its Columbus project and one license limited to the U.S., the finished work could only be distributed in the U.S. (otherwise the U.S.-only license would be violated).

b. The license grant

The developer must make sure that the copyright owner grants it all the rights necessary to use the material in the multimedia product. This should include the right to use, modify and distribute the material as part of the multimedia product. (For an example, see Clause 3 of the Multimedia License Agreement below. It's also contained on the forms disk under MULTILIC.)

If you intend to ever make your multimedia work available through the Internet, you should also obtain the copyright owner's display and performance rights. Although it's not entirely clear, transmission of a work over the Internet could involve exercise of both rights.

The license grant should also state whether it is exclusive or nonexclusive. An exclusive license means the developer is the only one permitted to exercise the rights granted in the license; obviously, a nonexclusive license means the opposite—in other words, the copyright owner will be able to license the same material on a nonexclusive basis to others.

Depending on the nature of the material being licensed, it may be important for a developer to obtain an exclusive license, since it means competitors will not be able to use the same material. For example, a developer of an entertainment program based on a unique cartoon character will likely wish to have the exclusive right to use the character. However, a nonexclusive license is usually adequate when dealing with less unique or important materials, such as run-of-the-mill photos, illustrations or stock footage.

Presumably, the copyright owner would require the developer to pay substantially more for an exclusive license, since it's giving up the right to grant multimedia licenses to others. Many copyright owners will simply refuse to grant an exclusive license. For example, stock photo houses rarely grant exclusive licenses to use their materials.

The copyright owner may wish to limit the license to a particular media format or configuration and/or platform. Obviously, this is not in the developer's best interests, since it limits the potential market for the product. Moreover, technological advances are rapidly changing the standard formats used for multimedia works.

Another important issue is whether the license allows the developer to use the licensed materials in future technologies, both known and unknown. Unless the license says so, it won't apply to technologies unknown when the license was entered into. Obviously, it's desirable for developers to have the right to use the materials in future technologies. The license agreement below specifically provides for this (see Clause 3).

c. Term

The developer should try to ensure that the term of the license lasts for the life of the multimedia product. When the license expires, the developer will have to negotiate a new one with the licensor or delete the material from its product.

A perpetual license is best, but the licensor may balk at this or demand substantially more money. A fixed term—five or ten years, for example—may be all the developer can obtain.

As with territory, the term of each license should be the same, because the license with the shortest term will govern the entire project.

d. Payment

Payment can take a variety of forms: for example, a fixed fee up-front, a fixed fee paid over time, an up-front fee combined with a royalty or a straight royalty. Royalties can be paid in a number of ways—for example, a fixed sum for each copy of the work that is sold or a percentage of the price of the product.

e. Use of licensed materials

If you intend to edit or otherwise alter the licensed material in any way, make sure the agreement specifically gives you permission to do so. Some copyright owners may demand control over how their materials appear in the multimedia work. This is a matter for negotiation.

As discussed in Section E5a, above, visual artists have certain moral rights in the United States under the Visual Artists Rights Act and all authors have much broader moral rights in many foreign countries. For this reason, a developer should seek to obtain wherever possible a written waiver of all moral rights held by the creator of the materials being licensed. The sample language in this clause provides such a waiver.

f. Representations and warranties

A representation and warranty is a legally binding promise about a statement of fact. If the promise turns out not to be true, the promisor can be sued for breach of contract.

The developer should seek to obtain a warranty from the copyright owner that it actually owns the rights to the materials it is licensing and that the use of the materials will not violate any third party's copyright or other proprietary rights. The language in this clause includes this kind of warranty.

Some copyright owners will refuse to grant such a warranty. Indeed, the copyright owner of the material a developer wishes to use may require the developer to provide it a warranty of noninfringement. In other words, to obtain permission to use the materials, the developer would guarantee the copyright owner that the use will not result in any copyright infringement claims or other intellectual property

infringement claims against the owner. The developer may also have to promise that it will obtain any necessary privacy/publicity and other releases. (See the discussion in Section F, above.)

g. Indemnification

An indemnification clause is frequently paired with representations and warranties. An indemnity is a promise by one person to pay specified costs and losses of another party under specified circumstances.

A developer should seek to require the copyright owner to indemnify it if any of the owner's representations and warranties turn out to be untrue. This means that the owner will have to bear or reimburse all costs and expenses, including attorney fees and damages, owed or paid by the developer if, for example, its use of the material results in a claim that it violated a third party's privacy or publicity rights. If a full-blown lawsuit results, these costs could be substantial.

As with warranties, the copyright owner of the material a developer wants to use may refuse to agree to indemnify the developer. Instead, the owner may demand that the developer indemnify it if the owner is sued by a third party as a result of the developer's use of the material in the multimedia work.

A multimedia developer should definitely consider obtaining insurance to cover any potential infringement claims. (See Section E1e for a discussion.)

2. Multimedia License Agreement

The Multimedia License Agreement presented in this section is favorable to the developer. It does not require the developer to make any warranties or indemnify the copyright owner. Some copyright owners may require that these items be added to the agreement. The Multimedia License Agreement is self-explanatory; see Section G1, above, for a discussion of key issues.

 The full text of the following agreement is on the forms disk under MULTILIC. See Chapter 1 for instructions on using the forms disk and preparing a final agreement.

H. Copyright Notice and Registration for Multimedia Works

1. Copyright Notice

Where a multimedia work consists of both written material and a computer disk, both should contain their own copyright notice. The computer disk should have a label containing a notice. In addition, it's a good idea to include a notice on the title screen on the computer when the disk is activated, or in an about or credit box. Alternatively, the notice could be displayed on screen continuously when the disk is used. (See Chapter 4 for detailed discussion.)

2. Copyright Registration

For all the reasons discussed in Chapter 4, multimedia works can and should be registered with the Copyright Office. It is always permissible to register each element of a multimedia work separately—manual, text, photos, video, etc. However, it may not be necessary to do so. An entire multimedia work can be registered at one time on one registration form for one $20 fee provided that:

- the copyright claimant is the same for all elements of the work for which registration is sought (the claimant is the original author of the item being registered or the person or entity to whom all the author's rights have been transferred; see Chapter 4, Section E, for detailed discussion), and
- all such elements are published together as a single unit—that is, they are distributed together as part of a single multimedia package (usually in the same package).

An example will help make these rules clear. Assume that AcmeSoft had developed a multimedia history of World War II. The multimedia package consists of a CD-ROM disk containing text, photos, video and music; and a printed manual explaining how to use the CD-ROM. Let's assume that AcmeSoft employees wrote the manual and some of the text on the CD-ROM. AcmeSoft employees also compiled all the materials together on the CD-ROM—that is, they chose which preexisting and new text,

Multimedia License Agreement

This Agreement is made as of June 19, 199X, between Argosy Productions, Inc. (the "Owner") and MultiSolutions Software, Inc. (the "Developer").

1. Background: Owner owns, controls or is in possession of the materials described in Exhibit 1 to this Agreement (the "Licensed Materials"). Developer desires to license all or part of these Licensed Materials for use in a multimedia program (the "Licensed Product"). Accordingly, the parties agree as follows.

2. Definitions: The following definitions shall apply to this Agreement.

"Licensed Materials" means the materials described in detail in Exhibit 1 to this Agreement.

"Licensed Product" means the following multimedia program: An interactive multimedia program entitled "Columbus 'Discovers' America" produced by MultiSolutions Software, Inc.

"Derivative Works" means a work that is based upon one or more preexisting works, such as a revision, modification, translation, abridgment, condensation, expansion or any other form in which such a preexisting work may be recast, transformed or adapted, and that, if prepared without authorization by the owner of the preexisting work, would constitute copyright infringement.

"Territory" means worldwide.

3. License Grant: Owner hereby grants Developer a nonexclusive license in the Territory defined in Clause 2 to:

- use and create Derivative Works from the Licensed Materials,
- incorporate the Licensed Materials and/or Derivative Works thereof within the Licensed Product,
- reproduce, publicly display and publicly perform the Licensed Materials, as incorporated in the Licensed Work, in any manner, medium or form whether now known or hereafter devised, and
- market, promote, sell, license and/or distribute copies of the Licensed Materials and Derivative Works thereof as part of the Licensed Product, both directly to end users and indirectly through distributors, dealers, resellers, agents and other third parties.

Developer shall not distribute or transfer in any way any copy of all or part of the Licensed Materials separate and apart from the Licensed Product.

4. Payment and Delivery: On execution of this Agreement, Developer agrees to pay Owner as follows: $2,000 cash.

Owner shall deliver the Licensed Materials to Developer within 10 days after execution of this Agreement.

5. Term of the License: This license commences on the date it is executed and shall continue for a period of four years unless earlier terminated in accordance with the terms of this Agreement.

6. Termination of the License: Each party has the right to terminate this Agreement if the other party has materially breached any obligation or warranty herein and such breach remains uncured for a period of 30 days after notice of such breach is sent to the other party. Upon termination of this Agreement, Developer shall promptly return to Owner all Licensed Materials and any other property of Owner held by it.

If this Agreement is terminated for any reason other than Developer's uncured material breach of its terms, Developer may continue to distribute existing Licensed Product already in inventory as of the effective date of termination.

7. Use of Licensed Materials: Owner acknowledges and agrees that Developer shall have sole discretion to determine the manner in which Licensed Materials are used in the Licensed Product. Developer may edit or otherwise alter the Licensed Materials and may combine them with other materials as it deems necessary for inclusion in the Licensed Product.

8. Moral Rights Waiver: Owner waives any and all moral rights or any similar rights in the Licensed Materials and agrees not to institute, support, maintain or permit any action or lawsuit on the grounds that the Licensed Product:

- constitutes an infringement of any moral right or any similar right
- is in any way a defamation or mutilation of the Licensed Materials
- damages Owner's reputation, or
- contains unauthorized variations, alterations, changes or translations of the Licensed Materials.

9. Copies of Licensed Materials: Owner acknowledges that in the course of preparing the Licensed Product, Developer may have to make copies and/or other reproductions of the Licensed Materials. Subject to the terms of this Agreement, Owner agrees that Developer shall have the right to possess and use such copies during the term of this Agreement. Developer shall not make any copies or other reproductions of the Licensed Materials after this Agreement terminates.

10. Copyright Notice and Credit Line: The following copyright notice and credit line must appear in connection with Developer's use of the Licensed Materials: "Documentary footage from 'The Logbook of Christopher Columbus,' courtesy of Argosy Productions, Inc. © 1988 by Argosy Production, Inc. All Rights Reserved."

11. Publicity/Privacy Releases: Developer shall obtain all necessary releases to enable Developer to utilize the Licensed Materials pursuant to this Agreement without violating any third party's privacy or publicity rights. This includes, but is not limited to, the releases of all persons or organizations whose name, voice, likeness, portrayal, impersonation or performance is included in the Licensed Materials.

12. Representations and Warranties: Owner hereby represents and warrants to Developer as follows:

- Owner is the owner of all right, title and interest, including copyright, in all the Licensed Materials, or has the authority to enter into this Agreement on behalf of the owner.

- Owner has not granted any rights or licenses to the Licensed Materials that would conflict with Owner's obligations under this Agreement.
- Owner will not enter into any agreement with any third party which would affect Developer's rights under this Agreement, or bind Developer to any third party, without Developer's prior written consent.
- Developer's use of the Licensed Materials as authorized by this Agreement will not infringe any existing copyright, trade secret, patent or trademark rights of any third party.

13. Indemnification: Owner shall indemnify Developer against all claims, liabilities and costs, including reasonable attorney fees, of defending any claim or suit arising by reason of Owner's breach of any condition, warranty or representation contained in this Agreement.

14. General Provisions: The following provisions shall apply.

(a) This Multimedia License Agreement is the sole and entire Agreement between the parties relating to the subject matter hereof, and supersedes all prior understandings, agreements and documentation relating to such subject matter. Any modifications to this Agreement must be in writing and signed by both parties.

(b) This Agreement will be governed by the laws of the State of California.

(c) Notices and correspondence to Owner should be sent to: Argosy Productions, Inc., 1411 Melrose Blvd., Hollywood, CA 90021.

(d) Notices and correspondence to Developer should be sent to: MultiSolutions Software, Inc., 18 North Bay Drive, Boston, MA 02110.

(e) This Agreement is not assignable by either party without the consent of the other.

Argosy Productions, Inc.

By: _____

Name: _____

Title: _____

Date: _____

MultiSolutions Software, Inc.

By: _____

Name: _____

Title: _____

Date: _____

Exhibit 1
The Licensed Materials are as follows: Up to two minutes of S-VHS video footage from documentary entitled "The Logbook of Christopher Columbus"; Argosy catalog #8293.

photos, videos and music to use, how much of each item to use and where to place each item in the multimedia work.

AcmeSoft is the copyright owner of the manual, which was written by its employees. AcmeSoft employees also wrote some of the text on the CD-ROM. All the other material on the CD-ROM was licensed by AcmeSoft—that is, it obtained permission to copy and distribute it on the CD-ROM from the copyright owners. AcmeSoft does not own the copyright in any of these individual bits of text, photos, video or music. However, AcmeSoft does own a compilation copyright in the multimedia work—that is, a copyright in the selection, arrangement and coordination of all the material on the CD-ROM disk, which was performed by AcmeSoft employees.

This selection, arrangement and coordination constitutes a work of authorship if it is original and minimally creative. (See Chapter 12 for detailed discussion of copyright protection for compilations.) This compilation copyright extends to all the material on the CD-ROM, both new and preexisting, both owned by AcmeSoft and licensed from third party copyright owners.

AcmeSoft may register all the elements to which it claims copyright ownership—the manual, the CD-ROM text it owns and the compilation copyright covering the selection and arrangement of all the CD-ROM material—on a single application for a single fee. Why? Because the copyright claimant for all the elements of the multimedia work for which protection is sought

by AcmeSoft is the same: AcmeSoft; and all these elements are being published together as a single unit at the same time.

What about registering all the individual bits of preexisting text, music, photos and video that AcmeSoft licensed? That's the province of the copyright owner of each individually licensed item. AcmeSoft may not register such material since it is not the copyright claimant (owner). But note that this preexisting material will end up being deposited with the Copyright Office by AcmeSoft when it deposits the whole CD-ROM (see below). However, this deposit will not result in registration of such material, since AcmeSoft is not the copyright claimant in this example.

a. Which form to use

Form PA is usually used for registration of multimedia works. Form PA is used to register any multimedia work containing an audiovisual element—photos, video, film clips, etc. A multimedia work consisting solely of text is registered on Form TX. If a multimedia work does not contain any audiovisual elements, but does contain sounds in which sound-recording authorship is claimed, Form SR is used.

b. Filling out Form PA

Chapter 4 contains a detailed discussion about how to fill out Form PA and Form TX. Following are the significant differences when registering a multimedia work on either form.

Space 1: Nature of This Work

State "audiovisual work" in the Nature of this Work box in Space 1.

Space 2: Name of Author

State only the name of the author(s) for the elements of the work for which copyright is claimed in this registration. If preexisting materials have been licensed from third parties, don't mention their names in Space 2. In our example above, AcmeSoft would be listed as the author in Space 2. The third parties from whom AcmeSoft licensed the material included in the work are not the authors of the work AcmeSoft is applying to register, and AcmeSoft's copyright does not cover their work.

Nature of Authorship. The elements of the multimedia work in which original authorship is claimed should be listed here. AcmeSoft in our example above could state "compilation and editing of preexisting text, photographs, video clips, film clips and music plus new original text."

Or, more broadly, if you are entitled to claim copyright in an audiovisual work, artwork on computer screens and the text of a computer program, all embodied on a CD-ROM, Space 2 of your application would read: "audiovisual work, artwork on computer screens and text of computer program."

If your CD-ROM claim consists solely of an original compilation of preexisting facts and data, the authorship in Space 2 would be described as "original compilation of preexisting data." Note that this nature of authorship statement is appropriate only where the applicant claims no authorship in the preexisting data, where the CD-ROM contains no computer program authorship the applicant is entitled to claim copyright in, and where the work is not marketed with a print manual. In this situation, you should submit a cover letter along with your application explaining what original selection, arrangement or ordering is present—that is, explaining what work was involved in selecting and arranging the preexisting material on the CD-ROM. Such selection and arrangement must rise to the level of original authorship to be copyrightable and therefore registrable. (See detailed discussion of compilation copyrights in Chapter 12.)

Space 6: Derivative Work or Compilation

If a multimedia work contains preexisting material such as photos, video and film clips, preexisting text, or music, Space 6 must be completed. If the work contains all new material, Space 6 can be left blank.

Space 6a must be filled in if the multimedia work is a derivative work; it is left blank if the work is just a compilation. A derivative work is a work that is created by adapting and recasting preexisting material into a new work of authorship. Most multimedia works containing preexisting material are derivative works—the preexisting material is edited and combined with other preexisting materials and new material to form a new original work of authorship. It's not necessary to individually list every preexisting work included in the multimedia work; a general description is sufficient. For example, AcmeSoft in our example above could state "previously published text, film and video footage, graphics and music."

Space 6b: Material Added to This Work Space 6b calls for a description of the new material added to the preexisting material in which copyright is claimed. You can simply repeat what you stated in the Nature of Authorship box in Space 2 above.

c. Deposit requirements

The Copyright Office has imposed special deposit requirements for multimedia works. One complete copy of the best edition of a multimedia work first published in the United States must be deposited with the Copyright Office. Everything that is marketed or distributed together must be deposited, whether or not you're the copyright claimant for each element. This includes:

- the ROM disk(s)
- instructional manual(s), and
- any printed version of the work that is sold with the multimedia package (for example, where a book is sold with a CD-ROM).

Multimedia works used on computers typically contain software that enables the user to operate the CD-ROM or other storage medium and access, search and retrieve the data and produce screen displays. The deposit must include identifying material for any such software in which copyright is claimed by the applicant. (But if the software is simply licensed from a third party, no such deposit is necessary.)

The software deposit must consist of a printout of the program source code or object code. However, the entire program need not be deposited. Instead, the applicant may deposit a printout of the first and last 25 pages of the source code. Or, if the program contains trade secrets, the applicant has the option of depositing:

- the first and last 25 pages of source code with the portions containing trade secrets blacked out
- the first and last ten pages of source code with no blacked out portions
- the first and last 25 pages of object code, together with any ten or more consecutive pages of source code with no blacked out portions, or

- for programs consisting of less than 25 pages, the entire program with the trade secret portions blacked out. (See Chapter 4 for detailed discussion of software deposit requirements.)

The Copyright Office wishes multimedia applicants to inform it as to whether the operating software is part of the multimedia work, and where it is embodied—for example, on a CD-ROM disk or other medium.

The Copyright Office has experienced some difficulty in viewing a number of CD-ROM products that have been deposited because it doesn't have the proper equipment. When this occurs, the Copyright Examiner will require the applicant to make a supplemental deposit of identifying material. For example, it might require a supplemental deposit of a video tape showing the audiovisual elements in which authorship is claimed. ■

Chapter 14

Employment Agreements

Part I. Employer's Guide to Drafting Employment Agreements

Part II. Employment Agreements From the Employee's Viewpoint

This chapter is about agreements between software developers and their employees. Typically, the employer presents a pre-drafted employment agreement to the prospective employee when a job offer is made, or soon afterward. Part I, below, provides employers with guidance on drafting such an agreement. Part II discusses the prospective employee's concerns when presented with such an agreement

Part I. Employer's Guide to Drafting Employment Agreements

It is essential that a software developer enter into written agreements with its employees. This should always be done before the employees commence work. Current employees who have not already done so should be asked to sign appropriate agreements, as discussed in Section D, below.

This chapter only covers agreements between employers and employees. If you're not sure whether a worker qualifies as an employee or an independent contractor, review Chapter 15.

A. Why Use Employment Agreements?

Employment agreements are used by software developers to help accomplish the following goals:

- to make clear to employees that they are in a confidential relationship with the employer and have a duty not to disclose confidential information to outsiders without the employer's permission
- to identify as specifically as possible what information the employer regards as confidential
- to assign to the employer, in advance, all proprietary rights (copyright, trade secret and patent) the employee may have in his or her work product, and
- where appropriate and legal, to impose reasonable restrictions on the employee's right to compete with the employer after the employment relationship ends.

B. Who Should Sign?

All employees who might have access to trade secrets should be required to sign an employment agreement. In order of priority, this includes:

- employees (programmers, systems engineers and other technical personnel) who play the key role in developing your software; in some companies, this is only a handful of employees
- other employees who help develop your software, such as technical writers and software testers
- marketing people, and
- administrative and clerical staff who can be expected to come into meaningful contact with trade secret materials.

C. When New Employees Should Sign

A developer should be sure to give a new employee the agreement before she starts work—preferably, at the same time a job offer is made. This way, the hiree can take the agreement home and study it and even have his or her lawyer look at it. Don't wait until the employee has actually started work. At this point, after quitting his or her old job (and perhaps even moving), the employee may feel he or she has no choice but to sign the agreement as written. If you later need to enforce the agreement, a court may conclude that it was not a freely bargained contract and refuse to enforce it.

D. Agreements With Current Employees

For an employment agreement with a continuing employee to be legally enforceable, you must give the employee something of value in return for agreeing to abide by the agreement. The fact that you pay the employee a salary and benefits may not be sufficient, because the employee was receiving these before you asked him or her to sign the agreement.

Give the employee a small cash bonus, a pay raise, stock options, vacation time or some other remuneration. This costs you something, but it ensures that the agreement will be enforceable. (It will also encourage the employee to sign the agreement.) The value of what you give a continuing employee for signing an employment agreement doesn't have to be enormous. But the greater the amount, the clearer it will be that there was a benefit to the employee and a binding contract was thereby created

EXAMPLE: Burt has been working as a staff programmer for Elite Software since its earliest days. When he was first hired, Elite did not have him sign any type of employment agreement. A few years later, Elite management realizes that Burt, a highly skilled programmer, has been exposed to valuable Elite trade secrets and has been intimately involved in the creation of some of Elite's most valuable products. Elite decides to ask Burt to sign an agreement containing nondisclosure and invention assignment clauses. To ensure that Burt receives something of value in exchange for his signing agreement Elite gives Burt a small pay raise.

Getting Current Employees to Sign Employment Agreements

One big problem software developers have with employment agreements is that they are usually not popular with employees, and some will refuse to sign them. Your employees may tell you that they know they can't divulge company trade secrets and view being asked to sign an agreement to that effect as unnecessary and an insult. This can be particularly true for small companies where the company owners and employees are (or view themselves as) friends.

Be sure to stress to any potentially offended employee that the use of such an agreement is no reflection on his character or trustworthiness. It is simply a standard legal precaution used by virtually all hi-tech businesses. Also, you may need to make the agreement as palatable as possible to the employee—for example, not attempt to impose post-employment noncompetition restrictions on the employee, as discussed in Section G, below. When dealing with a truly key employee, consider offering substantial monetary or other benefits in return for signing the agreement.

E. Selecting Employment Agreements You Need

The following two sections contain two employment agreements:

- Employment Agreement for Nontechnical Employee (EMPLOY1.TXT on disk), and
- Employment Agreement for Technical Employee (EMPLOY2.TXT on disk).

Be sure to read the instructions and discussion to draft the forms; not all the provisions in the agreements may be appropriate for your situation.

F. Employment Agreement for Nontechnical Employees

This is an employment and nondisclosure agreement for use with nontechnical employees—that is, employees who are not expected to help develop software. This includes clerical staff, production workers, personnel managers, marketing staff, sales staff and so forth. This agreement does not contain a copyright and invention assignment clause, since such employees are not being paid to help develop copyrightable or patentable works.

 The full text of the following agreement is on the CD-ROM forms disk under the file name EMPLOY1. See Chapter 1 for instructions on using the forms disk.

Introductory Paragraph

Select Alternative 1 if a new employee will be signing the agreement, and fill in the name of the company.

Select Alternative 2 if the agreement is with a current employee. Fill in the name of the company. To ensure that the agreement will be a legally binding contract, the employee should receive something of value over and above his or her normal salary and benefits for signing it—for example, cash or stock options. Specify the compensation to be provided.

1. Company's Trade Secrets

As discussed in Chapter 6, an employee who learns trade secrets as a result of a confidential relationship with his or her employer has a legal duty not to disclose them to others without the employer's permission. This clause defines the company's trade secrets; the next clause addresses the employee's nondisclosure obligations.

Like all provisions in an employment agreement (or any other contract), this clause must be reasonable. It should not cover everything in the employee's brain. A clause that attempts to do so will likely be unenforceable in court, because it is unreasonable. You don't need to add anything to this clause; it sets out the types of information and material that should be considered to be trade secrets.

2. Nondisclosure of Trade Secrets

This clause bars the employee from making unauthorized disclosures of the company's trade secrets. This makes clear to the employee that he or she has a duty to protect the employer's trade secrets. It also shows that the employer is serious about keeping trade secrets secret.

However, as explained in this clause, the employee's nondisclosure obligation does not extend to information the employee knew before coming to work for the company, information he learns from sources outside the company and information that is not confidential because it is public knowledge (so long as the employee didn't make it public).

3. Confidential Information of Others

It's a good idea to remind new employees that they have a duty not to disclose to the employer trade secrets learned from prior employers or others. Employers who take advantage of such information can easily end up being sued.

4. Return of Materials

It's important that employees understand their obligation to return all materials containing trade secrets when they leave the company. They should be reminded of this obligation in their employment agreement and before they leave.

Employment Agreement for Nontechnical Employee

In consideration of my continued employment with SOFTWARE OF AMERICA, INC. (the "Company") and also in consideration of stock options to purchase One Hundred (100) shares of the Company's stock, the receipt and sufficiency of which I hereby acknowledge, I agree as follows:

1. Company's Trade Secrets: I understand that in performance of my job duties with the Company, I will be exposed to the Company's trade secrets. "Trade secrets" means information or material that is commercially valuable to the Company and not generally known in the industry. This includes, but is not limited to:

(a) any and all versions of the Company's proprietary computer software, hardware, firmware and documentation;

(b) technical information concerning the Company's products and services, including product data and specifications, know-how, formulae, diagrams, flow charts, drawings, source code, object code, program listings, test results, processes, inventions, research projects and product development;

(c) information concerning the Company's business, including cost information, profits, sales information, accounting and unpublished financial information, business plans, markets and marketing methods, customer lists and customer information, purchasing techniques, supplier lists and supplier information and advertising strategies;

(d) information concerning the Company's employees, including salaries, strengths, weaknesses and skills;

(e) information submitted by the Company's customers, suppliers, employees, consultants or co-venturers with the Company for study, evaluation or use; and

(f) any other information not generally known to the public which, if misused or disclosed, could reasonably be expected to adversely affect the Company's business.

2. Nondisclosure of Trade Secrets: I will keep the Company's trade secrets, whether or not prepared or developed by me, in the strictest confidence. I will not use or disclose such secrets to others without the Company's written consent, except when necessary to perform my job. However, I shall have no obligation to treat as confidential any information which:

(a) was in my possession or known to me, without an obligation to keep it confidential, before such information was disclosed to me by the Company;

(b) is or becomes public knowledge through a source other than me and through no fault of mine; or

(c) is or becomes lawfully available to me from a source other than the Company.

5. Confidentiality Obligation Survives Employment

It's important to make clear that the employee's duty not to disclose her employer's confidential information does not end when she leaves the company, but continues for as long as the material remains a trade secret.

6. Conflict of Interest

This clause is intended to make clear to the employee that he shouldn't compete with the company while employed by it or engage in any activity that may harm the company.

7. Enforcement

This clause is intended to make it easier for the employer to obtain an injunction—a court order—to prevent the employee from breaching the agreement. For example, you may be able to obtain a court order preventing the employee from divulging your trade secrets to a competitor.

8. General Provisions

These general provisions are standard in many types of legal documents:

- **Successors.** This clause obligates all successors and heirs to the contents of the Agreement.
- **Governing Law.** Here you specify which state law governs the contract—usually either the state of incorporation or the company's business home. That way, you can hire an attorney locally to handle any legal problems that might arise under the Agreement.
- **Severability.** In the event that some part of the Agreement is declared invalid by a court, this clause ensures that the rest of the document is still valid.
- **Entire Agreement.** This clause clarifies that the Agreement supersedes any prior signed agreements.
- **Modification.** This clause stipulates that future modifications must be in writing, signed both by the company and the employee.
- **Assignment.** This clause prohibits the employee from assigning or delegating his or her duties under the agreement—for example, the employee may not get someone else to perform the work.

Signatures

Although not absolutely necessary, it's a good idea to have the employee's signature witnessed by a company representative. This is intended to prevent the employee from later claiming her signature was forged.

Skip to Chapter 1, Section D, for information about preparing the final agreement.

3. Confidential Information of Others: I will not disclose to the Company, use in the Company's business, or cause the Company to use, any information or material that is a trade secret of others.

4. Return of Materials: When my employment with the Company ends, for whatever reason, I will promptly deliver to the Company all originals and copies of all documents, records, software programs, media and other materials containing any of the Company's trade secrets. I will also return to the Company all equipment, files, software programs and other personal property belonging to the Company.

5. Confidentiality Obligation Survives Employment: I understand that my obligation to maintain the confidentiality and security of the Company's trade secrets remains with me even after my employment with the Company ends and continues for so long as such material remains a trade secret.

6. Conflict of Interest: During my employment by the Company, I will not engage in any business activity competitive with the Company's business activities. Nor will I engage in any other activities that conflict with the Company's best interests.

7. Enforcement: I agree that in the event of a breach or threatened breach of this Agreement, money damages would be an inadequate remedy and extremely difficult to measure. I agree, therefore, that the Company shall be entitled to an injunction to restrain me from such breach or threatened breach. Nothing in this Agreement shall be construed as preventing the Company from pursuing any remedy at law or in equity for any breach or threatened breach.

8. General Provisions:

(a) Successors: The rights and obligations under this Agreement shall survive the termination of my service to the Company in any capacity and shall inure to the benefit and shall be binding upon: (1) my heirs and personal representatives, and (2) the successors and assigns of the Company.

(b) Governing Law: This Agreement shall be construed and enforced in accordance with the laws of the State of New York.

(c) Severability: If any clause of this Agreement is determined to be invalid or unenforceable, the remainder shall be unaffected and shall be enforceable against both the Company and me.

(d) Entire Agreement: This Agreement supersedes and replaces all former agreements or understandings, oral or written, between the Company and me, except for prior confidentiality agreements I have signed relating to information not covered by this Agreement.

(e) Modification: This Agreement may not be modified except by a writing signed both by the Company and me.

(f) Assignment: This Agreement may be assigned by the Company. I may not assign or delegate my duties under this Agreement without the Company's prior written approval.

I have carefully read and considered all clauses of this Agreement and agree that all of the restrictions set forth are fair and reasonably required to protect the Company's interests. I acknowledge that I have received a copy of this Agreement as signed by me.

Date: _____

_____
Employee's Signature

_____
Typed or Printed Name

Witness: _____

Date: _____

_____
Signature

_____
Typed or Printed Name

_____
Title

G. Employment Agreement for Technical Employees

This agreement is for use with technical employees—programmers, systems analysts, employees who create documentation, software engineers and others whose job is to help the company develop software.

 The full text of the following agreement is on the CD-ROM forms disk under the file name EMPLOY2. See Chapter 1 for instructions on using the forms disk.

Introductory Paragraph

Select Alternative 1 if a new employee will be signing the agreement, and fill in the name of the company.

Select Alternative 2 if the agreement is with an existing employee. Fill in the name of the company. To be a legally binding contract, the agreement must be supported by consideration—that is, the employee must receive something of value for signing it. If the agreement is with a continuing employee, some additional consideration over and above her normal salary and benefits should be provided, such as cash or stock options. Specify the compensation to be provided.

1. Company's Trade Secrets

As discussed in Chapter 6, an employee who learns trade secrets as a result of a confidential relationship with his or her employer has a legal duty not to disclose them to others without the employer's permission. This clause defines the company's trade secrets; the next clause addresses the employee's nondisclosure obligations.

Like all provisions in an employment agreement (or any other contract), this clause must be reasonable. It should not cover everything in the employee's brain. A clause that attempts to do so will likely be unenforceable in court, because it is unreasonable. You don't need to add anything to this clause; it sets out the types of information and material that should be considered to be trade secrets.

2. Nondisclosure of Trade Secrets

This clause bars the employee from making unauthorized disclosures of the company's trade secrets. There are several good reasons for an employer to include a nondisclosure clause in its employment agreements. As we discussed in Chapter 6, software and other information qualifies as a trade secret only if reasonable precautions are taken to keep it secret. The use of nondisclosure clauses (or separate nondisclosure agreements; see Chapter 7) is perhaps the single most important reasonable precaution. Confidential information may not be deemed to be a trade secret where an employer does not use such agreements.

Including a nondisclosure clause in an employment agreement makes clear to the employee that he has a duty to protect the employer's trade secrets. It also shows that the employer is serious about keeping trade secrets secret.

This clause clearly defines employee obligations regarding trade secrets, which will also make it easier to obtain relief in court if an employee or ex-employee makes unauthorized disclosures.

However, as explained in this clause, the employee's nondisclosure obligation should not extend to information the employee knew before coming to work for the company, information he learns from sources outside the company and information that is not confidential because it is public knowledge (so long as the employee didn't make it public).

3. Confidential Information of Others

It's a good idea to remind new employees that they have a duty not to disclose to the employer trade secrets learned from prior employers or others. Employers who take advantage of such information can easily end up being sued.

4. No Conflicting Obligations

Many workers in the software industry have previously signed employment agreements or consulting agreements that may conflict with their ability to work for you—for example, because they contain noncompetition restrictions or restrictions on disclosure

of trade secrets that may touch upon the work the employee will perform for you. To make sure this isn't a problem, the agreement asks the employee to list any such prior agreements. If there are any, obtain copies and review them to make sure the employee isn't in any way barred from working for you.

5. Return of Materials

It's important that employees understand their obligation to return all materials containing trade secrets when they leave the company. They should be reminded of this obligation in their employment agreement and before they leave.

6. Confidentiality Obligation Survives Employment

It's important to make clear that the employee's duty not to disclose her employer's confidential information does not end when she leaves the company, but continues for as long as the material remains a trade secret.

7. Computer Programs Are Works Made for Hire

Where technical employees are involved, clauses that assign (transfer rights of ownership) intellectual property rights to the

Employment Agreement for Technical Employee

In consideration of the commencement of my employment with Elite Software, Inc. (the "Company") and the compensation hereafter paid to me, I agree as follows:

1. Company's Trade Secrets: I understand that in performance of my job duties with the Company, I will be exposed to the Company's trade secrets. "Trade secrets" means information or material that is commercially valuable to the Company and not generally known in the industry. This includes:

(a) any and all versions of the Company's proprietary computer software (including source code and object code), hardware, firmware and documentation;

(b) technical information concerning the Company's products and services, including product data and specifications, diagrams, flow charts, drawings, test results, know-how, processes, inventions, research projects and product development;

(c) information concerning the Company's business, including cost information, profits, sales information, accounting and unpublished financial information, business plans, markets and marketing methods, customer lists and customer information, purchasing techniques, supplier lists and supplier information and advertising strategies;

(d) information concerning the Company's employees, including their salaries, strengths, weaknesses and skills;

(e) information submitted by the Company's customers, suppliers, employees, consultants or co-venturers with the Company for study, evaluation or use; and

(f) any other information not generally known to the public which, if misused or disclosed, could reasonably be expected to adversely affect the Company's business.

2. Nondisclosure of Trade Secrets: I will keep the Company's trade secrets, whether or not prepared or developed by me, in the strictest confidence. I will not use or disclose such secrets to others without the Company's written consent, except when necessary to perform my job. However, I shall have no obligation to treat as confidential any information which:

(a) was in my possession or known to me, without an obligation to keep it confidential, before such information was disclosed to me by the Company;

(b) is or becomes public knowledge through a source other than me and through no fault of mine; or

(c) is or becomes lawfully available to me from a source other than the Company.

3. Confidential Information of Others: I will not disclose to the Company, use in the Company's business, or cause the Company to use, any information or material that is a trade secret of others. My performance of this Agreement will not breach any agreement to keep in confidence proprietary information acquired by me prior to my employment by the Company.

4. No Conflicting Obligations: I have no other current or prior agreements, relationships or commitments that conflict with this Agreement or with my relationship other than the following: [specify; if none, so state] _____ None. _____

_____

_____

_____

employer are even more important than nondisclosure clauses. This clause covers assignment issues, as do these clauses discussed below:

- "Disclosure of Developments" clause
- "Assignment of Developments" clause, and
- "Post-Employment Assignment" clause.

Computer programs, documentation and other copyrightable works created by employees within the scope of their employment are "works made for hire" to which the employer is considered the "author" for copyright purposes. (See Chapter 11.) However, it is dangerous for employers to rely solely on the work made for hire rule. This is because of possible legal uncertainty regarding who is an "employee" for copyright purposes, and when copyrightable works are created within the scope of employment. Therefore, the employee should be required to assign, in advance, all copyright rights in work-related works to the employer.

This clause makes clear that the employee may create copyrightable works as part of his or her job and that such works will be works made for hire. But if for some reason the work for hire rule does not apply, the employee assigns all copyright rights in work-related works to the employer.

8. Disclosure of Developments

The employee must be required to disclose promptly to the employer any and all work-related inventions and other developments she creates. This clause complies with state restrictions on invention assignments discussed in the "Assignment of Developments" clause, below.

In the state of Washington you must include the paragraph on disk that states that the Company will maintain a written record of all such disclosures for at least five years.

9. Assignment of Developments

Absent an assignment of rights to an employee's work-related inventions and other developments, the employer may not own what the employee creates. Or, at the very least, the employer may be subject to a costly and bitter legal fight over ownership rights. (See Chapter 11.)

An assignment is simply a transfer of ownership. An employee may transfer his ownership rights in any copyrights, trade secrets, patentable inventions or "mask works" (semiconductor chip designs) he creates on the employer's behalf before he actually commences work. This is when an assignment ideally should be made—before an employee begins his or her job. As discussed in Section D, above, if an assignment is executed long after an employee is hired, the employer must give the continuing employee a raise or other compensation to ensure that the assignment is enforceable.

5. Return of Materials: When my employment with the Company ends, for whatever reason, I will promptly deliver to the Company all originals and copies of all documents, records, software programs, media and other materials containing any of the Company's trade secrets. I will also return to the Company all equipment, files, software programs and other personal property belonging to the Company.

6. Confidentiality Obligation Survives Employment: I understand that my obligation to maintain the confidentiality and security of the Company's trade secrets remains with me even after my employment with the Company ends and continues for so long as such material remains a trade secret.

7. Computer Programs Are Works Made for Hire: I understand that as part of my job duties I may be asked to create, or contribute to the creation of, computer programs, documentation and other copyrightable works. I agree that any and all computer programs, documentation and other copyrightable materials that I am asked to prepare or work on as part of my employment with the Company shall be "works made for hire" and that the Company shall own all the copyright rights in such works. IF AND TO THE EXTENT ANY SUCH MATERIAL DOES NOT SATISFY THE LEGAL REQUIREMENTS TO CONSTITUTE A WORK MADE FOR HIRE, I HEREBY ASSIGN ALL MY COPYRIGHT RIGHTS IN THE WORK TO THE COMPANY.

8. Disclosure of Developments: While I am employed by the Company, I will promptly inform the Company of the full details of all my inventions, discoveries, improvements, innovations and ideas (collectively called "Developments")—whether or not patentable, copyrightable or otherwise protectible—that I conceive, complete or reduce to practice (whether jointly or with others) and which:

(a) relate to the Company's present or prospective business, or actual or demonstrably anticipated research and development; or

(b) result from any work I do using any equipment, facilities, materials, trade secrets or personnel of the Company; or

(c) result from or are suggested by any work that I may do for the Company.

The Company will maintain a written record of all such disclosures for at least five years.

9. Assignment of Developments: I hereby assign to the Company or the Company's designee, my entire right, title and interest in all of the following, that I conceive or make (whether alone or with others) while employed by the Company:

(a) all Developments;

(b) all copyrights, trade secrets, trademarks and mask work rights in Developments; and

(c) all patent applications filed and patents granted on any Developments, including those in foreign countries.

10. Post-Employment Assignment: I will disclose to the Company any and all computer programs, inventions, improvements or discoveries actually made, or copyright registration or patent applications filed, within six months after my employment with the Company ends. I hereby assign to the Company my entire right, title and interest in such programs, inventions, improvements and discoveries, whether made individually or jointly, which relate to the subject matter of my employment with the Company during the 12-month period immediately preceding the termination of my employment.

10. Post-Employment Assignment

Unfortunately, not all employees are honest when it comes to intellectual property rights. Some might try to steal materials they create that belong to their employer. Consider this scenario:

> EXAMPLE: Josephine, a programmer employed by Miracle Systems, has signed an enforceable, reasonable assignment agreement. While employed by Miracle, she develops a potentially valuable program that should be assigned to Miracle under the terms of the agreement. However, Josephine conceals her new program from Miracle. She leaves Miracle and two months later registers her program with the Copyright Office, listing herself as the sole owner. Does Miracle have any ownership rights in the program? Maybe, if it can convince a court she developed it while employed by Miracle. But a lengthy and expensive court battle would be required.

To help avoid these types of shenanigans, many hi-tech employers require inventive employees to agree to assign copyrightable or patentable works they create after the employment relationship ends. Such post-employment assignments are enforceable in most states if they are reasonable. To be reasonable, a post-employment assignment must:

- be for a limited time—probably no more than six months to one year after employment ends
- apply only to works that relate to the inventor's former employment, and
- apply only to works actually in existence, not to mere ideas or concepts in the employee's brain.

11. Notice Pursuant to State Law

A prospective or continuing employee and his or her employer are usually in an unequal bargaining position—the employer generally has the upper hand. Some hi-tech employers have attempted to take advantage of their leverage by requiring their employees to agree to very broadly worded assignments that purport to transfer to the employer in advance ownership of everything the employee creates, whether related to the job or not. In the words of one court, these employers try to obtain "a mortgage on a man's brain" (*Aspinwall Mfg. Co. v. Gill*, 32 F. 697 (3d Cir. 1887)).

To protect employees, several states, including California, impose restrictions on the permissible scope of assignments of employee-created inventions. Note that these restrictions apply only to "inventions" an employee creates—that is, software or other items for which a patent is sought. The restrictions apply only to employees, not to independent contractors.

The California restrictions are typical, and probably of most importance to the software industry. Under California law, an employee cannot be required to assign any of his or her rights in an invention he or she develops "entirely on his or her own time without using the employer's equipment, supplies, facilities, or trade secret information" unless:

- when the invention was conceived or "reduced to practice" (actually created or a patent application filed) it *related to the employer's business* or actual or "demonstrably anticipated" research or development, or
- the invention resulted from any work performed by the employee for the employer (California Labor Code, Section 2870).

The following states impose similar restrictions:

- Delaware (Delaware Code Annotated, Title 19, Section 805)
- Illinois (Illinois Revised Statutes, Chapter 140, Sections 301-303)
- Kansas (Kansas Statutes Annotated, Section 44-130)
- Minnesota (Minnesota Statutes Annotated, Section 181.78)
- North Carolina (North Carolina General Statutes, Sections 66-57.1, 66-57.2)
- Utah (Utah Code Annotated, Sections 34-39-2, 34-39-3)
- Washington (Washington Revised Code Annotated, Sections 49.44.140, 49.44.150).

Invention Assignment Restrictions in Other States

Employers doing business in states that do not have laws restricting invention assignments like the eight states discussed above should nevertheless not attempt to impose unreasonable invention assignments on their employees. Even in the absence of a state law like California's, a court could well refuse to enforce an assignment agreement that it deemed unreasonable—that is, that tried to obtain a "mortgage on a man's brain." Assignments complying with California law would probably be deemed reasonable in these states.

Here are examples that illustrates how these types of restrictions operate in practice.

EXAMPLE 1: Jim is a programmer employed by Orchid Development Co. Orchid is located in Northern California and is in the business of developing and marketing computer databases for business use. Before he began working for Orchid, Jim signed an employment agreement containing an invention assignment, complying with California law. An active computer game player, Jim creates a computer adventure game for children that uses revolutionary new methods to animate its characters in a very lifelike way. Portions of this program could well constitute a patentable invention.

Assume that Jim wrote his program at home, completely on his own time. Who owns Jim's invention, Orchid or Jim? Probably Jim. Since Orchid is not in the business of creating computer games, Jim's invention probably doesn't relate to its business or research and development; nor did Jim's game result from any work he performed for Orchid.

EXAMPLE 2: Assume the same facts above. But what if Jim created his game during working hours? In this event, Orchid's invention assignment would probably be effective—that is, it would own any inventions contained in the game.

EXAMPLE 3: Again, assume the same facts. What if Jim created the game at home, but his new animation method was a spin-off from work he performed for Orchid? Orchid's invention assignment would probably be effective because Jim's invention resulted from work he performed for Orchid.

If the employee will work in California, Illinois, Kansas, Minnesota or Washington State, state law requires that the employee be given written notice of state law restrictions on an employer's right to obtain an assignment of employee inventions. If this is not done, the assignment might be unen-

forceable. If the employee will work in any other state, delete this entire clause. Otherwise, include the appropriate state notice on the disk that states that an Exhibit A is attached, which sets forth written notice of state assignment restrictions. The applicable Exhibit A, setting forth the text of the state law, must also be attached to the agreement. (This is covered below.)

12. Execution of Documents

This clause simply requires the employee to execute any documents necessary to effect the assignment of intellectual property rights. If the employee is unable to do so because of sickness or for any reason, the company is appointed the employee's attorney-in-fact and may execute such documents on the employee's behalf.

13. Prior Developments

Unless the parties desire otherwise, the Agreement's assignment of intellectual property rights should not cover software, patents and other materials created and owned by the employee before commencing employment with the company. Since the employee wasn't working for the company when such items were created, the company shouldn't own them. This provision makes this clear and requires the employee to list all such prior developments.

11. Notice Pursuant to State Law: I understand that this Agreement does not apply to any invention that qualifies fully under the provisions of Washington Revised Code Annotated Section 49.44.140(1), the text of which is attached as Exhibit A. This section shall serve as written notice to me as required by Washington Revised Code Annotated Section 49.44.140(3).

12. Execution of Documents: Both while employed by the Company and afterwards, I agree to execute and aid in the preparation of any papers that the Company may consider necessary or helpful to obtain or maintain any patents, copyrights, trademarks or other proprietary rights at no charge to the Company, but at its expense.

If the Company is unable to secure my signature on any document necessary to obtain or maintain any patent, copyright, trademark or other proprietary rights, whether due to my mental or physical capacity or any other cause, I hereby irrevocably designate and appoint the Company and its duly authorized officers and agents as my agents and attorneys-in-fact to execute and file such documents and do all other lawfully permitted acts to further the prosecution, issuance and enforcement of patents, copyrights and other proprietary rights with the same force and effect as if executed by me.

13. Prior Developments: As a matter of record, I have identified below all prior developments ("Prior Developments") relevant to the subject matter of my employment by the Company that have been conceived or reduced to practice or learned by me, alone or jointly with others, before my employment with the Company, which I desire to remove from the operation of this Agreement. The Prior Developments consist of: _____ None. _____

_____

_____

I represent and warrant that this list is complete. If there is no such list, I represent that I have made no such Prior Developments at the time of signing this Agreement.

14. Conflict of Interest: During my employment by the Company, I will not engage in any business activity competitive with the Company's business activities. Nor will I engage in any other activities that conflict with the Company's best interests.

15. Post-Employment Noncompetition Agreement: I understand that during my employment by the Company I may become familiar with confidential information of the Company. Therefore, it is possible that I could gravely harm the Company if I worked for a competitor. Accordingly, I agree for two years following the end of my employment with the Company not to compete, directly or indirectly, with the Company in any of its business if the duties of such competitive employment inherently require that I use or disclose any of the Company's confidential information. Competition includes the design, development, production, promotion or sale of products or services competitive with those of the Company.

(a) Diversion of Company Business: For a period of 12 months from the date my employment ends, I will not divert or attempt to divert from the Company any business the Company enjoyed or solicited from its customers during the six months prior to the termination of my employment.

(b) Geographic Restrictions: I acknowledge and agree that the software developed by the Company is, or is intended to be, distributed to customers nationally throughout the United States. According, I agree that these restrictions on my post-employment competitive activity shall apply throughout the entire United States.

14. Conflict of Interest

This clause is intended to make clear to the employee that he shouldn't compete with the company while employed by it or engage in any activity that may harm the company.

15. Post-Employment Noncompetition Agreement

A post-employment noncompetition agreement (also called a "covenant not to compete" or "noncompete clause") is designed to discourage a former employee from competing for a given period of time in the market in which the employer does business.

a. States where post-employment noncompetition clauses are unenforceable

Post-employment noncompetition clauses are generally unenforceable under the laws of several states:

- Alabama (Alabama Code, Section 8-1-1 a)
- California (California Business & Professions Code, Section 16660)
- Colorado (Colorado Revised Statutes, Section 8-2-113- 3)
- Louisiana (Louisiana Revised Statutes Annotated, Section 23:921)
- Montana (Montana Code Annotated, Section 28-2-703 to 705)
- North Dakota (North Dakota Cent. Code, Title 9, Section 08-06)
- Oklahoma (Oklahoma Statutes Annotated, Title 15, Section 217-219).

However, even in these states, a covenant not to compete may be enforceable if it's reasonable and necessary to prevent a former employee from disclosing trade secrets to a competitor. For this reason, they are often included in employment agreements.

b. Why use post-employment noncompetition clauses?

From an employer's point of view, a noncompetition clause in an employment agreement can serve several highly useful functions:

- By making it difficult, if not impossible, for a key employee to leave the company, it helps ensure that the employer will receive full return on its investment in training the employee.
- It may help an employer maintain a competitive advantage by preventing key employees from working for—and thereby aiding—competitors.
- It can help keep the employer's valuable trade secrets out of the hands of competitors.

Indeed, where enforceable, noncompetition clauses are far more effective in protecting trade secrets than nondisclosure clauses. It can be very difficult for an employer to know whether an ex-employee has disclosed trade secrets to a competitor. Moreover, even if the employer is sure trade secrets have been disclosed, it can be difficult to obtain court relief for violations of a nondisclosure clause. The ex-employer

Alternatives to Noncompetition Restrictions

To put it mildly, noncompetition clauses are not popular with employees. Some potential (or continuing) employees will simply refuse to sign them. There are other, less drastic ways, to accomplish the same goals:

- **Deferred compensation.** Instead of forcing employees to sign an agreement with a noncompetition clause, many hi-tech companies give their employees stock options, pension benefits or other benefits that fully vest only after several years of employment. This gives the employee a strong financial incentive to stay.

- **Employment contracts for a definite term.** Normally, employment is "at will"—meaning the employer can fire the employee for any reason or no reason at all. Likewise, the employee can quit at any time. However, this can be changed by either a written or oral contract. One way a developer can help assure a key employee will stay with the company is to have him or her sign an employment contract guaranteeing employment for a definite term—say two or three years. This means the employer can't fire the employee during that time and the employee can't quit. If he or she does, the employer can sue for breach of contract.

These types of agreements are common in some businesses, for example, the entertainment industry and professional sports; but they can have a real down side. If the employee doesn't work out, keeping him or her on can be a horrible burden for the company. Moreover, if an employee really wants to be somewhere else, the quality of his or her work will inevitably suffer. Obviously, both parties need to consider carefully before making such a long-term commitment.

must prove that the employee actually disclosed confidential information or that there is an imminent threat of such an unauthorized disclosure. This can be an onerous task, especially where the ex-employee claims that the information allegedly disclosed didn't qualify as a trade secret.

These problems do not exist with noncompetition clauses. It's usually easy to discover whether an ex-employee has gone to work for a competitor. To enforce a noncompetition clause in court, the ex-employer need only show that the ex-employee went to work for a competitor in violation of the clause's terms.

The best part about a noncompetition clause from an employer's point of view is that it will deter both the employee from seeking employment with a competitor and the competitor from hiring him or her. This significantly reduces an employee's incentive and opportunity to divulge trade secrets.

Of course, noncompetition clauses can make it impossible for an employee to earn a living in her chosen line of work if he or she leaves his or her job. The right to earn a living is considered to be one of the most fundamental rights a person has. For this reason, courts generally look on such clauses with disfavor and will only enforce them if the terms are reasonable and enforcement serves a legitimate interest of the employer.

c. When to use post-employment noncompetition clauses

Don't try to use a post-employment noncompetition clause simply to chain an employee to his job or obtain an unfair advantage over your competitors. A noncompetition clause should be used only in states where it's allowed, when there is a legitimate business need for it. For example:

- **Protection of trade secrets.** An employer has a legitimate interest in preventing its trade secrets from being disclosed to competitors. Thus, a noncompetition clause may be called for where the employee has access to trade secrets.

- **Return on substantial investment in an employee.** Where an employer spends substantial time and money giving an employee special training, it has a legitimate interest in obtaining a fair return on its investment. Thus, an employer may legitimately insist that an employee sign an agreement with a noncompetition clause before making such an investment in him or her.

- **Key employees.** Particularly in the software industry, where highly valuable programs are often created by a few extremely talented individuals, an employer may have a legitimate interest in preventing employees with special, unique or extraordinary skills from working for competitors.

d. Reasonableness requirement

To be enforceable in the states that permit them, noncompetition clauses must be reasonable. If such a clause is found to be unreasonable, courts in some states will refuse to enforce it at all; others will ignore the unreasonable provisions and apply what they deem to be reasonable restrictions.

To be reasonable, a noncompetition clause must be limited as to time, scope and geographic region.

- **Time.** A noncompetition clause cannot last forever; it must have a definite time limit—the shorter the better. Such clauses typically last for no more than six months to two years.
- **Scope.** A noncompetition clause should be no more restrictive than necessary to accomplish the employer's legitimate objectives. The clause should define as specifically as possible exactly what types of activities the employee cannot perform for a competitor. Generally, these activities ought to be similar to those currently being performed by the employee.
- **Geography.** A noncompetition clause must specify the geographic region in which it applies. It should be limited to the geographic area in which the company does business or in which it has made definite plans to do business in the immediate future. Of course, most software developers market their work to customers throughout the United States, so their noncompetition clauses can apply to the entire country.

e. Choosing a noncompetition clause

The more limited a noncompetition clause is in scope and time, the more likely it will be deemed reasonable and therefore enforceable in court. Presented on disk are a range of options, from a fairly "stiff" noncompetition clause to a relatively mild one. Choose one of the following for paragraph (a):

Alternative 1. This is the strictest noncompete clause.

Alternative 2. This clause bars an ex-employee from taking competitive employment only if it requires him or her to disclose any of the company's confidential information. This is much weaker than Alternative 1, thus much more easily enforced.

Alternative 3. This clause is limited to products and services the employee actually worked on for a specified time period before leaving the company. It's the weakest and therefore the most "reasonable" clause of all.

In addition to the particulars of paragraph (a), each noncompete clause, should contain:

(b) Diversion of Company Business. This prohibits the employee from soliciting or diverting company business. This provision should apply only to the period six to 12 months before the employee left the company and for no more than six to 12 months after termination. Fill in the desired time periods.

(c) Geographic Restrictions. Most software companies do business throughout the United States, so their noncompetition covenants should apply in every state as well. This provision makes this clear.

16. Additional Post-Employment Noncompetition Terms

If you completed the Post-Employment Noncompetition Agreement clause above, you have the option to add any or all of the following:

(a) Written Consent. This lets the employee off the hook if he or she can convince the company that no confidential information will be disclosed to the new employer. It will help make the noncompete clause appear reasonable to a judge. This would be most appropriate where the employee's new duties wouldn't tempt him or her to disclose the prior employer's trade secrets.

(b) Inability to Secure Employment. An excellent way for an employer to make a noncompetition clause appear reasonable in the eyes of a court is for the employer to agree to pay all or part of the ex-employee's salary if the employee is unable to find work because of the noncompetition clause. This can be expensive, but it may be worth it to prevent a key employee from working for the competition and possibly divulging trade secrets.

17. Noninterference With Company Employees

It's pretty much impossible for an employee to quit and start a competitive business by himself or herself. He or she needs help, and will usually try to find it among co-workers. Indeed, it has been a common occurrence in the hi-tech field for groups of employees to leave a company to start a competitive company. This clause tries to prevent this by barring the employee from persuading other employees to leave the company.

This simple provision can be almost as effective as a covenant not to compete, while not presenting the difficult enforcement problems that noncompetition restrictions do. (But, of course, this clause will not prevent an employee from joining an already-established competitor.) This optional clause may be used in any state, including those that prohibit post-employment noncompetition clauses.

18. Enforcement

If the employee breaches, or threatens to breach the Agreement, this clause gives the employer the automatic right to an injunction to prevent such a breach. This clause does not preclude the employer's right to seek additional remedies.

19. General Provisions

These general provisions are standard in many types of legal documents:

- **Successors.** This clause obligates all successors and heirs to the contents of the Agreement.
- **Governing Law.** Here you specify which state law governs the contract—

16. Additional Post-Employment Noncompetition Terms: The following post-employment noncompetition terms shall apply:

(a) Written Consent: I understand that I will be permitted to engage in the work or activity described in this Agreement if I provide the Company with clear and convincing written evidence, including assurances from my new employer and me, that the contribution of my knowledge to that work or activity will not cause me to disclose, base judgment upon or use any of the Company's confidential information. The Company will furnish me a written consent to that effect if I provide the required written evidence. I agree not to engage in such work or activity until I receive the written consent from the Company.

(b) Inability to Secure Employment: If, solely as a result of this noncompetition agreement, I am unable to secure employment appropriate to my abilities and training despite my diligent efforts to do so, the Company shall either: (1) release me from my noncompetition obligations to the extent necessary to allow me to obtain such employment, or (2) pay me a periodic amount equal to my monthly base pay at termination for the balance of the term of this noncompetition agreement.

If and while the Company elects to pay me the amounts described above, I promise to diligently pursue other employment opportunities consistent with my general skills and interests. I understand that the Company's obligation to make or continue the payments specified above will end upon my obtaining employment, and I will promptly give the Company written notice of such employment.

17. Noninterference with Company Employees: While employed by the Company and for 12 months afterwards, I will not:

(a) induce, or attempt to induce, any Company employee to quit the Company's employ,

(b) recruit or hire away any Company employee, or

(c) hire or engage any Company employee or former employee whose employment with the Company ended less than one year before the date of such hiring or engagement.

18. Enforcement: I agree that in the event of a breach or threatened breach of this Agreement, money damages would be an inadequate remedy and extremely difficult to measure. I agree, therefore, that the Company shall be entitled to an injunction to restrain me from such breach or threatened breach. Nothing in this Agreement shall be construed as preventing the Company from pursuing any remedy at law or in equity for any breach or threatened breach.

19. General Provisions:

(a) Successors: The rights and obligations under this Agreement shall survive the termination of my service to the Company in any capacity and shall inure to the benefit and shall be binding upon: (1) my heirs and personal representatives, and (2) the successors and assigns of the Company.

(b) Governing Law: This Agreement shall be construed and enforced in accordance with the laws of the state of Washington.

(c) Severability: If any provision of this Agreement is determined to be invalid or unenforceable, the remainder shall be unaffected and shall be enforceable against both the Company and me.

usually either the state of incorporation or the company's business home. It's generally more convenient to choose the state in which you live. That way, you can hire an attorney locally to handle any legal problems that might arise under the Agreement.

- **Severability.** In the event that some part of the Agreement is declared invalid by a court, this clause ensures that the rest of the document is still valid.
- **Entire Agreement.** This clause clarifies that the Agreement supersedes any prior signed agreements.
- **Modification.** This clause stipulates that future modifications must be in writing, signed both by the company and the employee.
- **Assignment.** This clause prohibits the employee from assigning or delegating his or her duties under the agreement

—for, example, the employee may not get someone else to perform the work.

Signatures

Although not absolutely necessary, it's a good idea to have the employee's signature witnessed by a company representative. This is intended to prevent the employee from later claiming her signature was forged.

Exhibit A

To protect employees, several states impose restrictions on the permissible scope of assignments of employee-created inventions. If the employee will work in California, Illinois, Kansas, Minnesota or Washington State, include the appropriate notice of state law provided on the disk. Delete all state law notices that don't apply.

Skip to Chapter 1, Section D, for information about preparing the final agreement.

(d) Entire Agreement: This Agreement supersedes and replaces all former agreements or understandings, oral or written, between the Company and me, except for prior confidentiality agreements I have signed relating to information not covered by this Agreement.

(e) Modification: This Agreement may not be modified except by a writing signed both by the Company and me.

(f) Assignment. This Agreement may be assigned by the Company. I may not assign or delegate my duties under this Agreement without the Company's prior written approval.

I have carefully read and considered all provisions of this Agreement and agree that all of the restrictions set forth are fair and reasonably required to protect the Company's interests. I acknowledge that I have received a copy of this Agreement as signed by me.

Date: _____

_____
Employee's Signature

_____
Typed or Printed Name

Witness: _____

Date: _____

_____
Signature

_____
Typed or Printed Name

_____
Title

Exhibit A

Washington Revised Code Annotated Section 49.44.140 provides as follows:

(1) A provision in an employment agreement that provides that an employee shall assign or offer to assign any of the employee's rights in an invention to the employer does not apply to an invention for which no equipment, supplies, facilities, or trade secret information of the employer was used and that was developed entirely on the employee's own time, unless:

(a) the invention relates (i) directly to the business of the employer, or (ii) to the employer's actual or demonstrably anticipated research or development, or

(b) the invention results from any work performed by the employee for the employer.

Any provision that purports to apply to such an invention is to that extent against the public policy of this state and is to that extent unenforceable.

Part II. Employment Agreements From the Employee's Viewpoint

This section covers employment agreements from the employee's point of view. Hi-tech employees are commonly asked to sign various agreements either before or after they begin work. They may be told that these merely are "standard forms" that everyone signs. These forms may be quite lengthy and filled with difficult to understand legalese. Before you sign any agreement, read it carefully and make sure you both understand it and are comfortable signing it.

Of course, the extent to which the employer will be willing to alter any of the provisions in an employment agreement depends largely on how badly it wants you as an employee. And, the extent to which you may be willing to demand significant changes depends on how much you want the job.

Be sure to ask any prospective employer if you will be required to sign an employment contract, and, if so, ask for a copy before you accept the job. You don't want to be presented with a harsh agreement after you've already started work. At this point, having quit your old job, you may feel you have no choice but to sign it as written; or, at the very least, you will be in a much worse bargaining position than you were before accepting the new job.

Following are some of the key items you should look for when reviewing an employment agreement:

- confidentiality of trade secrets

- intellectual property ownership rights, and
- post-employment noncompetition restrictions.

H. Confidentiality of Trade Secrets

The agreement may contain a clause requiring you to keep the company's trade secrets confidential. There is nothing to object to here. Even without such a clause, you have a legal duty not to disclose your employer's trade secrets if you're routinely exposed to them as a part of your job. (See Chapter 6 for a detailed discussion.) This duty applies not only to your new employer, but to all past employers as well. In other words, do not bring to your new job or disclose to your new employer your old employer's trade secrets.

Be careful what you take from your prior employer. The best way to get your new employer and yourself involved in a trade secret suit is to take materials containing trade secrets belonging to your old employer when you leave for your new job. This includes not only documents but computer disks and even trade journal articles (you may have written valuable notes on these that belong to your old employer). The wisest policy is to ask your old employer's permission before taking any document, disk or other item that could conceivably contain the employer's trade secrets. It's best to get such permission in writing.

I.   Intellectual Property Ownership

If the employer knows what it is doing, the agreement should contain a provision by which you transfer your intellectual property ownership rights in the software and other materials you create as part of your job duties. (See the discussion in Section G9, above.) This is perfectly reasonable and unobjectionable. However, if you and your new employer are going to share ownership of any of your work product, make sure that the employment agreement (or perhaps another side agreement) spells out exactly what you've agreed to. The discussion of ownership of custom software in Chapter 17, Section B13, should be useful here as well. It discusses the various ways a software developer and customer can parcel out ownership rights. Rights in employee-created software can be handled in the same way.

1. Employee-Owned Materials

If you own any software development tools (for example, code you've created and used in all your software), patents or other valuable materials, and you want these items to remain your sole property, the agreement should make clear that your employer is not acquiring any ownership rights in them. Following is a sample clause for this; you'll need to type it yourself.

EXAMPLE: The following Developments *[if many, add:* "relevant to the subject matter of my employment by the Company"] have been conceived or reduced to practice or learned by me, alone or jointly with others, before my employment with the Company and I desire that they be removed from the operation of this Agreement: *[list all employee-owned materials]*.

2. Work Outside the Scope of Employment

You need to be very careful if you intend to create software or other potentially valuable products on your own time. An employer owns the intellectual property rights in software created by an employee within the scope of employment. Moreover, an employer may even have certain rights over works created outside the scope of employment if the employee used the employer's resources—for example, did a substantial amount of the work during business hours or used the employer's equipment. If an employee creates a valuable work on his or her own time, an unscrupulous employer might try to assert ownership over it by claiming that the work was within the scope of employment or the employee used its resources.

To avoid potential problems, if you plan to do work on your own, make sure you inform your new employer and obtain its written acknowledgment that it has no ownership interest in such work. (See Chapter 11, Section A2d, for sample form.)

3. Post-Employment Invention Assignments

Some employers seek to include a provision by which the employee agrees to assign to the employer copyrightable or patentable work the employee creates after the employment relationship ends. Such post-employment assignments are enforceable only if they are reasonable. (See the discussion in Section G9, above.) From your point of view, a post-employment assignment provision is just as undesirable as a noncompetition clause. (See Section J, below.) It can make it very difficult for you to get a new job, because your new employer may not be entitled to own anything you create during the period of the assignment provision.

Try to avoid signing agreements containing such provisions, or at least seek to keep the length of the restriction as short as possible. Also, make sure the assignment applies only to works actually in existence, not to mere ideas or concepts in your brain.

J. Post-Employment Restrictions on Competition

Post-employment restrictions on competition (also called "covenants not to compete") are contractual provisions that attempt to prevent an employee from competing with

the employer after the employment relationship ends. This is one area in which the interests of the employer and employee are diametrically opposed. Quite simply, you don't want to have any restrictions on your right to work for others if you leave the company. However, the more valuable your skills, the more likely it is that your employer will want to prevent you from working for the competition.

Fortunately for employees, post-employment noncompetition restrictions are highly disfavored by the courts. Moreover, several states, including California, have laws making employee covenants not to compete generally unenforceable. (See Section G15a, above, for a list.) If you're in a state that doesn't have such a law, this doesn't mean the employer may impose extremely harsh noncompetition restrictions on you. Covenants not to compete must be reasonable to be enforceable. A noncompetition clause that would prevent you from earning a living in your chosen occupation for a substantial time would likely be unenforceable in court. (See Section G15d, above, for detailed discussion.)

If your prospective employer absolutely insists on having a noncompetition clause, at least try to limit it as much as possible. Here are some pointers:

- **Time.** Seek to make the length of the restriction as short as possible. Try for six months or a year; anything over two years is probably unreasonable.
- **Scope.** Try to avoid promising not to work for any of the company's

competitors or for certain named competitors. Rather, agree not to help develop products or services competitive with or similar to products you actually worked on for the company.

• **Geography.** The noncompete clause should apply only to the geographic areas in which the company does business or has definite plans to do business when you terminate your employment. However, if the company distributes its software throughout the United States (as most do), a noncompete clause can apply to the entire country.

See Section G15e, above, for sample language incorporating these restrictions into a noncompetition clause. ■

Chapter 15

Consulting Agreements

Part I. Hiring Independent Contractors

Part II. Working As an Independent Contractor

This chapter is for people who hire independent contractors or consultants, those who work as independent contractors and the many people who do both. The terms "independent contractor" and "consultant" are used interchangeably. (For agreements between employers and employees, see Chapter 14.)

Part I is for people or companies who are hiring independent contractors or consultants. Part II is for people who work as independent contractors or consultants. You can skip to Part II if you're in the second category.

Part I. Hiring Independent Contractors

Part I explains all aspects of independent contractor agreements. A complete independent contractor agreement is contained in the forms disk at the back of this book. It is advisable, however, that you read the following discussion in conjunction with using the forms disk. The disk contains a number of options you'll have to choose from, and the rest of this chapter explains these options in detail.

A. Introduction

The software industry places heavy reliance on self-employed workers. Whether they are called "independent computer consultants," "dailies," "vendors," or nothing at all, such workers routinely provide software companies with a variety of services, including programming and software development and design, technical advice, software maintenance, training and software-related technical writing. The general term for a self-employed individual who offers services to the public is "independent contractor."

Independent contractors are treated very differently from employees for tax, insurance and other purposes. They must also be treated very differently from employees by the businesses that hire them. Significant savings can be realized by treating a worker as an independent contractor rather than as an employee. However, as we'll discuss below, there are significant risks as well. If the IRS or a state taxing authority concludes that a worker is really an employee and not an independent contractor, substantial penalties may be imposed on that worker's employer. There may also be significant and surprising consequences if an independent contractor creates a copyrightable work.

Various government agencies—the IRS, Department of Labor, state taxing authorities and unemployment insurance and workers' compensation agencies—may decide, independently of each other, whether a worker is an employee or independent contractor. Where disputes arise over the ownership of a work product—such as code, documentation or interface design—the courts may have to determine employment status for copyright purposes.

For a complete discussion of all the legal issues involved in hiring independent contractors, see *Hiring Independent Contractors,* by Stephen Fishman (Nolo Press).

B. Benefits and Drawbacks of Using Independent Contractors

A hiring firm that classifies workers as independent contractors obtains many financial and other benefits, but may face serious risks and drawbacks as well. Let's look at these in detail.

1. Benefits of Using Independent Contractors

Perhaps the main reason any business uses independent contractors is that it can save a great deal of money. A business that hires an employee incurs a number of obligations in addition to paying that employee's salary, including:

- **Federal tax withholding.** The employer must withhold federal income tax from the wages paid to an employee and pay them to the IRS. Each year, the employer must send the employee a Form W-2 showing how much he or she earned and how much was withheld.
- **Social Security and Medicare taxes.** Social Security and Medicare taxes (FICA) are levied on both the employer and employee and must be paid together with the withheld federal income tax.
- **Federal unemployment taxes.** Employers must pay federal unemployment taxes (FUTA).
- **State taxes.** Employers must also pay state unemployment taxes and, in many states, also withhold state income taxes from employees' paychecks.
- **Workers' compensation insurance.** Employers must provide workers' compensation insurance coverage for employees in case they become injured on the job.
- **Employment benefits.** Although not legally required, most employers give their employees health insurance, sick leave, paid holidays and vacations. More generous employers also provide pension benefits for their employees.
- **Office space and equipment.** An employer normally provides an employee with office space and whatever equipment he or she needs to do the job.

All of these items add enormously to the cost of hiring and keeping an employee. Typically, more than one-third of all employee payroll costs go for social security, unemployment insurance, health benefits and vacation.

By hiring an independent contractor instead of an employee, a business incurs none of these obligations. It need not withhold or pay any taxes. Perhaps most importantly, an independent contractor need not be provided with health insurance, workers' compensation coverage, a pension plan or any other employee benefits. The business need only report amounts paid to an independent contractor by filing a Form 1099-MISC with the IRS. (Even this form need not be filed if an independent contractor is incorporated or paid less than $600 in a calendar year.)

There is another important reason businesses often prefer to use independent contractors: It avoids making a long-term commitment to the worker. An independent contractor can be hired solely to accomplish a specific task, enabling a business to obtain specialized expertise only for a short time. The hiring firm need not go through the trauma, severance costs and potential lawsuits brought on by laying off or firing an employee.

2. Drawbacks and Risks of Using Independent Contractors

You might now be thinking, "I'll never hire an employee again; I'll just use independent contractors." Before doing this, you should know that there are some substantial risks involved in classifying workers as independent contractors.

a. Adverse tax consequences

The IRS and most states want to see as many workers as possible classified as employees, not independent contractors. This way, the IRS and states can immediately collect taxes based on payroll withholding. It also makes it far more difficult for workers to under-report their income or otherwise evade taxes.

In recent years, the IRS has mounted an aggressive attack on employers who, in the view of the IRS, misclassify employees as independent contractors. One of the industries the IRS appears to have targeted is the software business. If the IRS concludes that an employer has misclassified an employee as an independent contractor, it may impose substantial assessments, penalties and interest.

An employer's woes do not necessarily end with the IRS. The state version of the IRS and/or state unemployment or workers' compensation agency may also audit the employer and order that it pay back taxes and/or unemployment or workers' comp insurance.

Such assessments can easily put a small company out of business. Also, keep in mind that the owners of the business may be held personally liable for such assessments and penalties, even if the business is a corporate entity. If the business owners cannot pay the taxes or fees, other responsible company officials such as the controller or treasurer may be held personally liable for them.

b. Potential loss of intellectual property rights

Another potential drawback that may arise from using independent contractors instead of employees is that the hiring firm faces a possible loss of copyright ownership. Unless the hiring firm obtains a written assignment (transfer) of the contractor's copyright rights, the contractor may end up owning the copyright in the software or other materials the contractor creates—even though the hiring firm paid the contractor to do the work. To avoid this consequence, hiring firms must obtain written assignments from independent contractors. (See Chapter 11 for a detailed discussion.)

c. Loss of control over workers

By using independent contractors, the hiring firm gives up control of its workers. Independent contractors legally may not be treated like employees. For instance, the hiring firm may not supervise an independent contractor. He or she must more or less be left alone to perform the agreed-upon services without substantial guidance or interference. If you want to control how a worker performs, classify the worker as an employee.

C. Which Workers Qualify as Independent Contractors

Given the risks involved in misclassifying an employee as an independent contractor, it is important for those hiring in the software industry to clearly understand whether a worker qualifies as an independent contractor or should be treated as an employee. Stated simply, an independent contractor is a person who is in business for himself or herself. Anyone with an independent business qualifies.

To decide whether a worker is an independent businessperson or a mere employee, the IRS and courts assess the degree of control the hiring party has over the worker. An independent contractor maintains personal control over the way he or she does the work contracted for, including the details of when, where and how the work is done. The hiring party's control is limited to accepting or rejecting the final result of the independent contractor's work. An independent contractor is just that—independent.

If the person or company that hires a worker has the right to control the worker, that worker is an employee. This is so whether or not that right was actually exercised—that is, whether the worker was really controlled. If the right of control is present, the IRS will view the worker as an employee, even if you have a written agreement calling him or her an independent computer consultant, independent contractor, partner or co-venturer.

Part-time workers can be employees. If the right to control the worker exists, it also makes no difference whether a person only works part-time. Even a part-time worker will be considered an employee if he or she is not operating an independent business.

1. IRS Factors for Measuring Control

To help determine whether a worker is an employee or independent contractor, the IRS has developed a set of factors it uses to measure how much control the hiring firm has the right to exercise over the worker. These factors are an attempt by the IRS to synthesize the results of court decisions on who is and is not an independent contractor. They are intended to serve as flexible guidelines for IRS auditors, not as a strict series of tests. Not all the factors may apply to a given worker, and some may be more important than others. The factors are summarized in the following chart:

IRS Control Factors		
Behavioral Control	**A worker will more likely be considered an IC if you:**	**A worker will more likely be considered an employee if you:**
Factors that show whether a hiring firm has the right to control how a worker performs the specific tasks he or she has been hired to do.	• do not give him or her instructions how to work • do not provide training • do not evaluate how the worker performs.	• provide instructions that the worker must follow about how to work • give the worker detailed training • evaluate how the worker does the job (as opposed to evaluating the results of his or her work).
Financial Control	**A worker will more likely be considered an IC if he or she:**	**A worker will more likely be considered an employee if:**
Factors showing whether a hiring firm has a right to control a worker's financial life.	• has a significant investment in equipment and facilities • pays business or travel expenses himself or herself • markets his or her services to the public • is paid by the job, and • has opportunity for profit or loss.	• you provide equipment and facilities free of charge • you reimburse the worker's business or traveling expenses • the worker makes no effort to market his or her services to the public • you pay the worker by the hour or other unit of time • the worker has no opportunity for profit or loss—for example, because you pay by the hour and reimburse all expenses.
Relationship of the Worker and Hiring Firm	**A worker will more likely be considered an IC if:**	**A worker will more likely be considered an employee if:**
Factors showing whether you and the worker believe he or she is an IC or employee.	• you don't provide employee benefits such as health insurance • you sign an IC agreement with the worker • the worker performs services that are not a part of your regular business activities.	• you provide employee benefits • you have no written IC agreement' • the worker performs services that are part of your core business.

Microsoft Shows What Not to Do

A highly publicized case involving Microsoft shows how a software developer that uses ICs can get into trouble. Microsoft supplemented its core staff of employees with a pool of people it classified as ICs. These people worked as software testers, production editors, proofreaders, formatters and indexers. They all signed independent contractor agreements, worked on specific projects and submitted invoices for their services. But otherwise they were treated much the same as Microsoft's employees: they worked along with regular employees, sharing the same supervisors, performing identical functions and working the same core hours. They also received admittance card keys, office equipment and supplies from Microsoft. The IRS determined that the workers were really employees for Social Security and income tax purposes and Microsoft agreed to pay overdue employment and withholding taxes. To add insult to injury, several of the workers then sued Microsoft claiming that they were entitled to pension and stock ownership benefits Microsoft provided its employees. The court agreed, having been swayed by the IRS rulings and Microsoft's own admission that the workers should have been classified as employees all along. (*Vizcaino v. Microsoft*, ___ F.3d ___ (1997).)

2. Section 530—The Employer's "Safe Harbor"

Applying the factors discussed just above is a highly subjective exercise, leading to a great deal of uncertainty. Moreover, many employers and tax experts believe that IRS examiners often arbitrarily interpret the facts in order to find an employment relationship.

In an attempt to make life a little easier for hiring firms, Congress added Section 530 to the Internal Revenue Code in 1978. Section 530 serves as a "safe harbor" for a firm that classifies a worker as an independent contractor. Section 530 prohibits the IRS from retroactively reclassifying a worker from independent contractor to employee if the hiring firm satisfies three requirements:

- it filed all required 1099-MISC forms reporting to the IRS the payments to the workers in question
- it consistently treated the workers involved and others doing similar work as ICs, and
- it had a reasonable basis—that is, a good reason—for treating the workers as ICs—for example, treating such workers as ICs is a common practice in the software industry or an attorney or accountant said the workers qualified as ICs.

When the IRS audits a hiring firm, it will first determine whether the Safe Harbor applies; if it does, the auditor won't bother to consider the control factors discussed in the previous section.

a. Safe harbor cannot be claimed by brokers or consulting firms

It's very common in the software industry for hiring firms to obtain the services of temporary or highly specialized workers though brokers. In these situations, three parties are involved in the relationship: the client contracts with the broker who in turn contracts with the worker to provide services for the client. The broker is in effect a middleman. The client pays the broker who pays the worker after taking its own cut.

> **EXAMPLE:** Acme Technical Services is a broker that provides computer pro-grammers to others. Acme contracts with Burt, a freelance programmer, to perform programming services for the Old Reliable Insurance Company. Reliable pays Acme who in turn pays Burt after deducting a broker's fee.

Such brokers—also called technical services firms or consulting firms—may not use the Safe Harbor if they contract to provide third party clients with:

- engineers
- designers
- drafters
- computer programmers
- systems analysts, or
- other similarly skilled workers.

The provision in the Safe Harbor rules setting forth this limitation is often referred to as Section 1706. Section 1706 has engen-dered a great deal of fear, often bordering upon paranoia, among hi-tech firms. Many such firms refuse to hire ICs or will deal only with brokers who treat the workers as their own employees.

This fear is largely misplaced. The fact is that Section 1706 does not make anyone an employee. It just means that the broker or consulting firm that serves as the middle-man between them and their clients can't use the Safe Harbor. The workers may nevertheless be ICs under the IRS control test. (See Section C1.)

b. Section 1706 doesn't apply to clients

Moreover, Section 1706 applies only to the broker in the middle of a three-party rela-tionship, *not to the client.* The client could use the Safe Harbor if it was audited by the IRS and the examiner claimed the worker was the client's employee under the control test.

> **EXAMPLE:** AcmeSoft, Inc., contracts with Quickhelp Technical Services to obtain the services of Burt, a freelance programmer. AcmeSoft is then audited by the IRS. The examiner claims that AcmeSoft has the right to exert sufficient control over Burt for him to be Acme-Soft's employee under the control test. AcmeSoft can qualify for Safe Harbor protection if it meets the three require-ments discussed above—reasonable basis, consistency, 1099s.

In addition, the Safe Harbor can always be used where a firm contracts *directly* with a technical services worker, rather than going through a broker or consulting firm.

EXAMPLE: AcmeSoft, Inc., contracts with Burt directly to provide it with programming services—that is, it does not go through a broker. If AcmeSoft is audited, it can obtain Safe Harbor protection, provided that it satisfies the requirements.

c. State audits

No state has a counterpart to the IRS Safe Harbor. A state unemployment compensation or workers' compensation auditor will not be impressed by the fact that you've obtained Safe Harbor protection from the IRS. You'll need to convince the state auditor that the workers involved qualify as ICs under the state rules. These can be stricter than the IRS rules.

D. Independent Contractor Agreement Favorable to Hiring Firm

A hiring firm should develop a form IC agreement it can use over and over again with all the ICs it hires. The agreement provided in this section favors the hiring firm—that is, when it comes to those issues where the interests of the hiring firm and IC diverge, the agreement favors the hiring firm. The agreement is self-explanatory, with the following clarifications.

 If a consultant is being hired to help create computer software, you may be uncertain whether to use the independent contractor agreement contained in this chapter or the much longer custom software agreement discussed in Chapter 17. If an independent contractor is being hired to create an entire computer system, the custom software agreement should be used. The independent contractor agreement covered in this chapter is much simpler and is designed for more limited projects.

 The full text of the Consulting Agreement is on the CD-ROM forms disk under the file name CONSULT1. See Chapter 1 for instructions on using the forms disk.

Introductory Paragraph

Never refer to an IC as an employee or to yourself as an employer.

Do's and Don'ts for Software Companies That Use Independent Contractors

Software firms that classify workers as independent contractors need to remember that the workers must be treated like independent businesspeople, not like employees. Treat the worker the same way you would the accountant who does your company's taxes or the lawyer who handles your legal work. This means:

- **Sign a written contract with the independent contractor before the work begins.** The contract should specify the work to be performed and make it clear that the worker is an independent contractor. The contract should be for a term of no longer than three to six months. Even where extensive projects are involved, this can be accomplished by narrowly defining the work to be done and then drawing up new contracts to cover additional tasks.

- **Don't provide ongoing instructions or training.** If the independent contractor needs special training, he or she should procure and pay for it himself or herself.

- **Don't supervise the independent contractor or establish working hours.** It's up to the independent contractor to control when and how to accomplish the job.

- **Don't require formal written reports.** An occasional phone call inquiring into the work's progress is acceptable, but requiring regular written status reports indicates the worker is an employee. However, contracts for specific projects can (and should) have benchmarks for show-and-tell demonstrations or reports.

- **Don't invite an independent contractor to employee functions.** The exception is where outside vendors will be there as well.

- **Don't ever fire an independent contractor.** Instead, terminate the contract if he or she fails to meet the specifications or standards set forth in it.

- **Don't ever refer to an independent contractor as an "employee."** This should not be done verbally or in writing.

- **Set up a separate vendor file for each independent contractor you hire.** Keep in this file the independent contractor's contract, invoices, copies of 1099 forms and any other information that shows the worker is operating an independent business. This may include the independent contractor's business card and stationery, and evidence that the independent contractor has workers' compensation insurance coverage for her employees. Don't keep independent contractor records with your employee personnel files.

- **Don't pay independent contractors on a weekly, bi-weekly, or monthly basis like you pay your employees.** Rather, require all independent contractors to submit invoices, which are paid the same time you pay other outside vendors, such as your office supply company.

Initially, it's best to refer to the IC by his or her full name. If an IC is incorporated, use the corporate name, not the IC's own name. For example: "John Smith Incorporated" instead of just "John Smith." If the IC is unincorporated but is doing business under a fictitious business name, use that name. A fictitious business name or assumed name is a name sole proprietors or partners use to identify their business other than their own names. For example, if Al Brodsky calls his one-man marketing computer consulting business "ABC Consulting," use that name. This shows you're contracting with a business, not a single individual.

For sake of brevity, it is usual to identify yourself and the IC by shorter names in the remainder of the agreement. You can use an abbreviated version of the IC's full name —for example, "ABC" for "ABC Marketing Research." Or you can refer to the IC simply as "Consultant" or "Contractor."

Refer to yourself initially by your company name and subsequently by a short version of the name or as "Client" or "Firm."

Put the short names in quotes after the full names. Also include the address of the principal place of business of the IC and yourself. If you or the IC have more than one office or workplace, the principal place of business is the main office or workplace.

1. Services Performed by Consultant

The agreement should describe, in as much detail as possible, what the consultant is

expected to do. If a computer program is to be produced, describe it in as much detail as possible. Make sure to cover anything else the consultant should deliver, such as documentation.

It is often helpful to break down the project into discrete parts or stages—often called phases or "milestones." This makes it easier for the hiring firm to monitor the consultant's progress and may aid the consultant in budgeting her time. For example, the consultant's pay could be contingent upon the completion of each milestone. (Payment schedules are covered below, under "Consultant's Payment.")

You can include the description in the main body of the agreement. Or, if it's a lengthy explanation, put it on a separate document labeled "Exhibit A" and attach it to the agreement.

2. Consultant's Payment

There are a number of ways a consultant may be paid; choose the alternative that suits your needs:

Alternative 1: Fixed Fee. The simplest way for a consultant to be paid is to pay a fixed fee for the entire project. This way, you know exactly how much the work will cost you and the consultant won't have an incentive to pad the bill by working more hours.

Alternative 2: Installment Payments. Paying a consultant a fixed fee for the entire job, rather than an hourly or daily rate, supports a finding of independent contractor status. However, this can pose problems for the consultant due to difficulties in accurately estimating how long the job will take. One way to deal with this problem is to break the job down into phases or "milestones" and pay the consultant a fixed fee upon completion of each phase. If you use this approach, you must describe in the agreement what work the consultant must complete to receive each payment.

Alternative 3: Payment by the Hour/Day/Week/Month. If a fixed fee for the job is impractical, it doesn't make much difference for IRS purposes whether the consultant is paid by the hour, day, week or month. It's generally a good idea to place a cap on the consultant's total compensation. This may be a particularly good idea if you're unsure how reliable or efficient the consultant is.

3. Expenses

The IRS considers the payment of a worker's business or traveling expenses to be a mild indicator of an employment relationship. It's best not to reimburse an IC for expenses; instead, pay the IC enough so that he or she can pay his or her own expenses.

Select one of the two alternatives. Alternative 1 provides you will not pay any of the consultant's expenses. Alternative 2 provides that you will pay only those expenses you agree in writing to reimburse in advance.

4. Invoices

An independent contractor should never be paid weekly, bi-weekly or monthly the way an employee is. Instead, he or she should submit invoices, which should be paid at the same time and manner as you pay other vendors. You need to decide how long after you receive the invoice you will pay the consultant, 30 days is a common period.

5. Consultant an Independent Contractor

One of the most important functions of an agreement between a hiring firm and consultant is to help establish that the consultant is not the hiring firm's employee. In an audit of the hiring firm, an IRS examiner or similar official will almost surely want to see the firm's agreements with all workers classified as independent contractors. If the agreement indicates that the hiring firm has the right to control the worker, he or she will undoubtedly be viewed as an employee by the IRS. This will cause problems not only for the hiring firm, but for the consultant as well.

On the other hand, an agreement that indicates a lack of the right to control on the part of the hiring firm will contribute to a finding of independent contractor status. But such an agreement will not be determinative in and of itself. Simply signing a piece of paper will not make a worker an independent contractor. The agreement must reflect reality—that is, you must actually not have the right to control the worker.

The language in this clause addresses most of the factors the IRS and other agencies consider in measuring the degree of control of the hiring firm. (These factors are discussed in Section C.) All provisions show that the hiring firm lacks the right to control the manner and means by which the consultant will perform the agreed-upon services.

Include all of provisions a-j that apply to your particular situation. The more that apply, the more likely that the consultant will be viewed as an independent contractor.

6. Intellectual Property Ownership

Usually, you will want to obtain sole ownership of what the consultant creates, whether it be a computer program, documentation or other material. However, there is no rule that this has to be the case. Two different ownership alternatives are presented in the contract. Choose only one alternative and delete the other. Here's an explanation.

Alternative 1: Client Owns Consultant's Work Product. Obtaining ownership of the consultant's work product presents many advantages: you can do anything you want with the material and the consultant is prevented from giving the same material to your competitors. If you and the consultant agree that you will own the consultant's work product, you should obtain a written assignment of the consultant's intellectual

property rights in such work. Alternative 1 contains such an assignment. As discussed in detail in Chapter 11, a hiring firm can never be sure it owns what it pays an independent contractor to create unless it obtains such an assignment. Among the most important reasons to obtain an assignment from the IC is that otherwise the hiring firm may not have the right to create "derivative works" based on the original work product—for example, new versions of a program originally created by the consultant.

Alternative 2: Consultant Owns Work Product. You and the consultant may agree that the consultant will retain his or her ownership rights in the work product (perhaps in return for receiving reduced monetary compensation). In this event, instead of assigning his or her rights to the client, the consultant will grant you a non-exclusive license to use the work product.

This clause grants the client a nonexclusive license to use the consultant's work product in any of its products, but prevents it from selling the consultant's work to others. This is a generous license grant.

7. Ownership of Consultant's Materials

A software consultant will often have various development tools, routines, subroutines and other programs, data and materials that he or she brings to the job and that might end up in the final product. One term for these type of items is "Consultant's Materials."

You must make sure the consultant grants you a license to use these materials. This clause grants you a nonexclusive license to use such materials in any of your products. Try to have the consultant list in the agreement what these materials are. This avoids confusion later on.

8. Confidential Information

In the course of his or her work, the consultant may be exposed to your most valuable trade secrets. It is reasonable, therefore, for you to seek to include a nondisclosure provision in the agreement. Such a provision states that the consultant may not disclose the client's trade secrets to others without the client's permission.

These are the most important parts of the confidentiality provision in the agreement:

(a) This clause provides that the consultant has a duty not to disclose to others the work he or she creates for the hiring firm. This clause should be deleted from the agreement if the consultant retains ownership of her work product.

(b) This clause prevents the unauthorized disclosure by the consultant of any of your confidential information. Confidential information includes any written material you mark "confidential" or information disclosed orally that you later write down, mark as confidential and deliver to the consultant.

(c) A consultant should have no duty to keep material confidential if it does not qualify as a trade secret, is lawfully learned from persons other than the client, or is independently developed by the consultant.

(e) If you don't want to permit the consultant to disclose your business relationship, include this clause.

9. Noncompetition

A firm that hires a consultant naturally doesn't want the consultant to perform the same work for a competitor, thereby allowing the competitor to benefit from work originally paid for by the hiring firm. A hiring firm is protected from this problem to some extent where it obtains an assignment of all the consultant's rights in the work product. Theoretically, in this case the consultant can't use the work product on other projects because she doesn't own it. However, in practice it can be difficult to determine whether or not the consultant is using the client's work product on other projects.

A hiring firm obtains much greater protection by including a noncompetition clause in the independent contractor agreement. As discussed in Chapter 14, restrictions on competition are enforceable only if reasonable. To be viewed as reasonable by the courts, such restrictions must be drafted as narrowly as possible.

This optional clause only prevents the consultant from performing the exact same services for competitors that it performed for the hiring firm. This provision can be limited to the time the consultant is working for the client, or it can be extended for a limited period afterwards; no more than two years would be considered reasonable by most courts.

10. Term of Agreement

An independent contractor agreement should last no more than one or two years at most. Anything longer makes the consultant look like an employee. Successive agreements can be used if the project can't be completed in the time frame set out in this agreement.

11. Termination of Agreement

Many consultants and hiring firms want to have the right to terminate their agreements for any reason on two weeks' notice. Unfortunately, the IRS considers such an unfettered termination right to be an indicator of an employment relationship (an employee normally can quit or be fired at any time). This clause attempts to reach a compromise between the parties' desire to be able to get out of the agreement and at the same time satisfy the IRS and others that the consultant is an independent contractor. Of particular note are:

(a) This paragraph permits either party to terminate the agreement if the other has breached it and failed to remedy the breach within 30 days.

(b) Most software independent contractor agreements are basically contracts for personal services. If the client becomes dissatisfied with the service he or she is receiving and loses confidence in the consultant, the client should have the right to terminate the agreement. This paragraph permits the client to terminate the agreement only if in the client's "reasonable judgment" the consultant's performance is inadequate or unnecessary. This stops short of giving the client a completely unfettered right to fire the consultant at will.

12. Return of Materials

This clause requires both you and the consultant to return each others' materials at the end of the agreement.

13. Warranties and Representations

A warranty is a promise or statement regarding the quality, quantity, performance or legal title of something being sold. Software independent contractor agreements typically contain several warranty provisions.

(a) This clause provides that the consultant has the authority to perform as promised. This means, for example, that the consultant is not prevented from working for you because he or she has previously signed a noncompetition agreement for a previous client.

(b) In this clause, the consultant promises that the client will obtain free and clear ownership or license rights to consultant's work product and material. If the consultant has licensed any materials from third parties that are to be included in the work product, the licenses should be listed here.

(c) The consultant promises in this clause that his or her work product and materials will not infringe on others' copyrights, patents, trade secrets or other intellectual property rights.

(d) The consultant promises here that the work product will perform in substantial conformance with the specifications and will be free of reproducible programming errors. You need to state how long this warranty will last—it can be anywhere from 90 days to one year or longer.

14. Indemnification

Indemnification is a fancy legal word that means a promise to repay someone for their losses or damages if a specified event occurs. This clause requires the consultant to indemnify you or your business if someone sues or threatens to sue because the consultant breached any of the warranties made in the agreement. For example, if the consultant copied code from a third party and sold it to you, and that third party sued for infringement, the consultant would be required to pay for your legal defense and any damages a court awarded.

15. Employment of Assistants

Because independent contractor agreements are basically personal services contracts, it's often appropriate for you to have some control over who will do the work. If you've hired a consultant because of his or her particular skills, you may wish to have a say-so as to whether the consultant can get others to do the work you hired him or her to do. This is not exercising control over how the work will be done but rather agreeing on who will do the work.

(a) Alternative clauses

Choose the alternative Paragraph (a) that best suits you:

Alternative 1: Consultant May Employ Assistants. This clause leaves the issue up to the consultant.

Alternative 2: No Assistants Without Client's Consent. This clause requires the client's prior approval.

(b) Assignment of copyright by ICs used by your IC

The consultant promises in this clause that any independent contractors the consultant hires will assign their rights to the consultant so the consultant may in turn assign or license those rights to you. As discussed in detail in Chapter 14, the copyright in software, documentation and similar works created by an employee will automatically be owned by the employer only if created within the scope of employment. Software created by an independent contractor will be owned by the hiring party only if assigned to it by the independent contractor.

(c) Key employees of consultant

Paragraph (c) is optional. It should be used if the client has hired the consultant because the consultant has promised that certain key employees will be doing the work. If such employees quit working for the consultant, the client will want to have the option to terminate the agreement and hire someone else. Fill in the names of key employees and the amount of time the consultant will have to find acceptable replacements.

16. Mediation and Arbitration

As you doubtless know, court litigation can be very expensive. To avoid these costs, alternative forms of dispute resolution have been developed that don't involve going to court. These include mediation and arbitration.

In mediation, a neutral third person called a mediator meets with the parties and makes suggestions as to how to resolve their controversy. Typically, the mediator either sits the parties down together and tries to provide an objective view of their disputes, or shuttles between the parties as a hopefully cool conduit for what may be hot opinions. Mediation is nonbinding. That

means that if either party to the dispute doesn't like the outcome of the mediation, he or she can ask for binding arbitration or go to court.

Arbitration is usually like an informal court trial without a jury, but involves arbitrators instead of judges and is usually much faster and cheaper than courts. You may be represented by a lawyer, but it's not required.

No one can be forced into mediation or arbitration; one must agree to it, either in the contract or later when a dispute arises. Commercial contracts often include binding arbitration provisions. However, this is not a matter to be agreed to lightly. By submitting to binding arbitration, you're basically

giving up your constitutional right of access to the courts. Arbitration has many good points. It is usually faster and cheaper than court litigation. Also, because the parties choose the arbitrator, they can select someone who is familiar with computer and software law. Such a person might be expected to render a better decision than a judge or jury with no familiarity with the software business.

However, arbitration can also have a down side. Litigants have often found that arbitrators seek to reach a compromise between the parties' positions rather than ruling squarely in favor of one or the other. Moreover, arbitrators are under no obligation to follow established legal principles. Under the rules of the American Arbitration Association (which are most commonly used in arbitrations), no questioning of the parties or witnesses is allowed before the hearing (a process lawyers call discovery). This can lead to unfair results. Moreover, if you lose an arbitration there is essentially no right of appeal. A court can vacate (void) an arbitrator's decision only if it finds the arbitrator guilty of misconduct, bias, fraud or corruption. Proving this is extremely difficult. Finally, an arbitrator's decision is not self-enforcing; it must be entered with a court. In some cases (obtaining a quick restraining order, for example), you're better off going to court in the first place.

This optional clause requires you and the consultant to take advantage of these alternate forms of dispute resolution. You're first required to submit the dispute to mediation.

If mediation doesn't work, you must submit the dispute to binding arbitration.

You should indicate where the mediation or arbitration is to occur. You'll usually want it in the city or county where your office is located. You don't want to have to travel a long distance to attend a mediation or arbitration.

17. Attorney Fees

If you have to sue the consultant in court or bring an arbitration proceeding to enforce the agreement and win, you normally will not be awarded the amount of your attorney fees unless your agreement requires it. Including such an attorney fees provision in the agreement can be in your interest. It can help make filing a lawsuit economically feasible. It will also give the consultant a strong incentive to negotiate with you if you have a good case.

On the other hand, an attorney fees provision can also work against you. It may help the consultant find an attorney to sue you and make you more anxious to settle. If you think it's more likely you'll violate the agreement than the consultant will, an attorney fees provision is probably not a good idea.

Under this provision, if either person has to sue the other in court or bring an arbitration proceeding to enforce the agreement and wins—that is, becomes the prevailing party—the loser is required to pay the other person's attorney fees and expenses.

18. General Provisions

These general provisions are standard in many types of legal documents:

(a) This clause helps make it clear to a court or arbitrator that the parties intended the contract to be their final agreement. A clause such as this helps avoid claims that promises not contained in the written contract were made and broken. Always make sure that all documents containing any of the client's representations upon which you are relying are attached to the agreement as exhibits. If they aren't attached, they likely won't be considered to be part of the agreement.

(b) In the event that some part of the agreement is declared invalid by a court, this clause ensures that the rest of the document is still valid.

(c) This clause specifies which state law governs the contract. This should be the state in which you do business or are incorporated.

(d) When you want to do something important involving the agreement—terminate it, for example—you need to tell the consultant about it. This is called giving notice. This provision gives you several options for providing the consultant with notice: by personal delivery, by mail, or by fax or telex followed by a confirming letter.

If you give notice by mail, it is not effective until three days after it's sent. For example, if you want to end the agreement on 30 days notice and mail your notice of termination to the consultant, the agreement will not end until 33 days after you mailed the notice.

(e) This clause helps you to make sure that you and the consultant are separate legal entities, not partners or co-venturers. If a consultant is viewed as your partner, you'll be liable for its debts and the consultant will have the power to make contracts that obligate you to third parties without your consent.

(f) An assignment is the process by which rights or duties under a contract are transferred to someone else. For example, you may assign your right to receive the benefit of the consultant's services to someone else. This clause give you an unfettered right to assign your rights or obligations. However, the consultant may not make an assignment without your prior written approval. This prevents the consultant from getting someone else to do the work without your permission. This can be especially important where you've hired a consultant because of his or her particular skills or expertise. You probably don't want the consultant palming off the work on someone else who may not be as expert.

Signatures

It is not necessary for the parties to sign the agreement in the same room or on the same day. At least two copies should be signed, with each party retaining one.

Consulting Agreement

This Agreement is made between Earthworks Software Research Lab ("Client"), with a principal place of business at 1111 Silicon Lane, Fremont, CA, and Jack Aubrey ("Consultant"), with a principal place of business at 164 Fulton St., San Francisco, CA.

1. Services Performed by Consultant:

Consultant agrees to perform the services described in Exhibit A, which is attached to and made part of this Agreement.

2 Consultant's Payment:

Consultant shall be paid $10,000 upon completion of the work as detailed in Clause 1.

3. Expenses: Consultant shall be responsible for all expenses incurred while performing services under this Agreement.

4. Invoices: Consultant shall submit invoices for all services rendered. Client shall pay Consultant within 30 days after receipt of each invoice.

5. Consultant an Independent Contractor: Consultant is an independent contractor, and neither Consultant nor Consultant's staff is, or shall be deemed, Client's employees. In its capacity as an independent contractor, Consultant agrees and represents, and Client agrees, as follows:

(a) Consultant has the right to perform services for others during the term of this Agreement subject to noncompetition provisions set out in this Agreement, if any.

(b) Consultant has the sole right to control and direct the means, manner and method by which the services required by this Agreement will be performed.

(c) Consultant has the right to perform the services required by this Agreement at any place or location and at such times as Consultant may determine.

(d) Consultant will furnish all equipment and materials used to provide the services required by this Agreement, except to the extent that Consultant's work must be performed on or with Client's computer or existing software.

(e) The services required by this Agreement shall be performed by Consultant, or Consultant's staff, and Client shall not be required to hire, supervise or pay any assistants to help Consultant.

(f) Consultant is responsible for paying all ordinary and necessary expenses of its staff.

(g) Neither Consultant nor Consultant's staff shall receive any training from Client in the professional skills necessary to perform the services required by this Agreement.

(h) Neither Consultant nor Consultant's staff shall be required to devote full-time to the performance of the services required by this Agreement.

(i) Client shall not provide insurance coverage of any kind for Consultant or Consultant's staff.

(j) Client shall not withhold from Consultant's compensation any amount that would normally be withheld from an employee's pay.

6. Intellectual Property Ownership:

Work Product includes, but is not limited to, the programs and documentation, including all ideas, routines, object and source codes, specifications, flow charts and other materials, in whatever form, developed solely for Client under this Agreement.

Consultant hereby assigns to Client its entire right, title and interest, including all patent, copyright, trade secret, trademark and other proprietary rights, in the Work Product.

Consultant shall, at no charge to Client, execute and aid in the preparation of any papers that Client may consider necessary or helpful to obtain or maintain—at Client's expense—any patents, copyrights, trademarks or other proprietary rights. Client shall reimburse Consultant for reasonable out-of-pocket expenses incurred under this provision.

7. Ownership of Consultant's Materials:

"Consultant's Materials" means all programs and documentation, including routines, object and source codes, tools, utilities and other copyrightable materials, that:

- do not constitute Work Product,
- are incorporated into the Work Product, and
- are owned solely by Consultant or licensed to Consultant with a right to sublicense.

Consultant's Materials include, but are not limited to, the following: [DESCRIBE]

Consultant shall retain any and all rights Consultant may have in Consultant's Materials. Consultant hereby grants Client an unrestricted, nonexclusive, perpetual, fully paid-up worldwide license to use and sublicense the use of Consultant's Materials for the purpose of developing and marketing its products.

8. Confidential Information:

(a) Consultant agrees that the Work Product is Client's sole and exclusive property. Consultant shall treat the Work Product on a confidential basis and not disclose it to any third party without Client's written consent, except when reasonably necessary to perform the services under this Agreement.

(b) Consultant will not use or disclose to others without Client's written consent Client's confidential information, except when reasonably necessary to perform the services under this Agreement. "Confidential information" includes, but is not limited to:

- the written, printed, graphic or electronically recorded materials furnished by Client for use by Contractor
- Client's business plans, customer lists, operating procedures, trade secrets, design formulas, know-how and processes, computer programs and inventories, discoveries and improvements of any kind
- any written or tangible information stamped "confidential," "proprietary" or with a similar legend, and

- any written or tangible information not marked with a confidentiality legend, or information disclosed orally to Consultant, that is treated as confidential when disclosed and later summarized sufficiently for identification purposes in a written memorandum marked "confidential" and delivered to Consultant within 30 days after the disclosure.

(c) Contractor shall not be restricted in the use of any material which is publicly available, already in Contractor's possession or known to Contractor without restriction, or which is rightfully obtained by Contractor from sources other than Client.

(d) Contractor's obligations regarding proprietary or confidential information extend to information belonging to customers and suppliers of Client about whom Contractor may have gained knowledge as a result of Client's services to Client.

(e) All information concerning the existence of this Agreement and the existence of any business relationship between Consultant and Client shall be kept in confidence.

(f) Consultant will not disclose to Client information or material that is a trade secret of any third party.

(g) The provisions of this clause shall survive any termination of this Agreement.

9. Noncompetition: Consultant agrees that during performance of the services required by this Agreement, Consultant will not perform the same services for any competitor of Client in the specific field in which Consultant is performing services for Client.

10. Term of Agreement: This Agreement will become effective when signed by both parties and will end no later than March 1, 199X.

11. Termination of Agreement:

(a) Each party has the right to terminate this Agreement if the other party has materially breached any obligation herein and such breach remains uncured for a period of 30 days after notice thereof is sent to the other party.

(b) If at any time after commencement of the services required by this Agreement, Client shall, in its sole reasonable judgment, determine that such services are inadequate, unsatisfactory, no longer needed or substantially not conforming to the descriptions, warranties or representations contained in this Agreement, Client may terminate this Agreement upon 30 days' written notice to Consultant.

12. Return of Materials: Upon termination of this Agreement, each party shall promptly return to the other all data, materials and other property of the other held by it.

13. Warranties and Representations: Consultant warrants and represents that:

(a) Consultant has the authority to enter into this Agreement and to perform all obligations hereunder.

(b) The Work Product and Consultant's Materials are and shall be free and clear of all encumbrances including security interests, licenses, liens, or other restrictions except as follows: None.

(c) The use, reproduction, distribution or modification of the Work Product and Consultant's Materials does not and will not violate the copyright, patent, trade secret or other property right of any former client, employer or third party.

(d) For a period of 180 days following acceptance of the Work Product, the Work Product will be:

- free from reproducible programming errors and defects in workmanship and materials under normal use, and
- substantially in conformance with the product specifications.

14. Indemnification: Consultant agrees to indemnify and hold harmless Client against any claims, actions or demands, including without limitation reasonable attorney and accounting fees, alleging or resulting from the breach of the warranties contained Paragraph 12 of this Agreement. Client shall provide notice to Consultant promptly of any such claim, suit or proceeding and shall assist Consultant, at Consultant's expense, if defending any such claim, suit or proceeding.

15. Employment of Assistants:

(a) Consultant may, at Consultant's own expense, employ such assistants or subcontractors as Consultant deems necessary to perform the services required by this Agreement. However, Client shall have the right to reject any of Consultant's assistants or subcontractors whose qualifications in Client's good faith and reasonable judgment are insufficient for the satisfactory performance of the services required by this Agreement.

(b) Consultant warrants and represents that the Work Product shall be created solely by Consultant, Consultant's employees during the course of their employment or independent contractors who assigned all right, title and interest in the work to Consultant.

16. Mediation and Arbitration:

If a dispute arises under this Agreement, the parties agree to first try to resolve it with the help of a mutually agreed upon mediator in the following location: Fremont, CA. Any costs and fees other than attorney fees associated with the mediation shall be shared equally by the parties.

If it proves impossible to arrive at a mutually satisfactory solution through mediation, the parties agree to submit the dispute to binding arbitration at the following location—Fremont, CA—under the rules of the American Arbitration Association. Judgment upon the award rendered by the arbitrator may be entered in any court with jurisdiction to do so.

17. Attorney Fees: If any litigation or arbitration is necessary to enforce this Agreement, the prevailing party shall be entitled to reasonable attorney fees, costs and expenses.

18. General Provisions:

(a) Sole agreement: This is the entire Agreement between Consultant and Client.

(b) Severability: If any part of this Agreement is held unenforceable, the rest of the Agreement will continue in full force and effect.

(c) Applicable law: This Agreement will be governed by the laws of the State of California.

(d) Notices: All notices and other communications given in connection with this Agreement shall be in writing and shall be deemed given as follows:

- When delivered personally to the recipient's address as appearing in the introductory paragraph to this Agreement;
- Three days after being deposited in the United States mails, postage prepaid to the recipient's address as appearing in the introductory paragraph to this Agreement, or
- When sent by fax or telex to the last fax or telex number of the recipient known to the party giving notice. Notice is effective upon receipt provided that a duplicate copy of the notice is promptly given by first-class or certified mail, or the recipient delivers a written confirmation of receipt.

Any party may change its address appearing in the introductory paragraph to this Agreement by giving notice of the change in accordance with this paragraph.

(e) No partnership: This Agreement does not create a partnership relationship. Consultant does not have authority to enter into contracts on Client's behalf.

(f) Assignment: Consultant may not assign its rights or obligations under this Agreement without Client's prior written consent. Client may freely assign its rights and obligations under this Agreement.

Client: Earthworks Software Research Lab

By: _Sue Sanger_____
   (Signature)

Sue Sanger

Title: President

Consultant: Jack Aubrey

By: _Jack Aubrey_____
   (Signature)

Jack Aubrey

Social Security Number: 123-45-6789

Part II. Working As an Independent Contractor

Part II is for the huge number of people in the software industry who work as independent contractors. It provides an overview of the benefits and drawbacks of this lifestyle and includes a detailed consulting agreement favorable to the independent contractor.

For a complete discussion of all the legal issues involved in working as an independent contractor, see *Wage Slave No More: The Independent Contractor's Legal Guide,* by Stephen Fishman (Nolo Press).

E. Benefits and Drawbacks of Working As an Independent Contractor

Being an IC can give you more freedom than employees have and result in tax benefits. But there are also drawbacks.

1. Benefits of Being an Independent Contractor

- **You're your own boss.** When you're an IC you're your own boss, with all the risks and rewards that entails. This freedom from control is particularly appealing to many of the highly creative and independent people in the software industry.

- **You may earn more than employees.** You can often earn more as an IC than as an employee in someone else's business.

  According to *The Wall Street Journal,* ICs are usually paid at least 20% to 40% more per hour than employees performing the same work. This is because hiring firms don't have to pay half of ICs' Social Security taxes, pay unemployment compensation taxes, provide workers' compensation coverage or employee benefits like health insurance and sick leave. Of course, how much you're paid is a matter for negotiation between you and your clients. ICs whose skills are in great demand may receive far more than employees doing similar work.

- **Tax benefits.** Being an IC also provides you with many tax benefits that employees don't have. For example, no federal or state taxes are withheld from your paychecks as they must be for employees. Instead, ICs normally

pay estimated taxes directly to the IRS four times a year. Even more important, you can take advantage of many business-related tax deductions that are limited or not available at all for employees. This may include, for example, office expenses including those for home offices, travel expenses, entertainment and meal expenses, equipment and insurance costs and more.

2. Drawbacks of IC Status

Despite the advantages, being an IC is no bed of roses. Following are some of the major drawbacks and pitfalls.

- **No job security.** As discussed above, one of the best things about being an IC is that you're on your own. But this can be one of the worst things about it as well. When you're an employee, you must be paid as long as you have your job, even if your employer's business is slow. This is not the case when you're an IC. If you don't have business, you don't make any money.

- **No employer-provided benefits.** Although not required to by law, employers usually provide their employees with health insurance, paid vacations and paid sick leave. More generous employers may also provide retirement benefits, bonuses and even employee profit sharing. When you're an IC, you get no such benefits.

ICs also don't have the safety net provided by unemployment insurance. Nor do hiring firms provide them with workers' compensation coverage.

- **Risk of not being paid.** Some ICs have great difficulty getting their clients to pay them on time or at all. When you're an IC, you bear the risk of loss from deadbeat clients.

- **Liability for business debts.** If like most ICs you're a sole proprietor or partner in a partnership, you are personally liable for your business debts. An IC whose business fails could lose most of what he or she owns.

- **More complex tax returns.** Finally, your tax returns will likely be far more complex when you work as an IC than they were when you worked as an employee. In addition, you'll have to pay your own income and Social Security taxes directly to the IRS in the form of quarterly estimated taxes. Your clients will not withhold any taxes from your compensation.

F. Consulting Agreement Favorable to Independent Contractor

You should always use a written agreement whenever you work as an independent contractor. This can avoid innumerable headaches later on. The agreement need not be long or complex. A simple letter stating the services you'll perform, your compensation and the deadline for performance may be sufficient for small jobs.

However, for longer or more complex jobs, you'll probably want to use a more extensive agreement. The following agreement covers all the issues a software consultant may wish to include in a full-blown consulting agreement. This agreement is favorable to the consultant.

The text of a Software Consultants Agreement is in the CD-ROM forms disk under CONSULT2. See Chapter 1 for instructions on how to use the forms disk.

Names and Addresses

Here at the beginning of your contract, it's best to refer to yourself by your full business name. Later on in the contract, you can use an obvious abbreviation.

If you're a sole proprietor, use the full name you use for your business. This can be your own name or a fictitious business name or assumed name you use to identify your business. For example, if consultant Al Brodsky calls his software consulting business "ABC Consulting," he would use that name on the contract. Using a fictitious business name helps show you're a business, not an employee.

If you're business is incorporated, use your corporate name, not your own name— for example: "John Smith, Incorporated" instead of "John Smith."

Do not refer to yourself as an employee or to the client as an employer.

For the sake of brevity, it is usual to identify yourself and the client by shorter names in the rest of the agreement. You can use an abbreviated version of your full name—for example, ABC for ABC Marketing Research. Or you can refer to yourself simply as Contractor or Consultant.

Refer to the client initially by its company name and subsequently by a short version of the name or as Client or Firm.

Include the addresses of the principal place of business of the client and yourself. If you or the client have more than one office or workplace, the principal place of business is the main office or workplace.

1. Services You'll Perform

The agreement should describe in as much detail as possible what you're expected to accomplish. Word the description carefully to emphasize the results you're expected to achieve. Don't describe the method by which you will achieve the results. As an IC, it should be up to you to decide how to do the work. The client's control should be limited to accepting or rejecting your final results. The more control the client exercises over how you work, the more you'll look like an employee.

It's perfectly okay for the agreement to establish very detailed specifications for your finished work product. But the specs should only describe the end results you must achieve, not how to obtain those results.

You can include the description in the main body of the Agreement. Or if it's a lengthy explanation, put it on a separate attachment.

2. Payment

Software consultants can be paid in a variety of ways. Choose the alternative that suits your needs.

Alternative 1: Fixed Fee. In a fixed fee agreement, you charge an agreed upon amount for the entire project. This clause requires the client to pay you an initial sum when the work is commenced and the remainder when it's finished.

Alternative 2: Installment Payments. If the project is long and complex, you may prefer to be paid in installments rather than waiting until the project is finished to receive the bulk of your payment. One way to do this is to break the job into phases or milestones and be paid a fixed fee when each phase is completed. Clients often like this pay-as-you-go arrangement too.

To do this, draw up a schedule of installment payments tying each payment to your completion of specific services. It's usually easier to set forth the schedule in a separate document and attach it to the agreement as an exhibit. The main body of the agreement should simply refer to the attached payment schedule.

Following is an example of a schedule of payments. This schedule requires four payments: a down payment when the contract is signed and three installment payments. However, you and the client can have as many payments as you want.

Schedule of Payments

Client shall pay Contractor according to the following schedule of payments:

1) $[State sum] when this Agreement is signed.

2) $[State sum] when an invoice is submitted and the following services are completed:

[Describe first stage of services]

3) $[State sum] when an invoice is submitted and the following services are completed:

[Describe second stage of services]

4) $[State sum] when an invoice is submitted and the following services are completed:

[Describe third stage of services]

[ADD ANY ADDITIONAL PAYMENTS]

Alternative 3: Payment by Unit of Time.
Probably the majority of software consultants charge by the hour or other unit of time. This is by far the safest way to be paid if it's difficult to estimate exactly how long a project will take. However, many clients will wish to place a cap on your total compensation because they're afraid you'll "pad" your bill. If this is the case, include the optional sentence providing for a cap, but make sure it's large enough to allow you to complete the job.

3. Invoices

You should always submit an invoice to be paid. You need to fill in the time the client has to pay you after you send your invoice; 30 days is common, but you can shorten this period if you wish.

4. Late Fees

Many consultants charge a late fee if the client doesn't pay within the time specified in the consulting agreement or invoice. Charging late fees for overdue payments can get clients to pay on time. The late fee is normally expressed as a monthly interest charge—for example, 1% per month.

If you wish to charge a late fee, make sure it's mentioned in your agreement. You should also clearly state what your late fee is on all your invoices

5. Expenses

Expenses means the costs you incur that are directly attributable to your work for a client. It would include, for example, the cost of phone calls or traveling done on the client's behalf. Expenses do not include your normal fixed overhead costs such as your office rent or the cost of commuting to and from your office. They also do not include materials the client provides you to do your work.

Alternative 1: You pay own expenses.
Government agencies may consider payment of a worker's business or traveling expenses to be an indicator of an employment relationship. For this reason, it is usually best that you not be separately reimbursed for expenses. Instead, your compensation should be high enough to cover your expenses.

Setting your compensation at a level that covers your expenses has another advantage as well: It frees you from having to keep records of your expenses. Keeping track of the cost of every phone call or photocopy you make for a client can be a real chore and may be more trouble than it's worth.

However, if a project will involve expensive traveling, you may wish to separately bill the client for the cost. In this event, include the optional clause for this.

Alternative 2: Expenses Reimbursed. The second clause requires the client to reimburse you for your expenses. You need to provide how many cents per mile you'll charge for travel time.

6. Materials

If the client will provide you with any materials or equipment, list them in this clause. If you need these items by a specific date, specify the deadline as well.

7. Term of Agreement

The term of the agreement means when it begins and ends. Unless the agreement provides a specific start date, it begins on the date it's signed. If you and the client sign on different dates, the agreement begins on the date the last party signed. You normally shouldn't begin work until the client signs the agreement, so it's usually best that the agreement not provide a specific start date that might be before the client signs.

An IC agreement should have a definite end date. This ordinarily will mark the final deadline for your completion of your services. A good outside time limit is one or

at most, two, years. A longer term makes the agreement look like an employment agreement, not an IC agreement. If the work is not completed at the end of the term, you can negotiate and sign a new agreement.

8. Terminating the Agreement

When you sign a contract it doesn't mean you're irrevocably bound by it no matter what happens. Either you or the client can terminate a consulting agreement under certain circumstances. Termination means you cancel the agreement and you and the client go your separate ways. However, you could each still be liable to the other for any damages caused by failure to obey the contract before it was terminated.

It's important to clearly define the circumstances under which you or the client may terminate the agreement.

It's wise to place some limits on the client's right to terminate the contract. It's usually not in your best interest to give a client the right terminate you for any reason or no reason at all, since the client may unfairly abuse it. .

Instead, both you and the client should be able to terminate the agreement without legal repercussions only if there is reasonable cause to do so; or, at most, only by giving written notice to the other.

Alternative 1: Termination with reasonable cause. Termination with reasonable cause means either you or the client

TICK TOCK

have a good reason to end the agreement. A material—that is, serious—violation of the agreement is reasonable cause to terminate the agreement. What constitutes a material violation depends on the particular facts and circumstances. A violation is material if it impairs the value of the contract as a whole to the other party.

A minor or technical contract violation is not serious enough to justify terminating the contract for cause. For example, a slightly late payment by a client will normally be classified as minor and not justify terminating the agreement. However, if the client knows that you have cash flow problems, the late payment could constitute a material violation. Similarly, a minor delay in your performance wouldn't ordinarily be a material contract violation.

Unless your contract provides otherwise, a client's failure to pay you on time may not necessarily constitute reasonable cause for you to terminate the agreement. You may add a clause to your contract providing that late payments are always reasonable cause for terminating the contract. The following clause provides that you may terminate the agreement if the client doesn't pay you what you're owed within 20 days after you make a written demand for payment. For example, if you send a client an invoice due within 30 days and the client fails to pay within that time, you may terminate the agreement 20 days after you send the client a written demand to be paid what you're owed. This may help give clients incentive to pay you.

The clause also makes clear that the client must pay you for the services you performed before the contract was terminated.

Alternative 2: Termination without cause. Sometimes you or the client just can't live with a limited termination right. Instead, you want to be able to get out of the agreement at any time without incurring liability. For example, a client's business plans may change and it may no longer need your services. Or you may have too much work and need to lighten your load.

In this event, add a provision giving either party the right to terminate the agreement for any reason upon written notice. You need to provide at least a few days notice. Being able to terminate without notice tends to make you look like an employee. Thirty days is a common notice period, but less notice may be appropriate if the project is of short duration.

9. Independent Contractor Status

One of the most important functions of an agreement between a hiring firm and consultant is to help establish that you are not the hiring firm's employee. In an audit of the hiring firm, an IRS examiner or similar official will almost surely want to see the firm's agreements with all workers classified as independent contractors. If the agreement indicates that the hiring firm has the right to control you, you will undoubtedly be viewed as an employee by the IRS. This will cause problems not only for the hiring firm, but for you as well.

On the other hand, an agreement that indicates a lack of control on the part of the hiring firm will contribute to a finding of independent contractor status. But such an agreement will not be determinative in and of itself. Simply signing a piece of paper will not make you an independent contractor. The agreement must reflect reality—that is, you must actually not be controlled on the job by the hiring firm.

The language in this clause addresses most of the factors the IRS and other agencies consider in measuring the degree of control of the hiring firm. (These factors are discussed in Section C1.) All provisions show that the hiring firm lacks the right to control the manner and means by which you will perform the agreed-upon services.

Include all of provisions a-j that apply to your particular situation. The more that apply, the more likely that you will be viewed as an independent contractor.

10. Intellectual Property Ownership

Usually, the client will want to obtain sole ownership of what you create, whether it be a computer program, documentation or other material. However, there is no rule that this has to be the case. Two different ownership alternatives are presented in the contract. Choose only one alternative and delete the other. Here's an explanation.

Alternative 1: Client Owns Consultant's Work Product. If it's agreed that the client will own your work product, you should assign your rights to the client. But this assignment is expressly conditioned upon receipt of all your compensation from the client.

Optional sentence: An assignment of all rights means that you may not use the work you performed for the client without permission—for example, you may not include it in a program written for someone else. If desired, such permission can be included in the independent contractor agreement. The optional sentence in this clause grants you a nonexclusive license to use the work product. The license can be limited in any way—for example, as to term or area of use. If the client decides to grant the consultant such a license, it must decide if it will be "irrevocable"—that is, last forever; or be limited to a specified time period—for example, one or two years. The appropriate language in the optional clause should be used.

Alternative 2: Consultant Owns Work Product. In some cases, the consultant and client may agree that the consultant will retain his or her ownership rights in the work product (perhaps in return for receiving reduced monetary compensation). In this event, instead of assigning her rights to the client, the consultant will grant the client a nonexclusive license to use the work product.

This clause grants the client a nonexclusive license to use the consultant's work product in any of its products, but prevents it from selling the consultant's work to others. Such a license could be more restrictive— for example, it could limit the use to a particular product. If this is desired, modify the clause to indicate the restrictions.

11. Consultant's Materials

A software consultant will often have various development tools, routines, subroutines and other programs, data and materials that he or she brings to the job and that might end up in the final product. One term for these types of items is "Consultant's Materials."

Unless you want to transfer ownership of such materials to the hiring firm, you should make sure the independent contractor agreement provides that you retain all your ownership rights in this material. But, in this event, the agreement must also give the hiring firm a nonexclusive license to use the background technology that you include in your work product.

There are two clauses to choose from:

Alternative 1: Client's License Extends to All Products. The client would probably prefer to have the right to use the consultant's technology in any of its products. In this event, some sort of payment or royalty provision may be appropriate; if so, include the optional sentence and describe the compensation.

Alternative 2: Client's License Limited to Specific Products. This clause permits the hiring firm to use the background technol-

ogy only in a particular product or products. Make sure you describe any such products in detail.

Optional Clause: Identifying Materials. If you know what such materials consist of in advance, it's a good idea to list them in an exhibit attached to the agreement. Include this optional clause if you do this.

If possible, identify your background technology in the source code copies of the programs you deliver to the client and in any printouts of code delivered to the client. You might include a notice like the following where such material appears: "[Your Company Name] CONFIDENTIAL AND PROPRIETARY."

12. Confidentiality

Since software consultants often have access to their clients' valuable confidential information, hiring firms often seek to impose confidentiality restrictions on them. It's not unreasonable for a client to want you to keep its secrets away from the eyes and ears of competitors. Unfortunately, however, many of these provisions are worded so broadly that they can make it difficult for you to work for other clients without fear of violating your duty of confidentiality.

If, like most software consultants, you make your living by performing similar services for many firms within the computer industry, insist on a confidentiality provision that is reasonable in scope and defines precisely what information you must keep confidential. Such a provision should last for only a limited time—five years at the most.

The optional confidentiality provision in this agreement prevents the unauthorized disclosure by you of any written material of the client marked confidential or information disclosed orally that the client later writes down, marks as confidential and delivers to you within 15 days. This enables you to know for sure what material is, and is not, confidential.

13. Warranties

A warranty is a promise or statement regarding the quality, quantity, performance or legal title of something being sold. Everyone has some familiarity with warranties. Whenever you buy an expensive product such as a car, television or computer, the seller normally warrants—promises—that the product will do what it is supposed to do for a specific or reasonable time period. If it doesn't, the seller will repair or replace it.

Clients often expect software consultants to make some type of warranty regarding their services. If the software product or service you provide fails to live up to your warranty, the client can sue you in court for breach of warranty and obtain damages. The client doesn't have to prove that you were negligent—that is, failed to do your work properly. All it has to show is that your goods or services didn't perform the way you said they would. This makes it much easier for the client to obtain damages.

Alternative 1: Providing software as is. Many software consultants don't want to provide any warranties at all. To do this, you must include a clause in your agreement stating that your software goods or services are provided "as is." This means that if your goods or services are unsatisfactory, the client has no basis for a complaint.

The clause also disclaims—or disavows—certain implied warranties that can be assumed to be made even if no words are written or spoken. These are:

Implied warranty of merchantability. This warranty basically means that the seller promises that the goods are fit for their commonly intended use—in other words, they are of at least average quality. This warranty applies only to sales of new goods.

Implied warranty of fitness for a specific purpose. If a customer is relying on the seller's expertise to select suitable goods, and the seller is aware that the customer intends to use the goods for a particular purpose, the product becomes impliedly guaranteed for that purpose.

> **EXAMPLE:** A computer consultant is hired by a company to choose and install a new computer system. The consultant is told by the client that it needs the system to process new accounts within 12 hours. The system the consultant chooses and installs becomes impliedly guaranteed to do so.

However, this clause won't excuse you from failure to live up to the project specifications included in your written agreement. Nor will the clause protect you from charges of outright fraud if you lied to the client, or shield you from liability if your software is so defective it injures someone. To be effective, the as is clause should be printed in capitals so it won't be overlooked by the client.

Alternative 2: Limited warranty. Some clients may balk at having no warranty protection at all. In this event, you can use the following clause to give the client a limited warranty. It requires the client to report in writing any deficiencies in your work. You are then required to reperform your services; or, if you can't reperform, pay back the client what it paid you for your faulty work. The concluding paragraph states that this clause is the only warranty you're providing the client and disclaims the implied warranties discussed above. It's a good idea to print such a statement in capitals so the client won't overlook it.

may be included or excluded from the agreement; this is a matter for negotiation.

Under paragraph (a), the consultant is relieved from liability for any lost profits of the client, or special, incidental or consequential damages arising from defects in the work furnished by the consultant. These types of damages—lost profits in particular—can far exceed the consultant's total compensation and could even send the consultant into bankruptcy.

Paragraph (b), which is perhaps the most important, limits the consultant's total liability to the client to the amount of money actually received from the client, or, if desired, a specific dollar amount.

Paragraph (c) requires the client to indemnify the consultant against third party claims. These are claims brought by people or entities other than the client. Indemnification is a fancy legal work that means the client must pay attorney fees and other costs of defending such claims and any damages ultimately awarded against the consultant.

14. Limited Liability

Many consultants seek to include a provision in their agreements limiting their total liability to the client and/or third parties. Obviously, clients would prefer that there be no such clause, so we've included one only as an option. The clause contains four separate liability limiting provisions, any of which

15. Taxes

A few states require independent contractors to pay sales taxes, even if they only provide their clients with services. These states include Hawaii, New Mexico and South Dakota. Many other states require sales taxes to be collected and paid for certain specified services.

Whether or not you're required to collect sales taxes, include the following provision in your agreement making it clear that the client will have to pay these and similar taxes. States constantly change their sales tax laws, and more and more are beginning to look at services as a good source of sales tax revenue. So this provision could come in handy in the future even if you don't really need it now.

16. Contract Changes

It's very common for clients and software consultants to want to change the terms of an agreement after work has begun. For example, the client might want to make a change in the contract specifications which could require you to do more work for which you should be compensated. Or you might discover that you underestimated how much time the project will take and need to be paid more to complete it and avoid losing money.

This provision recognizes that the agreement may have to be changed. Although oral changes to contracts are enforceable, it's a very good idea to write them down. This provision states that you and the client must write down your changes and both sign the writing. Such a contract provision requiring modifications to be in writing is probably not legally enforceable—that is, both you and the client can still make changes without writing them down. How-

ever, it does stress the importance of documenting changes in writing.

Neither you nor the client is ever required to accept a proposed contract change. But because you are obligated to deal with each other fairly and in good faith, you can't simply refuse without attempting to reach a resolution. If you and the client can't agree on the changes, you're required to submit your dispute to mediation; and, if that doesn't work, to binding arbitration. This avoids expensive court litigation.

17. Dispute Resolution

As you doubtless know, court litigation can be very expensive. To avoid these costs, alternative forms of dispute resolution have been developed that don't involve going to court. These include mediation and arbitration.

In mediation, a neutral third person called a mediator meets with the parties and makes suggestions as to how to resolve their controversy. Typically, the mediator either sits the parties down together and tries to provide an objective view of their disputes, or shuttles between the parties as a hopefully cool conduit for what may be hot opinions. Mediation is nonbinding. That means that if either party to the dispute doesn't like the outcome of the mediation, he or she can ask for binding arbitration or go to court.

Arbitration is usually like an informal court trial without a jury, but involves arbitrators instead of judges and is usually much faster and cheaper than courts. You may be represented by a lawyer, but it's not required. See Section D16 above for a discussion of the pros and cons of arbitration.

This optional clause requires you and the client to take advantage of these alternate forms of dispute resolution. You're first required to submit the dispute to mediation. If mediation doesn't work, you must submit the dispute to binding arbitration.

You should indicate where the mediation or arbitration is to occur. You'll usually want it in the city or county where your office is located. You don't want to have to travel a long distance to attend mediation or arbitration.

18. Attorney Fees

If you have to sue the client in court or conduct and arbitration to enforce the agreement and win, you normally will not be awarded the amount of your attorney fees unless your agreement requires it. Including such an attorney fees provision in the agreement can be in your interest. It can help make filing a lawsuit economically feasible. It will also give the client a strong incentive to negotiate with you if you have a good case.

Under this provision, if either person has to sue the other in court to enforce the agreement and wins—that is, becomes the prevailing party—the loser is required to pay the other person's attorney fees and expenses.

19. General Provisions

These general provisions are standard in many types of legal documents:

(a) This clause helps make it clear to a court of arbitrator that the parties intended the contract to be their final agreement. A clause such as this helps avoid claims that promises not contained in the written contract were made and broken. Always make sure that all documents containing any of the client's representations upon which you are relying are attached to the agreement as exhibits. If they aren't attached, they likely won't be considered to be part of the agreement.

(b) In the event that some part of the agreement is declared invalid by a court, this clause ensures that the rest of the document is still valid.

(c) This clause specifies which state law governs the contract. This should be the state in which you do business or are incorporated.

(d) When you want to do something important involving the agreement—terminate it, for example—you need to tell the client about it. This is called giving notice. This provision gives you several options for providing the client with notice: by personal delivery, by mail, or by fax or telex followed by a confirming letter.

If you give notice by mail, it is not effective until three days after it's sent. For example, if you want to end the agreement on 30 days notice and mail your notice of termination to the consultant, the agreement will not end until 33 days after you mailed the notice.

(e) This clause helps you to make sure that you and the client are separate legal entities, not partners or co-venturers. If a client is viewed as your partner, you'll be liable for its debts and the client will have the power to make contracts that obligate you to others without your consent.

(f) An assignment is the process by which rights or duties under a contract are transferred to someone else. For example, you may assign your duty to perform services for the client to someone else. This clause give you an unfettered right to assign your rights or obligations.

Signatures

It is not necessary for the parties to sign the agreement in the same room or on the same day. At least two copies should be signed, with each party retaining one.

Consulting Agreement

This Agreement is made between AcmeSoft, Inc. ("Client"), with a principal place of business at 164 Techie St., Cambridge MA, and Sarah Goodrich ("Consultant"), with a principal place of business at 1000 Revere Ave., Boston MA.

1. Services Performed by Consultant:

Consultant agrees to perform the services described in Exhibit A, which is attached to and made part of this Agreement.

2. Consultant's Payment:

Consultant shall be compensated at the rate of $150 per hour. Unless otherwise agreed upon in writing by Client, Client's maximum liability for all services performed during the term of this Agreement shall not exceed $10,000.

3. Invoices

Consultant shall submit invoices for all services rendered. Client shall pay the amounts due within 30 days of the date of each invoice.

4. Late Fees

Late payments by Client shall be subject to late penalty fees of 1% per month from the due date until the amount is paid.

5. Expenses

Consultant shall be responsible for all expenses incurred while performing services under this Agreement.

6. Term of Agreement

This Agreement will become effective when signed by both parties and will end no later than January 15, 199x.

7. Materials

8. Terminating the Agreement

With reasonable cause, either party may terminate this Agreement effective immediately by giving written notice of termination for cause. Reasonable cause includes:

- a material violation of this agreement, or
- nonpayment of Consultant's compensation after 20 days' written demand for payment.

Consultant shall be entitled to full payment for services performed prior to the effective date of termination.

9. Consultant an Independent Contractor

Consultant is an independent contractor, and neither Consultant nor Consultant's staff is, or shall be deemed, Client's employees. In its capacity as an independent contractor, Consultant agrees and represents, and Client agrees, as follows:

(a) Consultant has the right to perform services for others during the term of this Agreement subject to noncompetition provisions set out in this Agreement, if any.

(b) Consultant has the sole right to control and direct the means, manner and method by which the services required by this Agreement will be performed.

(c) Consultant has the right to perform the services required by this Agreement at any place or location and at such times as Consultant may determine.

(d) Consultant will furnish all equipment and materials used to provide the services required by this Agreement, except to the extent that Consultant's work must be performed on or with Client's computer or existing software.

(e) The services required by this Agreement shall be performed by Consultant, or Consultant's staff, and Client shall not be required to hire, supervise or pay any assistants to help Consultant.

(f) Consultant is responsible for paying all ordinary and necessary expenses of its staff.

(g) Neither Consultant nor Consultant's staff shall receive any training from Client in the professional skills necessary to perform the services required by this Agreement.

(h) Neither Consultant nor Consultant's staff shall be required to devote full-time to the performance of the services required by this Agreement.

(i) Client shall not provide insurance coverage of any kind for Consultant or Consultant's staff.

(j) Client shall not withhold from Consultant's compensation any amount that would normally be withheld from an employee's pay.

10. Intellectual Property Ownership

Consultant shall retain all copyright, patent, trade secret and other intellectual property rights Consultant may have in anything created or developed by Consultant for Client under this Agreement ("Work Product"). Consultant grants Client a nonexclusive worldwide license to use and sublicense the use of the Work Product for the purpose of developing and marketing its products, but not for the purpose of marketing Work Product separate from its products. The license shall have a perpetual term and may not be transferred by Client. This license is conditioned upon full payment of the compensation due Consultant under this Agreement.

11. Consultant's Materials

Consultant owns or holds a license to use and sublicense various materials in existence before the start date of this Agreement ("Consultant's Materials"). Consultant may, at it's option, include Consultant's Materials in the work performed under this Agreement.

Consultant retains all right, title and interest, including all copyright, patent rights and trade secret rights in Consultant's Materials. Subject to full payment of the consulting fees due under this Agreement, Consultant grants Client a nonexclusive worldwide license to use and sublicense the use of Consultant's Materials for the purpose of developing and marketing its products, but not for the purpose of marketing Background Technology separate from its products. The license shall have a perpetual term and may not be transferred by Client. Client shall make no other commercial use of the Background Technology without Consultant's written consent.

Consultant's Materials include, but are not limited to, those items identified in Exhibit B, attached to and made part of this Agreement.

12. Confidentiality

During the term of this Agreement and for 6 months afterward, Consultant will use reasonable care to prevent the unauthorized use or dissemination of Client's confidential information. Reasonable care means at least the same degree of care Consultant uses to protect its own confidential information from unauthorized disclosure.

Confidential information is limited to information clearly marked as confidential, or disclosed orally and summarized and identified as confidential in a writing delivered to Consultant within 15 days of disclosure.

Confidential information does not include information that:

- the Consultant knew before Client disclosed it
- is or becomes public knowledge through no fault of Consultant
- Consultant obtains from sources other than Client who owe no duty of confidentiality to Client, or
- Consultant independently develops.

13. Warranties

Consultant warrants that all services performed under this Agreement shall be performed consistent with generally prevailing professional or industry standards. Client must report any deficiencies in Consultant's services to Consultant in writing within 90 days of performance to receive warranty remedies.

Client's exclusive remedy for any breach of the above warranty shall be the reperformance of Consultant's services. If Consultant is unable to reperform the services, Client shall be entitled to recover the fees paid to Consultant for the deficient services.

THIS WARRANTY IS EXCLUSIVE AND IN LIEU OF ALL OTHER WARRANTIES, WHETHER EXPRESS OR IMPLIED, INCLUDING ANY IMPLIED WARRANTIES OF MERCHANTABILITY OR FITNESS FOR A PARTICULAR PURPOSE AND ANY ORAL OR WRITTEN REPRESENTATIONS, PROPOSALS OR STATEMENTS MADE PRIOR TO THIS AGREEMENT.

14. Limitation on Consultant's Liability to Client

(a) In no event shall Consultant be liable to Client for lost profits of Client, or special, incidental or consequential damages (even if Consultant has been advised of the possibility of such damages).

(b) Consultant's total liability under this Agreement for damages, costs and expenses, regardless of cause, shall not exceed the total amount of fees paid to Consultant by Client under this Agreement.

(c) Client shall indemnify Consultant against all claims, liabilities and costs, including reasonable attorney fees, of defending any third party claim or suit arising out of or in connection with Client's performance under this Agreement. Consultant shall promptly notify Client in writing of such claim or suit and Client shall have the right to fully control the defense and any settlement of the claim or suit.

15. Taxes

The charges included here do not include taxes. If Consultant is required to pay any federal, state or local sales, use, property or value added taxes based on the services provided under this Agreement, the taxes shall be separately billed to Client. Consultant shall not pay any interest or penalties incurred due to late payment or nonpayment of such taxes by Client.

16. Contract Changes

Client and Consultant recognize that:

- Consultant's original cost and time estimates may be too low due to unforeseen events, or to factors unknown to Consultant when this Agreement was made
- Client may desire a mid-project change in Consultant's services that would add time and cost to the project and possibly inconvenience Consultant, or
- Other provisions of this Agreement may be difficult to carry out due to unforeseen circumstances.

If any intended changes or any other events beyond the parties' control require adjustments to this Agreement, the parties shall make a good faith effort to agree on all necessary particulars. Such agreements shall be put in writing, signed by the parties and added to this Agreement.

17. Dispute Resolution

If a dispute arises under this Agreement, the parties agree to first try to resolve the dispute with the help of a mutually agreed-upon mediator in the following location: Boston, MA. Any costs and fees other than attorney fees associated with the mediation shall be shared equally be the parties.

If it proves impossible to arrive at a mutually satisfactory solution through mediation, the parties agree to submit the dispute to binding arbitration in the following location—Boston, MA—under the rules of the American Arbitration Association. Judgment upon the award rendered by the arbitrator may be entered in any court with jurisdiction to do so.

18. Attorney Fees

If any legal action is necessary to enforce this Agreement, the prevailing party shall be entitled to reasonable attorney fees, costs and expenses in addition to any other relief to which it may be entitled.

19. General Provisions

(a) Sole agreement: This is the entire Agreement between Consultant and Client.

(b) Severability: If any part of this Agreement is held unenforceable, the rest of the Agreement will continue in full force and effect.

(c) Applicable law: This Agreement will be governed by the laws of the State of Massachusetts.

(d) Notices: All notices and other communications given in connection with this Agreement shall be in writing and shall be deemed given as follows:

- When delivered personally to the recipient's address as appearing in the introductory paragraph to this Agreement;
- Three days after being deposited in the United States mails, postage prepaid to the recipient's address as appearing in the introductory paragraph to this Agreement, or
- When sent by fax or telex to the last fax or telex number of the recipient known to the party giving notice. Notice is effective upon receipt provided that a duplicate copy of the notice is promptly given by first-class or certified mail, or the recipient delivers a written confirmation of receipt.

Any party may change its address appearing in the introductory paragraph to this Agreement by giving notice of the change in accordance with this paragraph.

(e) No partnership: This Agreement does not create a partnership relationship. Consultant does not have authority to enter into contracts on Client's behalf.

(f) Assignment: This Agreement is freely assignable.

Client: AcmeSoft, Inc.

By: _Jack Devlin_____

Jack Devlin

Title: President

Consultant: Sarah Goodrich

By: _Sarah Goodrich_____

Sarah Goodrich

Social Security Number:111-11-1111

Chapter 16

Software Licenses

This chapter is about software licenses. It includes sample agreements for individual negotiated licenses and licenses for mass-marketed software.

A. What Is a License?

In almost every country of the world, computer software is automatically protected by copyright law the moment it's created. Some software is also protected by patent law, but copyright has always been and remains the primary legal vehicle by which software ownership and use rights are defined and transferred.

A software author automatically becomes the owner of a complete set of exclusive copyright rights in any protected work he or she creates. These include the right to:

- reproduce the protected work
- distribute copies of the work to the public by sale, rental, lease or otherwise (but this right is limited by the first sale doctrine, which permits the owner of a particular copy of a work to sell, lend or otherwise dispose of the copy without the copyright owner's permission; see Section B2 below)
- prepare derivative works using the work's protected expression (that is, adapt new works from the original work), and
- perform and display the work publicly.

These rights are exclusive because only the owner of one or more particular rights that together make up copyright ownership may exercise it or permit others to do so. For example, only the owner of the right to distribute a program may sell it to the public or permit others to do so

A license is a grant of permission to do something. For example, when you get a driver's license the government gives you permission to drive a car. A copyright owner can give others permission to exercise one or more of the owner's exclusive rights listed above. Such a permission is also usually called a license. Licenses fall into two broad categories: exclusive and non-exclusive licenses.

1. Exclusive Licenses

When a software owner grants someone an exclusive license it means the recipient of the license becomes the only person entitled to exercise the rights covered by the license. The person or company granting a license is usually called the licensor, and the recipient is called the licensee.

Since the licensor is granting the licensee the exclusive right to exercise the rights covered by the license, an exclusive license is considered to be a transfer of copyright ownership. If you have the exclusive right to use something, you own it; that's what ownership is. Such an ownership transfer must be in writing to be legally valid.

EXAMPLE: AcmeSoft, a small software developer, creates a multimedia program on the history of World War

II. Since it lacks the resources to effectively market the program itself, AcmeSoft grants an exclusive license to distribute the program in the United States to Scrivener & Sons, a well established book publisher seeking entry into the electronic book market. Granting such an exclusive license means that only Scrivener may distribute the program in the U.S.; Scrivener owns this right. But AcmeSoft retains all its other copyright rights not covered by the license. For example, it retains the right to market the program outside the U.S. and to create derivative works based upon it (for example, a computer game).

A software owner's exclusive rights can be divided and subdivided and transferred to others in just about any way imaginable: by geographical area, computer platform, operating system, hardware, time or virtually any other way. Taking advantage of this sort of flexibility is often at the heart of a successful plan for getting a product distributed and sold in the marketplace.

EXAMPLE 1: AcmeSoft, a small start-up software developer, develops a new program and gives Behemoth Distribution, Inc., a software distribution company, an exclusive license to distribute the program for use on PCs in the United States. AcmeSoft also gives CDS, Inc., another distributor, the right to bundle the program with personal

computers in Europe. (This type of exclusive license is called an exclusive territorial license.) Finally, AcmeSoft grants an exclusive license to DigiTek, Inc., to create and distribute a Macintosh version of the program.

EXAMPLE 2: Jason grants Gameland an exclusive license to sell the Windows version of his computer game, *Kill or Die,* in the United States for three years. He grants Nintendo an exclusive license to sell a version of the game on Nintendo dedicated game machines throughout the rest of the world. He licenses the right to create a movie from the game (a derivative work) to Repulsive Pictures. He retains all his other rights and produces and sells a Macintosh version of the game himself.

Exclusive Licensee's Rights

Again, the holder of an exclusive license —the "licensee"— becomes the owner of the transferred rights. As such, unless the exclusive license provides otherwise, he or she is entitled to sue anyone who infringes on that right while the licensee owns it, and is entitled to transfer her license to others. The licensee may also record the exclusive license with the Copyright Office; this provides many valuable benefits. (See Chapter 11.)

2. Nonexclusive Licenses

A nonexclusive license gives someone the right to exercise one or more of a copyright owner's rights, but does not prevent the owner from giving others permission to exercise the same right or rights at the same time. A nonexclusive license is not a transfer of ownership; it's a form of sharing.

Nonexclusive licenses (like all other licenses) can be restricted in all sorts of ways. Thus, you can grant a nonexclusive license to use (or sell your program for use) on one particular microcomputer in one country (or county) for a set period of time.

Except in cases where custom software is created for a single customer, software licenses with end users normally take the form of nonexclusive licenses. This way, the software owner can give any number of end users the right to use the software.

> EXAMPLE: AcmeSoft creates a hot new program for identifying and locating lost cats. It grants nonexclusive licenses to dozens of fire departments and animal shelters throughout the country. These licenses give these end users the right to copy and use the program. Since these licenses are nonexclusive, there is no limit on the number AcmeSoft can grant.

As with exclusive licenses, nonexclusive licenses may be limited as to time, geography, media or in any other way. They can be granted orally or in writing. The much better practice, however, is to use some sort of writing.

B. Why Use Licenses to Sell Software?

Most works of authorship—such as books, magazines, records, photographs and artwork—are sold outright, either directly to end users or to middlemen such as bookstores who in turn sell the works to end users.

The transaction works like this: say you want to buy a book; you walk into a bookstore pay your money and you are sold a copy of the book. You now own the copy of the book. You don't have to sign a license agreement and the book doesn't contain any type of "shrink-wrap" license.

Software copyright owners are also free to simply sell copies of their software, that is, sell floppy disks, CD-ROMs or other media containing copies of the software to end users; or to sell digital copies to users over the Internet and commercial online services such as America Online.

Today, however, virtually all software is licensed to end users rather than sold outright like books are. Instead of owning the copy of the software they pay for, end users merely acquire permission to use it. A written license agreement—a contract—carefully defines and restricts the nature and extent of that permission.

Why should this be so? The answer is simple: money. Software owners believe that license agreements help them preserve their market share, obtain the maximum return on each transaction and help safeguard their intellectual property rights. All of this adds up, at least in theory, to greater profits.

To understand why software owners prefer to license their work to end users, you must first understand what rights the purchaser of a copy of a copyrighted work has. Software licenses are used to take away most of these rights.

Note carefully that a software user doesn't have any of the ownership rights discussed below unless the software license grants him or her such rights or the license turns out to be legally invalid.

1. What Is a Copy?

For copyright purposes, a "copy" is defined as any material object in which a work of authorship is "fixed." Software transferred to CD-ROMs, floppy disks, hard disks and other media certainly qualifies as a "copy." Thus, a person who downloads a program to a hard disk from the Internet, receives a "copy" of the program, just as person who buys the same program on a CD-ROM does.

Software contained in computer RAM may also qualify as a copy, so long as it stays in RAM for at least several minutes. Thus, copying occurs where a person downloads a program to RAM and uses it, even if it is never saved to a permanent storage medium such as a hard disk.

However, simply transmitting a computer program over the Internet probably doesn't involve making copies, even though temporary copies are stored in the RAM of various node computers on the Internet. These RAM copies likely exist for too short a time to be copies for copyright purposes. However, this is not a settled question.

2. Sales of Copies Do Not Transfer Copyright Ownership

Ownership of a copyright and ownership of a material object in which the copyrighted work is embodied—such as a computer disk—are entirely separate things. This means the sale or gift of a copy or copies of a program or other protected work does not operate to transfer the copyright owner's exclusive rights in the work. A copyright owner's exclusive rights can only be transferred by a written agreement. For example, a person who buys a CD-ROM or floppy disk containing a computer program owns the CD-ROM or disk and the copy of the software it contains, but acquires no copyright rights in the program. Likewise, a person who downloads a program from the Internet to his or her hard disk, owns the copy on his or her disk, but obtains no copyright rights in the program.

3. Rights of Owners of Software Copies

The fact that a person who purchases a copy of a computer program acquires no copyright rights does not mean, however, that the purchaser has no rights at all. On the contrary, there are a number of things the purchaser can do with his or her copy.

a. Unlimited use rights

First, a software copy purchaser can use the program copy any way he wants. He can run it on any single computer he chooses, in any location, for any purpose. If he so chooses, a purchaser is free to use a program copy to operate a service bureau and perform data processing for third parties. Or, he can permit third parties to use the software on a time-sharing basis. This is so even though these third parties might otherwise buy the program themselves from the copyright owner.

b. Right to copy the program into computer RAM

Of course, to utilize a program on a computer it is necessary to copy it from a permanent storage medium such as a CD-ROM into the computer's memory (also known as RAM or random access memory). Such copying is specifically permitted by Section 117 of the Copyright Act, which provides that "the owner of a copy of a computer program… [may] make or authorize the making of another copy … of that computer program provided that such new copy … is created as an essential step in the utilization of the computer program in conjunction with a machine and that it is used in no other manner." But courts have held that this provision does not permit permanent copies to be made on computer

disks or other permanent storage mediums. (*Allen-Myland, Inc. v. IBM Corp.*, 746 F.Supp. 520 (E.D.Pa. 1990).)

Of course, in the real world, end users usually copy the original copy of a program onto their computer's hard disk. This hard disk copy is what is then loaded into computer RAM. This copying onto a hard disk is apparently not allowed by Section 117. But making one copy of a lawfully possessed program onto a hard disk for use on one computer almost certainly constitutes a fair use of the original copy and is almost certainly permissible. (See Chapter 5, Section B3.)

c. Right to make archival copies

Because the magnetic media upon which computer programs are normally stored can easily be damaged and the program rendered unusable, it is highly advisable to make a back-up or archival copy of a program. Section 117 of the Copyright Act provides that program owners may make permanent copies of their programs "for archival purposes only." This means they can only be used internally and cannot be made accessible to third parties. If the original copy is transferred, the copy must also be transferred with it or destroyed.

d. Right to sell or give away the program

A software copy purchaser also has the right to sell his copy of the program to anyone he chooses, for any price he desires, without getting the copyright owner's permission. Or, the purchaser may give away his copy.

e. Adaptation right

Section 117 of the Copyright Act also gives the lawful owner of a program copy the right to create an adaptation of the program provided that it is "created as an essential step in the utilization of the computer program in conjunction with the [owner's] machine and in no other manner." (*Foresight Resource Corp. v. Pfortmiller*, 719 F.Supp. 1006 (D.Kans. 1989).)

Under this adaptation right, the lawful owner of a program copy is entitled to create enhancements or otherwise alter the program from the one he or she lawfully purchased. For example, the owner can perform his or her own upgrades and thereby avoid having to purchase upgrades from the software publisher or other copyright owner. The owner is completely within his or her legal rights, as long as he or she doesn't:

- Copy, distribute, display or perform the work itself for commercial purposes, or
- Sell the adapted copy or give it away.

EXAMPLE: The large accounting firm Gray & Grim buys one copy of a tax accounting program called Lie-R-s. Firm employees rewrite two program modules to improve the package's processing speed. So long as Gray & Grim uses this adapted work solely to improve the copies of Lie-R-s that it has legitimately purchased and uses in-house, no infringement of the copyright owner's exclusive right to prepare derivative works has occurred. However, if Gray & Grim distributes the software to other accounting firms without the copyright owner's permission, the owner's copyright in the original work, which includes the exclusive right to make adaptations (also called "derivative works"), would be infringed.

Software Licensees' Adaptation Rights

One question that has arisen is whether a software licensee has the right to make archival copies and adaptations as provided in Section 117 of the Copyright Act. By its own terms, Section 117 applies only to "the owner of a copy of a computer program." Most courts have interpreted this language literally and held that Section 117's back-up and adaptation rights apply only to program owners, not licensees. In other words, a person who purchases a program copy outright may make back-ups and adaptations, but a person who licenses a copy may not exercise such rights unless they are granted in the license agreement. (*S.O.S., Inc. v. Payday, Inc.*, 886 F.2d 1081 (9th Cir. 1988).) However, a few courts have held that Section 117 really applies to any rightful possessor of a program copy, and thus applies to licensees as well to purchasers. (For example, see *Foresight Resources Corp. v. Pfortmiller*, 719 F.Supp.1006 (D.Kan. 1989).)

f. Reverse engineering

Finally, a software purchaser is free to reverse engineer the program. That is, figure out how it works. Reverse engineering can take many forms. One form of reverse engineering is decompiling a program's unreadable object code into readable code. Whether or not such decompilation is permissible or is a copyright infringement has been hotly debated. But some courts have held that decompilation is permissible under some circumstances when the information is used to create a noncompeting product. (See Chapter 5.)

In any event, a purchaser of a software copy can use the information gained from reverse engineering not involving decompilation in any way he wishes. For example, he might create a competing program and go into competition with the seller of the original program.

4. Things Owners of Software Copies Can't Do

Since the purchaser of a copy of a program acquires no copyright rights, he can't exercise any of the copyright owner's exclusive rights listed at the beginning of this chapter.

a. No copies other than back-up and RAM copy

As mentioned above, a purchaser can't make any copies of the program other than archival copies, a copy loaded into a single computer's RAM and a permanent copy contained on the computer's hard disk. If the purchaser sells or gives away the program, he or she must destroy these copies or give the permanent archival copies to the new owner.

Of course a purchaser can't make copies of a program and sell them, give them away or otherwise distribute them.

b. Copy can only be used on a single computer at a time

A single program copy can only be used on a single computer at a time. This means, for example, that if a purchaser owns a desktop computer and a laptop, and wants to use his or her program on both, legally he or she must buy two copies. Similarly, a purchaser cannot load a program onto his or her hard disk and then give his or CD-ROM or floppy disk containing the program to someone else to run simultaneously on another computer.

Nor is it permissible for a program owner to make RAM copies for use in more than one machine simultaneously. For example, it would be impermissible for a user to insert a CD-ROM or floppy disk in his computer, load a program into RAM and then hand the disk to another user who would load the program into RAM on another computer.

c. No running the software on computer networks

Without permission from the copyright owner, the purchaser of a copy of a computer program may not use the program on a network. Remember, the purchaser may load a program into the RAM of only a single computer at a time. The multiple copies typically used in networks, although located only in volatile RAM, are not permissible without the copyright owner's permission. Persons or companies that want to use software on a network usually obtain a network/multi-user license from the copyright owner (see Section C); or, in the case of mass-marketed software intended to be used in networks, such licenses are already included in the package.

d. No software rentals or lending

Software developers and publishers have long feared that letting users lend or lease their software to the public would cause software piracy to increase (a potential pirate could simply rent a software package and copy it). After years of lobbying by the software industry, Congress added a special provision to the Copyright Act in 1990 expressly forbidding the owner of a copy of a computer program from renting, leasing or lending the copy to the public for "direct or indirect commercial advantage." (17 U.S.C. 109.)

However, there are four exceptions to this rental and lending prohibition:

- First, nonprofit libraries may lend software to the public for nonprofit purposes provided that the library affixes a copyright warning to the packaging of each copy lent.
- The rental prohibition also doesn't apply to "a computer program embodied in or used in conjunction with a limited purpose computer that is designed for playing video games." In other words, it is permissible to rent video game cartridges.
- The prohibition does not apply to "a computer program … embodied in a machine or product" that "cannot be copied during ordinary operation or use." For example, it is permissible to rent a car that contains on-board computer programs.
- Finally, the transfer of possession of a lawfully made copy of a computer program from one nonprofit educational institution to another or to faculty, staff and students does not constitute "rental, lease or lending for direct or indirect commercial purposes" and thus is not prohibited.

e. No derivative works

Other than making an adaptation for her personal use, the purchaser of a copy of a program may not make any derivative works based on the copy without the copyright owner's permission.

5. How Licenses Restrict Users' Rights

Because they don't want users to have the rights outlined in Section B3 above, software owners typically license their software rather that sell copies of it. The user does not acquire ownership of a copy of the software. Instead, he or she just obtains a license—permission—to use a copy of it. The user has only those rights provided in the license agreement. The license agreement normally includes provisions that effectively take away most of the rights that a purchaser of a copy would have. Such licenses typically include one or more of these restrictions:

- limiting use of the software to a particular computer with a particular serial number
- limiting use of the software to a particular model of computer
- limiting use of the software to computers with a particular processing capacity
- limiting use of the software to computers at a particular physical location
- limiting use of the software to a specified number of concurrent users
- limiting use of the software to a particular application within the licensee's business
- prohibiting use of the software to perform processing for third parties or even for other divisions of the licensee's business
- prohibiting transfer or sublicensing of the license without the licensor's prior written consent
- prohibiting the use of the software on a computer network
- prohibiting copying of the software for all but adaptation and archival purposes
- prohibiting modification of the software, and

- prohibiting the licensee from reverse engineering disassembling or decompiling the software.

C. Types of Software Licenses

Software licenses take a variety of forms:

- **Single user/CPU licenses:** This is a license giving permission to use the software on a single CPU/computer by a single user. The software may only be run on the computer designated in the license. Most single user licenses are for mass-marketed software. (See Section E.) However, negotiated licenses are drafted and signed for some high-end programs.

The other types of licenses discussed below all allow the user to make multiple copies of the software.

- **Site licenses:** As the name implies, a site license is a grant of permission to use software at a particular location. The location can be a single office address or an entire corporate division.

- **Enterprise licenses:** Rather than defining the scope of the licensee's use in terms of a physical location, enterprise licenses are based on the licensee's identity and the types of uses the licensee intends to make with the software. This approach leads to great flexibility regarding pricing. For example, the license price can be linked to the licensee's overall computing capacity or indexed to any other measure, such as the user's annual revenues. Many of the major software companies are experimenting with enterprise licenses.

- **Network/multi-user licenses:** These licenses permit the licensee to use the software on a computer network. Such licenses typically identify a series of computer/operating system combinations on which the software may be installed. The hardware platforms must be owned, leased to or under the sole control of the licensee. Such licenses do not limit the number of computers on which the software may be installed, but may limit the number of users of the programs.

D. How Licenses Are Formed

Software licenses are one type of contract, and the law generally applicable to contracts applies to them as well. There's no need for you to become an expert in contract law, but you should have a basic idea of how enforceable licenses are created.

A legally binding contract is created when one person agrees to do something for the other in exchange for something of value in return. To reach such an agreement, one person must offer to do something and the other must accept the offer. For example, a contract is formed when a software owner offers to license a program to a person or company for a specified price and the person or company accepts the offer—that is, promises to do pay the license fee. All the elements for an enforceable contract are present in such a transaction:

- the software owner has promised to do something for the licensee—license the software to him, her or it,
- the licensee has accepted the terms of the software owner's offer to license, and
- the licensee has promised to give the software owner something of value in return—a license fee.

However, negotiations aren't usually as simple as making an offer and having it immediately accepted. Often, there is some negotiation back and forth. For example, the prospective licensee will often accept part of the original offer but vary some important terms. An acceptance which varies the main terms of an offer serves as a rejection of the offer and becomes a counter-offer. The software owner then has the option of accepting or rejecting the counter-offer or making his or her own counter-offer. No contract is formed until one side's offer or counter-offer is fully accepted.

It's not necessary for a licensor and licensee to negotiate with each other face to face to form a contract. A license agreement can be formed over the phone, by fax, by e-mail, snail mail or by any other communications medium.

1. Do You Need a Writing?

The Copyright Act requires that all exclusive licenses be in writing and signed by the copyright owner to be valid.

The copyright law imposes no writing requirement for nonexclusive licenses. However, state laws governing the sale of goods require a writing for any sale involving goods worth more than $500. It's not entirely clear whether software constitutes "goods" under these laws or if a license is a "sale." But many courts have held that such licenses must be in writing.

Such a writing need not be a formal-looking contract printed on paper. Instead, it can consist of e-mail that is printed out or saved on disk or other electronic transmissions stored in computer memory, faxes or telexes.

2. Do You Need a Signature?

A license should be signed. The purpose of the signature is to authenticate the contents of the document. However, a "signature" need not consist of a handwritten ink signature on paper. A signature can also consist of symbols, codes or letters so long as it can be demonstrated to be authentic. For example, a typewritten name on a telex has been construed to constitute a signature as have faxed handwritten signatures. It's likely that clicking on an icon on a computer screen or entering a user ID number or other similar identification code, symbol or other information also qualifies as a signature.

In addition, software has been developed to create "digital signatures." The software is used to create a piece of data attached to

an electronic document indicating that a certain person created or agreed to the contents of the document. The data is encrypted using the signer's private key. To verify the signature, the encrypted signature is decrypted using that person's public key. If the signer's private key matches the public key, the signature is verified. Digital signatures have already been approved for use for certain government contracts.

E. Licenses for Mass-Marketed Software

Of course it's not practical to negotiate individual license agreements for mass-marketed software that is purchased and used by thousands or even millions of end users. Software developers and publishers typically have no contact in advance with the people who purchase their products from computer stores, mail-order houses, bookstores and other retail outlets. Nor is it possible to negotiate individual licenses when thousands or even millions of end users purchase a software product over the Internet and commercial online services.

This would seem to mean that copies of mass-marketed software must be sold—rather than licensed—to the public. However, software publishers really want to license their software, not sell it. So they developed the shrink-wrap license agreement. If you've ever bought a mass-marketed software package, you've probably seen a shrink-wrap license. They may be printed on an envelope inside the package in which the program disks are sealed or, in rare cases, printed in bold type on the outside of the software package under the clear plastic shrink-wrap. Some shrink-wrap licenses appear on the computer screen when the software is first installed. Their purpose is to turn what would otherwise be a simple consumer purchase of a copy of a computer program into a licensing transaction.

1. Are Shrink-Wrap Licenses Enforceable?

For years, copyright experts have questioned whether shrink-wrap licenses are legally enforceable. One of the requirements for an enforceable contract is a meeting of the minds. That is, the parties must knowingly agree on all the material terms of the contract. There would appear to be no meeting of the minds between most consumers of mass-marketed software and software publishers. Most consumers don't bother to read the shrink-wrap licenses before buying and opening the package. The vast majority undoubtedly assume that when they buy a software package in a store they own it, just as when they buy a book in a bookstore.

Because of such doubts, the software industry lobbied state legislatures in the mid-1980s to change existing state contract laws to permit enforcement of such licenses. Only two states ultimately enacted such laws—Illinois and Louisiana. The Illinois law was repealed in 1988 and a federal court held that most of the key provisions of the Louisiana law were invalid because they were preempted (superseded) by the federal copyright law. (*Vault Corp. v. Quaid Software Ltd.*, 847 F.2d 255 (5th Cir. 1988).)

However, shrink-wrap licenses received a huge shot in the arm in 1996, when for the first time a federal court ruled they were enforceable. This all happened when Matthew Zeidenberg bought a CD-ROM containing 95 million business telephone listings from ProCD. He downloaded the listings into his computer from the CD-ROM and made them available on his Website, averaging over 20,000 "hits" per day. Zeidenberg did not commit copyright infringement because phone listings are in the public domain. However, he did violate the terms of the shrink-wrap license that came with the CD-ROM. The license barred purchasers from copying, adapting or modifying the work. The license was contained in written form inside the box the CD-ROM came in. It was also splashed on the computer screen when the user started up the software. Zeidenberg had to agree to the license terms by clicking on an "I agree" box before he could access the data on the CD-ROM.

The court held that the license was an enforceable contract. ProCD had offered to form a contract with Zeidenberg—ProCD would allow him to use the CD-ROM subject to the terms of the enclosed license agreement in return for his payment. ProCD had invited Zeidenberg to accept the terms

of the contract by conduct—clicking on the "I agree" icon and using the software after having had an opportunity to read the license agreement. Zeidenberg had accepted and a valid contract was formed. Since Zeidenberg violated the terms of license, he was liable to ProCD for damages. (*ProCD v. Zeidenberg*, 86 F.3d 1447 (7th Cir. 1996).)

For a shrink-wrap license to be enforceable, however, the software licensor should take the following steps to alert the purchaser-licensee to the existence of the license prior to the sale:

- place a prominent notice on the outside packaging of the software stating that the purchaser will be bound by a shrink-wrap license
- when the purchaser first starts up the software, include an "I agree" routine in which the purchaser is required to scroll through the license terms and must then click on an "I agree" box or type in the words "I agree" before the software can be used, and
- give the purchaser the right to return the software and receive a full refund of the purchase price if he or she doesn't agree to the terms of the license.

2. Contents of Shrink-Wrap Licenses

As with negotiated end user licenses, shrink-wrap licenses take away or restrict most of the rights a purchaser of a software copy would have.

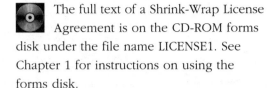 The full text of a Shrink-Wrap License Agreement is on the CD-ROM forms disk under the file name LICENSE1. See Chapter 1 for instructions on using the forms disk.

Open the file now. The sample form contains some blank spaces to fill in and several alternative provisions you must choose from. The following section explains each section of the agreement and provides guidance on how to complete it.

a. Notice provision

The first paragraph of the agreement is designed to alert the user that the software is being licensed, rather than sold. It is written in capitals to help ensure the user will read it. Two alternatives are provided; use the one that applies.

Alternative 1: This paragraph is used where the software includes an "I agree" routine in which the purchaser is required to scroll through the license terms and must then click on an "I agree" box or type in the words "I agree" before the software can be used. If the user doesn't agree to the license, he or she may return the software for a full refund.

Alternative 2: This paragraph should be used if there is no "I agree" routine. It provides that by opening the software package or the envelope containing the program diskettes, the user agrees to the terms of the license. If the user doesn't want to agree to the license, he is told to return the software for a full refund before opening the package.

b. License grant

The main purpose of using the shrink-wrap license, is for the publisher to retain ownership of the copy of the software stored on the disk. The user just gets a nonexclusive license to use the program, subject to various restrictions. This means the user does not have any of the rights of a software copy owner discussed in Section B3 above.

This license permits the user to load and use the software only on one computer at a time. An optional provision allows the purchaser to use the software on a portable or home computer if the software is permanently installed on the hard disk or other storage device of a computer (other than a network server) and one person uses that computer more than 80% of the time. A provision of this type is commonly included in shrink-wrap licenses, but there is no legal requirement that you include it.

c. Title

This clause make clear that you retain all intellectual property rights in the software.

d. Back-up copies

This provision allows the user to make back-up or archival copies. As discussed in Section B3, it's unclear whether licensees have this right unless the license gives it to them.

e. Things you may not do

This provision outlines all the things the licensee may not do with the software, including reverse engineering, decompiling or translating the software. The user is also not permitted to modify or adapt the software in any way, even for his or her own personal use. As discussed in Section B3, above, this is a right a software purchaser has. This means that if the user wants an upgrade he or she has to get it from the publisher.

Shrink-wrap licenses almost always contain a provision prohibiting the user from renting or leasing the software to the public, and one is included here. But, as discussed in Section B4 above, this is already prohibited by the Copyright Act.

The user is also barred from selling, sub-licensing, lending or giving away his or her copy of the software to any other person.

Computer disco

f. Limited warranty

The licensor promises in this clause that the program diskettes will be free from defects and the software will perform in substantial conformance with the documentation. The licensor makes no other warranties of any kind. You need to decide how long this warranty will last; 90 days is a common warranty period.

g. Limited remedy

If the software doesn't perform as promised, this clause gives the user the right to receive a replacement copy. If you can't provide a properly functioning copy, the user may return the software and receive a full refund.

The material in capitals is designed to limit your liability. It provides that you won't be liable for any damages arising from the licensee's use of the software.

h. Term and termination

The license automatically terminates if the licensee violates any of its terms. Upon termination, the licensee must return or destroy all copies of the software and documentation.

i. General provisions

These provisions are self-explanatory. You must fill in the state whose law will govern the agreement. This should be the state in which you have your principal place of business.

End User License Agreement

CAREFULLY READ THE FOLLOWING LICENSE AGREEMENT. BY OPENING THE PACKAGE OR CLICKING ON THE "ACCEPT" BUTTON, YOU ARE CONSENTING TO BE BOUND BY AND ARE BECOMING A PARTY TO THIS AGREEMENT. IF YOU DO NOT AGREE TO ALL OF THE TERMS OF THIS AGREEMENT, CLICK THE "DO NOT ACCEPT" BUTTON, AND, IF APPLICABLE, RETURN THIS PRODUCT TO THE PLACE OF PURCHASE FOR A FULL REFUND.

License Grant

The package contains software ("Software") and related explanatory written materials ("Documentation"). "Software" includes any upgrades, modified versions, updates, additions and copies of the Software. "You" means the person or company who is being licensed to use the Software or Documentation. "We" and "us" means AcmeSoft, Inc.

We hereby grant you a nonexclusive license to use one copy of the Software on any single computer, provided the Software is in use on only one computer at any time. The Software is "in use" on a computer when it is loaded into temporary memory (RAM) or installed into the permanent memory of a computer—for example, a hard disk, CD-ROM or other storage device.

If the Software is permanently installed on the hard disk or other storage device of a computer (other than a network server) and one person uses that computer more than 80% of the time, then that person may also use the Software on a portable or home computer.

Title

We remain the owner of all right, title and interest in the Software and Documentation.

Archival or Backup Copies

You may either:

- make one copy of the Software solely for backup or archival purposes, or
- transfer the Software to a single hard disk, provided you keep the original solely for backup or archival purposes.

Things You May Not Do

The Software and Documentation are protected by United States copyright laws and international treaties. You must treat the Software and Documentation like any other copyrighted material—for example a book. You may not:

- copy the Documentation,
- copy the Software except to make archival or backup copies as provided above,
- modify or adapt the Software or merge it into another program,
- reverse engineer, disassemble, decompile or make any attempt to discover the source code of the Software,
- Place the Software onto a server so that it is accessible via a pubic network such as the Internet, or
- sublicense, rent, lease or lend any portion of the Software or Documentation.

Transfers

You may transfer all your rights to use the Software and Documentation to another person or legal entity provided you transfer this Agreement, the Software and Documentation, including all copies, update and prior versions to such person or entity and that you retain no copies, including copies stored on computer.

Limited Warranty

We warrant that for a period of 90 of days after delivery of this copy of the Software to you:

- the physical media on which this copy of the Software is distributed will be free from defects in materials and workmanship under normal use, and
- the Software will perform in substantial accordance with the Documentation.

To the extent permitted by applicable law, THE FOREGOING LIMITED WARRANTY IS IN LIEU OF ALL OTHER WARRANTIES OR CONDITIONS, EXPRESS OR IMPLIED, AND WE DISCLAIM ANY AND ALL IMPLIED WARRANTIES OR CONDITIONS, INCLUDING ANY IMPLIED WARRANTY OF TITLE, NONINFRINGEMENT, MERCHANTABILITY OR FITNESS FOR A PARTICULAR PURPOSE, regardless of whether we know or had reason to know of your particular needs. No employee, agent, dealer or distributor of ours is authorized to modify this limited warranty, nor to make any additional warranties.

SOME STATES DO NOT ALLOW THE EXCLUSION OF IMPLIED WARRANTIES, SO THE ABOVE EXCLUSION MAY NOT APPLY TO YOU. THIS WARRANTY GIVES YOU SPECIFIC LEGAL RIGHTS, AND YOU MAY ALSO HAVE OTHER RIGHTS WHICH VARY FROM STATE TO STATE.

Limited Remedy

Our entire liability and your exclusive remedy shall be:

- the replacement of any diskette(s) or other media not meeting our Limited Warranty which is returned to us or to an authorized Dealer or Distributor with a copy of your receipt, or
- If we or an authorized Dealer or Distributor are unable to deliver a replacement diskette(s) or other media that is free of defects in materials or workmanship, you may terminate this Agreement by returning the Software and Documentation and your money will be refunded.

IN NO EVENT WILL WE BE LIABLE TO YOU FOR ANY DAMAGES, INCLUDING ANY LOST PROFITS, LOST SAVINGS, OR OTHER INCIDENTAL OR CONSEQUENTIAL DAMAGES ARISING FROM THE USE OR THE INABILITY TO USE THE SOFTWARE (EVEN IF WE OR AN AUTHORIZED DEALER OR DISTRIBUTOR HAS BEEN ADVISED OF THE POSSIBILITY OF THESE DAMAGES, OR FOR ANY CLAIM BY ANY OTHER PARTY.

SOME STATES DO NOT ALLOW THE LIMITATION OR EXCLUSION OF LIABILITY FOR INCIDENTAL OR CONSEQUENTIAL DAMAGES, SO THE ABOVE LIMITATION MAY NOT APPLY TO YOU.

Term and Termination

This license agreement takes effect upon your use of the software and remains effective until terminated. You may terminate it at any time by destroying all copies of the Software and Documentation in your possession. It will also automatically terminate if you fail to comply with any term or condition of this license agreement. You agree on termination of this license to either return to us or destroy all copies of the Software and Documentation in your possession.

Confidentiality

The Software contains trade secrets and proprietary know-how that belong to us and it is being made available to you in strict confidence. ANY USE OR DISCLOSURE OF THE SOFTWARE, OR OF ITS ALGORITHMS, PROTOCOLS OR INTERFACES, OTHER THAN IN STRICT ACCORDANCE WITH THIS LICENSE AGREEMENT, MAY BE ACTIONABLE AS A VIOLATION OF OUR TRADE SECRET RIGHTS.

General Provisions

1. This written license agreement is the exclusive agreement between you and us concerning the Software and Documentation and supersedes any and all prior oral or written agreements, negotiations or other dealings between us concerning the Software.

2. This license agreement may be modified only by a writing signed by you and us.

3. In the event of litigation between you and us concerning the Software or Documentation, the prevailing party in the litigation will be entitled to recover attorney fees and expenses from the other party.

4. This license agreement is governed by the laws of the state of California.

5. You agree that the Software will not be shipped, transferred or exported into any country or used in any manner prohibited by the United States Export Administration Act or any other export laws, restrictions or regulations.

3. Contents of Click-Wrap Licenses

"Click-Wrap" licenses serve the exact same function as shrink-wrap licenses except they are used for software that is distributed to end users over the Internet and commercial online services. The user downloads the software directly into his or her computer over phone lines, so there is no package or physical written license agreement the user can read. Instead, the user is asked to read the terms of the license on the computer screen and then click on an "accept" button to initiate the software download.

A click-wrap license may be easier to legally enforce than a shrink-wrap license because the user must take an active step—clicking on an accept button—to accept the license terms.

Moreover, the customer can be required to agree to the license before paying for the software. This avoids one of the principal legal objections to shrink-wraps: that they are not supported by consideration. Consideration is the value or quid pro quo that each party to a contract is supposed to receive from the other party in exchange for entering into the contract. Unless a contract provides some consideration for each party, the law will not usually recognize it as binding.

When a software consumer buys a software package containing a shrink-wrap license in a store or by mail order he or she gives consideration—the purchase price—and receives consideration in return—the software. The consumer assumes at this point that he or she owns the software copy. When the consumer then opens the software package he or she is supposed to enter into what seems a new agreement with the developer—the shrink-wrap license. The consumer is asked to provide consideration by giving up some of the ownership rights he or she would otherwise have, but gets no new consideration from the developer in return, since he or she already has the software. This can be avoided in an online transaction where the consumer must read and agree to the click-wrap license before purchasing the software.

The full text of a Click-Wrap License Agreement is on the CD-ROM forms disk under the file name LICENSE2. See Chapter 1 for instructions on using the forms disk.

The Click-Wrap license is virtually identical to the Shrink-Wrap license discussed in Section E2 above, except for some alterations to the first paragraph. The user is not asked to return the package if the license is unacceptable—obviously, there is no package.

End User License Agreement

CAREFULLY READ THE FOLLOWING LICENSE AGREEMENT. YOU ACCEPT AND AGREE TO BE BOUND BY THIS LICENSE AGREEMENT BY CLICKING THE ICON LABELED "I ACCEPT" THAT IS DISPLAYED BELOW. IF YOU DO NOT AGREE TO THIS LICENSE, CLICK THE ICON LABELED "CANCEL" AND YOUR ORDER WILL BE CANCELED, THE SOFTWARE WILL NOT BE DOWNLOADED AND YOU WILL NOT BE CHARGED.

License Grant

"You" means the person or company who is being licensed to use the Software or Documentation. "We," "us" and "our" means AcmeSoft, Inc.

We hereby grant you a nonexclusive license to use one copy of the Software on any single computer, provided the Software is in use on only one computer at any time. The Software is "in use" on a computer when it is loaded into temporary memory (RAM) or installed into the permanent memory of a computer—for example, a hard disk, CD-ROM or other storage device.

If the Software is permanently installed on the hard disk or other storage device of a computer (other than a network service) and one person uses that computer more than 80% of the time, then that person may also use the Software on a portable or home computer.

Title

We remain the owner of all right, title and interest in the Software and related explanatory written materials ("Documentation").

Archival or Backup Copies

You may copy the Software for back-up and archival purposes, provided that the original and each copy is kept in your possession and that your installation and use of the Software does not exceed that allowed in the "License Grant" section above.

Things You May Not Do

The Software and Documentation are protected by United States copyright laws and international treaties. You must treat the Software and Documentation like any other copyrighted material—for example a book. You may not:

- copy the Documentation,
- copy the Software except to make archival or backup copies as provided above,
- modify or adapt the Software or merge it into another program,
- reverse engineer, disassemble, decompile or make any attempt to discover the source code of the Software,
- place the Software onto a server so that it is accessible via a pubic network such as the Internet, or

- sublicense, rent, lease or lend any portion of the Software or Documentation.

Transfers

You may transfer all your rights to use the Software and Documentation to another person or legal entity provided you transfer this Agreement, the Software and Documentation, including all copies, update and prior versions to such person or entity and that you retain no copies, including copies stored on computer.

Limited Warranty

We warrant that for a period of 90 of days after delivery of this copy of the Software to you:

- the media on which this copy of the Software is provided to you will be free from defects in materials and workmanship under normal use, and
- the Software will perform in substantial accordance with the Documentation.

To the extent permitted by applicable law, THE FOREGOING LIMITED WARRANTY IS IN LIEU OF ALL OTHER WARRANTIES OR CONDITIONS, EXPRESS OR IMPLIED, AND WE DISCLAIM ANY AND ALL IMPLIED WARRANTIES OR CONDITIONS, INCLUDING ANY IMPLIED WARRANTY OF TITLE, NONINFRINGEMENT, MERCHANTABILITY OR FITNESS FOR A PARTICULAR PURPOSE, regardless of whether we know or had reason to know of your particular needs. No employee, agent, dealer or distributor of ours is authorized to modify this limited warranty, nor to make any additional warranties.

SOME STATES DO NOT ALLOW THE LIMITATION OR EXCLUSION OF LIABILITY FOR INCIDENTAL OR CONSEQUENTIAL DAMAGES, SO THE ABOVE LIMITATION MAY NOT APPLY TO YOU.

Limited Remedy

Our entire liability and your exclusive remedy for breach of the foregoing warranty shall be, at our option, to either:

- return the price you paid, or
- repair or replace the Software or media that does not meet the foregoing warranty if it is returned to us with a copy of your receipt.

IN NO EVENT WILL WE BE LIABLE TO YOU FOR ANY DAMAGES, INCLUDING ANY LOST PROFITS, LOST SAVINGS, OR OTHER INCIDENTAL OR CONSEQUENTIAL DAMAGES ARISING FROM THE USE OR THE INABILITY TO USE THE SOFTWARE (EVEN IF WE OR AN AUTHORIZED DEALER OR DISTRIBUTOR HAS BEEN ADVISED OF THE POSSIBILITY OF THESE DAMAGES OR FOR ANY CLAIM BY ANY OTHER PARTY.

SOME STATES DO NOT ALLOW THE LIMITATION OR EXCLUSION OF LIABILITY FOR INCIDENTAL OR CONSEQUENTIAL DAMAGES, SO THE ABOVE LIMITATION MAY NOT APPLY TO YOU.

Term and Termination

This license agreement takes effect upon your use of the software and remains effective until terminated. You may terminate it at any time by destroying all copies of the Software and Documentation in your possession. It will also automatically terminate if you fail to comply with any term or condition of this license agreement. You agree on termination of this license to destroy all copies of the Software and Documentation in your possession.

Confidentiality

The Software contains trade secrets and proprietary know-how that belong to us and it is being made available to you in strict confidence. ANY USE OR DISCLOSURE OF THE SOFTWARE, OR OF ITS ALGORITHMS, PROTOCOLS OR INTERFACES, OTHER THAN IN STRICT ACCORDANCE WITH THIS LICENSE AGREEMENT, MAY BE ACTIONABLE AS A VIOLATION OF OUR TRADE SECRET RIGHTS.

General Provisions

1. This written license agreement is the exclusive agreement between you and us concerning the Software and Documentation and supersedes any prior purchase order, communication, advertising or representation concerning the Software.

2. This license agreement may be modified only by a writing signed by you and us.

3. In the event of litigation between you and us concerning the Software or Documentation, the prevailing party in the litigation will be entitled to recover attorney fees and expenses from the other party.

4. This license agreement is governed by the laws of the state of California.

5. You agree that the Software will not be shipped, transferred or exported into any country or used in any manner prohibited by the United States Export Administration Act or any other export laws, restrictions or regulations.

F. Negotiated License Agreements

Negotiated license agreements are those individually agreed upon and signed by the user after negotiations between the user and software owner. Such agreements are not used for software sold online, in stores or by mail order. Rather, they are used when a software developer or owner deals personally with the end user.

> **EXAMPLE:** The Old Reliable Insurance Company wants to use a complex actuarial program developed by AcmeSoft, Inc. It contacts AcmeSoft and negotiates a deal: AcmeSoft agrees to license the program to Old Reliable for $10,000 per year for five years. AcmeSoft draws up a license agreement that is signed by both parties.

Negotiated end user licenses are normally nonexclusive licenses. As discussed in Section A2 above, the holder of a nonexclusive license acquires none of the licensor's exclusive copyright rights. All he or she has are the use rights granted in the license agreement. The licensor is free to enter into other nonexclusive licenses with as many other customers as it chooses.

The full text of a Negotiated License Agreement is on the CD-ROM forms disk under the file name LICENSE3. See Chapter 1 for instructions on using the forms disk.

Open the file now. The sample form contains a number of blank spaces to fill in and several alternative provisions you must choose from. The following section explains each section of the agreement and provides guidance on how to complete it.

Names and Addresses

List the names and addresses of the software owner and the customer. In the rest of the agreement, the owner will be called the licensor and the customer the licensee. Be sure to precisely name the licensee. For example, if you're licensing the software to a particular division within a large corporation, be sure to identify the division correctly.

1. Definitions

This section defines some key terms in the license. Subsection (a) requires that you identify the software you're licensing in a separate schedule and attach it to the license agreement.

2. Rights Granted Licensee

Several alternatives are provided as to how the licensee may use the software.

Alternative 1—single user license: The first alternative allows the licensee to use the software only on one computer at a time. This type of license is more common for mass-marketed software than for negotiated license agreements.

Alternative 2—multiple stand-alone computers: The second alternative allows the licensee to use the software on a stated number of separate stand-alone computers. You need to state the number of computers allowed.

Alternative 3—site license: This alternative permits the licensee to use the software on any number of computers at a given site. You need to provide the address or other identifying information for the site.

Alternative 4—network license: This alternative permits the license to use the software on a network. You have the option of limiting the total number of computers that can use the software at one time.

3. License Term

The license term means how long the license will last.

Alternative 1—perpetual term: The first alternative provides a perpetual license term. That is, the license lasts as long as the licensee continues to use the software and complies with the terms of the license—for example, continues to pay the license fee.

Alternative 2—term of years: The second alternative provides an initial term of a stated number of years. You need to provide how long the term will last. When the initial term expires, the license is automatically renewed unless the licensee discontinues it by sending you a notice of nonrenewal. This favors the licensor because the licensee must keep paying the licensor unless he or she takes an affirmative step to end the license when the term ends.

4. License Fee

You can set forth the license fee in the main body of the license or in a separate schedule attached to the agreement. Do whatever is most convenient.

5. Termination

This clause gives you the right to terminate the license if the licensee breaches any of its terms—for example, fails to pay you—or if the licensee goes bankrupt or becomes insolvent.

6. Return or Destruction of Software Upon Termination

When the license terminates, you don't want the licensee to keep any copies of the software. This provision requires the licensee to destroy all copies or return them to you. You have the right to inspect the licensee's premises to make sure all copies have been disposed of.

7. Title to Software

This provision makes clear that you retain all your intellectual property rights in the software.

8. Modifications and Enhancements

This provision bars the licensee from reverse engineering or modifying the software without the licensor's written consent.

9. Warranty

Licensors often provide some sort of guarantee for the software they license. However, there is no legal requirement that you do so. Two alternative warranty provisions are provided. These provisions are written in capital letters so the licensee can't later claim he or she overlooked them

Alternative 1—software provided "as is": Under the first alternative, you provide the software "as is"—that is, you make no guaranties or warranties about its performance.

Alternative 2—limited warranty: Alternative 2 provides a limited warranty. You promise that the software will function in substantial accordance with the documentation and specifications for a given time period. You need to state the period—for example, 90 days is a common period. If the software fails to perform adequately, you have the option of repairing or replacing it, or returning the licensor's license fee.

10. Confidentiality

This provision requires the licensee to maintain the software in confidence. This will help ensure that you won't lose any trade secret protection for the software. (See Chapter 6.)

11. Arbitration

Arbitration is a relatively low-cost alternative to expensive court litigation, in which an informal hearing is held before one or more arbitrators (usually attorneys or retired judges) who decide the merits of the issues and render a decision, which may or not be binding depending on the arbitration agreement. There are a number of professional arbitrators' organizations which conduct arbitrations, notably the American Arbitration Association, which has offices in most major cities. This clause requires you and the client to submit any dispute over the agreement to arbitration.

12. Attorney Fees

If you have to sue the licensee in court to enforce the agreement, and win, you normally will not be awarded the amount of your attorney fees unless your agreement requires it. Including such an attorney fees provision in the agreement can be in your interest. It can help make filing a lawsuit economically feasible. It will also give the licensee a strong incentive to negotiate with you if you have a good case.

Under this provision, if either party has to sue the other in court to enforce the agreement and wins—that is, becomes the prevailing party—the loser is required to pay the other party's attorney fees and expenses.

13. General Provisions

Following are several provisions that are customarily lumped together at the end of a license agreement. This does not mean they are unimportant.

(a) This clause helps make it clear to a court or arbitrator that the parties intended the contract to be their final agreement. A clause such as this helps avoid claims that promises not contained in the written agreement were made and broken.

(b) This clause, which is very important, states that any changes to the agreement must be in writing and agreed to by both parties to be effective. This provision protects both parties; reducing all modifications to writing lessens the possibility of misunderstandings. In addition, oral modifications may not be legally binding.

(c) This clause specifies which state law governs the contract. This should be the state in which you or the licensee do business or are incorporated.

(d) When you want to do something important involving the agreement—terminate it, for example—you need to tell the client about it. This is called giving notice. This provision gives you several options for providing the licensee with notice: by personal delivery, by mail, or by fax or telex followed by a confirming letter.

If you give notice by mail, it is not effective until three days after it's sent. For example, if you want to end the agreement on 30 days notice and mail your notice of termination to the licensee, the agreement will not end until 33 days after you mailed the notice.

(e) This clause helps you to make sure that the licensor and licensee are separate legal entities, not partners or co-venturers. If you are viewed as a licensee's partner, you will be liable for its debts and the licensee will have the power to make contracts that obligate you to others without your consent.

(f) An assignment is the process by which rights or duties under a contract are transferred to someone else. Unless the license prevents it, the licensee may assign its rights to someone else—that is, allow someone else to use the software. This clause does not allow the licensee to make such an assignment unless you agree in writing in advance. You are also allowed to charge a reasonable transfer fee for such an assignment.

Software License

This Agreement is made between Old Reliable Insurance Co. (the "Licensee") located at 145 Lonestar Ave., Austin, TX, and AcmeSoft, Inc. (the "Licensor") with a principal place of business at 10529 Naked Spur Place, Longview, TX.

1. Definitions:

(a) "Software" means the computer programs and documentation listed in Schedule A attached to this Agreement.

(b) "Install" means placing the Software on a computer's hard disk, CD-ROM or other secondary storage device.

(c) "Use" means (i) executing or loading the Software into computer RAM or other primary memory, and (ii) copying the Software for archival or emergency restart purposes.

2. Grant of Rights:

Licensor hereby grants to Licensee a nonexclusive nontransferable license to install and use the Software on any computer located at 145 Lonestar Ave., Austin, TX, provided such computers cannot be accessed from outside the site by a telecommunications network or otherwise.

3. License Term:

This License is effective when executed by both parties and the license granted to the Software remains in force until Licensee stops using the Software or until Licensor terminates this License because of Licensee's failure to comply with any of its terms and conditions.

4. License Fee:

Licensee agrees to pay Licensor the license fee set forth in the attached Schedule B.

5. Termination:

Licensor shall have the right to immediately terminate this License if Licensee fails to perform any obligation required of Licensee under this License or if Licensee becomes bankrupt or insolvent.

6. Return or Destruction of Software Upon Termination:

Upon termination of this License, Licensee shall return to Licensor or destroy the original and all copies of the Software including partial copies and modifications. Licensor shall have a reasonable opportunity to conduct an inspection of Licensee's place of business to assure compliance with this provision.

7. Title to Software:

Licensor retains title to and ownership of the Software and all enhancements, modifications and updates of the Software.

8. No Modification and Enhancements:

Licensee will make no efforts to reverse engineer the Software, or make any modifications or enhancements without Licensor's express written consent.

9. Warranty:

THE SOFTWARE IS PROVIDED "AS IS." LICENSOR DISCLAIMS ALL WARRANTIES, INCLUDING BUT NOT LIMITED TO, ALL EXPRESS OR IMPLIED WARRANTIES OF MERCHANTABILITY AND FITNESS FOR A PARTICULAR PURPOSE. LICENSOR ADDITIONALLY DISCLAIMS ALL OBLIGATIONS AND LIABILITIES FOR DAMAGES, INCLUDING BUT NOT LIMITED TO, SPECIAL, INDIRECT AND CONSEQUENTIAL DAMAGES, ATTORNEY FEES AND COURT COSTS ARISING FROM OR IN CONNECTION WITH THE USE OF THE SOFTWARE LICENSED UNDER THIS AGREEMENT.

SOME STATES DO NOT ALLOW THE EXCLUSION OF IMPLIED WARRANTIES, SO THE ABOVE EXCLUSION MAY NOT APPLY TO YOU.

10. Confidentiality:

Licensee will treat the Software as trade secrets and proprietary know-how belonging to Licensor that is being made available to Licensee in confidence. Licensee agrees to treat the Software with at least the same care as it treats it own confidential or proprietary information.

11. Arbitration:

The parties agree to submit any dispute under this License to binding arbitration in the following location: Austin, TX, under the rules of the American Arbitration Association. Judgment upon the award rendered by the arbitrator may be entered in any court with jurisdiction to do so.

12. Attorney Fees:

If any legal action is necessary to enforce this License, the prevailing party shall be entitled to reasonable attorney fees, costs and expenses in addition to any other relief to which it may be entitled.

13. General Provisions:

(a) Complete Agreement: This License together with all schedules or other attachments, which are incorporated herein by reference, is the sole and entire Agreement between the parties. This Agreement supersedes all prior understandings, agreements and documentation relating to such subject matter.

(b) Modifications to License: Modifications and amendments to this License, including any exhibit or appendix hereto, shall be enforceable only if they are in writing and are signed by authorized representatives of both parties.

(c) Applicable law: This License will be governed by the laws of the State of Texas.

(d) Notices: All notices and other communications given in connection with this License shall be in writing and shall be deemed given as follows:

- When delivered personally to the recipient's address as appearing in the introductory paragraph to this License;
- Three days after being deposited in the United States mails, postage prepaid to the recipient's address as appearing in the introductory paragraph to this License; or
- When sent by fax or telex to the last fax or telex number of the recipient known to the party giving notice. Notice is effective upon receipt provided that a duplicate copy of the notice is promptly given by first-class or certified mail, or the recipient delivers a written confirmation of receipt.

Any party may change its address appearing in the introductory paragraph to this License by giving notice of the change in accordance with this paragraph.

(e) No Agency: Nothing contained herein will be construed as creating any agency, partnership, joint venture or other form of joint enterprise between the parties.

(f) Assignment: The rights conferred by this License shall not be assignable by the Licensee without Licensor's prior written consent. Licensor may impose a reasonable license fee on any such assignment

AcmeSoft, Inc.

By: /s/

James Jones

Title: President

Date: Jan. 14, 199_.

Old Reliable Insurance Co.

By: /s/

Yolanda Allende

Title: Vice-President

Date: Jan. 30, 199_.

Chapter 17

Software Development Agreements

This chapter covers contracts for the developer of custom software. It is written primarily from the developer's point of view, but contains much useful information for custom software customers as well. There is no standard definition of "custom" software. In this chapter, the term is used to mean software—usually an entire system—created specially for a particular customer. But custom software need not be created entirely from scratch. Many of the components of the system may have been used by the developer before (and may be used again for other customers). As long as the system as a whole is unique, it fits the custom software definition.

A. Introduction

Creating a brand new piece of software (even one that contains much existing code) is a difficult and risky process. Without careful planning reflected in a thorough contract (written agreement), the parties may end up dissatisfied.

Contrary to conventional wisdom, a developer does not benefit by starting work immediately on the basis of a handshake or a brief letter that sets forth the contract price and a vague description of the project. Unfortunately, many development projects are handled in just this way. However, this approach is a recipe for disaster. If problems later develop—particularly if the customer had unrealistic expectations or failed to understand exactly what the developer agreed to do—the developer will have no contract to fall back on for help. That piece of paper—the development contract—is the developer's lifeline. If properly drafted, it will help prevent disputes by making it clear exactly what's been agreed to. If problems develop, the agreement will provide ways to solve them. If the parties end up in court, the agreement will establish their legal duties to each other.

Negotiating a contract can take some time and effort, but by using the phased approach advocated in Section A1, below, the delay should be minimized. Under this approach, the contract can be signed on the basis of a simple functional specification, without going to the time and effort of creating final detailed specifications or a delivery and payment schedule—usually the most time-consuming parts of a development agreement. These are created later as part of the first phase of the project.

1. Phased Agreements Work Best

It's almost always advisable to break down a custom software development project into discrete parts or stages, often called phases or "milestones." At the end of each stage, the developer delivers an acceptable product. Having the customer sign off on each phase of the project avoids claims of unsatisfactory performance by the customer at the conclusion of the project.

The phased approach also allows the developer an opportunity to deal with the customer's changing needs and wants. Few software projects ever completely follow the original specifications. The project usually grows as the work is done and the developer and customer get ideas for a better (and usually more complex) project. Moreover, continuous operating system improvements often guarantee major changes in the course of development, especially if the project takes more than a year. Developing in phases is a convenient way for the parties to meet and discuss changes and how much they will cost. The developer must make sure, however, that the overall delivery schedule is reasonable and provides some flexibility.

At the very least, a custom software development project should consist of two phases:

- **Specification phase.** The developer prepares a detailed design specification and proposes a completion schedule. In the model development agreement, the developer includes these items as part of a development plan to be provided to the customer. (See Section B3 below.)
- **Development phase.** If the customer is satisfied with the detailed specifications, the customer typically pays a specified sum and the developer commences to create the software.

If the customer is not satisfied with the detailed specifications, the developer either revises them or the contract is canceled. It's usually best for the parties to go their separate ways if they can't reach some sort of agreement upfront on detailed project specifications. If the contract is canceled, the developer is still entitled to be paid for the time and expense involved in creating the development plan.

Most custom software projects are too lengthy and complex to be divided into only two phases. After the initial specifications phase is completed, the customer will want the developer to deliver specified portions of the system as they are completed. In some cases, these system portions can run independently of each other so they can be tested as soon as they are completed.

2. Who Writes the Contract?

The most important rule of all contractual negotiations is that the party that creates the first draft of the contract usually obtains the best deal. It's always a good idea for a developer to present the customer with a form agreement to review. The initial draft may undergo many changes, but it serves as the basis for the final contract.

B. Contents of Custom Software Development Contracts

The full text of a Custom Software Development Agreement is on the CD-ROM forms disk under the file name CUSTSFT. See Chapter 1 for instructions on using the forms disk. This agreement favors the developer, but not unduly.

Open the file now. The sample form contains a number of blank spaces to fill in and several alternative provisions you must choose from. The following section explains each section of the agreement and provides guidance on how to complete it.

1. Identification of the Parties

Here at the beginning of the contract, both parties should list their full business names. Later on in the contract, you can use obvious abbreviations.

If you're a sole proprietor, use the full name you use for your business. This can be your own name or a fictitious business name or assumed name you use to identify your business. For example, if developer Al Brodsky calls his software consulting business "ABC Software Development," he would use that name on the contract. Using a fictitious business name helps show you're a business, not an employee.

If your business is incorporated, use your corporate name, not your own name—for example: "John Smith, Incorporated" instead of "John Smith."

If you're a limited liability company, use the name of your company—for example, John Smith, LLC, instead of just John Smith.

If you're a partner in a partnership, use your partnership name—for example, The Smith Partnership instead of John Smith..

For the sake of brevity, it is usual to identify yourself and the client by shorter names in the rest of the agreement. You can use an abbreviated version of your full name—for example, ABC for ABC Marketing Research. Or you can refer to yourself simply as Developer.

Refer to the customer initially by its company name and subsequently by a short version of the name or as Customer or Client.

Include the addresses of the principal place of business of the customer and yourself. If you or the customer have more than one office or workplace, the principal place of business is the main office or workplace.

2. Purpose of Agreement

It is customary to briefly state at the beginning the reason for the contract. This helps establish the parties' intent to create a legally binding contract, and may be helpful if the contract has to be interpreted and enforced by a judge or arbitrator, perhaps years after it was written. Note that the functional specifications, which describe the software in detail, should be attached to the agreement as an exhibit. (Functional specifications are discussed in Section A1, above.)

3. Preparation of Development Plan

The first phase of the project is the developer's preparation of a software development plan. The development plan should show the customer what the developer intends to do and how long it will take. In this clause, the customer's commitment to proceed with the project is contingent upon its acceptance of the development plan. This protects both the customer and developer. The customer's financial exposure is minimized: If the design fails to meet its original expectation, it can terminate the contract and seek a new developer without much loss. The developer is protected by having the customer agree in writing to the detailed specifications and delivery schedule before it actually starts to create the software. This prevents later claims that the finished product doesn't meet the customer's requirements.

This provision also gives the developer time to cure any deficiencies in the plan before the customer may terminate the contract. This seems only fair given the substantial investment of time and effort the developer will usually expend to create a development plan

Following are the key points the agreement addresses.

a. Specifications

Before the development agreement is signed, the customer (often with the aid of a computer consultant), or the developer, should create a functional specification describing the software in general terms. The developer will use the functional specifications as a guide in creating a far more technical detailed specification. The detailed specifications serve as the final project blueprint. They describe the project in a very precise technical manner and should provide the developer with all the information it needs to actually create the software. Drafting detailed specifications is beyond the scope of this book. See the sidebar below for further information.

Guides to Drafting Software Specifications

Some sources on how to draft specifications include:

- *An Introduction to Formal Specification and Z*, by Sinclair & Till (Prentice Hall)
- *Information Systems Development: Methodologies, Techniques and Tools*, by Avison and Fitzgerald (Blackwell Scientific Publications)
- *Software Engineering*, by Jones (John Wiley & Sons)
- *Software Requirements Analysis and Specification*, by Davis (Prentice Hall)
- *The Specification of Complex Systems*, by Harwood and Jackson (Addison-Wesley).

Creating a Prototype

It can be difficult or impossible for a technically unsophisticated customer to get a feel for how the proposed software will function from written specifications. For this reason, the developer may be asked to create a prototype of the actual system.

The prototype should include a complete set of proposed report formats, screen displays and menus so that the customer can review the program's customer interface. The prototype can be done either by hand on "storyboards" or on computer, using a tool like FILEMAKER PRO, HYPERCARD or MACROMIND DIRECTOR for the Macintosh or DESIGNER for MS-DOS computers.

b. Deliverables

The development plan should list all deliverables—that is, every item the customer wants the developer to provide. This includes not only the software itself, but the program and customer documentation as well.

Following is a checklist of deliverables for a typical software project.

- final specifications for the completed software showing any changes from the specifications contained in the Development Plan

- complete customer documentation, including a description of how to access and use each application, screen prints of menus and input/output screens, data input descriptions, sample output/report forms, error code descriptions and solutions where appropriate and explanations of all necessary disks and data used by the software
- complete program/technical documentation, including technical information about files and their locations, file names, file/database structure, record structure and layout and data elements
- if the customer will receive a copy of the source code, program source code listings with comments
- description of backup and recovery procedures, including process, medium for backup and number of diskettes or tapes to do a complete backup, and
- master copy of software on magnetic media, including all programs, online documentation and any documentation developed on computer.

c. Delivery schedule

The development plan should also include a schedule showing when each deliverable will be completed. The developer must take care that the delivery schedule provides sufficient time to complete the project. Developers tend to be incorrigible optimists, so they constantly underestimate how long development projects will take. It's best for the developer to be realistic up front, and not promise the customer what it can't deliver. Since delays are so common, the development agreement should state how delays will be dealt with. (See Section B9, below.)

d. Payment for development plan

Drafting a development plan—particularly the specifications—is difficult and time-consuming. Thus, the developer should be fairly compensated for its efforts. Where the developer is being paid a fixed price, it normally receives a portion as a down payment upon execution of the contract. If the plan is not accepted and the contract is canceled, the down payment may provide the developer with too little or too much money for the work it did on the plan.

This clause deals with this problem by providing that the developer will be paid on a "time and materials" basis for the development plan if the plan is not accepted and the contract is canceled. ("Time and materials" means the developer is paid for its time and actual costs.) If this amount is less than the down payment, the developer must return the excess to the customer. This paragraph need not be included in contracts in which the developer is to be paid on an ongoing hourly basis (see Section B4a, below). It would merely be redundant.

4. Payment

There are two basic ways to pay a developer for creating custom software:

- a pay per hour ("time and materials") agreement, or
- a fixed price agreement.

a. Alternative 1: "Time and materials" agreements

Under a "time and materials" agreement, the developer charges the customer by the hour, day or month at a flat hourly cost. This is by far the safest way to be paid if it's difficult to estimate exactly how long a project will take. However, many clients will wish to place a cap on your total compensation because they're afraid you'll "pad" your bill. If this is the case, include the optional sentence providing for a cap, but make sure it's large enough to allow you to complete the job.

b. Alternative 2: Fixed price agreements

The other payment option is for the customer to pay the developer a fixed price for the entire project. In theory, this payment scheme favors the customer by giving the customer certainty as to what the project will cost. Moreover, if payments are tied to the progress of the developer's work, it gives the customer substantial leverage to insist on timely and successful completion of the project.

At first glance, fixed price agreements would seem to be risky for developers: If the project takes much longer than originally anticipated, the developer could end up losing money. However, as a practical matter, fixed price agreements usually do not end up favoring the customer as much as one would think. If it turns out that the fixed price originally agreed upon will not provide the developer with fair compensation, because the project ends up taking too long, the customer will probably end up agreeing to pay the developer more money. Otherwise the developer may quit or end up delivering a hastily completed and shoddy product.

The developer's fixed price quote should be included in the Development Plan, which will also contain the detailed specifications, deliverables list and delivery schedule. Obviously, the developer should complete these last three items, particularly the detailed specification, before deciding how much to charge for the entire project. Only at this point can the developer have a reasonably accurate idea of how much time the project will require.

Fixed price contracts are normally paid in installments, with payment of each installment tied to completion and acceptance of a phase of the project. In addition, an initial down payment is usually made when the contract is signed. This provision requires that a payment schedule be included as part of the development plan, which will be attached to the contract as an exhibit. The developer should make sure that the schedule requires the customer to make regular periodic payments so that the developer can meet its own financial obligations.

The amount of the down payment is often a point of contention in fixed price contracts. Naturally, the developer should obtain as large a down payment as possible.

5. Payment of Developer's Costs

Whether a fixed price or time and materials payment arrangement is used, the developer is usually reimbursed by the customer for at least some out-of-pocket expenses incurred in performing its duties under the contract. The extent of such reimbursement is a matter for negotiation.

Alternative 1: Full reimbursement: The first alternative calls for payment of all the developer's out-of-pocket expenses; this may include items like communications charges (telephone, fax, postage, etc.).

Alternative 2: Partial reimbursement: One problem with the first alternative is that many government agencies consider payment of a worker's ordinary business expenses to be a mild indicator of an employment relationship. (See Chapter 15.) The second alternative clause limits reimbursement to extraordinary expenses, such as nonlocal travel, and will not be viewed as indicative of an employee-employer relationship.

6. Late Fees

Many developers charge a late fee if the customer doesn't pay within the time specified in the development agreement or invoice. Charging late fees for overdue payments can get customers to pay on time. The late fee is normally expressed as a monthly interest charge—for example, 1% per month.

If you wish to charge a late fee, make sure it's mentioned in your agreement. You should also clearly state what your late fee is on all your invoices.

7. Materials

If the client will provide you with any materials or equipment, list them in this optional clause. If you need these items by a specific date, specify the deadline as well.

8. Changes in Project Scope

It's quite common in the course of software development for the customer to wish to make changes—adding new features and/or deleting others. Of course, any changes to the specifications or any other provision of the contract should be in writing and signed by both parties to be effective. (This is required by Section 27(b), below.)

Major changes in the scope of the project may greatly increase—or decrease—the amount of work the developer has to do. If the developer is paid a fixed fee, it is only fair that its compensation should be increased or decreased to reflect the change in the workload. This usually is not an issue where the developer is paid by the hour; but if there is a cap on the total hourly compensation to be paid, the cap may have to be increased.

Changes in the scope of the project may also require changes in proposed delivery dates, and perhaps in the contract's warranty

provisions. (Warranties are discussed in Section 16.)

This provision sets forth a procedure for the parties to follow if the customer wants to change the specifications or other parts of the development plan. First, the customer must submit a written proposal to the developer showing the desired changes. The developer then responds to this proposal in writing, stating, among other things, what impact the desired changes will have on the contract price and delivery schedule. If the customer wants to go ahead with the changes, it submits a "Development Plan Modification Agreement" specifying all the agreed-upon changes and their effect on the provisions of the Agreement. The developer has ten days to accept or reject the Development Plan Modification Agreement.

In many instances, the developer, not the customer, will wish to alter the specifications. This may be because the specifications contain an error, do not accurately reflect the customer's true needs, or the project as originally agreed upon proves commercially unfeasible for a developer being paid a fixed fee. All such changes should be in writing and signed by both parties as required by the clause dealing with modifications to the agreement. (See Section 27(b) below.)

9. Delays

It is rare for custom software to be completed and delivered by the developer exactly on schedule. There are many reasons for this. Estimating how long it will take to create new software is an uncertain art at best (exacerbated by the fact that most programmers are incorrigible optimists and many customers are terminally impatient). Delays may also result if the developer has staffing changes or increased demands on existing staff.

The first paragraph of this section is designed to give the developer some leeway in the delivery schedule. Any deadline can be extended by the developer by giving the customer written notice. However, a cap is placed on the total of all the extensions. You need to decide how many days this cap should be.

Sometimes a project is delayed due to circumstances beyond the developer's control—for example, where an earthquake, fire or other act of God destroys or severely damages the developer's office and equipment. In this event, it is only fair that the developer's delay be excused. A special provision (often called a "force majeure" clause) is commonly included in development contracts to excuse a party's nonperformance due to circumstances beyond its control. The second and third paragraphs of this section contain such a provision.

10. Acceptance Testing of Software

"Acceptance testing" is a procedure by which the software is tested to see if it satisfies the detailed specifications set forth in the Development Plan. Acceptance testing is one of the most important phases of the software development process. The purpose is to determine whether the software does what it is supposed to do and is reliable. Particularly where safety is involved (for example, software implemented in a "911" service or designed to run an elevator), the software should be tested as thoroughly as possible.

The acceptance testing should force the software to perform repeatedly, without failure, on a variety of the customer's actual data, with speed and accuracy to match the specifications. It is also a good idea to stress test a system—that is, try to break it—to see how it recovers. Each section of the software should be tested independently and in combination with other sections.

The nature of the tests to be performed, the data to be used and the procedure to be followed should be defined by the parties before the testing begins. In many cases, the acceptance tests cannot be well defined until the final specifications are agreed upon or even until the software is completed. The specifications for acceptance testing should be included as part of the development plan. (See Section 3(a), above.) Of course, these specifications may be subsequently modified by the parties.

Unfortunately, many bugs will not be discovered during acceptance testing. Some bugs appear only after many hundreds or thousands of customer hours. For this reason, it's common for the developer to agree to fix bugs free of charge for a stated period after the software is accepted—usually

90 days to a year. (See Section 12, below, for a detailed discussion.)

Trivial Bugs

No software is absolutely perfect. It is impossible for a developer to create software of any complexity that is completely bug-free. However, there is a big difference between true bugs—defects that prevent the software from performing the customer's required tasks satisfactorily—and interface and peripheral glitches and other minor irritants that don't materially affect the software's performance. A developer should never promise that its software will be completely bug-free. (See the discussion in Section 16(d), below.) Moreover, the acceptance criteria should be designed so as to overlook trivial bugs that can simply be ignored.

---

a. Alternative 1: Acceptance testing provision for multi-phase projects

Complex software systems often consist of a number of independent units or "modules" that can be tested when completed. This way, the customer doesn't have to wait until the entire project is finished to test the software and see how the work is progressing. Of course, the schedule for delivery of each portion of the system should be set forth in detail in the development plan's delivery schedule.

If the software does not satisfy the acceptance criteria, the customer should explain the problems to the developer and then give it an opportunity to correct them. Developers are typically given 30 days to make corrections, but more time may be required if the software is extremely complex. If the developer cannot make the corrections, or re-delivers software that is still nonconforming, the customer should have the option of giving the developer more time or terminating the contract.

When all phases of development are completed, the software should be tested in its entirety. The same acceptance procedure is used as for testing each phase, except that optional language allows the time periods for the developer's corrections and the customer's review and reevaluation to be increased beyond the 30 days allowed for acceptance of each phase 30 days may simply not be enough time to test and evaluate the entire program.

b. Alternative 2: Testing when project completed

Some types of software really can't be tested until the entire system is completed and running, except perhaps the print and display functions. This clause is a simpler acceptance testing provision designed to be used where serious testing won't be conducted until the software is delivered in final form. This provision should also be used for projects where the entire program will be delivered at one time, rather than in phases.

11. Training

The customer and/or its employees will usually have to be trained how to use the software. This provision requires the developer to conduct training. Where the developer is paid a fixed fee, the cost of training can be included in the overall fee. However, where the developer is paid on an hourly basis, it will have to be paid extra for training. In either event, the customer should be responsible for its own costs associated with such training.

12. Maintenance of Software

"Maintenance" is a term used for upkeep of software after it has been put into operation. There are two types of maintenance:

- fixing bugs (sometimes called "remedial maintenance"), and
- modifying and/or enhancing software because the customer's needs have changed (sometimes called "adaptive maintenance").

It can cost far more to maintain software than to develop it in the first place. Many developers consider maintenance to be a nuisance and would prefer to use their re-sources on other new development projects. Such developers want to terminate their work for the customer upon delivery and acceptance of the software. The customer, on the other hand, needs someone to main-tain the software. It is often most efficient for the persons who originally create a piece of software to maintain it. Their familiarity with the original software's design should enable them to do a better job than someone who is completely new to the software.

Typically, custom software development agreements contain a warranty in which the developer promises to fix any bugs for free for a limited time—usually 90 days to a year. (See Section 16, below, for a detailed discus-sion.) The following provision addresses post-warranty remedial maintenance (bug correction) only. Adaptive maintenance (enhancements and modifications) should be handled in a separate agreement.

This provision requires the developer to perform remedial maintenance and provide telephone hot line support after the warranty expires. The customer pays the developer an annual fee for this service. Note that the provision applies only to "reproducible errors ... so that the Software is brought into substantial conformance with the Specifications." This protects the developer from committing to fix trivial errors or errors that may occur only once in many thousands of hours of operation and that cannot be readily reproduced.

13. Ownership of Software

The moment computer code is written, it is protected by copyright and someone becomes the owner of that copyright. Similarly, patent and trade secret ownership rights may come into existence. Many software developers and customers harbor the misapprehension that, since the developer is being paid to create the software by the customer, the customer will automatically own all rights to it. This is not the case. Absent a written contract transferring ownership from the developer to the customer, the developer will most likely own the copyright in the software (unless the developer is considered the customer's employee or, perhaps, if it was part of a larger work and was prepared under a written work for hire agreement. See Chapter 11.)

One of the most important functions of a software development agreement is to establish exactly who will own the intellectual property rights to the software to be created. This is often one of the most hotly contested issues between the developer and customer, and can easily become a "deal breaker." Ownership rules for intellectual property are covered in detail in Chapter 11. This section focuses on how to handle these issues in a custom software development agreement.

Floppy Disk Ownership Isn't Intellectual Property Ownership

Owning the material object in which software is embodied—whether a floppy disk, hard disk or ROM—is separate and distinct from intellectual property ownership. When a customer is given a floppy disk containing a software program written by the developer, the customer owns that disk—no one can legally take it away from him—but the customer cannot exercise any of the developer's exclusive copyright rights in the software contained on that disk absent a transfer (license or sale) of such rights from the developer to the customer.

This means that the customer could not legally make more than one archival copy of the software, could not distribute it to the public, and could not create derivative works based upon it—modified versions, for example. This is what we're talking about when we discuss software ownership—ownership of intangible intellectual property rights—not ownership of floppy disks or other media.

Ownership issues are critically important for the developer. If a developer signs a contract with a customer transferring its ownership of the intellectual property rights in the software, the developer can never use, sell or license that software again. A developer who signs such a contract may end up giving up far more than it actually realized or intended—it may lose the ability to do similar work for other customers in the future.

We emphasized the "may" above because no one knows exactly to what extent computer software is protected by the law. It is clear that copyright protects source code, so a developer who relinquishes copyright ownership in a program may not use that same source code again unless provisions for such use are made as part of the transaction (or in a later license). But copyright protection might go beyond a program's literal source code—for instance, to the structure, sequence and organization of the code.

The potential problems do not end here. Copyright does not protect ideas, concepts, know-how, techniques, formulae or algorithms. However, these items may be protected by trade secrecy or, in some instances, patents. Thus, a developer that relinquishes all its intellectual property rights in the software it creates for a customer could conceivably be barred by trade secrecy or patent law from using similar ideas, techniques and so forth in other programs.

The moral is this: A developer should make sure that it either retains enough ownership rights in what it creates to allow it to continue to do similar development work for other customers, or, obtains enough money from the customer to compensate it for the possible lost future business.

One way a developer can protect its future business is to obtain a nonexclusive license to use the software. Another is to retain ownership of the software and provide the customer with a license to use the software. Both these options are discussed below. In addition, the developer should be careful to retain ownership of its "background technology." That includes the programs and materials that the developer uses over and over again in most or all of its projects—such as routines for displaying menus, document assembly and printing. (See Section 14 for a detailed discussion.)

Four ownership alternatives are provided:
- sole ownership by the customer
- ownership by developer with an exclusive license to customer
- ownership by developer with a non-exclusive license to customer, and
- joint ownership.

a. Alternative 1: Ownership by customer

Because they are paying the developer to create the software, some customers insist on receiving sole ownership. The following clause grants all ownership rights in the software to the customer, with no restrictions. Typically, a developer that relinquishes all its ownership rights will demand more payment than if it were allowed to retain at least some ownership and profit from the software by licensing it to others.

As mentioned above, an assignment of all of the developer's rights means that the developer may not use the software created for the customer, for example, by including part of it in a program created for someone else. This can work a substantial hardship on the developer, especially one that regularly works on similar types of software.

One way a developer can make such an ownership transfer more palatable is to have the customer grant the developer back a nonexclusive license to use the software. A nonexclusive license gives someone the right to use software or other copyrighted work, but does not prevent the copyright owners from granting others the same rights at the same time.

The license can be limited in any way—such as in duration or the type of software in which it can be used. For example, the developer can be barred from using the software to help the customer's named competitors or from developing similar types of products. The optional provision granting a license to the developer would be used in addition to the assignment from developer to customer.

b. Alternative 2: Ownership by developer with exclusive license to customer

Another option is for the developer to retain ownership of the software and give the customer an exclusive license to use it. (Nonexclusive licenses are covered below, in Alternative 3.)

With an exclusive license, only the customer has the right to use it—within the scope of the license. If an exclusive license gives the customer the right to use the software in every possible context at every possible location, it would be the functional equivalent of ownership. In practice, however, the parties usually agree to limit the customer's use rights. For example, the customer's right to use the software may be limited as to duration, area (worldwide or domestic), market or hardware (the customer could be permitted to use the software only on a particular platform). Under this type of license, the developer would have the exclusive right to modify the software and could sell or license it to others outside the customer's area of exclusivity.

This type of arrangement often benefits both the customer and developer: The customer is assured that the developer will not sell or license the software to competitors during the term of the exclusive license. At the same time, the developer retains control over the software and will have the opportunity to earn income by licensing it to others outside the area of the customer's exclusivity and/or after the exclusive license expires.

This provision grants an exclusive license that is limited as to time. When the exclusive license expires, the customer receives a perpetual nonexclusive license, meaning that the developer is free to license the software to others. This license is nontransferable—it does not permit the customer to sub-license the software to others, but this can be permitted if the parties desire. The license permits the customer to use the software on any number of computers for internal purposes and to make as many back-up copies as it needs.

c. Alternative 3: Ownership by developer with nonexclusive license to customer

The most favorable ownership arrangement for the developer may be for the customer to be given only a nonexclusive license to use the software. This means that the developer is free to license the software to anyone else, including the developer's competitors. This type of ownership arrangement would likely result in the lowest possible price to the customer, because the developer may earn additional income by licensing the software to others.

d. Alternative 4: Joint ownership

Yet another option is for the customer and developer to jointly own the software. Under a joint ownership arrangement, each party is free to use the software or grant non-exclusive licenses to third parties without the other's permission (unless they agree to restrict this right). Normally, joint owners must account for and share with each other any monies they earn from granting such licenses. This is probably not desirable in the developer-customer situation, so this provision specifically provides that neither party need account to the other—in other words, they need not share any money they earn from the software.

14. Ownership of Background Technology

A software developer will normally bring to the project various development tools, routines, subroutines and other programs, data and materials. One term for these items is "background technology." It's quite possible that background technology may end up in the final product. For example, this may include code used for installation, window manipulation, displaying menus, data searching, data storing and printing.

If the developer transfers complete ownership of the software to the customer, the customer also may end up owning this background technology. Such an arrangement would prohibit the developer from using the background technology in other projects without obtaining the customer's permission (and perhaps paying a fee). A developer is usually well advised to avoid this problem by making sure the agreement provides that the developer retain all ownership rights in background technology. In this event, the agreement also should give the customer a nonexclusive license to use the background technology that's included in the customer's software.

This provision permits the customer to use the background technology as included in the software, but keeps ownership in the hands of the developer. The developer should prepare a separate exhibit that identifies in as much detail as possible the background technology to be included in the software.

This provision need not be included in a contract in which the developer retains ownership of the software.

Identify background technology. If possible, identify your background technology in the source code copies of the programs in any printouts of code you deliver to the customer. You might include a notice like the following where such material appears: "[Your Company Name] CONFIDENTIAL AND PROPRIETARY."

15. Source Code Access

If the customer obtains ownership of the software, it should receive the source code and system/program documentation created by the developer. But if the developer retains ownership and merely grants the customer a license to use the software, source code access can become an important issue.

Some clients insist on having access to the developer's source code. They're afraid the original developer won't be around months or years down the line when the software needs to be maintained, modified or enhanced. They're afraid it will be difficult or impossible to do such work without the source code. However, as a practical matter, access to the source code is greatly overrated as a benefit for a software customer. The fact is, even with decent documentation, the expense involved in picking up somebody else's code is often greater than programming from scratch.

Software developers are understandably reluctant to give a customer a copy of their proprietary source code. A software developer's most important asset is usually its source code, which may contain highly valuable trade secrets. One way for a developer to deal with a client who demands access to the source code is to agree to a source code escrow.

Under a source code escrow agreement, the developer gives a copy of the source code and documentation to a neutral third party for safekeeping. The third party will release the source code to the customer only upon the occurrence of specified conditions, such as the developer's bankruptcy or failure to maintain the software. This keeps the developer's source code confidential while, in theory, assuring the customer access to it should it become necessary.

So long as the customer pays for the escrow and the conditions for its release are reasonable, this arrangement works well for the developer. It avoids giving the customer the source code outright.

Literally anybody can serve as the escrow agent. In the past, attorneys, accountants and bank escrow departments have frequently been used. In recent years, though, a number of houses specializing in software escrows have been established. (See the sidebar below.)

Using an escrow firm that specializes in software affords several advantages. First, these companies provide a carefully controlled environment for storage of magnetic media, assuring that the deposited material is undamaged. In addition, some software escrow houses also provide a verification service. This may consist of simply making sure the materials deposited match the requirements of the escrow agreement. However, for an additional charge, some escrows will take the source code provided by the developer and compile it (turn it into object code) to see if it is identical to the object code given to the customer. Software escrow companies normally supply detailed form escrow agreements for the parties to sign. These agreements attempt to evenly balance the interests of both parties.

Professional Software Escrow Companies

The following is professional software escrow houses provide nationwide service. There may be other software escrow houses near your local area. It pays to shop around, since fees vary widely.

Data Securities International
6165 Greenwich Drive #220
San Diego, CA 92122
619-457-5199

Fort Knox Safe Deposit Inc.
235 DeKalb Industrial Way
Decatur, GA 30030
404-292-0700; 800-875-5669

National Escrow Corporation
P.O. Box 190810
Dallas, TX 75219
214-526-8383; 800-383-1800

National Safe Depository
2109 Bering Drive
San Jose, CA 95131
408-453-2753; Fax 408-441-6826

Zurich Depository Corporation
1165 Northern Blvd.
Manhasset, NY 11030
516-365-4756

Since there is no guarantee when a development project is commenced that the software will be satisfactorily completed, it makes sense to delay spending the time and money involved in setting up a source code escrow until the software is actually written. This optional clause obliges the parties to set up an escrow with a software escrow house to be determined later. The escrow agreement is also to be negotiated later. This clause makes clear that the customer will pay for the escrow. This is fair because the escrow is really for the customer's benefit. It also sets forth the circumstances under which the escrowed materials will be released to the customer by the escrow company; this should also, of course, be spelled out in detail in the escrow agreement.

16. Warranties

A warranty is a promise or statement regarding the quality, quantity, performance or legal title of something being sold. We all have some familiarity with warranties. Whenever we buy an expensive product from a car, to a television to a computer, the seller normally warrants that the product will do what it is supposed to do for a specific or reasonable time period, otherwise the seller will fix or replace it.

When goods are sold in the course of business, they generally are warranted. If the goods later prove defective and the seller fails to repair or replace them in accordance with the warranty, it is called a "breach of warranty" and the buyer can seek relief in the courts. In many states, hefty damages can be obtained against sellers who fail to live up to their warranties. These may include not only the cost of replacing the defective software, but any economic losses suffered by the customer as a result of the defect, such as lost profits.

Custom software developers are naturally hesitant about giving a warranty for something that is not yet in existence when the warranty is made. However, some customers usually demand assurance that the product will work.

Because this is an area of active bargaining between the developer and customer, warranty provisions vary widely. Before we discuss sample warranty provisions for custom software development contracts, let's take a quick look at the various types of warranties.

a. Express warranties

When a developer makes an actual promise about how the software will work, whether orally or in writing, it is making an "express warranty." An express warranty can be created by using formal words such as "guarantee," "affirm," or "warrant." However, it is important to understand that no magic words are necessary to create an express warranty. Representations make by salespeople, sales literature, statements at product demonstrations, proposals, manuals or contractual specifications can all constitute express warranties. And this can even be true where the developer did not intend to create a warranty. Express warranties can last for any period of time, ranging from a few months to the lifetime of the software.

Customers often seek an express warranty from software developers guaranteeing that the software is free from defects and will meet the functional and design specifications set forth in the development plan. (See Section 16(d), below.) Another common express warranty is a guarantee that the software will not infringe any third party's copyright, patent or trade secret rights.

b. Implied warranties

In every commercial transaction involving the sale of movable goods, certain representations by the seller are assumed to be made, even if no words are written or spoken. These representations are implied by state laws based on the Uniform Commercial Code ("U.C.C."), a set of model laws designed by legal scholars that have been adopted by every state but Louisiana. The U.C.C. establishes uniform rules governing the sale of goods and other commercial transactions. In the past, a number of courts have disagreed on whether custom software qualifies as a "good" governed by these state U.C.C. laws, but today the trend appears to be that these laws apply to custom software sales transactions. (There is no question that the U.C.C. applies when software is bundled with hardware, or when standard off-the-shelf software is customized.)

This book can't provide a whole course on the U.C.C. but you should be aware that

there are four implied warranties that automatically exist in contracts for the sale of goods unless they are expressly disclaimed (disavowed). These are:

- **Implied warranty of title.** All sellers warrant that they are transferring good legal title to the goods; that they have the right to make the transfer; and, as far as they know, the goods are not subject to any liens, encumbrances or security interests. This warranty is particularly important for software development agreements because the software often contains elements that have been licensed from or to third parties.

- **Implied warranty against infringement.** The seller warrants that the product will be delivered free of any rightful claim by any third party that the product infringes such person's patent, copyright, trade secret or other proprietary rights.

- **Implied warranty of fitness for a specific purpose.** If a customer is relying on the seller's expertise to select suitable goods, and the seller is aware that the customer intends to use the goods for a particular purpose, the product becomes impliedly guaranteed for that purpose. For example, if a developer knows that the customer needs software to operate an assembly line at a particular speed, and agrees to develop software for that purpose, there is an implied warranty that the software will operate the line at the proper speed even if this specification isn't made a part of the contract. This warranty almost always applies in custom software transactions.

- **Implied warranty of merchantability.** The seller promises that the goods are fit for their commonly intended use— in other words, they are of at least average quality. This means that software must perform so as to satisfy most customers' expectations. The software need only perform in a minimally acceptable manner to satisfy this warranty; it need not satisfy the highest function, speed or other performance criteria.

c. Alternative 1: Disclaimer of all warranties

There is no requirement in most states that the seller of goods provide any warranties at all. The implied warranties discussed above (and any express warranties) may be expressly disclaimed by the seller. This means that the goods are sold "as is." While an "as is" statement will protect a seller from many types of claims, it won't protect it from charges of outright fraud (if it lied about the goods in question). To be effective, "as is" statements must be "conspicuous"— for instance, printed in boldface capitals and large type—so they won't be overlooked by the customer (no proverbial "fine print").

d. Alternative 2: Providing express warranties

Although creating custom software is a difficult and often uncertain process, it is reasonable for the customer to expect the developer to stand behind its product. In a custom software development agreement, the developer typically gives the customer certain express warranties and disclaims any and all implied warranties. The parties need to negotiate exactly what type of express warranties the developer will make. Naturally, the customer wants the developer's warranties to be as expansive as possible, while the developer wishes them to be narrowly drawn. A compromise must be reached.

Alternative 2 contains the following express warranties commonly found in custom development agreements. Include whichever warranties are desired.

- **Warranty of Software Performance:** Under a warranty of software performance, the developer guarantees that the software will function properly. The developer promises that the software is free from material defects (but not absolutely perfect) and will perform in substantial conformance with the specifications.

This warranty is usually limited in time, to anywhere from 90 days to one year. During the warranty term, the developer is required to correct any defects and modify the software as necessary, free of charge. Normally excluded from coverage are any defects caused by the customer's misuse of the software or from causes beyond the developer's control, such as a power failure.

- **Warranty of title:** The developer warrants that it has the legal right to grant the customer all rights specified in the contract. This normally means that no intellectual property rights to the software have been licensed to others on an exclusive basis. In addition, if the developer has used any code covered by another's copyright, patent or trade secret protections, it has the legal right to do so.

- **Warranty against disablement:** Developers who are concerned that they might not be paid fully or that the customer may breach the terms of the development contract have been known to include "computer viruses" and disabling devices in their software. These devices are intended to disable the software, either automatically with the passage of time or under the developer's control. The purpose, obviously, is to prevent the customer from using the software if the customer fails to uphold its end of the agreement.

Is this legal? One court has indicated it might be, but only if the developer tells the customer in advance that disabling devices will be included in the software and the customer agrees (F*rank & Sons v. Information Solutions,* (N.D. Okla. No. 88C1474E), Computer Indus. Lit. Rep., Jan. 23, 1989, at 8927-35). In the absence of such notice and consent, a developer who disables a customer's software could be liable for all the customer's resulting damages. These could be substantial, especially if the customer's entire computer system is affected.

In one well-known case, a developer included a disabling device in an inventory control system it created for cosmetics manufacture for Revlon, Inc. When Revlon stopped paying the developer because it was dissatisfied with the system's performance, the developer sent Revlon a letter warning that it would disable the software if payment was not forthcoming. The developer then activated the disabling device by dialing into Revlon's computer system. As a result, two of Revlon's distribution centers were completely shut down for several days. Revlon estimated its losses at $20 million. Revlon sued the developer, who settled for an undisclosed amount (*Revlon, Inc. v. Logisticon, Inc.,* No. 705933 (Cal. Super. Ct., Santa Clara Cty., complaint filed Oct. 22, 1990)). The lesson is clear: A developer should absolutely never include any disabling device in software without informing the customer and obtaining its consent in advance. Even then, the developer should think twice if a customer does consent—the customer might sue the developer anyway if activation of a disablement device causes it substantial losses.

Not only will most customers refuse to allow inclusion of a disabling device in their software, they will often demand that the developer expressly guarantee that none has or will be included.

- **Warranty of compatibility:** The warranty of compatibility provides that the software will be compatible with the hardware on which it will run and with any non-custom software included

Warranties a Developer Should Not Make

A developer should only provide a warranty as to those matters within its control. This is a matter of fairness and common sense. Matters beyond a developer's control include:

- **Error-free software.** A developer cannot realistically warrant that the software will be completely bug-free. All software, particularly custom software, inevitably contains some bugs. But there is a big difference between true bugs—defects that prevent the software from performing the customer's required tasks satisfactorily—and interface and peripheral glitches and other minor irritants that don't materially affect the software's performance. The most a developer should promise is that the software will not contain "material" defects. A developer should never promise to fix trivial bugs free of charge. Fixing minor bugs can be just as difficult and expensive as fixing major ones. Moreover, the customer really doesn't need to have trivial bugs fixed at all. All the customer needs is stable software that performs satisfactorily. Trivial bugs that don't prevent the software from performing satisfactorily can simply be ignored.

- **Software will be free from defects in materials and workmanship.** This type of warranty is commonly found in contracts for machinery, including computer hardware. However, it does not belong in software development contracts. Again, no developer can safely guarantee that custom software will be perfect.

- **Software will perform in exact conformance with specifications**. Developers shouldn't promise this unless they're absolutely sure it will be true. It's far better for the developer to warrant that the software will perform "in substantial conformance" with the specifications, meaning that trivial variations will not violate the warranty.

in the customer's system. This warranty is particularly important where a customer is acquiring a system from multiple vendors—that is, hardware from one or more vendors, and software from others.

- **Disclaiming warranties not in agreement:** In return for the express warranties included in the contract, the customer typically agrees to allow the developer to disclaim any and all other warranties, whether express or implied. Such a disclaimer should be typed in capitals, preferably boldface, to be enforceable.

17. Intellectual Property Infringement Claims

"Intellectual property" is a catch-all term that includes copyrights, patents, trade secrets and trademarks. (See Chapter 2 for a detailed discussion.) Most software development agreements contain some kind of express warranty against intellectual property infringement. The extent of such a warranty is subject to negotiation.

In this highly litigious world, intellectual property infringement is an issue the developer must think about carefully. In some cases, the developer may even choose to lower its price or make other concessions to the customer to avoid making a broad warranty of noninfringement. Three alternative warranty provisions are provided in the agreement.

Insurance Coverage for Infringement Claims

Your business may be insured for intellectual property infringement claims and you may not even know it. The Comprehensive General Liability Insurance ("CGL") policies typically obtained by businesses may provide such coverage. Several courts have held that the "advertising injury" provision included in many CGL policies covers infringement claims. However, not all CGL policies provide such coverage, particularly those written after 1986. Ask your insurance broker whether your policy covers infringement claims. If the broker doesn't know, you may need to consult with an insurance attorney who represents policyholders. If your CGL policy doesn't cover infringement claims, you may be able to obtain such coverage by purchasing umbrella or excess policy coverage from your insurer.

a. Alternative 1: Limited warranty against infringement

In this clause the developer warrants that it will not knowingly violate the copyright or trade secrets rights of any third party. However, no warranty is made as to patent infringement. This is because it is very difficult for a developer to know for sure whether its software might violate a patent, primarily because pending patent applications are kept secret. Instead, the developer simply promises that to the best of the developer's knowledge the software will not infringe any existing patent.

Some customers absolutely insist that the developer indemnify (repay) them if a third party brings a lawsuit claiming the software infringed on the party's intellectual property rights. An optional indemnification provision is provided here. It is as narrowly drafted as possible. The developer must indemnify the customer only if the third party intellectual property rights involved were known to the developer prioxr to delivery of the software. This means, for example, the developer won't be liable if a patent issued covering some element contained in the software after the software was delivered.

b. Alternative 2: "No-knowledge" representation

Even better for the developer is to provide no warranty of noninfringement at all, and instead extend the "no-knowledge representation" to copyrights and trade secrets as well as patents. Because there are no uniform national rules, it remains far from clear exactly how far copyright protection for software extends. (See Chapter 5.) As a result, it can be difficult or impossible to know for sure if custom software violates the copyright in any similar preexisting programs. In fact, there have been many instances in which a developer's employees have included software elements belonging to a prior employer; as a practical matter, it can be impossible for a developer to know about or prevent this.

c. Alternative 3: No warranties or representations

Best of all, from the developer's point of view, is a provision in which the developer states that it makes no warranties or representations of any kind regarding intellectual property infringement and will not indemnify the customer if an infringement claim is made (see discussion of indemnification below). This alternative is most logical when the developer retains ownership of the software; it's unlikely a customer who is to obtain ownership of the software would agree to it. If you use this clause, it should be printed in boldfaced, capital letters.

18. Limits on Developer's Liability

Although it may be rather frightening and depressing to think about, custom software developers face potentially enormous liabilities. Improperly designed or bug-ridden software can cause the customer serious financial losses for which the customer may look to the developer to make good.

> EXAMPLE: BioWorkware creates a custom software system designed to automate a biotechnology laboratory. A few weeks after installation, the system crashes. While BioWorkware tries to find out went wrong, the lab is forced to purchase software from another vendor to get the lab up and running. As a result of all this, the lab is shut down for a week and loses several

experiments potentially worth hundreds of thousands of dollars. The lab demands that BioWorkware repay the losses caused by the crash. To pay this amount, BioWorkware would have to liquidate its business. BioWorkware refuses to pay, and the lab sues.

To prevent a nightmarish scenario of this type from driving them out of business, developers are wise to insist on the following provisions limiting their liability to the customer. These provisions are optional, but can be very helpful for developers.

a. No liability for consequential damages

The consequential damages arising out of even a modest problem can easily bankrupt a developer. At the very least, the developer should insist that the agreement include a provision excluding it from any liability for incidental or consequential damages arising out of the agreement. Such damages include lost profits or other economic damages arising from a malfunction where the developer had reason to know that such losses could occur if the software malfunctioned. This could include, for example, the value of the experiments lost by the biotech lab in the example above.

b. Limit on developer's liability to customer

Another way to limit the developer's potential liability limits the developer's total liability to the customer to a specified amount. A typical liability limit is the amount paid by the customer for the software. This amounts to a money-back guarantee for the customer, while getting the developer off the hook for a potentially much larger liability. If desired, a liability standard not based on the contract price can be set. Obviously, such a provision highly favors the developer.

c. Developer's liability for third party claims

The harm caused by malfunctioning software is not necessarily limited to the customer; it may economically or even physically damage third parties as well.

> **EXAMPLE:** SafeSoft writes a custom software package designed to operate a chemical factory. The software crashes and so does the factory, resulting in a chemical spill costing hundreds of thousands of dollars to clean up. Dozens of suits are brought against the chemical company by property owners affected by the spill. The chemical company demands that SafeSoft pay off these claims.

To avoid this type of scenario, the developer may seek to include in the development agreement a clause providing that it is not liable for any claim made against the customer by any third party (other than for intellectual property infringement if it is providing a warranty against infringement).

d. Indemnification of developer for third party claims

If third parties are harmed by malfunctioning software, they'll likely sue everyone involved, including the developer. Both the customer and the developer may be liable for the full amount of such claims. Indemnification provisions are used to require one party to pay the other's attorney fees and damages arising from such claims. Indemnification provisions don't affect the third party claimant. They simply straighten liability between the developer and the customer.

In the example above, property owners affected by the chemical spill would undoubtedly sue not only the chemical factory, but SafeSoft as well, claiming that it negligently designed the software. A developer in this situation could find itself faced with defending itself against suits brought by persons and entities it never heard of. Its attorney fees alone could far exceed what it was paid to create the software.

Ideally, the developer would like the customer to agree to indemnify the developer against such third party claims. Realizing that their software may adversely affect many people they never contracted with, more and more developers are seeking provisions like this which, of course, highly favor the developer. A developer of software that poses an obvious risk of potential financial and/or physical damage to third parties—for example, software implemented in banking hardware or airline radar—should seriously consider seeking such a provision in the development agreement.

19. Confidentiality

Since software developers often have access to their customers' valuable confidential information, customers often seek to impose confidentiality restrictions on them. It's not unreasonable for a customer to want you to keep its secrets away from the eyes and ears of competitors. Unfortunately, however, many of these provisions are worded so broadly that they can make it difficult for you to work for other clients without fear of violating your duty of confidentiality.

If, like most software developers, you make your living by performing similar services for many firms within the computer industry, insist on a confidentiality provision that is reasonable in scope and defines precisely what information you must keep confidential. Such a provision should last for only a limited time—five years at the most.

The confidentiality provision in this agreement prevents the unauthorized disclosure by the developer of any written material of the customer marked confidential or information disclosed orally that the customer later writes down, marks as confidential and delivers to you within 15 days. This enables the developer to know for sure what material is, and is not, confidential.

The clause also makes clear that the developer does not have any duty to keep confidential material that does not qualify as a trade secret, is legitimately learned from persons other than the customer or is independently developed.

- **Optional provision: Software confidentiality:** If the developer retains ownership of the software, it wants to make sure that the customer treats it as confidential. In this event, this optional clause should be included in the development agreement:

20. Term of Agreement

The term of a software development should run from the date it is executed (signed by both parties) until full performance or earlier termination or cancellation.

21. Termination of Agreement

The language governing how the contract may end is very important to both parties. The provision in this agreement is fairly standard. It permits either party to terminate the agreement if the other materially breaches any of its contractual obligations and fails to remedy the breach within 30 days. A "material" breach means a breach that is serious, rather than minor or trivial. Missing a deadline by one day is not "material"; missing it by three months is. For developers, the material breach most likely to result in termination is the customer's failure to pay the developer in a timely

fashion. If the developer terminates the agreement because of the customer's default (usually because the customer has failed to pay the developer), the customer should return any software or other materials received from the developer and should pay the developer for the work it has done.

- **Optional provision: early customer termination:** The customer may want the option to terminate the agreement at its convenience if it decides for some reason it doesn't want to go through with the project. In this event, the customer should have to pay the developer all amounts due for accepted work and relinquish any rights in the software.

22. Taxes

It is customary in custom software development agreements for the customer to pay any required state and local sales, use or property taxes. Whether or not the developer is required to collect sales taxes, the following provision should be included in the agreement making it clear that the customer will have to pay these and similar taxes. States constantly change their sales tax laws and more and more are beginning to look at services as a good source of sales tax revenue. So this provision could come in handy in the future even if the developer doesn't really need it now.

23. Developer an Independent Contractor

One of the most important functions of the agreement is to help establish that the developer is not the customer's employee. A developer will be considered the customer's employee if the customer has the right to control the developer. This will cause problems not only for the customer, but for the developer as well. (See Chapter 15.)

A development agreement that indicates a lack of control on the part of the hiring firm will contribute to a finding of independent contractor status. But such an agreement will not be determinative in and of itself. Simply signing a piece of paper will not make a developer an independent contractor. The agreement must reflect reality—that is, the developer must actually not be controlled on the job by the customer.

The language in this clause addresses most of the factors the IRS and other agencies consider in measuring the degree of control of the hiring firm. (These factors are discussed in Chapter 15, Section C.) All provisions show that the hiring firm lacks the right to control the manner and means by which the developer will perform the agreed-upon services.

Include all of provisions a-j that apply. The more that apply, the more likely that the developer will be viewed as an independent contractor.

24. Optional Provision: Nonsolicitation of Developer's Employees

One of a software developer's fears is that a customer will hire away a star programmer or other key employee and do future work on program enhancements and modifications in-house. This optional provision is designed to prevent this. It may give the developer some peace of mind.

25. Mediation and Arbitration

Mediation and arbitration are two forms of "alternative dispute resolution"—means for settling disputes without resorting to expensive court litigation. Mediation is relatively informal, and by its nature is never binding. Typically, the mediator either sits the parties down together and tries to provide an objective view of their disputes, or shuttles between the parties as a cool conduit of what may be red-hot opinions. Where the real problem is a personality conflict or simple lack of communication, a good mediator can keep a minor controversy from shattering the relationship between software developer and customer. Where the argument is more serious, a mediator may be able to lead the parties to a mutually satisfactory resolution that will obviate time-consuming and expensive litigation.

In arbitration, an informal hearing is held before one or more arbitrators (usually attorneys or retired judges) who decide the merits of the issues and render a decision, which may or not be binding depending on the arbitration agreement. There are a number of professional arbitrators' organizations which conduct arbitrations, notably the American Arbitration Association which has offices in most major cities.

No one can be forced into mediation or arbitration; one must agree to it, either in the contract or later when a dispute arises. Commercial contracts often include binding arbitration provisions. However, this is not a matter to be agreed to lightly. By submitting to binding arbitration, you're basically giving up your constitutional right of access to the courts. Arbitration has many good points. It is usually faster and cheaper than court litigation. Also, because the parties choose the arbitrator, they can select someone who is familiar with computer and software law. Such a person might be expected to render a better decision than a judge or jury with no familiarity with the software business.

However, arbitration can also have a down side. Litigants have often found that arbitrators seek to reach a compromise between the parties' positions rather than ruling squarely in favor of one or the other. Moreover, arbitrators are under no obligation to follow established legal principles. Under the rules of the American Arbitration Association (which are most commonly used in arbitrations), no questioning of the parties or witnesses is allowed before the hearing (a process lawyers call discovery). This can lead to unfair results. Moreover, if you lose an arbitration there is essentially

no right of appeal. A court can vacate (void) an arbitrator's decision only if it finds the arbitrator guilty of misconduct, bias, fraud or corruption. Proving this is extremely difficult. Finally, an arbitrator's decision is not self-enforcing; it must be entered with a court. In some cases (obtaining a quick restraining order, for example), you're better off going to court in the first place.

This optional clause requires the developer and customer to take advantage of these alternate forms of dispute resolution. They're first required to submit the dispute to mediation. If mediation doesn't work, they must submit the dispute to binding arbitration. Indicate where the mediation or arbitration is to occur. You'll usually want it in the city or county where your office is located. You don't want to have to travel a long distance to attend a mediation or arbitration.

If you don't want to give up your right to go to court, don't use this clause.

26. Attorney Fees

If you have to sue the client in court to enforce the agreement, and win, you normally will not be awarded the amount of your attorney fees unless your agreement requires it. Including such an attorney fees provision in the agreement can be in your interest. It can help make filing a lawsuit economically feasible. It will also give the customer a strong incentive to negotiate with you if you have a good case.

Under this provision, if either person has to sue the other in court to enforce the agreement and wins—that is, becomes the prevailing party—the loser is required to pay the other person's attorney fees and expenses.

27. General Provisions

Following are several provisions that are customarily lumped together at the end of a software development agreement. This does not mean they are unimportant.

(a) This clause helps make it clear to a court or arbitrator that the parties intended the contract to be their final agreement. A clause such as this helps avoid claims that promises not contained in the written contract were made and broken. The developer should make sure that all documents containing any of the customer's representations upon which the developer is relying are attached to the agreement as exhibits. If they aren't attached, they likely won't be considered to be part of the agreement.

(b) This clause, which is very important, states that any changes to the agreement must be in writing and agreed to by both parties to be effective. This provision protects both parties; reducing all modifications to writing lessens the possibility of misunderstandings. In addition, oral modifications may not be legally binding.

Contract Changes in the Real World

In the real world, people make changes to their contracts all the time and never write them down. If the changes are very minor, this might not pose a problem. But be aware that a contract alteration might not be legally binding if it is not written down. And, of course, if a dispute develops, the lack of a writing will make it difficult to prove what you actually agreed to.

If you agree to a minor contract change (over the phone, for example) and don't want to go to the trouble of dealing with a formal signed contract modification, at least send a confirming letter to the other party setting forth the gist of what you've agreed to. This isn't as good as a signed contract modification, but it will be helpful if a dispute later develops.

(c) This clause specifies which state law governs the contract. This should be the state in which the developer does business or is incorporated.

(d) When you want to do something important involving the agreement—terminate it, for example—you need to tell the client about it. This is called giving notice. This provision gives you several options for providing the client with notice: by personal delivery, by mail, or by fax or telex followed by a confirming letter.

If you give notice by mail, it is not effective until three days after it's sent. For example, if you want to end the agreement on 30 days notice and mail your notice of termination to the consultant, the agreement will not end until 33 days after you mailed the notice.

(e) This clause helps you to make sure that the developer and customer are separate legal entities, not partners or co-venturers. If a customer is viewed as a developer's partner, the developer will be liable for its debts and the customer will have the power to make contracts that obligate the developer to others without the developer's consent.

(f) An assignment is the process by which rights or duties under a contract are transferred to someone else. For example, you may assign your duty to perform services for the client to someone else. This clause gives both parties an unfettered right to assign their rights or obligations.

28. Signatures

The end of the main body of the agreement should contain spaces for the parties to sign.

29. Exhibits

Make sure that all exhibits are attached to all copies of the agreement. Each exhibit should be consecutively numbered or lettered ("A,B,C" or "1,2,3"). Also, the references to the exhibits in the main body of the agreement should match the actual exhibits. The exhibits to the agreement will include:

- the Functional Specification (see Section 3(a), above)
- the Development Plan (see Section 3, above), and
- the developer's list of Background Technology (see Section 14, above).

Refer to Chapter 1, Section D, for information about how to put the agreement together.

Custom Software Development Agreement

1. Identification of the Parties: This Agreement is made between Old Reliable Insurance Co. (the "Customer") with a principal place of business at 123 State St., Chicago, Ill., and AcmeSoft, Inc. (the "Developer") with a principal place of business at 111 Dally Place, Chicago, Ill.

2. Purpose of Agreement: Customer desires to retain Developer as an independent contractor to develop the computer software (the "Software") described in the Functional Specifications contained in Exhibit A attached to and made part of this Agreement. Developer is ready, willing and able to undertake the development of the Software and agrees to do so under the terms and conditions set forth in this Agreement. Accordingly, the parties agree as follows:

3. Preparation of Development Plan: Developer shall prepare a development plan ("Development Plan") for the Software, satisfying the requirements set forth in the Functional Specifications. The Development Plan shall include:

(a) detailed Specifications for the Software;

(b) a listing of all items to be delivered to Customer under this Agreement ("Deliverables");

(c) a delivery schedule containing a delivery date for each Deliverable; and

(d) a payment schedule setting forth the amount and time of Developer's compensation.

Developer shall deliver the Development Plan to Customer by April 1, 199_. Customer shall have 30 days to review the Development Plan. Upon approval of the Development Plan by Customer, it will be marked as Exhibit B and will be deemed by both parties to have become a part of this Agreement and will be incorporated by reference. Developer shall then commence development of Software that will substantially conform to the requirements set forth in the Development Plan.

If the Development Plan is in Customer's reasonable judgment unsatisfactory in any material respect, Customer shall prepare a detailed written description of the objections. Customer shall deliver such objections to Developer within 30 days of receipt of the Development Plan. Developer shall then have 30 days to modify the Development Plan to respond to Customer's objections. Customer shall have 30 days to review the modified Development Plan. If Customer deems the modified Development Plan to be unacceptable, Customer has the option of terminating this Agreement upon written notice to Developer or permitting Developer to modify the Development Plan again under the procedure outlined in this paragraph. If this Agreement is terminated, the obligations of both parties under it shall end except for Customer's obligation to pay Developer all sums due for preparing the Development Plan and the ongoing obligations of confidentiality set forth in the provision of this Agreement entitled "Confidentiality."

Payment for Development Plan: If the Development Plan is not accepted by Customer and Customer terminates this Agreement, Developer shall be entitled to compensation on a time and materials basis at an hourly rate of $100 plus expenses to the date of termination. Developer shall submit an invoice detailing its time and expenses preparing the Development Plan. If the invoice amount is less than the amounts paid to Developer prior to termination, Developer shall promptly return the excess to Customer. If the invoice amount exceeds the amounts paid to Developer prior to termination, Customer shall promptly pay Developer the difference.

4. Payment:

The total contract price shall be set forth in the Development Plan. Customer shall pay the Developer the sum of $10,000 upon execution of this Agreement and the sum of $10,000 upon Customer's approval of the Development Plan. The remainder of the contract price shall be payable in installments according to the payment schedule to be included in the Development Plan.

Each installment shall be payable upon completion of each project phase by Developer and acceptance by Customer in accordance with the provision of this Agreement entitled "Acceptance Testing of Software."

5. Payment of Developer's Costs:

Customer shall reimburse Developer for all out-of-pocket expenses incurred by Developer in performing services under this Agreement. Such expenses include, but are not limited, to:

(a) all communications charges;

(b) costs for providing conversion services for converting Customer's database;

(c) media costs;

(d) travel expenses other than normal commuting, including airfares, rental vehicles, and highway mileage in company or personal vehicles at __ cents per mile; and

(e) other expenses resulting from the work performed under this Agreement.

Developer shall submit an itemized statement of Developer's expenses. Customer shall pay Developer within 30 days from the date of each statement.

6. Late Fees:

Late payments by Customer shall be subject to late penalty fees of 1% per month from the due date until the amount is paid.

7. Changes in Project Scope: If at any time following acceptance of the Development Plan by Customer, Customer should desire a change in Developer's performance under this Agreement that will alter or amend the Specifications or other elements of the Development Plan, Customer shall submit to Developer a written proposal specifying the desired changes.

Developer will evaluate each such proposal at its standard rates and charges. Developer shall submit to Customer a written response to each such proposal within 10 working days following receipt thereof. Developer's written response shall include a statement of the availability of Developer's personnel and resources, as well as any impact the proposed changes will have on the contract price, delivery dates or warranty provisions of this Agreement.

Changes to the Development Plan shall be evidenced by a "Development Plan Modification Agreement." The Development Plan Modification Agreement shall amend the Development Plan appropriately to incorporate the desired changes and acknowledge any effect of such changes on the provisions of this Agreement. The Development Plan Modification Agreement shall be signed by authorized representatives of Customer and Developer, whereupon Developer shall commence performance in accordance with it.

Should Developer not approve the Development Plan Modification Agreement as written, Developer will so notify Customer within 10 working days of Developer's receipt of the Development Plan Modification Agreement. Developer shall not be obligated to perform any additional services prior to its approval of the Development Plan Modification Agreement.

For purposes of this Agreement, each Development Plan Modification Agreement duly authorized in writing by Customer and Developer shall be deemed incorporated into and made part of this Agreement. Each such Development Plan Modification Agreement shall constitute a formal change to this Agreement adjusting fees and completion dates as finally agreed upon.

8. Delays:

Developer shall use all reasonable efforts to deliver the Software on schedule. However, at its option, Developer can extend the due date for any Deliverable by giving written notice to Customer. The total of all such extensions shall not exceed 30 days.

Any delay or nonperformance of any provision of this Agreement caused by conditions beyond the reasonable control of the performing party shall not constitute a breach of this Agreement, provided that the delayed party has taken reasonable measures to notify the other of the delay in writing. The delayed party's time for performance shall be deemed to be extended for a period equal to the duration of the conditions beyond its control.

Conditions beyond a party's reasonable control include, but are not limited to, natural disasters, acts of government after the date of the Agreement, power failure, fire, flood, acts of God, labor disputes, riots, acts of war and epidemics. Failure of subcontractors and inability to obtain materials shall not be considered a condition beyond a party's reasonable control.

9. Acceptance Testing of Software:

Customer shall have 30 days from the date of delivery of the Software in final form to inspect, test and evaluate it to determine whether the Software satisfies the acceptance criteria in accordance with procedures set forth in the Development Plan, or as established by Developer and approved by Customer prior to testing.

If the Software does not satisfy the acceptance criteria, Customer shall give Developer written notice stating why the Software is unacceptable. Developer shall have 30 days from the receipt of such notice to correct the deficiencies. Customer shall then have 30 days to inspect, test and evaluate the Software. If the Software still does not satisfy the acceptance criteria, Customer shall have the option of either (1) repeating the procedure set forth above, or (2) terminating this Agreement pursuant to the section of this Agreement entitled "Termination." If Customer does not give written notice to Developer within the initial 30-day inspection, testing and evaluation period or any extension of that period, that the Software does not satisfy the acceptance criteria, Customer shall be deemed to have accepted the Software upon expiration of such period.

10. Ownership of Software:

Developer assigns to Customer its entire right, title and interest in anything created or developed by Developer for Customer under this Agreement ("Work Product") including all patents, copyrights, trade secrets and other proprietary rights. This assignment is conditioned upon full payment of the compensation due Developer under this Agreement.

Developer shall execute and aid in the preparation of any documents necessary to secure any copyright, patent, or other intellectual property rights in the Work Product at no charge to client. However, Customer shall reimburse Developer for reasonable out-of-pocket expenses.

11. Ownership of Background Technology: Customer acknowledges that Developer owns or holds a license to use and sublicense various preexisting development tools, routines, subroutines and other programs, data and materials that Developer may include in the Software developed under this Agreement. This material shall be referred to as "Background Technology." Developer's Background Technology includes, but is not limited to, those items identified in Exhibit B, attached to and made a part of this Agreement.

Developer retains all right, title and interest, including all copyright, patent rights and trade secret rights in the Background Technology. Subject to full payment of the consulting fees due under this Agreement, Developer grants Customer a nonexclusive, perpetual worldwide license to use the Background Technology in the Software developed for and delivered to Customer under this Agreement, and all updates and revisions thereto. However, Customer shall make no other commercial use of the Background Technology without Developer's written consent

12. Warranties:

THE SOFTWARE FURNISHED UNDER THIS AGREEMENT IS PROVIDED ON AN AS "AS IS" BASIS, WITHOUT ANY WARRANTIES OR REPRESENTATIONS EXPRESS, IMPLIED OR STATUTORY; INCLUDING, WITHOUT LIMITATION, WARRANTIES OF QUALITY, PERFORMANCE, NONINFRINGEMENT, MERCHANTABILITY OR FITNESS FOR A PARTICULAR PURPOSE. NOR ARE THERE ANY WARRANTIES CREATED BY A COURSE OF DEALING, COURSE OF PERFORMANCE OR TRADE USAGE. DEVELOPER DOES NOT WARRANT THAT THE SOFTWARE WILL MEET CUSTOMER'S NEEDS OR BE FREE FROM ERRORS, OR THAT THE OPERATION OF THE SOFTWARE WILL BE UNINTERRUPTED. THE FOREGOING EXCLUSIONS AND DISCLAIMERS ARE AN ESSENTIAL PART OF THIS AGREEMENT AND FORMED THE BASIS FOR DETERMINING THE PRICE CHARGED FOR THE SOFTWARE.

13. Intellectual Property Infringement Claims:

Developer warrants that Developer will not knowingly infringe on the copyright or trade secrets of any third party in performing services under this Agreement. To the extent any material used by Developer contains matter proprietary to a third party, Developer shall obtain a license from the owner permitting the use of such matter and granting Developer the right to sub-license its use. Developer will not knowingly infringe upon any existing patents of third parties in the performance of services required by this Agreement, but Developer MAKES NO WARRANTY OF NON-INFRINGEMENT of any United States or foreign patent.

14. Limitation of Developer's Liability to Customer:

(a) In no event shall Developer be liable to Customer for lost profits of Customer, or special or consequential damages, even if Developer has been advised of the possibility of such damages.

(b) Developer's total liability under this Agreement for damages, costs and expenses, regardless of cause, shall not exceed the total amount of fees paid to Developer by Customer under this Agreement [OPTIONAL: "or $[AMOUNT], whichever is greater"].

(c) Developer shall not be liable for any claim or demand made against Customer by any third party except to the extent such claim or demand relates to copyright, trade secret or other proprietary rights, and then only as provided in the section of this Agreement entitled Intellectual Property Infringement Claims.

(d) Customer shall indemnify Developer against all claims, liabilities and costs, including reasonable attorney fees, of defending any third party claim or suit arising out of the use of the Software provided under this Agreement, other than for infringement of intellectual property rights. Developer shall promptly notify Customer in writing of any third party claim or suit and Customer shall have the right to fully control the defense and any settlement of such claim or suit.

15. Confidentiality: During the term of this Agreement and for 6 months afterward, Developer will use reasonable care to prevent the unauthorized use or dissemination of Customer's confidential information. Reasonable care means at least the same degree of care Developer uses to protect its own confidential information from unauthorized disclosure.

Confidential information is limited to information clearly marked as confidential, or disclosed orally that is treated as confidential when disclosed and summarized and identified as confidential in a writing delivered to Consultant within 15 days of disclosure.

Confidential information does not include information that:

- the Developer knew before Customer disclosed it
- is or becomes public knowledge through no fault of Consultant
- Developer obtains from sources other than Customer who owe no duty of confidentiality to Customer, or
- Developer independently develops.

16. Term of Agreement: This Agreement commences on the date it is executed and shall continue until full performance by both parties, or until earlier terminated by one party under the terms of this Agreement.

17. Termination of Agreement: Each party shall have the right to terminate this Agreement by written notice to the other if a party has materially breached any obligation herein and such breach remains uncured for a period of 30 days after written notice of such breach is sent to the other party.

If Developer terminates this Agreement because of Customer's default, all of the following shall apply:

(a) Customer shall immediately cease use of the Software.

(b) Customer shall, within 10 days of such termination, deliver to Developer all copies and portions of the Software and related materials and documentation in its possession furnished by Developer under this Agreement.

(c) All amounts payable or accrued to Developer under this Agreement shall become immediately due and payable.

(d) All rights and licenses granted to Customer under this Agreement shall immediately terminate.

18. Taxes: The charges included here do not include taxes. If Developer is required to pay any federal, state or local sales, use, property or value added taxes based on the services provided under this Agreement, the taxes shall be separately billed to Customer. Developer shall not pay any interest or penalties incurred due to late payment or nonpayment of such taxes by Customer.

19. Developer an Independent Contractor:

Developer is an independent contractor, and neither Developer nor Developer's staff is, or shall be deemed, Client's employees. In its capacity as an independent contractor, Developer agrees and represents, and Customer agrees, as follows:

(a) Developer has the right to perform services for others during the term of this Agreement subject to noncompetition provisions set out in this Agreement, if any.

(b) Developer has the sole right to control and direct the means, manner and method by which the services required by this Agreement will be performed.

(c) Developer has the right to perform the services required by this Agreement at any place or location and at such times as Developer may determine.

(d) Developer will furnish all equipment and materials used to provide the services required by this Agreement, except to the extent that Consultant's work must be performed on or with Customer's computer or existing software.

(e) The services required by this Agreement shall be performed by Developer, or Developer's staff, and Customer shall not be required to hire, supervise or pay any assistants to help Developer.

(f) Developer is responsible for paying all ordinary and necessary expenses of its staff.

(g) Neither Developer nor Developer's staff shall receive any training from Customer in the professional skills necessary to perform the services required by this Agreement.

(h) Neither Developer nor Developer's staff shall be required to devote full-time to the performance of the services required by this Agreement.

(i) Customer shall not provide insurance coverage of any kind for Developer or Developer's staff.

(j) Customer shall not withhold from Developer's compensation any amount that would normally be withheld from an employee's pay.

20. Non-Solicitation of Developer's Employees: Customer agrees not to knowingly hire or solicit Developer's employees during performance of this Agreement and for a period of one year after termination of this Agreement without Developer's written consent.

21. Mediation and Arbitration: If a dispute arises under this Agreement, the parties agree to first try to resolve the dispute with the help of a mutually agreed-upon mediator in the following location: Chicago, Ill. Any costs and fees other than attorney fees associated with the mediation shall be shared equally be the parties.

If it proves impossible to arrive at a mutually satisfactory solution through mediation, the parties agree to submit the dispute to binding arbitration in the following location—Chicago, Ill.—under the rules of the American Arbitration Association. Judgment upon the award rendered by the arbitrator may be entered in any court with jurisdiction to do so.

22. Attorney Fees

If any legal action is necessary to enforce this Agreement, the prevailing party shall be entitled to reasonable attorney fees, costs and expenses in addition to any other relief to which it may be entitled.

23. General Provisions:

(a) Complete Agreement: This Agreement together with all exhibits, appendices or other attachments, which are incorporated herein by reference, is the sole and entire Agreement between the parties. This Agreement supersedes all prior understandings, agreements and documentation relating to such subject matter. In the event of a conflict between the provisions of the main body of the Agreement and any attached exhibits, appendices or other materials, the Agreement shall take precedence.

(b) Modifications to Agreement: Modifications and amendments to this Agreement, including any exhibit or appendix hereto, shall be enforceable only if they are in writing and are signed by authorized representatives of both parties.

(c) Applicable law: This Agreement will be governed by the laws of the State of Illinois.

(d) Notices: All notices and other communications given in connection with this Agreement shall be in writing and shall be deemed given as follows:

- When delivered personally to the recipient's address as appearing in the introductory paragraph to this Agreement;
- Three days after being deposited in the United States mails, postage prepaid to the recipient's address as appearing in the introductory paragraph to this Agreement, or
- When sent by fax or telex to the last fax or telex number of the recipient known to the party giving notice. Notice is effective upon receipt provided that a duplicate copy of the notice is promptly given by first-class or certified mail, or the recipient delivers a written confirmation of receipt.

Any party may change its address appearing in the introductory paragraph to this Agreement by giving notice of the change in accordance with this paragraph.

(e) No Agency: Nothing contained herein will be construed as creating any agency, partnership, joint venture or other form of joint enterprise between the parties.

(f) Assignment: The rights and obligations under this Agreement are freely assignable by either party. Customer shall retain the obligation to pay if the assignee fails to pay as required by this Agreement.

24. Signatures: Each party represents and warrants that on this date they are duly authorized to bind their respective principals by their signatures below.

Customer: Old Reliable Insurance Co.

By: /s/

Jane Daniels

Title: Vice-President

Date: Feb. 28, 199_

Developer: AcmeSoft, Inc.

By: /s/

Stuart Simon

Title: President

Date: March 3, 199_

Chapter 18

Help Beyond This Book

Hopefully, this book provides you with most of the information you need about software law and contracts. But you may need additional help, either in the form of more advanced legal resources or an attorney's advice.

Section A introduces you to resources that contain comprehensive information on each area of intellectual property law. Section B lists several resources that provide additional software contracts. Finally, Section C gives some tips for finding a lawyer specializing in computer law.

A. Further Information on Intellectual Property Law

If you have any questions about intellectual property law (copyright, trade secret, patent or trademark law) that have not been answered by this book, a three-step process is suggested.

- If you have access to the World Wide Web, check one or more of the sites listed below to see if there is an article or other discussion answering your question.
- If you need more in-depth information, take a look at one or more discussions by experts in the field to get a background and overview of the topic being researched. You will already have obtained a basic background from this book and will be looking for additional details on a particular topic. You'll probably need to go to a law library to find these materials.

- If you need still more information, read the law itself (cases and statutes) upon which the experts base their opinions. The accompanying sidebar discusses how to research case law in more detail.

1. Using the Law Library

Many law libraries are open to the public and can be found in most federal, state and county courthouses. Law school libraries in public universities also routinely grant access to the public. In addition, it is also often possible to use private law libraries maintained by local bar associations, large law firms, state agencies or large corporations if you know a local attorney or are willing to be persistent in seeking permission from the powers that be.

Law libraries may seem intimidating at first. It may be helpful to know that most librarians have a sincere interest in helping anyone who desires to use their library. While they won't answer your legal questions, they will often put your hands on the materials that will give you a good start.

After you locate a law library, your approach to legal research should proceed along these lines:

Legal Research: How to Find and Understand the Law, by Stephen Elias and Susan Levinkind (Nolo Press), or another basic legal research guide, can help you understand legal citations, use the law library, and understand what you find there.

Researching Court Decisions

Throughout this book, legal treatises and law review articles are referred to in citations like this: *Apple Computer v. Franklin,* 714 F.2d 1240 (3rd Cir. 1983). This identifies a particular legal decision and tells you where the decision may be found and read. Any case decided by a federal court of appeals is found in a series of books called the Federal Reporter. Older cases are contained in the first series of the Federal Reporter or "F." for short. More recent cases are contained in the second series of the Federal Reporter or "F.2d" for short. To locate the *Apple v. Franklin* case, simply find a law library that has the Federal Reporter, Second Series (almost all do), locate volume 714 and turn to page 1240.

Opinions by the federal district courts (these are the federal trial courts) are in a series called the Federal Supplement or "F.Supp." For example, a case that appears in the Federal Supplement is *Lotus Dev. Corp. v. Paperback Software Int'l.* 740 F.Supp. 37 (D. Mass. 1990).

Cases decided by the U.S. Supreme Court are found in three publications, any of which is fine to use: United States Reports (identified as "U.S."), the Supreme Court Reporter "identified as "S.Ct.") and the Supreme Court Reports, Lawyer's Edition (identified as "L.Ed."). Supreme Court case citations often refer to all three publications—for example—*Diamond v. Diehr,* 450 U.S. 174, 101 S.Ct. 1048, 96 L.Ed. 187 (1985).

2. Copyright Law

The first place to go for more information on copyright law is *The Copyright Handbook: How to Protect and Use Written Works,* by Stephen Fishman (Nolo Press). This book discusses copyright protection for writings, but the principles are applicable to software as well. It also has a chapter on copyright on the Internet.

a. Internet resources

If you have access to the Internet's World Wide Web you can find valuable information about copyright by using any of the following sites:

- **The U.S. Copyright Office at lcweb. loc.gov/copyright** This site offers regulations, guidelines, forms and links to other helpful copyright sites.
- **Findlaw at www.findlaw.com** This search engine offers a comprehensive list of copyright resources on the Web. Click intellectual property under the topic heading on the home page and click copyright from the subcategory list on the intellectual property page.
- **Law Journal Extra Copyright Law Center at www.ljx.com/copyright** This site offers articles, recent copyright cases and links to further copyright information on the Web.
- **Kuesterlaw at www.kuesterlaw.com** The Jeffrey R. Kuester law firm provides an online reference service that will lead you to other copyright resources on the World Wide Web.

b. Legal treatises

Software copyrights are discussed in many outstanding legal treatises.

- *Scott on Computer Law*, by Michael D. Scott (Prentice Hall Law & Business). This two-volume treatise contains a detailed discussion of copyright protection for software, including copyright protection in foreign countries.
- *Software, Copyright, & Competition*, by Anthony Lawrence Clapes (Quorum Books), gives one lawyer's view on how software should be protected by the copyright law.
- *Nimmer on Copyright*, by Melville and David Nimmer (Matthew Bender), is the leading treatise on all aspects of copyright law. This four-volume work covers virtually every legal issue concerning U.S. and foreign copyright law. Its coverage of computer software has recently been expanded, but it is not concerned exclusively with software, like the two treatises cited above.
- *The Law and Business of Computer Software*, edited by D.C. Toedt III (Clark Boardman Callaghan), contains a useful article providing a country-by-country analysis of international copyright protection for software.
- *International Copyright Protection*, edited by David Nimmer and Paul Geller (Matthew Bender), provides exhaustive coverage of copyright protection in other countries.

c. Law review articles

If you have a very unusual copyright problem that is not covered by books on copyright and/or computer law, or you have a problem in an area in which the law has changed very recently, the best sources of available information may be law review articles. You can find citations to all the law review articles on a particular topic by looking under "copyright" in the Index to Legal Periodicals or Current Law Index. A key to the abbreviations used in these indices is located at the front of each index volume. Substantial collections of law reviews are usually kept in large public law libraries or university libraries.

A number of articles dealing with copyright are available on the World Wide Web. Many are listed on the Findlaw site at www.findlaw.com/01topics/23intellectprop/01copyright/publications.html.

d. Statutes

The primary law governing all copyrights in the United States after January 1, 1978, is the Copyright Act of 1976. A copy of the complete Copyright Act is located on the World Wide Web at www.law.cornell.edu/usc/17/overview.html.

The United States Copyright Office has issued regulations which implement the copyright statutes and establish the procedures which must be followed to register a work. These regulations are located on the World Wide Web at www.law.cornell.edu/copyright/regulations/regs.overview.html.

e. Court decisions

There are several ways to find court decisions on a particular legal issue. This book, legal treatises and law review articles contain many case citations. In addition:

- The United States Code Annotated and United States Code Service both cite and briefly summarize all the decisions relevant to each section of the Copyright Act of 1976. These are located just after each section of the Act.
- Federal Practice Digest (West Publishing Company) provides short summaries of copyright law decisions under the term "copyright." The digest contains a detailed table of contents and a very detailed subject matter index at the end of the set.

To understand how court decisions are named and indexed, see instructions in the sidebar, above.

After you find the name of a decision you want, you'll need to obtain a copy. You can get copies of many recent decisions from the World Wide Web. The Findlaw site at www.findlaw.com contains links to sites containing legal decisions. For older decisions, you'll need to go to a law library.

For the most recent information available on copyright, consult the Copyright Law Reporter, a weekly loose-leaf service published by Commerce Clearing House (CCH). It contains the full text or summaries of recent copyright-related court decisions and relevant discussions of new developments in copyright law. The first volume of the set contains easy-to-follow instructions on how to use this valuable resource.

If you have Web access, recent copyright decisions can also be found at the Law Journal Extra Copyright Law Center at www.ljx.com/copyright.

3. Patent Law

The first source to consult if you have any questions about patent law is *Patent It Yourself*, by David Pressman (Nolo Press). This book explains in detail how the patent system works and how to prepare and file a patent application yourself.

a. Internet resources

If you have access to the Internet's World Wide Web you can find valuable information about patent law by using any of the following sites:

- **Findlaw at http://www.findlaw.com** This general purpose legal search engine is a good place to start for researching patent law. Click on intellectual property in the topics section of the homepage and then click on the patent subcategory when the intellectual property page appears. From there you can find patent statutes, regulations, the Manual of Patent Examination Procedures (MPEP), other PTO materials and articles of general interest.
- **Kuesterlaw at http: //www.kuesterlaw. com/** This site, maintained by an Atlanta, Georgia, intellectual property law firm, also is an excellent springboard for finding patent statutes, regulations, court cases and articles on

recent patent law developments, such as software patents and the provisional patent applications.

- **The U.S. Patent and Trademark Office at http://www.uspto.gov** This is the place to go for recent policy and statutory changes and transcripts of hearings on various patent law issues. You may also use this site to conduct a search of the first pages of patents (that include the patent abstracts) for patents issued since 1971.

- **IBM Patent Search Site at http://patent.womplex.ibm.com** This site offers free patent searching for patents issued since 1971.

- **The Shadow Patent Office at http://www.spo.eds.com/** This site, operated by Electronic Data Systems, lets you search recently issued patents for free and also offers an excellent patent search service (for patents back to 1972) for a per-search fee.

- **Software Patent Institute at http://www.spi.org** This site lets you search for previous software developments that may affect whether a particular software item qualifies for a patent.

b. Legal treatises

Legal treatises on patents include:

- *Patent Law Fundamentals*, by Peter Rosenberg (Clark Boardman Callaghan), is the best legal treatise for patent law. This publication is generally considered by patent attorneys to be the bible of patent law. Because it is written for attorneys, it might be somewhat difficult sledding for the non-lawyer. However, if you first obtain an overview of your topic from the Pressman book, you should do fine.

- *Patent Law Handbook*, by C. Bruce Hamburg (Clark Boardman Callaghan), is another useful book. A new edition of this book is issued every year.

c. Law review articles

As mentioned earlier, law review articles are an excellent way to keep abreast of recent legal developments. By looking under "Patents" in the Index to Legal Periodicals or Current Law Index, you will find frequent references to articles on current patent law developments. A key to the abbreviations used in these indexes is located at the front of each index volume. Substantial collections of law reviews are usually located in large public law libraries or university libraries.

A number of useful articles can be found through the Findlaw and Kuesterlaw sites mentioned above.

d. Statutes

The basic U.S. Patent Law is located in Title 35, United States Code, Section 101 and following. This can be found in the United States Code Annotated (U.S.C.A.) or United States Code Service, Lawyers Edition (U.S.C.S.). A copy of the complete Patent Law is located on the World Wide Web at www.law.cornell.edu/usc/35/i_iv/overview.html.

e. Court decisions

You'll find citations to relevant court decisions in Patent Law Fundamentals or a law review article. In addition, the U.S. Code Annotated and U.S. Code Service both refer to and briefly summarize all the decisions relevant to each section of the patent law. You can also find short summaries of patent law decisions in West Publishing Company's Federal Practice Digest under the term "patent."

To understand how court decisions are named and indexed, see instructions in the sidebar, above.

After you find the name of a decision you want, you'll need to obtain a copy. You can get copies of many recent decisions from the World Wide Web. The Findlaw site at www.findlaw.com contains links to sites containing legal decisions. For older decisions, you'll need to go to a law library.

Recent patent law court decisions can be found at the Law Journal Extra Patent Law Center at www.ljx.com/patents/.

4. Trade Secret Law

There isn't quite as much information available on trade secrets as on the other areas of intellectual property.

a. Internet resources

If you have access to the Internet's World Wide Web you can find valuable information about trade secrets by using the Trade Secret Home Page [www.execpc.com/~mhallign/]. This site provides discussions of recent developments and general background information on trade secrets. Also visit Findlaw [www.findlaw.com], a general purpose legal search engine. Click on intellectual property in the topics section of the homepage and then click on the tradesecret subcategory when the intellectual property page appears. From there you can find appropriate statutes and discussions of tradesecret principals.

b. Treatises

Treatises on trade secret law include:
- *Milgrim on Trade Secrets*, a comprehensive treatment of trade secret law published by Matthew Bender as Volume 12 of its Business Organizations series, is probably the most complete resource regarding trade secret issues, especially if you have a specific or detailed question.
- *Trade Secret Law Handbook*, by Melvin F. Jager (Clark Boardman Callaghan), contains mini-discussions of most trade secret related concepts, a number

of sample agreements and licenses, as well as references to cases and statutes where appropriate.

- *Trade Secrets*, by James Pooley (Unacom), is an excellent book written for nonlawyers. You will find this book more accessible than the treatises cited above. It does not contain the extensive citations to primary resource materials (cases and statutes) that the Milgrim and Jager books have, but it does include sample trade secret agreements.

c. Law review articles

Law review articles are often a good place to find information about recent software protection developments. Look under "Trade Secret" in the Index to Legal Periodicals or Current Law Index. A key to the abbreviations used in these indexes is located at the front of each index volume. Substantial collections of law reviews are usually located in large public law libraries or university libraries.

d. Statutes

There is no national trade secret law; instead, it consists of individual laws for each state. For direct access to state statutes governing trade secrets, look under "Trade Secret," "Proprietary Information," or "Commercial Secret" in the index accompanying the statutes of the state in question.

In addition, the Uniform Trade Secrets Act, a model statute designed by legal scholars, has been adopted in one version or another by some 46 states.

e. Court decisions

For summaries of cases involving trade secret principles, consult the West Publishing Company state or regional digests under "Trade Regulation," "Contracts," "Agency" and "Master and Servant."

To understand how court decisions are named and indexed, see instructions in the sidebar, above.

After you find the name of a decision you want, you'll need to obtain a copy. You can get copies of many recent decisions from the World Wide Web. The Findlaw site at www.findlaw.com contains links to sites containing legal decisions. For older decisions, you'll need to go to a law library.

5. Trademark Law

Before consulting any of the resources cited below, first read *Trademark: How to Name Your Business & Product*, by Kate McGrath and Stephen Elias (Nolo Press). This guide provides an overview of trademark law and explains how to select and register a trademark and conduct trademark searches.

a. Internet resources

If you have access to the Internet's World Wide Web you can find valuable information about trademarks by using any of the following sites:

- **Nolo Press at http://www.nolo.com** Nolo Press offers self-help information about a wide variety of legal topics, including trademark law. (See the Intellectual Property topic in the Legal

Encyclopedia, which incidentally includes selected entries from this part of the book.)

- **Findlaw at http://www.findlaw.com** This search engine offers an excellent collection of trademark-related materials on the Web, including trademark statutes, regulations, classification manuals and articles of general interest. Click the intellectual property link in the topics section on the Findlaw home page and then click trademark in the subcategory section on the intellectual property page.

- **GGMARK at http://www.ggmark.com/** This site, maintained by a trademark lawyer, provides basic trademark information and a fine collection of links to other trademark resources.

- **Sunnyvale Center for Invention, Innovation and Ideas at http://www.sci3. com** This site, maintained by the Sunnyvale Center for Innovation, Invention and Ideas (a Patent and Depository Library), provides information about their excellent, low cost trademark search service conducted by the Center's librarians.

- **Micropatent at http://www.micropat. com/trademarkwebindex.html** This site, maintained by Micropatent, lets you do your own search of the federal trademark register for $20 a day (text) and $30 a day (text and images). You can get a lot of searching done within a 24 hour period if you're adequately prepared.

- **Kuesterlaw at http: //www.kuesterlaw. com/** This site, maintained by an Atlanta, Georgia, intellectual property law firm, also is an excellent springboard for finding trademark statutes, regulations, court cases and articles on such recent trademark law developments as domain name disputes.

- **Law Journal Extra Trademark Law Center at www.ljextra.com/trademark/** contains recent trademark decisions, articles and links to many other trademark sites.

- **U.S. Patent and Trademark Office at http://www.uspto.gov** The U.S. Patent and Trademark Office is the place to go for recent policy and statutory changes and transcripts of hearings on various trademark law issues.

b. Treatises

For truly in-depth information on trademarks, consult the following treatises:

- *Trademarks and Unfair Competition*, by J. Thomas McCarthy (Clark Boardman Callaghan), is the most authoritative book on trademark law. This multi-volume treatise discusses virtually every legal issue that has arisen regarding trademarks.

- *Trademark Registration Practice*, by James E. Hawes (Clark Boardman Callaghan), provides a detailed guide to trademark registration.

- *Trademark Law—A Practitioner's Guide*, by Siegrun D. Kane (Practicing Law Institute), contains practical advice about trademark disputes and litigation.

c. Law review articles

You can find law review articles on trademark law by looking under "trademark" or "unfair competition" in the Index to Legal Periodicals or Current Law Index. A key to the abbreviations used in these indexes is located at the front of each index volume. Substantial collections of law reviews are usually located in large public law libraries or university libraries. You can also find a number of articles on the Web. You can access many articles on the Web through the Findlaw and Kuesterlaw sites mentioned above.

d. Statutes

The main law governing trademarks in the United States is the Lanham Act, also known as the Federal Trademark Act of 1946 (as amended in 1988). It is codified at Title 15, Chapters 1051 through 1127, of the United States Code. You can find it in either of two books:

- United States Code Annotated (U.S.C.A.), or
- United States Code Service, Lawyers Edition (U.S.C.S.).

All law libraries carry at least one of these series. To find a specific section of the Lanham Act, consult either the index at the end of Title 15, or the index at the end of the entire code.

A copy of the complete Lanhan Act is located on the World Wide Web at www.law.cornell.edu/uscode/15/ch22.html.

e. Court decisions

You'll find citations to relevant court decisions in *Trademarks and Unfair Competition* or a law review article. In addition, the U.S. Code Annotated and U.S. Code Service both refer to and briefly summarize all the decisions relevant to each section of the Lanham Act. You can also find short summaries of trademark law decisions in West Publishing Company's Federal Practice Digest under the term "trademark."

To understand how court decisions are named and indexed, see instructions in the sidebar, above.

After you find the name of a decision you want, you'll need to obtain a copy. You can get copies of many recent decisions from the World Wide Web. The Findlaw site at www.findlaw.com contains links to sites containing legal decisions. For older decisions, you'll need to go to a law library.

Recent patent law court decisions can be found at the Law Journal Extra Trademark Law Center at www.ljx.com/trademark/

B. Further Information on Software Contracts

If you need a software contract not contained in this book, consult the following sources:

- *Vendor's Guide to Computer Contracting*, by Friedman, Hildebrand and Lipner (Prentice Hall Law & Business). This one-volume guide contains a number of sample contracts designed with a software developer's interests in mind. It includes a sample software license agreement, development agreement, employment and consulting agreements, maintenance and service agreements, marketing/distributing agreements and software escrow agreements. The book was written for nonlawyers and contains clear discussions of what is in the forms and how to use them.

- *Allen & Davis on Computer Contracting: A User's Guide with Forms and Strategies*, by Don A. Allen and Lanny J. Davis (Prentice Hall Law & Business). This book discusses software and hardware contracting from the customer's point of view. It has an extensive discussion of how a customer should organize a system for software contracting and negotiate software and hardware contracts. It includes sample annotated software licensing, development, maintenance and escrow agreements. It also has sample hardware purchase and lease agreements. All the agreements are designed to protect the customer's interests.

- *Computer Software Agreements*, by Ridley, Quittmeyer and Matuszeski (Warren, Gorham & Lamont). This book was written for lawyers and is not as accessible as the two listed above; but it contains a huge number of sample agreements, including multiple development, employment, marketing, distribution, end user, service bureau, database and backup services agreements.

You may be able to find these books in a large university library or law library; otherwise, you'll probably have to order them direct from the publisher. They can all be ordered on 30-day approval, so you can send them back if you don't like them.

C. Finding a Lawyer

If you're faced with a problem you cannot or do not want to handle yourself, you may need to see a lawyer. A large number of lawyers hold themselves out to the public as "computer lawyers." Many of them have a background in intellectual property litigation; others may have worked for a computer software or hardware company or for a law firm that does extensive business advising such companies.

A lawyer with a solid background either working for or advising hi-tech businesses is probably your best bet if you need help with contract drafting. But if you need help filing a patent application or (God forbid) with patent litigation, be aware that patent law is a separate legal specialty. Only lawyers admitted to the federal patent bar can practice patent law. Many patent lawyers specialize in a particular industry; be sure to ask any patent lawyer you considering hiring whether he or she has experience handling software patent applications and/or litigation.

Patent lawyers may also be able to help you with trademark, copyright and trade secret matters. But some patent lawyers don't put much effort into these other areas.

So, if you are shopping for a copyright, trademark or trade secret lawyer, do your best to find someone who specializes primarily in these fields.

Finding a good lawyer is no different than finding any other professional to help your business. The best way is always to ask for referrals from friends or colleagues in your industry. If your company has a general business lawyer, ask for a referral as well. Your county bar association may also be able to refer you to someone. If all else fails, look in your local Yellow Pages under attorneys specializing in "computer law" and "patent, trademark & copyright." ■

Index

CATALOG

	PRICE	CODE

BUSINESS

	PRICE	CODE
The California Nonprofit Corporation Handbook	$29.95	NON
The California Professional Corporation Handbook	$34.95	PROF
The Employer's Legal Handbook	$29.95	EMPL
Form Your Own Limited Liability Company	$34.95	LIAB
▣ Hiring Independent Contractors: The Employer's Legal Guide, (Book w/Disk—PC)	$29.95	HICI
▣ How to Form a CA Nonprofit Corp.—w/Corp. Records Binder & PC Disk	$49.95	CNP
▣ How to Form a Nonprofit Corp., Book w/Disk (PC)—National Edition	$39.95	NNP
▣ How to Form Your Own Calif. Corp.—w/Corp. Records Binder & Disk—PC	$39.95	CACI
How to Form Your Own California Corporation	$29.95	CCOR
▣ How to Form Your Own Florida Corporation, (Book w/Disk—PC)	$39.95	FLCO
▣ How to Form Your Own New York Corporation, (Book w/Disk—PC)	$39.95	NYCO
▣ How to Form Your Own Texas Corporation, (Book w/Disk—PC)	$39.95	TCOR
How to Handle Your Workers' Compensation Claim (California Edition)	$29.95	WORK
How to Market a Product for Under $500	$29.95	UN500
How to Mediate Your Dispute	$18.95	MEDI
How to Write a Business Plan	$21.95	SBS
The Independent Paralegal's Handbook	$29.95	PARA
Legal Guide for Starting & Running a Small Business, Vol. 1	$24.95	RUNS
▣ Legal Guide for Starting & Running a Small Business, Vol. 2: Legal Forms	$29.95	RUNS2
Marketing Without Advertising	$19.00	MWAD
▣ The Partnership Book: How to Write a Partnership Agreement, (Book w/Disk—PC)	$34.95	PART
Sexual Harassment on the Job	$18.95	HARS
Starting and Running a Successful Newsletter or Magazine	$24.95	MAG
▣ Taking Care of Your Corporation, Vol. 1, (Book w/Disk—PC)	$29.95	CORK
▣ Taking Care of Your Corporation, Vol. 2, (Book w/Disk—PC)	$39.95	CORK2
Tax Savvy for Small Business	$28.95	SAVVY
Trademark: Legal Care for Your Business and Product Name	$29.95	TRD
Wage Slave No More: The Independent Contractor's Legal Guide	$34.95	WAGE
Your Rights in the Workplace	$19.95	YRW

CONSUMER

	PRICE	CODE
Fed Up With the Legal System: What's Wrong & How to Fix It	$9.95	LEG
How to Win Your Personal Injury Claim	$24.95	PICL
Nolo's Everyday Law Book	$21.95	EVL
Nolo's Pocket Guide to California Law	$11.95	CLAW
Trouble-Free Travel...And What to Do When Things Go Wrong	$14.95	TRAV

ESTATE PLANNING & PROBATE

	PRICE	CODE
8 Ways to Avoid Probate (Quick & Legal Series)	$15.95	PRO8
How to Probate an Estate (California Edition)	$34.95	PAE
Make Your Own Living Trust	$21.95	LITR
▣ Nolo's Will Book, (Book w/Disk—PC)	$29.95	SWIL
Plan Your Estate	$24.95	NEST
The Quick and Legal Will Book	$15.95	QUIC
Nolo's Law Form Kit: Wills	$14.95	KWL

FAMILY MATTERS

	PRICE	CODE
A Legal Guide for Lesbian and Gay Couples	$24.95	LG
California Marriage Law	$19.95	MARR

▣ Book with disk

● Book with CD-ROM

CALL 800-992-6656 OR USE THE ORDER FORM IN THE BACK OF THE BOOK

	PRICE	CODE
Child Custody: Building Parenting Agreements that Work	$24.95	CUST
Divorce & Money: How to Make the Best Financial Decisions During Divorce	$26.95	DIMO
Get A Life: You Don't Need a Million to Retire Well	$18.95	LIFE
The Guardianship Book (California Edition)	$24.95	GB
How to Adopt Your Stepchild in California	$22.95	ADOP
How to Do Your Own Divorce in California	$24.95	CDIV
How to Do Your Own Divorce in Texas	$19.95	TDIV
How to Raise or Lower Child Support in California	$18.95	CHLD
The Living Together Kit	$24.95	LTK
Nolo's Law Form Kit: Hiring Childcare & Household Help	$14.95	KCHLO
Nolo's Pocket Guide to Family Law	$14.95	FLD
Practical Divorce Solutions	$14.95	PDS
Smart Ways to Save Money During and After Divorce	$14.95	SAVMO

GOING TO COURT

Collect Your Court Judgment (California Edition)	$24.95	JUDG
How to Seal Your Juvenile & Criminal Records (California Edition)	$24.95	CRIM
How to Sue For Up to 25,000...and Win!	$29.95	MUNI
Everybody's Guide to Small Claims Court in California	$18.95	CSCC
Everybody's Guide to Small Claims Court (National Edition)	$18.95	NSCC
Fight Your Ticket ... and Win! (California Edition)	$19.95	FYT
How to Change Your Name (California Edition)	$24.95	NAME
Mad at Your Lawyer	$21.95	MAD
Represent Yourself in Court: How to Prepare & Try a Winning Case	$29.95	RYC
The Criminal Law Handbook: Know Your Rights, Survive the System	$24.95	KYR

HOMEOWNERS, LANDLORDS & TENANTS

The Deeds Book (California Edition)	$16.95	DEED
Dog Law	$14.95	DOG
⌷ Every Landlord's Legal Guide (National Edition)	$34.95	ELLI
Every Tenant's Legal Guide	$24.95	EVTEN
For Sale by Owner (California Edition)	$24.95	FSBO
Homestead Your House (California Edition)	$9.95	HOME
How to Buy a House in California	$24.95	BHCA
The Landlord's Law Book, Vol. 1: Rights & Responsibilities (California Edition)	$34.95	LBRT
The Landlord's Law Book, Vol. 2: Evictions (California Edition)	$34.95	LBEV
Leases & Rental Agreements (Quick & Legal Series)	$18.95	LEAR
Neighbor Law: Fences, Trees, Boundaries & Noise	$18.95	NEI
Safe Homes, Safe Neighborhoods: Stopping Crime Where You Live	$14.95	SAFE
Tenants' Rights (California Edition)	$19.95	CTEN
Stop Foreclosure Now in California	$29.95	CLOS

IMMIGRATION

How to Get a Green Card: Legal Ways to Stay in the U.S.A.	$24.95	GRN
U.S. Immigration Made Easy	$39.95	IMEZ

● MONEY MATTERS

● 101 Law Forms for Personal Use: Quick and Legal Series (Book w/disk)	$24.95	101LAW
Chapter 13 Bankruptcy: Repay Your Debts	$29.95	CH13
Credit Repair (Quick & Legal Series)	$15.95	CREP
The Financial Power of Attorney Workbook	$24.95	FINPOA
How to File for Bankruptcy	$26.95	HFB
Money Troubles: Legal Strategies to Cope With Your Debts	$19.95	MT
Nolo's Law Form Kit: Personal Bankruptcy	$14.95	KBNK

⌷ Book with disk

● Book with CD-ROM

	PRICE	CODE

Stand Up to the IRS .... $24.95 — SIRS

PATENTS AND COPYRIGHTS

The Copyright Handbook: How to Protect and Use Written Works .... $29.95 — COHA
Copyright Your Software .... $39.95 — CYS
 License Your Invention (Book w/Disk) .... $39.95 — LICE
The Patent Drawing Book .... $29.95 — DRAW
Patent, Copyright & Trademark: A Desk Reference to Intellectual Property Law .... $24.95 — PCTM
Patent It Yourself .... $44.95 — PAT
Software Development: A Legal Guide (Book with disk—PC) .... $44.95 — SFT
The Inventor's Notebook .... $19.95 — INOT

RESEARCH & REFERENCE

Government on the Net, (Book w/CD-ROM—Windows/Macintosh) .... $39.95 — GONE
Law on the Net, (Book w/CD-ROM—Windows/Macintosh) .... $39.95 — LAWN
Legal Research: How to Find & Understand the Law .... $19.95 — LRES
Legal Research Made Easy (Video) .... $89.95 — LRME

SENIORS

Beat the Nursing Home Trap .... $18.95 — ELD
Social Security, Medicare & Pensions .... $19.95 — SOA
The Conservatorship Book (California Edition) .... $29.95 — CNSV

SOFTWARE
Call or check our website for special discounts on Software!

California Incorporator 2.0—DOS .... $79.95 — INCI
Living Trust Maker 2.0—Macintosh .... $79.95 — LTM2
Living Trust Maker 2.0—Windows .... $79.95 — LTWI2
Small Business Legal Pro Deluxe CD—Windows/Macintosh CD-ROM .... $79.95 — SBCD
Nolo's Partnership Maker 1.0—DOS .... $79.95 — PAGI1
Personal RecordKeeper 4.0—Macintosh .... $49.95 — RKM4
Personal RecordKeeper 4.0—Windows .... $49.95 — RKP4
Patent It Yourself 1.0—Windows .... $229.95 — PYP12
WillMaker 6.0 .... $69.95 — WD6

Special Upgrade Offer
Get 25% off the latest edition off your Nolo book

It's important to have the most current legal information. Because laws and legal procedures change often, we update our books regularly. To help keep you up-to-date we are extending this special upgrade offer. Cut out and mail the title portion of the cover of your old Nolo book and we'll give you 25% off the retail price of the NEW EDITION of that book when you purchase directly from us. For more information call us at 1-800-992-6656. This offer is to individuals only.

Book with disk
Book with CD-ROM

CALL 800-992-6656 OR USE THE ORDER FORM IN THE BACK OF THE BOOK

ORDER FORM

Code	Quantity	Title	Unit price	Total
		Subtotal		
		California residents add Sales Tax		
		Basic Shipping ($6.00 for 1 item; $7.00 for 2 or more)		
		UPS RUSH delivery $7.50–any size order*		
		TOTAL		

Name

Address

(UPS to street address, Priority Mail to P.O. boxes)

* Delivered in 3 business days from receipt of S.F. Bay Area use regular shipping. order.

FOR FASTER SERVICE, USE YOUR CREDIT CARD & OUR TOLL-FREE NUMBERS

Order 24 hours a day	1-800-992-6656
Fax your order	1-800-645-0895
e-mail	cs@nolo.com
General Information	1-510-549-1976
Customer Service	1-800-728-3555, Mon.-Fri. 9am-5pm, PST

METHOD OF PAYMENT

☐ Check enclosed

☐ VISA   ☐ MasterCard   ☐ Discover Card   ☐ American Express

Account #   Expiration Date

Authorizing Signature

Daytime Phone

PRICES SUBJECT TO CHANGE.

VISIT OUR STORES

You'll find our complete line of books and software, all at a discount.

BERKELEY
950 Parker Street
Berkeley, CA 94710
1-510-704-2248

SAN JOSE
111 N. Market Street, #115
San Jose, CA 95113
1-408-271-7240

VISIT US ONLINE

on the Internet

www.nolo.com

NOLO PRESS 950 PARKER ST., BERKELEY, CA 94710